HANDBOOKS

D1562078

NAPA & SONOMA

PHILIP GOLDSMITH

NAPA & SONOMA

LAKE COUNTY

Middletown

BUTTS CANYON RD

NAPA COUNTY

Capay

YOLO COUNTY

NAPA VALLEY APPELLATION

Pope Valley

Lake Berryessa

CALISTOGA

Calistoga

HOWELL MOUNTAIN

DIAMOND MOUNTAIN DISTRICT

CHILES VALLEY DISTRICT

CHILES POPE VALLEY RD

SPRING MOUNTAIN DISTRICT

ST. HELENA

Napa River

St. Helena

Lake Hennessey

SILVERADO TRAIL

RUTHERFORD

CAPELL VALLEY RD

SONOMA VALLEY

OAKVILLE

ATLAS PEAK

NAPA VALLEY WINE TRAIN

BENNETT VALLEY

Kenwood

STAGS LEAP DISTRICT

Yountville

SONOMA MOUNTAIN

Glen Ellen

YOUNTVILLE

WOODEN VALLEY

HWY

MOUNT VEEDER

OAK KNOLL DISTRICT OF NAPA VALLEY

WILD HORSE VALLEY

SOLANO COUNTY

SONOMA

NAPA

Fairfield

PETALUMA HILL RD

OLD ADOBE RD

LOS CARNEROS/ SONOMA

Napa River

LOS CARNEROS

Petaluma

SONOMA VALLEY

American Canyon

Cordelia

Novato

Petaluma River

Vallejo

San Pablo Bay

Grizzly Bay

Contents

Discover Napa & Sonoma

It's the end of another perfect summer day in Wine Country: Relax on a winery terrace, glass of glorious cabernet in hand, fragrant lavender wafting in the warm air and the golden glow of the late afternoon sun casting long shadows in the endless green corduroy of the vineyards. It's hard not to dream of living in this part of the world.

You wouldn't be the first. Over the centuries, people from all around the world have been lured by the lush forests, tall mountains, abundant rivers, and warm valleys that make up Napa and Sonoma. They've created a rich historical, cultural, and agricultural tapestry that continues to grow and evolve even in the 21st century.

Back in the 1800s, early winemakers chose this geographically diverse and largely unpopulated area of the state to grow grapes – a testament to the conditions and climate here. Ever since, Napa and Sonoma have remained the center of California's wine industry, flourishing as other wine-growing regions came and went.

Though it only produces about 4 percent of the state's wine, the Napa Valley puts on one of the greatest wine shows on earth, with ever-more-elaborate wineries turning out some of the best wines in California along with world-class restaurants.

Neighboring Sonoma County is where the true diversity of the region is most visible. Wineries – generally smaller than in the

Napa Valley — coexist in the valleys and on mountain slopes with farms, quirky small towns (and their diverse inhabitants), and vast expanses of forest, grassland, and wetland. Such varied geography gives rise to just about every kind of food and wine imaginable.

Before your head starts spinning thinking of all the wine tasting you'll be doing, keep in mind that both regions offer an array of opportunities for peace and relaxation. Take a long, slow drive on quiet country roads that showcase stunning redwoods, an eternity of rolling hills, the satisfying symmetry of vineyards, and sunny, vibrant mustard flowers. Soak in the restorative natural hot springs of Calistoga. Rent a canoe and drift down the Russian River. Or hike through the cool, damp old-growth forest at Armstrong Redwoods State Park.

Within the decadence of the Napa Valley and the rustic charms of hidden Sonoma, there's sure to be a place that will fire your imagination and feed your dreams.

Planning Your Trip

The mind-boggling range of activities, wines, scenery, and food that makes this such a diverse part of the world also ensures that seeing and doing the Wine Country will mean different things to different people.

The key to visiting the region is planning. In the hedonistic Wine Country it's hard not to have fun, but your trip can be made all the more enjoyable if there's a plan of action—any plan, however rudimentary; otherwise it's easy to feel overwhelmed. Often it's fun to let tasting room staff, hotel concierges, or fellow travelers help flesh it out with local knowledge and experiences. After all, a crucial part of Wine Country lifestyle is relaxation and indulgence, neither of which should be worked at too hard.

If you're wine-tasting and try to visit too many wineries, the day will seem like a blur with few lasting memories except frustration when heavy traffic wrecks an overly optimistic schedule. Take note of how long tours last or how many wines there are to taste, and allow plenty of time to linger and chat with the winemaker or tasting-room staff. Be sure to mix both big and small wineries into a schedule to experience the full spectrum of California's wine heritage. And, of course, pepper any visit with healthy doses of non–wine-related activities, such as hiking, shopping, or perhaps cooking classes.

► WHERE TO GO

Napa Valley

This *is* California Wine Country, as far as many people are concerned—arguably the most important wine-making region in the state with a name that is recognized around the world. The 30-mile-long Napa Valley is a valley of contrasts. Some 15 distinct appellations are home to hundreds of wineries, ranging from the historic big names that make millions of cases of wine per year down

Wild mustard blankets a Napa Valley vineyard in February.

Landmark Vineyards is known for its pinot noir.

to more modest wineries turning out some of California's best cabernet sauvignons. It can be expensive and crowded in Napa, yet it's not hard to find pockets of rural tranquility as you venture off the beaten path.

Southern Sonoma

Although it now lives in the cultural shadow of the Napa Valley, this is ground zero not only for California's modern wine industry but for California itself. The notable town of Sonoma is thoroughly at peace with itself, as though worn out from the tumultuous series of events more than 150 years ago that gave birth to the state. Life is more laid-back (and cheaper) than in the larger, more famous neighboring valley, yet there are still plenty of cultural, culinary, and outdoor attractions alongside the first-class wines, from the sleepy town of Glen Ellen to the cool flatlands of Los Carneros.

Northern Sonoma

If any region epitomizes the diversity of California's Wine Country, it is northern Sonoma, where scenery and wines from the multitude of hills and small valleys often have little in common other than their Sonoma County address. The cool, lush Russian River Valley has forests, rivers, small farms, and some of the best pinot noir and chardonnay in California. The warmer Dry Creek Valley and Alexander Valley are home to big red wines from small family-owned wineries. Bordering all three regions is the fascinating town of Healdsburg, itself a mix of the upscale and down-home.

▶ WHEN TO GO

Summer and fall are the most popular seasons to visit, and for good reason. This is when the weather is at its best and the wineries are at their most active, laying out lavish food and wine events, preparing for harvest, and releasing new vintages.

The problem is, everyone seems to be here at this time of year. Hotel prices surge, traffic clogs the roads, and getting a restaurant reservation is like a game of roulette. Weekends can be particularly bad, as day-trippers from San Francisco and other Bay Area cities swell the already bulging tourist traffic, potentially turning a weekend getaway into a weekend in purgatory.

Visiting midweek at this time of year can make a huge difference. St. Helena, Healdsburg, and Sonoma can feel positively deserted on an August or September weekday. After October, things quiet down a little bit, hotel rates drop, and the weather can still be fine as the vineyards turn glorious hues of red and gold.

Winter is the wettest but also the quietest period, when wineries can be blissfully devoid of visitors and enable plenty of one-on-one time with tasting-room staff. In spring the weather warms up and the valley and mountains are a fresh, vivid green after the winter rains, making this one of the best times to visit the Wine Country ahead of the worst summer crowds.

harvesting the grapes

▶ BEFORE YOU GO

Transportation

Almost everyone gets around by car in California, and it's no different in Napa and Sonoma, most of which is rural and therefore has little, if any, public transportation. You might be able to park the car to explore some of the bigger towns such as Napa or Healdsburg by foot for a day, visiting urban tasting rooms, shops, and sights. Ultimately, however, you'll need two wheels or four to fully appreciate Wine Country.

There's one obvious problem with this scenario—drinking wine and driving (or cycling) is not the best combination. If you're wine-tasting, planning a designated driver each day or for the duration of the trip is a good idea, or look in to several companies that offer daylong tours either in a private vehicle with driver or as part of a group in a small bus. If you must drive, having the discipline (and skill) to spit out wine in the tasting room is essential.

As you plan an itinerary, be aware that driving times can be slower than you expect. Average speeds can be very low on rural roads, especially mountain roads and in busy areas like Napa during rush hour. Distances between wineries and summer heat can also make biking more exhausting than you might think, so plan accordingly.

What to Take

Wine Country is generally a rather civilized place to visit, but nature likes to keep everyone guessing. Visit November through April, and almost every part of Wine Country, from the coast to the heart of the Napa Valley, will be about the same temperature—usually 55–65°F during the day. Summer is a different story. The coast tends to be cool June–October, while the inland valleys are hot, with significant temperature differences often occurring in just a half-hour drive.

The key to staying comfortable in such conditions is to wear layers of clothing that can be shed during the drive from the cool coast to the cauldron of Calistoga. Be prepared to put some back on in the evening, as temperatures can drop sharply after dark, particularly in the fall.

Sunscreen, hats, and sunglasses are essential wear in the summer heat, especially with alcohol thrown into the mix to accelerate dehydration. This is essentially an outdoorsy, agricultural area, so casual clothing and good walking shoes are recommended for tramping up to picnic spots or through vineyards on tours. The more adventurous may want hiking boots and binoculars to explore the mountain and forest trails.

Very few restaurants require anything more than smart casual attire, so unless you're planning to eat at the more upscale establishments in the Napa Valley or Healdsburg area, leave cocktail dresses and sport coats behind.

Explore Napa & Sonoma

▶ BEST OF NAPA AND SONOMA

There's more than wine to the Wine Country, and some of the best sights and activities are not wine-related at all. This weeklong tour of the major wine regions will give a taste of the diversity on offer, taking in a mix of wineries, sights, and outdoor activities. Driving is the best way to get around, but you could also rent a bike in Sonoma or Healdsburg to explore some of the local attractions.

Day 1

In the city of Napa, grab some breakfast at one of the many eateries in the Oxbow Public Market and get your first taste of gourmet Wine Country food. Drive north on the Silverado Trail, stopping first at the spectacular Persian palace Darioush. Continue north to the organic champion Robert Sinskey Vineyards, where food is as much a part of the visitor experience as wine. A few miles farther north, stop at the sparkling wine

specialist Mumm and take a look around its photography galleries before chilling with a glass of bubbly on the terrace overlooking the Napa Valley. If you time it right, the sun might be just starting to set over the western hills. Continue to Calistoga for a creek-side dinner at the Calistoga Hotel.

Day 2

After a hearty breakfast at the cozy Café Sarafornia, learn more about Calistoga's colorful Victorian history at the Sharpsteen Museum. Buy picnic supplies in the town before heading south for a tour of the caves at the nearby Schramsberg winery, a champagne house with its own unique Victorian history. Alternatively you could experience some fake Tuscan history with a tour of the spectacular Castello di Amorosa. Continue south to Bothe-Napa Valley State Park for a short hike through the redwoods followed by

Darioush, a winery noted for its Bordeaux-style estate wine

VARIETAL TOURS

Many wineries are particularly well known for one or two varietals. If you're a fan of a particular type of wine, it's worth planning a trip to the wineries – and regions – that specialize in it.

CLASSIC CABERNETS

Cabernet sauvignon is the king of California wines, and the Napa and Sonoma Valleys are where some of the best Californian cabs are made.

- **Stags Leap District,** where beautifully structured cabernets are made.
- **Shafer Vineyards,** tucked away in its own private canyon, where you might be lucky enough to taste its Hillside Select cabernet.
- **Stag's Leap Wine Cellars,** home to the vineyards that beat the best in the world in the famous Paris tasting of 1976.
- **Beaulieu Vineyard,** where bigger, bolder cabernets are laced with the Rutherford appellation's distinct flavor of "Rutherford dust."
- **Rubicon Estate,** one of the best winery shows in the valley, courtesy of owner and filmmaker Francis Ford Coppola.
- **Pride Mountain Vineyards,** an ideal place for a picnic, with panoramic views of both the Napa and Sonoma Valleys. A taste of

the elegant cabernet up here will reveal how different these powerful mountain wines can be from their valley-floor competitors.

PLEASURES OF PINOT

Santa Barbara County might have had the best pinot publicity in recent years from the movie *Sideways,* but the cooler parts of Northern California, and particularly Sonoma, are home to arguably the best pinot noirs and pinot-based sparkling wines in the state.

- **Domaine Carneros,** and its flagship Avant Garde pinot noir, a Carneros classic.
- **Landmark Vineyards,** for the highly regarded Kastania and Grand Detour pinot noirs, sourced from coastal vineyards.
- **Siduri Wines,** to taste cult-favorite pinots from just about every major growing region on the West Coast.
- **Dutton-Goldfield Winery,** one of the valley's best pinot vineyards.
- **Hartford Family Winery,** as beautiful a location as any; sample some highly praised, vineyard-designate Russian River pinots.
- **Davis Bynum,** offering vineyard-designate pinot noirs in an old hop kiln building.

a picnic under the trees. Drive farther south to St. Helena, stopping off for one of the cooking demonstrations at the Culinary Institute of America if you have time. From St. Helena, take the scenic drive up Spring Mountain Road to the very top to experience the sweeping views and wonderful mountain wines of Pride Mountain Vineyards. Continue west and spend the night down in Sonoma Valley.

Day 3

Take a fun, motorized tour around the Benziger Family Winery vineyards in Glen Ellen, one of the few biodynamic wineries in California. After

tasting some of their classic Sonoma cabernets, head for nearby Figone's Olive Oil Company just south of Glen Ellen to taste some diverse olive oils. After lunch at one of the many great restaurants in Glen Ellen, hike around the scenic Jack London State Historic Park, once part of the Victorian author's giant ranch and now full of fascinating ruins. Those with enough energy can expend plenty of it in Sugarloaf Ridge State Park on the other side of the valley, where redwoods and sunny ridges offer ample outdoor choices and spectacular views. End the day tasting reserve wines on the peaceful patio overlooking the valley at Chateau St. Jean.

Day 4

Browse the shops and sights around the historic Sonoma Plaza, perhaps tasting some crisp chardonnay at the Charles Creek Vineyards tasting room or on the patio of the Roche Winery tasting room. If you have time, consider exploring some of the historic wineries nearby, including Sebastiani Vineyards and Gundlach Bundschu. Have lunch in Sonoma before heading south to Carneros for a prebooked afternoon Discovery Tour at the artistic wonderland of the di Rosa Preserve. Finish your afternoon relaxing on the terrace at the château-like Domaine Carneros, sampling some of the fine sparkling wines, or visit the modern, minimalist tasting room of neighboring Cuvaison Estate to sample some classic chardonnay and pinot noir while overlooking the vineyards. Inspired by the wines, make the short drive back up to Sonoma to dine at one of the town's many superb restaurants.

Day 5

Drive north through the Sonoma Valley, stopping at tiny Loxton Cellars to taste the wonderful syrah and, if owner Chris Loxton

has the time, a short tour of the vineyards. Contrasting the modest wine-making operation at Loxton a little further north is the splendor of the Ledson Winery. Continue up-valley to Santa Rosa and then head west into the Russian River Valley for a change of scenery and a change of wines. After lunching in the tiny town of Graton, head up to Iron Horse Vineyards for some afternoon champagne overlooking the rural scenery. Drive north to the funky riverside town of Guerneville and, if you have time, continue up to the Armstrong Redwoods State Reserve for a late afternoon hike in the cool shade of the majestic redwoods. Chose from cheap and cheerful or gourmet dining options in Guerneville, perhaps ending the day at one of the colorful local bars.

Day 6

With a breakfast from Guerneville's River Inn Grill preparing you for a busy day, head east to Korbel Champagne Cellars for a tour of the historic winery. Stop at the Korbel deli to pack a picnic, then continue along the river to spend an hour or two lounging by the Russian River at Sunset Beach or Steelhead Beach. Gather up

guarding the tasting rooms at Sebastiani Vineyards

MORE THAN JUST WINE

Tasting wines is certainly not the only reason to visit Napa and Sonoma. To lure more people through their doors, wineries have become skilled at differentiating themselves with attractions besides wine.

STANDOUT TOURS

- Architecture buffs should check out the free tour at the futuristic **Opus One** winery to see the opulence that comes from being created by two of the world's most famous winemakers.

- Farther north in the valley, the angular **Clos Pegase** winery has a bolder style. Tour the Greek-inspired architecture and the founder's big art collection.

- At the historic **Far Niente** winery, car fanatics can admire the private vintage car collection of late owner Gil Nickel and visit the huge network of caves under the main house.

- The newest touring spectacle is the massive medieval castle of **Castello di Amorosa,** where towers, banquet halls, and dungeons are as much a part of the fun as the Diamond Mountain wines.

- To visit **Long Meadow Ranch** high in the hills above Rutherford, visitors are driven in a curious-looking Swiss military vehicle called a Pinzgauer.

- To reach the monastery-like **Sterling Vineyards,** perched on a knoll outside Calistoga, visitors board gondolas that would be more at home at a ski resort.

- If you prefer to venture below ground, make an appointment to visit the massive cave complex at **Palmaz Vineyards** just east of Napa.

HISTORY HIGHLIGHTS

- The **Buena Vista Winery** and neighboring **Bartholomew Park Winery** are both on land originally farmed by wine-making pioneer Agoston Haraszthy. Both have fascinating small museums with plenty to keep history buffs happy.

- The **Gundlach Bundschu Winery** was winning awards for its wines more than 100 years ago.

- **Sebastiani Vineyards & Winery** was founded in 1904 by Italian immigrant Samuele Sebastiani, who also built many buildings in the town.

WINE EDUCATION

- For a thorough understanding of how to appreciate wine, sign up for one of the Saturday morning Wine Basics classes at **Goosecross Cellars** in Yountville.

- Just outside Calistoga, the historic **Schramsberg Winery** offers one of the more entertaining and educational champagne tours through its spooky Victorian caves.

- If you can find the **Medlock Ames** winery in the Chalk Hill region near Healdsburg, Ames Morrison would be happy to take you around his vineyard to explain how everything is done.

CULINARY ADVENTURES

- Visit one of the many farms that sell seasonal fruit and vegetables, such as **Kozlowski Farms** in the Russian River Valley.

- Many of the region's top chefs shop at **farmers markets,** and two of the best are held weekly in Healdsburg and Sonoma during the summer and fall.

- Several urban marketplaces also bring farm-fresh produce and gourmet food to the masses, including the **Oxbow Public Market** in Napa and **Plaza Farms** in Healdsburg.

- Do some olive oil tasting at the **Olive Press** at the Jacuzzi winery in Carneros or at the **St. Helena Olive Oil Company** in the Napa Valley.

- Some of the secrets to cooking with these ingredients can be learned at the **Culinary Institute of America** near St. Helena; this leading West Coast cooking school offers several cooking demonstrations every day Friday–Monday.

FREE TOURS AND TASTINGS

follow the sign to the pinot noir

Wine tasting in the Napa Valley can be expensive – but it doesn't have to be. Although free wine is getting harder to come by, a handful of wineries still offer free tasting as part of a tour, sometimes by appointment only. They include **Frog's Leap** (which also offers free organic produce if you're lucky), **Caymus Vineyards, Mayacamas Vineyards,** and **Reverie Winery** on Diamond Mountain. Free tasting without a tour is available at **V. Sattui Winery,** though you'll have to endure crowds most of the year.

At **Goosecross Cellars,** for the the $10 Napa-standard tasting fee you can also enroll in the educational and entertaining Wine Basics class offered on the winery lawn every Saturday morning during the summer, which includes a couple of tastings as part of the fun.

Another way to save money is to forsake wine and instead take the free tours offered by some wineries, which are often entertaining enough even without wine. Some wineries that schedule free tours (often by appointment only) include **The Hess Collection, Trefethen Vineyards,** and **Clos Pegase.** At smaller boutique wineries, simply asking will often get visitors a quick unofficial tour.

A third way to save money is to go coupon hunting. Drop in to the local chamber of commerce or any other tourist information center; they sometimes have vouchers for free tastings at various wineries hidden among the piles of free brochures and magazines. Or, browse a few of the free magazines, like *The Vine* and *Wine Country This Week,* available at wineries and information centers: The winery ads often include vouchers or offers for free or two-for-one tastings.

Similarly, if you have the chance, trawl the websites of the wineries you want to visit and see if they have printable vouchers for discount tasting (Beringer, for example, nearly always has two-for-one coupons). Or check out NapaValley.com and WineCountry.com, which often have pages dedicated to discounts and promotions. Even social networking sites like Facebook and Twitter, or review sites like Yelp, often offer two-for-one tasting coupons from wineries with an online presence.

Another idea is to talk to the concierge or owner wherever you're staying. Many hotels and inns arrange free or discount tastings for their guests at local wineries, or at least have a few vouchers they can give you.

If you can't avoid paying to taste the wines at a favorite winery, then check if the cost of the tasting can be deducted from any wine purchases you make. Many wineries offer this courtesy, especially with their more expensive reserve tasting fees. As a last resort, tag along with a local – many wineries offer free tasting to Napa Valley residents.

the energy to continue up the Westside Road to visit some of the region's best pinot noir producers, including Thomas George Estates and C. Donatiello Winery, perhaps stopping off at Hop Kiln Winery along the way to see the see the giant kilns that once dried hops for beer making. Finish up in the pretty town of Healdsburg, where there are ample dining, lodging, and entertainment options.

Day 7

Explore the many downtown tasting rooms of Healdsburg, then drive or bike into the nearby Dry Creek Valley to visit some small wineries that produce some big zinfandels. Ridge

Vineyards has an environmentally friendly winery building that is as organic as its wines, and the Timber Crest Collective is home to a handful of small innovative wine producers. If you're on four wheels rather than two, cross over into neighboring Alexander Valley, where cabernet is king. Visit Alexander Valley Vineyards, one of the most historic in the valley, and drive to the far northern end of the valley to visit the historic Asti Winery, once home to the Italian-Swiss Colony and now home to Souverain. Finish the day with a pizza and local wine at Diavola Pizzeria & Salumeria, perhaps taking home some locally made salami as an unusual Wine Country gift.

▶ A ROMANTIC WEEKEND

What better way to spend a long weekend in the Wine Country than by experiencing the best champagne, food, art, and pampering that the Napa and Sonoma Valleys have to offer? This long-weekend trip illustrates the diversity and hedonism of Wine Country,

and most locations are within easy drives of the countless inns, B&Bs, and resorts in the southern end of the Napa Valley.

Depending on what time your day gets started, there are plenty of opportunities to stop in at additional wineries. Alternatively,

the winery terrace at Domaine Chandon

REDWOODS AND RIVERS

Much of the Napa and Sonoma is rural, and excellent opportunities for outdoor recreation abound. Escaping the winery crowds in summer is surprisingly easy in one of the many parks and preserves, or even on the rivers and lakes of the region.

HIKING

Just a few miles from the bars and restaurants of Guerneville in the Russian River Valley, the 800-acre forested **Armstrong Redwoods State Reserve** offers some of the most diverse hiking in the area. Take a stroll through the cool, damp redwoods and take in some local history on the **Pioneer Trail,** or continue on to the 5,700-acre wilderness of **Austin Creek State Recreation Area.**

SWIMMING AND BOATING

The Russian River has plenty of beaches, most unmarked but still easily accessible from the road. The best place to swim is in the roped-off area at **Memorial Beach** in Healdsburg, while the best place for a summer beach party is Guerneville's **Johnson's Beach.** In between, there are countless other beaches (some clothing-optional) and swimming holes, including the family-friendly **Sunset Beach** near Rio Nido.

Another way to reach the Russian River beaches is by renting an aluminum canoe at **Burkes Canoe Trips** in Forestville and paddling up- or downstream through the forests and vineyards. The more adventurous can rent a kayak at **Russian River Outfitters** in Duncan's Mill and paddle all the way to the ocean.

Or head for **Lake Sonoma** at the top of Dry Creek Valley; there are several swimming beaches and powerboat rentals at the marina.

BIKING

Several parts of Wine Country offer relatively flat and quiet roads well suited to biking between wineries. The **Dry Creek Valley** in northern Sonoma is compact, easy to navigate, and full of wineries (though it gets hot in the summer); rent bikes in nearby Healdsburg. Just as flat, but a little cooler and with longer distances between wineries, is **Carneros.** Rent bikes in Sonoma and take a 35-mile loop past some of the best wineries in the wetlands, or simply explore Sonoma's handful of wineries.

Experienced mountain bikers have plenty of world-class trails to choose from. In the Sonoma Valley, many head for the trails of **Annadel State Park,** including the fast downhill single-track Lawndale Trail and the rocky, technical Orchard Trail. Just south of Napa, **Skyline Wilderness Park** has hosted several mountain-biking world cup competitions, and much of the competition loop can still be ridden today, including the Manzanita Trail, described as one of the best single-tracks on the World Cup circuit.

Armstrong Redwoods State Reserve in Guerneville

the view from Domaine Carneros

cut out a few wineries from the itinerary and spend more time soaking up the atmosphere—or in a mud bath.

Day 1

Get acquainted with the Napa Valley, its history, and its wines at the Napa Valley Museum just outside Yountville before toasting your arrival in the Wine Country with some luxuriously rich blanc de noirs champagne at nearby Domaine Chandon. Have lunch at the winery's renowned restaurant, then take a tour or simply explore the sculpture-filled gardens.

In the evening, head down to the old red-brick Napa Mill on the river in downtown Napa for a classic Wine Country dinner on the patio at the charming French bistro Angèle, followed by an after-dinner cocktail and dancing at Silo's jazz and blues bar right next door.

Day 2

Drive south into Carneros to the di Rosa Preserve to see some whimsical contemporary art at the Gatehouse Gallery. Before you get to Napa, make an appointment for one of the morning tours of all the galleries and gardens, home to one of California's biggest collections of contemporary art.

Afterward, head across the road to the palatial Domaine Carneros and contemplate art with a glass of fruity brut rosé champagne and hors d'oeuvres on the terrace overlooking the vineyards, or in front of a blazing fire on a chilly winter day.

Drive a little farther west to Sonoma and enjoy a light gourmet lunch before spending the afternoon exploring the sights and boutiques around pretty Sonoma Plaza, perhaps even taking a stroll past flower-filled front yards to the Sebastiani winery to taste some of its more unusual Italian-varietal wines.

In the evening, enjoy a glass of wine while watching the plaza's wildlife—from ducks to humans—at the Ledson Hotel before driving north for dinner in Glen Ellen at the cozy and romantic bistro Saffron. If you're in the mood for some nighttime stargazing, drive east from Glen Ellen up into the dark Mayacamas Mountains on Trinity Road, then descend back into the Napa Valley via the Oakville Grade.

Day 3

Begin the day with breakfast or brunch at Gordon's Café & Wine Bar in Yountville. If it's not too late in the morning, drive north to the winery that has come to symbolize the Napa Valley like no other—the Robert Mondavi Winery. Take one of the regular tours to see the best of the sprawling mission-style buildings and taste some classic Napa wines.

Continue north to the V. Sattui Winery just outside St. Helena to buy a cheap, fruity bottle of gamay rouge and picnic supplies (including a corkscrew) before continuing north to the Bothe-Napa Valley State Park, where you can be in the redwoods within minutes and find a perfect picnic spot.

After a relaxing lunch, and perhaps a short hike to appreciate some of the park's valley views, it's time for some pampering, Calistoga-style. Drive north to the famous spa town in time for your appointment for a couple's restorative mud bath at the Lincoln Avenue Spa. Since it's a wine-themed weekend, choose the antioxidant-laden mud containing wine, grapeseed oil, and green tea.

Later in the afternoon, head south from Calistoga along the rural Silverado Trail to Rutherford and the Mumm Napa Valley winery, where there's usually a fascinating exhibition of art or photography that can be enjoyed with a glass of bubbly in hand.

Stay in Rutherford or return later in the evening for the culinary highlight: a sunset dinner overlooking the valley at the Auberge du Soleil resort, high up in the hills. Book well in advance to secure a table on the terrace for a memorable experience.

Robert Mondavi Winery

NAPA VALLEY

Mention California wines and most people will think of the Napa Valley, usually abbreviated to simply "Napa." Mention that you're writing a travel guide to Northern California's Wine Country and almost everyone will ask about your favorite Napa wineries. There's no escaping it—the Napa Valley is regarded as the center of everything wine in California, no matter how Sonoma, Santa Barbara, or Mendocino might jump up and down for attention.

The oft-mentioned Paris tasting of 1976, which pitted the valley's wines in a blind tasting against France's best, put the Napa Valley—and California—firmly on the international wine map: Napa Valley wines won both the red and white tasting, while other Californian wines placed in the top five.

The Napa Valley led the premium wine revolution in the 1980s and saw the building of some of California's most ostentatious wineries in the last two decades, most recently a grandiose castle near Calistoga and, coming soon, a Frank Gehry–designed winery near St. Helena. This little valley is now home to more than a quarter of all the wineries in California, despite the fact that it accounts for only about 4 percent of all the wine made in the state. The statistics speak for themselves—the Napa Valley turns out some of the best wine in California.

The valley is also a marketing manager's dream. Natural beauty, colorful history, some of the biggest names in world wine, and $100 bottles of cabernet all serve to draw hordes of visitors—almost 5 million a year at last count. They in turn are entertained by top chefs, luxury pampering, and lavish winery shows like

HIGHLIGHTS

The Hess Collection: Located in the mountains above Napa, this part gallery, part winery brings new meaning to the expression "the art of wine making" (page 41).

Frog's Leap Winery: Revel in the laid-back vibe at this organic winery. In addition to good wine, there's an organic garden, and it's one of the few places left in the valley where tasting is free (page 75).

Pride Mountain Vineyards: Straddling the Napa and Sonoma border, this mountain-top winery has some of the best views in the valley and some of the best mountain wines (page 93).

Culinary Institute of America: The West Coast's next star chefs are born inside this fortresslike former winery, and you can get a taste of their training at regular cooking demonstrations (page 95).

Bothe-Napa Valley State Park: Take a break and stroll back in time through the red-woods in this gem of a park (page 97).

Schramsberg Vineyards: If you plan to visit just one champagne cellar, why not make it the most historic one in the valley? Take a tour through the spooky cellars once visited by Robert Louis Stevenson (page 109).

Castello di Amorosa: Just down the road from the Victorian splendor of Schramsberg, step back even further in time and visit this astonishing replica of a medieval castle. They make wine here too (page 110).

Sharpsteen Museum: Learn about Calistoga's early days at this quirky little mu-seum. It's right next to one of the original cot-tages from the first-ever hot springs resort in the town (page 115).

LOOK FOR ◖ TO FIND RECOMMENDED SIGHTS, ACTIVITIES, DINING, AND LODGING.

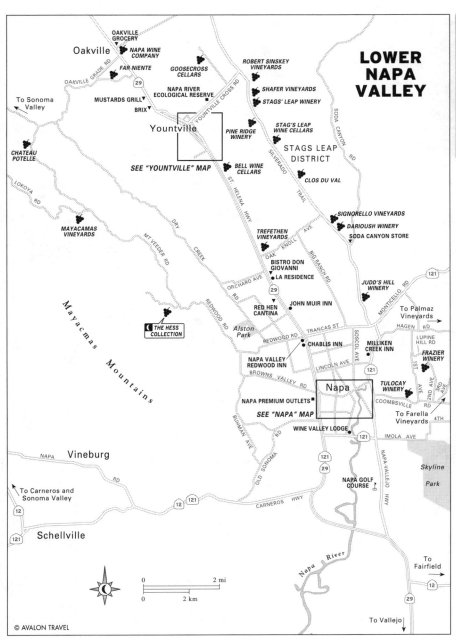

© AVALON TRAVEL

NAPA VALLEY

UPPER NAPA VALLEY

To Pope Valley Winery
and Hubcap Ranch

Angwin

HOWELL MOUNTAIN RD

CHILES POPE VALLEY RD

CATACULA LAKE WINERY

Howell
Mountain

HOWELL MTN RD

EHLERS
ESTATE

SPANISH
VILLA INN

Deer
Park

To Rust Ridge Winery
and B&B and Brown
Estate Winery

LODI LN

DEER PARK RD

SEE DETAIL

MEADOWOOD
NAPA VALLEY

0   2 mi

0   2 km

SEE
"ST. HELENA"
MAP

MAIN ST

St. Helena

CHILES POPE VALLEY RD

SPRING MOUNTAIN
VINEYARDS

SILVERADO TRAIL

RUTHERFORD
HILL WINERY

Lake Hennessey
City Recreational
Area

To Kuleto
Estate Winery

LOUIS M.
MARTINI
WINERY

AUBERGE
DU SOLEIL

Lake
Hennessey

PRAGER WINERY
& PORT WORKS

V. SATTUI WINERY

ZINFANDEL LN

SAGE CANYON RD

128

HALL WINES

DEAN &
DELUCA

CONN CREEK RD

INK HOUSE
B&B

FROG'S LEAP
WINERY

MUMM NAPA VALLEY

LONG MEADOW RANCH/
RUTHERFORD GARDENS

RANCHO
CAYMUS
INN

128

ZD WINES

BEAULIEU
VINEYARD

RUTHERFORD RD

CAYMUS
VINEYARDS

SILVERADO TRAIL

Rutherford

RUTHERFORD GRILL

ST. HELENA OLIVE OIL CO.

RUBICON ESTATE WINERY

29

PEJU PROVINCE WINERY

ST HELENA HWY

NICKEL & NICKEL

OPUS ONE

OAKVILLE CROSS RD

ROBERT MONDAVI WINERY

Oakville

© AVALON TRAVEL

no others in California, or probably anywhere else in the world.

It can all seem a bit like a giant wine theme park at times, especially when lining up at yet another ticket booth to empty your wallet for the privilege of being herded around another winery by guides who are probably as bored as they look. It's not a great stretch to imagine that one day there will be giant gates at either end of the valley where all-inclusive passes will be sold to the "Greatest Wine Show on Earth" (the Sonoma Valley would be the parking lot if some competitive types had their way).

But though many visitors flock lemming-like to the same big wineries, there are hundreds of others to choose from in the valley, big and small, glamorous and rustic. Such diversity is one of Napa Valley's big draws and the reason so many people keep coming back for more.

Art lovers could easily spend an entire vacation visiting the many wineries with art or sculpture displays. Photosensitive souls can hunt down all the wineries with cool, dark underground caves. Architecture buffs will have a field day at some of the more outlandish facilities with design influences in the valley ranging from medieval to avant-garde.

And that's before even considering wine itself. The valley is home to boutique wineries making just a few hundred cases of wine a year and to corporate behemoths turning out millions. The multitude of microclimates has given rise to a patchwork of 15 (and counting) distinct appellations, or AVAs, where just about every major type of grape can be grown. Although this is a red wine–lover's paradise, there's a wine made here for almost every palate.

The valley's diversity extends well beyond wine: At one end of the valley are the hot springs and spas of Calistoga, while Napa at the other end contains some big-city entertainment. In between, nature offers plenty of diversions from wine, and restaurants turn out delicacies that would put many in world capitals to shame.

The locals are remarkably sanguine about the endless stream of visitors clogging their valley. Clearly, they are wise enough not to discourage the hands that ultimately feed them. But they also get to experience the beauty and diversity of the valley, the quality of the food, and the strong sense of community when the rest of us have long since gone home.

And, of course, they get to toast their good fortune with some of the best wines in the world.

ORIENTATION

The Napa Valley, including Carneros, is roughly 35 miles long, with two main roads running up each side of the valley and about half a dozen roads traversing the 2–4 miles between them. As far as the world's major wine-making regions go, this is baby sized, so don't be intimidated.

Just north of Carneros is the city of **Napa** itself, the biggest settlement in the valley, home to many of the workers who keep the wine industry humming. The city was called Nappa City when it was laid out in grand style by Nathan Coombs in 1848 on a bend in the Napa River. The river connected the city to San Francisco and was pivotal to its rapid growth over the subsequent decades. It has also been pivotal to the city's ongoing modern revival since Napa embarked on the huge $300 million flood defense program after disastrous floods wiped out downtown businesses in the 1980s and 1990s and even as recently as December 2005.

It's not the most attractive city and has traditionally been bypassed by tourists speeding to the big-name wineries and trendy towns farther north, but Napa has been making more of an effort to cash in on its Victorian history, riverside setting, and namesake valley.

There are decades of neglect and terrible architecture to counter, however, and the downtown revitalization is definitely a work in progress, not helped by the 2009 recession that resulted in a new crop of empty storefronts, shuttered restaurants, and the bankruptcy of Napa's cultural shrine to wine and food, COPIA.

Napa also still lacks the compactness and style of other Wine Country destination towns like Sonoma, Healdsburg, or even St. Helena farther north. That is changing, however, as the city completes its massive flood-defense program and luxury hotels and condo developments sprout along the newly secured riverbanks. The Westin hotel chain opened a luxury hotel on the riverbank in 2009, and more hotels are on the way that will generate some much-needed tourist traffic and revenue. Even the Ritz-Carlton Company won approval in 2008 for a $200 million riverside resort development, although the recession has reportedly put that project on hold.

From Napa, the two main valley roads begin. The St. Helena Highway—more commonly known as Highway 29—is the well-beaten path up the valley. It passes the town of **Yountville,** dominated by increasingly upscale shops, restaurants, and hotels, then whistles past sleepy **Rutherford** before hitting what has become almost the spiritual heart of the valley, **St. Helena.** This is the town that all others in Wine Country aspire to be: pretty, upscale, full of boutiques and restaurants, yet still a fairly down-to-earth, functional place—except on those weekends when the world comes to visit and traffic slows to a crawl.

St. Helena and the surrounding big-name wineries are the main draw in this part of the valley, and rural tranquility quickly returns as Highway 29 continues north to the narrow top of the valley, where sleepy **Calistoga** has an almost frontier-town feel—seemingly torn between maintaining its slumber and being awakened by attracting more tourists to its up-and-coming wineries and famous volcanic hot springs.

Calistoga is also where the other main valley

NAPA'S SILLY-MONEY WINES

At the Napa Valley Wine Auction in 2008, six bottles of 1992 Screaming Eagle sold for $500,000. They were magnums, but that still works out to more than $40,000 per bottle or about $7,000 per glass. Granted, the auction is a charity event and therefore encourages big spending for a good cause, but there are probably no other wines that would be bid so high, whatever the occasion.

Make that *few* other wines. There were 10 magnums of Harlan Estate wine that sold for $340,000. And then there was an eight-magnum vertical of Bryant Family Vineyards wine that sold for $290,000 and six bottles plus one Methuselah (6 liters) of the latest vintage from Dalla Valle that went for a mere $200,000. Just those four lots illustrate the power of Napa's so-called cult wines to open the wallets of both serious collectors and those simply with more money than they know what to do with.

The cult wine phenomenon started in the early 1990s and reached a crescendo during the dot-com boom years, when a lot of people really did have more money than they knew what to do with. They bought the beautifully made, limited-production Napa Valley cabernets, like those from Screaming Eagle and Harlan Estate, probably as much to gain the cachet of owning something so rare as to resell for a profit a few years later. As with any rare commodity, lots of bidders will push up the price.

The dot-com bubble burst, but the cult wine bubble never really did. Retailers report that sales of such silly-money wines remain as solid as their prices. There's no doubting that they are good wines, made by some of the best winemakers and sourced from some of the best vineyards. Whether they're worth hundreds of dollars or more is a question often asked – though it's ultimately irrelevant, because there are plenty of people still willing to pay and to wait years to get on the exclusive mailing lists to even get a chance to pay.

A little more troubling is that the term "cult wine" is now bandied about a little too casually. It is commonly used as a marketing tool or for bragging rights, so it's no surprise that calling even the Screaming Eagles of the world a cult wine these days is as likely to elicit a roll of the eyes as an opening of the wallet.

road, the Silverado Trail, ends. Named for a silver mine that it once served north of Calistoga, it runs from Napa along the foot of the eastern hills and is the shortcut used to get up and down the valley by locals in the summer when the other side of the valley is clogged. Anyone in a hurry to get to a spa appointment in Calistoga or a restaurant in Napa should consider cutting across the valley to the Silverado Trail if there is heavy traffic on Highway 29.

This undulating, winding two-lane road remains almost eerily quiet at times and feels like it's in another valley altogether. It's a road along which smaller wineries turn out some of the best wines in the valley, with little of the hoopla of the big showoffs farther west. It's also a road down which serious wine lovers might prefer to travel, sampling famous cabernet sauvignons in the Stags Leap or Rutherford appellations before heading up into the hills to some hidden gems on Howell Mountain or in the rural Chiles Valley.

Napa Valley Wines

The Napa Valley probably has more microclimates and soil types along its 35-mile length than any other valley in the Wine Country. The climates and the soils drew the attention of wine-loving European settlers in the 1800s, and the seeds of the modern day wine industry were sown.

As you drive from the city of Napa north to Calistoga in the middle of summer, the temperature can rise by up to 20 degrees. Although the northern end of the valley is significantly hotter than the southern end, throughout the length of the valley there are dozens of unique microclimates created by small hills on the valley floor as well as the canyons and slopes of the mountains that define its eastern and western sides.

In addition, geologists have identified a staggering 33 different types of soil in the valley, laid down over millions of years by volcanoes, rivers, and the earth's shifting crust. The combined soils and microclimates create a patchwork of growing conditions that could keep winemakers happy for centuries more, and that

is why there are so many distinct, recognized growing regions within the Napa Valley.

The Napa Valley north of Carneros is predominantly a red wine–growing region, thanks primarily to a warm climate that ensures the most popular red grape varietals can easily ripen and attain the sugar levels needed to make the big, powerful wines for which the valley is known. White grapes and some red varietals like pinot noir can get by in cooler climates because they generally reach their desired ripeness more easily while retaining high enough acid levels desired by winemakers.

The one red grape for which Napa is most famous is cabernet sauvignon. There were about 45,000 acres of vineyards planted in Napa County in 2008, about three-quarters of which were planted with red grape varietals, according to the U.S. Department of Agriculture. Just over half that red grape acreage was cabernet, which means that one varietal accounts for 40 percent of all the vineyards in Napa County (about 19,000 acres). The figure is probably closer to 50 percent of all the vineyards in the Napa Valley north of Carneros, where pinot noir and chardonnay are the more dominant varietals.

That's not to say that other wines are not important here; far from it. The Napa Valley is where some of California's most distinctive chardonnay and sauvignon blanc are produced, together with increasing amounts of syrah, sangiovese, and many other minor varietals. But cabernet always has dominated the vineyards and probably always will, with chardonnay a distant second in terms of vineyard acreage, followed closely by merlot.

Most of the big Napa Valley wineries own vineyards all over the valley. They and smaller wineries also often buy fruit from other growers outside Napa Valley, so white wine drinkers need not despair—there will usually be plenty of whites on offer, even at wineries in the big-cab appellations like Rutherford and Stags Leap. But ultimately this is a valley dominated by cabernet and chardonnay, and those looking for more unusual types of wine will want to choose the wineries they visit carefully.

PLANNING YOUR TIME

So how can visitors make sense of all those wineries and avoid all the crowds? It's a $10,000 question with about 10,000 different answers. Many visitors seem to follow a similar pattern, never making it much farther north than St. Helena and sticking to the western side of the valley. If you can avoid that pattern, you're halfway to lowering your blood pressure.

The other key to enjoying the valley rather than being frustrated by it is plenty of planning. There's so much to do and so many wineries to visit that anyone simply turning up without a plan, however vague, will end up with a headache even before drinking too much wine in the sun. Visitors can get away with no preplanning in many other parts of Wine Country, but not in such a tourist mecca as the Napa Valley.

Research the type of wine that wineries specialize in before choosing which to visit, especially if you're not a big red wine drinker. This is, after all, the land of endless cabernet sauvignon, but it is also a land where plenty of stunning white wines, including champagne, are made. And if you are a big cabernet drinker, this can be the place to learn much more about the king of wines—how and why a Spring Mountain cabernet is different from a Stags Leap cabernet, for example.

Alternatively, pick a theme not related to wine for a day of touring. Wineries in Napa have necessarily become adept at distinguishing themselves from their competitors to try to attract increasingly jaded visitors, a form of Wine Country evolution. Some rely on the reputation of their wines, others on art, caves, car collections, architecture, gardens, tours, caves, history—the list is almost endless and provides endless employment opportunities for marketing folks.

When the crowds or choices get to be too much, simply head for the hills, where healthy doses of nature help make the hidden wineries in the Mount Veeder, Spring Mountain, and Chiles Valley appellations that much more enjoyable. Even the sleepy Coombsville area right outside the city of Napa has plenty to offer wine lovers.

If possible, avoid the peak season that runs roughly July–October. It brings peak crowds, particularly on weekends; peak hotel prices; and peak daytime temperatures. April–June is perhaps the best time to visit, when the wet winter season is finally drying out, the temperatures mild, the creeks flowing, the hills green, and the vineyards full of vivid yellow wild mustard.

TOURS

One way to visit wineries without having to worry about traffic, drinking, or cooking an expensive wine in a sun-baked car is to take a daylong organized wine tour. Someone else does the driving, you can drink until you can no longer stand, and any precious wine purchases will get transported back to your hotel probably in better shape than you.

Another advantage is that the local tour guides are knowledgeable about the valley, the wineries, and often about wines as well, making an organized tour an option worth considering if you have no idea where to start.

There are two tour companies, each offering different experiences. The **Napa Winery Shuttle** (707/257-1950, www.wineshuttle. com) is basically a hop-on, hop-off minibus that picks up at any of a long list of local hotels at about 10 A.M. (though they can often pick up at any hotel not on the list) and runs among 10 wineries between Oakville and St. Helena, plus a couple of Yountville restaurants for those who want a sit-down lunch. Those wineries represent a good cross section of the valley and include a handful of smaller producers, a champagne house, and some of the big names, including Mondavi, Niebaum-Coppola, and Beaulieu Vineyard. Visit as many or as few as you like during the day for $75 per person.

Beau Wine Tours (707/257-0887 or 800/387-2328, www.beauwinetours.com) is more of a custom touring company and is often the owner of the limos seen parked at some of the bigger wineries. Rent a chauffeured car, SUV, or limousine for 3–14 people for $55–135 an hour plus tax, tip, and (depending on gas prices) a fuel surcharge, and plan your own itinerary. Note that the size of the stretch limos and vans means they sometimes cannot visit smaller wineries at all, or only by prior arrangement. Beau Wine Tours has plenty of knowledge of the valley, however, and can offer lots of advice. It also offers private, preplanned, daylong tours starting and finishing in either the Napa Valley or San Francisco from $99.

Napa Valley Wine Train

The age of the steam trains that first brought the masses to the valley's Victorian spas and early wineries has long gone, but a modest reminder remains in the Napa Valley Wine Train (1275 McKinstry St., Napa, 707/253-2111 or 800/427-4124, www.winetrain.com). It has been kept alive by providing what the valley does best—good food and wine. The train runs 20 miles from downtown Napa up to St. Helena and back, and reservations are essential.

The idea of being cooped up on a glorious fall day watching the vineyards and wineries through the windows of a restored Pullman rail car might not seem appealing, but it's better than it sounds. The only problem is that it eats into your day. Think of it as taking a four-hour lunch or dinner at a gourmet, if slightly unusual, restaurant with entertainment often thrown in for free. The food is beautifully prepared, the wine first-class, and the restaurant dripping with brass and mahogany. There are no comparisons to Amtrak here.

Lunch and dinner trips are offered daily, as well as a brunch excursion on weekends. The basic fare of $50 gets you on the train, but food is extra. Those additional rates range from $45 for the Gourmet Express lunch menu up to $75 for a four-course dinner with specially paired wines, with plenty of dining options in between. In reviving the old rail cars, the Wine Train also revived the old railroad class system too—each car caters to a different class of diner, so you won't be jealously eyeing your neighbor's five-course spread when you've already polished off your three courses.

GETTING THERE

There were far more ways to get to the Napa Valley a century ago, when trains and riverboats

Wine, dine, and see the valley on the Wine Train.

© PHILIP GOLDSMITH

brought the visitors and goods that made the valley so successful. The car has long since become the main transportation mode, though the more adventurous can still get here on public transportation.

By Car

The Napa Valley is almost the same driving distance from three major international airports—Oakland, San Francisco, and Sacramento. Driving from the airports to the city of Napa itself will take 1–2 hours, depending on traffic; from downtown San Francisco or Oakland, it's closer to an hour of driving time.

The most direct route from Oakland and Sacramento is on I-80 (west from Sacramento, east from Oakland). Exit at Marine World Parkway (Highway 37), then take Highway 29 north into Napa and beyond. From Sacramento, a slightly more direct route is to exit at Jameson Canyon Road (U.S. 12), a little farther north of American Canyon. This also heads west and meets Highway 29 at the Napa airport.

From the San Francisco airport and city (especially downtown), it takes about the same amount of time to drive across the Bay Bridge to I-80 and north to Napa as it does to go the prettier route through Marin. This route crosses the Golden Gate Bridge on U.S. 101 to Marin County, past Novato, then west on Highway 37, which links with U.S. 121 through Carneros, past the turnoff to the Sonoma Valley, and eventually to Highway 29 just south of Napa.

The Napa Valley is also easily accessible from other parts of the Wine Country, thanks to the numerous roads that cross the Mayacamas Mountains down the western side of the valley.

From the Sonoma Valley, just north of Glen Ellen, Trinity Road winds its way east into the mountains, becoming Dry Creek Road in the Mount Veeder appellation, before coming down into the Napa Valley to Oakville as the Oakville Grade. Farther north in the Sonoma Valley, just east of Santa Rosa, Calistoga Road heads to the hills and eventually to Calistoga,

or you can turn off on St. Helena Road after about three miles to cross into the Napa Valley down through the Spring Mountain appellation and into St. Helena.

From the Russian River Valley, just north of Santa Rosa, take Mark West Springs Road east, eventually turning onto Porter Creek Road, which leads down into Calistoga. And from the Alexander Valley, U.S. 128 runs south through Knights Valley to Calistoga.

Try not to be in a rush if you take these routes, because they are narrow, winding, and slow, but a lot of fun if time is not of the essence.

By Boat and Bus

The most unusual way to get to the valley without driving, short of an epic bicycle ride, is on the **Baylink Ferry** from San Francisco via Vallejo. The speedy catamarans leave San Francisco's Ferry Building about every hour 7 A.M.–10 P.M. during the week and every couple of hours 9 A.M.–10 P.M. on weekends for the 55-minute crossing to Vallejo, which is about 12 miles south of Napa. The one-way fare is $13. For a detailed seasonal schedule, contact Baylink Ferries (707/643-3779 or 877/643-3779, www.baylinkferry.com).

From the Vallejo ferry terminal, route 10 of Napa Valley's **VINE** bus service runs directly to downtown Napa about every hour until 8 P.M. during the week, every two hours until 6:50 P.M. on Saturday, and just four times a day on Sunday, with the first bus leaving at 10:15 A.M. and the last at 5:30 P.M. It's about a 65-minute journey to Napa (except for a few times of the day when the bus makes stops) and is a bargain at $2.15. Route 10 also continues to the valley through Yountville and St. Helena to Calistoga; check the schedule for details on this route. For more information on schedules and routes contact VINE (707/255-7631 or 800/696-6443, www.napavalleyvine.net).

Taking the ferry and bus to the valley and then renting a bike in downtown Napa, St. Helena, or Calistoga for a couple of days would certainly make for a memorable Wine Country experience, but it might not be for the impatient.

GETTING AROUND
By Car

Seemingly everyone drives to the Napa Valley, so you'd think everything would be geared up for the cars transporting those 5 million annual visitors to this part of the world. Wrong! This is essentially agricultural land that its custodians battle to protect, so the mighty vine and strict planning laws limit a lot of development—including, evidently, road widening.

The 28-mile drive from Napa to Calistoga up Highway 29 can take less than 45 minutes in the middle of a winter day. Try that same drive on a summer weekend or a weekday during the evening rush hour and it might take close to double that. The sheer volume of traffic is really what slows things down, especially with so much traffic coming and going from the multitude of wineries and the traffic bottleneck of St Helena's Main Street.

Heading north on Highway 29, you can be lulled into a false sense of security as you zip towards St. Helena, only to hit a wall of traffic about a mile south of the town caused by traffic lights that seem to meter only a dozen cars at a time onto Main Street. Heading south from St. Helena from mid-afternoon until evening on many days, your average speed is likely to be less than 20 mph until well after Rutherford. The mid-valley traffic situation is not helped by the countless turnoffs for wineries from Rutherford to St. Helena that also slow traffic. Make your life easier and use the empty center lane of the road to turn left into wineries or when turning left out of wineries to merge into traffic. That's what it's there for.

The almost constant traffic jams on Highway 29 are also a reason to discover the Silverado Trail, running north–south on the other side of the valley. There might be the occasional slowdown caused by a valley visitor unfamiliar with its dips and bends or who is simply lost. Usually, however, this is the domain of merciless local speed demons zipping up and down the valley at 60 mph, a feat usually possible even when the road through St. Helena across the valley is at a standstill. Many locals will use the Silverado to bypass St. Helena altogether, cutting back to Highway 29 when necessary using one of the many small cross-valley roads.

Napa is the only city in the valley to have made an effort to ease traffic flows, with its brief stretch of smooth-flowing freeway and frustrating yet effective one-way system downtown. The irony, of course, is that so many valley visitors bypass the city for destinations up-valley, so traffic is usually light anyway.

By Bike

Picking the right route at the right time of the day and exploring a section of the valley by bike can be one of the most enjoyable ways to experience the Wine Country. Whether you plan a long bike ride up the Silverado Trail or a short hop around a handful of Rutherford-area wineries, there are a handful of established places to rent well-maintained bicycles in St. Helena, Calistoga and Napa. All know the area from a biker's perspective and so will have plenty of suggestions on routes from easy rides of a few miles to epic loops through some of the best mountain appellations. Helmets, locks, bottle cages, and puncture repair kits are always included with rentals. It's also worth asking about free roadside assistance should you get a flat.

St. Helena Cyclery (116 Main St., St. Helena, 707/963-7736, www.sthelenacyclery.com, 9:30 A.M.–5:30 P.M. Mon.–Sat., 10 A.M.–5 P.M. Sun.) rents basic hybrid bikes for $10 per hour or $35 per day and more advanced road bikes from $65 per day but only takes reservations for groups of 10 or more wanting road bikes. Check the website for coupons and other specials. **Calistoga Bike Shop** (1318 Lincoln Ave., Calistoga, 707/942-9687 or 866/942-2453, www.calistogabikeshop.com, 10 A.M.–6 P.M. daily) does take reservations and rents hybrids for $35 per day and both road and mountain bikes from $45 per day. **Napa River Velo** (680 Main St., Napa, 707/258-8729, www.naparivervelo.com, 10 A.M.–6 P.M. Mon.–Sat., 10 A.M.–5 P.M. Sun.) is on the river side of the new Riverside Plaza development near the Napa Mill and rents bikes in the city of Napa for $35–75 per day, depending on whether you want a basic hybrid or a fancy road or mountain bike. Also in the city of Napa, Napa Valley Bike Tours (6795 Washington St., Building B, Yountville, 800/707-2453, www.napavalleybiketours.com) offers rentals by the day along with its all-inclusive tours and might also drop off and pick up its bikes at your hotel.

Touring on a bike is easy in almost every part of the valley thanks to the flat landscape (on the valley floor, at least) and the proximity of all the wineries. The only place you might want to avoid is the stretch of Highway 29 between Oakville and St. Helena, which is the scene of regular car accidents—probably caused by inattentive, lost, or simply drunk visitors. It's also such a busy stretch of road that you might not want the hassle of car-dodging anyway.

The best stretches of valley to explore on a bike include the Silverado Trail in the Stags Leap District, where big-name wineries like Clos du Val, Pine Ridge, Shafer, Stag's Leap, and Robert Sinskey are all along a three-mile stretch of winding road. Just beware the speed demons on the Trail. Other easy rides include many of the cross-valley roads, which sometimes have fewer wineries per mile but also have far less traffic. Biking the Rutherford Road from Highway 29 to the Silverado Trail, for example, takes in Beaulieu, Frog's Leap, and Caymus. Then a few hundred yards down the Silverado Trail are Mumm and ZD.

The Coombsville area east of the city of Napa is also worth exploring on bike, not only because it has relatively quiet and flat roads but also because of its proximity to the hotels and amenities of the city. You could leave your hotel after breakfast, visit a couple of small wineries and have a relaxing picnic, then be back in Napa by mid-afternoon.

A couple of companies can do all the work and planning for your bike tour. All you need to do is show up and pedal. To plan an entire vacation centered around biking in the valley, try **Getaway Adventures** (2228 Northpoint Pkwy., Santa Rosa, 707/568-3040 or 800/499-2453, www.getawayadventures.com), which offers day, weekend, and weeklong all-inclusive packages, including hotel, meals, bike, tour guide, and shuttle van. Weekend packages are $899–1,000, and 4–6-day packages run $1,299–2,499, with prices depending on both luxury and the number of days. Tours are usually offered once a month and take in the Napa Valley and parts of northern Sonoma. The day trips cost $149 and include the bike, helmet, water, lunch, and a guided tour of about five wineries in the Calistoga area.

Napa Valley Bike Tours (6795 Washington St., Building B, Yountville, 800/707-2453, www.napavalleybiketours.com), based at the other end of the valley, offers three- and four-day all-inclusive packages that stay within Napa Valley. The two-night, three-day Romantic Getaway packages are $705–840, depending on accommodations and time of the week (weekends are more expensive), and the longer packages start at $800. Day tours are also offered at $139–149 for the day, lunch and group tour guide included. If the sight of all the lovely straight rows of vines snaking up and down hills with pristine dirt between them appeals to your inner mountain biker, there's even a day trip offered that takes you biking through the vineyards of Bouchaine Winery in Carneros for $150. Plain old bike rentals to go it alone start at $24 for two hours or $35 per day for hybrids. The company also offers free delivery and pickup of two or more bikes to hotels and B&Bs south of St. Helena.

NAPA VALLEY

Napa and Vicinity

Many people bypass Napa, heading up to the middle of the valley to start their wine-tasting day, but there's plenty happening this far south as well. Napa is chock-full of tasting rooms, and the city is bordered by one of the best mountain appellations in the valley as well as the newest valley appellation, both home to historic and modern wineries, small and large.

Just north of the city of Napa is one of the newest of the Napa Valley's 14 appellations, **Oak Knoll.** As in the Yountville appellation farther north, the climate is a blend of the cooler weather in Carneros, south of Napa, and the hotter mid-valley temperatures. Just about every major grape varietal is grown here, though the appellation is probably best known for whites such as chardonnay and sauvignon blanc. Being such a new appellation it does not yet have much name recognition, so don't expect to see many wines with Oak Knoll identified on the label.

West of the Oak Knoll appellation is the **Mount Veeder** appellation, stretching all the way from Napa up the middle of the valley on the slopes of the Mayacamas Mountains to the highest ridges and the Sonoma County line. Compared to Spring Mountain and Diamond Mountain subappellations further north on the slopes of the same mountain range, Mount Veeder wines have a leaner, more mineral edge to them. The thin volcanic soils provide little nourishment for the struggling vines, and the region is far enough south to feel the cooling effects of the bay. The conditions result in elegant, age-worthy cabernets with good acidity and an earthiness lacking from mountain appellations farther north. Syrah and zinfandel are also grown on the mountain slopes and produce wines with a distinct sense of place.

Just a few miles east of the city itself, meanwhile, is an area that could become the next official AVA in the valley—Coombsville. Small in terms of vineyard acreage (under 1,000 acres) and the number of wineries, it is nevertheless starting to turn out some noteworthy wines as distinct as any in the valley thanks to a patchwork of different soils and microclimates, from sun-soaked hillsides to cool, breezy lowlands. It is an ideal place to grow both bordeaux varietals as well as cooler-climate varietals like pinot noir and riesling. The cabernets and merlots made have a more restrained, Old World style than those from warmer up-valley vineyards, so lovers of big, burly Napa Valley wines might be disappointed.

TASTING ROOMS IN NAPA

You could spend a whole day, or even two, sampling wines from the dozen tasting rooms in the city of Napa itself—a process that's made a lot cheaper with the **Taste Napa Downtown wine-tasting card.** Available at any of the 10 participating tasting rooms and shops, the card costs only $20 and is valid at all the bigger tasting rooms and many stores that offer wine tasting, including JV Wine, Bounty Hunter, and the Napa General Store—and gets you initial tastes for only $0.10.

Without the card, tasting prices range from a couple of dollars up to $25 at the larger collectives (though you can keep the quality Riedel tasting glass at the Vintner's Collective). The three main tasting rooms are the only places to taste the wine of some of the valley's smallest wineries, and the winemakers themselves will sometimes be pouring the wines on weekends.

One of the most central participating tasting venues is the café-style **Wineries of Napa Valley** (1285 Napa Town Center, 707/253-9450 or 800/328-7815, www.napavintages.com, 11 A.M.–6 P.M. Mon.–Thurs., 10 A.M.–7:30 P.M. Fri.–Sat., 10 A.M.–6 P.M. Sun.) in the Napa Town Center shopping mall on 1st Street. Managed by Goosecross Cellars, it is also the outpost of a half-dozen other small valley producers, including Burgess Cellars and Ilona, both of which make some good wines from the Howell Mountain appellation. You

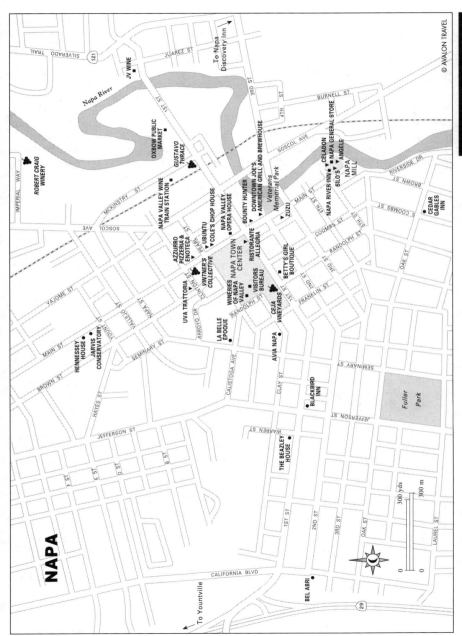

NAPA VALLEY

© AVALON TRAVEL

NAPA

SILVERADO TRAIL

121

JV WINE

JUAREZ ST

To Napa Discovery Inn

Napa River

3RD ST

BURNELL ST

4TH ST

OXBOW PUBLIC MARKET

GUSTAVO THRACE

SOSCOL AVE

Veterans Memorial Park

CELADON
NAPA GENERAL STORE
NAPA RIVER INN
SILO'S
ANGÈLE
NAPA MILL

RIVERSIDE DR

BROWN ST

ROBERT CRAIG WINERY

IMPERIAL WAY

McKINSTRY ST

NAPA VALLEY WINE TRAIN STATION

COLE'S CHOP HOUSE

UBUNTU

NAPA VALLEY OPERA HOUSE

BOUNTY HUNTER

DOWNTOWN JOE'S AMERICAN GRILL AND BREWHOUSE

ZUZU

MAIN ST

1ST ST

S COOMBS ST

CEDAR GABLES INN

SOSCOL AVE

AZZURRO PIZZERIA & ENOTECA

VINTNER'S COLLECTIVE

PEARL ST

CLINTON ST

RISTORANTE ALLEGRIA

NAPA VALLEY TOWN CENTER

BETTY'S GIRL BOUTIQUE

COOMBS ST

RANDOLPH ST

OAK ST

UVA TRATTORIA

WINERIES OF NAPA VALLEY

VISITORS BUREAU

CEJA VINEYARDS

FRANKLIN ST

3RD ST

YAJOME ST

VALLEJO ST

NAPA ST

COOMBS ST

ARROYO DR

RANDOLPH ST

LA BELLE ÉPOQUE

AVIA NAPA

CLAY ST

BLACKBIRD INN

SEMINARY ST

HENNESSEY HOUSE

JARVIS CONSERVATORY

SEMINARY ST

CALISTOGA AVE

Fuller Park

MAIN ST

BROWN ST

HAYES ST

JEFFERSON ST

WARREN ST

THE BEAZLEY HOUSE

JEFFERSON ST

E ST

D ST

B ST

300 yds
300 m

1ST ST

2ND ST

3RD ST

OAK ST

LAUREL ST

CALIFORNIA BLVD

BEL ABRI

To Yountville

29

can also buy wine by the glass here and take advantage of the free wireless Internet access.

A stone's throw away is Napa's newest downtown tasting room, the public outpost of Carneros-based **Ceja Vineyards** (1248 1st St., 707/226-6445, www.cejavineyards.com, noon–6 P.M. Sun.–Fri., noon–11 P.M. Sat.). The large space is part wine-tasting bar and part art and entertainment venue, featuring a rotating display of works from local Hispanic artists and free salsa lessons on Saturday evenings. Both reflect the Mexican roots of the Ceja family, the eldest generation of which epitomized the American dream as children of immigrant farm workers who worked their way to becoming vineyard owners and finally winery owners in less than three decades. At least one member of the extended Ceja family is likely to be behind the bar to tell the story. Ceja makes only 5,000 cases of wine a year, but all the major varietals are represented from Ceja's cool-climate vineyards in Carneros and further west near Petaluma. The Carneros Chardonnay and Pinot Noir, along with the bargain-priced red blend Vino de Casa, are among the standouts. The white house blend has the flavor and price to be a great summer picnic wine. If you're looking for a Saturday night of entertainment, have an early dinner and head over to Ceja for happy hour (5.30–7:30 P.M.). A few glasses of wine will quickly remove your inhibitions for the salsa and free-style dancing to follow.

Just across McKinstry Street from the Oxbow Public Market is the spacious tasting room of **GustavoThrace** (1021 McKinstry St., 707/257-6796, www.gustavothrace.com, 11 A.M.–5:30 P.M. daily), another boutique Napa Valley winery established in the 1990s by Mexican American winemaker Gustavo Brambila, a Napa Valley wine veteran who started his storied career as the Chateau Montelena assistant winemaker in the 1970s, and his business partner, Thrace Bromberger. If you're lucky, at least one of them is likely to be in the tasting room to recommend some wines to taste and places to visit. If not, you can't go wrong with any of the cabernets, the spicy barbera, the powerful petite sirah, or the clean and crisp sauvignon blanc. Also check out the two proprietary red blends, Tessera and the bargain-priced 3rd Bottle.

The biggest tasting room is the **Vintner's Collective** in the historic stone Pfeiffer Building (1245 Main St. at Clinton St., 707/255-7150, www.vintnerscollective.com, 11 A.M.–6 P.M. daily, tasting $25). A house of ill repute during its Victorian youth, it is now the public face of 15 different wineries and winemakers, most notably the zinfandel specialist D-Cubed; Gregory Graham, a winemaker with a résumé that reads like a who's who of Napa wineries; the pinot noir specialist Ancien Wines; and the single-vineyard wines of Chiarello Family Vineyards, founded by the chef behind St. Helena's Tra Vigne restaurant. The regular tasting includes a flight of five wines, while the more expensive tasting adds four more-expensive wines. Parking is free, although limited.

Fans of mountain-grown cabernet sauvignon should make an appointment for a tasting at **Robert Craig Winery** (625 Imperial Way, 707/252-2250, www.robertcraigwine.com, 10 A.M.–4:30 P.M. Mon.–Sat., tasting $20), which is a little off the beaten path in Napa yet still only a short drive (or long walk) from the Oxbow Market or downtown area. Craig got his start in the wine industry by buying a vineyard on nearby Mount Veeder in the late 1970s (it was later bought by Donald Hess, founder of the Hess Collection), and since those early days his focus has been on mountain-grown cabernets. Tasting Robert Craig wines from Mount Veeder, Howell Mountain, and Spring Mountain alongside the more approachable Affinity proprietary blend sourced from lower-elevation vineyards illustrates the astounding difference in characteristics that each mountain appellation creates—differences that are more obvious than those between cabernets from different valley floor appellations, for example. Mountain-grown cabernets are not for the faint-hearted, and the wines aren't cheap, but even at $50–70 per bottle, any cabernet lover would be hard-pressed not to leave with at least one.

COOMBSVILLE WINERIES

The rolling hills and country lanes to the east of the city of Napa are home to an increasing number of small wineries that coexist alongside horse farms, sheep pasture, and the giant Napa Valley Country Club. In a valley of big wineries and big traffic jams, exploring this area by car or on a bike is a welcome respite from the more hectic parts of the valley. Due to local planning codes, all the wineries in this area require an appointment.

Frazier Winery

At the end of a small paved road nestled among rolling hills, Frazier (70 Rapp Ln., Napa, 707/255-3444, www.frazierwinery.com, tours by appointment 10 A.M.–4 P.M. Mon.–Sat.) is one of the larger wineries in this area yet is still small by Napa Valley standards. It makes about 3,000 cases of mainly cabernet sauvignon and merlot that consistently seem to receive good ratings from the major wine magazines and are worth a visit to Coombsville to try.

Founder and former airline pilot Bill Frazier moved here in the early 1980s and by the end of the decade had caught the wine bug and planted merlot and cabernet on his small estate, becoming a pioneer in this cooler part of the valley, which had yet to become a major wine-producing area, let alone a place where cabernet was grown. After selling the grapes for a few years, the estate vineyard was expanded and Frazier started to make his own wine at customer crush facilities before converting an old barn on the estate into his own winery in 2000. The winery remains very much a family affair with several of Bill's children helping run the operation today. You're more than likely to have a Frazier as your tour guide if you visit.

The flagship wine is a powerful and complex reserve cabernet sauvignon called Memento that is made in very limited quantities and only in the best vintages. It has been favorably compared to some of the top cult cabernets in the valley, although at over $100 per bottle it might not be in everyone's price range. The equally intense nonreserve cabernet wins almost as much acclaim and is half the price.

The merlot has a lot in common with merlots from Carneros, having more subtle and earthy characteristics compared to some of the fruit bombs made up-valley. All three can usually be tasted from either bottle or barrel, accompanied by cheeses and chocolate, on the appointment-only tour of the winery and caves.

The slightly cheaper Lupine Hill label cabernet and merlot accounts for about half the winery's output and is made from the juice deemed not quite good enough for the Frazier label. The style is a little more fruit-forward and approachable, and the price is more palatable. There are no white wines made here, although Frazier recently planted a new vineyard to chardonnay, so expect that to be added to the portfolio in the coming years.

Farella Vineyard

Tom Farella has been a grape grower in this part of the Napa Valley for decades, so to say he knows Coombsville fruit well is perhaps an understatement. He still sells most of his estate fruit to other wineries, but also makes about 1,200 cases of his own wines a year under the Farella and Farella-Park labels, with a more varied portfolio than many small producers. The small winery (4111 Redwood Rd., Napa, 707/255-1144, www.hesscollection.com, by appointment 10 A.M.–5:30 P.M. daily, tasting $10 Mon.–Fri., $10–30 weekends) is nestled in the trees at the end of a long driveway cutting through the vineyards and, depending on the time of year, Tom's personalized tour might involve a walk through the vineyards or a tasting of some barrel samples.

Very reasonably priced estate cabernet sauvignon, merlot, and syrah account for about half the production here, but the standouts are the 19 Block Cuvee ($36) and 2008 Sauvignon Blanc ($19).

Palmaz Vineyards

With a 100,000-square-foot four-story cave system extending underground and complete with its own elevators and a computerized carousel of giant fermentation tanks, this winery could be in a James Bond movie. It's actually the home of Palmaz Vineyards (4029 Hagen Rd., Napa, 707/226-5587, www.palmazvineyards.com, tours and tasting by appointment only, $60) and was hailed as an architectural and engineering marvel when it was completed in 2009 after a reported eight years of construction costing $20 million. This is not just a wine aging cave like so many others in the Napa Valley; it's a huge gravity-flow winery facility built entirely underground with its own water treatment plant and the world's largest reinforced underground structure at its center. Only in the Napa Valley could you have a reproduction of a medieval castle at one end of the valley and an underground castle at the other.

In 1997 the Palmaz family bought the historic Cedar Knoll Winery, founded by Henry Hagen in 1881 but abandoned since Prohibition, and began work on creating a modern winery operation funded by the sale of the lifesaving coronary stent technology developed by Dr. Julio Palmaz during his long medical research career. Estate vineyards were replanted, and plans were drawn up to build the underground winery, taking advantage of the cool temperatures underground and the less stringent planning rules for caves in Napa County.

The resulting structure is certainly impressive. The wines are also pretty impressive, and most can be tasted as part of the pricey, appointment-only tour that takes place with a family member and includes small bites of gourmet food to pair with the wines. Book well in advance because every tour is private, so only a handful of visitors can visit each week.

About 7,000 cases of wine are made here each year (although the winery has a far larger capacity). Most is cabernet sauvignon that costs upwards of $100 per bottle. Typical of Coombsville cabernets, it is a more Old World style with more elegance and less sheer power than cabernets from elsewhere in the Napa Valley. A very Burgundian style of chardonnay is also made here with less buttery oak and more crispness than many in Napa Valley. If you're lucky, you might also get to taste the very limited production riesling, sourced from a cool spot in the nearby Oak Knoll district, and the wonderfully aromatic Muscat Canelli dessert wine.

Tulocay Winery

Bill Cadman has been making wines in this part of the world under the Tulocay label since 1975 and previously worked at some of the biggest wineries in the valley, making him one of the Napa Valley's modern pioneers and his winery the oldest in Coombsville. Yet he still manages to fly under the radar in this valley of superstar winemakers and super egos, quietly going about his business making a few hundred cases each of chardonnay, cabernet sauvignon, syrah, and pinot noir from locally grown grapes as well as a big, bold merlot and monster zinfandel from further afield in the Sierra foothills. This is a refreshingly down-home winery operation.

Tulocay (1426 Coombsville Rd., Napa, 707/255-4064, www.tulocay.com, tasting by appointment) is perhaps best known for its elegant, age-worthy pinot noir and both a traditional (for Napa, at least) barrel-fermented chardonnay and a unoaked, stainless steel fermented version. Both are sourced from the nearby Haynes vineyard. Bill also makes two cabernets, one from the nearby Rancho Sarco vineyard and one a blend from vineyards further up-valley. Taste both with him under the oak trees at his tasting table and you'll better understand what makes this part of the Napa Valley such a unique spot for growing cabernet. You'll also likely hear plenty of local history and gossip.

Bill's more recent claim to fame has been as a spoiler to attempts by local wineries to have the area designated an AVA called Tulocay, a name that is derived from an 8,000-acre parcel of land called Rancho Tulocay that was granted to a local land manager by the Mexican government in 1841 (Tulocay is said to have been a Native American word for "red clay earth"). Cadman's use of the Tulocay label for his wines made from grapes outside the region would have fallen foul of labeling laws if the AVA was granted, and that conflict caused the federal government to scrap the application in 2008. Local wineries have since reapplied to have the area designated an AVA under the Coombsville name instead.

OAK KNOLL AREA WINERIES
Judd's Hill

With the founder of Whitehall Lane Winery behind the scenes and a novel business plan, this small winery at the southern end of the Silverado Trail is beginning to make a big reputation. Judd's Hill (2332 Silverado Trail, Napa, 707/255-2332, www.juddshill. com, 10 A.M.–4 P.M. daily, appointments recommended) is named for Judd Finkelstein, the ukulele-playing son of Art Finkelstein, who was one of the founding partners of St. Helena's Whitehall Lane Winery. After selling the Whitehall business in the late 1980s, Art established Judd's Hill, and it has since become a thoroughly family affair. His wife, Bunnie, together with Judd and his wife, Holly, all take active roles, with Art and Judd the resident winemakers.

Only 3,000 cases of wine are made here, but the portfolio has grown rapidly in recent years. An approachable, complex cabernet sauvignon remains the mainstay and accounts for about half the production and many rave reviews. The flagship wine is a cabernet sourced from the hillside estate vineyards and exhibiting dusty tannins and a long finish. A few hundred cases of a rich, juicy petite sirah from Lodi-area vineyards are produced, along with a rustic Napa Valley syrah and a light, elegant pinot noir from the vineyards around the winery. Judd's Hill also makes a proprietary red blend called Magic, so named because Judd not only works his magic on wines and the ukulele but also on audiences as an amateur magician.

Tasting at the small modern visitors center, completed in 2006, gives a chance to talk to the winemaker about the wines and learn more about the other side of the business. As well as a producer of its own wines, Judd's Hill is also a micro-crush facility that enables small producers and wine enthusiasts to make as little as one barrel of wine using the winery's equipment. Walking around the barrel room, it quickly becomes evident that there are more barrels of other producers' wines than there are of Judd's Hill wines, but Judd still knows what's in just about every barrel whether it's his or not.

Darioush

This Persian palace rising from the vineyard flatlands just north of Napa is one of the more unusual recent additions to Napa Valley's ever-colorful architectural mash-up. Darioush and Shahpar Khaledi came to the United States from Iran in the 1970s, and after a stint making cartloads of money in the grocery business, they set about creating their dream winery. They made their first wines in 1997; the palatial visitors center, with its unique mix of Persian and contemporary architecture, opened in 2004.

Darioush (4240 Silverado Trail, Napa, 707/257-2345, www.darioush.com, 10:30 A.M.–5 P.M. daily, tasting $25) is a hard-to-miss winery, thanks in part to the 16 giant sandstone pillars, each topped with a double-headed bull, that take the place of more traditional trees in front of the main entrance. The theme is continued in the luxurious interior, where carved sandstone looks like it's straight from the set of *Raiders of the Lost Ark,* but it still manages to blend seamlessly with designer furnishings, architectural lighting, and stainless steel trim. If you have to wait for the crowds to thin out at the glass-topped tasting bar, take a seat on what looks like (and probably is) a Le Corbusier leather sofa.

About half the winery's total production of 10,000 cases is the Signature cabernet sauvignon, a luxurious wine made with all five bordeaux varietals. Other wines include, appropriately, a shiraz—the grape is named for the Shiraz region of Iran, where it was once believed to have originated (recent DNA analysis disproved this); coincidentally, Shiraz is also where the Khaledis grew up. Merlot, chardonnay, and viognier round out the wines sourced

© JAMES GATELEY

Darioush and its dramatic sandstone pillars

from the winery's 75 acres of Napa Valley vine-yards. Darioush also makes a small amount of pinot noir from the Russian River Valley.

Signorello Vineyards

Originally a grower of predominantly white grapes, Signorello (4500 Silverado Trail, Napa, 707/255-5990, www.signorellovineyards.com, general tastings 10:30 A.M.–5 P.M. daily by appointment) started making its own wine in the mid-1980s and by the early 1990s had planted red grapes and started making the bordeaux-style wines that it is best known for today. Visiting here is a nice reassurance that small wineries can still thrive in the big-time Napa Valley even without attaining cult status.

The estate cabernet sauvignon now dominates the winery's 5,000-case annual production, but limited-production estate chardonnay and syrah are also made, together with some highly rated pinot noir from the Las Amigas vineyard in Carneros, and zinfandel from hotter vineyards up near Calistoga. The winery is set back from the road on a hill with an idyllic view from its sunny poolside patio, making

it a pleasant enough stop on a daily tasting schedule.

The best way to experience the winery, its wines, and the wonderful patio, however, is through the various food-related tastings offered every day. The appointment-only Enoteca Experience is a 1.5 hour tour and tasting offered twice a day (11 A.M. and 2:30 P.M., $65) that includes gourmet appetizers paired with various Signorello wines that vary by the season. On Saturdays and Sundays April–October there are other foodie options, most recently Kobe beef and Cabernet ($55) and Pizza Sundays ($35). Check the website for current food and wine activities.

Trefethen Vineyards

One of the southernmost of Napa Valley's historic 19th-century wineries lies just a stone's throw from Highway 29 and is worth the short detour even if you're heading for the more famous wineries further north. Trefethen (1160 Oak Knoll Ave., Napa, 707/255-7700, www.trefethen.com, 10 A.M.–4:30 P.M. daily) is one of the oldest wineries in the valley, and unusually for the valley, is made entirely of wood. Originally called the Eshcol winery, it was built by a couple of well-to-do Napa bankers in the 1880s and designed by the legendary Victorian winery designer Hamden McIntyre—the man behind many other historic valley winery buildings, including Far Niente and Greystone.

Like most of the big Victorian wineries, Eshcol originally used a gravity-flow winemaking system on its three floors, a minimalist approach now increasingly fashionable in modern wineries. The Trefethen family bought the place in 1968 and still owns it today. It was also briefly used by Domaine Chandon to produce sparkling wine while the champagne house built its current home near Yountville.

The old Eshcol name graces the approach road to the winery and a cheaper range of wines not sold at the winery, but the building, with its large brick patio and pretty gardens (including a 100-year-old cork-oak tree), is lovingly preserved and appears on the National Register of Historic Places. The original winemaking equipment is long gone, and wines are made in an adjacent modern facility. The historic structure is primarily used for barrel storage and hospitality, yet it's still worth taking the appointment-only tour offered each morning to see the upper levels in all their musty wooden glory. Otherwise you can get a peek at the solid redwood beams and trusses from one of the barrel rooms open to the public on the ground floor, right next to the cozy tasting room.

Trefethen is perhaps best known for its chardonnay, which grows well in the slightly cooler southern end of the valley. It also makes a good dry riesling, a decent cabernet sauvignon, and a host of other wines. Tasting four of the estate wines costs $10. Double your money and you can taste some of the reserve wines in the wood-paneled Wine Library. All told, the winery now makes about 65,000 cases of wine a year.

The Trefethen family was the driving force behind the decade-long quest to have Oak Knoll designated as an official AVA in the Napa Valley—the title was finally bestowed in 2004.

MOUNT VEEDER WINERIES
◖ The Hess Collection

The art is probably going to be more memorable than the wines at this mountain estate (4111 Redwood Rd., Napa, 707/255-1144, www.hesscollection.com, 10 A.M.–5:30 P.M. daily, tasting $10 Mon.–Fri., $10–30 weekends) just 15 minutes from downtown Napa and right next door to the Christian Brothers' Mont LaSalle Novitiate. That's not to say the art of winemaking has not been perfected here. It certainly has, but the soaring four-story gallery linking the two historic stone winery buildings is the biggest draw. It houses part of the private contemporary art collection of winery founder and Swiss entrepreneur Donald Hess.

Most of the contemporary paintings and sculptures are by lesser-known European artists discovered by Hess through his artistic grapevine, though works by some big names like Francis Bacon and Frank Stella are also there. While lost in the art, it would be easy to forget this is a winery but for a couple of large windows looking from the gallery onto the inner workings of the winery itself, one framing a bottling line that could be called a piece of industrial art.

There are no organized tours, so take yourself on a free iPod-guided tour of the gallery and also the cool dark barrel room off the lobby, which is open to visitors and offers a glimpse at the inside of one of the original winery buildings. A winery was built here in 1903 and later sold to Christian Brothers in 1930. Hess secured a 99-year lease on the property in the 1980s and rebuilt the winery to produce wine from the mountain vineyards he had started planting in the 1970s.

Hess now owns about 300 acres of vineyards in the Mount Veeder appellation that provide the core of the Hess Collection wines, augmented by hundreds more acres elsewhere in the Napa Valley and farther south in Monterey County that provide grapes for the cheaper Hess Estate and Hess Select labels.

A few of the Hess Collection wines, including the cabernet and chardonnay, are the only ones usually available to taste, but on weekends you might be treated to impromptu tastings of some of the rest of the huge portfolio here, including perhaps the beautifully structured Mountain Cuvée red blend or even some of the Peter Lehman wines from South Australia that are distributed in the United States by Hess and sold at the winery.

Mayacamas Vineyards

Down the road from Chateau Potelle is tiny Lokoya Road, leading to the historic stone winery of Mayacamas Vineyards (1155 Lokoya Rd., Napa, 707/224-4030, www.mayacamas.com, tasting and tours by appointment 8 A.M.–4 P.M. Mon.–Fri. only), which dates from the 1880s but was abandoned soon after. It was bought in 1941 by Jack Taylor, who brought the winery back to life and named it after the Mayacamas Mountains it stands on. He is said to have issued stock and paid dividends of winery picnics and chardonnay, a concept that might not fly so well in today's cash-driven world.

The current owners, Robert and Elinor Travers, bought the winery in 1968 and now produce an earthy and concentrated cabernet sauvignon with great aging potential as well as a crisp, oak-free chardonnay that will also mellow with a couple of years of aging. Those two wines account for the bulk of the 4,000-case production. Mayacamas also produces smaller quantities of outstanding sauvignon blanc, merlot, and (unusually for this appellation) pinot noir from its mountain vineyards. Rising up to 2,400 feet, the vineyards are some of the highest in the region, giving the wines a cool mountain character that few other Napa Valley wineries can match.

SIGHTS

In an attempt to lure St. Helena–bound visitors to the valley, Napa has recently made a big push to recast itself as a hip and historic place that's a Wine Country destination rather than a series of exits off the freeway. In doing so, however, it has also had to avoid alienating its big population of local residents and valley workers, who would prefer that the city remain as cheap and functional as possible.

It's a tough balancing act, and the results to date have been mixed. The main anchor downtown is the Napa Town Center shopping mall, a pastel-colored 1980s concoction generally worth avoiding other than for the city's visitors center and neighboring Wineries of Napa Valley tasting room. In the streets around the Town Center, the sense of being in the center of any sort of dynamic downtown area quickly fizzles. That might change in years to come as the flood-control project along the river is completed and new developments start to sprout. The Oxbow Public Market next to Copia will undoubtedly lure food fans, and a number of new luxury hotels being built or planned downtown will bring in much-needed tax revenues and free spenders. A sign of the potential that developers see in Napa came in early 2007 when Ritz-Carlton announced its intention to build a 350-room resort just east of downtown.

One attempt by the city to liven up the downtown scene in the meantime is an ongoing program to have local artists paint **murals** depicting scenes from the valley's history. The effort is noble, but the sites could be better. Look for them on walls on Randolph Street at 1st Street (opposite a gun exchange), outside the visitors center hidden at the back of Napa Town Center, and opposite the Opera House on Main Street.

Napa River Front District

The most obvious result of the flood-defense work is the revitalization of the historic commercial area along Main Street, both north and south of the downtown area. Despite almost a decade of work that has seen historic properties renovated and new complexes built, Napa still struggles to create a self-sustaining downtown economy, a task not helped by the 2009 recession that resulted in a new crop of empty storefronts and shuttered restaurants.

The cultural anchor of the River Front District is the recently restored **Napa Valley**

© PHILIP GOLDSMITH

Napa's Italianate opera house now hosts theater, not opera.

Opera House (1030 Main St., 707/226-7372, www.napavalleyoperahouse.com). La Scala it isn't, but the 1880 Italianate building is a reminder of Napa's Victorian boom times. The opera house is one of a handful of pre-1890 buildings scattered around downtown. In fact, Napa has more buildings that survived the 1906 earthquake than any other city or town in this part of the Wine Country. At one end of the spectrum is the fabulous Gothic Victorian **First Presbyterian Church** (1333 3rd St., 707/224-8693, www.fpcnapa.org) at 3rd and Randolph Streets, built in 1875, and at the other is the 1888 **Semorile Building** (975 1st St.), just around the corner from the opera house and now home to the Bounty Hunter restaurant. An easy-to-follow walking tour of Napa's historic buildings is available from the Napa Valley Conference & Visitors Bureau.

Farther south, right at the end of Main Street, is the southern anchor of the River Front District, the restored **Napa Mill** (www. historicnapamill.com). This riverside complex in a redbrick Victorian building used to be where steamships docked before the automobile age. It now houses upscale restaurants and shops, including the Napa General Store. The Riverbend Performance Plaza here hosts free music and art shows on weekends.

The biggest casualty of Napa's fluctuating economy in recent years has been the American Center for Wine, Food, and the Arts, also known as COPIA. It was the first museum-like establishment in the country devoted entirely to the culture of food and wine, the brainchild of the late Napa Valley wine-making legend Robert Mondavi, who bought the land and donated it to the nonprofit organization that was charged with running the center. Its out-of-the-way location within Napa and a mission that was hard to define meant visitor numbers never reached the level required to sustain the venture, and it declared bankruptcy in late 2008, closing its doors to the public and beginning a politically charged debate about what to do with the impressive contemporary building and its gardens just up the road from the vibrant Oxbow Public Market. As this book went to press in early 2010 a sale of the property by the creditors looked increasingly imminent, but there was still no indication of potential buyers or what attraction, if any, will take COPIA's place in the building.

ENTERTAINMENT

There's usually something going on in the bars and restaurants along bustling Main Street in downtown Napa's River Front District, especially on the **Third Thursday Night on the Riverfront** each month, when many places stay open until 9 P.M. with accompanying music and other events. In general, however, Napa is not a city with much active nightlife, and there are only a handful of small venues that cater to live entertainment, mainly of the jazz variety.

A popular casual jazz venue is **Uva Trattoria** (1040 Clinton St. at Brown St., Napa, 707/255-6646, www.uvatrattoria.com, lunch and dinner weekdays, dinner weekends, dinner entrées $14–26)—not a bad place to eat either. There is music from the Leo Cavanaugh Trio and the big-band sound of the Gentlemen of Jazz (6:30–9 P.M. Wed.–Sat.), together with some occasional visiting artists, mainly on Saturday nights. Another Napa eatery with live music is **Downtown Joe's** brewery and grill (902 Main St. at 2nd St., 707/258-2337, www.downtownjoes.com). Music is varied and ranges from rockabilly to Latin to jazz.

At the Napa Mill complex, **Silo's** (530 Main St., 707/251-5833, www.silosjazzclub.com, 5–10 P.M. Wed.–Thurs., 5 P.M.–midnight Sat.–Sun.) has become as popular for evening wine tasting or a predinner drink as it has for its live jazz and blues, featured almost every night. Cover charges vary from free to $25 depending on the band. Wines on the decent wine list have far lower markups than at most local restaurants, and there is

also a small food menu of appetizers, pizza, and desserts.

Napa might not be the center of the valley's wine scene, but it is the cultural center. The **Napa Valley Opera House** (1030 Main St., Napa, 707/226-7372, www.napavalleyoperahouse.com) is home to just about every performance art except opera. It is the base of the **Napa Valley Repertory Theater** (707/251-9126, www.naparep.com), which usually presents about four programs each season, and schedules its own wide range of music, dance, and theater throughout the year. Call for more information, or check the website for a schedule of programs.

The first Saturday of every month is Opera Night at Napa's **Jarvis Conservatory** (1711 Main St., Napa, 707/255-5445, www.

NAPA VALLEY FESTIVALS AND EVENTS

JANUARY–APRIL

The year in the Napa Valley kicks off with the **Napa Valley Mustard Festival,** a celebration of food and wine in the valley that lasts from the end of January to early April, roughly coinciding with the blazing yellow flowers of wild mustard that brighten up the otherwise bare, leafless vineyards.

The festival is as much about drumming up business for valley businesses during the tourism off-season as raising dollars for local charities. There are countless events throughout the two months in towns up and down the valley, most notably **Mustard, Mud, and Music** in Calistoga on the first Saturday in March; and the **Taste of Yountville,** usually held on the third Saturday of March. All are essentially big street parties featuring local restaurants, entertainment, wineries, and stores. For more information and tickets for these events and others during the Mustard Festival, contact the festival organizers in Yountville (707/938-1133, www.mustardfestival.org).

MAY

It might seem strange to have a wine festival

in the Napa Valley, a place where wine seems to be celebrated every day of the year. But the **Napa Valley Wine Festival,** held in early May in Yountville, has a higher purpose than simply indulgence – it raises money for local schools. Some 50 wineries pour their wines to accompany food from countless valley restaurants, making it the best place to sample the wines of the valley without spending hours in a car. Tickets ($35-45) and information can be obtained from the festival sponsor, Napa Valley Unified Education Foundation (707/253-3563, www.nvef.org).

JUNE

Summer begins with big blowout sales at the **Napa Valley Wine Auction,** usually a three-day event over the first weekend in June. The annual charity event brings together the valley's biggest wine names and some very big wallets to wine, dine, and bid sometimes crazy prices for barrels and bottles of wine, all for a worthy cause. Most of the pricey tickets are sold by invitation only, and the few available to the general public usually sell out early in the year. Contact the Napa Valley Vintners jarvisconservatory.com), a few blocks north of the opera house, opposite the grounds of a rather bleak-looking high school. It's a casual night of entertainment provided by local Bay Area singers accompanied by the conservatory's musicians, a bit like a greatest hits of opera. The $15 ticket price includes wine and snacks during the intermission, and the entertainment usually starts at 8 P.M.

SHOPPING

The city of Napa is a slightly schizophrenic place as far as shopping goes, having to cater to its large working-class population, downtown office workers, and visitors alike. Many locals frequent the car-friendly big box stores and supermarkets that line Trancas Street north of downtown Napa. Many visitors make a beeline

for the outlet mall west of downtown next to Highway 29. Food-loving locals and visitors alike frequent the Oxbow Public Market east of downtown. That leaves the downtown area itself feeling like a ghost town for much of the week and downtown merchants struggling for business.

The situation was not helped by the 2009 recession and the scrapping of an ambitious downtown redevelopment plan that left the area in limbo for years. By early 2010 there were dozens of empty storefronts in the downtown area. Even a free trolley service that for seven years linked all these disparate parts of the city was scrapped in 2009 because ridership was so low and local businesses no longer wanted to give it financial support. As a result, a car, bike, or good pair of legs will be

---

for more information (707/963-3388, www.napavintners.com/auctions).

JULY-SEPTEMBER

The **Robert Mondavi Summer Music Festival** (888/769-5299, www.robertmondaviwinery.com) in July and August has become a summer institution in the Napa Valley and features big-name rock, jazz, blues, and Latin music artists (Julio Iglesias, Tears for Fears, Aimee Mann, and India.Arie, for example). The outdoor concerts are held Saturday evenings on the Robert Mondavi winery grounds, usually from the beginning of July through mid-August. Tickets cost $60-115 depending on the concert.

The celebration of music continues in August with the monthlong **Music in the Vineyards** (707/258-5559, www.napavalleymusic.com) series of chamber music concerts. The festival kicks off in early August and features a concert every couple of days at wineries and other venues up and down the valley.

Downtown Napa is also host to a couple of other annual fairs. The **Napa Town & Country Fair** in August at the Napa Valley Expo

Fairgrounds (www.napavalleyexpo.com) is a kid-friendly arts, crafts, and (of course) culinary celebration, though distinct from the free **Annual Napa Wine and Crafts Faire** (call 707/257-0322 for information) that takes over streets in downtown Napa in early September.

OCTOBER

Not to be left out of the music action, Calistoga throws a big blues party in October. **Calistoga Downtown Blues** (866/306-5588, www.calistogajazz.com) includes local and national blues artists playing on stages set up along Lincoln Avenue. This being Wine Country, wine tasting is a big part of the fun too. It's free to attend, though the wine tasting and the biggest evening events require tickets.

NOVEMBER-DECEMBER

The valley's wine caves are great for aging wine but also have pretty good acoustics, as you can discover at one of the weekend **Carols in the Caves** concerts from late November through December. Visit www.cavemusic.net or call 707/224-4222 for more information on the wineries hosting the concerts.

needed to visit the handful of shopping locations worth visiting.

Head across the freeway on 1st Street from downtown and it's hard to miss the **Napa Premium Outlets,** a typical modern outlet mall with 50 stores that include Ann Taylor, Timberland, J Crew, Bennetton, and Izod (629 Factory Stores Dr., right off Highway 29, 707/226-9876, www.premiumoutlets. com, all stores 10 A.M.–8 P.M. Mon.–Thurs., 10 A.M.–9 P.M. Fri.–Sat., 10 A.M.–6 P.M. Sun.). Despite its lack of Wine Country charm and distinctly suburban feel, this is about as vibrant as the shopping experience gets in the city of Napa.

The anchor development for downtown Napa is the **Napa Town Center,** a rather forlorn-looking 1980s open-air shopping center that is now home to a motley collection of unremarkable chain and local stores. It is, however, home to the Napa Valley Conference & Visitors Bureau and the Wineries of Napa Valley tasting room, so you might find yourself walking through it anyway. After failing to win permission for a big redevelopment plan, the owner of the mall embarked on a new marketing and leasing program in late 2009 that should help to revitalize the retail environment and bring some life back to the downtown area in 2010 and beyond.

There are still some quirky local shops in the downtown area that continued to thrive through the downturn, however. One of the more original is the women's vintage clothing store **Betty's Girl Boutique** (1239 1st St., 707/254-7560, 11 A.M.–6 P.M. daily except Wed. and Sun.), on 1st Street opposite the shopping center and far more original than most of the clothing stores you'll find downtown.

Continue east on 1st Street and cross the river to the Oxbow Public Market (644 1st St.), a food mecca that is also home to the charming antique and gift store **Heritage Culinary Artifacts** (610 1st St., Stall 14, 707/224-2101, www.heritageartifacts.com, 9 A.M.–7 P.M. Mon.–Sat., 9 A.M.–6 P.M. Sun.). Some of the culinary treasures from around the world are so unusual that you might be tempted despite their high price tags. Continue east on 1st Street to one of the best wine shops in town, **JV Wine** (301 1st St., 707/253-2624, www.jvwine.com, 8 A.M.–9 P.M. Mon.–Sat., 9 A.M.–8 P.M. Sun.). It's a Napa institution that sells a huge selection of wine and beer and can ship wine to states that allow it. It also offers afternoon tasting of wine every Friday for $5, and takes part in the Taste Napa Downtown wine-tasting card program.

Although it's a short walk from downtown, the best place to find a gift in Napa is probably the **Napa General Store** (540 Main St., Napa, 707/259-0762, www.napageneralstore. com, 8 A.M.–5 P.M. daily) in the redbrick Napa Mill complex. Alongside the café and wine bar, the store sells a huge range of Wine Country products including cookbooks and cooking supplies, specialty foods, wine accessories, soaps from the Napa Soap Company, and even some furniture, all with some link to the Napa Valley. If you're looking for a Napa gift for anyone, this should be your first stop.

RECREATION
Skyline Wilderness Park

Most people don't associate Napa Valley with serious mountain biking, but just outside the city of Napa is Skyline Wilderness Park (707/252-0481, www.skylinepark.org, 8 A.M.–7 P.M.), which hosted the U.S. round of the Mountain Bike World Cup three years in a row in the late 1990s. It's not the prettiest park in the valley—that distinction goes to Bothe-Napa Valley State Park near St. Helena—but it does offer 16 miles of trails for bikers, hikers, and horseback riders through its 850 acres of meadows and woodland. Spring is probably the best time to come, when the meadows are full of wildflowers doing their thing before the dry season turns the grassland to golden brown.

The park is reached from downtown Napa on Imola Avenue. The day-use fee is $5, and be sure to pick up a map when you arrive because the trail system is more complex than most. Hikers should look out for bikers and horses—all users share all the trails.

MORE THAN JUST HOT AIR

Hot-air balloons have become so synonymous with the Napa Valley that locals barely even blink when they float overhead in the early morning. There are still plenty of people willing to pay to get up before dawn for this unique adrenaline rush followed by a serene aerial view of the valley and its spectacular wineries, though perhaps fewer than in recent years; mergers between ballooning companies have reduced the number offering rides to less than half a dozen.

Most are farther south in the valley, especially around Yountville, but a couple farther north can float the bleary-eyed over some of the volcanic scenery at the northern end of the valley. Early-morning winds tend to be southerly, so pick a company that launches north of any place you really want to see from the air, but also bear in mind that balloons generally don't float far – often only a few miles over the course of a flight.

The drill is more or less the same for any ballooning adventure, whatever the company: get up before the sun rises and its rays start to generate unstable warm air that balloon pilots hate; get to a prearranged pickup point by 6-7 A.M. (depending on the season), usually a hotel or restaurant near the launch site (some companies will also collect customers staying locally); drive to the launch site and watch, sometimes take part in, the inflation of the balloon; then finally take off with the roar of the burners for an hour-long, silent drift at elevations ranging from treetop to several thousand feet, depending on the conditions. Brunch usually follows, either at a local restaurant or alfresco in a meadow, and the whole experience usually lasts about four hours.

Plenty of variables, however, can make a balloon trip less than perfect. The obvious one is the weather, which can either cancel a trip outright (fog, rain, and high winds especially), or, in the case of more localized fog, the launch site might be moved to somewhere where the skies are clearer, sometimes even outside the valley.

Some companies will do a "double hop," leaving those unfortunate enough to be assigned to the second hop, or flight, of the day following behind the balloons in a van to the landing spot before finally getting a flight. The drawback of the second flight (apart from the feeling of having woken up early for nothing) is that air currents can die down after the sun rises and the balloon might not float very far. Ask if a double hop is planned – they tend to be more common during the busy summer and fall seasons. If it is, insist on hopping on board with the first group.

Ask how big the basket is and how many groggy souls will be crammed in with you. Some companies limit riders to eight or even four people; others take up to 16 per flight. For a large premium, most also offer the option of a private flight for two.

Farthest north in the valley is **Calistoga Balloons** (888/995-7700, www.calistogaballoons. com, $225), which launches from the Calistoga area and offers brunch afterward at the Hydro Grill in town. **Napa Valley Aloft** (www.napavalleyaloft.com) owns three Yountville-area ballooning companies with three different prices, and can be visited in the Vintage 1870 Marketplace building in Yountville. One of the three is **Above the West Ballooning** (800/627-2759, $295), which offers a free shuttle from anywhere in the valley, guarantees no more than four people to a basket, and in summer has its postflight brunch alfresco in a vineyard. The cheapest is **Balloon Aviation** (800/367-6272, $225), which has no shuttle but still guarantees no double hops.

The **Bonaventura Balloon Company** (707/944-2822 or 800/359-6272, www. bonaventuraballoons.com, $215-250) offers flights in the northern half of the valley and a variety of brunch options, from the most expensive at the Meadowood Resort to a cheaper picnic option. Also check the website for special rates. **Balloons Above the Valley** (707/253-2222 or 800/464-6824, www.balloonrides. com, $230) usually launches from near the Domaine Chandon winery in Yountville and offers a private brunch after the flight. It also sometimes has good online deals, including no-frills flights that are shorter, foodless, and cheaper.

Mountain bikers wanting to try their skills on the world cup route should ride from near the park's entrance for about a mile up Lake Marie Road before turning right onto the murderous ascent of Passini Road and then descending on the rocky, sometimes steep single-track of the Bayleaf Trail. The next stage of the cup was the Manzanita Trail, reached by climbing back up Lake Marie Road to the fig tree. The undulating two-mile trail was described as one of the best single-tracks on the cup circuit.

Disc golf offers some less traditional exercise. You might know it as Frisbee golf, but the Professional Disc Golf Association would prefer you use the D word instead. It is played exactly as you might think, like golf but throwing a Frisbee instead of hitting a little white ball. There is an 18-hole course, and (in case you don't always travel with one) Frisbees (sorry, discs) are available at the entrance kiosk, along with course maps. The dress rules are a little more relaxed than on most traditional golf courses—no collared shirts or fancy shoes are required. In fact, you don't even have to wear shirts or shoes.

Those who'd prefer to expend less energy can find **picnic areas** near the park entrance and about 2.5 miles up the Lake Marie Road at the lake itself.

Alston Park

Untouched by either vineyards or development, Alston Park instead has sweeping views of both from the western fringe of the city of Napa. The park is off Dry Creek Road, reached by driving west from Highway 29 from either Redwood Road or Trower Avenue. There's no entrance fee, and the park is open dawn to dusk, although the only map is on an information board.

It's not on quite the same scale as Skyline but still offers plenty of picnicking, hiking, and biking possibilities in its 150 acres of rolling hills and meadows and along five miles of trails. There are picnic tables and a canine common where dogs can be let off the leash—a rarity in the relatively dog-unfriendly valley.

Just avoid the park during the middle of hot summer days unless you're training for a desert trek, because there are few trees and little shade.

Golf

The southern end of the valley is where all the biggest and most exclusive golf courses are, many of them not open to the public. Among those that are, the biggest is the 18-hole **Napa Golf Course** (2295 Streblow Dr., Napa, 707/255-4333, www.playnapa.com, call for tee times) at Kennedy Park a couple of miles south of downtown on Soscol Avenue, which eventually becomes the Napa-Vallejo Highway. The 6,500-yard, par-72 championship course costs $25–35 to play during the week for non-residents and $34–46 on weekends. Rates vary depending on time of day. It has a driving range, practice putting greens, and a fully stocked golf shop.

ACCOMMODATIONS

Although it feels a little removed from all the wine action in the valley, and is not the most attractive Wine Country town in this part of the world, the city of Napa provides the widest choice of accommodation options. Many major chain hotels can be found here (including some recent upscale additions) as well as cheap independent motels, Victorian B&Bs, and a couple of modern boutique hotels. Best of all, rooms are generally cheaper here than anywhere else in the valley, especially at the low end of the market.

Another advantage of staying in Napa, particularly if you're not a cabernet sauvignon fan, is its proximity to the Carneros region, the land of pinot noir and chardonnay. It's just a 15-minute drive south to many wineries in the eastern half of Los Carneros, or a 15-minute drive north to some of the Napa Valley's best cabernet producers. And for those traveling to or from Oakland or San Francisco, Napa has the shortest drive time of any of the valley's towns—a full 45 minutes closer to San Francisco than Calistoga, for example.

The city is also home to a good selection of

restaurants, most within a short walk of most downtown hotels and B&Bs. Indeed, if you don't want to drive to dinner and still have the choice of more than a handful of restaurants, then Napa is the probably the best place to stay in the valley.

Under $100

There are more lodging options at the low end of the price spectrum in and around Napa than anywhere else in the valley. The **Wine Valley Lodge** (200 S. Coombs St., Napa, 707/224-7911, www.winevalleylodge.com) is a simple, clean, and bargain-priced independent motel let down only by its location about a mile south of downtown Napa, putting it just out of walking distance to most good restaurants and shops. It is just off Imola Avenue, however, which provides a quick connection to Highway 29 and wineries to the north and south. The guest rooms are simply but tastefully furnished, though with the ubiquitous motel-standard floral bedspreads made of some sort of synthetic material that feels like it could stop a bullet. All have TVs, air-conditioning, and private bathrooms with showers, and cost $50–80 midweek, depending on the season, and $80–130 on weekends.

A little north of downtown Napa is **Napa Valley Redwood Inn** (3380 Solano Ave., off Redwood Rd., Napa, 707/257-6111, www.napavalleyredwoodinn.com). Some big-hotel touches (newspapers, free high-speed Internet access, HBO, a decent-sized outdoor pool) sweeten the appeal of the otherwise small and well-worn motel-style rooms. Its location right next to the St. Helena Highway (Highway 29) puts it in easy reach of wineries but also means there's some traffic noise to contend with, and you must drive to reach local restaurants in Napa and Yountville. A new mall across the street, Redwood Plaza, at least puts decent coffee within easy reach, and nothing is too unbearable considering the rates are as low as $80–90 midweek and $80–150 on weekends, depending on the season.

Right next door to the Redwood Inn is the **Chablis Inn** (3360 Solano Ave., off Redwood Rd., Napa, 707/257-1944 or 800/443-3490, www.chablisinn.com). It's a bit more upscale than its neighbor but is still a glorified motel with prices that squeak in at just under $100 midweek for the basic rooms (with the bullet-proof bedspreads). The deluxe rooms are only $20 more per night and a little more luxurious, with comforters, CD players, and whirlpool tubs in the bathrooms. Weekend rates are considerably higher, starting at $140 per night.

Across town and a little off the beaten track is the **Napa Discovery Inn** (500 Silverado Trail, 707/253-0892, www. napadiscovery-inn.com), a small and relatively clean motel with a decent list of amenities and rooms starting at $85 midweek, rising to almost $200 on summer weekends. It's in a quiet part of town but not really close to any major attractions, so you'll definitely need a car if you plan to stay here.

$100-200

For just a few dollars more a night than the nearby motels you could stay in, the more hotel-like **John Muir Inn** (1998 Trower Ave., Napa, 707/257-7220 or 800/522-8999, www.johnmuirnapa.com) is a sprawling building just off Highway 29 on the northern edge of Napa. The bland building is nothing much to look at, but it has nice gardens and plenty of clean and comfortable rooms that are a step up from most motel rooms. Standard amenities include Internet access, air-conditioning, and enough room for a desk. Some have refrigerators and microwaves or full kitchenettes, and three of the deluxe king rooms have whirlpool tubs. Standard rooms start at $140–210 per night midweek, depending on the season, and $170–220 on weekends. Deluxe rooms are usually only $10 more per night. As with most inns and hotels, a free continental breakfast is included, but guests can instead choose a money-off voucher for breakfast or brunch at the neighboring Marie Callender's restaurant.

Napa's first and still most unique boutique hotel, the **Napa River Inn** (500 Main St., Napa, 707/251-8500 or 877/251-8500, www.napariverinn.com) has perhaps the best location in the city at the historic redbrick Napa Mill, a small riverside food and entertainment complex only a 10-minute walk to more shops and restaurants in downtown Napa. The 66 guest rooms are spread among three buildings—two are part of the historic mill itself and one (the Embarcadero building) was built in 1997. All rooms are furnished in an eclectic mix of contemporary and either Victorian or nautical style, many with fireplaces, balconies, or views, though the views vary wildly from a parking lot to the river, which still bears some scars of recent flood-control construction work. Staying here is not as pricey as the location and luxury might suggest. Smallish standard rooms cost $180–200 midweek and only about $20 more on weekends. The most expensive deluxe rooms in the historic buildings are double that, though there are plenty of options in between. The larger rooms tend to be in the main historic building.

The Napa Mill itself has everything a hotel guest might need: Choose between two of the city's best restaurants (Celadon and Angèle) for dinner. In the morning, after the hotel breakfast from Sweetie Pies bakery, buy picnic supplies at the Napa General Store and book an evening spa treatment before setting off for a day of wine tasting.

Giving the Napa River Inn a run for its money is the **Avia Napa** (1450 1st St., 707/224-3900 or 866/644-2824, www.aviahotels.com) hotel, which opened in 2009 in a brand new building on 1st Street, bringing some much-needed modern energy to the tired downtown accommodation and architecture scene. Touted as a boutique hotel, it is actually a new addition to a rapidly expanding national chain of affordable and stylish hotels, featuring lots of polished wood, crisp linens, and modern amenities from iPod docks to massive plasma-screen TVs. Some aspects of the service will not be up to the same levels of more established or expensive local hotels, but the location and quality of amenities are hard to beat for the price. The smallest king rooms with walk-in showers start at $130 midweek in the spring, rising to $280 on a busy summer weekend, but

as with most chains there are often discounts available. Prices increase about $30 per night with every additional luxury room feature, such as soaking tubs, balconies, fireplaces, and views.

The choice of Victorian B&Bs in Napa can be a bit bewildering. One establishment that has some of the cheaper rates and plenty of room options is **Hennessey House** (1727 Main St., Napa, 707/226-3774, www.hennesseyhouse.com), about six blocks north of downtown Napa. The only downside to the location is the particularly ugly high school across the road. Six rooms in the main Queen Anne–style Victorian house cost $139–239, depending on season, all with private bathrooms and some with four-poster beds and claw-foot tubs. Four larger, more ornate rooms, with fireplaces, whirlpool tubs, and CD players, are in the Carriage House and cost $189–299. The full gourmet breakfast is enough to soak up plenty of wine during those morning wine tastings, and the sauna is a place to relax tasting-weary feet at the end of a winter day. Allergy sufferers be warned: The resident cat has free rein of the common areas.

Anyone fed up with Victorian frills should check out the **€ Blackbird Inn** (1755 1st St., 707/226-2450 or 888/567-9811, www.blackbirdinnnapa.com), an arts and crafts–style shingled house dating from the 1920s with furnishings to match the era's relatively clean and simple lines. It's just a few blocks from downtown Napa, right opposite the West Coast home of *Wine Spectator* magazine, making it probably the most conveniently located B&B in Napa. The teddy bears on each bed are a trademark of the Four Sisters group, which owns this and a handful of other small Wine Country inns—although there's no corporate feel to the place. The only disadvantage is that there are no owners living there to take care of any late-night problems, but there are advantages too. Unusually for a B&B, there are TVs in every room with DVD players (the walls supposedly have some decent sound-proofing, unlike those at many B&Bs) and free wireless Internet access in addition to the more common fireplaces and whirlpool tubs in some rooms. Rates range from $145 midweek to $185 on weekends for the smallest room, though most are in the $200–285 range.

Just a couple of blocks from the Blackbird Inn and touted as Napa's first B&B when it opened in the 1980s, **The Beazley House** (1910 1st St., Napa, 707/257-1649 or 800/559-1649, www.beazleyhouse.com), with its own feline resident, is in another squat shingled mansion, this one dating from 1906 and adorned with rather garish blue-and-white canopies over the windows. Rooms contain the usual mix of what look like your great-grandmother's best furnishings. The five guest rooms in the main house have private bathrooms, though only one of the five has a claw-foot tub, and cost $180–260. The other five rooms are in the Carriage House and are more luxurious, with whirlpool tubs, fireplaces, individual air-conditioning, and views of the lush garden; they cost $255–340.

Despite being somewhat marooned right next to the freeway opposite the outlet stores, the **Bel Abri Inn** (837 California Blvd., off 1st St. at Hwy. 29, Napa, 877/561-6000, www.belabri.net) offers good value for money and convenience but is not the most stylish accommodation in the city. The clean, modern building is furnished in a faux French country style and has 15 rooms, including a few with patios or fireplaces, starting at $140 in winter and about $50 per night higher in winter. Midweek and weekend prices are usually the same, but there is the usual two-night minimum at the weekend. In terms of amenities and services it lies somewhere between a motel and a hotel, but it does offer a few luxury touches like concierge service and an evening wine and cheese tasting. Downtown Napa is a little too far to walk comfortably, but it is only a few minutes' drive.

Over $200

Arguably one of the finest Victorian B&Bs in Napa is **La Belle Époque** (1386 Calistoga Ave., Napa, 707/257-2161 or 800/238-8070, www.labelleepoque.com), a glorious Queen Anne–style mansion built in 1893 with an antique-stuffed interior that looks like the movie set for an Agatha Christie mystery. The six guest rooms are all unique, most with stained-glass windows, some with canopy beds, and others with fireplaces or whirlpool tubs. Standard amenities include TVs with VCRs, high-speed Internet access, and CD players, and all guests are invited to evening wine receptions featuring wines from local wineries or from the inn's own big wine cellar. All this pampering and history, plus a very central yet tranquil location, comes at a cost. Rates range from $180 for a couple of the rooms midweek in midwinter up to $275–329 on summer weekends. Two suites in a separate Victorian house across the street go for $199–439 more.

Like a set for a real-life game of Clue, the sprawling mansion that is home to the **Cedar Gables Inn** (486 Coombs St. at Oak St., Napa, 800/309-7969, www.cedargablesinn.com) might have you wondering if you'll bump into Colonel Mustard in the study. Built in 1892 by a renowned English architect, the huge Tudor-style mansion covered in cedar shingles was one of the grandest houses in Napa County in its heyday and the site of many lavish balls and gatherings. Today the labyrinth of stairways, passages, and secret doors is home to a lavish B&B with nine guest rooms, all exquisitely furnished with Victorian finery. All have private bathrooms, four have fireplaces, and four have whirlpool tubs. Other amenities include free wireless Internet access and a gourmet breakfast befitting the surroundings. They range in price $209–359. The Inn has an ideal location in a peaceful residential neighborhood about a 10-minute walk to downtown Napa and a similar distance from the restaurants at the Napa Mill.

Less chintz and more privacy than at most B&Bs are part of a stay at **La Residence** (4066 Howard Ln., Napa, 707/253-0337 or 800/253-9203, www.laresidence.com), on the northern edge of the city. It's actually more of a luxury country inn, with 25 guest rooms contained in four buildings set on two acres of wooded grounds with a hot tub and a small heated pool.

In early 2006 the property was bought by the owners of Hall Winery, who plan to upgrade and possibly expand the hotel, but meanwhile it's business as usual. The smallest and cheapest rooms ($175–235, depending on the season) are in the main mansion house, dating from 1870 and furnished with queen beds, original antiques, CD players, and TVs. Readers report that the plumbing in the old house can be temperamental, but all the bathrooms are nicely modernized. Larger rooms in the more modern French Barn building ($225–275) have a touch of French country style, plus balconies or patios and working fireplaces. The newest and biggest rooms ($300–350) are in the new Cellar House, with LCD TVs, wet bars, and giant bathrooms added to the already long list of amenities. A couple of unique suites are similarly luxurious. Although the inn is nowhere near downtown Napa, it does offer easy access to the rest of the valley and is virtually next door to the excellent Bistro Don Giovanni. There is free wireless Internet access, a gourmet breakfast, and a casual reception every evening featuring wines from Hall Winery.

There are luxurious resorts in the valley with views, others with wooded privacy, some with vineyards, but the **Milliken Creek Inn** (1815 Silverado Trail, Napa, 707/255-1197 or 888/622-5775, www.millikencreekinn.com) has another twist—its riverside setting, understated mix of Victorian and colonial Asian furnishings, relaxing earth tones, and the sense of exclusivity that comes from having just 12 guest rooms to share the lush gardens and fountains.

Relax on the lawn by the riverbank or lounge in the room in front of a fireplace or on a private deck and have yourself a peaceful Zen experience. All rooms come with full entertainment systems, luxurious linens, and wireless Internet access. The cheapest are the two Milliken rooms at $275–650, depending on the season and the time of the week. The premium rooms, starting at $450 a night (and going up to $775), include extras ranging from Jacuzzis and canopied beds to plasma-screen TVs and expansive private decks.

Worth noting is that the inn is a gratuity-free zone, but as a reminder that nothing is free in the Napa valley, a 12 percent service fee is added to your bill each day. Unless you want to complain and have the fee removed or reduced (and feel like a grinch), be sure to make full use of the helpful staff and the evening wine tastings to get your money's worth.

FOOD
River Front District and Downtown

"Global comfort food" is how the culinary creations at **Celadon** (500 Main St., Napa, 707/254-9690, www.celadonnapa.com, lunch Mon.–Fri., dinner daily, dinner entrées $16–34) have been described, and the surroundings in the historic Napa Mill buildings are equally comfortable. The shabby-chic exterior and huge sheltered patio give way to a pure bistro-chic interior, the perfect match for the internationally influenced Californian menu. The wine list offers about the same balance of California and the rest of the world.

At the other end of the mill is the pocket of Francophone charm **Angèle** (540 Main St., Napa, 707/252-8115, www.angelerestaurant. com, lunch and dinner daily, dinner entrées $18–36). The rustic interior and canopied riverside patio are perfectly romantic settings for the classic French bistro food that has won plaudits from critics. Adding to its sophistication is an outstanding Californian and French wine list that includes about a dozen wines available by the half-bottle.

Sandwiched between Celadon and Angèle, the Napa General Store is home to the **General Café** (540 Main St., 707/259-0762, breakfast and lunch daily, www.napageneralstore.com, entrées $8–14), serving a wide range of Asian-inspired entrées as well as sandwiches and pizza from the wood-fired oven. There are a handful of tables in the store, but the main draw is the riverside patio. The accompanying wine bar is open until 6 P.M. and is an ideal place to whet your dinner appetite with a glass of bubbly by overlooking the river.

Cole's Chop House (1122 Main St., Napa,

© PHILIP GOLDSMITH

The Napa Mill complex is a food and entertainment hub along Napa's waterfront.

707/224-6328, dinner daily, entrées $18–46) is the baby brother to Celadon, offering a slightly less refined but equally well-designed (though short) menu featuring steakhouse dishes, from oysters to well-aged beef, in a classic steakhouse setting rich with dark wood and contrasting white tablecloths. It doesn't quite stack up to the best steakhouses up-valley, but it is a credible alternative if you crave a hunk of meat in downtown Napa.

Those craving some hearty Italian food have several choices. **Ristoriante Allegria** (1026 1st St., 707/254-8006, www.ristoranteallegria. com, lunch and dinner daily, dinner entrées $14–28) is a cozy, leafy oasis tucked into a corner of the rather desolate First Street Plaza and is housed in a historic Italianate bank building that creates an air of Old World elegance. The restaurant is far larger than the exterior suggests, however, and can get noisy inside, so reserving a table on the small patio bordering the plaza is recommended. There's nothing terribly inventive about the menu, and the dining experience is not quite up to par with some of the more famous Italian restaurants up-valley, but with reasonable prices, a huge wine list, and competent cooking, it's a solid choice.

Uva Trattoria (1040 Clinton St. at Brown St., Napa, 707/255-6646, www.uvatrattoria. com) has become a Napa institution for its rustic Italian food and lively bar and as one of the few live music venues in the city.

The River Front District is the main food center in downtown Napa, and one of its most inventive establishments is (**Bounty Hunter** (975 1st St., off Main St., Napa, 707/226-3976 or 800/943-9463, www.bountyhunterwinebar. com, lunch and dinner daily, plates and entrées $6–18), a wine shop, tasting bar, and (most recently) casual restaurant serving small plates to help the wine go down. The setting, in a historic brick-walled Victorian building with knotty wood floors, a copper ceiling, and wine barrels for table bases, is as relaxed as the comfort food served. It includes gumbo, the beer-can chicken (a Cajun-spiced chicken impaled on a Tecate beer can), and chili. Alternatively, just order some cheese and settle down at the wine bar with one of the 400 wines sold here (40 by the glass) or a tasting flight. Since it's a wine shop too, you'll pay retail prices for wines bought with a meal, and there'll be plenty of advice available from the fun-loving staff.

The best pizza in town can be found at **Azzurro Pizzeria & Enoteca** (1260 Main St., Napa, 707/255-5552, www.azzurropizzeria.com, lunch and dinner daily, pizzas $13–16), which earned a loyal local following at its former modest location on Second Street before moving to its current fancier digs in 2008. The thin-crust pizzas from the wood-fired oven are some of the best in this part of the world—not surprising considering the founder of this popular restaurant honed his pizza skills at the famous Tra Vigne restaurant in St. Helena. The menu includes classic Italian starters, salads, and a handful of pasta dishes alongside the dozen or so pizzas, and there are plenty of choices for vegetarians. The wine list is dominated by thoughtfully chosen Napa and Sonoma wines, yet another sign that this is a no-nonsense and hassle-free dining experience favored by locals.

With the amount of critical praise heaped on **ZuZu** (829 Main St. at 2nd St., Napa, 707/224-8555, www.zuzunapa.com, lunch weekdays, dinner daily, plates $5–13), you'd think it was competing with French Laundry for title of the valley's best restaurant. Thankfully, it's a refreshingly down-to-earth tapas bar that's a great place to end a stressful day of touring without having to worry about reservations or the bill. The cozy interior with its exposed brick, beams, and tile is the perfect setting for the Spanish-inspired small plates, none of which (except the Moroccan glazed lamb chops) costs over $10. Lunch is only served during the week, when it's a popular local hangout.

Downtown Joe's American Grill and Brewhouse (902 Main St., 707/258-2337, lunch and dinner daily, breakfast weekends, dinner entrées $9–21) is a hopping alternative to the swanky restaurants and endless wine of the Napa Valley. Sure, it has a wine list (a short one), but most people come here for the more

than half-dozen microbrews with the usual comical microbrew names, like Tantric India Pale Ale and Catherine the Great Imperial Stout. The menu is pretty standard if slightly pricey grill fare, but there's also a cheaper pizza and pub grub menu. There is live music in the evening Thursday–Sunday.

Throw all preconceptions of vegetarian restaurants out of your mind when you visit **Ubuntu** (1140 Main St., 707/251-5656, lunch weekends, dinner Mon.–Sun., dinner entrées $9–16). The upstairs yoga studio might suggest this place is a little "granola," but the restaurant has garnered rave reviews and a Michelin star, and there is barely a chunk of tofu to be seen in the sleek Zen-like interior. Cofounder and executive chef Jeremy Fox had a philosophy of celebrating locally grown produce rather than actively shunning meat, and with such an abundance of vegetables in the Napa Valley (including from Ubuntu's own nearby farm) he has plenty to work with. The main dishes on the seasonal menu are small, but most are under $15, so buying a handful to share at the table is the best bet. Their richness and sophistication, however, should satisfy even the most ardent meat eaters. The well-thought-out international wine list is, naturally, dominated by wines from organic or biodynamic vineyards, although the options are on the pricey side. In early 2010 both Jeremy Fox and pastry chef Deanie Fox left Ubuntu, and it remains to be seen how the restaurant will fare without them.

Oxbow Public Market

Right next door to COPIA is a new development showcasing local artisanal food suppliers and local restaurants that's a one-stop shop for anyone looking for a quick fix of Napa Valley cuisine. The Oxbow Public Market (610 1st St., Napa, www.oxbowpublicmarket.com) is designed along the same lines as the highly successful Ferry Building Marketplace in San Francisco, which quickly became a magnet for city's foodies after it opened in 2003. Oxbow, on a smaller scale, has a similar mix of restaurants and food vendors in a farm stand–like setting. All the tenants in the market are generally open at least 10 A.M.–7 P.M. weekdays and 10 A.M.–6 P.M. on weekends, but many are open later, as noted below.

Some of the restaurants that anchor the new development include outposts of St. Helena's gourmet burger joint **Gott's Roadside Tray Gourmet** (10:30 A.M.–9 P.M. daily)—formerly Taylor's Automatic Refresher—together with popular bakery and café **Model Bakery** (7 A.M.–7 P.M. daily). Another interesting addition to the Napa food scene that has proven to be very popular is **Pica Pica,** said to be one of the first restaurants in California to offer Venezuelan street cuisine, which is known for its unique combinations of sweet and savory flavors, such as shredded skirt steak with black beans, cheese, and sweet plantains. The specialty dish is *arepas,* a corn flour–based flatbread filled with your choice of almost a dozen savory fillings and grilled to a crisp. Two other bread options are also offered, and all cost $8–9. The kitchen is open until 8 P.M. Monday–Thursday, until 9 P.M. Friday–Saturday, and until 5 P.M. Sunday.

Almost next to Pica Pica is the **Folio Enoteca & Wine Bar,** which serves Mediterranean-inspired food that complements the many Californian and international wines available to buy or taste. The only problem, if you want a more substantial meal, can be finding somewhere to sit at one of the few tables or the four-seat bar. The best options are the mouth-watering panini or pita sandwiches, which can be ordered to go and cost $8–10.

Restaurants are only half the story at Oxbow, however. One of the biggest draws is the cornucopia of Napa Valley food, from organic ice cream and olive oil to cheese and meats. **Five Dot Ranch** sells every cut of grass-fed beef and every other meat imaginable, while the **Oxbow Cheese Market** is a pungent tribute to local artisanal cheese makers. There's also an outpost of Sonoma's **Olive Press** and more meats at the charcuterie **The Fatted Calf** at the side of the market on McKinstry Street. Finish shopping or dining with a delectable organic dessert from **Three Twins Ice Cream** or with

one of everyone's favorite treats from **Kara's Cupcakes,** which is hard to miss at the front of the main market building thanks to its giant pink menu board.

Vicinity of Napa

A few miles north of downtown Napa is the popular Italian restaurant **Bistro Don Giovanni** (4110 Howard Ln., next to Hwy. 29, Napa, 707/224-3300, lunch and dinner daily, dinner entrées $14–28). It's hard to miss on the east side of Highway 29 (though you might miss the turn for Howard Lane) and is a favorite of locals looking for moderately priced Italian bistro food with a bit of Californian flair, all in a relaxed and vibrant setting. On a warm summer night, ask for a table on the huge bustling outdoor patio. Anything from the wood-fired oven is worth trying here, especially the pizzas and oven-roasted fish. The wine list is dominated by Napa and Sonoma, but there's a good choice from the mother country too, and an unusually wide selection by the half-bottle.

If the relentless Wine Country–themed activities and food gets to be a bit too much, you can escape it all at the **Red Hen Cantina** (4175 Solano Ave., 707/255-8125, most dishes under $12), a colorful and sometimes raucous Mexican bar and restaurant right off Highway 29. Just look for the giant red hen on the roof of the building; it used to grace a nearby barn containing an antique store. The food is by no means gourmet, and the bar can get packed, but if you stick to basics on the menu like enchiladas or a burrito, have a margarita or two, and sit out on the patio, you'll have an experience that is refreshingly devoid of Wine Country pretension.

Picnic Supplies

If you're in Napa and heading to the hills for lunch, the **Napa General Store** (540 Main St., 707/259-0762) in the Napa Mill complex is about as gourmet as you can get for takeout food in the town. You'll have to battle your way past all the other nonfood trinkets and gifts it sells, though. At the **Oxbow Public Market**

(610 1st St., Napa, www.oxbowpublicmarket.com) there are plenty of options for take-out food, from Pica Pica's Venezuelan food to gourmet sandwiches from the Model Bakery or Fatted Calf charcuterie.

Just south of the Darioush winery is the **Soda Canyon Store** (4006 Silverado Trail, at Soda Canyon Rd., Napa, 707/252-0285), just about the only decent place to buy deli food, cheeses, and wine along the Silverado Trail.

Farmers Markets

Downtown Napa might not instantly bring to mind bucolic country farms, but farm-fresh produce (and craft stalls) can be found at **Napa Downtown Market** May–October, on Tuesday and Saturday mornings until noon in the parking lot of the Wine Train just down McKinstry Street from the Oxbow Public Market.

Music, chef's demonstrations, wine tasting, and food from local restaurants fill several blocks of downtown Napa one evening a week during the summer as part of the **Napa Chef's Market** (at 1st St. and Napa Town Center,

707/257-0322, 5–9 P.M. Thurs. Memorial Day–early Aug.). It's like a mini Taste of Napa event and a fun predinner diversion, especially if you have bored kids in tow.

INFORMATION AND SERVICES

First stop for any visitors without a plan—whether staying in Napa, heading up to Calistoga, or simply doing some online research—should be the **Napa Valley Conference & Visitors Bureau** (1310 Napa Town Center, 707/226-7459, www.napavalley.com, 9 A.M.–5 P.M. daily). The staff know the valley like the backs of their hands and can usually rustle up some useful printed information.

The nearby **Napa Chamber of Commerce** (1556 1st St., Napa, 707/226-7455, www.napachamber.com, 8:30 A.M.–5 P.M. Mon.–Wed. and Fri., 10:30 A.M.–5 P.M. Thurs.) sells packages of information from maps to directories and touring guides, although you might be able to find some of the same information for free at the visitors bureau.

Yountville and Vicinity

The appellations in the southern half of the Napa Valley encompass some of the best cabernet-growing regions in California. They can also be cool enough for growing many other varietals, both red and white, most notably in the **Yountville** appellation, where chardonnay, sangiovese, zinfandel, sauvignon blanc, and even some pinot noir seem to thrive. Although wines from the Yountville AVA are certainly worthy of the Napa Valley pedigree, there is no one particular trait for which they are known. Indeed, you rarely see the Yountville name mentioned on bottles, and the appellation certainly lacks the cachet of the hilly region to its east.

The **Stags Leap District** appellation on the eastern side of the valley along the Silverado Trail is perhaps one of the most recognizable Napa AVAs to wine lovers, particularly red wine lovers. This fairly cool, hilly 1,300 acres

of land rising up to the mountain crags (across which the legendary stag leapt to escape its hunters) is without doubt the land of cabernet sauvignon, and few other varietals get a look in. The cabernets have been famously described by the founder of Stag's Leap Wine Cellars as "an iron fist in a velvet glove," and they certainly have a gentle elegance that belies their sometimes astonishing aging potential. The combination of volcanic soils and cool air channeled between the handful of knolls that make up the district are thought to play a role in making this such a good place to create some of Napa Valley's best cabernets. Despite the fame of the Stags Leap District, most wineries here are refreshingly low-key.

North of Yountville is the **Oakville** appellation, warmer and home to some of the most famous cabernet sauvignon vineyards and

YOUNTVILLE

To Silverado Trail

To St. Helena and Calistoga

MAISONRY

THE FRENCH LAUNDRY
LAVENDER INN
BOUCHON
MAISON FLEURIE
PETIT LOGIS
BARDESSONO HOTEL
V MARKETPLACE
HURLEY'S
CHAMBER OF COMMERCE
NAPA VALLEY RAILWAY INN
BISTRO JEANTY
YOUNTVILLE DELI
VILLAGIO INN & SPA
REDD
AD HOC
DOMAINE CHANDON
VINTNER'S GOLF CLUB
NAPA VALLEY MUSEUM

To Napa

© AVALON TRAVEL

0 — 300 yds
0 — 300 m

wineries, including Robert Mondavi and Far Niente. Although this is where the land of big bold Napa cabernets begins in the valley, the appellation also turns out some excellent sauvignon blanc and chardonnay. Oakville is often compared to Rutherford just to its north, and both appellations have very similar growing conditions and a similarly long list of famous wineries stretching back to the 1800s. Both also turn out rich, meaty cabernets that have helped give Napa Valley its reputation for powerhouse wines. Oakville just does it with slightly less fanfare than its more famous neighbor, Rutherford.

YOUNTVILLE WINERIES
Domaine Chandon

The first big French champagne house to come to California was Moët-Hennessy in 1973, and its Domaine Chandon winery (1 California Dr., off Hwy. 29, Yountville, 707/944-2280, www.domainechandon.com, 10 A.M.–6 P.M. daily, tasting $18–22) is still one of the most impressive wineries in terms of architecture and landscaping. The buildings blend into the hillside beneath towering trees next to a giant (if slightly murky) pond and are almost invisible from the road. It's not the sort of modesty that one expects from such a big glamorous operation producing several hundred thousand cases of sparkling and still wines each year; the surroundings are more earth-mother than youthful bling.

Once across the bridge and into the cavernous reception, skip the PR presentations and head upstairs to the spacious tasting bar and salon, with its cozy club-like atmosphere and doors out onto a leafy terrace and lawn area. Art is everywhere, both inside and out in the gardens, and you can buy pieces from some of the ever-changing exhibitions. The basic half-hour tour, which costs $12, takes in all stages of champagne making but runs only once daily at 11:30 A.M. For an additional $18 you can combine the tour with a tasting of both still and sparkling wines.

The tastings alone start at $18, free glass included, for the Classic flight that includes the popular bone-dry Riche and some lower-end bubblies. At the other end of the tasting spectrum is the Prestige flight ($22), which includes the more expensive vintage brut and Étoile sparklers that are bottle-aged for years to give them a rich, toasty aroma.

If you plan to take home a bottle or two, some of the reserve wines offer perhaps the best bargains, with far more complexity than the nonreserve wines for not much more money. Domaine Chandon also makes still wines from the three most important champagne grapes— pinot noir, chardonnay, and petit meunier. They're a little overpriced but worth trying if champagne is not your thing. All can be tasted as part of the Varietal flight ($15).

Unless you are into some serious champagne, however, pick the Classic tasting flight and kick back on the terrace with one of the tasty, if meager, appetizers. The terrace and the sometimes energetic atmosphere are as much reasons to come here as the champagne. Another big draw is the acclaimed restaurant, Étoile, which is as unashamedly high-end and stylish as the champagnes with which it shares the name. Gold cards and restrained elegance are the themes at this destination eatery—there is no written dress code, but you'll have a hard time getting beyond the concierge if you're wearing shorts.

Goosecross Cellars

Anyone lamenting that everything wine-related in the Napa Valley costs too much should head on over to Goosecross (1119 State Ln., Yountville, 707/944-1986 or 800/276-9210, www.goosecross.com, 10 A.M.–4:30 P.M. daily, tasting $10) on a Saturday morning for the fun, informative, and free Wine Basics class (10:30 A.M. Sat., reservations essential). The hour-long session is held on a shady lawn and pitched at just the right level for novices and wine buffs alike to learn some fascinating facts (and myths) about wines and the best ways to savor them. Of course, there are a couple of wines to taste as part of the education.

The cozy Goosecross tasting room itself is squeezed in next to the barrels and offers all 10 wines that this family-owned winery makes, including the standout Howell Mountain cabernet sauvignon, the juicy syrah sourced from vineyards in southern California, and the crisp but fruity Napa Valley chardonnay. The flagship wine is the Aeros, a powerfully flavored red blend made only in the best vintages. From the minimal metal winged label this is clearly a special wine, and chances are you won't be able to taste it because only a couple of hundred cases are made of each vintage. It's worth looking out for, nevertheless.

In total, Goosecross produces only about 9,000 cases of wine, making it one of the valley's smaller wineries that is open to the public. The laid-back family vibe is refreshing, especially considering its location in the heart of the Napa Valley, and if you can't get to the Wine Basics class, the standard tasting fee here is only $10, which is half what you'd pay at most nearby wineries.

Bell Wine Cellars

It's not surprising that a former assistant winemaker at Rutherford's Beaulieu Vineyard now makes his own critically acclaimed cabernet sauvignon from Rutherford-area vineyards. Anthony Bell established Bell Wine Cellars (6200 Washington St., Yountville, 707/944-1673, www.bellwine.com, tastings daily by appointment, tasting $15) in the early

1990s, first making wine at other wineries before buying the former Plam Vineyards winery near Yountville in 1998. Since then, new partners have provided an injection of money, and the winery has started to expand, all the while keeping its reputation for outstanding cabernet.

The cab from Baritelle Vineyards in Rutherford, Bell's signature wine since 1991, is famous for being the valley's first-ever single-vineyard cabernet made from just one clone of the vine. Clone 6 cabernet is one of a handful of cabs made here that together account for the majority of the 10,000-case production. True cabernet lovers might want to splurge on the $75 clonal tasting, which includes cheese and a chance to try to distinguish the characteristics of four wines each made from a distinct clone of cabernet, including the clone 6 version.

Bell has also made a name for his syrah, sourced from the Sierra foothills, and offers a couple of reasonably price red blends, including a classic cabernet-based claret that understandably sells out fast considering its quality and modest $30 price. Whites are represented by Yountville chardonnay and several sauvignon blancs from vineyards in Lake County and Bell's native South Africa. The appointment-only tastings offer the chance to talk to people who really know their wines.

STAGS LEAP WINERIES
The Stags Leap Duo

A trip down the Silverado Trail would not be complete without visiting at least one of the two wineries that share the name of one of the best-known Napa appellations—one that helped put California on the international wine map in the 1970s.

If you're wondering how two unrelated wineries can use such a well-known name in this age of fiercely guarded trademarks, it will be no surprise to learn there was a lengthy legal battle involved. These neighbors fought over the use of the Stags Leap name as it became associated with world-class wines in the 1970s and 1980s, and the case was finally settled in 1985 when the court ruled that the term Stags

© PHILIP GOLDSMITH

the Stags Leap district, home of blockbuster cabernets

Leap referred simply to a geographical area, and each winery agreed to let the other use it (each also kept the apostrophe in a different position). Not long after the dust had settled, Stags Leap became an official appellation with no apostrophe in its name at all. Confused? You should be!

The more famous of the duo is **Stag's Leap Wine Cellars** (5766 Silverado Trail, Napa, 707/261-6422 or 866/422-7523, www. cask23.com, 10 A.M.–4:30 P.M. daily), which made the cabernet sauvignon that beat out the best French bordeaux in the now-famous 1976 blind tasting in Paris, and followed it up with another win in the anniversary tasting 30 years later in 2006. It still makes outstanding single-vineyard cabernet from that same SLV vineyard as well as the older Fay vineyard next to it. Such renowned wines command high prices, none more so than the Cask 23 cabernet, which uses the best grapes from both vineyards.

These three estate cabernets, together with an equally impressive chardonnay, can be tasted for $30. Nonestate wines from other

Napa vineyards offer a cheaper tasting option ($15) and might include the excellent Artemis cabernet, which has some Fay vineyard grapes in it; the merlot; or the sauvignon blanc (you might also be able to steal a taste of these non-estate wines if you indulge in the more expensive tasting option). Appointment-only tours ($40) take in the pristine-looking cave system and its fascinating Foucault pendulum (for measuring the earth's rotation), and they conclude with the estate tasting.

Although a magnet for serious wine enthusiasts, and a fairly large producer (about 50,000 cases, including the cheaper Hawks Crest label), this family-run winery exudes an unassuming and friendly atmosphere, making it far less intimidating for the casual day-tripper than many of the valley's other big names. The small tasting room is off to the left of the main winery building and can get crowded, so plan to get here early.

Farther north on the Silverado Trail, down a long driveway lined with ancient walnut trees, is the first winery to bear the area's name, **Stags' Leap Winery** (6150 Silverado Trail, Napa, 707/944-1303 or 800/640-5327, www.stagsleap.com). Its wines might be less famous than those of the other Stag's Leap, but its history and setting are far more impressive. The winery was founded in 1893, taking its name from the old Native American legend of a stag that evaded hunters by leaping across the craggy cliffs towering above the winery. The Victorian splendor remains fully intact today.

In 1909 the winery's original owner sold out and the stone Manor House went through many incarnations, including a hotel and a navy camp, before being abandoned in 1953. It wasn't until 1970 that it was brought back to life as a winery and the vineyard was replanted to include cabernet sauvignon, merlot, and petite sirah, alongside some of the original sirah vines, said to be some of the earliest plantings of that grape in the United States. Those three varietals still dominate the winery's production of about 60,000 cases today.

Perhaps the most noteworthy wines are the inky, full-bodied petite sirah (spelled "petite syrah" here) and the proprietary Ne Cede Malis, a true Rhône-style field blend dominated by petite sirah that gets its name from the Latin phrase "Don't give in to misfortune," the motto of winery founder Horace Chase.

Since 1997 the winery has been owned by multinational Fosters Wine Estates, but the Victorian splendor of the manor house and tranquility of the lush surroundings far from the valley crowds certainly don't hint at corporate ownership. Few people realize it's open to the public, but appointment-only tours (10:30 A.M. and 2:30 P.M.) are available during the week for a limited number of people. They fill up fast, so book early. The tours take in the Manor House, wine-making facilities, and wonderful gardens including the apothecary, full of medicinal plants, and the sensory garden, devoted to flavorful and aromatic plants. Tie a visit here in with a tour of Shafer Vineyards, which shares the same driveway off the Silverado Trail.

Clos Du Val

Although it has long since become a well-known Stags Leap District winery, Clos Du Val (5330 Silverado Trail, Napa, 707/259-2200 or 800/993-9463, www.closduval.com, 10 A.M.–5 P.M. daily, tasting $10–20) is said to have come about thanks to a Frenchman sticking his arm out of a moving car window. The Frenchman was Bernard Portet, and he was searching for a patch of land on which to create a winery to rival the best in Bordeaux, where he grew up and learned his wine-making skills. In 1970, on that fateful road trip through the valley, he settled on this prime 120-acre chunk of Napa Valley because, he said, the cooler air signified it could produce wines of a more reserved, French style than the hotter appellations du jour of Rutherford and Oakville. The winery was established by Portet and American business partner John Goelet in 1972 and later purchased more land down in Carneros.

The winery has always produced wines to rival some of the best of Bordeaux, though the rather plain, concrete winery building itself seems to take more inspiration from 1970s design aesthetics than a Bordeaux château. It looks best in the summer when its walls are softened by ivy and the pretty gardens are in bloom. The showmanship here is definitely in the wines rather than the buildings or interior.

Almost half the 80,000 cases of wine made here each year are cabernet sauvignon, and this is the wine Clos Du Val is best known for. The generic Napa cabernet is good, but the Stags Leap estate cabernet is outstanding and comes from the vineyard right outside the winery door. Chardonnay is the other large-production wine in the portfolio and comes from the Carneros vineyard, as does a pinot noir. Another estate wine worth trying is the white bordeaux blend of semillon and sauvignon blanc called Ariadne.

There's plenty to do here other than taste wine, from a self-guided tour around the demonstration vineyard that illustrates all the different trellis systems used in vineyards (the tour provides an accompanying explanation) to playing a game of *pétanque,* the French version of boccie. Tours are available by appointment only.

Pine Ridge Winery

Nestled in a small dell with its trademark ridge of pine trees above is another of the Stags Leap District's big cabernet houses, established by Gary Andrus in 1980. He has since expanded the winery to 65,000 cases and increased his vineyard holdings to about 200 acres throughout the valley, helping make Pine Ridge (5901 Silverado Trail, Napa, 707/252-9777 or 800/575-9777, www.pineridgewinery.com, 10:30 A.M.–4:30 P.M. daily, tasting $15 or $25, tours by appointment $25, barrel tasting $30) one of the few wineries to make highly rated wines from most of Napa's finest cabernet appellations—Stags Leap, Rutherford, Oakville, and Howell Mountain. The flagship is the Andrus Reserve, a bordeaux-style blend made with grapes from almost all those appellations.

The smallish tasting room is virtually devoid of merchandise, putting the wines firmly center stage as long as a tour bus has not just disgorged its passengers. The regular tasting option ($15) covers the white wines and cheaper reds, and might include a Carneros- or Rutherford-sourced chardonnay, viognier, merlot, or cabernet franc. The reserve and some of the cabernets can only be tried with the more expensive tasting option ($25) or as part of the appointment-only barrel tasting in the Hillside Room, offered three times a day for $30.

Tours of the vineyard and aging caves, followed by a barrel tasting with cheese accompaniment, are offered three times a day by appointment (10 A.M., noon, and 2 P.M., $25), and there's a small picnic area under the trees above the winery.

Shafer Vineyards

Tasting wine at Shafer (6154 Silverado Trail, Napa, 707/944-2877, www.shafervineyards.com, sales 9 A.M.–4 P.M. weekdays, tasting by appointment 10 A.M. and 2 P.M. weekdays, $45) is about as close as many visitors might get to one of Napa's much-hyped cult wines without forking over hundreds of dollars for the rare bottles that do make it beyond the waiting lists. Schafer's limited-production Hillside Select cabernet sauvignon is regularly compared to the highly extracted wines from small producers like Screaming Eagle, Harlan Estate, and Bryant Family that are critically acclaimed and rare enough to command their cult status. About 2,000 cases of Hillside Select are made each year, out of about 32,000 for the winery as a whole.

The secrets to success here are the rocky hillside vineyards behind the modest winery, which produce limited quantities of powerfully flavored grapes that go into the Hillside Select cabernet. Some of these grapes also make it into the lower-priced but equally plush cabernet, supplemented by grapes from vineyards farther south that also provide fruit for the acclaimed syrah (called Relentless) and merlot. Shafer's chardonnay is sourced from the winery's Carneros vineyards. A small vineyard on the hillside behind the winery is planted to sangiovese, which provides the fruit for the limited-production Firebreak blend of sangiovese and cabernet.

An informative sit-down discussion and tasting is offered twice a day on weekdays by appointment only, but the $45 price tag is a bit steep considering a tour of the facility is no longer included. The price could be worthwhile if the Hillside Select is available for tasting, but sometimes it has already sold out for the year. The consolation is that an excellent cabernet port that is only available at the winery usually is available for tasting. Visitors will also probably meet John Shafer's canine grape tester, Tucker, and perhaps John himself.

Space is limited to 10 people and demand is high, so booking weeks in advance is sometimes necessary, as is a tolerance of the serious oenophiles who tend to flock here. There's no sign for the winery on Silverado Trail, so look for the cluster of property numbers at the end of the private road almost opposite the entrance to Silverado Vineyards.

Robert Sinskey Vineyards

It might be part of the elite group of Stags Leap wineries, but the reputation of Robert Sinskey Vineyards (6320 Silverado Trail, Napa, 707/944-9090 or 800/869-2030, www.robertsinskey.com, 10 A.M.–4:30 P.M. daily, tasting $25–50) was built on wines from Carneros. It is now at the forefront of the organic and biodynamic movement in the valley and is almost as well known for its culinary reputation as its wines. Founder Robert Sinskey planted his first vineyard on land in Carneros and for many years sold the grapes to the neighboring Acacia winery. When Acacia changed hands, Sinskey embarked on his own wine-making odyssey, buying more Carneros land and eventually a five-acre parcel in Stags Leap on which he built his winery in the late 1980s. His son, Rob Sinskey, eventually took over running the business, and the winery now produces about 25,000 cases of wine per year.

The elegant stone and redwood winery with its lofty cathedral-like tasting area is a feast for the senses in many different ways. Visitors are greeted by a field of lavender, an organic

the gardens at Robert Sinskey Vineyards

© PHILIP GOLDSMITH

vegetable garden, and parking lot arbors covered in aromatic jasmine. The spacious tasting bar and demonstration kitchen are in the slender, tall main room that's reminiscent of a cathedral nave.

As early as 1991 the winery started championing organic growing practices, and now all 170 acres of its vineyards (most in Carneros) are certified organic, making Sinskey the second-largest organic farmer in the Napa Valley (the largest is the Napa Wine Company). The next step was biodynamic certification, which the winery finally obtained in 2007 (and explains the photos of sheep in vineyards you will see around the winery). Organic farming principles were embraced by Rob Sinskey's wife, Maria, who is a well-known chef and author of one of the better Napa Valley cookbooks, *The Vineyard Kitchen.*

In fact, food is as important as wine here. The demonstration kitchen at the back of the tasting room is a key stop on the culinary tour ($50) offered by appointment daily at 11 A.M. On summer weekends, the sheltered terrace beyond the kitchen hosts the white wine bar, and food from the kitchen is often part of the fun, but you can also bring your own picnic to eat with a glass of Sinskey wine. Even at the tasting bar there are always morsels of food to accompany the wines, to illustrate the food-friendliness of the wines and perhaps to make the relatively high tasting fees easier to swallow. Better value is the $30 appointment-only cave and cellar tour, which ends with a similar tasting.

The wine that Robert Sinskey Vineyards is best known for is pinot noir, and there are three versions, all from Carneros—two from single vineyards and a slightly cheaper blend. Carneros vineyards are also the source of the merlot, cabernet, and cabernet franc that go into the elegant, bordeaux-like Vineyard Reserve, a wine that tastes like it should cost far more than its sub-$40 price tag (which is why it usually sells out fast). Sinskey also makes some nice white pinots, including an unoaked pinot blanc and a heady Alsace blend of pinot gris, pinot blanc, riesling, and gewürztraminer called Abraxas. The Stags Leap District is represented by the estate cabernet sauvignon, which is every bit as good as wines from Sinskey's neighbors.

OAKVILLE WINERIES
Napa Wine Company

The modest Cellar Door tasting room of the Napa Wine Company (7830 Hwy. 29, Oakville, 707/944-1710 or 800/848-9630, www.cultwinecentral.com, 10 A.M.–4:30 P.M. daily, tasting $20), just across the road from the Oakville Grocery, does not suggest that this is a huge wine-making and grape-growing operation. The tasting room is a cooperative of 25 small wineries, all of which use the Napa Wine Company's custom crush facilities to make their wines. In fact, the venture makes more than 1.5 million cases of wine for wineries ranging from tiny boutiques making a few hundred cases up to some of the giants of the valley that would probably prefer that people didn't know they outsource some production.

Between all those jobs, the Napa Wine Company manages to make about 10,000 cases of its own wine as well, including a highly regarded cabernet sauvignon. It manages all this wine making using equipment bought from the wine conglomerate Heublein in 1993, including what used to be the white-wine production facility for the Inglenook Winery. But wine making is just part of its business. Grape

THE TALE OF THE MISSING VINTAGES

If you decide to splurge at Napa Valley wineries to taste some older library vintages, be aware that some wineries have unexpected gaps in their collections. A huge fire in 2005 at the giant Wines Central warehouse on Mare Island near Vallejo, just south of Napa, wiped out an estimated 6 million bottles of California wines that were stored there. Both current vintages and rare library collections belonging to more than 90 wineries were destroyed. Many Napa Valley wineries, both large and small, were affected, and it's sad now to see gaping holes in the lineup of older vintages at some of them today. Long Meadow Ranch, for example, lost its entire library collection going back to 1994. Smaller wineries that stored all their wines at the warehouse were particularly hurt, and some lost almost an entire year of sales. Even larger wineries will take a long-term financial hit due to their inability to fulfill future orders from restaurants and other buyers. But for everyone, the loss is more than financial – older vintages are essential for winemakers to assess how their wines age, enabling them to adjust blends or other aspects of the wine-making process.

What makes it harder to swallow for those affected is that the fire is believed to have been started deliberately. Federal prosecutors alleged that the man trusted with running the business and safeguarding the wines started the fire in the warehouse to hide evidence that he'd been illegally selling his clients' wines. In 2009 he pleaded guilty as part of a plea agreement with prosecutors.

growing has been the foundation on which the wine business was built. The Pelissa family has been supplying grapes to wineries in the valley for three generations and owns more than 600 acres in the Oakville and Yountville appellations, all now farmed organically.

Some of the small wineries represented in the tasting room have links to some major valley figures like Karen MacNeil Fife, the Beckstoffer family, and David Abreu. Other wineries here are simply small or medium-sized family affairs, making a stop here the best way to taste some outstanding Napa Valley wines made without the usual Napa Valley fanfare.

Opus One

Only serious wine lovers need go out of their way to visit Opus One (7900 Hwy. 29, Oakville, 707/944-9442, www.opusonewinery.com, 10 A.M.–4 P.M. daily, tours 10:30 A.M., tasting $30), the monolithic tribute to red bordeaux that was formed in 1979 by Robert Mondavi and the late legendary French winemaker Baron Philippe de Rothschild, head of famed Château Mouton-Rothschild in France. In a valley filled with ever more bold architectural statements, the building housing this grand winery is still one of the most fascinating and looks like it will stand the architectural test of time.

This is a proudly appointment-only winery. The concierge escort to the tasting room and $30 tasting fee to taste just the single type of wine made here are reminders that Opus One was California's very first ultrapremium winery. It still tries hard to retain that edge with its attitude and its wines, including among the best cabernet in the valley. It's not a place for those easily intimidated by posh exclusivity. The tasting fee is made easier to swallow because it buys you virtually an entire glass of the current vintage of the signature wine, which retails for $160 a bottle, and gets you access to the rooftop terrace with its fantastic views. Opus One also makes a cheaper nonvintage cabernet called Overture that sells for about a third that price, not that you'll see much evidence of it at the winery.

The hour-long appointment-only tour ($35) is well worth taking if you can get a reservation. It takes in some of the striking features and technology of the building. Completed in 1991, the winery is a half-buried architectural tribute to the contemporary and old-school

Opus One: for serious wine (and architecture) aficionados

© JAIME PHARR/123RF.COM

heritages (and wines) of the two founders, and from afar it resembles a giant limestone spaceship landed in the vineyards. Inside, antique European furniture blends with minimalist design touches and state-of-the-art wine-making elements like the giant semicircular barrel-aging room. Despite the opulence, this is a relatively small winery by Napa standards, making about 35,000 cases of wine a year.

Far Niente

One of the most highly regarded wineries in the valley opened to the public only in 2004, but the appointment-only tour and tasting is among the best in the valley, not least because Far Niente (1350 Acacia Dr., off the Oakville Grade, Oakville, 707/944-2861, www.farniente.com, tours by appointment 11 A.M.–3 P.M. daily, $50) makes only two highly regarded (and expensive) wines—cabernet sauvignon and chardonnay—so the tasting of five wines will always include some older library vintages. Despite the $50 price tag, the tour is extremely popular and booking in advance during the summer is essential.

Far Niente was established as a winery in the late 1800s, and the name is Italian for "without a care," which was appropriate considering the place was abandoned before Prohibition in 1919. Oklahoma businessman Gil Nickel bought the elegant old stone buildings in 1979 and has since transformed the winery into a Napa wine-making powerhouse (he also established the nearby Nickel & Nickel winery). Far Niente now produces just over 30,000 cases of wine per year, around a third of it cabernet from the Oakville appellation, and is known for its consistently high ratings from critics.

Among the highlights of the tour are a walk through the aging caves under the main house, which have been extended into a 40,000-square-foot labyrinth over the decades, and a chance to see Nickel's classic cars in the Carriage House, many of which he raced at some point, including a rare prototype Ferrari known as the Yellow Beast. Those lucky enough to visit in April and May will also see some of the 8,000 azaleas in bloom in the 13 acres of gardens with a sweeping view of the valley.

Nickel & Nickel

Almost opposite the lavish Mondavi winery is the rather quaint Victorian farmstead of Nickel

PHILIP GOLDSMITH

Behind the Victorian charms of Nickel & Nickel is a state-of-the-art winery.

& Nickel (8164 Hwy. 29, Oakville, 707/967-9600, www.nickelandnickel.com, tasting and tours by appointment 10 A.M.–3 P.M. Mon.–Fri., 10 A.M.–2 P.M. weekends, $40), sister winery to Far Niente just down the road. Gil Nickel, of Far Niente fame, founded the winery in the mid-1990s to make 100 percent varietal wines (made entirely from one type of grape rather than containing small percentages of blending grapes that never get mentioned on the bottle). Many of the buildings in the complex date from the late 1800s, but there is also a cunningly disguised state-of-the-art winery hidden in the huge barn built recently using Victorian building methods. The barn sits atop a huge underground barrel room with vaulted ceilings that would make any Victorian engineer proud.

The collection of beautifully restored cottages and barns and the centerpiece 1884 Sullenger House opened to the public in 2003 and can be seen on the appointment-only tour, a sedate and classy affair that culminates in the tasting of five of the wines. The winery now makes about 30,000 cases of wine a year, and all of them are vineyard-designate from just about every Napa Valley appellation as well as the Russian River and Dry Creek Valleys in Sonoma. There are more than 10 different cabernet sauvignons, for example. Sadly, tasting them all is out of the question, but you can often try four as part of the Terroir Tour tasting. Although cabernet dominates the production, there are some outstanding chardonnays from Napa Valley and the Russian River Valley made in varying styles, as well as syrah, merlot, and zinfandel.

Robert Mondavi Winery

This sprawling mission-style complex with its distinctive giant archway and bell tower is considered by some to be the temple of modern Napa wine-making, with the late Robert Mondavi the high priest. Others are of the opinion that it's a classic example of the over-commercialization of the Napa wine industry—and judging by the crowds and limos that throng the winery, they have a point.

The winery (7801 Hwy. 29, Oakville, 707/226-1395 or 888/766-6328, www.robert-mondaviwinery.com, 10 A.M.–5 P.M. daily) was once the crown jewel of the Robert Mondavi Corporation, which started life as the more modest winery Mondavi established in the 1960s, ushering in the valley's modern-day wine industry. Decades later, after swallowing many California and international wineries, the Mondavi Corporation was acquired by the multinational giant Constellation Brands and has since shed some of its former acquisitions, most notably Arrowood in the Sonoma Valley. The core brands remain, however, including the Woodbridge winery in central California, which makes vast quantities of cheaper wines, and the share of the exclusive Opus One winery just down the road. Annual production for all the Mondavi labels is measured in the millions of cases rather than the thousands, but the best Napa Valley wines that can be tasted at the winery account for only a fraction of that total.

At the time it was built in 1966, this was the first new winery in the valley since Prohibition, and as Robert Mondavi grew his business, he blazed a trail down which many of the valley's more recently established wineries have followed. Some go so far as to credit Mondavi with helping create the modern Napa Valley wine industry. Although the Mondavi family accumulated an enviable portfolio of vineyards over the decades, many critics believe the quality of the wines has never lived up to the hype, particularly after the company went public in the 1990s to fund its massive expansion.

Touring the impressive grounds and buildings and learning about their history and about wine-making are certainly the highlights of visiting the winery and give the wines a lot to live up to. Despite the naysayers (and there are plenty), the wines are still rather special, particularly if you stick to the classic cabernet, chardonnay, and sauvignon blanc on which Mondavi has historically focused. Opportunities to taste more wines are somewhat limited.

The comprehensive $25 tour of the vineyards and winery includes a tasting of three wines and is offered by appointment on the hour 10 A.M.–4 P.M. You can usually sign up for a same-day tour at the reception desk. The number of other tours is quite bewildering, numbering almost a dozen in the summer, so check the website for options. Highlights include the Twilight Tour, which is perfect for the end of a hot summer day, and the Wine Basics tasting, which is a bargain at $15 for wine tasting "beginners."

Without a tour the tasting options are limited to $5–15 per wine in the Le Marche tasting room or $30 for a flight of four reserve wines in the To Kalon Room. Of course, if the modern-day Napa Valley that Mondavi helped create has already bankrupted you, it's always free to wander around the courtyard to admire the architecture and views, and imagine a time in the 1960s when this was virtually the only winery in the area.

SIGHTS

More about the history of Napa and the entire valley can be found at the **Napa Valley Museum** (55 Presidents Circle, off California Dr., Yountville, 707/944-0500, www.napavalleymuseum.org, 10 A.M.–5 P.M. Wed.–Mon., adults $5, children under age 7 free). It usually has a fascinating mix of exhibits exploring the valley's natural and cultural heritage, from the modern wine industry back to Native American life, together with an interactive high-tech exhibit on the science of wine making. From the St. Helena Highway (Highway 29) north of Napa, take the Veteran's Home exit and head west on California Drive.

SHOPPING

Yountville, population about 3,500, is the little Napa Valley town that has become a big draw for diners and shoppers, with more restaurants per capita than seemingly any other place in the valley. Most of the action is in and around the giant brick **V Marketplace** building (6525 Washington St., Yountville, 707/944-2451, 10 A.M.–5:30 P.M. daily) that was once a winery and distillery. It was built in 1870 by German immigrant Gottlieb Groezinger, who made most of his fortune decades earlier in the California gold rush.

His huge winery was left abandoned following Prohibition, and just over a century after it was built, the giant building was transformed from a temple of wine to a temple of consumerism. Groezinger might turn in his grave if he saw it today, but not every shopping center can boast of being on the National Register of Historic Places.

The building has been tastefully restored inside, with the exposed brick and giant wooden beams lending an air of sophistication to the 36 generally unsophisticated little boutique shops selling everything from clothes and accessories to toys, art, and the usual Wine Country gifts.

Most of the stores clearly thrive on tourist dollars, but it's still fun to get lost for half an hour exploring the nooks and crannies of the three floors. Some of the more memorable shops include **Cravings,** on the ground floor near the back entrance, which sells some gourmet food that could be useful for a picnic as well as some interesting gourmet cookware; **Domain Home & Garden** and **Gami's Scandia Imports,** which both sell fun items for the home and garden; and **Napa Style,** just off the courtyard, which is a home chef's cornucopia and a slightly overdone homage to local celebrity chef Michael Chiarello—it's a challenge to find any item sold here that is not in some way branded with his name (a few steps away you can even eat at his newest restaurant, Bottega). Just across the courtyard is the **V Wine Cellar,** a decent and fairly large wine shop that sells a lot of local and international wines and has occasional tastings.

Arts and crafts lovers should cross Washington Street to the rather undistinguished and equally touristy **Beard Plaza,** which is where some of the town's galleries can be found, including **RAS Galleries** (707/944-9211), which features contemporary ceramic, glass, and sculpture artists.

A short walk away at the northern end of Washington Street, art and design meets wine tasting at one of the most unique shopping experiences in the valley, **Maisonry** (6711 Washington St., 707/944-0889, 10 A.M.–6 P.M. Sun.–Wed.,

© PHILIP GOLDSMITH

Maisonry pairs wine with art.

than the flocks of tourists more commonly sighted in these parts. Almost 150 types of bird and 40 types of butterfly call this peaceful 70-acre patch of the valley home. The reserve has no specific hours but is probably best avoided during the rainy season (December–April) when it can be too wet to be accessible.

The small paved parking lot is on the north side of Yountville Cross Road, about halfway between Highway 29 and the Silverado Trail just west of the small bridge over the river. There's just one trail, about a mile long, that dives into woodland, crosses the river (only possible during the dry summer and fall months), and eventually loops back on itself, but not before affording a unique view of the valley's native wildlife and plant life.

Golf

Just south of the Domaine Chandon winery is the nine-hole, 2,800-yard **Vintner's Golf Club** (7901 Solano Ave., off California Dr., Yountville, 707/944-1992, www.vintnersgolfclub.com, call for tee times). Fees for nonresidents range from $25 midweek to $35 weekends for nine holes, and up to $45 to play 18 holes.

ACCOMMODATIONS

The small town of Yountville, just eight miles north of Napa, halfway to St. Helena, not only has an impressive number of restaurants and shops but also a lot of hotel rooms for its size. Being right next to Highway 29 and a major cross-valley road, it is within easy reach of just about every winery.

Those advantages make the town both blessed and cursed, however. Easy access and plentiful services make it a great base from which to explore the valley, but Yountville also attracts hordes of visitors during the day and suffers from almost constant traffic noise near Highway 29, destroying much of the rural charm and often making it feel more like a suburban mall than a historic town of 3,000 residents. You might wonder where all the locals actually are—they tend to emerge at night after the shops close.

10 A.M.–8 P.M. Thurs., 10 A.M.–10 P.M. Fri.–Sat.). Housed in a historic Victorian-era stone house, the concept for Maisonry is to be a living gallery, where the work of both contemporary and classical artists and designers is part of the decor and also happens to be for sale. The reality is that it can be a little intimidating stepping into such a rarefied atmosphere with its immaculately dressed staff, but just pretend you have several thousand dollars to blow and you'll quickly feel relaxed poking around the imaginative and beautifully made home furnishings and design pieces. There are a few reasonable priced items that would make good souvenirs of the Napa Valley, from antique wine bottles to Native American arrows, and the beautifully designed garden is a relaxing refuge in which to taste the many wines on offer.

RECREATION
Napa River Ecological Reserve

A small patch of land next to the river in Yountville has been saved from the vineyards, and it's now a great place to see wildlife other

For years, the character of Yountville could best be described as Mediterranean pastiche, but as the Napa Valley continues to reinvent itself and go upmarket, Yountville's character has changed, and several new contemporary high-end hotels have opened or were slated to open as this edition went to press.

Under $150

The Orient Express it is not, but this is the only place in the valley where you can sleep on a train. Sort of. The nine railcars and cabooses that constitute the affordable **Napa Valley Railway Inn** (6523 Washington St., Yountville, 707/944-2000) took their last trip many decades ago and are now fitted out with king or queen beds, air-conditioning, skylights, flat-screen TVs, and private bathrooms, making surprisingly comfortable accommodations right in the middle of Yountville (ranging $125–185, depending on the season and the time of week). The downside is that they are stranded in the middle of a sea of blacktop that is the parking lot for the V Marketplace (no problem parking here), and the inn is only staffed during daylight hours with just an emergency number for any nighttime mishaps. The odd-numbered red rooms have nice views of vineyards and the hills beyond, if you can overlook the large parking lot and Highway 29. The blue rooms are a bit quieter and back onto a smaller parking lot and downtown Yountville. There's enough tall greenery planted to offer some privacy from late-night parkers, but it's still wise to remember to draw the curtains when it gets dark.

$150-200

In the heart of Yountville is the 【 **Maison Fleurie** (6529 Yount St., Yountville, 707/944-2056 or 800/788-0369, www.maisonfleurie-apa.com), which also does its best to be more French than Californian. The old ivy-covered stone-and-brick buildings around a pretty courtyard certainly evoke the French countryside, as do the vineyards almost across the street (if you ignore the contemporary Bardessono Hotel that sprouted up next to the vines). Inside the cozy lobby and the 15 guest rooms the French country theme continues, though it tends to go a little over the top with the flowery fabrics and faux antiques. Cozy is also the word used by the hotel to describe its smallest and cheapest rooms—the Cozy Double is just 80 square feet. They start at $140 and at that price sell out quickly despite their diminutive floor space. If you do get one, plan on spending time outside by the small pool to prevent claustrophobia. The biggest rooms ($235–300) are in the adjoining Carriage House and Bakery buildings and include fireplaces, views, and spa tubs in some.

The French theme continues (in name, at least) at the tiny **Petit Logis** (6527 Yount St., Yountville, 877/944-2332, www.petitlogis.com), tucked away in a one-story building next to Maison Fleurie. The five rooms in a row of former shops have their own outside entrances and are decorated in fairly minimal but comfortable France-meets–New England country style. They include private bathrooms with whirlpool tubs ($150–200 per night midweek, depending on the season; $215–275 on weekends). Rates are $20 more with breakfast, but the extra is worth paying because the inn smartly defers to the cooking skills of two nearby restaurants—Pacific Blues across the street or Gordon's Café a short drive (or long walk) away—far better than picking over the less-than-impressive breakfast options at many other inns in the valley.

Over $200

The Yountville area has more than its fair share of upscale lodgings, many of which seem to be competing for conference and meeting business. That roughly translates to some slightly unjustified prices for the average visitor. Two that are probably more worth the top dollar they charge than most are Villagio Inn & Spa and Vintage Inn, large resort-style properties on either side of the V Marketplace shopping center that are spacious, luxurious, and far more service-oriented than lower-priced inns. The concierges are actually able to get reservations at the best local restaurants when your own attempts might fail.

The **Vintage Inn** (6541 Washington St., Yountville, 707/944-1112 or 800/351-1133, www.vintageinn.com) has a French theme and is the smaller and more attractive of the two, with rooms arranged around gardens, fountains, and pools. The **Villagio Inn & Spa** (6481 Washington St., 707/944-8877 or 800/351-1133, www.villagio.com) has Tuscan-themed decor and similar amenities, plus an on-site spa (that can also be used by Vintage Inn guests), but it is in a cluster of buildings that looks like an extension of the neighboring apartment complex despite the faux Roman gardens. Neither Euro-theme is terribly convincing, but both inns have very similar spacious rooms with fireplaces, sunken tubs, and a small outdoor patio or balcony. Rates are identical at both properties and are determined in part by position. A ground-floor exterior room starts at $340 midweek ($555 on weekends) and the price increases for courtyard rooms, peaking with the giant suites ($505–1,295).

The teddy bears on the beds are a feature of the small chain of hotels owned by Four Sisters Inns, which owns the **Lavender Inn** (2020 Webber St., Yountville, 707/944-1388 or 800/522-4140, www.lavendernapa.com). The nine spacious rooms here are themed in French country style, though with a little more of a contemporary feel, and cost $225–300 per night. All have fireplaces, and a few have private hot tubs and patios to take in the smell of the lavender gardens on warm summer nights. Guests can use the pool at Maison Fleurie down the road.

If you're looking for some contemporary luxury with plenty of green cred, the sprawling **Bardessono Hotel** (6526 Yount St., 707/204-6000, www.bardessono.com) is the newest member of the Napa Valley's growing collection of super-resorts catering to those with money to burn for the ultimate in pampering. The 62-room hotel is one of only a few worldwide to be LEED-Platinum certified, thanks to a laundry-list of nature-friendly design and operational features, but its much-touted environmental credibility is dented somewhat when you consider the fact that part of the vineyard farmed by the Bardessono family for three generations was ripped out to build the place. Arranged around multiple courtyards with its own meandering streams, it resembles a contemporary luxury condo development more than a traditional hotel, but the amenities and services are what you'd expect when every room is a suite and costs upward of $600 per night—massive TVs, private patios, fireplaces, outdoor showers, giant Jacuzzi tubs, countless spa treatments, and the finest linens money can buy.

FOOD

Anchored by The French Laundry, Yountville has become something of a restaurant mecca in the Napa Valley in recent years as the town continues to transform itself and move further upmarket. Several old stalwarts have closed, including the much-loved breakfast spot Gordon's, the Napa Valley Grille, and Compadres Mexican restaurant, while new upscale dining places have opened, including one at the new super-resort Bardessono as well as Bottega, the flagship restaurant of celebrity chef Michael Chiarello. Much of the new action on the restaurant scene is likely to take place at the northern end of Yountville on Washington Street, however, where there has been significant redevelopment. As this edition went to press, rumors suggested both the former Napa Valley Grille site and redeveloped property on the former PJ Steak site were being eyed by other well-known chefs, and the new Hotel Luna right next door was poised to open its upscale Italian restaurant, Cantinetta Piero. Even the venerable Gordon's opposite the Hotel Luna could reopen, according to locals.

Downtown Yountville

Good luck trying to get a reservation at **The French Laundry** (6640 Washington St., Yountville, 707/944-2380, dinner daily, lunch Fri.–Sun.). The famous restaurant is usually booked up two months in advance thanks to its world renown, limited seating, and strict reservations system. Reservations can only be made two months in advance, and such is the

© PHILIP GOLDSMITH

The French Laundry offers memorable meals for a memorable price.

© PHILIP GOLDSMITH

a hidden courtyard for two near the Bouchon bakery in Yountville

demand that all the slots for the two evening seatings two months hence are usually snapped up the first morning they are made available. This is the case for much of the year, particularly on weekend nights and despite the astronomical price tag, so either be prepared to hit redial for the best part of a morning or persuade your hotel to make a reservation for you. If you are one of the lucky few to get in, you'll probably remember the seven- or nine-course prix fixe dinner as your best meal all year, but you'll want to forget the $250 price in a hurry. If you can't get a reservation, you can at least see some of the ingredients growing in the restaurant's own organic vegetable garden just across the street.

Touched by the same magic, however, is French Laundry's little cousin down the road, **Bouchon** (6534 Washington St., Yountville, 707/944-8037, lunch and dinner daily until 12:30 A.M., entrées $16–33), a French bistro. There's a little more bustle here than at the similar Bistro Jeanty nearby, perhaps because of the French Laundry connection or proximity to Yountville's thriving downtown scene (if there is such a place as downtown Yountville), but the brief menu still evokes a relaxed Parisian hole, helped by a smattering of French wines on the otherwise Napa-dominated list.

A few doors down the street is the down-to-earth **Hurley's** (6518 Washington St., Yountville, 707/944-2345, lunch and dinner daily, entrées $10–28). It might lack the Gallic charm of some of its neighbors, but the spacious restaurant with a large, heated patio has won a loyal following for its Mediterranean-inspired food prepared by renowned Valley chef Bob Hurley. It also stays open far later than other local restaurants, serving from a smaller bar menu 9 P.M.–midnight daily.

What was once Yountville's most popular casual breakfast hangout, The Diner, closed in 2004 (to much local dismay), and in its place a wine bar opened. That lasted about a year and was replaced in 2006 by **Ad Hoc** (6476 Washington St., Yountville, 707/944-2487, early dinner Thurs.–Mon., prix fixe menu $49). The name is apt due to the high turnover of businesses in this airy modern building, although it was reportedly chosen because owner Thomas Keller wanted only a temporary name while he worked out the restaurant's style. The name has stuck, the style has settled at rustic family style, and the popularity has soared. That's probably due to the Keller name—the same Thomas Keller who is behind French Laundry and Bouchon just up the road. The four-course menu changes nightly, and you'll get no choices, but considering the quality of the rustic seasonal fare, that's not necessarily a bad thing. The only certainty is that there'll be either soup or salad followed by a meat or fish main course, a cheese course, and dessert. The casual family-style dining suits the food better than the wine. The wine list is suitably endowed with moderately priced Californian and international wines, but markups are higher than is usual in this part of the wine world, and glasses are simple tumblers rather than stemware, which makes the prices even more egregious. Reservations are not quite as hard to get as at the Laundry, but don't expect to walk in and get a table most evenings either.

Next door to Ad Hoc is the sleek modern home of **Redd** (6480 Washington St., Yountville, 707/944-2222, www.reddnapavalley.com, lunch Mon.–Sat., dinner daily, dinner entrées $20–32), a critically acclaimed restaurant opened in 2005 by renowned Bay Area chef Richard Reddington, who made a name for himself at Auberge du Soleil before turning his attention across the valley to Yountville. The minimalist contemporary dining room oozes with luxurious fabrics, fixtures, and furniture, a style that is mirrored by the modern American cooking that has been compared favorably to the food at French Laundry. If you're in the mood to splurge, the $70 five-course taster menu will leave you with a lasting memory of the Napa Valley.

A visit to the classy restaurant at the Bardessono super-resort (6526 Yount St., 707/204-6030, www.bardessono.com, breakfast and dinner daily, lunch weekdays, breakfast dishes $5–20) needn't break the bank if you plump for its best-value meal—breakfast. Dinner prices are at the high end even for pricey Yountville, but for breakfast it is a great place to start the day with a small menu of classic dishes from a full cooked breakfast to simple coffee and pastries served inside or out.

Along St. Helena Highway (Highway 29)

One of the first big roadside restaurants north of Napa is **Brix** (7377 St. Helena Hwy., Yountville, 707/944-2749, lunch and dinner daily, entrées $12–31), a cavernous place with a little bit of an expense-account atmosphere but that serves some interesting Asian-American food—somewhat of a rarity in the valley. A standout feature of the restaurant is the big patio overlooking vineyards.

Mustards Grill (7399 St. Helena Hwy., Yountville, 707/944-2424, lunch and dinner daily, dinner entrées $17–26) is considered the king of the valley grills, having been around for over 25 years and having seen many more fashionable restaurants in the valley come and go. Such longevity and fame, however, have also put it firmly on the tourist map, as illustrated by the line waiting for tables on busy weekends. It might not look like much from the outside and resembles a fancy roadhouse on the inside, but unlike the Napa Valley Grille and the Rutherford Grill that are both now part of a chain, Mustards is a thoroughly Napa Valley affair, run by Cindy Pawlcyn, who also owns a couple of unique restaurants in St. Helena. It has spawned a cookbook and grows many of its own vegetables in its garden, as only a Napa restaurant could. The menu is filled with the sort of rich roasted and grilled meats that scream for a powerful Napa cabernet sauvignon, of which there are several dozen on the international wine list.

Picnic Supplies

In Yountville, the **Bouchon Bakery** (6528 Washington St., Yountville, 707/944-2253), opposite the V Marketplace, has a limited selection of very good sandwiches for under $10, as well as fresh bread and some sweeter bakery delights (try the macaroons). Right at the back of the **Napa Style** store, itself at the back of the V Marketplace, a small deli

offers gourmet made-to-order sandwiches, although they tend to be on the pricey side. A limited selection of soft drinks is also available. Locals are usually to be found ordering lunch at the **Yountville Deli**, which is on the north side of the Yountville Ranch Market (6498 Washington St., 707/944-2002, 6 A.M.–10 P.M. daily, deli 6 A.M.–3 P.M. daily). A full range of sandwiches is available in the deli for $6–8, and the market itself has everything else you might need for a picnic, from bread and cheese to beverages, including plenty of half bottles of local wine.

Farther up the St. Helena Highway (Highway 29) is the hard-to-miss **Oakville Grocery** (7856 St. Helena Hwy., Oakville, 707/944-8802, 7 A.M.–5 P.M. Mon.–Thurs., 7 A.M.–6 P.M. Fri.–Sat., 8 A.M.–5 P.M. Sun.). Just look for the line of cars parked at the side of the road next to a rather underwhelming-looking building with only a giant vintage Coca-Cola sign on one wall to brighten it up. Although it lacks the modern glamour of its spin-offs in Healdsburg and Palo Alto, this original is one of the best picnic supply stops

The Oakville Grocery is one of the Napa Valley's best picnic stops.

in the valley (some say in the entire country) and has certainly stood the test of time.

Farmers Market

Those who really want to assemble a picnic from scratch might want to pick through **Yountville's farmers market,** which operates May–October in the giant V Marketplace parking lot (where else?) 4 P.M.–dusk Wednesday.

INFORMATION AND SERVICES

The tiny **Yountville Chamber of Commerce** (6484 Washington St., Suite F, Yountville, 707/944-0904, www.yountville.com, 10 A.M.–5 P.M. daily) is awash with guides, leaflets, magazines, and advice about the local area. The concierge desk at the **V Marketplace** shopping center is also worth stopping at for some local tips and information.

Rutherford

This is a part of the valley where the weather starts to get seriously warm in the summer and the cabernets get seriously muscular. In fact, 71 percent of the vineyards in this appellation are planted to cabernet sauvignon, and the area was home to some of the pioneering wineries in the Napa Valley.

Like Oakville, Rutherford is a big appellation that spans the width of the valley. Some critics suggest there is not a great deal of difference between the two neighboring appellations—both have similar soils and weather, and both are capable of producing rich, muscular cabernets with exceptional balance. How Rutherford earned the bigger name over the years for cabernets might be partly due to the historic and influential wineries that made wine here, such as Inglenook and Beaulieu. Indeed, it was Beaulieu's famous winemaker, André Tchelistcheff, who made the connection between the distinctive soils of the region and their influence on the characteristics of the equally distinctive wines. "It takes Rutherford dust to grow great cabernet," he famously said.

You might also often hear the term "Rutherford Bench," a section of the AVA down the western side of the valley that is not benchland in the traditional sense and was never granted its own appellation status. It has become an oft-used marketing term nonetheless, normally used to suggest the best part of the Rutherford region.

RUTHERFORD WINERIES
Peju Province Winery

The slightly overstated French provincial architecture here hints at the roots of owner Anthony Peju, who arrived in the Napa Valley in the 1980s from his homeland of Azerbaijan by way of France, England, and Los Angeles. He was initially a grape grower in the valley, selling fruit to other valley winemakers before finally making his own wine. He also inadvertently helped smaller winemakers in the late 1980s by successfully suing Napa County when it tried to prevent him from selling wine out of his garage before his new winery had been completed. He won, thanks to a state law that allows a grower to sell his product where it is grown, and his victory subtly redefined what the term "winery" actually meant.

Peju's winery (8466 Hwy. 29, Rutherford, 707/963-3600 or 800/446-7358, www.peju. com, 10 A.M.–6 P.M. daily, tasting $10), with its manicured gardens, koi pond, curiously shaped trees, and lofty tasting room in a tower replete with giant stained-glass window, was finally completed in 1990, and the result is like a French country estate viewed through a hallucinogenic haze. It now produces about 35,000 cases of wine, and for years there has been talk of increasing this dramatically, but that has yet to happen. The trees lining the driveway make this an easy winery to spot from a distance, and their curved trunks are slowly but surely being trained to form arches over the road.

Apart from the curious trees, Peju is perhaps best known for its cabernet franc, but that's one wine that's usually not available for tasting due to its almost cultlike status. It sells out within months of its release each year, but Peju eventually plans to expand production and offer both reserve and vineyard-designate cabernet franc in the tasting room. Instead, visitors can taste the equally outstanding estate cabernet sauvignon and the unusual Provence table wine, a dark rosé blend of almost all the other varietals Peju grows—merlot, cabernet franc, and syrah, plus the white colombard and sauvignon blanc. Those varietals, together with zinfandel, are also available as separate wines, many sold only through the winery.

Peju is open later than most in the area, but during particularly crowded times you might find getting into the tasting room involves a bit of a wait. Once inside, however, the tasting fee is low for Napa Valley standards, and there might be some additional entertainment by the "Yodelmeister," a uniquely talented tasting room server.

◖ Frog's Leap Winery

Unlike many of his haughty neighbors, owner John Williams injects some fun into the often staid Napa wine scene, from the name of the winery and its classy black-and-white deco-style wine labels to a wine called Leapfrogmilch (a blend of riesling and chardonnay, and a perfect picnic wine) and the ever-present winery motto "Time's fun when you're having flies."

Frog's Leap (8815 Conn Creek Rd., off Silverado Trail, Rutherford, 707/963-4704 or 800/959-4704, www.frogsleap.com, 10 A.M.–4 P.M. Mon.–Sat., last tasting at 3:30 P.M., free tours at 10:30 A.M. and 2:30 P.M.) was formed by Williams and partner Larry Turley in 1981 near St. Helena on a former frog farm that once supplied the little amphibians' legs to restaurants throughout California. The winery's name was also a take on Stags Leap, that famous winery farther south

where Williams was once winemaker. It was not until 1994, when the partnership ended, that Williams moved the winery to Rutherford and restored the huge red barn that was home to the Adamson winery 100 years before.

Williams has used organic farming practices all along, and Frog's Leap is now regarded as a champion of organic practices in the valley. It also has a big organic vegetable and fruit garden, and visitors can usually help themselves to produce. The red barn is still the landmark to look out for, not least because there are precious few signs identifying the winery from the road, but it is no longer the main destination for visitors. In 2006 the winery opened a new tasting and hospitality building on what was once a huge expanse of grass beloved by picnickers. Thankfully the spacious lounge-like interior and wrap-around veranda of the new building are just as relaxing for tasting wine as soft grass, although the modernity is not quite in keeping with the rustic ramshackle charm of the older buildings and gardens.

No appointment is needed to visit the winery, and you can often taste the wine of the day for free (and perhaps some freshly harvested produce in the box by the main door). Regular tastings for $15 offer four wines and a few morsels to eat, all served inside or out. The best reason to visit, however, is for one of the free tours offered twice daily by appointment only. They highlight the organic farming principles for which the winery is famous and end with a free tasting.

Almost half the 60,000 cases of wine made here each year are the excellent and well-priced sauvignon blanc, but Frog's Leap is also known for its cabernet sauvignon, zinfandel, and the flagship Rutherford, a bordeaux-style red blend that highlights the unique fruit-meets-earth characteristics of Rutherford appellation wines. The portfolio also includes merlot, chardonnay, syrah, and a wine called (appropriately enough) Pink, which is another fun and cheap picnic wine.

Caymus Vineyards

This is a great example of how wineries on

TAKING TOURS TO ANOTHER LEVEL

There are already cable cars and castles, modern art and historic architecture, Hollywood connections and classic car collections. What could possibly upstage such a diverse collection of attractions in this giant theme park of viticultural egotism and hedonism?

One candidate is a six-wheel-drive vintage Swiss military vehicle called a Pinzgauer, which looks like no other vehicle in the valley. It is the transport of choice at **Long Meadow Ranch,** a tranquil ranch and winery high up in the Mayacamas range above Rutherford, which is itself unlike any other winery you're likely to visit in the bustle of Napa Valley.

Visiting the 650-acre ranch and tasting the grass-fed beef, olive oil, and wines does not come cheap, but for a change of pace it might be worth the price. The trip from Rutherford up the narrow mountain roads in the open-sided Pinzgauer is rather like going on a safari – one that provides a refreshing escape from the Napa Valley zoo.

Once at the ranch, it no longer feels like the Napa Valley. The stress of Highway 29 traffic is just a distant memory. Horses munch contentedly in the paddock, the smell of sagebrush wafts through the crisp air (perhaps mingling with a hint of manure), and only the rows of vines struggling up distant mountainsides are a reminder that this is still Wine Country.

Ted Hall, a former management consultant who grew up on a farm in Pennsylvania, bought the historic ranch in 1989 and has since transformed it into a farming and ranching business that could probably keep restaurants up and down the valley supplied with ingredients all year long. Grass-fed beef, eggs, vegetables, and fruit are all part of the organic bounty. The ranch also breeds and sells horses, cattle, and the occasional rooster, so you might be able to pick up an unusual souvenir. This being Wine Country, however, it is olive oil and wine that visitors learn most about on the tours.

Vineyards were planted up here as far back as the late 1800s, by some accounts, and today there are about 25 acres of vines farmed at the ranch, producing about 5,000 cases of wine. The cabernet sauvignon has taken its place alongside some of the best in the valley in recent years and is a softer, earthier style of wine more reminiscent of bordeaux than the wines made on the hotter valley floor. A sauvignon blanc is the only white wine produced. Sangiovese was added to the portfolio in 2000, though it is made in such limited quantities that it usually sells out within a few months of being released in early summer. The couple of acres of merlot grapes planted in the late 1990s go into the proprietary Ranch House Red blend, a relative bargain at under $20 a bottle.

The olive oil history goes back just as far. A grove of some 200 olive trees dating from about 1870 was discovered shortly after Hall

---

this side of the valley turn out some of the best wines with little fanfare. The Caymus family has been farming in the valley for more than 100 years but was ahead of the modern wine rush when they ripped up their prune orchards to plant vines in the early 1970s.

Since then, Caymus (8700 Conn Creek Rd., Rutherford, 707/967-3010, www.caymus.com, tasting by appointment 10 A.M.–4 P.M. daily, $25) gained a reputation under the ownership of the late Charlie Wagner for producing one of the best Napa cabernets, the Special Selection, made with the best grapes from the estate vineyard in Rutherford. It garners regular praise from all the major critics and is usually on the tasting flight at the sit-down, appointment-only tasting. The other well-known Caymus wine, now made by Charlie's son, Chuck, is a nonreserve cabernet that is equally impressive and half the price. A less-well-known wine, but one to look out for nonetheless, is the outstanding zinfandel that is sold only at the winery.

Don't come expecting a flashy Napa-style spectacle for the money. This is definitely a winery tasting experience for those serious about their wines, but gardening aficionados will also get a kick from the pretty surroundings.

bought the land; it had been overgrown by a forest of taller trees. The grove has since been brought back to productive life and is the source of the flagship oil, Prato Lungo. Another 2,000 olive trees were planted, and the ranch is now home to one of only two oil presses in the Napa Valley.

Sustainable farming is the byword here, as the huge piles of compost suggest. Even the winery building is a model of sustainable practices. Walls are made from compressed earth dug out during construction of the caves, and all power is provided by solar panels.

Tasting the wines, olive oil, and perhaps some local cheese and beef is the culmination of the various tours offered at Long Meadow Ranch. A Pinzgauer ferries visitors up ever-narrower mountain roads to the ranch, passing vineyards, olive orchards, and meadows (sit on the right side on the way up for the best views of the valley below). The safari-like excursion continues up into vineyards and olive groves, where principles of grape and olive growing and organic farming practices are explained, before returning to the winery building for a look at the olive press and barrel-aging caves, and the all-important tasting.

The cheapest tour lasts about two hours, costs $35, and is offered every Saturday at 11 A.M. during the summer. During the week, daily tours cost $50 but are slightly longer, and the tasting at the end includes more oils and wines. There's also a self-propelled tour – following a hiking trail around the ranch to work up an appetite for the tasting. For $150, you can taste just about everything the ranch produces with a gourmet picnic after the main tour.

All the tours are appointment-only and are limited to 10 people, which is the seating capacity of the Pinzgauer. That means they book up fast during the summer but also ensures they are always fairly intimate and relaxing.

The ranch has an organic outpost down on the valley floor called **Rutherford Gardens** (1796 St. Helena Hwy., Rutherford, just opposite Grgich Hills winery), from where all the tours begin. Ted Hall bought a six-acre parcel of land next to Highway 29 and, instead of planting vines like all his neighbors, turned it into an organic fruit and vegetable farm. Produce is sold to local restaurants, at the St. Helena farmers market, and at the farm stand that's open Saturdays May–October.

Whether you have a tour booked or not, take a few minutes to wander around the gardens for an aromatic and mouthwatering reminder that there's more to Napa Valley than grapes – and, perhaps, to snag a spot at the secluded picnic table hidden under the giant fig tree.

For more information about the tours and to book a spot, contact Long Meadow Ranch (707/963-4555, www.longmeadowranch.com) at least 48 hours in advance.

Beaulieu Vineyard

A giant ivy-clad winery building that looks as dominant as any in the Napa Valley is a reminder of the huge role Beaulieu Vineyard (BV, 1960 Hwy. 29, Rutherford, 707/967-5200, www.bvwines.com, tastings and tours 10 A.M.–5 P.M. daily) played in the modern Californian wine industry. Founded in 1900 by Frenchman Georges de Latour, BV was one of the few wineries to maintain production during Prohibition. After repeal, Latour brought a young wine expert over from France to help him refine his wines and ensure they would not spoil while being shipped to the East Coast markets. That man was the late André Tchelistcheff, a Russian émigré who ended up transforming the way wine was made in California while he was winemaker at Beaulieu 1938–1973.

Tchelistcheff helped modernize the winemaking process and improved vineyard management at Beaulieu, introducing new principles of cellar hygiene, improving fermentation techniques, and even introducing those giant wind machines you still see in the valley today that are designed to prevent frost damage to vines. Where he led, others followed. BV wines were soon winning awards, and the quality of the valley's other wines drastically improved as Tchelistcheff's methods became commonplace. He is said to have coined the term "Rutherford dust," for the area's soils, an expression still used today by critics who claim to be able to taste the soil's characteristics in the wines.

The winery has long since passed into the hands of multinational wine conglomerates (it is currently owned by Diageo) and now makes well over 1 million cases of wine per year, although the best Napa Valley wines available here represent only a fraction of the total. BV is perhaps best known for its powerful, dusty cabernet sauvignons, in particular the flagship Georges Latour Private Reserve and the more approachable Tapestry blend, plus the cheaper nonreserve Rutherford. It also makes a full range of other red and white wines from its Napa Valley vineyards, four of which can be sampled on the red-only or white-only tasting menu.

The best option, however, are the two cabernet-focused tasting options. One includes some clonal bottlings and the Tapestry blend ($20)

and the other is a horizontal or vertical $30 tasting of the single-vineyard reserves, including the Latour, that is offered in the impressive new reserve tasting room, which has rich stonework, subdued lighting, and a marble-topped tasting bar that does a good job of conveying the appropriate degree of gravitas for wines that helped put California on the world wine map. A tasting of some of BV's best cabernets is also part of the $40 appointment-only tour of the historic winery and its cellars.

Rutherford Hill

One of the best merlots for the price and certainly the best winery picnic grounds in the valley can be found at Rutherford Hill Winery (200 Rutherford Hill Rd., off Silverado Trail, Rutherford, 707/963-1871, www.rutherfordhill.com, 10 A.M.–5 P.M. daily, tasting $15–30), housed in a giant barnlike redwood building just a mile up the hill from the Silverado Trail (and neighboring the Auberge du Soleil resort). The winery was created in the early 1970s, and the Rutherford Hill name dates from 1975, when a group of investors

© PHILIP GOLDSMITH

Rutherford Hill winery makes some fine merlot and is a great spot for a picnic.

bought the winery. It changed hands again the mid-1990s, but the decades-long reputation for making excellent and consistent merlot has remained. That varietal now accounts for about three-quarters of the approximately 100,000 cases of wine made here.

Rutherford Hill also makes small quantities of a lot of other wines that never seem to garner quite the same praise as the merlot. They include cabernet sauvignon and a couple of chardonnays, syrah, and sangiovese, all from Napa Valley vineyards.

A chilled bottle of sauvignon blanc or rosé of merlot are perhaps the best wines to grab for a picnic in one of the two oak-shaded picnic grounds, both of which offer tantalizing glimpses through the trees of the valley far below. The view also takes in the rooftops of the exclusive Auberge du Soleil resort just down the hill, so even if you can't afford to stay there, you can at least see what some of the fuss is about.

In the 1980s the winery carved out some of the most extensive aging caves in the valley, with more than a mile of tunnels that can store about 8,000 barrels of wine. They can be seen as part of the short tour offered three times a day at 11:30 A.M., 1:30 P.M., and 3:30 P.M. for $5 on top of the regular tasting fees.

Rubicon Estate Winery

When a fabled Hollywood director buys one of the most storied of the historic Napa Valley wineries, it's somewhat inevitable that the result would be one of the most ostentatious winery shows in the valley. And so it is at Rubicon Estate (1991 Hwy. 29, Rutherford, 707/968-1100, www.rubiconestate.com, 10 A.M.–5 P.M. daily, tour only $25, tasting and tour $25–50), where stretch limos idle in the parking lot and an eager group of valets relieve visitors of their cars before they are sent down the red carpet to the historic ivy-clad stone mansion nestled at the foot of the scenic hills.

Try to ignore the pergolas and fountains outside—they are modern additions that add a bit of film-set drama to the otherwise beautiful mansion. Instead, take your small green

visitor's passport inside the mansion house and sign up for the next hour-long Legacy Tour to learn more about the winery's colorful history and explore the new storage caves, or sidle up to the bar in the cavernous tasting room for a taste of five wines (possibly more if the entertaining pourers are in a jovial mood). Both the tour and tasting are included in the $25 entrance fee, which everyone (except valley residents) must pay just to get beyond the gatehouse. It's a policy that might prevent a surplus of gawkers, but it doesn't seem to prevent huge crowds flocking here on the busiest days.

While waiting for the tour to start, you can browse the small museum that highlights the history of the former Inglenook Estate, which Francis Ford Coppola and his wife, Eleanor, bought in sections between 1975 (a year after *The Godfather II* was released) and 1994 and have since transformed into a huge tourist and wine-making presence in the valley. With this being part Hollywood production, there's also plenty of ego-massaging museum space devoted to the Coppolas themselves, including the film careers of Francis, Eleanor, and their children Sofia and Roman.

The Inglenook Estate was established in 1871 by the son-in-law of George Yount, the first white settler in Napa Valley, who is also credited with planting the first vineyard in the valley in 1838. Inglenook, its vineyard, and some surrounding land were bought in 1879 by Alaskan fur trader Gustave Niebaum, who set about becoming a serious wine producer, albeit as more of a hobby than a business. Niebaum died in 1908, but the winery and its mission to make world-class wines lived on in fits and starts in the hands of Niebaum's widow, friends, and relatives (including Niebaum's great-nephew, renowned valley winemaker John Daniel), until it was sold to United Vintners in 1964, which eventually became Heublein in 1969.

What the Coppolas bought in 1975 was not actually the Inglenook winery operation but part of the estate's land and Niebaum's mansion. Nevertheless, a new winery was born in 1978 and called Niebaum-Coppola in homage to Gustave Niebaum and his pursuit of wine perfection. Legendary winemaker André Tchelistcheff helped the Coppolas create their first wine, called Rubicon, a powerful bordeaux blend that is still made today. The entire Inglenook Estate was eventually reunited almost 20 years later when the Coppolas bought much of the rest of the Inglenook winery and its vineyards from Heublein in 1994 (one of the Inglenook production facilities was sold to the Napa Wine Company in Oakville).

Despite its grand surroundings and history, Rubicon Estate makes a modest 35,000 cases of estate wines, including the flagship Rubicon and its white equivalent, called Blancaneaux. Other wines from the Rutherford estate vineyards include the Edizione Pennino zinfandel, named after Coppola's maternal grandmother; the blockbuster Cask cabernet sauvignon; an aromatic cabernet franc; and an unusual sparkling wine called Sofia blanc de blancs, which is made using pinot blanc, muscat, and sauvignon blanc, giving it a richer fruit flavor than traditional sparklers (there's no mention of whether the wine's character matches Sofia Coppola's). The cheaper Captains Reserve wines, available only at the winery, account for about a third of the production and are sourced from other Napa Valley vineyards. They include a Carneros pinot noir, a crisp sauvignon blanc from the Pope Valley, and merlot with a dash of petite sirah added to the blend.

If you like the wines, you can get more than a taste at the small wine bar down the end of the long passage to the left of the entrance. In addition to wines by the glass, the bar offers coffee and some food-friendly appetizers that can be enjoyed at one of the cozy tables under the vaulted ceilings of the cellar or on the sunny patio.

The Coppola name is also attached to many other cheaper wine labels, however, and those are the focus at a winery the Coppolas bought in 2005 near Geyserville in the Alexander Valley. Production of Coppola-branded wines amounts to about 750,000 cases a year, with the Rubicon Estate representing the cream of the crop.

Mumm Napa Valley

A late starter among the French champagne houses to set up in California, Mumm Napa (8445 Silverado Trail, Rutherford, 707/967-7700, www.mummcuveenapa.com, 10 A.M.–5 P.M. daily, tasting $5–25) was established in 1985 by France's G. H. Mumm and Seagram, though it has been owned by several other multinationals since then, including Allied Domecq and currently Pernod Ricard. There is definitely a corporate air about the operations here, but not really more so than many other large valley wineries. The unassuming redwood winery building, completed on the Silverado Trail in 1988, is certainly lower key than you would expect for a winery that makes about 200,000 cases of sparkling wine and owns more than 50 vineyards all over Carneros and the Napa Valley.

The wines range from the classic and reasonably priced Brut Prestige, a dry blend of pinot noir and chardonnay, up to the more fruit-forward and expensive DVX, which comes in white and rosé styles. Mumm also makes a winery-only pinot gris still wine, which is perfect for a picnic but tends to sell out quickly.

Like all the big champagne houses in the valley, Mumm puts on quite a show for visitors, but the tasting options are by the glass and can prove to be pricey. The upside is that you can relax on the big terrace overlooking the vineyards and have someone bring your bubbly of choice, whether you want to spend just $5 or splurge $15 for the best as you watch the sun set on a balmy summer evening. Be prepared to wait on holiday weekends or at other busy times because lines often snake out the door. A seat is not essential; you can stroll over to the small art gallery, glass in hand, to see the permanent collection of about 30 original Ansel Adams prints as well as other photography exhibits that change several times a year. Large windows in the gallery give tantalizing views of the barrel and triage rooms below.

Those who prefer to learn more about what they are drinking and seeing should take the informative (and free) tour, which runs on the hour from 10 A.M. until 3 P.M. and illustrates the art and science behind the bubbles. Private tours are available by appointment.

ZD Wines

People leave all sorts of professions to establish wineries, though perhaps one of the more unusual is the rocket engineering business that Gino Zepponi (the Z in the name) and Norman de Leuze (the D) left to concentrate on the winery they had started as a hobby in Carneros in 1969. By the time they had put ZD on the map as a producer of high-quality chardonnay and pinot noir, wine-making was a full-time job. Their winery moved to its current location in Rutherford in 1979. It's an unassuming winery and tasting room that offers a relaxing change of pace in the often frenetic valley along with a chance to actually have a meaningful conversation about wine with the staff. The basic fee of $10 for tasting some consistently good wines is also a refreshing change from the many pricier, hit-and-miss tasting-room experiences elsewhere in the valley.

ZD is now owned by the De Lueze family and still makes outstanding chardonnay and pinot from its Carneros vineyards, including reserves. Those two varietals still account for the majority of the 30,000 cases made each year but have been joined by a rich cabernet sauvignon from other Napa appellations along with a reserve cabernet from ZD's own three acres of vineyards in Rutherford. All are available in the tasting room and can also be tried at the $20 wine-and-cheese pairing offered every Saturday morning by appointment. Tours of the winery, including a barrel tasting, are also available by appointment for $25, but the better touring option is the $30 ecotour that takes visitors out into an organic cabernet vineyard to discuss the principles of Wine Country organic farming.

Taking pricey Napa cabernet to the extreme, ZD also makes limited quantities of its Abacus wine each year from a blend of all its previous vintages of reserve cabernet, starting from 1992. In 2010, Abacus XII was released,

containing 17 former vintages. The idea is to combine the best aspects of aged wine with the fruit of more youthful wine. You'll have to pay upwards of $450 per bottle to find out if it succeeds, however, because Abacus is not available for tasting (8383 Silverado Trail, Napa, 800/487-7757, www.zdwines.com, 10 A.M.–4:30 P.M. daily, regular tasting $10, reserve $15).

SHOPPING

Yountville and St. Helena have done a pretty good job of sucking the retailing life from elsewhere in the mid-valley area, with the exception of the **St. Helena Olive Oil Company** (8576 St. Helena Hwy. S., Rutherford, 707/967-1003 or 800/939-9880, www.sholiveoil.com, 10 A.M.–5 P.M. daily), which is orphaned a few miles south of its namesake town in Rutherford. Don't be put off by the modest storefront while tooling up the road toward St. Helena. This place has a cavernous interior and sells far more than olive oils. In fact, almost every condiment a gourmet cook might need (and some they never knew they needed) is probably here, from balsamic vinegar to honey by way of strange concoctions like apricot pepper and stone-ground cabernet mustard. Take a break from wine tasting and try some of the 20 or so olive oils lined up on the counter. Then end the break and wash the oils down with more wine at the tasting counter of **Off the Map Wines** (tasting fee $10), which represents more than a dozen of the valley's small high-end wine producers.

ACCOMMODATIONS

High up in the eastern hills of the valley, bathed in afternoon sun and buzzing with the sound of the golf carts used to ferry guests around, is (**Auberge du Soleil** (180 Rutherford Hill Rd., Rutherford, 707/963-1211 or 800/348-5406, www.aubergedusoleil.com), or the Inn of the Sun, one of the valley's most luxurious resorts, famous for being the hangout of the rich, the famous, and lucky honeymooners. This is a place totally at ease with itself, where the decor plays a relaxed second fiddle to the stunning location rather than competing with it. Terracotta tiles, natural woods, fireplaces, leather, and earth tones hint at some French country style, but it's the views from almost everywhere that dominate. Work out in the gym with views, eat with views at the acclaimed restaurant, swim with views, or step out of your room's French doors onto a balcony with views. Just be prepared to pay dearly for those views, the amenities, and the exclusivity of the whole place. Whether they're worth the money is open to debate, but Auberge regularly shows up on lists of the world's top hotels, and its rates have climbed significantly in recent years, suggesting there is no shortage of people willing to empty their bank accounts for the privilege of staying here.

There are 50 rooms and suites in cottages spread throughout the 33 lush acres of this former olive grove, and all have the word *view* in their descriptions. The cheapest and smallest are the Hilltop View rooms ($575 in winter, $725–750 summer–fall) in the main building upstairs from the restaurant and bar, though they "may be inappropriate for light sleepers," the resort suggests. Slightly larger rooms in better locations start at $625, and the mammoth suites that are the size of a typical apartment run $1,150–1,625 per night.

Slightly more down-to-earth than Auberge in terms of price, altitude, and attitude is the cozy **Rancho Caymus Inn** (1140 Rutherford Rd., Rutherford, 707/963-1777 or 800/845-1777, www.ranchocaymus.com). Wood beams and floors, adobe walls, and quirky design elements, including hand-dyed South American rugs and carved headboards, give this 26-room Spanish-style inn a rustic hand-crafted charm. Modern amenities are somewhat lacking, but the rooms all have private bathrooms, small patios overlooking the lush gardens, wet bars and refrigerators, and a separate seating area that make them more like junior suites. All but the smallest Caymus Suites have fireplaces. Some of the more expensive suites also have whirlpool tubs. Rates for the Caymus Suites start at $155 midweek in winter and reach $260 per night on fall weekends. The larger Rancho Suites run $185–310 per night and the Master Suites are $215–410 a night.

FOOD

If a special occasion requires a special restaurant (and French Laundry is not answering the phone), there's probably no better place in this part of the valley than **Auberge du Soleil** (180 Rutherford Hill Rd., off Silverado Trail, Rutherford, 707/967-3111 or 800/348-5406, reservations required, lunch and dinner daily, four-course prix fixe $105, chef's tasting six-course prix fixe $125). You don't need to be a guest to see why this resort restaurant has been wowing diners with its menu and stunning views of the valley since 1981. The wow factor is still as strong as ever and might make you want to stay at the resort on your next visit (after saving up, that is).

The exquisitely prepared French-Californian food is not as expensive as you'd think—the $105 set price buys you a four-course dinner with plenty of choices for every course (although that doesn't include wine, of course). Just make sure you choose a fine day, and try to get a table out on the terrace for the best views, especially at sunset. And casual as it might be, this is still a fancy restaurant, so don't turn up in baggy shorts and flip-flops.

For some more down-to-earth dining, often without the need for a reservation, the **Rutherford Grill** (1180 Rutherford Rd., next to Beaulieu Vineyard's winery, Rutherford, 707/963-1792, lunch and dinner daily, dinner entrées $15–40) offers traditional steakhouse fare in a slightly corporate setting that hints at the fact that it is owned by the Houston's restaurant chain. Nevertheless, it has become one of the most popular steakhouses among Napa Valley residents and is a great place for a reliably cooked and aged steak to pair with a well-aged Rutherford cabernet. This is not the place to go for cutting-edge California cuisine, but it is the place for a classic steak dinner. There's also a nice shady patio, although it's a little too close to the road to be classified as peaceful.

St. Helena and Vicinity

St. Helena has been the center of the valley's wine industry from the very beginning. George Crane first planted grapes in the area in 1861, followed by Charles Krug a few years later. With the new wine industry springing up all around, the town grew rapidly and was incorporated in 1876, only a few years after Napa and many years before Calistoga in 1885.

St. Helena's history has been inextricably linked to the valley's wine industry ever since. Calistoga to the north had its spas to draw visitors, and Napa to the south became a thriving commercial port city, gateway to the valley, but to a certain extent St. Helena has always been a tourist town. Wealthy weekenders came here to wine and dine in the early 1900s, an influx of European immigrants created the thriving Italian and French heritage, and the town was the epicenter of the valley's bootlegging industry during Prohibition, making the St. Helena Highway (Highway 29, to locals) almost as busy in the 1930s as it is today.

This might be a town with the dubious distinction of having a name used disparagingly as a verb—"St. Helena–ization" being the process of a historic pretty town selling its soul to tourism—but it also boasts active civic leaders who fight hard against overdevelopment in an attempt to keep some semblance of the town's historic and rural charm intact.

The Wines

As the Napa Valley gets narrower farther north and the mountains ever more sheltering, the weather gets hotter. The **St. Helena** appellation includes the narrowest point of the valley and also some of the biggest and most historic winery names, like Beringer, Charles Krug, and Louis Martini. The heat and rich alluvial soils are responsible for wines that help give the Napa Valley its name for rich and highly extracted wines. You'll know a St. Helena cabernet when you taste one—big, bold, and powerful.

West of St. Helena, up the slopes of the Mayacamas mountains, is the **Spring Mountain** appellation, an area with almost as much wine-making history as the valley floor below. The region gets its name from the many springs and creeks—there's actually not a peak called Spring Mountain. The mountain wineries here make cabernet sauvignon and merlot with uncommon density and power. White wines are less common but include sauvignon blanc with a classic mountain minerality. As with many mountain-grown wines, however, the reds can be less approachable when young than those from the valley floor, but they tend to be more consistent year to year and usually only need a few years of aging to reach their full potential.

ST. HELENA WINERIES
V. Sattui Winery

To say this place gets crowded in the summer is like saying the Napa Valley is an undiscovered wine region. Sattui (1111 White Ln., St. Helena, 707/963-7774, www.vsattui.com, 9 A.M.–6 P.M. daily spring–fall, 9 A.M.–5 P.M. winter) has become a victim of its own success, and can resemble a supermarket the night before Thanksgiving as hordes descend on the pretty winery for its extensive deli and even more extensive list of well-priced wines. This is picnic central (and often party central) in this part of the valley, though after eating enough free deli samples, you might not need to buy picnic supplies. The pungent smell of the dozens of cheeses and countless other gourmet foods fills the tasting room of the stone winery building, while on summer weekends hardly an inch of grass is visible outside in the two-acre picnic area as tour buses disgorge their stumbling passengers.

The reason for its popularity is simple—this is the only place in the valley where you can buy good food and cheap wines, then plop yourself down on the grass right outside to eat and drink. You just have to ignore the constant drone of traffic from the main road and the shrieks of drunken visitors. It's also

To **C** CULINARY INSTITUTE
OF AMERICA and Calistoga

29 128

BERINGER
VINEYARDS

MAIN ST

PRATT AVE

ELMHURST AVE

OAK AVE

SPRING MOUNTAIN RD

MADRONA AVE

To **C** PRIDE MOUNTAIN VINEYARDS,
Spring Mountain and Santa Rosa

© AVALON TRAVEL

FULTON LANE

RAILROAD AVE

SILVERADO MUSEUM/
PUBLIC LIBRARY
★
LIBRARY LANE

HUNT AVE

POPE ST

TERRA
CAMEO   CINDY'S
Lyman   THEATER   BACKSTREET
Park ODD   KITCHEN
FELLOWS   LOLO'S
HALL GIUGNI'S   SECOND
WOODHOUSE   GILLWOODS GROCERY   TO NONE
CHOCOLATE   CAFÉ   & DELI
NAPA VALLEY   ANA'S
COFFEE ROASTING   MARKET   CANTINA   SUNSHINE
COMPANY   FOODS
MODEL   HOTEL   MARTINI
BAKERY   ST. HELENA   HOUSE

PINE ST

KEARNEY ST

ADAMS ST

SPRING ST

MITCHELL DR

STOCKTON ST

one of only three wineries in the entire valley with an exemption to a planning law banning wineries from hosting weddings or wedding receptions, so don't be surprised to see the occasional bride.

V. Sattui is an old wine-making business, but the winery itself is not that old. Vittorio Sattui started making wine in San Francisco in the late 1800s using grapes from St. Helena vineyards. It wasn't until 1975 that a winery was built here by great-grandson Daryl Sattui, and its combination of cheap wines and a well-stocked delicatessen was an instant hit. As the winery became swamped in the 1990s, Sattui embarked on a new venture to fulfill his dreams of creating a Tuscan wonderland and high-end wines. Opened in 2007, his Castello di Amorosa near Calistoga is a tranquil contrast from V. Sattui and should be the destination for those wanting to taste the best Sattui wines.

The V. Sattui operation now makes about 45,000 cases of wine each year, with many bottles costing less than $20, and has won several "Winery of the Year" awards from the State Fair. You will not find any reviews from magazine critics, however, because Sattui wines

cannot be bought at any wine shop. The entire production is sold at the winery and through the Sattui wine clubs, making this one of the most successful direct-to-consumer wineries in California. The huge portfolio includes a host of great picnic wines, like the popular Gamay Rouge rosé (both still and sparkling forms), a dry riesling, and a tangy sangiovese. Cabernet sauvignon in both blended and vineyard-designate styles is what the winery is perhaps best known for. All can be tasted for a modest $5 (which also adds to the popularity), but despite the size of the tasting bar you might have to wait a while for space to open up.

Also worth trying are the dessert wines, including delicious madeira and juicy muscat. Buy a case of any wine and you instantly become a member of the Cellar Club, which has its own tasting bar. The winery also has some of the longest opening hours in the valley, making it an ideal stop if you're an early riser or late eater.

Hall

This is the classy public face of one of Napa Valley's rising stars and has been snapping up

ST. HELENA

prime vineyards since it was established in Rutherford in 1995 by entrepreneurs Kathryn and Craig Hall. By 2006 the Halls were the third-largest land owners in the valley, and the Hall winery (401 St. Helena Hwy. S., St. Helena, 707/967-2626 or 866/667-4255, www.hallwines.com, 10 A.M.–5:30 P.M. daily, tasting $15–25) is set to become the talk of the valley in a couple of years when a new winery, designed by Frank Gehry and local architect John Lail, is finally completed.

Behind the modest tasting room is the former Napa Valley Cooperative Winery, a warehouse-like facility built around an old stone winery dating from 1885. The original winery is an important piece of valley history that will be uncovered and form the centerpiece of the new winery complex. The trademark Gehry flourishes had to be toned down before approval was granted by the city of St. Helena in early 2006, but it will still be a unique, modern addition to the architectural mash-up of the Napa Valley winery scene.

Once the new winery is completed, production of Hall wines will probably increase from the current 25,000 cases to take full advantage

of the growing portfolio of vineyards in the Napa and Alexander Valleys. Until then, the relaxed tasting room is in what looks like a shabby-chic cottage-style building with a large shaded patio. But as you approach the entrance with its bright red awning, don't be fooled by the peeling paint on the exterior—it was hand-painted to look shabby-chic and is just another artistic addition to the many sculptures in the grounds from the Halls' private collection.

The Halls have another winery, the exclusive Hall-Rutherford, in the hills above Auberge du Soleil across the valley, which is open to the public by appointment only and is where a high-end cabernet sauvignon is made from the Sacrashe estate vineyard. You might be lucky enough to taste this along with more reasonably priced Hall wines, including cabernet sauvignon, merlot, and sauvignon blanc.

Louis M. Martini Winery

The hulking winery of Louis M. Martini (254 St. Helena Hwy., St. Helena, 707/968-3362, www.louismartini.com, 10 A.M.–6 P.M. daily, tasting $15–30) just north of V. Sattui is another piece of Napa's wine-making history, established here after the repeal of Prohibition in the 1930s by Louis Martini, an Italian immigrant who had been making wine at his small family winery and later at a larger facility in the Central Valley. Shortly after setting up in the Napa Valley he also bought 240 acres of vineyards in the Mayacamas Mountains above the Sonoma Valley. That Monte Rosso vineyard has been responsible for Martini's best wines ever since.

The winery was family owned right up to 2002, when it was bought by the even bigger family wine business, the giant E&J Gallo, and became Gallo's first Napa Valley outpost. Gallo pumped millions into upgrading the rather tired old winery, and by all accounts the wines have improved as a result. This is very much a winery for red wine drinkers—the two white wines made here don't generally feature on the tasting menu, although you might get a free taste of the muscat and gewürztraminer blend during the summer.

The 300,000 cases of wine made here each year are dominated by various iterations of cabernet sauvignon, from appellation-specific bottlings to vineyard-specific and right down to lot-specific. The few other noncabernet wines on the list include a petite sirah and meritage blend that is arguably better value and more approachable than some of the cabs. Many of the best wines come from the Monte Rosso vineyard, including cabernets, a zinfandel, and a syrah. Several vintages of the Monte Rosso cabernet are usually featured on the priciest of the tasting menus. A sheltered patio has tables and chairs for those who want to linger, and Martini is open at least half an hour later than most neighboring wineries, making it a good last stop.

Prager Winery & Port Works

Right opposite the entrance to Martini is the little wooden sign and driveway leading to Prager Winery (1281 Lewelling Ln., St. Helena, 707/963-7678 or 800/969-7678, www.pragerport.com, 10 A.M.–4:30 P.M. daily, tasting $15), a funky, family-owned port producer that is a refreshing change from the commercial

atmosphere of most wineries in the area. The closest you'll find to a winery museum here is the Web Window, a masterpiece of spiderweb engineering that's supposedly been untouched since 1979.

The Prager family makes a few regular wines here (a couple are usually included in the tasting), but most of the 3,500-case annual production is an unusual selection of ports and late-harvest dessert wines, including a fruity white port made from chardonnay and the more usual vintage and tawny ports made predominantly with cabernet sauvignon and petite sirah grapes. Bring a cigar to enjoy with port out in the garden.

Beringer Vineyards

The oldest continuously operated winery in Napa Valley is now a huge tourist attraction that often contributes to St. Helena's summer traffic jams, though it is still worth a visit (ideally midweek, when it's a bit quieter) for its significance in the valley's wine history and for some outstanding reserve wines.

Beringer Vineyards (2000 Main St., St. Helena, 707/963-7115, www.beringer.com, 10 A.M.–6 P.M. daily summer, 10 A.M.–5 P.M. daily fall–spring) was started by a couple of German brothers, Jacob and Frederick Beringer, who already knew a bit about winemaking by the time they reached California. Jacob arrived first, working briefly for Charles Krug before he bought land nearby. By 1878 his winery was said to be making 100,000 gallons of wine a year (about 45,000 cases by today's measure), and he was eventually joined by his brother, who built the lavish and ornate Rhine House to remind him of home.

The winery operated through Prohibition and shortly after repeal was making an astonishing 200,000 gallons of wine a year. It was good wine too: Beringer is one of a handful of historic wineries in the valley (others include Inglenook, Beaulieu, and Larkmead) credited with helping modernize the wine industry after Prohibition by introducing European-style production techniques and quality control rather than making cheap bulk wines. The entire

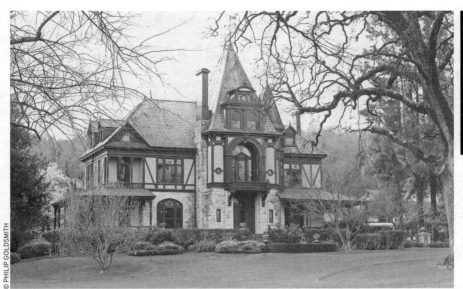

The Rhine House at Beringer Vineyards is a reminder of the winery's German roots.

© PHILIP GOLDSMITH

estate was placed on the National Register of Historic Places in 2001.

Successive corporate owners have poured millions into restoring both the property and the reputation of the winery. Most recently its current owner, Fosters Wine Estates, restored and upgraded the Rhine House, making it an even more impressive location to taste some of Beringer's best wines. Overall the winery is a huge operation, making several million cases of wine each year (at a modern facility over the road) under numerous labels, but it owns many prime vineyards and is still known for turning out some of the best and most consistent premium wines in California, most notably its Private Reserve chardonnay and cabernet sauvignon, which are both beloved by well-known U.S. wine critics.

Beringer was the first Napa winery to offer reserve wine tasting, back in the 1980s, and continues the tradition in the Rhine House, where $25 buys you a flight of any four wines from the dozen usually on the menu, including some outstanding single-vineyard cabernets as

well as the Private Reserve cabernet and chardonnay that are considered among the best in the Napa Valley. You can also make an appointment for a more civilized and relaxing reserve tasting on the porch of the Rhine House surrounded by greenery for the same price. The regular tasting in the old winery building up the hill costs just $10 for one of several themed flights of wine, but the atmosphere is far less enjoyable than the wood-paneled and stained-glass charm of the Rhine House unless you draw a particularly entertaining and generous pourer.

The half dozen different tours at Beringer are also well worth experiencing, offering plenty of wine education, history, and a tasting for not much more than a tasting alone would cost. They are generally offered four times a day. Check the website for exact times. The two best are the Taste of Beringer Tour ($20), which has a wine-making focus and takes in vineyards, the 19th-century hand-dug caves, and a tasting; and the Rhine House tour ($25), a must for history buffs that includes a sit-down tasting. Reservations are strongly recommended for these tours, particularly in the summer, but you might be able to buy tickets on the same day during quieter times of the year. The shorter Family Tour takes you deep inside the old stone winery and caves, finishing with a tasting of a couple of wines, and is a bargain at $15 (no reservations are taken, so come early to buy tickets for a later tour that day).

The popularity of the winery along with the ticket booths adjacent to the parking lot tend to make the place feel more like a wine theme park in the summer, but the grounds are expansive enough that you can escape the worst of the crowds and take a self-guided stroll around the Rhine House and gardens to get a sense of how grand the estate must have been in its heyday. In the summer you might also be able to help yourself to the succulent fruit from the numerous peach trees growing near the parking lot.

Charles Krug Winery

It's probably fitting that the winery founded by the grandfather of the Napa Valley wine industry, Charles Krug, was also the winery that helped start the modern-day wine dynasty of the Mondavis. Krug arrived in California in the heady days after the gold rush and fell in with the likes of Agoston Haraszthy, credited with being the first serious winemaker in the state. He planted his first vineyard in the Sonoma Valley in the 1850s next to Haraszthy's ranch and was soon making wine for friends and acquaintances in the Napa Valley, including George Yount (father of Yountville) and Edward Bale (who built the nearby Bale Grist Mill). He eventually sold up in Sonoma and moved to the winery's present-day location in the 1860s, using the land belonging to his new wife, Carolina Bale, to set up the valley's first large-scale winery.

Krug made a lot of wine there, and he made quite a reputation for himself as both a winemaker and a pillar of the local community. When he died in 1892, his winery was run by his business associate, local banker James Moffit, who maintained its reputation before Prohibition sent it reeling.

Enter the Mondavis. In 1943, the Krug winery was saved from its post-repeal life as a bulk wine producer when Cesare Mondavi bought it and built a new family wine business around it, creating one of the leading wineries in the valley. After his death in 1959, however, there was a bitter feud between his two sons, Robert and Peter, that resulted in Robert establishing his own separate winery (which has since become an empire), while Peter's side of the family held on to and still controls the Charles Krug business.

With a history like that, it's hardly surprising that parts of the Charles Krug Winery (2800 Main St., St. Helena, 707/967-2200 or 800/682-5784, www.charleskrug.com, 10:30 A.M.–5 P.M. daily, tasting $10–20) are historical landmarks, including the stately old Carriage House and giant redwood cellar building. Tours were curtailed in 2007 in order to renovate some of the earthquake-unsafe buildings, but the promised reopening has yet to materialize as of early 2010. At some point the tasting room will move to the restored winery, but until then the experience of visiting a winery so steeped in history can be a little anticlimactic because the tasting room is in a small cottage standing in the shadows of the historic structures and ancient trees. That cottage has a bit of history itself, however. It is said to have been the first dedicated tasting room in the valley when it was built in the 1950s. Once inside, the wines rather than the surroundings are very much the focus.

The winery owns more than 800 acres of vineyards throughout Napa and produces about 80,000 cases of wine, including just about every major varietal but specializing in cabernet sauvignon. The wines have never achieved the critical acclaim of those from the other Mondavi-related winery further south, but recent replanting in the vineyards should eventually pay dividends. Krug does produce a handful of approachable and well-priced wines, however, including a sauvignon blanc and a rosé (both great summer picnic wines), a Russian River pinot noir, and one of the better value Napa Valley cabernets you'll find in this area. Hardcore cabernet lovers should focus on the reserve tasting, however, which includes some of the vineyard-specific and small-lots wines, as well as the flagship Voltz blend.

St. Clement Vineyards

After passing the big boys of Napa wine like Beringer, Krug, and Markham, it's hard not to miss the quaint turreted Victorian house perched on the side of the hill west of the main road. That is St. Clement (2867 St. Helena Hwy. N., St. Helena, 800/331-8266, www. stclement.com, 10 A.M.–5 P.M. daily, tasting $10–25), a small winery that used to be Spring Mountain Winery before those owners moved their operation farther up the hill in the 1970s and sold this place.

It is now owned by Fosters Wine Estates, making it the little sister to Beringer Vineyards just down the road. The winery is as small as its home suggests, making about 25,000 cases of wine per year, three-quarters of which is cabernet sauvignon and the flagship Orropas red meritage blend (a backwards spelling of Sapporo, the Japanese company that owned the winery until 1999). The two tasting rooms in

the mansion itself can feel a little cramped and are not terribly representative of the charm of the Victorian estate, but for $25 you can taste some of the excellent single-vineyard and library wines in the old winery building behind the house, a far more relaxed setting.

The old winery and stone cellars under the house, where its original owner used to make wine, can also be seen as part of the appointment-only tour offered twice a day. There's also a pretty porch overlooking the valley, though traffic noise is ever-present. Nevertheless, it's a good place to enjoy the company of the winery cat along with a bottle of the rosé wine called La Vache, which is a steal and perfect for picnics.

Freemark Abbey

Despite the name, there is no religious connection with the weathered stone barn sandwiched between a brewpub and an unremarkable group of small office buildings. Freemark Abbey (3022 St. Helena Hwy. N., St. Helena, 800/963-9698, www.freemarkabbey.com, 10 A.M.–5 P.M. daily, regular tasting $10, reds only $20) instead got its current identity in the 1940s from the

© PHILIP GOLDSMITH

the Victorian home of St. Clement Vineyards, the sister winery to neighboring Beringer nickname of Albert "Abbey" Ahern and the names of partners Charles Freeman ("Free") and Markquand Foster ("Mark"), who bought the former Lombarda Winery and its stone building, which date from 1899.

That wine-making era lasted only 20 years, however. After a brief stint as a candle factory and a restaurant, the place once again became a winery in 1967 when it was bought by a new set of partners. Today, Freemark Abbey is probably best known for its cabernet sauvignon, from the generic Napa Valley version to a couple of vineyard-designates, including the flagship from the Bosche Vineyard near Rutherford.

Plenty of other wines are available to try in one of the more relaxing and spacious tasting rooms in the valley, though it's in the decidedly unhistoric building next to the winery. The portfolio includes merlot, sangiovese, chardonnay, and viognier, which may or may not be on the five-wine tasting menu. Cabernet lovers should consider the red-only tasting option, which offers a chance to compare some of the single-vineyard cabernet sauvignons along with the cabernet franc.

Duckhorn Vineyards

Adjacent to Freemark Abbey is Lodi Lane, which cuts across the valley to the Silverado Trail and the impressive farmhouse-style home of Duckhorn (1000 Lodi Ln. at Silverado Trail, St. Helena, 888/354-8885, www.duckhorn. com, 10 A.M.–4 P.M. daily, tasting $15–25), a winery known for some outstanding merlot and cabernet sauvignon. Those two wines were the first to be made when the winery was established in the mid-1970s, and they still account for most of the 50,000 cases of wine made each year. Sauvignon blanc is the only white wine in the portfolio. Duckhorn also makes about 10,000 cases of its Paraduxx wine, a proprietary blend of zinfandel, cabernet, and merlot, and they built a custom Paraduxx winery to the south near Yountville that opened at the end of 2005.

The stylish entrance lounge of the winery and the big circular tasting bar beyond,

surrounded by neatly arranged tables and chairs, resemble an upscale club or restaurant so it's no surprise that trying the wines can be pricey. But the personal service, quality wines, and peaceful veranda overlooking the vineyards make the tasting experience far more relaxing and fulfilling than at some other wineries.

Although you can visit the winery whenever you want, tastings require an appointment. During the week it's usually possible to get on the list right away, but for weekends it's best to call ahead. The flight of four wines in the basic tasting includes both Napa Valley–designated wines, while the more expensive Enhanced tasting includes estate wines from the Howell Mountain and St. Helena appellations. More of the estate wines, including the best merlots, can be tasted with food pairings following a tour for an additional $10.

Ehlers Estate

Moderate wine consumption might be good for the heart, according to some researchers. Moderate consumption of Ehlers Estate wines is most certainly good for hearts in general. The historic stone Ehlers Estate winery (3222 Ehlers Ln., St. Helena, 707/963-5972, www. ehlersestate.com, 9:30 A.M.–4:30 P.M. Tues.– Sat. by appointment, tasting $25–45), just north of St. Helena, is owned by the Leducq Foundation, a French charity that funds cardiovascular research at high-profile medical schools around the world including Harvard, Columbia, and the University of California at San Diego. Visiting such a nonprofit enterprise is a refreshing idea in a valley known more for unashamed hedonism.

The winery was established in 1886 by Bernard Ehlers but lasted only until Prohibition. It languished until the 1960s, when the first of a series of well-intentioned owners brought the estate back to life as a winery under various names for the next two decades. French businessman Jean Leducq and his wife, Sylviane, bought part of the estate in the late 1980s and continued acquiring other parts as they became available. In 2001 they bought the winery building, thus reuniting the entire 42-acre estate for the first time since Prohibition. (Jean died the following year.) Since then, the beautiful stone building has been enhanced by a tasteful architectural makeover and now sits peacefully among the vines in the middle of the valley.

Unlike many valley wineries, Ehlers Estate makes only estate wines from the surrounding organic and biodynamic vineyards, many of which have been replanted over the past decade. About 10,000 cases of wine are made now, including a worthy cabernet sauvignon, merlot, and sauvignon blanc, but that will undoubtedly increase. One thing that won't change: a portion of the sales generated by the winery go to the Leducq Foundation to support its research programs. Tasting is by appointment only, and the best option is to sign up for one of the twice-daily tours of the vineyard and winery followed by a sit-down tasting accompanied appetizers and perhaps the company of winemaker, Kevin Morrisey.

Benessere Vineyards

The family that established Benessere (1010 Big Tree Rd., St. Helena, 707/963-5853, www. benesserevineyards.com, 10 A.M.–5 P.M. daily, tasting $15) in 1994 does not publicize the fact that the winery used to be owned by **Charles Shaw,** a name that will forever be associated with the Two-Buck Chuck phenomenon of cheap and cheerful wines. Shaw owned the winery from the early 1970s but eventually sold up when he and his wife divorced. The brand was bought by the Bronco Wine Company, which now churns out those cheap wines, but the winery property itself and 42 acres of neglected vineyards were eventually bought by John and Ellen Benish in the early 1990s.

They have since transformed it into a producer of increasingly well regarded Italian varietal wines with the help of some expert Italian wine-making consultants. The lively and light Italian wines here are a nice diversion from the more intense cabernet and chardonnay that dominate the scene in this part of the Napa Valley, and the winery itself is at the end of a small road far off the beaten path of the St.

Helena Highway (Highway 29), surrounded by aromatic gardens and guarded by a hefty Newfoundland dog.

Sangiovese and zinfandel dominate the 5,000-case production, but Benessere also makes a small amount of pinot grigio, a unique and picnic-friendly sparkling muscat, and some unique blended reds that incorporate both French and Italian varietals. The flagship wine is called Phenomenon and is a rich blend of sangiovese, cabernet sauvignon, syrah, and merlot. The Sorridente is a blend of cabernet, merlot and aglianico, a dark and powerfully flavored grape normally grown in southern Italy. An appointment for tasting is technically necessary, but calling ahead by even an hour is usually fine during the week.

SPRING MOUNTAIN WINERIES

Exploring this lesser-known appellation makes an interesting diversion from St. Helena and is a beautiful drive. From Highway 29, turn onto Madrona Road, and Spring Mountain Road is three blocks further on the right. Alternatively, just south of Beringer Vineyards, Elmhurst Road also leads to Spring Mountain Road. From there the road follows a creek as it climbs steeply through redwoods and oak trees, past terraced mountain vineyards and orchards, to the many small wineries that often have stunning views of the valley far below.

If you're on a schedule, be sure to leave plenty of time to visit wineries up here because the drive is slow and quickly becomes frustrating (and potentially dangerous) if you're in a hurry. Allow at least a half hour to drive one way from St. Helena to Pride Mountain Vineyards, for example. All the wineries on Spring Mountain are appointment-only (thanks to a county ordinance that aims to prevent the small road becoming too busy), but with the exception of Pride you can usually secure an appointment a day or two ahead.

Spring Mountain Vineyards

Not far out of St. Helena is one of the oldest Spring Mountain wineries, one that is almost as famous for its Hollywood connection as for its history and wines. It was established in the 1880s as the Miravalle estate by businessman Tiburcio Parrot, who also constructed the ostentatious Victorian mansion that is said to have been inspired by the Rhine House built down the hill by his friends the Beringer brothers.

The estate became Spring Mountain Vineyards (2805 Spring Mountain Rd., St. Helena, 877/769-4637 or 707/967-4188, www.springmtn.com, tour and tasting $25) when it was bought in the 1970s by Michael Robbins. He built a modern winery on the grounds, but his wines were somewhat forgotten when the grounds and mansion became better known as the set for the 1980s television soap opera *Falcon Crest*. Although Robbins tried to cash in by releasing wines under the Falcon Crest label, the winery never regained its former glory and eventually went bankrupt in 1990.

It has since been brought spectacularly back to life after it was bought in 1992 by a Swiss banker, Jaqui Safra, who bought several surrounding vineyards (including part of the historic La Perla vineyard) and built a new winery. The winery reopened to the public in 2003 after Safra's investments had paid off and the quality of the wines, along with the glory of the estate, had been restored. Spring Mountain's vineyards stretch from the valley floor almost to the top of Spring Mountain, giving the winery a huge variety of soils and microclimates to work with. It is perhaps best known for its sauvignon blanc and cabernet sauvignon, in particular the meritage blend called Elivette, which is both predominantly cabernet and gets consistently high ratings. The winery also makes a Spring Mountain syrah that has won plenty of critical praise in recent years, and thanks to a cool spot in the mountain vineyards it also grows and produces a few hundred cases of pinot noir, a wine not normally made this far north in the valley.

Tours of the beautiful grounds and some of the historic buildings, including the famous Miravalle mansion and caves, are offered just once a day by appointment at 2 P.M. Tours are followed by a tasting of four wines, though there's also a tasting-only option offered four times a day, and the fee can be applied to any purchase.

Terra Valentine

One man's remarkable stone folly of a building is reason alone to visit this winery, which was established in 1999 on the former Yverdon Vineyards property. Yverdon itself was founded in the 1970s by a reclusive eccentric, Fred Aves, who built himself a Gothic-style drystone and concrete winery replete with stained-glass windows (which he made as well), statues, and curious features like fish-shaped doorknobs and a sculpted spiral staircase. Any home improvement aficionado will be in awe of his handiwork.

Terra Valentine (3787 Spring Mountain Rd., St. Helena, 707/967-8340, www.terravalentine.com, open daily, tour and tasting $30) still makes wine in the building and is known mainly for its cabernet sauvignon, which accounts for much of the 7,000-case annual production, and the best cabernet is the flagship bottling from the Wurtele vineyard. It also makes a Russian River Valley pinot noir and a couple of limited-production wines, including a sangiovese-and-cabernet blend called Amore.

Appointment-only tours are offered twice a day (10:30 A.M. and 2:30 P.M.); they can be on the short side depending on the time of year but are worth it to see the fabulous building and for the sit-down tasting of wines paired with cheese and chocolate.

Schweiger Vineyards

Toward the top of the hill on the right is another of Spring Mountain's small makers of highly regarded cabernet sauvignon and another with spectacular views from its vineyards. Schweiger (4015 Spring Mountain Rd., St. Helena, 707/963-4882 or 877/963-4882, www.schweigervineyards.com, tours and tasting by appointment 10 A.M.–3:30 P.M. daily, $10) used to sell its fruit to other wineries in the Napa Valley but started making its own wines in the mid-1990s, gradually increasing production to the current level of about 5,000 cases and building a new winery along the way.

Winemaker Andy Schweiger used to ply his trade at Chateau St. Jean in the Sonoma Valley and Cain Vineyards near St. Helena before he started making wine for his family's label. He is also the winemaker for several of Napa Valley's smallest boutique wineries.

The vast majority of the wine is cabernet, but Schweiger also makes small amounts of merlot and chardonnay, all from the estate vineyards at about 2,000 feet in elevation, and a nice sauvignon blanc from a vineyard over the hill in the Sonoma Valley. The flagship wine is the reserve cabernet, called Dedication, which competes with the best from Spring Mountain. Another perennial favorite is the cabernet port, which is made in true nonvintage style by blending wines dating back more than a decade.

Barnett Vineyards

It's a long and winding driveway leading to Barnett Vineyards (4070 Spring Mountain Rd., St. Helena, 707/963-7075, www.barnettvineyards.com, by appointment 10 A.M.–4:30 P.M. daily, $35) from the main road, but the reward is worth the few wrong turns you might take along the way. This appointment-only boutique winery, established by the Barnett family in the late 1980s, takes care to keep guests to a minimum to ensure the wines and the tranquility of the panoramic Napa Valley view can be enjoyed in all their glory. It's one of the best views from a vineyard you'll find in this part of the world.

A visit to the winery starts at the tasting bar, tucked away in a corner of the cool dark barrel room, where most of the half-dozen wines are usually available to taste. Spring Mountain vineyards account for about half the 5,000-case production here and are the source of Barnett's cabernet and merlot, both of which exhibit the classic concentration and robust tannins of Spring Mountain fruit. The tangy chardonnay is sourced from the famous Sangiacomo Vineyard in southern Sonoma, and the pinot noir comes from the cool Green Valley appellation in the Russian River Valley, but it often sells out within six months of its

release. Another wine that sells out fast despite its $125 price tag, probably due to the glowing reviews it gets almost every year, is the flagship Rattlesnake Hill cabernet, sourced from vines on a small knoll above the winery at 2,400 feet elevation.

If the weather is cooperating, guests can often continue tasting the wines and learn more about the winery and its vineyards on one of the two small decks perched at the end of rocky paths among the terraced vineyards. You feel a little like a mountain goat traversing the terraces, and heels are not recommended. A wood-burning pizza oven on the top deck might one day be pressed into action for hungry visitors, but until then the panoramic views across the Napa Valley and the almost uncanny silence are perfect accompaniments to the outstanding wines.

◖ Pride Mountain Vineyards

When you reach the line on the road that marks the border of Napa and Sonoma Counties, you're as far up Spring Mountain as you can go and just outside the estate of Pride Mountain (4026 Spring Mountain Rd., St. Helena, 707/963-4949, www.pridewines.com, by appointment 10 A.M.–3:30 P.M. Mon. and Wed.–Sat., tasting $10), a winery that has been receiving wine reviews almost as lofty as its location 2,000 feet up in the Mayacamas Mountains. The former Summit Ranch was bought by the Pride family in the late 1980s and has since grown to make about 15,000 cases of wines per year, most notably some powerful and intense examples of cabernet sauvignon and merlot that account for about two-thirds of the winery's production. Other wines that regularly score over 90 points with the critics include an aromatic cabernet franc, chardonnay, and viognier. Many Pride wines sell out quickly, particularly the limited-production reserves.

Grapes have been grown here since 1870, by some accounts, and the size of the burned-out shell of the old Summit winery building, constructed in 1890, suggests that a fair amount of wine was produced until Prohibition ended the party. The 80 acres of vineyards that Pride owns straddle the Sonoma-Napa border on these mountain ridges that afford panoramic views over the two valleys and beyond. Some wines are made from Napa grapes, others from both Napa and Sonoma grapes—the winery has to take great care to keep Napa and Sonoma grapes separate during harvest to ensure it doesn't put Sonoma grapes in a bottle that's designated Napa (or vice versa) and fall afoul of the strict labeling laws.

The views and wines are best sampled on the tour and tasting ($15) offered once a day at 10 A.M., for which you must book well in advance even at relatively quiet times of the year. Appointment-only tastings are offered the rest of the day and cost only $10, a relative bargain considering the quality of the wines that generally cost upwards of $50 a bottle and the attentive, often entertaining service. Visitors can also book picnic tables and eat at what is probably the highest picnic ground in Wine Country. With views across the vineyards to distant mountains there's definitely a feeling of being on top of the world.

SIGHTS

Much of St. Helena's Victorian heyday is on display on Main Street (mainly between Hunt and Adams Streets), in the residential area stretching a few blocks west and just one block east on Railroad Avenue. Even the unusual street lamps on Main Street are antiques, dating from 1915.

At **1302 Main Street** (at Hunt Street), a brass inlay in the sidewalk is the only sign that the wonderfully named Wonderful Drug Store had its home for half a century in this building constructed in 1891 by local businessman Daniel Hunt (as a sign of the times, the building is now home to a plus-size clothing store and a real estate agent).

North up that block is the retro-looking **Cameo Cinema** (1340 Main St., www.cameocinema.com), the latest in a long line of theaters to inhabit the 1913 building with its pressed-steel ceilings and classy deco exterior, both now complemented by state-of-the-art seating, sound, and projection.

At the end of that block is the former **Odd Fellows Hall** (1350 Main St.), built in 1885 as Lodge 167 of the Independent Order of Odd Fellows, the social fraternity established in 1810 in England. The building is said to have a sealed granite memorial stone containing a time capsule of articles from the era. It was also once home to the neighboring **Steves Hardware,** itself founded in 1878.

Almost opposite at 1351 Main Street is what used to be the **Bank of St. Helena,** established and built in the 1880s by a group of local winemakers, including Charles Krug. A lot of the original interior features and stone walls are still evident, though the building, until recently the 1351 Lounge, is now an olive oil store. Farther south is another 1880s building (this one made of wood) that is home to the **Hotel St. Helena** (1305–1309 Main St.).

Silverado Museum

One of the Valley's most famous literary visitors, the Scottish writer Robert Louis Stevenson, spent his honeymoon in the valley just as St. Helena's Victorian building boom was getting under way in 1880. His life and visit is celebrated in the compact Silverado Museum (1490 Library Ln., off Adams St., 707/963-3757, www.silveradomuseum.org, noon–4 P.M. Wed.–Sun., free), right next to the small library a few blocks from Main Street.

There are more than 9,000 of Stevenson's personal artifacts on display, including original manuscripts of some of his many books. The most famous in these parts is *The Silverado Squatters,* published in 1883, which chronicles his Napa Valley travels and meetings with early wine industry pioneers. Stevenson is probably best known elsewhere in the world for some of his other books, including *Treasure Island* and *The Strange Case of Dr. Jekyll and Mr. Hyde.*

Bale Grist Mill

About two miles north of St. Helena is one of the more unusual sights in a valley dominated by the wine industry, the Bale Grist Mill (3801 St. Helena Hwy. N., 707/942-4575, mill grounds open 10 A.M.–5 P.M. daily, tours

11:30 A.M. and 1, 2:30, and 3:30 P.M. Sat.–Sun., $3). The small rickety-looking redwood mill building with its oversized, 36-foot-high waterwheel is now part of a small State Historic Park. It was built in 1846 by Edward Bale on a tiny part of the 10,000 acres of land he was granted by the Mexican government as thanks for his role as surgeon-in-chief for the Mexican army in California (it also probably helped that he had married the niece of the army's regional commander, General Mariano Vallejo, a few years earlier).

He bartered away chunks of his land for money and services to help build both this mill and a separate sawmill not far away. It originally had a 20-foot waterwheel, but a later owner made a few power upgrades, adding the bigger wheel and iron cogs in the 1850s, a few years after Bale died. This was all before the age of wine, so the mill became a big part of valley life, and people from far and wide brought their grist (grain) to be milled here.

The weekend-only tours shed more light on both the man and the milling. The wheel turns sporadically these days, subject to the vagaries of its age and park budget cuts. When it is operating (usually only during the summer), there is usually some "run of the mill" flour for sale, ground between the giant millstones that literally weigh a ton. If it's not operating, the only real reason to visit (unless you're a water mill junkie) is the setting. The mill itself and a handful of picnic tables are reached from the parking lot along a quarter-mile trail that ends looping back to the main road, so traffic noise and the rather sad state of the mill building itself make for a bit of an anticlimax. Instead, turn left before reaching the mill to take the pretty mile-long hike through the madrone woods, past the remains of the valley's first church and the old Pioneer Cemetery, and into neighboring Bothe-Napa Valley State Park.

ENTERTAINMENT
◖ Culinary Institute of America
The Napa Valley takes food very seriously, so it's fitting that the West Coast outpost of the CIA is housed in one of the grandest old

winery buildings in California, the fortresslike former Greystone Winery just north of downtown St. Helena (2555 Main St., St. Helena, 707/967-2320). Built in 1890, it later found fame as the Christian Brothers winery until a new corporate owner put it up for sale in the late 1980s. The institute bought the building in 1992 and spent $15 million renovating it to its former glory. It still makes some wine under the Greystone label from a small estate vineyard nearby.

Chefs and sommeliers are busy being trained behind the imposing stone walls, but you don't need the dedication they have to learn a secret or two from the Napa Valley's top chefs. Hour-long cooking demonstrations are open to the public (reservations 707/967-2320, 10:30 A.M. and 1:30 P.M. weekends, $15) and include a tasting of the finished dish, so the fee makes it worthwhile, especially at lunchtime. Don't expect to go more than once over a weekend, though, because the same demonstration is given on both days.

A small exhibit just beyond the huge, carved redwood entrance doors illustrates the history of the Greystone Winery with some of the original Christian Brothers barrels, casks, and brandy-making stills. Most intriguing of all is a display of more than a thousand corkscrews, some of them hundreds of years old and miniature marvels of engineering, all collected by Brother Timothy, a wine chemist and renowned winemaker at Christian Brothers 1935–1989.

Nightlife
It might seem like this part of the valley goes to sleep after the restaurants have closed down for the evening, and sadly that's more or less true. The popular 1351 Lounge, a little piece of cocktail heaven in St. Helena, closed in 2005 and was turned into an olive oil store. It was one more small step in the "St. Helena–ization" of St. Helena.

Now the job of keeping the locals lubricated at night falls to the casual hangout **Ana's Cantina** (1205 Main St., 707/963-4921). It's a Mexican restaurant by day and a bar by night, when beer and margaritas are the drinks of choice, and pool, karaoke, and live weekend music provide the entertainment, usually until 1 A.M. Although the bartenders know how to mix some good cocktails, this falls just shy of being a dive bar, so don't expect to see much, if any, of the usual "Wine Country" ambience.

Having to drive for an evening's entertainment is by no means perfect, but the best live music options in the valley are down in the city of Napa, at Silo's jazz club and Uva Trattoria, or eight miles up the road in Calistoga at the Calistoga Brewery.

SHOPPING

It's hardly surprising in a valley that was built on the guilty pleasures of consumption that shopping is a close third to eating and drinking for many visitors. St. Helena is dominated by small boutiques that tend to cater to tourists—locals head south to the big-box stores around Napa or Santa Rosa for any significant shopping. Nevertheless, St. Helena is by far the best place for shopaholics to get their fix in the Napa Valley.

The short stretch of Main Street in downtown St. Helena is quick and easy to explore, with an eclectic mix of shops that draw crowds and help create some horrendous traffic jams as visitors look for parking. Countless gift shops sell everything from soap to wine trinkets; some of the more eclectic gifts are to be found at **Findings** (1269 Main St., 707/963-6000, www.findingsnapavalley.org, 10 A.M.–6 P.M. daily). Fashionable St. Helena dogs must shop for gifts and clothes at **Fideaux** (1312 Main St., 707/967-9935, 10 A.M.–5 P.M. daily), which sells the latest fashions for Fido as well as other pricey pet-related paraphernalia. Down the southern end of Main Street next to the gas station is **Lolo's Second to None** (1120 Main St., 707/963-7972, www.lolosconsignment.com, 10:30 A.M.–5:30 P.M. Tues.–Sat., 10:30 A.M.–4 P.M. Sun.–Mon.), a consignment store stuffed with St. Helena's version of pre-owned junk, from designer labels to collectible crockery.

High-end contemporary art and design is gradually supplanting the more traditional Wine Country paraphernalia in the valley, as illustrated by two eclectic galleries that opened right next to each other in 2009 in the historic Independent Order of Odd Fellows building on Main Street. The **Martin Showroom** (1350 Main St., 707/967-8787, www.martinshowroom.com, 10 A.M.–6 P.M. Mon.–Sat., noon–4 P.M. Sun.) is a showcase for designer Erin Martin, who fashions contemporary pieces with a rustic or industrial chic from natural and reclaimed materials. While you may not take home a $15,000 table or bronze statue as a souvenir of the Wine Country, there is nonetheless plenty of inspiration on offer from the works of Erin and a handful of other artists and designers represented here, along with plenty of more affordable, whimsical items for sale, from jewelry to housewares. Right next door is the St. Helena outpost of the **I Wolk Gallery** (1354 Main St., 707/963-8800, www.iwolkgallery.com, 10 A.M.–5:30 P.M. daily), which is represented at four locations in the Napa Valley, including Maisonary in Yountville and at the Auberge du Soleil resort. Unlike the Martin showroom, this is a more traditional gallery with rotating exhibitions of contemporary works from Bay Area artists and sculptors.

Probably the valley's best kitchen store, the **Spice Islands Marketplace** (2555 Main St., St. Helena, 707/967-2309, 10 A.M.–6 P.M. daily) in the Culinary Institute of America supplies all those trainee chefs and sommeliers (and you) with the best culinary equipment, spices, and other essentials from around the world. It is also the place to go to pick up a cookbook memento of the Wine Country. It carries thousands of wine bibles and cookbooks, including every Napa Valley title under the sun. Some might even be signed by the authors, if they teach a course here.

Foodies might drool on entering the only West Coast outpost of New York's superdeli **Dean & Deluca** (607 St. Helena Hwy. S., 707/967-9980, www.deandeluca.com, 7 A.M.–7 P.M. Sun.–Thurs., 7 A.M.–8 P.M. Fri.–Sat.), just south of downtown St. Helena. This being the Wine Country, of course, it stocks some 1,400 wines plus countless local cheeses, meats, and produce, all alongside the already unmatched selection of gourmet foods from around the world.

Chocoholics might get a sugar rush just by looking at the neat rows of dozens of handmade bonbons at **Woodhouse Chocolate** (1367 Main St., 707/963-8413 or 800/966-3468, www.woodhousechocolate.com, 10:30 A.M.– 5:30 P.M. daily). It's a good old-fashioned chocolatier with interior decorations as sumptuous as the confectionery made by Tracy Wood Anderson, a former pastry chef. Indulging is not as expensive as you'd think, particularly in this valley of pricey wine tasting. For less than a flight of wines at a local winery, you can walk out of here with a small box of chocolate bliss.

The best olive oil in town is undoubtedly at the **Napa Valley Olive Oil Manufacturing Company,** though it no longer presses its oils here (835 Charter Oak Ave., St. Helena, 707/963-4173, 9 A.M.–5:30 P.M. daily). Despite being in the heart of the valley's food scene, it retains a decidedly small-time family feeling, selling its organic oils and thoroughly Italian deli items out of a colorful and chaotic small barnlike store.

RECREATION

The Napa Valley might seem to be covered with vineyards, but around its fringes there are still hundreds of acres as yet untouched by the mighty vine, some only minutes away from the Wine Country hordes.

◖ Bothe-Napa Valley State Park

This is the most accessible place up-valley to escape anything wine-related and also the inside of the car, just a few miles north of St. Helena and right off the main highway (3801 St. Helena Hwy. N., 707/942-4575, sunrise– sunset, $8 day-use fee). Proximity to the wineries and shops of St. Helena makes the park a popular picnic spot, but most people packing a lunch don't venture far beyond the shady picnic area just beyond the parking lot near the Pioneer Cemetery (and the road). They miss

the best reason to come here, which is to experience the relative wilderness that's so close to the beaten path and home to some of the most easterly stands of coastal redwood trees.

Most of the best hiking trails start from the **Redwood Trail,** which runs from the main parking lot through the cool redwood forest along Ritchey Creek for just over a mile before meeting the **Ritchey Canyon Trail.** That trail more or less follows the creek for about another mile to the site of an old homestead, an ideal destination for adventurous picnickers.

More strenuous hikes start from the Redwood Trail and climb steeply into the heat to some rewarding lookout points. The closest is Coyote Peak, accessed via the **Coyote Peak Trail** and just under a mile from the creek. From the lookout spur, the trail continues to the **South Fork Trail.** Turn right here to head back down to the creek for a loop of about four miles, or go left to climb again to another lookout. These trails are not for the faint-hearted, especially in the summer when it can get very hot, so don't underestimate the dehydrating power of too many glasses of wine.

Mountain bikers (or anyone on a Wine Country bike tour tired of dodging weaving rental cars) also have a few miles of trails to explore here, but only those that start north of the creek near the campground. Those same trails are also open for horseback riding, offered during the spring and summer by the **Triple Creek Horse Outfit** (reservations 707/887-8700, www.triplecreekhorseoutfit. com) for those without their own steed; a one-hour ride costs $60.

Golf

There are a couple of nine-hole golf courses up-valley, but serious golfers should head south to the Napa area, where all the valley's 18-hole courses are.

The **Meadowood Country Club & Resort** (900 Meadowood Ln., off Silverado Trail, St. Helena, 707/963-3646, www.meadowood. com) has a nine-hole par-62 course open only to guests or guests of guests of this exclusive 250-acre hideaway.

ACCOMMODATIONS

This part of the valley has a far wider range of accommodations than Calistoga, but at far higher prices, justified perhaps by the convenient location in the middle of the valley, the pretty Main Street, the thriving restaurant scene, or maybe because, in world-famous St. Helena, they can get away with it.

Prices are all relative, of course. The cheapest accommodations in this area might be pricier than the low end in either Napa or Calistoga, but don't expect that extra money to buy more luxury. The low end of this scale is the same as the low end on any other scale, where rooms will generally be clean and comfortable but not as luxurious as their price might suggest. At the other end of the scale are some truly luxurious rooms but at prices that might make you choke on a glass of cabernet, especially on summer weekends.

Under $150

The 1940s-era **El Bonita Motel** (195 Main St., St. Helena, 707/963-3216 or 800/541-3284, www.elbonita.com), with its retro neon sign, is not the most glamorous place to stay in St. Helena but is one of the cheaper options and still pretty fancy for a motel. The cheapest rooms are laid out around a small pool but suffer from less privacy and more road noise than the pricier Homestead and Garden rooms set further back on the property. All contain modern but fairly sparse furnishings and include air-conditioning and microwave ovens. Rates for the Poolside rooms start at $90 on winter weekdays and go as high as $269 on summer and fall weekends ($209 during the week). The Garden and Homestead rooms are quieter but less of a bargain, with rates starting at $120 during winter weeks and rising to $269 on peak-season weekends.

$150-250

The **Hotel St. Helena** (1309 Main St., St. Helena, 707/963-4388 or 888/478-4355, www.hotelsthelena.net) is about as central as can be, down a little alley off Main Street right in the middle of town. The old Victorian building is full of original features and stuffed with knick-knacks, including a lot of dolls. The 18 guest rooms get some of the same treatment (minus the dolls), with brass beds, a smattering of antiques, plush carpeting and fabrics, but limited modern touches—air-conditioning is included, but you'll have to ask for a TV. You might also have to tolerate some less charming Victorian traits such as temperamental plumbing and poor sound insulation. The four smallest and cheapest rooms share a bathroom and run $105 midweek, $195 weekends. The best deals are the North Wing rooms, which are still on the small side but have private bathrooms and start at $145 midweek, $235 weekends. The larger Windsor rooms start at $165 midweek, $275 weekends, and the single suite starts at $250 midweek, $375 weekends.

Right next to El Bonita Motel is the **Vineyard Country Inn** (201 Main St., St. Helena, 707/963-1000, www.vineyardcountryinn.com), a combination of hotel and motel with 21 spacious suites that all cost the same, ranging from a relative bargain of $185 in winter months to less of a bargain at $325 during peak summer and fall seasons. All are in a main two-story building or several cottages around the pool and pleasant brick patios—just be sure to ask for a room away from the main road, which is noisy enough to render the balconies of some suites next to useless. All suites have either two queens or one king bed, vaulted or beamed ceilings, fireplaces, refrigerators, and comfortable but unexceptional country-style furniture.

One of the more reasonably priced B&Bs in the area is **Ink House** (1575 S. St. Helena Hwy., St. Helena, 707/963-3890, www.inkhouse.com), an 1884 Victorian just south of the town with an unusual observatory room perched on top of the roof where guests can sip wine and watch the world (and the wine train) go by. The common areas are chock-full of unusual antiques, from the grand piano and pipe organ to the stained glass in the observatory. The six bedrooms continue the theme and have been lovingly decorated with a mix of antiques, and most have a view of either hills or vineyards. Standard queen rooms start at $175, and larger rooms with king beds start at $225. Midweek discounts are usually offered during the winter. Rates include a full gourmet champagne breakfast each morning, wine and appetizers each evening, and Winery VIP tasting passes.

For some true peace and quiet, skip the valley floor and head for the hills. Northeast of St. Helena near the small community of Deer Park is secluded **Spanish Villa Inn** (474 Glass Mountain Rd., St. Helena, 707/963-7483, www.napavalleyspanishvilla.com), a small Mediterranean-style B&B set in several acres of beautifully tended grounds with boccie and croquet courts as well as roses galore. The six rooms and two suites start at $150 during the winter (sometimes there's a 20 percent discount during slow weeks) and $199 during the summer. All have private bathrooms and unusual touches like hand-painted sinks, plantation-style shutters, and carved headboards but, alas, an overabundance of floral prints. Downstairs rooms open onto a patio overlooking the garden, while one of the upstairs suites has its own balcony.

Over $250

On the southern edge of St. Helena, hidden from the road behind a thicket of trees, is the mock-Tudor mansion of the **Harvest Inn** (1 Main St., St. Helena, 707/963-9463 or 800/950-8466, www.harvestinn.com), set in eight acres of lush gardens shaded by mature trees. The place is crammed with stylish antiques, fancy brickwork, and other often-surreal English country features. There's nothing surreal about the luxury of the 74 rooms and suites, however: All have CD players and VCRs, featherbeds, and minibars; some have their own private terrace or views of neighboring vineyards. The smallest queen and king rooms cost from about $250 midweek during the winter and $315 in the summer. The priciest deluxe rooms with vineyard views start at $400 in the winter and $435 in the summer. Add about $50 to those rates for weekend nights. There are some good deals during

the winter at more reasonable rates. The more expensive Vineyard rooms are furthest from the main road, and many have vineyard views. The Fountain rooms are the newest and were opened in 2005 around a new conference center.

The **Inn at Southbridge** (1020 Main St., St. Helena, 800/520-6800, www.innatsouthbridge.com) doesn't even try to pretend it's in the middle of Wine Country and instead offers luxurious urban sophistication with barely a hint of faux Tuscan decor or Victorian antiques, all in a refreshingly modern building opposite the Taylor's Automatic Refresher diner. The 20 spacious rooms have vaulted ceilings, understated modern furniture, DVD players, down comforters, and high-speed Internet access. A few also have fireplaces and balconies with a view of either the highway or vineyards. They start at $275 midweek in winter ($350 weekends), though there are often deals that take the rate closer to $200 midweek. Summer rates start at $325 midweek for the cheapest king rooms ($425 weekends) and shoot up to more than $500 for the suite. In the same complex of buildings is the bargain Pizzeria Tra Vigne, and right next door is the Napa Valley Health Spa, with a fitness center and heated outdoor pool (both free for inn guests) and a full-service luxury spa.

Its location surrounded by vineyards a few miles north of St. Helena makes the **Wine Country Inn** (1152 Lodi Ln., St. Helena, 707/963-7077 or 888/465-4608, www.winecountryinn.com) a slightly cheaper alternative to some of the other luxury resorts out in the wilds. This family-run establishment offers an unusual down-home atmosphere, good amenities, and a decent breakfast. Rooms are decorated with a mix of modern and rustic; CD players and handmade quilts enhance the sometimes unremarkable furniture. You'll either love the combination or wonder why you're paying so much for a riot of flowery fabric. Splurge on a room with a view, though, and there'll be no questioning it. The cheapest rooms start at $194, but rooms with views or a private patio cost about $275–405 for most of the year, increasing about $30 during the harvest season (Aug.–Oct.). Small suites with added features like balconies with a view, whirlpool tubs, and double-headed showers cost $315–450 most of the year. There are five luxury cottages with 800 square feet of lounging space starting at $465 a night.

The luxurious **Meadowood Napa Valley** (900 Meadowood Ln., off Silverado Trail, St. Helena, 707/963-3646 or 800/458-8080, www.meadowood.com) resort is a bit past its prime and facing increasing competition in this astronomical price bracket, but it's still worth considering if you're planning to splurge, not least because of its spectacular setting on 250 lush acres in the hills above the Silverado Trail. The rooms are in 20 country-style lodges spread around the grounds and range from simple two-room studios ($475–575, depending on the season) up to spacious suites ($675–2,500). All have fireplaces, beamed ceilings, private decks or terraces, and every conceivable luxury trapping. For those who actually venture out of the rooms, there are plenty of distractions, including miles of hiking trails, two swimming pools surrounded by vast expanses of lawn, tennis courts, a nine-hole golf course, and croquet. And to make sure visitors never have to venture down into the valley, there's a small spa, wine-tasting events, and two highly regarded restaurants on-site.

Camping

The Napa Valley might be touted by every marketing brochure as a bank-breaking hedonistic playground, but it actually has a couple of remarkably good campgrounds where two people can stay for less than it would cost them to taste wine at most of the nearby wineries. So forget about matching a Napa cabernet with the latest in-season gourmet produce—instead see how it goes with s'mores around a campfire under a warm summer night sky.

You can light your fire and unpack the marshmallows just a few miles north of St. Helena in the leafy **Bothe-Napa Valley State Park** (3801 St. Helena Hwy., 707/942-4575). There are 50 sites, 42 of which can

accommodate RVs up to 31 feet long (though there are no hookups). The other eight sites are tent-only, and all cost $35 per night. Sites can be reserved through Reserve America (www.reserveamerica.com or 800/444-7275) April–October, and the rest of the year they are available on a first-come, first-served basis. Most sites offer some shade beneath oak and madrone trees, and there's a swimming pool in which to cool off, as well as flush toilets, hot showers, and that all-important fire ring at every site. The park itself stretches up into the hills and offers miles of hiking trails through the redwoods along the creek or up into the sun for some great views.

Further north in Calistoga is a slightly less appealing camping location at the **Napa County Fairgrounds** (1435 Oak St., Calistoga, 707/942-5221). It's ostensibly an RV park with 78 sites, 32 with sewer hookup ($33 per night) and the other 46 with only water and electricity ($30). Tent campers are corralled onto a grassy area with 20 tent-only sites ($20). Showers and a restroom are provided, but for most other amenities you'll have to head to downtown Calistoga.

FOOD

There's an ongoing tug-of-war between up-valley and down-valley restaurants for the limited tourist food dollars, and the balance seems to shift almost every time one restaurant closes and a new one opens—both common occurrences in the Napa Valley. St. Helena's ever-changing restaurant scene with its big-name chefs continues to do battle with towns down south, competing with Yountville for the title of Napa Valley's culinary epicenter.

Californian

The lush gardens, waterfalls, and twinkling lights outside might make it seem like a curious Zen center or fancy private house, but **Martini House** (1245 Spring St. at Oak St., 707/963-2233, www.martinihouse.com, dinner entrées $17–35, prix fixe $63 or $109 with wine pairing) is actually another popular venture by super-restaurateur Pat Kuleto that celebrates the valley's wine-making and Native American heritages. That roughly translates to some beautifully designed dishes prepared by chef Todd Humphries, who has a tendency to go foraging in the local woods for some of the ingredients (or so we're told), like the wild mushrooms used in the restaurant's popular mushroom soup. The wine list is suitably stocked with cult classics, but this place has become such a classic itself that it is usually tough to get a reservation, even though it recently lost its Michelin star. The curious craftsman-style house just off Main Street is worth a look, however. It was built by an opera singer turned bootlegger named Walter Martini, and Kuleto seems to have spared no expense restoring it. If you have no reservation but want to sample the namesake martinis, head downstairs to the cellar bar. You can also order food downstairs, but the rustic atmosphere is not as enjoyable as the main restaurant upstairs.

A couple of restaurants are worth discovering on Railroad Avenue, just a block east of Main Street but a world away from the bustle. The eponymous owner of **Cindy's Backstreet Kitchen** (1327 Railroad Ave. at Hunt St., 707/963-1200, www.cindysbackstreetkitchen. com, lunch and dinner daily, dinner entrées $15–26) is Cindy Pawlcyn, the woman behind the ever-popular Mustards Grill in Yountville. She has created a charming hole-in-the-wall here with a side entrance that makes it feel like you're walking into someone's house. The quiet patio is a hive of activity at lunchtime. The menu goes for the same homey charm, with large plates including meatloaf, wood-oven duck, and *steak frites*. The small plates and sandwiches for lunch can be ordered to go.

A few doors from Cindy's in the historic stone Hatchery Building is **Terra** (1345 Railroad Ave., 707/963-8931, www.terras-restaurant.com, dinner Wed.–Mon., entrées $20–36), a romantic restaurant that competes with the best restaurants in the valley (with its food and spin-off cookbook) thanks to chef Hiro Sone, who won the prestigious James Beard Foundation award for Best Chef in California. The menu is French and

Californian with Asian flourishes, and might include such eclectic creations as sake-marinated Alaskan black cod with shrimp dumplings. The prices, however, are on the high side, befitting the Michelin star awarded to Terra every year since 2007, but are by no means astronomical. The best value (assuming you are hungry) is the seasonal four-course tasting menu for $65.

When three partners with résumés that read like the greatest hits of Bay Area restaurants got together in 2002 to create **Market** (1347 Main St., St. Helena, 707/963-3799, www.market-sthelena.com, lunch and dinner daily, dinner entrées $12–24), the result could well have been another quality Napa Valley dining experience ending with an astronomical bill. That's certainly what the stone walls, Victorian bar, and elegant tables might suggest. Instead, the prices and atmosphere are very down-to-earth, and jaded locals have grown to love the place. The American bistro–style food is sophisticated yet familiar, with dishes like pan-roasted crispy chicken sharing the menu with mac and cheese made, of course, with the best artisanal cheeses. The wine list manages to keep a lid on prices, with none of the wide selection more than $14 above retail, beating even the corkage fee of most local restaurants. The lunch menu is even more of a bargain, with most of the gourmet sandwiches and salads under $15. All are also available to go, providing an instant gourmet picnic.

In a sleek modern building with a giant outdoor patio on the southern edge of St. Helena is the most recent of Cindy Pawlcyn's culinary adventures, **Go Fish** (641 Main St., St. Helena, 707/963-0700, www.gofishrestaurant.com, lunch and dinner daily, dinner entrées $17–30, sushi $5–20). You can have your meal battered, fried, grilled, or raw, but the only caveat is that it has to be fish. There are a couple of nonfish items on the menu, but the biggest draw here is the daily fresh fish listed on the board that can be cooked and sauced any way you want—the wood-fired grill offers the most tempting choice in many cases. Or let the kitchen make the choice with the "Fish Our Way" menu option, a little cheaper because it includes the sides. An accompanying raw bar offers oysters and clams, and the small sushi bar has the rest of the raw options covered.

Almost opposite Go Fish is **Farmstead** (738 Main St., St. Helena, 707/963-9181, dinner daily, entrées $15–26), which takes the idea of farm-fresh to a new level. Opened in 2010, it is the newest venture from Long Meadow Ranch, a winery and farm based in the hills above Rutherford that supplies many of the ingredients, including vegetables, herbs, olive oil, eggs, and grass-fed beef (a specialty). The rustic restaurant is housed in the barn of the former Whiting Nursery, where salvaged farm equipment and even old tree stumps have found new life as fixtures, fittings, and furnishings. Even the booths are covered in leather sourced from the Ranch's cattle. The former executive chef of the Rutherford Grill brings just the right balance of sophistication and familiarity to the simple menu, and if none of the well-priced wines in the varied California-heavy wine list appeals, the restaurant imposes only a $2 charitable donation to open a bottle of your own. To escape the echo-chamber noise in the barn, ask for one of the coveted tables on the outdoor patio surrounded by fruit trees.

Italian

Tra Vigne (1050 Charter Oak Ave., 707/963-4444, www.travignerestaurant.com, lunch and dinner daily, dinner entrées $16–29) is a rarity in the valley—a restaurant that has been around since the early 1990s without ever really changing its formula (it has changed chefs a few times, however). This is a thoroughly Italian place with a classic Italian-American menu, lots of cool stone and terracotta tile, and a wonderful enclosed leafy patio straight out of Tuscany. The wine list reflects the California-inspired Italian menu, with a good selection of local and Italian wines to go with the exquisite pizzas, pastas, and dinner entrées prepared with the usual high-quality local ingredients. As well as a cookbook, Tra Vigne has spawned a deli, wine bar, and pizzeria in St. Helena.

If getting a reservation at Tra Vigne is a problem, there are still plenty of ways to experience its winning formula, thanks to its numerous offspring. One is **Pizzeria Tra Vigne** (1016 Main St., 707/967-9999, lunch and dinner until 9 P.M. Sun.–Thurs., until 9:30 P.M. Fri. and Sat., pizzas $13–20), which, like any adolescent, has had many incarnations over the years, but always the same parent. This being Napa, the pizzas have some unusual and exotic toppings on the perfect thin crusts, and are best enjoyed on the patio. Look for the giant tomato outside the front door opposite the entrance to the Merryvale winery—left over from the restaurant's previous incarnation as Pizzeria Tomatina. There is no corkage fee here, so bring your own wine, or choose from more than two dozen local wines by the glass or bottle.

Casual Dining

Although St. Helena's food scene is constantly changing, there is one place that the term "institution" could apply to, and that's the half-century-old **Gott's Roadside**, formerly Taylor's Automatic Refresher (933 Main St., 707/963-3486, www.gottsroadside.com, lunch and dinner until 10 P.M. daily spring–fall, until 9 P.M. daily in winter, $3–13). This unmistakable old diner just south of downtown is home of the ahi burger and other diner delights, many given a Wine Country gourmet twist but also with prices that have been given a Wine Country lift. A big grassy picnic area with plenty of tables gives a little respite from the traffic, or perch on a stool at the counter. It's a unique experience, but after dropping $30 or more for lunch for two people in the summer, and waiting in a long line for the restrooms, you might wish you'd gone to a more traditional restaurant with more traditional air-conditioning and facilities. New outposts of Taylor's that are more civilized have opened in Napa and San Francisco, but this is the original and still the best if you want some old-school kid-friendly outdoor fun.

The **Model Bakery** (1357 Main St., 707/963-8192, www.themodelbakery.com, 7 A.M.–6 P.M. Tues.–Sat., 7 A.M.–4 P.M. Sun., lunch items

$4–10) is known for baking some of the best bread in the valley and is the latest incarnation of a bakery that has existed here since the 1920s. It's a great place for quick and easy lunches, including gourmet sandwiches, salads, and pizza cooked in the same brick ovens as the bread. Most can be ordered to go, but you might also be lucky enough to snag one of the few tables dotted around the black-and-white tiled floor like strategically placed chess pieces.

For the best breakfasts and no-nonsense lunches in St. Helena, head to **Gillwoods Café** (1313 Main St., 707/963-1788, 7 A.M.–3 P.M. daily, most dishes $8–12). It's a friendly, no-frills diner popular with locals and perfect for some good old fashioned hearty food to prepare you for a day of exploring or to help you recover from yesterday's overconsumption of wine.

If quick refreshment is all you need to keep going, the **Napa Valley Coffee Roasting Company** (1400 Oak Ave., 707/963-4491, www.napavalleycoffee.com, 7 A.M.–6 P.M. weekdays, 7:30 A.M.–6 P.M. weekends) offers some peace and quiet on its patio a block from Main Street.

A couple of miles north of St. Helena is the **Silverado Brewing Company** (3020 St. Helena Hwy. N., 707/967-9876, www.sthelenabrewingcompany.com, dinner daily, entrées $7–18), sprawling right next to the historic stone winery of Freemark Abbey. The menu won't win awards for originality, but it uses quality local produce and is generally well priced. The main attraction here is the beer, which is complemented by an unexpectedly generous wine list. Relaxing on a warm evening on the patio with a cool India pale ale helps you understand how the old Wine Country cliché came about: "it takes good beer to make good wine."

Picnic Supplies
The ease of finding picnic food in this part of the valley is matched only by the ease of finding a place to eat it, whether at the countless wineries with big and small patches of grass or among the redwoods in the Bothe-Napa Valley State Park.

Several of St. Helena's restaurants offer almost all their lunch menu items to go, including **Cindy's Backstreet Kitchen, Market,** and the **Model Bakery.** But even they cannot compete with the gourmet paradise of **Dean & Deluca** (607 St. Helena Hwy. S., 707/967-9980). Just don't lose track of time while browsing the food you never knew existed. A cheaper and altogether quirkier place to buy sandwiches is the old-fashioned deli counter at **Giugni's Grocery & Deli** (1227 Main St., St. Helena, 707/963-3421), an old St. Helena institution that's chock-full of fascinating family memorabilia. Be sure to ask for some Giugni juice, a trademark marinade that's delicious. Those planning to build their own sandwich can also battle through the crowds to the well-stocked deli at the **V. Sattui Winery** (1111 White Ln., St. Helena, 707/963-7774, www.vsattui.com, 9 A.M.–6 P.M. daily spring–fall, 9 A.M.–5 P.M. daily winter).

And don't shun the ugly strip mall home of **Sunshine Foods** (1115 Main St., 707/963-7070, 7:30 A.M.–8:30 P.M. daily), next to the Wells Fargo bank at the southern end of the downtown zone. It's a quality grocery store with a remarkably broad range of deli sandwiches and salads, wines, and even freshly made sushi.

Farmers Market
The place to buy local produce direct from the farmers is the **St. Helena Farmers Market,** held 7:30 A.M.–noon every Friday, May–October, at Crane Park, west of Main Street via Sulphur Springs Road or Mills Lane.

INFORMATION AND SERVICES
Just about every brochure, free magazine, and coupon can be found at the **St. Helena Chamber of Commerce** (1010 Main St., 707/963-4456 or 800/799-6456, www.sthelena.com, 10 A.M.–5 P.M. Mon.–Fri.) at the southern end of Main Street.

Those who need to look up some obscure wine fact on the fly should head to the small wine annex of the modest **St. Helena Public Library** (1492 Library Ln., off Adams St.,

707/963-5244, open daily), a few blocks off Main Street, though it's not nearly as comprehensive as the Sonoma County Wine Library in Healdsburg. Just across the street from Library Lane, on the 2nd floor of the modern office building, is the **Napa Vintners Association** (707/963-3388, www.napavintners.com). You can usually pop in to buy one of the excellent maps it publishes of the valley and its wineries.

If you're in town for a few days, the local *St. Helena Star* newspapers are worth picking up at any local café, as much for the latest Wine Country gossip as for information about local events and some entertaining wine-related columns.

Calistoga

No other town in the Napa Valley retains a sense of its pioneer Victorian roots more than Calistoga, with the remaining stretch of its old boardwalk and Victorian storefronts framed by views in all directions of mountains and forests. Replace the cars and paving with horses and mud, and things would probably look much like they did a hundred years ago when the spa town was at its peak, drawing visitors from far and wide to its natural hot springs and mud baths.

The town was built on mud, literally and figuratively. San Francisco businessman Sam Brannan bought up thousands of acres of land here in the 1850s, drawn by the development potential of the hot springs. He opened a very profitable general store in the late 1850s (now a historic landmark at 203 Wapoo Ave.) followed by his lavish Hot Springs Resort in 1868. He was also instrumental in bringing the railroad this far up the valley to transport visitors to his new resort, making the town a destination for the masses and gateway to Sonoma and Lake Counties to the north.

What Brannan is perhaps best known for, however, is an alcohol-induced slip of the tongue. Legend has it that in a speech promoting his resort he planned to say that it would become known as the "Saratoga of California," referring to the famous New York spa town, but his words instead came out as "the Calistoga of Sarafornia."

Calistoga's modern fortunes have been mixed, and the town has struggled in recent years to keep pace with the frenetic development activity further south in the Napa Valley. Some well-known restaurants have closed, and the eastern edge of downtown looks rather forlorn and neglected, a situation that is supposed to be remedied at some point by the city's redevelopment plan. Whatever ends up being built, Calistoga will likely never lose its relaxed, homely feeling.

The Wines

Many visitors never really explore the wineries this far north in the valley, and they are missing out. Not only are the crowds thinner up here (and the food cheaper), but the area was a historic hub of wine-making in the valley. There's still plenty of wine-making action at both small boutique wineries and grand architectural palaces. The area's latest claim to fame is the impressive Tuscan castle built by valley son Daryl Sattui just south of Calistoga.

Although the Calistoga area was one of the first places that grapes were grown in the Napa Valley, it has been one of the last to be granted its own subappellation status. Chateau Montelena led the charge to get the Calistoga AVA officially designated, and the process took far longer than anticipated, but finally, in December 2009, after six years, the "Battle of Calistoga" was won, and the area became the 15th AVA in the Napa Valley. One reason it took so long is that a nearby winery called Calistoga Cellars does not use grapes from the region in its wine, so would be unable to continue using the world "Calistoga" on its labels. It tried and failed to get an exception to the

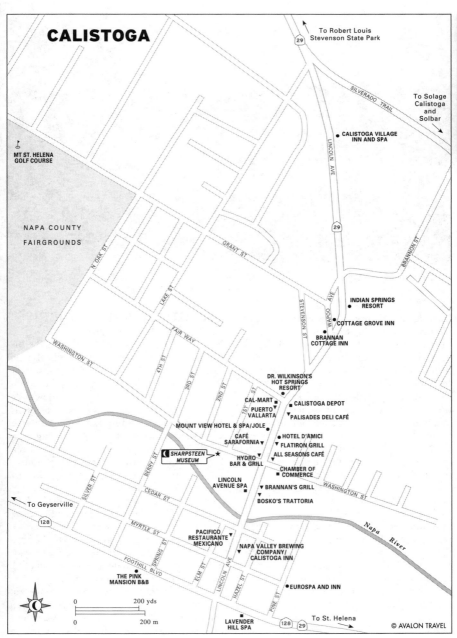

CALISTOGA

To Robert Louis
Stevenson State Park
29

SILVERADO TRAIL

To Solage
Calistoga
and
Solbar

MT ST. HELENA
GOLF COURSE

NAPA COUNTY
FAIRGROUNDS

LINCOLN AVE

CALISTOGA VILLAGE
INN AND SPA

N. OAK ST

LAKE ST

GRANT ST

29

STEVENSON ST

WAPOO AVE

BRANNON ST

INDIAN SPRINGS
RESORT

COTTAGE GROVE INN

BRANNAN
COTTAGE INN

FAIR WAY

WASHINGTON ST

4TH ST

3RD ST

2ND ST

ST ST

DR. WILKINSON'S
HOT SPRINGS
RESORT

CAL-MART
PUERTO
VALLARTA

CALISTOGA DEPOT

PALISADES DELI CAFÉ

MOUNT VIEW HOTEL & SPA/JOLE

BERRY ST

CAFÉ
SARAFORNIA

HOTEL D'AMICI

FLATIRON GRILL

ALL SEASONS CAFÉ

SHARPSTEEN
MUSEUM

HYDRO
BAR & GRILL

CHAMBER OF
COMMERCE

LINCOLN
AVENUE SPA

WASHINGTON ST

BRANNAN'S GRILL

To Geyserville

SILVER ST

CEDAR ST

BOSKO'S TRATTORIA

128

Napa River

MYRTLE ST

SPRING ST

PACIFICO
RESTAURANTE
MEXICANO

FOOTHILL BLVD

ELM ST

LINCOLN AVE

NAPA VALLEY BREWING
COMPANY/
CALISTOGA INN

THE PINK
MANSION B&B

HAZEL ST

EUROSPA AND INN

0   200 yds

0   200 m

PINE ST

LAVENDER
HILL SPA

128 29

To St. Helena

© AVALON TRAVEL

© PHILIP GOLDSMITH

Calistoga is the northern frontier of the Napa Valley, where life goes a little slower.

labeling rule, and must now either change its name or start buying local grapes.

On the western slopes, home of the historic Schramsberg winery and the pseudo-historic Castello di Amorosa, is the **Diamond Mountain** AVA. It was designated in 2001 as the first subappellation in the northern part of the Napa Valley. Winemakers there are already making a name for Diamond Mountain wines as they learn to tame and soften the powerful tannins of the mountain grapes to create increasingly impressive and intense wines with trademark hints of dark chocolate.

Not many white-wine grapes are grown on Diamond Mountain, but on the valley floor, in the Calistoga AVA, whites are common and as impressive as anywhere else in the valley, while the reds have an intensity and power indicative of the warm climate this far up-valley. Indeed, Calistoga temperatures in the summer are often a good 20 degrees warmer than down in Carneros, and nights are not nearly as cold, creating ripening conditions closer to those in Sonoma's Alexander Valley than in some parts of the Napa Valley.

CALISTOGA AREA WINERIES
Frank Family Vineyards

The imposing sandstone building of the historic Larkmead Winery (1091 Larkmead Ln., Calistoga, 707/942-0859 or 800/574-9463, www.frankfamilyvineyards.com, 10 A.M.–5 P.M. daily, tasting $10) a few miles south of Calistoga has had a more colorful history than most, finding fame for still wines and sparkling wines as well as surviving many identities and a big fire in 2000. In its current incarnation it is now perhaps as well known for an unpretentious and slightly quirky tasting experience as for its wines.

The Larkmead area was christened by Lillie Hitchcock Coit (memorialized by San Francisco's Coit Tower) in the 1870s for the many larks in the area, and a winery was first established here in 1884. It was not until the wine-making operation found fame under the ownership of the Italian-Swiss Salima family that the big stone winery building was constructed in 1906, and Larkmead went on to be known for making some of the valley's best wines in huge quantities, right up until 1940 when Felix Salima died.

After changing ownership several times, Larkmead was bought by the Solari family in 1948, and the winery building was sold so they could concentrate on managing the hundreds of acres of vineyards. Kornell Champagne Cellars bought the building, and went on to become one of the biggest producers of sparkling wines in the valley. At one point Kornell made close to 80,000 cases of mainly sweeter, German-style bubbly before bankruptcy ended its run in the early 1990s.

The most recent incarnation of the winery has also had its ups and downs. In the early 1990s, the Rombauer family (a name familiar to food lovers for Irma Rombauer's book *The Joy of Cooking*) bought the winery in partnership with Hollywood executive Rich Frank. Both partners made wine there and ran a custom crush business for small wineries up and down the valley—until a disastrous warehouse fire in 2000 destroyed an estimated 85,000 barrels of stored wine, wiping out the entire stock of many of those clients.

Now the winery makes about 15,000 cases of Frank Family Vineyards still and sparkling wines. The increasing emphasis is on still wines, particularly cabernet sauvignon from Rutherford-area vineyards and chardonnay from Carneros. Sparkling wine remains an important part of the portfolio, however, and a dry blanc de blancs and blanc de noirs are offered as the first part of the tasting in the new tasting room that opened in 2008 in the original craftsman bungalow on the property. Free tours are offered twice a day for most of the year, except when the winemakers are particularly busy around bottling or crush time. If there are no tours, while away some time in the shady picnic area behind the winery.

Larkmead Vineyards

When Larry and Polly Solari bought the historic Larkmead Winery in 1948, keeping the vineyard and quickly selling the old stone winery building (now the home of Frank Family Vineyards across the road), they could not have imagined that more than half a century later their daughter would be producing critically

acclaimed wines at a brand-new winery. For decades the Solaris were known more as grape growers than winemakers, but in the past few decades Kate Solari Baker and Cameron Baker have been quietly perfecting wines sourced from their 110 acres of vineyards just on the other side of Larkmead Lane.

Until the smart new Larkmead Vineyards (1100 Larkmead Ln., Calistoga, 707/942-0167, www.larkmead.com, 10 A.M.–3 P.M. daily, tasting $30) winery building became functional in 2005 (it was completed in 2006), the wines were made at the Napa Wine Company in Oakville with the help of experienced winemakers Paul Hobbs and Andy Smith. With new winemakers and a new winery, Larkmead has gone from strength to strength in recent years and won particular praise for its opulent and elegant cabernets made in a classic European style. Anyone wondering just how good the red wines from the new Calistoga AVA can be should give these a try.

Larkmead still sells about two-thirds of its fruit to other winemakers but keeps the cream of the crop for the 8,000 cases of wine it makes each year, almost half of which is accounted for by the opulent estate cabernet sauvignon that critic Robert Parker seems to like, judging by some recent reviews. The bordeaux-like blends are just as impressive. They include the merlot-dominated Firebelle Meritage, a powerfully flavored wine named for the nickname given to Lillie Hitchcock Coit, who christened the Larkmead area back in the 1800s, and the cheaper 60/40, which is a more straightforward blend of cabernet sauvignon (60 percent) and merlot. All three are usually available to taste, along with a crisp sauvignon blanc. The two flagship wines, Salon and the Solari Reserve, are made in such small quantities that almost the entire production goes to wine club members, a canny move that maintains the exclusivity of Larkmead wines.

The cottage-style winery surrounded by aromatic native plants is modest by Napa Valley standards, a sign that it is more serious about wines than tourists. It's also usually pretty quiet during the week, and that's when it's possible to get a tasting appointment with just a few hours' notice. If you're the only visitors, you might also be treated to a quick tour of the wine-making facilities.

Sterling Vineyards

When it opened in 1973, this contemporary, monastery-like winery, perched high on a wooded knoll rising straight from the valley floor just south of Calistoga, was hailed as one of the most spectacular wineries in the valley by some and lambasted by others. Sterling Vineyards (1111 Dunaweal Ln., Calistoga, 707/942-3345 or 800/726-6136, www.sterlingvineyards.com, 10:30 A.M.–5 P.M. daily, visitor fee $25–40) remains one of the most striking to this day, with whitewashed walls and bell towers that look like they're straight from a Greek travel brochure—hard to miss driving north on Highway 29 into Calistoga.

Such an unusual building, with its aerial gondola whisking visitors 300 feet up to the winery, was bound to become a serious tourist attraction, and so it has. At first glance the gondola, ticket booths, and giant parking lot make it feel more like an out-of-season ski resort than a winery, but once at the top of the hill it's all about wine and views.

Sterling was established in the late 1960s by executives Peter Newton and Michael Stone, who owned the Sterling Paper Company that gave the winery its name. Newton even added some sounds of his homeland by shipping over the bells rescued from the old St. Dunstan's Church in London, which was destroyed during World War II.

Since then, Sterling has built up its production and vineyards. It now makes about 400,000 cases of wine per year and has more than 1,200 acres of vineyards in just about every Napa appellation, from Los Carneros, where it owns the Winery Lake vineyard in the Di Rosa Preserve (source of some highly rated pinot noir and chardonnay), to high up in the Diamond Mountain appellation (source of grapes for some powerhouse cabernet sauvignon). Its growth was helped by the deep pockets of the multinational corporations that have owned the winery since the late 1970s, most recently Diageo.

Once visitors have paid the $25 to get up the hill, everything is pretty much free, including a fun self-guided tour of the winery on elevated walkways, the views, and a sit-down tasting of five wines either inside or out on the patio (weather permitting). It's a unique experience, but one that involves more walking that at most wineries. Those more interested in the wines than the views should opt for one of the pricier tasting options that includes the limited release and single-vineyard wines for which Sterling is better known (those fees can be put toward a purchase). The only thing sometimes missing is the sort of personal service found at smaller wineries, so you might have to persevere to get any detailed information from the staff about what you're drinking.

Clos Pegase

Sterling might be easy to spot perched atop its nearby hill, but just down the road, Clos Pegase (1060 Dunaweal Ln., Calistoga, 707/942-4981, www.clospegase.com, 10:30 A.M.–5 P.M. daily, tasting $15) is truly hard to miss. If the giant pink-and-yellow boxy creation reminds you partly of the whimsical home appliances in your local Target store and partly of a 1980s shopping mall, there's good reason. Clos Pegase was designed in the 1980s by postmodernist architect Michael Graves, better known to most consumers these days as the designer of cheerful teakettles, toasters, and other household paraphernalia.

Graves won a competition sponsored by the San Francisco Museum of Modern Art to design a "temple to wine and art" for entertaining owner Jan Schrem's wine-making passion and displaying his sizable art collection. The original design, which included a giant statue of the winged horse Pegasus, after which the winery is named, had to be toned down, but the resulting building, completed in 1987, is still pretty garish against the bucolic backdrop. It could be mistaken for the Napa outpost of a modern art museum; giant sculptures lurk around every corner, and postmodern design touches grace almost every part of the building. It's a place that's a lot easier to admire up close than from afar.

Look for art and sculpture, both ancient

© PHILIP GOLDSMITH

Clos Pegase, modern architecture amid the vines

and modern, by Kandinsky, Ernst, Moore, and other big names during one of the free tours offered here at 11:30 A.M. and 2 P.M. Despite the fact that the tour tends to be pitched more toward the less artistically inclined among us, it's really the only way to fully appreciate the winery, its art, and the building's ancient Greek design influences. The tour also takes in the fermentation room and maze of caves burrowed into the hillside behind the winery—nothing particularly notable compared to the arty stuff, but fun nonetheless.

Schrem, who made his fortune in the publishing business, also bought hundreds of acres of vineyards in the Calistoga area and down in Carneros. Much of the fruit is sold to other winemakers, and only about a third goes into the 40,000 cases of wine made each year at Clos Pegase, from the high-end Homage reserves down to a local cabernet sauvignon and some reasonably priced, approachable pinot noir, merlot, and chardonnay from Carneros.

◖ Schramsberg Vineyards

If you plan to visit just one of the valley's big champagne makers, the historic Schramsberg

winery (1400 Schramsberg Rd., via Peterson Dr. off Hwy. 29, Calistoga, 707/942-4558 or 800/877-3623, www.schramsberg.com, 10 A.M.–4 P.M. daily, tour and tasting $40) should be high on the list. The winery was established high on the wooded slopes of Diamond Mountain in 1862 by German immigrant Jacob Schram, who had soon made such a name for himself as a maker of high-quality wines that he was paid a visit by a vacationing Robert Louis Stevenson in 1880, a visit memorialized in Stevenson's book *Silverado Squatters.*

In those days, Schram made still wines mainly from German grape varietals, and the winery pretty much died with Schram in 1905. Its fame as a sparkling winemaker didn't begin until the 1960s, when the Davies family bought the rundown property. Rather than compete with the makers of sweeter sparkling wines like the nearby Kornell winery (long since gone) and Korbell in the Russian River Valley, the new owners opted to make drier wines from traditional French champagne grapes—a risk, considering the American palette was more accustomed to sweet white zin than bone-dry champagnes at the time.

The Davies's 1965 blanc de blancs was the first American-made champagne to use chardonnay grapes. The 1969 vintage was served to President Richard Nixon and Chinese Premier Zhou Enlai in Beijing in 1972 for a toast to the normalization of diplomatic relations. In fact, the sales room is full of photos and menus from various White House events at which Schramsberg wines have been served.

Today Schramsberg makes about 45,000 cases of wines, ranging from that historic blanc de blancs and a rich, creamy blanc de noirs up to its flagship J. Schram wine, regarded as one of the best Californian champagnes. To taste them, however, you must sign up for one of the appointment-only tours of the winery, which include a visit to the Victorian mansion, a trip into the spooky bottle-lined caves that date from the late 1800s, and a lesson on the art of champagne making, all culminating in a sit-down tasting. The price is on the high side, but the setting, the history, and the quality of the wines you taste make it worthwhile.

If the wines taste complex, that could be because the grapes come from 67 different vineyards in four California counties, with many in Carneros and the Anderson Valley in Mendocino. The hotter estate vineyard around the winery was replanted mainly to cabernet sauvignon in the late 1990s, and Schramsberg now makes a cabernet (the 2001 vintage was the first release) under the J. Davies label.

Even if you cannot book yourself on a tour, it's worth a quick detour from Highway 29 up the perilously narrow wooded road (with almost invisible speed bumps) just to see the mansion and the ornate gardens that are like a Victorian oasis hidden in the forest. You can also buy any of the wines and look at the old photos in the sales room, which is open all day.

C Castello di Amorosa

Daryl Sattui's Tuscan wonderland, Castello di Amorosa (4045 N. St. Helena Hwy., Calistoga, 707/942-8200, www.castellodiamorosa.

Castello di Amorosa brings some outlandish Tuscan heritage to the Napa Valley.

© PHILIP GOLDSMITH

A MAGIC KINGDOM OF WINE

Whether or not you think a replica medieval castle in the Napa Valley is just a bit over the top (and there are many in the valley who do), it's hard not to be impressed when the fairytale turrets and massive stone walls rear into view as you round a curve on the steep driveway. The product of one man's dream, **Castello di Amorosa** finally opened in 2007, some 14 years and a reported $30 million after the painstaking construction began. As its Italian name implies, this castle was a labor of love.

Despite its rather unfortunate symbolism to critics of the Disneyfication of the Napa Valley, Castello di Amorosa is in many ways no different from other lavish structures that have been built in the valley over the centuries by eccentric winemakers honoring their family roots or simply realizing grand ambitions. The trend started in the 1880s when the Beringer brothers painstakingly recreated an ornate Gothic mansion modeled on their German home. In the following 120 years the valley has become host to extravagant buildings inspired by architecture in Greece (Sterling Vineyards), Persia (Darioush), France and Italy (countless wineries), as well as some fascinating modern interpretations of classic structures like Opus One and Clos Pegase. Many of those architectural imposters created quite a stir when first completed, but all have now settled into the valley's cultural and architectural blend. The Castello simply adds a touch more Tuscany to the mix – 121,000 square feet of Tuscany, to be precise.

This latest Napa winemaker to build his dream is Daryl Sattui, a fourth-generation Italian American winemaker and medieval history buff who had already made a name for himself in the valley with the highly successful V. Sattui winery in St. Helena. His monumental castle is an architectural mash-up, built in just over a decade to resemble the various additions that were commonly made to castles over centuries. It's not based on any particular castle in Tuscany but was inspired by features of many, distilled into a final design by Sattui himself.

Cross the dry moat on the drawbridge, enter through the iron gates into the stone passageway, and sign up for the two-hour tour and tasting ($31-68, no children under 5) to get the most from a visit here. The basic wine-tasting option ($16-26) gives you barely a hint at the history lessons that lie in the towers rising four stories above and passageways that plunge four stories below. First stop on the tour is the Great Hall, a two-story marvel of frescos, coffered ceilings, and stone walls fit for any wine-fueled banquet. The cloistered main courtyard beyond, with its tiny chapel and colorful planters, could be out of almost any ancient French or Italian village. The towers offer strategic views over the valley and even have chutes to pour hot oil on the advancing hordes below.

The best parts of the castle, though, are underground. A warren of cool, damp passageways descend to catacombs and vaulted cellars, including the breathtaking, 130-foot-long main barrel room with its vast cross-vaulted ceiling. There's even a dungeon, stocked with some particularly heinous torture instruments – including an original iron maiden, which looks rather like an upright mummy case but is lined with spikes to impale hapless victims inside. Next door is an aptly named pit of despair, into which victims were thrown to starve to death with only the company of rats.

Everything was painstakingly recreated using traditional materials and a small army of artisans. Every piece of iron, from the elaborate gates and dragon-head sconces down to the nails in the massive wooden doors, was hand-forged in Italy, where the antique bricks and tiles were also sourced. Much of the stone used in the walls was quarried locally, and the pieces were hand-shaped onsite to fit together like a giant three-dimensional jigsaw.

com, tours 9:30 A.M.–4:30 P.M. Mon.–Fri., 9:30 A.M.–5 P.M. weekends, tasting $16–26, two-hour tour and tasting $31, no children under age 5), is a sight for the eyes. Surrounded by such a fantastic structure, it's easy to forget that this is also a working winery. At the back of the castle and in a neighboring building designed to resemble a Tuscan farmhouse, there's a state-of-the-art gravity-flow winery where Sattui creates limited-production Italian-inspired wines from his Diamond Mountain vineyards together with a handful of acres in Mendocino's Anderson Valley and elsewhere in the Napa Valley. Current production is a modest 10,000 cases.

The 38 acres of vineyards planted to cabernet sauvignon, sangiovese, merlot, and primitivo (a relative of zinfandel) around the castle produce intensely flavored red wines typical of Diamond Mountain, but some also with the typical tannic bite that can take a few years to mellow in the bottle. They include the excellent-value Il Brigante, a blend of cabernet, merlot, and sangiovese that's a bit like a baby super-Tuscan but with a baby price to go with it. Its big sister is the supple and opulent super-Tuscan blend called La Castellana, named for the traditional lady of the castle. The flagship Diamond Mountain wine is Il Barone, a powerhouse mountain cabernet. Other reds include well-priced and limited-production sangiovese and merlot. The highlights of the white wines are the Mendocino gewürztraminers, made in both a slightly sweet (dolcino) and bone-dry style. Other whites include several chardonnays and the classic Italian white wine, pinot grigio.

In terms of both the wines produced and the number of visitors, Sattui plans to make Castello di Amorosa a far more exclusive experience than his crowded V. Sattui winery. There has been talk of setting some limits on the number of people allowed up the driveway to the castle, but judging by summer crowds, that has not yet happened. Those crowds do mean it's worth calling ahead, particularly on busy weekends, to reserve a spot on a tour and ensure you're able to experience Daryl Sattui's kingdom of wine.

Reverie Vineyard & Winery

At the end of the long driveway off Diamond Mountain Road, Reverie (1520 Diamond Mountain Rd., Calistoga, 707/942-6800 or 800/738-3743, www.reveriewine.com, by appointment 10 A.M.–4 P.M. daily) shares a hidden sun-drenched valley surrounded by terraced vineyards that are key to its success as well as the success of the neighboring wineries that share this little part of wine-growing heaven. Reverie released its first wine in 1995 and now produces about 2,500 cases of mainly bordeaux-style red wines, together with small amounts of a delicious cabernet franc, from its 40 acres of rocky mountain vineyards, with the help of consultant winemaker Ted Lemon, better known for his sought-after Littorai pinot noir and chardonnay wines.

These big ripe reds with muscular tannins are classic Diamond Mountain wines, enhanced (at least mentally) by the alfresco tasting experience under towering redwood trees. With help from a different winemaker, Reverie also makes small quantities of crisp, nonmalolactic chardonnay from Diamond Mountain fruit, and a sauvignon blanc sourced from vineyards down in the valley, both under the Daydream label. Of all the wines, however, it's hard not to go home with a bottle of the fun proprietary red blend called AsKiken, named after winery founder (and former PR guru) Norm Kiken.

A quick tour of the small low-key winery followed by a tasting in the caves or under the redwoods can easily be arranged by calling first. There's no real tour schedule—if someone's there, they will probably be happy to show you around, although in recent years Reverie has suspended its tours during the winter months, so call before you plan your itinerary.

Von Strasser Winery

To get to Reverie, the driveway off Diamond Mountain Road first passes the unobtrusive home of the Von Strasser winery (1510 Diamond Mountain Rd., Calistoga, 707/942-0930, www.vonstrasser.com, 10:30 A.M.–4:30 P.M. daily, tour and tasting $20), established in 1990 by Rudy von Strasser, who was instrumental in putting Diamond Mountain on the wine map. He spearheaded the alliance of local growers that finally succeeded in having Diamond Mountain declared its own subappellation within Napa Valley in 2001, after almost a decade of trying.

Von Strasser offers plenty of memorable examples of what can be done with Diamond Mountain grapes. It makes a selection of intense, vineyard-designate cabernet sauvignons from its own estate and adjacent vineyards, together with a chardonnay and a few hundred cases of the appellation's only zinfandel. Total production of about 9,000 cases makes it one of the largest of Diamond Mountain's handful of wineries.

The Estate Vineyard cabernet is the wine that Von Strasser is probably best known for, balancing powerful tannins with equally powerful fruit, resulting in high ratings from critics almost every year. This and a couple of other cabernets are usually available to taste by appointment as part of a flight of five wines at the low-key tasting room. Also ask about tours of the winery, and you might be lucky enough to have Rudy as your tour guide.

Zahtila Vineyards

Across the valley from Diamond Mountain, where the Silverado Trail meets Highway 29 just east of Calistoga, is a little cluster of modest buildings belonging to this family-owned boutique winery. Zahtila (2250 Lake County Hwy., Calistoga, 707/942-9251, www.zahtilavineyards.com, 10 A.M.–5 P.M. daily, tasting $10) makes some fine cabernet sauvignon and zinfandel. Its relaxed atmosphere and smooth-drinking wines offer a nice change of pace (and price) from the Napa Valley crush. Staff in the cozy tasting room are also a mine of information about other

small local wineries. Just don't trip over the chewed toys left lying around by the friendly winery dog.

The specialty here is zinfandel, which is grown in the small Oat Hill Vineyard next to the winery, planted in the 1970s by the previous owners. Most of the fruit, however, is bought from other growers for its 2,000 cases of wine. Cabernet sauvignon comes from the Rutherford and Calistoga areas and goes into the rich, smooth Napa cabernet and flagship Beckstoffer cabernet. Additional zinfandel is bought from the Russian River Valley and sometimes the Dry Creek Valley. Chardonnay was added to the portfolio in recent years and is sourced from vineyards near St. Helena.

Chateau Montelena

This beautiful French- and Chinese-inspired Chateau Montelena (1429 Tubbs Ln., Calistoga, 707/942-5105, www.montelena. com, 9:30 A.M.–4 P.M. daily, tours 9:45 A.M. Tues., Thurs., and Sun., $40; tasting $20 or $40) wine estate will forever be remembered for putting Napa Valley on the map when its 1973-vintage chardonnay trounced the best French white burgundies at the famous 1976 Paris tasting. The winery is by no means resting on its past achievements, however, and is still a top Napa winemaker today. Yet even before the Paris tasting it had quite a colorful history.

Chateau Montelena dates back to the 1880s, when Alfred Tubbs (after whom Tubbs Lane is named) bought land and built the imposing stone château, eventually naming it after Mount St. Helena, which looms in the distance. The winery prospered until Prohibition, after which it made limited amounts of wine and sold grapes to other growers before the estate was broken up in the 1950s.

The giant five-acre Jade Lake and Chinese flourishes like the lacquered bridges and pavilions were added by Yort Wing Frank, who bought a chunk of the estate in 1958 for a bit of retirement fun. Serious wine-making didn't start again until just over a decade later, when the château and original vineyards were re-united by James Barrett and partner Leland Paschich, signaling the start of Chateau Montelena's modern-day wine-making heritage. In an ironic twist to the story of a winery that humiliated some of the finest French wine châteaus in the 1970s, Chateau Montelena was destined to be acquired by the Bordeaux wine château Cos d'Estournel in 2008, but the deal fell through and left the Barrett family still firmly in charge.

James' son, Bo Barrett, has been Montelena's winemaker since 1982 and was famously portrayed as a long-haired renegade in the semi-fictitious 2008 movie *Bottle Shock,* about the 1976 Paris tasting. Not surprisingly, there is a "behind the scenes" tour offered three times a week that includes a tasting of the latest vintage of chardonnay and a movie souvenir; check the website for times.

Soft, plush cabernet sauvignon is now just as acclaimed as the rich chardonnay at Montelena, and together they account for the bulk of the 35,000-case production. An excellent estate zinfandel is also made, and all are usually available to taste. Cabernet fans can also try a vertical Library tasting of the age-worthy but pricey estate cabernet in the intimate stone-walled Estate Room. Reservations for this twice-daily sit-down tasting are essential.

THE EASTERN MOUNTAINS WINERIES

The oak-studded peaks and valleys hidden in the Vaca Mountains on the eastern side of Napa Valley offer a relaxing diversion and a total change of pace. Grapes have been grown here for more than 100 years, and the area was ripe for a new wave of viticultural development until the valley's biggest growers recently turned their attention farther north to Lake County, where land is cheaper and the promise greater.

Nevertheless, there are still some great wines made in these hills, most notably in the Chiles Valley appellation, where zinfandel

and sauvignon blanc enjoy the warmer growing conditions, and on Howell Mountain, where cabernet sauvignon reigns supreme in the thin volcanic soils.

The Chiles Valley offers the best touring possibilities and is easy to reach. Take Highway 128 (Sage Canyon Road) up into the hills from the Silverado Trail at Rutherford, past Lake Hennessey, and go either left or right at the junction. Both roads lead to the valley. Just be sure to leave plenty of time to drive there and back on the mountain roads and to take lunch because there's very little apart from farmland and vineyards up there.

Catacula Lake Winery

Turn left at the Lake Hennessey junction onto Chiles Pope Valley Road and continue for about six miles into the Chiles Valley to this former summer camp. The first vintage from Catacula Lake (4105 Chiles Pope Valley Rd., St. Helena, 707/965-1104, by appointment daily, tasting $5) was in 1999, and it now makes about 5,000 cases of wine per year, including some increasingly good zinfandel and sauvignon blanc, at bargain prices.

Considering so few wines are made here, none costing more than $20 a bottle, the $5 fee for the appointment-only tasting might seem a little steep, but a couple of library wines are thrown in, and there's also sometimes a two-for-one tasting offer on the winery's website. The peaceful setting next to the lake with an outdoor patio and picnic area also makes it a worthwhile outlay.

RustRidge Ranch & Winery

About three miles from Lake Hennessey on Chiles Pope Valley Road, turn right onto Lower Chiles Valley Road to get to this very rustic part-winery, part-ranch, where thoroughbred horses are just as important as wine. Tastings at RustRidge (2910 Lower Chiles Valley Rd., St. Helena, 707/965-9353, www.rustridge.com, 10 A.M.–4 P.M. daily, tour and tasting $20) are held in an old cattle barn that now houses the winery workings, and a visit here is as much about smelling the horses as the wine.

About 55 of the ranch's 440 acres are planted with grapes, and the winery makes about 2,000 cases of zinfandel, both barrel- and tank-fermented chardonnay, cabernet sauvignon, and sauvignon blanc. The rest of the fruit is sold to other wineries. Tours and tastings are offered every day by appointment only, but with life up here so relaxed, all that's usually required is a call to check that someone's home.

Brown Estate Vineyards

At the far southern end of the Chiles Valley appellation is a relative newcomer to the wine business, but one that is already making a name for its zinfandels.

The Brown family bought the land as a vacation home in 1981, and by 1990 had planted 40 acres of vineyards on the former Victorian homestead. The Browns sold their fruit to other wineries until 1996, when they made their first zinfandel vintage. It was lauded by critics, as were many of the subsequent vintages. Since then Brown (3233 Sage Canyon Rd., St. Helena, 707/963-2435, www.brown-estate.com, open to Wine Club members only) has added chardonnay to the mix and blasted a 6,500-square-foot cave complex out of the hillside behind the winery.

Brown makes about 4,000 cases of predominantly zinfandel but also small quantities of cabernet sauvignon and chardonnay from the estate vineyards, though it still sells some fruit to other local wineries.

Kuleto Estate

When one of the Bay Area's most successful restaurateurs turns his hand to wine-making, you can be sure the resulting winery is going to be quite a destination. Pat Kuleto's hillside estate does not disappoint, from the secret gate code given to visitors who make an appointment to the Tuscan-style house, Villa Cucina, with its infinity pool framing a view of Lake Hennessey and the valley beyond.

Kuleto is the man behind such swank San Francisco restaurants as Boulevard and Farallon as well as the popular Martini House down the hill in St. Helena. The Kuleto Estate winery (2470 Sage Canyon Rd., St. Helena, 707/302-2200, www.kuletoestate.com, tours by appointment at 10:30 and 11:45 A.M. and 1 and 2:30 P.M. daily, $35), completed in 2002, will likely be just as successful if recent ratings are any indication, particularly as Kuleto works his culinary contacts to get his wines on the lists of some of the country's top restaurants.

The 90 acres of vineyards planted on the twists and turns of these 800 acres of former grazing land are planted predominantly to cabernet sauvignon and sangiovese, with small blocks of zinfandel, syrah, pinot noir, and chardonnay. Production is about 8,000 cases now but will undoubtedly grow if the success of Kuleto's other ventures is anything to go by.

Tours of the diverse vineyards and modern winery, together with a comprehensive tasting of wines with cheeses, are available four times a day by appointment. And as you enter the gate code and drive onto the estate, you can imagine for a fleeting moment that you've arrived at your own personal Wine Country estate.

SIGHTS
◖ Sharpsteen Museum

The quirky little Sharpsteen Museum (1311 Washington St., Calistoga, 707/942-5911, www.sharpsteen-museum.org, 11 A.M.–4 P.M. daily, donations requested) was donated to the city in the 1970s by its creators, Ben and Bernice Sharpsteen, and depicts up-valley life from the days of the Wappo people to the early 1900s. Its main claim to fame is a beautifully painted diorama depicting Calistoga in its hot springs heyday, but it also has some more traditional exhibits, many no doubt enhanced by the skills of Ben Sharpsteen, who was an Academy Award–winning animator.

Next door is one of the frilly little cottages built by Sam Brannan in the 1860s for his groundbreaking Hot Springs Resort in Calistoga. It was moved here in the 1970s, leaving only one of Brannan's cottages where

An ornate Victorian cottage that was once part of Sam Brannan's original Calistoga spa resort is now part of the Sharpsteen Museum.

© PHILIP GOLDSMITH

it was built—at the Brannan Cottage Inn on Wapoo Avenue.

Old Faithful Geyser

Although it may not really be worth the time or money, visitors continue to flock to Calistoga's Old Faithful Geyser (1299 Tubbs Ln., Calistoga, 707/942-6463, www.oldfaithfulgeyser.com, 9 A.M.–6 P.M. daily spring–fall, 9 A.M.–5 P.M. daily winter, adults $10, children $3), one of only three geysers in the world reliable enough to get the "Old Faithful" moniker. There must be something hypnotic about the thought of watching water shoot 60 feet or more into the air that keeps people coming. Or perhaps it's the free mud bath into which you can unwittingly sink if you get too close to the edge of the pools. Just hope you don't get there right after an eruption has finished, or it could be as long as a 45-minute wait until the next one (the gap between eruptions varies depending on

Old Faithful Geyser

© SUSAN LEONARD/123RF.COM

the season, so check the website for the latest updates). Still, that's time enough to open your faithful old wallet for some overpriced and tacky Old Faithful gifts. Even the famous fainting goats near the entrance seem bored by all the fuss and rarely faint on cue, as their "genetic defect" is supposed to guarantee.

Petrified Forest

Another natural attraction nearby that illustrates the area's volcanic past but with far more scenic value (though no goats) is the Petrified Forest (follow the signs to Santa Rosa, 707/942-6667, 9 A.M.–7 P.M. daily summer, 9 A.M.–5 P.M. daily winter, $8), a couple of miles up Petrified Forest Road from Calistoga. Like the Geyser down the hill, the experience feels very homespun with little in the way of glossy corporate tourist facilities. You also might start wondering what you paid for, because the short trails meander through what seem like recently fallen redwood trees. In fact, they were long ago turned to stone at such a microscopic level that they still look almost like real wood rather than the fossils they are. In the distance looms Mount St. Helena, believed to have been the source of the volcanic eruption that buried the trees millions of years ago and started the long petrification process. Guided tours are available on weekends at 11 A.M., and there are plenty of chunks of petrified wood for sale in the wonderfully tacky visitors center under a very old oak tree (no one knows how old, but probably over 600 years).

Pope Valley

Sleepy Pope Valley is the unlikely setting for California Historic Landmark No. 939. Even more unlikely is that California would designate a collection of thousands of hubcaps strung from posts, fences, and trees as a historic landmark. But such is the importance of this strange collection to the state's eclectic folk-art scene (or so someone thought) that the **Hubcap Ranch,** created by Emanuel "Litto" Damonte

from the 1950s to his death in 1985, was given its lofty status, and Litto was immortalized as the Pope Valley Hubcap King.

It is still a private ranch, so don't expect any Wine Country–style tours, though you're welcome to leave a hubcap from the rental car or your own to ensure the collection keeps growing. The ranch's dogs seem to love trying to scare visitors, so don't be surprised when they hurl their snarling bodies at the fence behind the landmark plaque.

Litto's grandson, Mike Damonte, has kept up the folk-art tradition that his grandfather inadvertently started when he hung lost hubcaps on his fence in case their hapless owners wanted them back. The growing collection proved to be a magnet, and soon neighbors and anonymous visitors were leaving hubcaps rather than taking them. Now, half a century later, there are, it is said, about 5,000 of the things glinting in the sun, from lavish chrome 1960s trim to the present-day plastic wannabes.

Hubcap Ranch is easy to get to and easy to spot. From the Silverado Trail, head up Deer Park Road, through the small college town of Angwin, and down through the forest to the auto-repair shop, junkyard, and general store that constitute downtown Pope Valley. At that intersection, turn left onto Pope Valley Road. From the Catacula Lake Winery, continue east along Chiles Pope Valley Road, then bear right at the general store. Hubcap Ranch is about two miles farther, at 6654 Pope Valley Road just past the Pope Valley Winery, though you certainly won't need to look for the number on a mailbox.

While you're in the area, the **Pope Valley Winery** (6613 Pope Valley Rd., 707/965-1246, www.popevalleywinery.com, 11 A.M.–5 P.M. Thurs.–Sun., call ahead Mon.–Tues., free tasting) is worth a stop, despite its sprawling scrappy-looking setting. The original three-story winery building was built in 1909 and operated as the Sam Haus Winery until 1959. Since then a variety of owners have tried to make a go of it in this remote location, the latest being

© PHILIP GOLDSMITH

Donations are always welcome at the Hubcap Ranch.

a group of valley residents who bought the old buildings in 1998 and now make about 4,000 cases of mainly red wines from the 80 acres of Pope Valley vineyards, including zinfandel, cabernet sauvignon, and sangiovese.

ENTERTAINMENT

For the sleepiest and most mellow town in the Napa Valley, Calistoga has some of the best nightlife. This is still Wine Country, however, so don't expect too much beyond live local bands and the ability to buy a beer after 11 P.M. The **Hydro Bar & Grill** (1403 Lincoln Ave., 707/942-9777) sometimes hosts local live music on weekend nights, and the **Napa Valley Brewing Company** at the Calistoga Inn (1250 Lincoln Ave., 707/942-4101, www.calisto-gainn.com) offers live jazz or blues every night of the week on the creek-side patio during the summer and often on weekends in the winter. There's also a popular open mike night on Wednesday and themed music on most other weekday nights hosted by the house DJ. More information is available online or by phone from the Calistoga Inn.

SHOPPING

Like many things in Calistoga, shopping is a little more down-to-earth here than elsewhere in the valley. Sure, there are plenty of gift shops, but there's a decidedly artisanal feel to most of them, like the **American Indian Trading Company** (1407 Lincoln Ave., next to the Hydro Bar & Grill, 707/942-9330, 10 A.M.–6 P.M. daily), which sells arts, crafts, and jewelry from Native American tribes all over the country, including a few local groups. On Highway 29 just south of Lincoln Avenue is **Calistoga Pottery** (1001 Foothill Blvd., 707/942-0216, 9 A.M.–5 P.M. daily), another good place to buy something original from local artists who have supplied some of the valley's biggest wineries and restaurants with their stoneware.

At the eastern end of Lincoln Avenue is the historic **Calistoga Depot** (1458 Lincoln Ave.), the second-oldest remaining railroad depot in the country, built by Sam Brannan in 1868 and crucial to the early success of Calistoga's Victorian spas. It is now home to a handful of funky little stores, some of them in six old railroad cars parked on the tracks that lead to nowhere. **Calistoga Wine Stop** (707/942-5556, 10 A.M.–6 P.M. daily) is in the main depot building and has a good selection of wines from both Napa and Sonoma, including a few rarities.

Wine aficionados will also probably enjoy sniffing around the small **Enoteca Wine Shop** (1348 Lincoln Ave., 707/942-1117, 11:30 A.M.–5:30 P.M. daily), which specializes in smaller (sometimes cult) producers of wines from California and beyond. Another fascinating wine shop, one that prides itself on selling hard-to-find boutique California wines, is the **Wine Garage** (1020 Foothill Blvd., Calistoga, 707/942-5332, 11 A.M.–6:30 P.M. Mon.–Sat., 11 A.M.–4:30 P.M. Sun.) on Foothill Boulevard just south of Lincoln Avenue. Owner Todd Miller travels throughout the lesser-known wine regions of Northern California trying and buying wines from small wineries, loading them onto his truck, and bringing them back to the shop. No bottle costs over $25, and many are under $15—a refreshing change in a valley of big wine names and big prices.

If your visit to Calistoga is too brief to get immersed in a mud bath, you can buy a jar of the stuff to take home with you at **Mudd Hens** (1348 Lincoln Ave., 707/942-0210, www.mud-dhens.com, 10:30 A.M.–6 P.M. Sun.–Thurs., 10:30 A.M.–9 P.M. Fri.–Sat.). In addition to the (rather expensive) Calistoga mud, you'll find countless other body-care related products, from teas to potions.

RECREATION
Robert Louis Stevenson State Park

By far the best views in the valley, and perhaps the entire Wine Country, are from the top of Napa's highest peak, Mount St. Helena, which is at the northern end of the valley in the park named for the mountain's most famous Victorian visitor.

Stevenson honeymooned in a cabin here after traveling from his native Scotland to marry Fanny Osbourne, the woman he met at an artists' retreat. The area had just been abandoned by silver miners following the rapid rise

and fall of the **Silverado mine** in the 1870s, after which the Silverado Trail is named, along with Stevenson's account of his brief stay in the valley, *Silverado Squatters.*

The happy couple's cabin is long gone, marked only by a small monument partway up the five-mile trail to the summit. Look out for two big dirt parking lots on either side of the road about eight miles north of Calistoga on Highway 29. The **Mount St. Helena Trail** starts from the western lot and has virtually no shade, together with some particularly steep sections—it climbs about 2,000 feet in five miles to the 4,339-foot summit of the mountain—so hiking it in the middle of a hot summer day is not recommended. On the clearest days, usually in spring, the 360-degree views stretch for more than 100 miles, and in winter there is often a dusting of snow near the peak. Those not so determined to get to the summit can take a spur off the main trail at about the 3.5-mile point to the 4,000-foot South Peak, which has impressive views of the valley.

The eastern parking lot marks the start of the **Table Rock Trail,** a shorter and less strenuous 2.2-mile trail that climbs out of the woodland and past volcanic rock outcroppings to a ridge overlooking the flat moonscape known as Table Rock and the entire valley to the south. The more adventurous can connect to the **Palisades Trail,** which crosses Table Rock and eventually meets the Oat Hill Mine Road leading down into the valley, though that turns the hike into a daylong expedition and ends miles from the parking lot.

Calistoga Spas

During his stay here in 1880, Robert Louis Stevenson observed that Calistoga "seems to repose on a mere film above a boiling, sub-terranean lake." That mineral-laden boiling water fueled the growth of one of the biggest spa destinations in California. Railroad baron Samuel Brannan first cashed in on the endless hot water supply in 1862 with his Hot Springs Resort, and by the late 1860s the new railroad was bringing the fashionable and well-heeled from San Francisco to immerse themselves.

The emphasis of the dozens of spas these days has broadened to include everything from restorative volcanic mud to mineral soaks, wraps, and facials. The clientele has also broadened to include the less well-heeled, drawn by the straightforward, no-nonsense spa treatments here that dispense with the more luxurious frills offered by the bigger Napa Valley and Sonoma super-resorts. Don't go expecting glamorous establishments straight out of a glossy magazine spread—some of the places look like decidedly unglamorous motels in need of some restorative work themselves.

The region's Wappo people were the first to discover the unlikely pleasure of soaking in the local mud (one wonders who first had the idea and why). These days the mud is usually a mixture of dark volcanic ash, peat (for buoyancy), and hot mineral water that suspends your body, relaxes muscles, and draws out impurities in the skin, all accompanied by a rather off-putting sulfurous smell. A 10–15-minute soak is usually followed by a rinse in crystal-clear mineral water and a steam wrap with or without piped music. Aromatherapies, massages, and other hedonistic treatments can be added afterward but will quickly run up the price. Those worried about lying in someone else's

LEAVE WINE (AND CLOTHES) BEHIND

Put away the camera, forget about wineries, leave your cynicism behind, and take off all your clothes (if you want to) at the historic and decidedly alternative **Harbin Hot Springs,** about a half hour north of Calistoga, beyond Mount St. Helena in rural Lake County (Harbin Springs Rd., off Big Canyon Rd., Middletown, 707/987-2477 or 800/622-2477, www.harbin.org).

In some sense, this place could be described as a hot springs resort. It has the natural springs and the history of its Calistoga spa cousins to the south, dating from the late 1800s when the sick and infirm sought out the natural waters here. A more accurate description these days, however, would be a New Age ecoresort still running on 1960s flower power. It's a place where you're far more likely to hear about the joy of finding a higher state of consciousness than the joy of savoring the best cabernet in Napa. That's if you hear anything. In some parts of the resort, even a whisper will elicit gentle but firm rebukes that might conjure up fears of some bizarre karmic retribution. It also has a bit of a reputation for being a pickup joint, both gay and straight, which makes you wonder how one hooks up in silence.

Nevertheless, there's enough on offer within the 1,200 acres to please even a wine-soaked cynic – from hiking trails in the hills to the series of indoor-outdoor hot and cold pools among the trees; from the organic food store to the communal kitchen. Best of all is the end-less flow of free classes and workshops ranging from dance and yoga to meditation and massage. Harbin is perhaps best known for its Watsu massage – a form of Shiatsu massage performed while you float in a pool.

Nearly all the activities are free after paying a day-use fee of $25 (weekdays) or $35 (weekends), though at least one person in your party will need to buy a $10 trial membership to the nonprofit organization that runs Harbin. If you only want to sunbathe naked (or clothed) for half a day or take a yoga class, the six-hour fee is $5-10 less. Check the website for a full schedule of events and classes.

Another reason to come here is for the wide range of accommodations. They range from dorm rooms ($35-50, bring your own towels and bedding) and basic rooms with shared baths ($60-140) up to rooms with full baths (from $130 midweek, $190 weekends) and three cottages tucked away in the woods ($170-190 midweek, $230-260 weekends). The most bizarre rooms are in a space-age domed complex perched on a hillside that look as though they were designed by an architect on acid. The double rooms with wacky windows and shared bathrooms cost from $110 midweek and $150 weekends. Camping in the meadows is also an option and is free with the day-use fee ($25-35), though no fires or camping stoves are allowed, so you'll be eating in one of the on-site vegetarian restaurants or using the communal kitchen.

impurities can take comfort from the claims that the mud is regularly flushed with fresh spring water. There is evidently such a thing as "clean" mud.

Wherever and whatever the treatment, remember that the heat can rapidly dehydrate your body, so lay off the wine beforehand and don't plan to hike to the top of Mount St. Helena afterward. Reservations are usually needed, but you might luck out just by walking in, especially midweek. Most spas are also open late, making them an ideal way to wrap up a long day of touring (pun intended).

On the site of Brannan's original resort is the **Indian Springs Resort** (1712 Lincoln Ave., 707/942-4913, www.indianspringscalistoga. com, 9 A.M.–8 P.M. daily), which specializes in 100 percent volcanic mud bath treatments ($85), using the volcanic ash from its 16 acres of land, and mineral baths ($70). It also has what is said to be California's oldest continuously operating swimming pool, an Olympic-sized version built in 1913 and fed by warm spring water. In fact, you can usually see the puffs of steam from the natural hot springs onsite. Spa customers can lounge by the pool as long as they want, though it can get crowded and the water is a little too warm for any serious swimming.

Another muddy Calistoga institution announced by its big, red neon sign is the funky **Dr. Wilkinson's Hot Springs** (1507 Lincoln Ave., 707/942-4102, www.drwilkinson.com, 8:30 A.M.–3:45 P.M. daily), founded by an eccentric chiropractor in the 1950s who developed his own secret recipe for the mud that his children still guard closely today. "The Works," a 1.5-hour pampering with mud bath, facial, mineral soak, and blanket wrap, costs $89. For $40 more, you can finish with a 30-minute massage, and there are plenty of other competitively priced packages available.

The **Lincoln Avenue Spa** (1339 Lincoln Ave., 707/942-5296, www.lincolnave-nuespa.com, 10 A.M.–6 P.M. Sun.–Thurs., 10 A.M.–8 P.M. Fri.–Sat.) offers couples the chance to float in twin tubs of mud in a private room ($85). There is a choice of four types

of mud, including an Ayurvedic herbal mud and an antioxidant-laden wine mud containing wine, grape seed oil, and green tea. It also offers salt scrubs, with or without accompanying mud, and a full range of massages and facials. No jokes about spa treatments breaking the bank here—this spa is in an impregnable-looking stone building that was a Victorian-era bank.

At the **Lavender Hill Spa** (1015 Foothill Blvd., 707/942-4495, www.lavenderhillspa. com, 9 A.M.–9 P.M. daily) the mud is used only once before being discarded and is an international affair, containing Calistoga volcanic ash, French sea kelp, Dead Sea salt, and the trademark lavender oil. Like most treatments here, the mud bath ($85) is available for singles or couples. For the same price there is also a Thai milk bath with sea kelp and some fruity essential oils that is part of a whole range of other Thai-inspired massages and facials, all in a relaxing gardenlike setting.

There is an equally diverse selection of ways to immerse yourself **Mount View Spa** (1457 Lincoln Ave., 707/942-5789 or 800/816-6877, www.mountviewhotel.com, 9 A.M.–9 P.M. daily) in the namesake hotel, including mineral mud baths, aromatherapy baths and saunas, mud- and seaweed-wraps, massages, and facial treatments in perhaps the classiest setting in Calistoga. The mineral mud baths ($70, couples $80) and wraps might contain grape seeds, aromatherapy essences, as well as Moor mud added to the water. Massages start at $99, and the huge selection culminates with a three-hour $360 extravaganza called the Head to Toe package, which includes a mineral bath, body polish, Swedish massage, and facial. The hotel's pool can also be used by spa customers.

ACCOMMODATIONS

Calistoga is one of the cheapest places in the valley for most purchases, from food and gas to a place to stay. This is still Wine Country, however, so "cheap" is a relative term, and prices have risen faster than the valley average in the past few years. Calistoga might finally be cashing in on its charms, or at least cashing in on the fact that a fancy resort, Solage, opened in 2007 and promises to bring a flood of tourist dollars to town.

Some of the Victorian B&Bs strung along the Highway 29 and Foothill Boulevard seem downright reasonable during the week, but rates can almost double on summer weekends, much like everywhere else in the valley. The best bargains are probably the numerous spa resorts that offer slightly less elegant motel-style rooms for slightly more reasonable prices. All generally offer free continental breakfast, though with some you might be left wondering which continent manages to function on such meager morning sustenance.

Whatever the accommodation, remember that this end of the valley is the hottest, and sleeping without air-conditioning in the height of summer can be a challenge. As in the rest of the valley, there is also a penalty to pay for wanting to stay during a weekend, when rates are often 50 percent higher than midweek and a two-night minimum is pretty standard. And that's if you can find a room. As always, book plenty of time in advance from July through October.

Under $100

To use the term "bargain" to describe the **Calistoga Inn** (1250 Lincoln Ave., Calistoga, 707/942-4101, www.calistogainn. com) might be a bit of an overstatement, but this no-nonsense inn right on the creek in the center of town does offer some of the cheapest, if not the most luxurious, accommodations in town. The 18 rooms are Spartan compared to those of the Victorian inns in the surrounding blocks—no air-conditioning, no televisions, shared bathrooms (but an in-room sink), a dose of street or restaurant noise, and often not enough room to swing a proverbial cat. Still, they are clean, comfortable, even stylish in their minimalist way, and cost from only $69 a night midweek year-round—that's about as cheap as it gets in Calistoga. On summer weekends the price shoots up to $119, making the basic rooms far less of a bargain, though there is no minimum-stay requirement. One of

Calistoga's better restaurants and a microbrewery are right downstairs, making for a night of good food, entertainment, and (hopefully) sleep, all in a charming Victorian package.

A more rustic accommodation option is at the **Mountain Home Ranch** (3400 Mountain Home Ranch Rd., off Petrified Forest Rd., Calistoga, 707/942-6616, www.mountainhomeranch.com), up in the hills about a 10-minute drive from Calistoga. This is a down-home family B&B and working ranch with rooms in the main house and separate cottages that are more practical than stylish. The cheapest, with a shared bathroom, squeak in at just under $100 March–November (less during the winter), while regular rooms with private bathrooms are just over $100 during the high season and $80 during the winter. The two- and three-room cabins scattered among the oak trees start at $140 for double occupancy, though there's an additional $20 charge per person for more than two guests. They are fairly cheap and private but a little run-down and by no means luxurious. Part of the charm of the ranch, however, is its peaceful rural setting. Hiking trails lead from the accommodations to the farm and down to a creek—just be sure to get directions because the trail is not obvious. It's a great place for outdoorsy types who don't want the hassles of camping and for families with adventurous kids.

Within walking distance of downtown Calistoga is motel row, the eastern stretch of Lincoln Avenue where the chains and cheapies are located. One of the best of the cheap options is the **Calistoga Village Inn and Spa** (1880 Lincoln Ave., Calistoga, 707/942-0991, www. greatspa.com), which has a variety of rooms starting at $75 midweek and $95 on the weekends. All are decorated in the style of Anywhere, USA, with the ubiquitous flowery synthetic bedspreads and plain furniture, though they also have air-conditioning and pools, two essential extras for hot Calistoga summers. An on-site spa offers 60-minute massages for $165 plus tax.

$100-200

This is the price range into which many of

Calistoga's spas and B&Bs fall. One of the best values is the Calistoga institution **Dr. Wilkinson's Hot Springs Resort** (1507 Lincoln Ave., Calistoga, 707/942-4102, www.drwilkinson.com). Best known for its mud baths, the doctor also has 42 basic rooms just a few steps from all the shops and restaurants of Lincoln Avenue. From the outside this looks like a 1950s motel, but the rooms have a little more going for them, with modern and tasteful (if slightly sparse) furnishings, including comfortable beds, air-conditioning, and fairly standard motel levels of equipment. Don't expect luxury at this price, although the charm of the lively resort more than compensates. The cheapest rooms are arranged around the courtyard or pool and cost from $149 midweek during the winter up to $235 on summer weekends. A small neighboring Victorian cottage houses some more expensive rooms that run $279–299, though there's little in the way of additional creature comforts to justify the higher prices.

Also at the low end of the price range is the **EuroSpa and Inn** (1202 Pine St., Calistoga, 707/942-6829, www.eurospa.com), a motel-style establishment on a peaceful residential street just a block from Lincoln Avenue. Rooms in the small bungalows arranged around a central parking lot are fairly tastefully furnished and come with a long list of standard features including whirlpool tubs, air-conditioning, gas stoves (certainly not needed in summer), Internet access, and refrigerators. They start at $140 midweek during the summer and $200 on weekends, and go up to $190 midweek ($260 weekends) for the largest rooms with two beds. Winter rates are generally 20 percent lower. Being on the edge of town, the inn's pool looks onto vineyards and is where the continental breakfast is usually served in summer.

Staying in a little piece of history is cheaper than you might think at the **Brannan Cottage Inn** (109 Wapoo Ave., Calistoga, 707/942-4200, www.brannancottageinn.com). The Victorian cottage with its white picket fence is the only cottage from Sam Brannan's original Calistoga resort that still stands where it was built, on a quiet street just off Calistoga's main drag. It is now on the National Register of Historic Places and contains six rooms furnished in tasteful and restrained Victorian style, all with air-conditioning, private bathrooms, views of the pretty gardens, and a private entrance from the wraparound porch. The smallest room with a four-poster bed costs $185 midweek and $210 weekends. The biggest room, an upstairs mini-suite, costs $230 midweek and $255 weekends. Knock about $30 off those prices during the winter.

One of the biggest old buildings in downtown Calistoga (though that's not saying much) is home to the **Mount View Hotel** (1457 Lincoln Ave., Calistoga, 707/942-6877 or 800/816-6877, www.mountviewhotel.com), which brings a bit of urban style within walking distance of almost everything Calistoga has to offer. The cheapest queen and king rooms ($199 weekdays, $249 weekends during the high season) can be a bit on the small side, but all 29 rooms and suites have a slightly eclectic mix of modern furnishings with Victorian antique and art deco touches harking back to the hotel's 1920s and 1930s heyday. The list of standard features is impressive for Calistoga and stretches to CD players in some rooms and free wireless Internet access. The more expensive suites ($329 midweek, $429 on weekends during the high season) have claw-foot tubs and wet bars, and the pricier suites have balconies overlooking the street. Best of all are the three separate cottages, each with its own small outdoor redwood deck and hot tub, though expect to pay upward of $400 a night during the summer. The hotel used to be home to one of Calistoga's best restaurants, Stomp, but that closed in 2006 and was replaced by a more modest wine and tapas bar called BarVino.

If you're able to get a reservation for one of the four rooms at the **Hotel d'Amici** (1436 Lincoln Ave., Calistoga, 707/942-1007, www.hoteldamici.com), consider yourself lucky. The charming hotel above the Flatiron Grill offers spacious and comfortable junior suites in the heart of Calistoga for very reasonable rates, which makes it very popular. The two smaller suites at the back of the hotel are the cheapest, with official rates starting at $185 per night but often available for $40 less midweek in winter. The larger suites at the front of the building have fireplaces and share a balcony looking over Lincoln Avenue. They start at about $200 off-season and go up to about $300 on summer weekends. All the rooms are decorated in simple, clean style and offer private bathrooms with soaking tubs, down comforters, cable television, and a bottle of Rutherford Grove wine (the Pestoni family owns both the winery and the hotel). A continental breakfast appears as if by magic outside the door every morning, but the lack of on-site staff can make late-night arrivals challenging. Be sure to keep the confirmation letter for the code to get into the hotel.

Over $200

Hats off to the owners of **The Pink Mansion** (1415 Foothill Blvd., Calistoga, 707/942-0558 or 800/238-7465, www.pinkmansion. com) for not even attempting to come up with a clever name for their bright pink Victorian pile, which dates from 1875. The honest name is matched by some unique features that were added by the last person to live there full-time, the eclectic Alma Simic—like the small heated pool in what looks like a Victorian parlor. She's the one who painted the house pink in the 1930s, the color it has been ever since. The woodsy surroundings, quaint but not overly frilly furnishings, and features like claw-foot tubs and air-conditioning make this one of the pricier establishments along this stretch of road, however. The smallest rooms start at $225 a night, and the gargantuan and luxurious Master Suite, dripping with period features and exotic woods, goes for $345. At $245, the Wine Suite is perhaps the best value, with a fireplace, private garden entrance, and separate sitting area.

One of the prettiest spa resorts in Calistoga with among the most tastefully decorated rooms and a giant spring-fed pool is **Indian Springs** (1712 Lincoln Ave., Calistoga, 707/942-4913, www.indianspringscalistoga.com). The cheapest

rooms are in the two-story mission-style lodge building, which used to be a neighboring hotel but was bought and renovated by Indian Springs in 2005. They start at $185 midweek in winter, rising to $225 midweek in the summer. Weekend rates are $50–75 higher. The 1940s-era cottages that the resort is best known for are on the pricey side, but are made more palatable by the plank flooring, kitchenettes, and barbecues on their back porches. At one end of the spectrum are Sam's Bungalows, named for Sam Brannan, who set up his Victorian-era resort on the land that Indian Springs now occupies. They start at $285 during the summer (Jul.–Oct.) and on winter weekends but are only $195 midweek in winter. The palm-lined driveway is surrounded by the cozy one- and two-bedroom Palm Row cottages that start at $410 during the summer ($215 midweek in winter) and are probably the best bargains, with their separate sitting area with a sofa-bed. Ask for numbers 16 or 17—they back onto open fields for some extra isolation. Both the Sam's and Palm Row bungalows share front porches and a wall with the neighboring unit, but the more expensive Colbert bungalows are totally detached and can comfortably sleep four. They cost $355 during the summer ($225 midweek in winter).

As its name suggests, the **Cottage Grove Inn** (1711 Lincoln Ave., Calistoga, 707/942-8400 or 800/799-2284, www.cottagegrove. com) is actually 16 private cottages strung along a small road under a pretty grove of old elm trees on the edge of Calistoga. The cottages were built in 1996 and offer some modernity along a strip dominated by older motels. Despite their individual names, all 16 are furnished in a similar Mediterranean style with vaulted ceilings, beautiful antique wood floors, and a long list of luxury features including a double Jacuzzi tub, CD and DVD player, fireplace, and front porch on which to sit, sip, and watch the world go by. The price for such personal space and luxury starts at $295 midweek and $360 on weekends during the summer and runs $250–295 the rest of the year.

Calistoga was chosen to host the first resort created by Solage Hotels, a new brand from the exclusive Auberge Resorts chain that owns the staggeringly expensive Auberge du Soleil down in Rutherford. Opened in 2007, **Solage Calistoga** (755 Silverado Trail, Calistoga, 866/942-7442, www.solagecalistoga.com) is best thought of as a baby Auberge, offering stylish contemporary accommodation for far less money. Being Calistoga, there's also a spa, but this one shares the resort's chic, modern style, although you'll pay extra to use it if you're not a hotel guest. Touted as the Napa Valley first "affordable" resort, Solage is clearly targeted at a younger, more urban crowd than places like Auberge and Meadowood. Fashionable materials like polished concrete, pebbled floors in the steam showers, and plenty of dark wood complement the abundant technology in every room, from flat-screen TVs and CD players to wireless Internet access and iPod docks. A couple of cruiser bikes are parked outside each room; they're not touring quality, but they'll certainly get you into downtown Calistoga, a half mile away, and maybe to a few nearby wineries. Arriving here can be a little underwhelming because the trees planted here have yet to grow large enough to create a feeling of an oasis on what is otherwise a rather featureless patch of land bordering a trailer park, but once you're settled in this self-contained resort it's easy to forget the world outside. "Affordable" is a relative term for the resort, however. It's certainly affordable compared to Auberge du Soleil, but it's the top end of the scale for sleepy Calistoga. The 89 studio-style rooms have winter rates starting at $395–495, rising to $495–595 in summer. Suites will set you back $725–895 depending on the season and day.

Nearby is another member of the exclusive Auberge chain of resorts, this one hidden away on a wooded hillside with super-resort prices to match the glorious setting. The **Calistoga Ranch** (580 Lommel Rd., off Silverado Trail, Calistoga, 707/254-2800, www.calistogaranch.com) is like a collection of exclusive lodges with a country-club atmosphere. Guests are relieved of their cars upon entering and whisked off up the hill to their rooms in golf carts. The accommodations consist of a series of rooms

joined by a deck, with every conceivable luxury bell and whistle, from indoor-outdoor fireplaces and showers to plasma-screen TVs and wet bars. The smallest are 600 square feet, about double the average hotel room size and also double the average price around here, starting at $550 in winter and $750 in the peak fall season. Expect to pay more for views of any kind, and for one of the apartment-sized one-bedroom lodges (starting at $790 without hot tub, $890 with). For those who can bear to leave their luxury hideaways, there's the exclusive Bathhouse spa (treatments $75–260), outdoor pool, classes and seminars, and miles of hiking trails around the grounds.

FOOD

Calistoga is often overlooked in the valley's food scene, eclipsed by the culinary destinations of Yountville and St. Helena. High-end restaurants have struggled to survive here, as illustrated by the seemingly endless stream of restaurants that have tried, and failed, to make money in the town's fancy Mount View Hotel. Even the venerable Wappo Bistro, a favorite of many valley residents and frequent visitors, could not survive the 2009 recession. The new Solage resort, which opened in 2007, could bring back some much-needed culinary cachet to this part of the valley as well as some much-needed big spenders. Meanwhile, there remains a diverse selection of mid-priced bistros and grills that should satisfy all but the pickiest diners.

Breakfast

The old-fashioned **Café Sarafornia** (1413 Lincoln Ave., 707/942-0555, www.cafesarafornia.com, 7 A.M.–2:30 P.M. daily, entrées $6–13), named for the famous verbal blunder by the town's founder, Sam Brannan, is the favorite destination of locals, serving downhome, no-nonsense breakfast and brunch at the bar, booths, or tables. It also sells sandwiches to go ($8–10).

Fine Dining

The latest tenant to try to make a go of it in the

Mount View Hotel is **JoLe** (1457 Lincoln Ave., 707/942-5938, www.jolesrestaurant.com, dinner Wed.–Mon., small plates $6–20), where the emphasis is on small plates of locally-sourced, Mediterranean-inspired food in a contemporary setting. Select two or three dishes per person, such as sea scallops and sweetbreads with a parsnip puree or roasted quail with fingerling potatoes and Italian black cabbage, or try the four-course tasting menu. The list of local and international wines is well priced, and all but the most expensive wines are available by the glass and by the Pichet, which is about a half bottle.

Walking past the ▌ **Calistoga Inn** (1250 Lincoln Ave., 707/942-4101, www.calistogainn.com, dinner and lunch daily, dinner entrées $15–28) on a cool dark winter evening, it's tempting to go into the restaurant just for the cozy rustic atmosphere exuded through its Victorian windows. During the warmer months the draw is the creek-side patio, but all year the cuisine would probably best be described as reliable bistro-style comfort food. Next door to the restaurant is an equally relaxed pub that's home to the **Napa Valley Brewing Company,** founded in 1989 and said to be the first brewery established in the valley since Prohibition. The inn also usually has some sort of evening entertainment, from open mike nights to jazz.

The menu at the **All Seasons Café** (1400 Lincoln Ave., 707/942-9111, lunch 11:30 A.M.–2:30 P.M., dinner 5–9 P.M. Tues.–Sun., dinner entrées $17–27) is, as the name suggests, inspired by local produce currently in season, and the sophisticated dishes attract food lovers from all over the valley, though recent reports suggest quality has slipped a bit. The small wine list at the table is just a sampling of the hundreds of labels available in the wine store at the back of the main restaurant. Buy a bottle to take home, or pay the $15 corkage fee to drink it at the table, saving plenty on the usual markup for wines.

Bosko's Trattoria (1364 Lincoln Ave., 707/942-9088, www.boskos.com, 11:30 A.M.–10 P.M. daily, dinner entrées $10–18) is another Calistoga institution with a reputation for its Italian comfort food as solid as the stone building it calls home. The simple salads, some of the valley's best pastas, and wood-fired pizzas served in the homey surroundings all cost less than $16, and there's a good selection of delicious, well-stuffed panini sandwiches for less than $9.

At the eastern edge of town is the trendy **Solbar,** part of the luxurious Solage Calistoga resort (755 Silverado Trail, 707/226-0850, breakfast, lunch, and dinner daily, lounge menu available until 11 P.M., dinner entrées $18–30, small plates $11–15). It was already an increasingly popular outdoor dining destination up-valley after opening in 2007, and that was before it was awarded a Michelin star in 2009. The sleek and contemporary indoor dining room is a fine backdrop for the innovative cuisine with Asian and Latin influences, like grilled salmon with coconut rice, bok choy, and pickled ginger, or the chili-rubbed pork-cheek tacos, but the spacious outdoor patio with its floating fireplace is the biggest draw in summer and fall. With a couple of appetizers and a bottle of wine on a warm summer night there's no better place for some up-valley people-watching and stargazing.

Grills

Brannan's Grill (1374 Lincoln Ave., 707/942-2233, lunch and dinner daily, dinner entrées $19–35) brought the big-time Napa food scene right to the heart of Calistoga when it opened in 1998, though its reputation is said to have slipped a bit in recent years. White tablecloths, the 19th-century dark-wood bar, and the giant murals of the valley's past lend an air of elegance to accompany the pricey all-American menu, which usually includes two or three steaks. The wine list offers a smattering of choices from Oregon, Europe, and Australia alongside Napa and Sonoma regulars. Lunch or brunch ($7–12) is a cheaper way to experience the sumptuous interior.

A few doors down the road is Brannan's sister restaurant, **Flatiron Grill** (1440 Lincoln Ave., 707/942-1220, lunch weekends, dinner daily, dinner entrées $12–26), which is an altogether cheaper dining option. In terms of both the food and decor it's a bit like a baby Brannan's, serving slightly less sophisticated food from the grill in stylish, but not quite as elegant, surroundings.

Mexican

Traditional Mexican food can be found at the spacious **Pacifico Restaurante Mexicano** (1237 Lincoln Ave., 707/942-4400, lunch and dinner daily, dinner entrées $13–18), including some regional specialties and weekend brunches. Those who prefer more of a hole-in-the-wall Mexican experience should walk to the other end of Lincoln Avenue to **Puerto Vallarta** (1473 Lincoln Ave., 707/942-6563, lunch and dinner until 9 P.M. daily, $5–10), right next to the supermarket. The traditional food comes with equally traditional plastic surroundings both inside and out on the patio leading to the entrance.

The roomy, exposed-brick interior of the **Hydro Bar & Grill** (1403 Lincoln Ave., 707/942-9777, dinner entrées $9–15) hints at its other life as a live-music venue, but it's also a place to get quick meals at the bar, ranging from traditional burgers to Mexican-themed small plates ($4–10), together with plenty of microbrews. It stays open well after most other restaurants have closed.

Picnic Supplies

Although Calistoga's Palisades Market has long since closed, The Depot is now home to its offspring, the **Palisades Deli Café** (1458 Lincoln Ave., 707/942-0145, 7 A.M.–6 P.M. daily). In addition to coffee and other café staples, it sells a range of cold and hot sandwiches to eat in or take out ($6–9), including a decadent tri-tip sandwich. Just across the road is the less glamorous **Cal Mart** supermarket (1491 Lincoln Ave., 707/942-4545, 7 A.M.–9 P.M. daily), which sells even cheaper deli sandwiches, though it has a more limited selection.

Drop in to **Café Sarafornia** (1413 Lincoln Ave., 707/942-0555) to pick up one of its sandwiches, or for a gourmet alternative you could go to **Bosko's Trattoria** (1364 Lincoln Ave., 707/942-9088) and order a panini to go.

Farmers Market

The **Calistoga Farmers Market** (Lincoln Ave. at Washington St.), which sells crafts as well as produce, is held 8:30 A.M.–noon on Saturday June–September.

INFORMATION AND SERVICES

The **Calistoga Chamber of Commerce** (1133 Washington St., 707/942-6333, www.calistogafun.com, 9 A.M.–5 P.M. daily) has just about every brochure and flyer for the Calistoga area and much of the rest of the Napa Valley, as well as helpful staff on hand to answer any questions.

SOUTHERN SONOMA

Southern Sonoma is one of those places that doctors should send the hypertensive, because there's something about the place that makes your blood pressure drop despite having plenty of visitors. The Sonoma Valley and neighboring Carneros region are just so laid-back and slow-going that even finding parking is unnervingly easy, and sitting in what passes as rush-hour traffic here will barely get you tapping your fingers.

Apparently it has always been a pretty good, stress-free life in these parts. Mother Nature might mix things up a bit with the occasional fire or earthquake, but she also provides hot springs, redwood forests, burbling streams, fertile soils, and a friendly climate. In terms of climate, scenery, and growing conditions, the Sonoma Valley is a mini Napa Valley, but it has

been spared the same level of development by some favorable rolls of the historical dice.

In a sense, southern Sonoma is fairly close to paradise: a place where wine, history, scenery, and some of the best California produce combine in an area small enough to tour in a day or two. A visitor can spend the morning sipping splendid wine and be strolling through historic Victorian splendor by the afternoon, or might traverse a muddy mountain one hour and spend the next relaxing in a spa covered in therapeutic mud. There are few other parts of the Wine County as compact yet packed with opportunity.

Hundreds of years ago, these same natural attributes attracted numerous Native American tribes, who lived peacefully side by side without the turf battles common elsewhere. Even

HIGHLIGHTS

🌙 Gundlach Bundschu Winery: Witness Shakespeare or Mozart performed on a summer day at the outdoor amphitheater of this historic winery (page 136).

🌙 Benziger Family Winery: See Benziger's biodynamic vineyards from a tractor-drawn tram, the most entertaining tour in the valley (page 140).

🌙 Chateau St. Jean: It's worth it to pay a little extra for the reserve tasting and learn about wine while relaxing on the patio overlooking the valley (page 146).

🌙 Sonoma Plaza: Spend an afternoon exploring the eclectic shops and historic sites of the notable Sonoma Plaza (page 152).

🌙 Sonoma Mission: The last Californian mission has been immaculately restored, and its museum sheds light on the important role it played in the region's history (page 153).

🌙 Sugarloaf Ridge State Park: Meander down the short nature trail or hike to the top of Bald Mountain for the best valley views (page 158).

🌙 Jack London State Historic Park: Scenic hiking trails surround the former residence of the valley's prolific author and adventurer, Jack London (page 158).

🌙 Domaine Carneros: Take a private tour and learn how champagne is made, all with a glass of bubbly in hand (page 174).

🌙 Cline Cellars: Enter an oasis of green at this historic winery next to a natural spring and explore all of California's missions in miniature (page 179).

🌙 The di Rosa Preserve: Enter a wonderland of art and leave the Wine Country behind (page 183).

LOOK FOR 🌙 TO FIND RECOMMENDED SIGHTS, ACTIVITIES, DINING, AND LODGING.

author Jack London sensed something intoxicating in the air. He relocated from Oakland to put down deep roots in the Sonoma Valley, transforming himself from working-class hero to gentleman farmer and land owner. The main characters in his 1913 novel *Valley of the Moon* spend months wandering up and down California in search of their nirvana, the Sonoma Valley.

The lucky locals have worked hard against the odds to keep their valley and flatlands so inviting. In the 1960s, they fought off a plan developed by car-crazed California to drive a freeway down the middle of Sonoma Valley. Instead it was built through the middle of Santa Rosa to the west. While fame and freeways brought the heaving masses to Napa and northern Sonoma, the valley became the land that development forgot.

By 1980 there was a grand total of two sets of traffic lights—and there aren't many more now. One of the busiest intersections in the valley, on the south side of Sonoma plaza, is still very politely controlled by four simple stop signs. The valley's modern custodians are still a potent force, even defending a few local chickens in the downtown Sonoma threatened with resettlement. Such is the passion here to keep the "slow" in this place the locals call Slownoma.

Can the valley keep its identity amid modern population and development pressures? It's trying hard, but is swimming against the tide of tourism. Wineries and hotels are being mopped up by bigger and bigger conglomerates. The succulent local food is transforming into ever more expensive "cuisine." An average family home in the valley now costs more than $1.5 million. Visit quickly before Napa hops over the mountains, pushes up the prices, and ends the mellow fun.

In the long term, there's more hope for Carneros, simply because there is no "there" there. The vineyards that are slowly covering any remaining pastureland (that is, the land that's not already underwater) are effectively spiking future development. Chances are that nothing much will change here anytime

soon—except perhaps that rush-hour traffic on the two-lane roads may worsen as more people visit or move to the Napa and Sonoma Valleys.

PLANNING YOUR TIME

The Sonoma Valley and Carneros are two of the easiest parts of Wine Country to visit, each having just one main road running its entire length. A visit to Carneros can be slightly harder to plan due to the lack of major towns, but it's easy enough to stop there for a few hours on the way to or from Sonoma and Napa.

Within the 17-mile-long Sonoma Valley, the wineries, shops, and hotels are generally centered around the towns of **Glen Ellen** and neighboring **Kenwood,** and Sonoma itself. Without a well-planned strategy, it can be time-consuming to try to visit wineries at both the northern and southern ends of the valley, especially when the Sonoma Highway (Highway 12) slows down with northbound rush-hour traffic in the afternoon.

If you do find yourself traveling slower than you like on Highway 12, it's worth heading a few miles west at Glen Ellen or Boyes Hot Springs to pick up Arnold Drive, an alternative north-south route in the valley. It runs mainly through residential areas, but sticking to the 30 mph speed limit on this quiet road might be more relaxing than being tailgated on Highway 12. It runs right down to the junction with Highway 121 in **Carneros.**

It can easily take a full day to visit about five wineries around Sonoma and Kenwood, or in Carneros, and still have enough time for lunch without getting indigestion. An alternative strategy might be to pick four or five wineries that specialize in a particular wine. Or spend a full day exploring the shops and historic sights of Sonoma while tasting wine at several dedicated tasting rooms on the Sonoma Plaza. There are also four wineries just outside downtown.

If you do plan to visit wineries throughout the valley, get an early start. Their busiest times are mid–late afternoon, especially for the wineries around Kenwood that most visitors only get to toward the end of the day. Most wineries are open at 10 A.M. (a few from 11 A.M.) and close between 4:30 and 6 P.M., depending on the season.

Wineries along the Carneros Highway (Highway 121) are generally clustered at the eastern and western ends of Carneros. Those at the western end include Viansa, Gloria Ferrer, and Cline, on the way from San Francisco to Sonoma. Those farther east are more spread out and generally lie between the road to Sonoma (Napa Road or Highway 12) and the city of Napa. They include Artesa, Mahoney, and Bouchaine.

For some reason very few wineries have any sizable trees in their parking lots, preferring instead to plant trees that either look stunted or have minimal leaf cover. Consequently there's usually no shade, and for the nine months of the year that the sun shines, parked cars quickly heat up to the temperature of an oven. Take a cooler if you plan a picnic or want to prevent that $100 bottle of wine from trying to become vinegar.

Compared to the Napa Valley, wine tasting in the Sonoma Valley is refreshingly cheap. Most wineries charge a tasting fee of either $5 or $10, perhaps more for tasting the more expensive reserve wines. It's a refreshing change from the Napa Valley, where $25 tasting experiences have become the norm. As in many other parts of the Wine Country, the tasting fee can sometimes be recouped when you buy one or more bottles of wine.

GETTING THERE

A century ago there were more ways to get to Sonoma than there are today—by ferry, train, stagecoach, automobile, or plane. The train is long gone, ferries come nowhere near, the tiny local airports have no scheduled services, and there is no direct bus service to Sonoma, just some local connections to Santa Rosa and Petaluma—all of which leaves the car with a monopoly.

Getting there by car, however, is straightforward. From San Francisco the most traveled route is via U.S. 101, Highway 37, and Highway 121, which leads to the heart of Carneros and to the junction of Highway 12 to Sonoma and the Sonoma Valley. The drive from the bridge to Sonoma takes just under an hour, longer if you have to navigate San Francisco local traffic.

To avoid Sonoma and go straight to Glen Ellen, go straight on Arnold Drive at the junction and gas station about five miles after joining Highway 121. It is a slower road but avoids heavy traffic and leads to the heart of Glen Ellen.

Other routes to the area from the north and east include Highway 12 east into the valley from U.S. 101 at Santa Rosa, or Highway 37 west from I-80 at Vallejo to the junction of Highway 121. Be warned that Highway 121 through Carneros is infamous for nasty accidents due to its unexpected bends and dips, dawdling tourists, and high volume of commuter (in other words, speeding) traffic.

GETTING AROUND

Once again, the car is how most people get around Carneros and the Sonoma Valley. The only real alternative to the tiring car-to-winery-to-car relay is a tiring bike ride. Rent a **bicycle** in either Glen Ellen or Sonoma and stick to the wineries in those areas to avoid long distances, summer heat, and tipsy drivers. Cruising around the empty flatlands of Carneros on two wheels is a rewarding way to get off the beaten track and visit less-crowded wineries, but only for those with the stamina for long distances.

Some hotels and B&Bs have their own bicycles for rent. Otherwise, two shops rent bikes and supply tour maps. **Sonoma Valley Cyclery** (20093 Broadway, Sonoma, 707/935-3377, 10 A.M.–6 P.M. Mon.–Sat., 10 A.M.–4 P.M. Sun.) rents bikes for $25 per day. For $10 more it offers a self-guided tour from the shop to local Sonoma wineries or a 35-mile round-trip trek to some Carneros wineries. The area around Sonoma is perfect for exploring by bike. If you're staying downtown, park the car, rent a bike, and visit the historic downtown sites as well as the Ravenswood, Buena Vista, and

Gundlach Bundschu wineries that are within a mile or two of the plaza.

There is no physical address for the **Goodtime Touring Company** (707/938-0453 or 888/525-0453), but it will deliver bikes to your hotel. It rents basic bikes for $25 per day, road bikes for $40, and tandems for $45. The closest thing to biking luxury (short of having someone else pedal) is Goodtime's half-day guided tour of Sonoma-area or Kenwood-area wineries, which includes a gourmet lunch and wine-tasting fees. Those tours are $135 and start at 10:30 A.M.

Sonoma Valley

They must feed the ducks of Sonoma Plaza something special to make them stick around the car-choked plaza rather than flying a few miles north to the serenity of the valley, even with the nice new plaza ponds completed in 2006. Getting out of Sonoma, as fascinating and historic as it is, is the only way to really get an idea of what valley residents are fighting to preserve.

The road north out of Sonoma passes fast-food outlets and a strip mall, about as close to urban sprawl as there is. In keeping with the valley's laid-back nature, it's a spaced-out, relaxed sort of sprawl linking Sonoma and three spring towns: Boyes Hot Springs, Fetters Hot Springs, and Agua Caliente, all of which look like they could do with a rejuvenating spa treatment themselves.

The towns end abruptly, and the serene valley lies ahead. Plum, walnut, and peach orchards once shared the valley with cows that must have thought they'd died and gone to heaven to be grazing here. Now the mighty vine has taken over the valley floor. There's really little else but green things along the Sonoma Highway, except the loose-knit community of **Kenwood** (with the valley's cheapest gas) and, at the border of Santa Rosa, the retirement community of Oakmont.

Slightly off the main road southeast of Kenwood, the town of **Glen Ellen** is a Wine Country town with plenty of fancy restaurants and inns hidden in the surrounding woods yet still with the valley's nice laid-back vibe. It's truly a one-street town, with a curious dogleg halfway down the main street that is the real center of it all—not that there's all that much

happening. It has managed to remain quaint without succumbing to the fake frills that so many other old towns in the United States get wrapped in. One of the biggest buildings is an auto shop, a sign that real life still takes place in this part of the valley.

The Wines

The volcanic soils of the hot mountainsides and the rich alluvial plains of the valley floor make Sonoma an ideal place to grow a plethora of grape varietals, a fact the missionaries and immigrants of the 1800s quickly discovered. The valley doesn't have quite the number of different growing conditions and soils of the larger Napa Valley, but winemakers maintain that its wines can be just as good.

In many ways the Sonoma Valley and Napa Valley are more alike than different. Both have productive mountain growing regions, both are proportionally similar, face the same direction, and are affected by the same wind and rain patterns. The fact that Sonoma's early head start in winemaking in the mid-1800s petered out by the early 1900s seems to have had more to do with chance and bad business decisions by the early pioneers like Agoston Haraszthy. The larger Napa Valley wineries established in the late 1800s gained more commercial traction, perhaps due the greater availability of land. Once a critical mass of winemaking had been reached, there was no turning back.

Climate-wise, the Sonoma Valley has three distinct appellations. The **Sonoma Valley** AVA is the largest and includes some or all of the other two. It stretches from the top of the valley near Santa Rosa all the way down to the

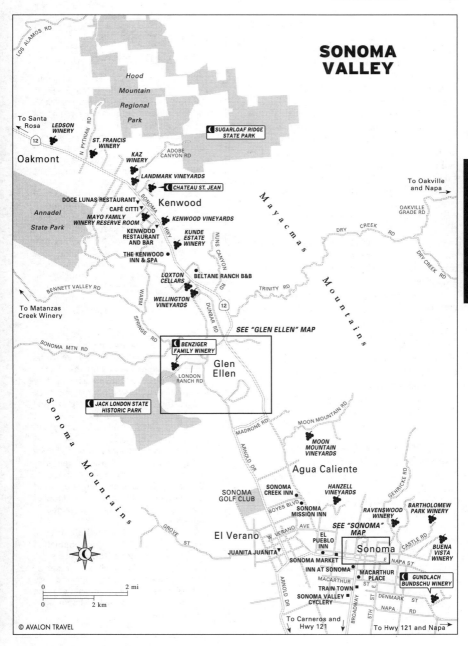

SOUTHERN SONOMA

SONOMA VALLEY

Hood Mountain Regional Park

To Santa Rosa

LEDSON WINERY

12

Oakmont

N PYTHIAN RD

LOS ALAMOS RD

ST. FRANCIS WINERY

KAZ WINERY

ADOBE CANYON RD

SUGARLOAF RIDGE STATE PARK

LANDMARK VINEYARDS

CHATEAU ST. JEAN

Kenwood

DOCE LUNAS RESTAURANT
CAFÉ CITTI
MAYO FAMILY WINERY RESERVE ROOM

KENWOOD VINEYARDS

Annadel State Park

KENWOOD RESTAURANT AND BAR

KUNDE ESTATE WINERY

THE KENWOOD INN & SPA

SONOMA HWY

NUNS CANYON RD

Mayacmas Mountains

To Oakville and Napa

OAKVILLE GRADE RD

DRY CREEK RD

DRY CREEK RD

BENNETT VALLEY RD

LOXTON CELLARS

BELTANE RANCH B&B

WELLINGTON VINEYARDS

WARM SPRINGS RD

DUNBAR RD

TRINITY RD

12

To Matanzas Creek Winery

SONOMA MTN RD

SEE "GLEN ELLEN" MAP

BENZIGER FAMILY WINERY

Glen Ellen

LONDON RANCH RD

JACK LONDON STATE HISTORIC PARK

Sonoma Mountains

MADRONE RD

ARNOLD DR

MOON MOUNTAIN RD

MOON MOUNTAIN VINEYARDS

Agua Caliente

HANZELL VINEYARDS

GEHRICKE RD

SONOMA GOLF CLUB

SONOMA CREEK INN

BOYES BLVD

SONOMA MISSION INN

RAVENSWOOD WINERY

BARTHOLOMEW PARK WINERY

SEE "SONOMA" MAP

GROVE ST

El Verano

W VERANO AVE

EL PUEBLO INN

Sonoma

CASTLE RD

BUENA VISTA WINERY

JUANITA JUANITA

SONOMA MARKET

INN AT SONOMA

E NAPA ST

MACARTHUR PLACE

GUNDLACH BUNDSCHU WINERY

ARNOLD DR

MACARTHUR ST

TRAIN TOWN

SONOMA VALLEY CYCLERY

BROADWAY

5TH ST E

DENMARK ST

NAPA RD

0   2 mi

0   2 km

To Carneros and Hwy 121

To Hwy 121 and Napa

© AVALON TRAVEL

bay, bordered by 3,000-foot-high mountains on each side and encompassing 116,000 acres of land and about 13,000 acres of vineyards (compare that to the Napa Valley's 35,000 acres of vineyards).

The valley acts like a giant funnel, channeling cooler air (and sometimes fog) up from the bay, leaving the mountainsides to bask in warm sunshine. Zinfandel loves the higher, hotter elevations, while cabernet and merlot ripen well on hillsides and the warmer north end of the valley. Pinot noir, chardonnay, and other white varietals prefer the slightly cooler valley floor, especially farther south toward Carneros.

The 800 acres of vineyards in the cooler and rockier **Sonoma Mountain** appellation just up the hill from Glen Ellen vary widely depending on their exposure, but the region is known mostly for its cabernet, although chardonnay, pinot noir, and other white varietals are also grown here.

The newest appellation is **Bennett Valley,** created in 2003, which stretches northeast from the Sonoma Mountains toward Santa Rosa and only just overlaps with Sonoma Valley. Its 700 acres of vineyards are primarily planted with merlot and chardonnay and generally have rocky, volcanic-based soils. A gap in the low mountains west of the Bennett Valley lets ocean air and fog through and keeps growing conditions cool compared to the Sonoma Valley and the mountains.

SONOMA WINERIES
Bartholomew Park Winery

There seems to be a history competition between Bart Park (1000 Vineyard Ln., Sonoma, 707/935-9511, www.bartpark.com, 11 A.M.–4:30 P.M. daily, tasting $5), as it's known, and the neighboring Buena Vista Winery. Both have links to the Sonoma wine pioneer Agoston Haraszthy, and both are equally entitled to brag about it since they share what used to be Haraszthy's land. While Buena Vista has the original press house and caves from Haraszthy's winery, Bart Park has the site of Haraszthy's Romanesque home (a reproduction now stands there and is open on

BATTLE OF THE CHICKENS

They are sometimes there, but officially they're not. The saga of the Sonoma Plaza chickens perfectly illustrates Sonoma's enduring small-town quirkiness in the face of the creeping invasion of expensive hotels, restaurants, and other newcomers.

At one point there were more than 100 chickens scratching out a living in the plaza, and they had plenty of local fans who appreciated the hick character they brought to the city. Letters to local newspapers told newcomers to "go home" if they didn't like the chickens. A city plan to cull the birds and keep their numbers to a more manageable 40 was met with squawks of protest from supporters.

"You'd see them crossing on the crosswalk. I think they learned from watching people," a reporter at the *Sonoma Index-Tribune* newspaper recalls. There was even one that regularly laid eggs in a plaza crafts store.

In 2000, however, the roosters were implicated in several pecking and scratching attacks on small children, marking the beginning of the end for the chicken population. In May that year, citing safety and liability issues, the city council voted to evict the chickens from the plaza and resettle them at local farms, a move that prompted a "roost-in" protest by 100 chicken lovers in front of City Hall.

There was an attempt to reintroduce some friendlier breeds of chicken later that year, together with an "egg patrol" to ensure their numbers didn't get out of hand, but four of them quickly fell foul of local dogs, and the rest were rounded up and whisked off to safety.

Now there are officially no chickens, just the plaza's friendly duck population to occasionally hold up traffic. But a small group of unofficial chickens can sometimes be seen scratching around City Hall, especially at night, perhaps trying to undermine the council that sent them packing years ago.

SONOMA

SOUTHERN SONOMA

Wednesdays and weekends) and most of the vineyard land. Neither of the two wine-making operations that exist today has been operating very long.

Since Haraszthy's day, Bart Park has been home to a cat-loving widower, a home for "delinquent women," a hospital, and finally the home of the Bartholomew family, which bought it in the 1940s and soon started making wine again under Haraszthy's defunct Buena Vista label. They later sold the winery and the Buena Vista name, keeping a large chunk of the vineyards and creating the Hacienda Winery, which they operated until their deaths. In 1994 it became the Bartholomew Park Winery and is now owned by the nearby Gundlach Bundschu Winery and operated as a boutique sibling.

Bart Park's colorful history is detailed in a small but packed museum housed in the old hospital building, along with the small tasting room where you can taste the estate chardonnay, cabernet sauvignon, and merlot, as well as several wines from other vineyards around Sonoma. Only 4,000 cases are produced a year, though for such limited-production wines, they're not too expensive.

The real charm of Bart Park, however, has nothing to do with history or wine. The winery sits in some glorious open space, including what remains of the formal gardens of an old mansion that was burned down (reportedly by the delinquent women) and the small garden of the reproduction Haraszthy home. You can wander freely throughout as if it's your own private garden and find great shaded picnic spots with sweeping views of the valley. Miles of hiking trails start from the winery and wind up the nearby hillsides. Where they start is not obvious, however, so ask someone in the winery for directions.

Buena Vista Winery

Buena Vista (18000 Old Winery Rd., Sonoma, 800/926-1266, www.buenavistacarneros.com, 10 A.M.–5 P.M., tasting $10) boasts that it was California's first premium winery, but the claim sounds more grandiose than it actually is. Today's Buena Vista sits on some of the land used by the original Buena Vista Winery, established by Agoston Haraszthy in 1858. Among the old winery structures that remain are the original hand-dug caves (now unsafe and closed), the original champagne cellar, and the old stone press-house, which is today the visitors center and helps the site qualify as a California Historic Landmark.

The original Buena Vista Winery did not survive Prohibition, however, and the current winery is a modern incarnation. Some land and the Buena Vista label were bought in 1968 from the Bartholomew family (former owners of the Bartholomew Park winery), and ownership of Buena Vista has changed many times since then. One could also argue that Haraszthy's original Buena Vista Winery wasn't actually the first premium winery in California. It all depends on the definition of premium.

The winery has been owned by various multinational conglomerates for decades (the current owner is Ascentia Wine Estates) and is a thoroughly commercial operation (as it was in Haraszthy's day), producing half a million cases of wine a year and attracting an estimated 120,000 visitors. Despite the fact that it gets very crowded in the summer, the leafy complex of stone buildings is still worth visiting for its historical importance. The plentiful hillside picnic tables are well shaded, though none of them offer much privacy on summer weekends when the winery tends to be swamped by busloads of visitors.

Although Buena Vista is in the Sonoma Valley, its 1,000 acres of vineyards are now about seven miles south in the Carneros area, apart from a few acres used for demonstrations and tours. The mid-priced Carneros estate wines include pinot noir, cabernet, merlot, chardonnay, and a newly released syrah that are all pretty good value for money. The flagship Ramal Vineyard wines are available only at the winery and include cabernet, pinot noir, and chardonnay.

◖ Gundlach Bundschu Winery

Not many wineries in California can boast that they won awards for their wines almost 100 years ago, but GunBun (2000 Denmark St., Sonoma, 707/938-5277, www.gunbun.com, 11 A.M.–4:30 P.M. daily, tasting $5–10), as it's known, is one of them. The 19 Gundlach Bundschu wines entered into the 1915 Panama-Pacific International Exhibition in

San Francisco all won medals, and the winery today focuses on squeezing the highest quality wines possible out of its estate vineyards without buying grapes from anywhere else. The other aspect of the estate that makes this a winery worth visiting are the ample outdoor picnicking and entertainment opportunities in a peaceful part of the valley.

Grapes have been grown in the winery's Rhinefarm vineyard since they were first planted in 1858 by Bavarian-born Jacob Gundlach, a pioneer of the early California wine industry who is credited with planting Sonoma County's first riesling vines. He was joined in the business by his son-in-law, Charles Bundschu, in 1868, and the next generation of Gundlachs and Bundschus established the Gundlach Bundschu Wine Company in the early 1900s. Wine production was stopped during Prohibition and was restarted in 1973 by Jim Bundschu, Gundlach's great-great-grandson, who runs the winery today with his son Jeff.

Today the 300 acres of Rhinefarm vineyards principally grow cabernet sauvignon, merlot, pinot noir, chardonnay, and gewürztraminer, together with some zinfandel, tempranillo, and a few other minor varietals. The winery's emphasis is on red bordeaux- and burgundy-style wines, and the cabernets and merlots tend to have plenty of tannic backbone. Some of the cheaper wines are available only from the winery and include the nonvintage Bearitage red blend and the unusual Kleinberger, an aromatic, fruity German wine.

The tasting room is housed in one of the original stone winery buildings, which can feel cramped when full of visitors—but the fun atmosphere makes it more bearable. Browse the historical memorabilia, including old wine posters from the 1800s. A short walk away is the 430-foot-long hillside cave, which is often part of the seasonal tours offered once daily (Thurs.–Mon., $20). The focus of the tours changes with the seasons, however, so check to see what you'll be seeing when you make a reservation. In winter it might be the cave and in summer the wine-making facilities. In all cases, the price includes a sit-down tasting. During the summer months, on Friday or Saturday mornings, GunBun also offers a tour of the estate vineyards in a quirky former Swiss military vehicle called a Pinzgauer, followed by a tasting of some of the best Estate wines.

GunBun also provides a shady patio, a picnicking area at the top of Towles' Hill overlooking the valley, and even a grassy amphitheater where you can see performances of Shakespeare or Mozart during the summer. Overall it has one of the nicest outdoor spaces of any winery in the valley. Check the website for event schedules or just pack a picnic before visiting.

Sebastiani Vineyards & Winery

A visit to Sonoma would not be complete without a trip to the Sebastiani winery (389 4th St. E., Sonoma, 707/933-3230 or 800/888-5532, ext. 3230, www.sebastiani.com, 10 A.M.–5 P.M. daily, tasting $10–15), founded by one of the city's most important benefactors and philanthropists, Samuele Sebastiani. It's the only large winery within walking distance of the Sonoma Plaza and has both wines and a history worth exploring.

Samuele Sebastiani arrived in Sonoma from northern Italy in 1895 and worked in local stone quarries before gathering enough money to buy an old winery in 1904. The business grew rapidly and was one of only 10 wineries that stayed open during Prohibition, when it made sacramental and medicinal wines as well as a fortune for Samuele. He spent money lavishly around town, building the Sebastiani Theater on the plaza and countless other commercial and residential buildings, most of which survive today in some form or another.

Samuele's son August took over the business in 1934 and transformed Sebastiani into a huge wine empire before his death in 1980. The winery was then managed by August's son, Sam Sebastiani, but a family dispute forced him out in the 1980s, and he went on to establish the Viansa winery in Carneros with his wife (this fact is airbrushed out of the official winery history). For many years the Sebastiani winery was run by August's daughter, Mary Ann

Sebastiani Cuneo, but in late 2008 the family ties came to an end with the sale of the winery and most of its vineyards to the Foley Wine Group.

Sebastiani pioneered the sale of cheap and cheerful half-gallon bottles of wine in the 1970s and developed a slew of additional wine brands in the 1980s, eventually producing a mind-boggling 8 million cases (96 million bottles) of wine per year. With the new millennium came a new strategy to focus only on premium Sebastiani-labeled wines, and all the other brands were sold off in 2001, reducing production to less than 200,000 cases.

The flagship wine is the Cherryblock cabernet sauvignon, sourced from an old vineyard near the winery, but the best value is another proprietary wine called Secolo, a bordeaux blend first made in 2001 to celebrate the winery's 100th anniversary. Both regularly garner 90-plus-point ratings from wine critics, but the Secolo is half the price of the $75 Cherryblock. Most of the other wines come from vineyards throughout Sonoma County and are reds, including merlot, pinot noir, zinfandel, and cabernet, together with a barbera that reflects Sebastiani's Italian heritage. One standout is the Alexander Valley cabernet sauvignon. The only white offered, in both vineyard-designate and Sonoma County versions, is a chardonnay. Several wines are available exclusively at the winery, including a Napa Valley cabernet, the Italian-style red blend Dolcino Rosso, and Eye of the Swan, a pinot noir–based wine with a pale pink color that reminded August Sebastiani (who was an avid amateur ornithologist) of the eyes of a black swan.

The cool, vaulted visitors center is chock-full of Italian-themed gifts but is on a scale that can feel slightly impersonal, with more of a corporate than a family atmosphere. It's worth taking one of the three daily historical tours of the cellars and old stone buildings to see some of the original wine-making equipment from the early 1900s and learn more about the history of the winery and its family. Alternatively you can hop on a trolley and see some of the oldest family vineyards together with key Sebastiani buildings in Sonoma. Complimentary tours are given daily at 11 A.M., 1 P.M., and 3 P.M. Other tours and seminars are available by appointment.

Ravenswood Vineyards

"To err is human but to zin is divine" is just one of the many droll mottos you'll find at the tasting room of this fun and friendly zinfandel specialist a few blocks north of downtown Sonoma. To use a wine industry pun, visiting here is a barrel of laughs; you're as likely to leave with a zin-inspired bumper sticker as a bottle of the jammy wine.

Bordeaux-style wines were the original inspiration of founder, Joel Peterson, but in the 1970s he discovered the joys of zinfandel and instead of heading down the path of Old World subtlety he ended up in the new world of powerhouse reds. Ravenswood (18701 Gehricke Rd., Sonoma, 707/933-2332 or 888/669-4679, www.ravenswood-wine.com, 10 A.M.–4:30 P.M. daily, tasting $10–15) now makes about a half million cases of wine a year, some three-quarters of which is accounted for by more than a dozen different zinfandels.

If you're a zinfandel fan or just after a bit of wine-tasting fun, this will be heaven. The vineyard-designate zins at Ravenswood exhibit the full range of flavors and styles that the humble zinfandel is capable of producing, from the full-throttle fruitiness of Dry Creek and Amador County zins to the more subtle spiciness of cooler-climate versions from Mendocino and the Russian River Valley. In case none of those help you see the light, there's always the Zen of Zin, a zinfandel-dominated field blend that might help you on your journey of discovery.

Despite being known for zinfandel, Ravenswood also makes some remarkably good Rhône-style wines with the same rustic appeal as the zinfandels, from the peppery Sonoma County carignane to the bold, syrah-dominated blend called Icon. The most expensive wines are the vineyard designates, which include plenty of zinfandels but also cabernet sauvignon, merlot, and the flagship Pickberry meritage, a lush yet elegant blend of cabernet sauvignon, merlot, and cabernet franc from the slopes of Sonoma Mountain and so named

Ravenswood Vineyards: a barrel of laughs

because the vineyard owner's kids used to pick blackberries there.

It's worth opting for the pricier tasting, which includes many of the best single-vineyard wines. If you're up early enough, the daily tour at 10:30 A.M. ($15) is an entertaining start to the day and usually includes tasting of barrel samples. As Ravenswood grew and was eventually bought by Constellation Brands in 2001, the winemaking operations were moved to a more modern facility further south, but the rustic old stone winery with its patios, picnic tables, and pretty gardens still has plenty of atmosphere today, and Joel Peterson is still very much in charge.

Plaza Tasting Rooms

A homey 1940s craftsman-style cottage just off the Sonoma Plaza with flower-filled gardens and street-front outdoor tasting patio is the new tasting location of the Carneros-based winery **Roche Winery & Vineyards** (122 W. Spain St., Sonoma, 707/935-7115, www. rochewinery.com, 11 A.M.–6:30 P.M. daily, free tasting). The winery opened its tasting room here in 2009 after the family sold its existing winery in Carneros and embarked on the development of a new facility on the 500-acre estate it retained in the area. The wines are all sourced from the estate vineyards and include several pinot noirs and some nice chardonnays (including a unique late-harvest version) as well as syrah and merlot. Taste them indoors or outdoors while sitting at a patio table watching the street life go by.

At the southeast corner of the Plaza next to the Ledson Hotel is the tasting room for the latest venture of Michael Sebastiani, member of Sonoma's famed Sebastiani wine-making clan and former winemaker at Viansa, **Highway 12 Vineyards & Winery** (498 1st St. E., 707/939-1012, www.highway12winery. com, 10:30 A.M.–5:30 P.M. daily). Along with partners Paul Giusto and Doug Offenbacher, Sebastiani has helped propel Highway 12 from humble beginnings in 2003 to a producer of several thousand cases of highly regarded and well-priced wines, dominated by cabernet blends and chardonnays. As the name implies, Highway 12 makes wines from vineyards along the highway that runs through the Sonoma Valley and Carneros. The bulk of the wines are sourced from just three vineyards, including Serres Ranch at the southern end of the Sonoma valley and the famed Sangiacomo Family vineyard on the border of Carneros. Highlights include both the chardonnays, which are made in a plush, full-bodied style. Among the reds, the most interesting wines are the blends, from the traditional Bordeaux blend to the La Piazza blend of sangiovese, primitivo, and zinfandel.

Outstanding chardonnays, and a large cow sculpture made entirely of wine corks, are the specialties of **Charles Creek Vineyards** (483 1st St. W., 707/935-3848, www.charles-screek.com, 11 A.M.–6 P.M. daily, tasting $5) at its small storefront tasting room and gallery space on the west side of the plaza. The winery was established in 2002 by Bill Brinton, a descendent of tractor pioneer John Deere, after many years as a grape grower on his Sonoma Mountain estate. It now makes about 12,000 cases of mainly chardonnay and cabernet sauvignon from vineyards across Sonoma and Napa, including the renowned Sangiacomo Vineyard just south of Sonoma and Dutton Ranch in the Russian River Valley. Fruit from both features strongly in many of the chardonnays, including the bright and tangy Las Patolitas ("little ducks") and the mellower La Sorpresa ("the surprise"). The flagship chardonnay is Las Abuelas ("the grandmothers"), a lightly oaked and intensely flavored wine sourced from various Carneros vineyards with far more spring in its step than its name would suggest. The several cabernets are also subtly different blends from famous-name vineyards all over Napa, many of them in mountain appellations that give the wines intensity and earthiness. The En Casa label of wines, which includes cabernet and a syrah, offer the best vales at under $25 a bottle, but none of the wines cost more than $40.

Wineries by Appointment

Many of the wineries open to the public in the

Sonoma Valley are those of big producers that can attract big crowds. For a more personal (and free) experience of some valley wines, call ahead to visit one of these historic, appointment-only wineries on the eastern mountain slopes of the valley.

Moon Mountain Vineyard (1700 Moon Mountain Dr., Sonoma, 707/996-5870, tour and tasting $20) is high up in the Mayacamas Mountains on a site that has been planted with vines since the 1800s. The winery's current 74 acres of organic vineyards grow bordeaux varietals for its cabernet sauvignon, sauvignon blanc, and cabernet franc wines, as well as grapes for its dense, concentrated zinfandel. The drive up to the winery is pretty, and if you have the time you can hike up to the top of the estate for some spectacular views of the valley.

Hanzell Vineyards (18596 Lomita Ave., Sonoma, 707/996-3860), just north of Sonoma, was established in 1948 by industrialist James D. Zellerbach and is today renowned for its luxury-priced but limited-production chardonnays and pinot noirs that regularly score over 90 points in reviews. The secret to its success are its very own Hanzell clones of both pinot and chardonnay. In fact, the pinot noir vineyard on the mountain slopes is said to be the oldest in California. A new winery was recently opened, enabling Hanzell to double its existing production to 7,000 cases a year from its 42 acres of estate vineyards. The tour and tasting fee is pricey for Sonoma ($45) but buys a very personalized experience, including a jaunt into the vineyards, a tour of the winery and caves, and a sit-down tasting.

GLEN ELLEN WINERIES
◖ Benziger Family Winery

With vines poking out from the hillside grass, free-range cockerels crowing, and its collection of rustic wooden buildings hidden among the trees, the mountainside Benziger Family winery (1883 London Ranch Rd., Glen Ellen, 888/490-2739, www.benziger. com, 10 A.M.–5 P.M. daily, regular tasting $10, reserves and estate wines $15) seems like an

Benziger Family Winery, which features biodynamic farming

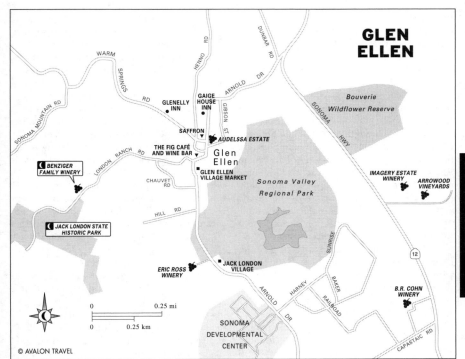

old family farm rather than a commercial wine business. In some ways it is. The Benziger family came from New York in the 1980s to this former hippie ranch and transformed it into the valley's only biodynamic winery while managing to keep three generations of Benzigers happy on its 800 acres. Some 30 Benziger folk now call this land their home, many of them working in the winery.

Biodynamic farming principles go beyond organic. Instead of simply ensuring no harmful chemicals pollute the land, biodynamic principles attempt to recreate the natural interactions among all aspects of the environment, from earth to sky. The overgrown look of the vineyards is deliberate (they are cover crops, in biodynamic terms), as are the 30 acres of woods and wetlands. The colorful Insectory is a garden in the middle of the vineyards planted with native flowers to attract dynamic pest-fighting insects. Cows and sheep help mow the grasses and fertilize the land, but the more entertaining (and nonnative) peacocks had to be fenced in because they were playing havoc with the vines. Benziger, along with a handful of Mendocino wineries, was ahead of the curve, and biodynamic principles are now catching on across Wine Country.

All the wildlife and more can be seen on an entertaining 45-minute tractor-drawn tram tour that winds through the vineyards, giving information on vines, local nature, and biodynamic principles before delivering visitors to the wine-making facility and hillside storage cave. It's the best tour in the valley for the money (only $15) and culminates with a basic tasting back at the winery. Tours are offered four times daily, but the tram isn't big, so in the summer you should buy a same-day ticket as far in advance as possible. Call the winery for the seasonal schedule. If you only want to taste the wines, the best option is the $15 reserve tasting that includes many of the best biodynamic wines.

Almost two-thirds of the 45 biodynamic acres at Benziger is planted with cabernet sauvignon, taking advantage of the natural sun trap created by the surrounding hillsides. Other Bordeaux varietals are also planted, plus some zinfandel and sauvignon blanc. The Sonoma Mountain estate wines are biodynamic and are priced from about $25 and up. The Family and Reserve ranges of wines, together with some more pricey vineyard designates, are made with grapes from vineyards all over Sonoma and Northern California, including a couple of interesting clone-specific pinot noirs from Los Carneros. Most can be tried in the spacious but sometimes crowded tasting room. Benziger's Imagery brand of small-lot wines, with its unique label art, has its own home in the nearby Imagery Winery.

B. R. Cohn Winery

If you're a cabernet lover, then you have something in common with Bruce Cohn, founder and owner of B. R. Cohn winery (15000 Sonoma Hwy., Glen Ellen, 800/330-4064, www.brcohn.com, 10 A.M.–5 P.M. Mon.–Thurs., 10 A.M.–6 P.M. Fri.–Sun., tours by appointment, tasting $10–15). He is so fond of cabernet that he has planted all 100 acres on a former dairy with cabernet sauvignon. His Olive Hill vineyard has its own microclimate warmed by an underground geothermal aquifer (the same one that feeds the valley's hot springs) and shielded from cool air by Sonoma Mountain.

Cohn used to sell his grapes to other wineries in the valley, but started bottling under his own label after an Olive Hill vineyard wine produced by the Gundlach Bundschu Winery was chosen to accompany President Reagan on a trip to China in the 1980s. In the early days, Cohn received advice and help from famed winemaker Charlie Wagner at Napa's Caymus Winery. The rest, as they say, is history.

Cohn buys chardonnay from Carneros

vineyards together with merlot, zinfandel, and syrah from elsewhere in Sonoma for some of his other wines, including an interesting syrah-cabernet blend that incorporates some Olive Hill vineyard fruit. Also look out for Moose, a huge black bulldog-Labrador cross, in the winery and on the label of a bold red blend.

The olive trees surrounding the buildings and lining the driveway give the vineyard not only its name but also some award-winning olive oil that is available in the tasting room. The French picholine olive trees are relatively young by olive standards—only 140 years old—and the eight acres around the winery form the largest picholine orchard in the valley. The estate oil is 100 percent picholine, and various blended oils are also available, together with some unusual vinegars, such as raspberry champagne vinegar and cabernet vinegar. Many can be tasted at the winery.

As you walk from the parking lot up to the tasting room, you might also hear Doobie Brothers songs wafting over the patio, giving away Bruce Cohn's other profession as the manager of the Doobies since the early 1970s and some other bands in the 1980s, including Bruce Hornsby and Night Ranger. The music connection continues to this day—the winery hosts an annual fall music festival charity event featuring members of the Doobies plus countless other rock and country musicians.

Imagery Estate Winery

The world's largest collection of wine label art by some well-known contemporary artists (including Sol LeWitt and Terry Winters) is one reason to visit Imagery (14335 Sonoma Hwy., Glen Ellen, 707/935-4515 or 877/550-4278, www.imagerywinery.com, 10 A.M.–4:30 P.M. daily fall–spring, 10 A.M.–4:30 P.M. Mon.–Fri., 10 A.M.–5:30 P.M. Sat.–Sun. summer, tasting $10). Another is the wide variety of small-lot wines that are available only at the winery itself. Imagery was established as a boutique offshoot of the Benziger Family Winery in the 1980s when art labels were catching on and winemaker Joe Benziger met the art director at nearby Sonoma State University, Bob Nugent.

That relationship helped spawn the Imagery brand and the unique labels.

Artists have free rein apart from two rules: There can be no nudity on the label (for legal reasons), and every label has to include an image, however abstract or small, of the Greek Parthenon, a small replica of which stands on a hillside at parent winery Benziger and was evidently the site of some wild parties before the Benziger family bought the ranch in the 1980s. The Parthenon is also now the symbol for Imagery, and a Greek theme seems to have been worked into almost every aspect of the winery.

Nugent, who has painted some of the labels himself, is now curator of the collection, charged with finding new up-and-coming artists. Benziger focuses on creating unusual wines from vineyards on the 20-acre estate and other vineyards throughout Sonoma, including Ash Creek, which is the highest-altitude vineyard in Sonoma County. Imagery produces fewer than 8,000 cases of wine per year. The Artist Series includes sangiovese, barbera, malbec, petite sirah, viognier, and a white burgundy, while the Vineyard Collection includes more traditional wines like cabernet sauvignon, merlot, and zinfandel. Most are priced $20–40.

Matanzas Creek Winery

It's worth the 10-minute drive up scenic Bennett Valley Road (off Warm Springs Road) from Glen Ellen to visit Matanzas Creek (6097 Bennett Valley Rd., Santa Rosa, 707/528-6464 or 800/590-6464, www.matanzascreek.com, 10 A.M.–4:30 P.M. daily, tasting $5), especially in May and June when the lavender is in full bloom and is quite a sight (and smell) to behold. The winery is in Sonoma's newest appellation, nestled at the foot of the hills surrounded by woods, flower-filled gardens, and the largest planting of lavender in California. Like the fields outside, the tasting room is filled with the scent of lavender in the form of soaps, oils, cut stems, and all sort of other aromatic products for pampering and cooking.

The former dairy became a winery in 1977, although the current barnlike winery building was built in 1985. Former owners Sandra and Bill MacIver led the application to get the Bennett Valley classified as its own appellation, and in December 2003 it became the 13th AVA in Sonoma County, encompassing only four wineries (including Matanzas Creek) and 850 acres of vines.

The winery's own 280 acres of Bennett Valley vineyards are planted with chardonnay, merlot, cabernet sauvignon, sauvignon blanc, and syrah, all benefiting from cooling influences of the ocean air that never really makes it over the mountains into the Sonoma Valley. More grapes are now brought in from elsewhere in Sonoma and Mendocino Counties as the new owner, Kendall-Jackson, ramps up production to 60,000 cases per year. All the estate's grape varietals are represented in the wines, but the winery is particularly well known for its chardonnays and limited-production merlots.

Tours are available by appointment twice a day, and printed guides to the surrounding flower and lavender gardens are available in the tasting room. Although no food is sold at the winery, this is a great place for a picnic accompanied by a bottle of Matanzas rosé or sauvignon blanc. The lavender is harvested each year right before the winery holds its annual Wine & Lavender event, usually on the last Saturday in June. Tickets for the wine, food, and lavender party are $75 and should be booked in advance.

Audelssa Estate Winery

The former tasting room of Navillus Birney was revamped in 2007 to reflect the winery's merger the previous year with another local family winery, Audelssa Estate. The small downtown space now resembles more of an upscale café, with neat rows of tables and a tasting menu that includes morsels of food as well as wine.

The Audelssa Estate Winery (13647 Arnold Dr., Glen Ellen, 707/933-8514, www.audelssa. com, 11 A.M.–5 P.M. Thurs.–Mon., tasting $15) is a small family-run operation started in the late 1990s that now makes a modest 3,000 cases of wine per year, sourced predominantly from its highly regarded mountain vineyards

THE HUNGARIAN CONNECTION

Although German and Italian families founded some of the oldest wineries still operating in this part of Sonoma, it was a Hungarian immigrant named **Agoston Haraszthy** who became the area's first big commercial winemaker, and in doing so he helped change the face of the Californian wine industry.

Within a decade of arriving in the state, he had established the pioneering Buena Vista Winery in the Sonoma Valley and was producing some of the best wines in the United States. A decade later he was gone. While his contribution to California's wine industry was important, it was not quite as important as might be suggested by some of the accolades heaped upon him over the centuries.

Haraszthy is often called the Father of California Viticulture, for example, despite the fact that by the time he started bottling wine at Buena Vista the state was already producing about 240,000 gallons of the stuff. He is also sometimes credited with introducing the ubiquitous zinfandel grape to California, but there is some evidence that it arrived in the state even before he did.

One thing that is safe to say is that Haraszthy helped introduce European grapes and European-style commercial wine production to an industry still dependent on its missionary roots. He also had an entrepreneur's sense of self-promotion, which might explain his larger-than-life image.

His wine odyssey started in Wisconsin, of all places. He arrived there from Hungary and helped create what is now Sauk City, but the harsh Wisconsin winter quickly killed the vines he tried to cultivate. In 1849, like modern-day snowbirds, he headed west to the kinder, gentler climate of Southern California.

In San Diego, Haraszthy entered politics as a state legislator, and a combination of political and agricultural aspirations gradually drew him north. The 560-acre plot of land he bought in the Sonoma Valley in 1856 was quickly planted with many European grape varietals, and soon the Buena Vista Winery, with its hand-dug caves, boasted the largest vineyard in the United States and was producing award-winning wines.

He also reportedly helped plant vineyards for other Sonoma families that became (and still are) big names in the wine industry themselves, including Krug, Gundlach, and Bundschu.

By the 1860s, Haraszthy was combining his political and viticultural interests, promoting Californian wine across the country and getting state funding to travel around Europe to study wine-making techniques.

He returned in 1862 with thousands of vine cuttings collected in almost every European country, from Spain to Turkey. Among them are believed to be the cabernet sauvignon, pinot noir, sauvignon blanc, riesling, and semillon varieties that have become mainstays of the California wine industry.

Exactly what he brought back is open to debate, however, since cataloging and naming conventions in those days were unreliable. Some of those well-known grapes might also have stealthily arrived in California long before, and many others that he brought back never took hold.

Haraszthy's downfall was as sudden as his success. In 1863, facing financial problems, he sold his wine business to the Buena Vista Viticultural Society, a conglomerate in which he held almost half the shares, and took a management position. But within three years he was accused of mismanagement and Enron-style fraud in an attempt to create the biggest winemaker in California; in 1866 he quit.

What happened after this is still a bit of a mystery. Haraszthy left California in 1868 to run a sugar plantation in Nicaragua, but he disappeared in the rain forest and is believed to have been killed by a crocodile.

It's hard not to raise a glass to an immigrant who, in the space of 25 years, had been the co-founder of a Wisconsin town, a businessman, a politician, and a crocodile's meal. But as you raise that glass of mass-produced Sonoma Valley red wine, also consider that it might not taste quite the same (or be as cheap) if not for Agoston Haraszthy.

on the other side of the Sonoma Valley. Since the early 1990s the Schaefer family has farmed a steep 120-acre vineyard known as Mountain Terraces near the top of the Mayacamas Mountains on the eastern side of Sonoma Valley, and the fruit has become much sought-after as some of the best in Sonoma.

Like many growers with quality vineyards, the family eventually chose to make its own wines from a small portion of the vineyard. The result was an impressive collection of accolades from national wine critics for its cabernet sauvignon, syrah-based blends, and a bordeaux blend called Summit, all exhibiting the intensity that's unique to mountain-grown fruit. Originally called Schaefer Sonoma Vineyards, the winery was forced to change its name to avoid confusion with Napa Valley's Schafer Vineyards. Dan Schaefer came up with the word Audelssa, using parts of his three daughters' names.

There are plenty of tasting options, but be aware that the tasting room is closed midweek and is small, so there might be standing room only on busy days. Despite those drawbacks and a tasting fee on the high side for this part of the valley, the intimate atmosphere and outstanding wines make it a worthwhile stop.

Eric Ross Winery

You can almost imagine author Jack London himself relaxing with a book in the cozy tasting room of the Eric Ross winery (14300 Arnold Dr., Glen Ellen, 707/939-8525, www.ericross. com, 11 A.M.–5 P.M. Thurs.–Mon., tasting $5), across the street from the Jack London Village complex. The bright red–painted rustic building throngs with visitors on summer weekends, but during the week you'll likely have the comfy leather sofa inside to yourself. On winter days the fireplace makes it all the more homey; just imagine a few artfully crammed bookcases, and this could be Jack London's living room.

The metal-topped corner tasting bar almost seems like an afterthought, but it's where all the action is to be found. The Eric Ross winery was created in the mid-1990s by two photographers, Eric Luse and John Story Ross, both of whom had come to know wine and the Wine

Country very well through their assignments on the two main San Francisco daily newspapers. Their previous careers explain the abundance of photographs on display in the tasting room. The winery itself is located in Marin, but this is the winery's only tasting room and the place to sample the range of pinot noirs, chardonnays, zinfandels, and other wines, all sourced from Russian River Valley vineyards.

The pinots in particular are worth trying, and there are usually two or three available to taste, each from a different vineyard and each with a distinct character featuring classic Russian River complexity and smoothness. The syrah and zinfandel also offer some of the same cool-climate elegance and a refreshing alternative to more exuberant examples from the warmer Sonoma Valley at other wineries. One of the more unique offerings is the white Rhône-style Marsanne-Roussanne, a full-bodied white that balances wonderful aromatics with a refreshing acidity. The winery recently added a nice cabernet sauvignon sourced from a valley vineyard near Glen Ellen to its portfolio. All the wines are made in limited quantities; total production at Eric Ross is only about 3,000 cases per year.

Loxton Cellars

Although it's officially an appointment-only winery, visiting Loxton Cellars (11466 Dunbar Rd., Glen Ellen, 707/935-7221, www.loxtoncellars. com, 11 A.M.–5 P.M. daily, free tasting) is usually as easy as checking to see if the sign is out on the road at the end of the driveway. If it is, then someone's home to pour some wines on the makeshift tasting bar set up in the corner of the spotless, warehouse-style barrel room. Visiting here is as unpretentious an experience as you can have in a valley that is already pretty laid-back.

Owner and winemaker Chris Loxton used to be assistant winemaker at neighboring Wellington Vineyards and had plenty of experience before that in his native Australia, so he knows Sonoma well and knows how to make distinctive red wines. He focuses mainly on syrah and zinfandel made from both Sonoma Valley and Russian River Valley grapes, including a shiraz from Australian vine clones, an earthy syrah from hillside fruit, a robust syrah port, and a dry rosé syrah. More recently he added cabernet sauvignon and a cabernet-shiraz blend—a sure sign that there's an Aussie at work.

Loxton owns no vineyards, instead working through lease agreements with established growers and helping them manage the vineyards. With just 2,000 cases made each year, the small-lot wines from quality vineyards offer outstanding value for money with most costing $20–30 a bottle. Call ahead and arrange a personal tour of the vineyards and winery from Chris himself to gain more insight into the wines and his winemaking style.

KENWOOD AREA WINERIES
Kunde Estate Winery

The Kunde Estate (9825 Sonoma Hwy., Kenwood, 707/833-5501, www.kunde.com, 10:30 A.M.–4:30 P.M. daily, tasting $10–20) sprawls across 2,000 acres of valley land, making it the largest family-owned winery in the west and providing enough space for a whopping 800 acres of estate vineyards where 20 varietals of grape are grown from the valley floor up to elevations of 1,000 feet on the terraced hillsides. In fact, the winery has enough vineyards, and varied enough growing conditions, to make only estate wines and still have enough fruit left to sell to neighboring wineries.

Grapes have been grown here by the Kunde family since 1904, when Louis Kunde acquired the historic Wildwood Vineyard, which was first planted in 1879 by some of the valley's wine pioneers. There is still a patch of zinfandel vines dating from 1882 happily growing here, grapes from which go into the limited-production Century Vines zinfandel.

The current incarnation of the winery was built in the late 1980s to resemble a giant version of an old dairy barn that stood nearby and is run by the fourth wine-making generation of the family. Kunde makes fine examples of just about every wine that can be made from Sonoma Valley grapes, though it is perhaps best known for its zinfandel, cabernet sauvignon,

and vineyard-designate chardonnays. It also makes a few unusual wines among its bargain-priced Tasting Room series, available only at the winery, including a fruity gewürztraminer, a strawberry-laced grenache rosé (both perfect picnic wines), and an intriguing blend of cabernet and zinfandel called Bob's Red. There are plenty of good picnic wines to complements an alfresco lunch in shady lakeside picnic area.

The spacious tasting room rarely seems crowded, but the best tasting option here is in the Kinneybrook Room, where you can taste the more expensive Grand Estate reserve wines along with a small cheese plate while relaxing in one of the leather club chairs. Free tours of the aging caves stretching half a mile under the hillside behind the winery are offered on the hour Friday–Sunday. Groups of six or more can also go on one of many appointment-only tours to see parts of the huge estate. Contact the winery for more information.

◖ Chateau St. Jean

If you were to build your own personal château in the Sonoma Valley, you couldn't pick a much better location than this. A long driveway through the vineyards leads up to Chateau St. Jean (8555 Sonoma Hwy., Kenwood, 707/833-4134, www.chateaustjean.com, 10 A.M.–5 P.M. daily, tasting $10–15), a white turreted mansion at the foot of the mountains. The walk from the parking lot to the tasting rooms leads through a manicured formal garden, and on the other side of the reserve tasting room is a patio and expanse of lawn overlooking the valley and its vineyards.

The winery itself was once a private residence surrounded by walnut groves, built as a palatial summer home by a family of Michigan mining barons in the 1920s. The château was almost bought by Bruce Cohn, founder of B. R. Cohn Winery, in the 1970s but ended up being acquired by a group of investors who opened it as a winery in 1975 with Richard Arrowood as the winemaker. He went on to establish his own Arrowood Vineyards & Winery just down the road, and St. Jean is now owned by the multinational Fosters Wine Estates.

The winery pioneered the production of vineyard-designate wines in Sonoma in the 1970s and now has almost a dozen in its portfolio, including several pinot noirs and chardonnays, a pinot blanc, a fumé blanc, and a syrah. Grapes for all the wines are sourced from vineyards all over Sonoma County, including the Russian River Valley and Los Carneros, but 80 acres of estate vineyards around the château are planted principally with chardonnay.

Although St. Jean is best known for its white wines (which include multiple chardonnays, viognier, gewürztraminer, pinot blanc, riesling, and fumé blanc), it also has its share of big reds, including Cinq Cepages, a Bordeaux-style red blend of five varietals—some grown in a tiny vineyard perched on a steep slope above the winery—that is always rated highly by critics. Other red wines are Sonoma County cabernet sauvignon, merlot, and pinot noir, as well as some powerhouse reserve and estate versions priced $50–100. The Reserve malbec in particular is worth trying just for its heady aroma

of blueberries. Tasting-room staff love to boast that this is the only California winery (as of 2006) that has had five wines in the *Wine Spectator* Top 100 in one year (1996).

The spacious main tasting room has a small deli and countless Wine Country gifts, but it's worth spending a little extra to taste wines in the more comfortable and intimate reserve tasting room, especially in summer when its sun-drenched patios and petanque courts are open. Upstairs from the reserve tasting room, there's a small gallery featuring the work of local artists. An educational Terroir Tour gives some insight into growing grapes, making wine, and then tasting wine. St. Jean also offers VIP reserve tasting in a private room and an hour-long sensory analysis class—just some of the additional educational courses and tours offered.

Kaz Vineyard & Winery

This is the one winery in the valley where it's guaranteed that the owner will be pouring the wine in the tasting room. Kaz (a.k.a.

The crazy world of Kaz Vineyard & Winery lurks in this modest barn.

Richard Kasmier) is also as close as you'll get to a renegade winemaker, producing just 1,000 cases per year of bizarrely named wine blends and ports, some dominated by relatively rare grapes for California, such as the red alicante bouschet and lenoir, which is a varietal more commonly found in Texas or in tiny amounts in some California blends. The wines will not be to everyone's taste, but it's unlikely that you won't find at least one that tickles your fancy.

Kaz also grows syrah, cabernet franc, chardonnay, and dechaunac in his 2.5-acre organic vineyard (he once grew an unimaginable 15 varietals on five acres) and buys other grapes from neighboring wineries. A winery motto, "No harm in experimenting," ensures that many blends will change each year, though some are pretty much constant, including the ZAM (zinfandel, alicante, mourvèdre), Sangiofranc (sangiovese and cabernet franc), and Mainliner (100 percent lenoir). For added interest, all the wine labels are vintage photos hand-colored by Kaz's wife, Sandi.

Kaz Vineyard (233 Adobe Canyon Rd., Kenwood, 707/833-2536, www.kazwinery. com, 11 A.M.–5 P.M. Fri.–Mon. or by appointment, tasting $5) is open Friday–Monday only and is four driveways up the road from Landmark Vineyards on the left (drive slowly because it's easy to miss). The tiny tasting room doubles as a barrel storage area, and it doesn't take many people to fill it up, but Kaz keeps the crowd entertained and you'll quickly get to know everyone around you. The unmarked door at the back of the tasting room opens onto a small garden with just enough room for a private picnic.

Landmark Vineyards

Landmark (101 Adobe Canyon Rd., Kenwood, 707/833-1144, www.landmarkwine.com, 10 A.M.–4:30 P.M. daily, tasting $5–15) was one of the first California wineries to make only chardonnay, though it has since expanded to pinot noir and most recently syrah, all made using grapes from the 11 acres of estate vineyards and others sourced from all over California.

Enjoy a game of boccie ball while sipping wine at Landmark Vineyards.

Chardonnay still accounts for the majority of the 25,000-case production, and the wines range in price from the $28 Overlook chardonnay up to the most expensive Lorenzo Reserve and Damaris Reserve, named after the winery's founder, Damaris Deere Ethridge, the great-granddaughter of John Deere (inventor of the steel plow and a name now associated with tractors). Another well-regarded Sonoma County chardonnay producer, Charles Creek Vineyards, also has some Deere family heritage. There must be something in the genes.

The red wines at Landmark include the single-vineyard Kanzler pinot, the Grand Detour (named after John Deere's home town in Michigan), and the limited-production Steel Plough syrah, named for John Deer's first farming invention. Like the chardonnays, all three reds are generally well-liked by critics.

A large mural behind the tasting bar livens up an otherwise drab room, but the best aspects of the Spanish-style buildings are outside. The large shady courtyard outside the tasting room leads to a fountain and gardens with a view straight over the vineyards to Sugarloaf Mountain in the distance. A few picnic tables are available, as is a free boccie ball court to test how straight you can throw after a few glasses of wine.

Mayo Family Winery Reserve Room

Forgo a picnic and instead try to get a lunchtime reservation at this tasting room with a resident chef. Seven wines are served with seven different small appetizers exquisitely prepared by the chef and served at tables in the small, intimate Mayo Family winery reserve tasting room (9200 Sonoma Hwy., Kenwood, 707/833-5504, 10:30 A.M.–6:30 P.M. daily). Instead of traditional wine tasting with crackers or perhaps breadsticks at the bar, this is a thoroughly gourmet affair with seasonal morsels such as seared scallops with oyster mushrooms and applesauce-braised short ribs paired with red and white wines from Mayo's Russian River and Sonoma Valley vineyards. The "meal" ends with a delectable dessert paired with Mayo's zinfandel port. The $35 tasting fee is easier to swallow considering the food and wine education you'll receive, and especially if you treat the tasting as a lunch substitute.

Mayo Family Winery was established in the early 1990s by Diane and Henry Mayo and is now run by their son, Jeff. From the beginning, the Mayo's goal was to make small quantities of vineyard-specific wines. They own small vineyards in the Sonoma Valley and Russian River Valley and over the years have sourced fruit from other vineyards in those two areas. Since their current winery opened in 2000, production has ramped up to about 10,000 cases of about 30 different wines, although not all will be available year-round. Most of the production is sold direct to consumers, so reviews in magazines are rare, but the success of the winery is a testament to the popularity of its wines.

Mayo is perhaps best known for its zinfandels and Rhône-varietal wines like syrah and carignane sourced from Russian River Valley vineyards, but it also makes some nice Bordeaux-style red blends and several white wines sourced from nearby vineyards, including a gewürztraminer from the Kunde estate

FIGHTING FIRE WITH WINE

On a breezy day in September 1911, a stove exploded in a cobbler's shop on the east side of Sonoma Plaza, setting off what the *Sonoma Index-Tribune* newspaper described as a "disasterous fire" that was eventually extinguished with the help of a quick-thinking wine merchant.

The town's fire truck and 100 firefighters were quickly on the scene of the original fire, but were soon overwhelmed when changing winds spread the flames to buildings up and down the street and, at one point, set fire to the grass on the plaza.

When the roof of Agostino Pinelli's wine cellars on Spain Street caught fire and he saw the fire truck was too far away to help, he and some firefighters connected a hose and pump to a 1,000-gallon tank of his wine and, as reported by the *Index-Tribune*, "A powerful stream of red wine was directed on the burning wine cellar."

Although the fire eventually destroyed most of the other buildings on 1st Street East, Pinelli's red wine was credited with helping firefighters prevent the fire from spreading to even more buildings on the south side of the plaza.

The Pinelli building is still standing today on 1st Street East near Spain Street. It was built in 1891 from local stone quarried by the Pinelli family, which also helped Samuele Sebastiani get his start in the quarrying business before he went on to establish the Sebastiani Winery. Today, the building is home to offices and shops, including (rather appropriately) the **Sonoma Wine Shop** (412 1st St. E., Sonoma, 707/996-1230, 11 A.M.–6 P.M. daily).

that has a hint of sweetness. If the Reserve Room tasting is too much to bite off, many of the Mayo wines can be sampled in a more traditional environment at the winery's main tasting room (13101 Arnold Dr., 707/938-9401, 10:30 A.M.–6:30 P.M. daily, tasting $6–12), which is open later than most, just down the road near Glen Ellen.

Ledson Winery & Vineyards

It's worth driving almost all the way to the top of the valley just to see the "Castle," as it's known to locals—a description that at first was meant more in a derogatory sense but has now been embraced by the Ledson winery (7335 Sonoma Hwy., Kenwood, 707/537-3810, www.ledson.com, 10 A.M.–5 P.M. daily, tasting $15–25). This is about as ostentatious as the Sonoma Valley gets, and it's still a far cry from the palaces (and actual castles) in the Napa Valley.

Steve Ledson made his money in the local contracting business and set about building this 16,000-square-foot Gothic dream home to

get back to his childhood roots of farming and ranching in the Sonoma Valley (and it's literally a dream home—Ledson says its design came to him in dreams). By the time it was finished in 1999 he had decided that it was attracting a little too much attention for his family, so he turned it into a winery and hospitality property and continued to live near Sonoma, where he has another vineyard.

Enter through the grand front door, pass the sweeping staircase, polished oak accents, and marble fireplaces, and you almost feel like you're walking onto the set of some Wine Country soap opera. There are no fewer than six tasting bars in various rooms, together with a small marketplace stocked with wines and a pungent selection of cheeses, sandwiches, and other picnic supplies. You can picnic on the grounds in the shade of a giant oak tree, although there's limited space and you can only eat food bought at the winery itself.

The house is surrounded by 17 acres of merlot vineyards, but Ledson also owns about 20 acres of zinfandel near his home just south of

© SONOMA COUNTY TOURISM BUREAU

Ledson Winery & Vineyards, known locally as the "Castle"

Sonoma and thousands of acres in Mendocino County, where he grows chardonnay, pinot noir, and syrah. In addition, he sources grapes from all over the Wine Country to make a huge portfolio of red and white wines, all of which are available only from the winery and the exclusive Ledson Hotel on Sonoma Plaza. There's no need to bother selling them anywhere else, because the entire 35,000-case output of the winery is sold directly to visitors and the winery's club members.

Almost every grape varietal is represented in the portfolio, including the estate merlot; cabernet sauvignon from Northern Sonoma; chardonnay, pinot grigio, and pinot noir from the Russian River Valley; Rhône varietals from Sonoma and Mendocino; and the unusual orange muscat from the Monterey area that's worth tasting. It's a case of pick your poison—there's bound to be a wine to please everyone—but the highlights include the estate merlot, both the Russian River and Carneros chardonnays, and the red meritage blends.

St. Francis Winery & Vineyards

Named to honor the Franciscan monks who are widely credited with planting California's first wine grapes, St. Francis (100 Pythian Rd., Santa Rosa, 800/543-7713, www.stfranciswine. com, 10 A.M.–5 P.M. daily, tasting $10–15) is a place for red-wine lovers, and particularly merlot fans. Merlot grapes have been grown here since the winery was established in 1971, and St. Francis was one of the first California wineries to bottle merlot as a stand-alone wine rather than as part of a Bordeaux-style blend.

The winery has expanded from the original, historic 100-acre Behler Ranch vineyard and now has more than 600 acres of vineyards in the Sonoma Valley and Russian River Valley that supply grapes for its chardonnay, cabernet, merlot, zinfandel, and syrah wines. They include the Nun's Canyon vineyard high up in the Mayacamas Mountains, which produces some of St. Francis's best cabernets and merlots. All the reserve wines are from single vineyards, while the cheaper Sonoma County wines include grapes from multiple vineyards.

The spacious tasting room is one of the best-designed in the valley, not surprising considering the mission-style winery complex was opened in 2001, making it one of the newer rooms in the valley. Windows running the length of the room look out onto the vineyards and mountains, and you can easily escape into the garden if it gets too crowded.

Tasting the reserve wines costs $15, though for $20 more the winery throws in some food at the appointment-only food and wine pairing session with appetizers from the winery's chef, Todd Muir.

Family Wineries

Perhaps the cheapest wine-induced buzz in the Sonoma Valley can be had at Family Wineries (9380 Sonoma Hwy., Kenwood, 888/433-6555, www.familywines.com, 10:30 A.M.–5 P.M. daily, tasting $5), a cooperative tasting room on a busy Kenwood corner. Four wineries are featured, and there are usually plenty of tastes for the regular tasting fee, including a very varied selection of pinot noirs and chardonnays. All the wineries represented are small family-owned affairs, and on weekends some of the winemakers themselves often do the pouring.

David Noyes Wines is a producer of mainly pinot noir, chardonnay, and zinfandel sourced from some well-known vineyards in the Dry Creek and Russian River Valleys and made using spare production capacity at some equally well-known wineries. In some respects it's a virtual winery, except David clearly knows his vines and wines, having started his wine-making career at Ridge Vineyards and having helped the Kunde family establish the Kunde Estate Winery in the late 1980s. He started his own label in 2001 and now also works as part of the wine-making team at nearby Wellington Vineyards.

The Macrae Family Winery also specializes in Russian River Valley pinot noir and chardonnay, but also has some full-throttle reds in its portfolio, including merlot and cabernet sauvignon sourced from the Stagecoach Vineyard on the slopes of Napa Valley's Atlas Peak appellation. S. L. Cellars is a small producer of pinot noir and chardonnay sourced from the Carneros and Russian River Valley regions, but it also makes a Brut sparkling wine as well as a Syrah from Dry Creek Valley. Another winery represented at the tasting room is Collier Falls Vineyards, which is based in the Dry Creek Valley and produces a few thousand cases a year of zinfandel, cabernet sauvignon, primitivo, and petite sirah from its estate vineyards.

SIGHTS

Sonoma is not the only Wine Country town with a rich history stretching back hundreds of years, but it holds the distinction of being ground zero both for the turbulent events that led to the creation of the state of California in the 1840s and for the beginnings of California's booming wine industry. Many of the most important buildings from that active period in the mid-1800s are still standing, making Sonoma one of the most historically alive Wine Country towns in Northern California.

◖ Sonoma Plaza

Sonoma Plaza (Spain St. between 2nd St. and 4th St., 707/996-1090), the eight-acre square that over the past 180 years has seen religious uprisings, revolution, fires, and now large numbers of tourists, is at the center of the region's history and is the heart and soul of the valley. Fascinating shops and boutiques selling everything from designer clothes to African handicrafts fill the streets around the plaza, along with galleries and some of the valley's best restaurants, many of them in historic buildings that date from the 1800s.

Sonoma Plaza was created in 1835 by General Vallejo for troop maneuvers and for a long time was little more than a muddy patch of grazing land surrounded by a picket fence. It is now the largest town square in California, and despite being thoroughly gentrified and besieged by cars, still maintains a sense of grace that only somewhere with such a rich history can pull off.

An excellent self-guided walking tour of the plaza's many Victorian-era buildings is buried between the endless pages of advertisements in the free *Sonoma Valley Guide*, copies of which are usually in the **Sonoma Valley Visitors Bureau** on the plaza.

Sonoma City Hall was built to look the same from every direction.

© PHILIP GOLDSMITH

A few yards north of the visitors bureau is the **Bear Flag Monument,** a bronze statue that is roughly where the flag was raised by settlers in 1846 heralding the eventual creation of the State of California and the demise of Mexican rule. Smack in the middle of the plaza is **Sonoma City Hall,** built from locally quarried stone with four identical sides—to give equal importance to traders on all four sides of the plaza, so the legend goes. Like most civil construction projects today, the building project came in late and way over its budgeted cost of $15,000, delayed by stonemason strikes and the ballooning price of materials following the 1906 San Francisco earthquake. It took five years to build and was finally completed in 1909.

Almost opposite the mission entrance on Spain Street, the wobbly-looking adobe building with a long first-floor veranda is the **Blue Wing Inn,** a gold rush–era saloon and stagecoach stop that is thought to be one of the oldest unaltered buildings in the city and the oldest hotel north of San Francisco. It is now a private residence.

◖ Sonoma Mission

The north side of the plaza was the first to be developed in the early days of Sonoma and is where the oldest buildings can be found, many now part of the Sonoma State Historic Park. The **Mission San Francisco Solano de Sonoma** (corner of 1st St. and E. Spain St., 707/938-9560, 10 A.M.–5 P.M. Fri.–Wed., $3), established in 1823, was the last of California's 21 missions but had a short religious life. Its land and buildings were seized by the Mexican government in 1834 along with all the other missions on the West Coast. By the end of the 1800s, Sonoma's once-proud mission had suffered the ignominy of being used as hay barn and a winery, and of having a saloon built right in front of it.

Enter the unlikely figure of newspaper magnate William Randolph Hearst, who helped provide funding that enabled a preservation society to buy the mission in 1903 for $5,000. Restoration didn't start until 1911, however, by which time various collapses had left the building in ruins. The reconstructed building open to the public today has a large cross on the roof where an old bell tower used to be

© PHILIP GOLDSMITH

Sonoma Mission, the last of the Spanish missions built in California but is otherwise largely the same as the original. The $3 entrance fee buys access to a small museum and the large dusty courtyard full of giant prickly pear cactus plants said to be as old as the mission itself. Just don't touch the cacti or you'll be pulling tiny hairlike spikes out of your hands for the rest of the day.

The Vallejo Connections

Many of the historic sights in Sonoma that date from the turbulent mid-1800s were built for or by General Mariano Vallejo, the Mexican army commander who later became an important state politician.

Across 1st Street from the mission is the two-story adobe **Sonoma Barracks** building (10 A.M.–5 P.M. Fri.–Wed., $3), which was constructed in stages between 1834 and 1841 by Native American slaves captured by the same Mexican army it eventually housed. In 1860 it was converted to a winery by General Vallejo (many plaza buildings saw service as wine cellars or wineries over the years) and in the late 1800s became a store with an ornate Victorian facade tacked on the front. It was partly restored in the 1930s and was used for private residences and offices until being bought by the state in 1958 and fully restored. The small museum housed there today contains artifacts from its military history. The courtyard was once the scene of grisly staged animal fights.

Next to the barracks is the old **Toscano Hotel,** which was built in the 1850s. Just across the small square behind the 1940s building that contains the Sonoma Cheese Factory is the site of Vallejo's first home, **La Casa Grande,** built in 1840 and where Vallejo was arrested by the Bear Flag party in 1846. The house itself burned down long ago, and just the two-story, adobe-brick servants quarters remain.

Vallejo's next home, built in 1850, reflected his new status as a state senator and is on 20 acres of parkland about a 10-minute walk west of the plaza on Spain Street at 3rd Street West. Vallejo called this new home **Lachryma Montis,** Latin for "tear of the mountain," the name given by Native Americans to a nearby spring that once supplied much of the town's water. The Mission, Barracks, and Lachryma Montis are all part of the Sonoma State Historic Park (707/938-9560).

In a display of excess that would put many of today's movie stars to shame, Vallejo spent $150,000 (in 1850 dollars) to build and decorate the ornate Gothic-style Victorian house, construct numerous summer houses, and plant the huge 250-acre estate where he lived until his death in 1890. Even the wood-framed **Swiss Chalet** next to the house, originally used to store the estate's fruit (and, of course, used as a winery), was built from materials imported from Europe. Today it is a visitors center and museum (10 A.M.–5 P.M. Fri.–Wed., $3). The house itself is open during museum hours and is still full of Vallejo's decadent marble fireplaces, rosewood furniture, chandeliers, and frilly lace.

The Sebastiani Theatre

Not only was California born in Sonoma, but so was California theater. What was believed to be California's first theatrical presentation,

© PHILIP GOLDSMITH

The Sebastiani Theatre dominates Sonoma Plaza.

Benjamin Webster's *The Golden Farmer,* was put on by American soldiers in an old adobe storehouse converted to a theater in 1849.

Today, a theater of the silver screen era is one of the most prominent buildings on the plaza. The Sebastiani Theatre (476 1st St. E., 707/996-2020, www.sebastianitheatre.com), built to replace the burned-down Don Theatre, was funded by Samuele Sebastiani, city benefactor and founder of the eponymous winery. It opened its doors in April 1934 with the film *Fugitive Lovers* and today hosts films or live entertainment almost every night.

Although it was the most striking, the theater was only one of many buildings Sam Sebastiani built for the city. Others include an apartment building still standing at 28–34 Spain Street, a bus station next door, and a combined bowling alley and skating rink not far away that was called the Sebastiani Rollatorium in the 1940s but has long since been replaced by a strip mall.

Depot Museum and Train Town

The scale-model trains that haul passengers around a 1.25-mile track at the Train Town amusement park in Sonoma are the only reminders of the once-thriving railroad that brought visitors to Sonoma Valley.

The first stretch of the original Sonoma Valley Railroad opened in 1879 and ran from Vineburg just south of Sonoma to Wingo, three miles south of present-day Schellville, where it connected with boats to San Francisco. It was soon extended down to San Pablo Bay and north to Sonoma Plaza. From the plaza it followed Spain Street and turned right on present-day Highway 12, running all the way up the valley to Glen Ellen.

Back in 1890, taking the ferry and train from San Francisco's Ferry Building to Sonoma took about two hours, not much longer than it takes by car now. But the rising popularity of cars in the early 1900s and the opening of the Golden Gate Bridge in 1937 eventually led to the demise of the region's railroads.

More about the history of the Sonoma railroads can be found at the small Depot Museum (270 1st St. W., 1–4:30 P.M. Wed.–Sun., 707/938-1762, free admission), a block north of the plaza. The museum is an exact replica of the original railroad depot, which burned down in 1976, and is surrounded by Depot Park, popular with the city's drunks except on Friday when the farmers market takes over.

Riding the only trains left in town requires a visit to the brightly painted station of Train Town (20264 Broadway, 707/938-3912, www.traintown.com). The strange and often crowded combination of amusement park, model railway, and petting zoo is open 10 A.M.–5 P.M. daily June–Labor Day, and 10 A.M.–5 P.M. Friday–Sunday only for the rest of the year. The fare is $4.75 for all ages, but adults should be warned that the mandatory stop at the petting zoo at the halfway point can be a little tedious. The amusement park rides, which include a Ferris wheel and vintage carousel, each cost $2.50.

ENTERTAINMENT AND EVENTS

The Sonoma Valley is as much about olives as wine during the winter when the annual **Sonoma Valley Olive Festival** (www.olivefestival.com) is in full swing. The festival kicks off with the Blessing of the Olives at Sonoma's mission and the Olive Harvest Tasting in early December, then runs through February. Check the website for a full list of the 30 or more events, including plenty of fun cooking demonstrations organized at wineries, restaurants, and outdoors to celebrate the oily fruit. Many are free, but the biggest events usually require tickets, available at the Sonoma Valley Visitors Bureau on Sonoma Plaza.

Late May through June is lavender season in the Sonoma Valley, and the aromatic purple flower is celebrated with the annual **Lavender Festival** (usually the third weekend in June, 707/523-4411, www.sonomalavender.com, $5 per car) next to the Chateau St. Jean winery in Kenwood. Learn about growing countless varieties of lavender, how to use the oil, and even how to cook with lavender. There's also a lavender festival held in early June at the Matanzas Creek Winery near Glen Ellen.

Shakespeare in Sonoma celebrates the town's theatrical heritage and its great summer weather July–September with Sunday-evening performances of Shakespeare's plays put on by the local Avalon Players group in the outdoor amphitheater at the Gundlach Bundschu Winery. Tickets cost $15–20. For more information, contact the Avalon Players (707/996-3264, www.sonomashakespeare.com).

If the silver screen is more your thing, August brings the annual **Wine Country Film Festival** to the historic Sebastiani Theatre on Sonoma Plaza and several valley wineries. Film screenings are usually accompanied by a range of other Wine Country events during the month, all involving plenty of food and wine. For a schedule of events and ticket prices, visit www.winecountryfilmfest.com.

Among the big wine events in the valley during the year is the annual **Passport to Sonoma Valley,** usually held on the third weekend in May, when 40 wineries up and down the valley throw themed parties with free food, wine, and entertainment for those lucky enough to have a festival passport. They can be bought ahead of time for either the whole weekend or just one day from the Sonoma Valley Vintners & Growers Alliance (707/935-0803, www.sonomavalleywine.com). Some passports might also be available from select wineries on the day.

Earlier in the year is the **Savor Sonoma Valley** event (707/431-1137, www.heartofthevalley.com), hosted by the Heart of Sonoma Valley Association, usually the third weekend in March at wineries around Glen Ellen and Kenwood.

Ramekins Sonoma Valley Culinary School

The Napa Valley has the famous Culinary Institute of America, but the Sonoma Valley, not to be outdone, has its own renowned culinary school in Ramekins (450 W. Spain St., Sonoma, 707/933-0450, www.ramekins.com), just four blocks from the plaza and voted 2005 Cooking School of the Year by the International Association of Culinary Professionals.

Ramekins has far more in the way of a hands-on cooking experience for casual visitors than the CIA over in St. Helena, including classes and demonstrations, sometimes by well-known chefs, that don't cost much more than a meal at many local restaurants, making the evening classes a fun alternative to eating a meal that someone else prepared. Check the website for a constantly updated schedule.

RECREATION

Outside the town of Sonoma and its environs, there is little in the way of development—the two other major valley towns of Kenwood and Glen Ellen are compact, to say the least. Vineyards are counted as important residents in this part of the world, and large swaths of the mountains are protected parkland, creating a giant playground for the valley's residents and visitors to bike, hike, and trot to their heart's content (and also creating a planning nightmare for would-be developers and wineries wanting to expand their vineyards). Even the town of Sonoma has its own little hiking paradise within walking distance from the plaza.

The three largest year-round park areas are the 5,000-acre Annadel State Park, with almost 40 miles of trails; the 2,700-acre Sugarloaf Ridge State Park, with 25 miles of trails; and the neighboring 1,400-acre Hood Mountain Regional Park. All three are just minutes from the wineries at the north end of the Sonoma Valley, though be warned that they all get hot in the summer; come prepared to battle dehydration.

Also worth noting is that dogs are not allowed on any major trails in any of the state parks but are allowed on short leashes in Sugarloaf's neighbor, Hood Mountain Regional Park (although this park is closed during the fire season, June–October, so you can only walk Fido here in the rainy season).

Annadel State Park

Redwoods, oaks, meadows, and a large well-stocked lake make Annadel State Park (6201

Channel Dr., Santa Rosa, 707/539-3911, sunrise–sunset, $6 per car) one of the most diverse of Sonoma Valley's parks. It's easily accessible from both Santa Rosa and Kenwood. Most trails start from Channel Drive, which is reached by driving north from Kenwood on Highway 12; just before the road becomes four lanes, turn left on Melita Road, then left on Montgomery Drive, and left on Channel Drive.

The rocky trails that make Annadel a bone-jarring ride for mountain bikers today also give away its previous life as an important source of obsidian for Native American tools and rock for cobblestones for cities up and down the West Coast in the early 1900s. There's still some evidence of quarrying on many of the trails, including the aptly named Cobblestone Trail, which used to be the route of a tramway carrying rock down the hill to the railroad.

Mountain bikers love the fact that most of the trails are either single-track or double-track

More than 35 miles of hiking, biking, and horseback riding trails weave through Annadel State Park.

© SONOMA COUNTY TOURISM BUREAU

and strewn with rocks for a bit of added fear. This is probably not the best place for novice bikers to find their wheels, but it offers some of the best midlevel mountain biking in the Bay Area, with plenty of technical trails and an elevation gain and drop of about 1,000 feet for most loops.

Popular downhills include the Lawndale Trail from Ledson Marsh, a smooth, fast single-track through the forest; the Upper Steve's Trail and Marsh Trail loop; and the rockier Orchard and Cobblestone Trails (including the Orchard Loop). Lake Ilsanjo is pretty much the center of the park and a good start and end point for many biking loops, although it can be relatively crowded on summer weekends. The best way to reach it from the main parking lot is to ride up the Warren Richardson fire road, saving the single-track for going downhill.

An alternative entrance that avoids the fee and is popular with mountain bikers is on Lawndale Road. From Highway 12, take a left just north of the Landmark Winery; the unmarked dirt parking lot is on the right about a mile down the road. Farther up Lawndale Road, forking off to the right, is Schultz Road, leading to the Schultz Trailhead. It's better to bike up the Schultz Trail and come down Lawndale.

The best time to go **hiking** in Annadel is spring or early summer when the wildflowers are in full bloom in the meadows around Lake Ilsanjo, named after two former landowners, Ilsa and Joe Coney. The two-mile trek from the parking lot up the Warren Richardson Trail to the lake gives a good cross section of the park's flora, starting in a forest of redwoods and Douglas fir and climbing up through oaks to the relatively flat area around the lake where miles of other trails converge.

Lower Steve's Trail, which branches off and then rejoins the Richardson trail, is one of the few trails off-limits to bikes and therefore worth taking if you've been harassed by speeding bikers. Allow about four hours to make the round-trip and explore the lake area.

The Cobblestone Trail to Rough Go Trail is an alternative but rockier and longer ascent to

SOUTHERN SONOMA

the lake, and one on which you're more likely to meet bikers hurtling down the hill or some of the park's wild turkeys ambling across your path. At the lake there are picnic areas and restrooms, plus access to the rest of the trail network.

Fishing at the lake is also popular, with black bass and bluegill the most common catch. The Park Service suggests the purple plastic worm as the best bait for bass, and garden worms or grubs are favored by bluegills. Anyone over 16 must have a California fishing license.

(Sugarloaf Ridge State Park

Sugarloaf Ridge State Park (2605 Adobe Canyon Rd., Kenwood, 707/833-5712, $8) is perfect for either a quick fix of shady redwood forests or for hikes to some of the best views, both terrestrial and extraterrestrial, in the valley. It's about a 10-minute drive up Adobe Canyon Road from the Landmark Winery, putting it within easy reach of the valley floor for picnics and short day hikes. The park is open from sunrise until about two hours after sunset, but hours change depending on the time of year. Call to check times. It also has the only campground in the valley.

The somewhat barren hillside near the entrance is deceiving. From winter to early summer, a 25-foot waterfall tumbles just a few hundred yards from the parking lot along the Canyon Trail, and the 0.75-mile-long shady Creekside Nature Trail runs from the picnic area.

The big **hiking** draw is the seven-mile round-trip slog up to the summit of 2,729-foot Bald Mountain, rewarded by sweeping 360-degree views of the North Bay. It starts off on paved fire roads, but the paving soon ends as the trail climbs 1,500 feet in about three miles with no shade at all, so take a hat and plenty of water in the summer. From the summit, the Grey Pine Trail offers an alternative route downhill, and on the way up there's a short detour to the peak of neighboring Red Mountain.

To get 12 inches closer to the sun, there's an equally long and hot hike from the parking lot to the 2,730-foot summit of Hood

Mountain, which actually lies in neighboring Hood Mountain Regional Park. The dirt parking lot for the Goodspeed Trailhead is on the left of Adobe Canyon Road next to a stand of redwood trees just before the road starts climbing steeply.

From the lot, the trail crosses and follows Bear Creek through the forest, eventually crossing the creek again and steepening for the next three miles into exposed grass and scrubland. Eventually it reaches a ridge where you can bear left for the sweeping views west from the Gunsight Rock Overlook, or turn right and trek the remaining half mile up to the Hood Mountain summit. Allow at least five hours round-trip. During fire season (June–Oct.) the trail is closed about halfway up but is still a good place to go for a picnic.

Sugarloaf is also home to the **Robert Ferguson Observatory** (707/833-6979, www.rfo.org, $3 for night viewing, under age 18 free, daytime solar viewing free), the largest observatory open to the general public on the West Coast. It's just a short walk from the main parking lot. Check the website or call for a schedule of daytime solar viewing and regular stargazing through 8-, 14-, and 24-inch telescopes. There are usually at least two public day- and night-viewing sessions per month, plus regular astronomy classes throughout the year. Ask about the huge 40-inch refractor telescope, which opened in 2005.

(Jack London State Historic Park

The 800-acre Jack London State Historic Park (2400 London Ranch Rd., Glen Ellen, 707/938-5216, 10 A.M.–5 P.M. daily, $8 per car) is a short distance past the Benziger Family Winery and offers a unique combination of scenic hiking and self-guided history tours around the buildings that once belonged to one of the valley's best-known authors, Jack London.

From the entrance kiosk, turn left to visit the **House of Happy Walls** (10 A.M.–5 P.M. daily, free), the former residence of Jack London's widow, Charmian, and now a museum about the author's life. From there it's only a half-mile

© PHILIP GOLDSMITH

the ruins of Jack London's imposing
Wolf House

including a barn, an old distillery building, and the ruins of the winery itself. Others, like the piggery known as the Pig Palace, were built by London himself.

From the Beauty Ranch Trail, the Lake Trail goes uphill past the vineyards and through the redwoods for about half a mile to the forest-fringed lake created by London, where there are picnic spots and restrooms.

From there, explore the oak woods and meadows on a series of looping trails, or take the long Mountain Trail to the park summit next to Sonoma Mountain. That hike is about seven miles round-trip but can be lengthened by taking loops off the main trail. Another long hike is the Ridge Trail, which leaves the Mountain Trail and twists through forests and clearings with sweeping views before reaching the connecting Vineyard Trail leading back to the lake.

Mountain biking is allowed on all the trails in the park except the Cowan Meadow, Fallen Bridge, and Quarry Trails, plus a few around the lake. You might see a member of the Benziger family from the winery down the road hurtling by, but be aware that all trails are shared with hikers and some with horses. The Ridge Trail loop is recommended over the Mountain Trail to the summit, which is a steep uphill and perilously rocky downhill.

Sonoma Overlook Trail

Nowhere is the spirit of Slow-noma better represented than in this three-mile trail just north of Sonoma Plaza that winds through woods and meadows to the top of Schocken Hill, with fine views over the town below. The site almost became home to another Wine Country resort in 1999, but residents banded together to ensure it was instead preserved as a city-owned open space.

Grab picnic supplies and head for the trailhead near the entrance to the Mountain Cemetery on West 1st Street about a half mile north of the plaza beyond Depot Park. Within an hour you'll feel like you're in the middle of nowhere. Dogs, bikes, and smoking are not allowed on the trail.

walk on a paved trail to London's grave and the ruins of the spectacular **Wolf House,** his 17,000-square-foot dream home that burned down accidentally just before it was completed in 1913. There was speculation that it was arson, but modern-day investigators conducted a forensic arson investigation in 1995 and concluded the fire was probably caused by spontaneous combustion of rags soaked in highly flammable turpentine and linseed oil used during construction. Today, only the monumentally thick stone walls remain in the dappled shade of the surrounding redwoods, but in the House of Happy Walls there's a model of just how impressive the house would have looked had it not met such a fiery fate.

The parking lot for the miles of **hiking** trails is to the right after the entrance. From there, the Beauty Ranch Trail winds around the buildings on London's former ranch, including the cottage where he wrote many of his later books and died at a youthful 40 years old. Many of the other buildings once belonged to the 19th-century Kohler and Frohling winery,

SOUTHERN SONOMA

In spring, the **Sonoma Ecology Center** (707/996-0712, www.sonomaecologycenter. org) offers docent-led weekend hikes along the trail to identify the abundant spring wildflowers and other natural highlights. Contact the center for more information.

Golf

An alternative to hiking miles up a hot dusty trail is to meander around a lush golf course never far from a glass of crisp chardonnay.

The grande dame of the valley golf scene is the **Fairmont Sonoma Mission Inn Golf Club** (17700 Arnold Dr., Sonoma, 707/996-0300), opened in 1928 and planned by the original investors to rival the famous Del Monte course in Monterey. The 18-hole, par-72 course is on 170 acres bordered by the Sonoma Mountains and vineyards. Only club members and guests at the neighboring Fairmont Sonoma Mission Inn can play here, however.

The closest public course is in Petaluma, a 15-minute drive from Sonoma, at the **Adobe Creek Golf Club** (1901 Frates Rd., Petaluma, 707/765-3000, www.adobecreek.com). The 18-hole, par-72 links course has tee rates from $20 midweek afternoons up to $60 on the weekends, and rents clubs and carts. Be sure to check the website for last-minute discounted greens fees that can save you up to half off the regular fee.

Horseback Riding

Rides of 1–3 hours, together with more expensive private rides that include lunch, are available in Sugarloaf Ridge and Jack London State Parks through the **Triple Creek Horse Outfit** (707/887-8700, www.triplecreekhorseoutfit.com). Rates start from $60 for one hour, and groups don't usually exceed six riders. Reservations must be made in advance, and rides are limited to those over eight years old and weighing less than 220 pounds. Wear appropriate footwear, and arrive at the stable (located at the end of the main parking lots in both parks) about a half hour before your date with the horse. Rides in Sugarloaf State Park are offered year-round, and on the half dozen nights during the summer when the moon is full there are two-hour rides offered at dusk for $90. In Jack London State Park, the ride takes you past some of Jack London's favorite haunts.

Sonoma Valley Spas

Aware that local Native American tribes had long talked about the healing properties of Sonoma Valley's numerous hot springs, Captain Henry Boyes spent two years drilling all over his property at the southern end of the valley in search of them. In 1895 he hit what would turn out to be liquid gold—a 112°F gusher that ushered in decades of prosperity for the valley's hotel owners.

Within a few months, another source of the hot water had been tapped by the owner of the neighboring Agua Caliente Springs Hotel. By 1900 thousands of visitors were bathing in the new hot mineral baths every year, and developers saw the potential for mass tourism, especially with the increasing popularity of the new railroad that ran from San Pablo Bay to Sonoma and up to Glen Ellen.

Soon the Boyes Springs mineral baths and the Agua Caliente Springs Hotel were transformed into first-class resorts. By 1910 many other hotels and resorts had opened, including Fetters Hot Springs and Verano Springs, complete with vaudeville shows, dances, and concerts. The *Sonoma Index-Tribune* newspaper reported that 23,000 people came in on the railroads for the Fourth of July weekend in 1916, close to the peak of the resort boom. Just seven years earlier there had been no one to witness the annual Fourth of July parade except local residents.

Boyes Hot Springs Hotel (along with several other resorts) burned down in a huge valley fire in September 1923, and an exclusive new resort, the **Sonoma Mission Inn** (100 Boyes Blvd., Sonoma, 707/938-9000, www.fairmont. com/sonoma), with its mission-style architectural touches, opened on the site in 1927.

Today, the inn is the only spa hotel in the valley with its own natural source of hot mineral water. Even if you're not a guest at the

Fairmont-owned hotel, basic spa packages are available for $49–89, depending on how many extra salon pamperings are added on. The basic spa includes an exfoliating shower, warm and hot mineral baths, and herbal steam room and sauna, interspersed with various cold showers and baths. Various add-on massages, stone treatments, and mud baths are also available to purify and relax you (until you see the bill).

The Kenwood Inn & Spa (10400 Sonoma Hwy., Kenwood, 707/833-1293 or 800/353-6966, www.kenwoodinn.com/spa.php) might not have its own source of mineral water, but its Caudalie Vinotherapie Spa makes full use of the surrounding vineyards, and it was voted one of the top resort spas in the United States by readers of *Condé Nast Traveler* in 2009. The wraps, baths, and other treatments use vine and grape seed extracts to purify body and mind. Some might make you feel like a grape yourself, such as the wine barrel bath that exfoliates using bubbling water enriched with crushed grape seeds, skin, stalks, and pulp. For non-hotel guests there's a $35 day-use fee on top of the regular fees, which range from $70 for 20 minutes in a wine barrel to almost $200 for longer massages and facials. Complete packages incorporating body treatments, massages, and facial treatments (plus lunch) cost upward of $300.

Just south of the Sonoma Plaza, the **Garden Spa** at the luxurious MacArthur Place inn is a good place for some luxury pampering with a list of spa treatments that could cause you to tense up with indecision (29 E. MacArthur St., Sonoma, 707/933-3193, www.macarthurplace.com/spa.php). Facials, wraps, and massages featuring all sorts of therapeutic herb, flower, and vegetable extracts and essential oils start at $120, with longer treatments incorporating mineral baths starting at $225. Couples can get their treatments together, and all spa guests also have full use of the inn's tranquil outdoor pool and fitness center.

ACCOMMODATIONS

Anyone expecting cheap and cheerful accommodation over the hills from overpriced Napa Valley establishments will be sadly disappointed. The cheapest place to sleep in the valley is with Mother Nature in a campground. The second cheapest is more than $100 per night.

Like the wine made here, the Sonoma Valley is increasingly marketed as a luxury destination with luxury bells and whistles that command premium prices. The pressure to keep the small-town feel of Sonoma doesn't help either, ensuring that most hotels and inns stay small and planning hurdles remain high, thus limiting the number of rooms available. As in Napa, many places here sell a Wine Country lifestyle that mixes Mediterranean with Victorian influences, but there are some new options that throw a little more contemporary inspiration into the mix.

Apart from a few big resort or chain hotels, the accommodation scene in Sonoma Valley is one of small, usually independent establishments with a handful of rooms. The smaller the hotel or inn, the more likely there is to be a two-night minimum over weekends, especially during the busiest summer and early fall months. Cancellation policies might also be less than flexible. The peak hotel season is generally from the end of May through October, roughly corresponding to the best weather in the region.

The closest place for true bargain-priced accommodations is along the U.S. 101 freeway corridor across the Sonoma Mountains, where most of the chain motels can be found. Stay around Petaluma or in the Rohnert Park and Santa Rosa areas, and it's only a 10–15-minute drive into the valley.

Under $150

The ◖ **Sonoma Hotel** (110 W. Spain St., Sonoma, 707/996-2996 or 800/468-6016, www.sonomahotel.com) is one of the rare bargains in the valley, offering some of the cheapest rooms and a superb location in a historic building right on Sonoma Plaza next to the highly rated Girl & the Fig restaurant. Even the four cheapest rooms ($99–110 depending on the season) have views of something worthwhile, though don't expect luxury. The rooms are small, dark, and sparsely (though tastefully) furnished, but for this price in this location there's really nothing to complain about. More expensive rooms and junior suites get more light and floor space, plus some additional French country–style furniture, and cost $140–220 in winter, $150–245 in summer. In keeping with the price and the hotel's heritage (the building dates from 1880), there are few amenities, and you're likely to hear your neighbor's nighttime antics. Also be warned that the bathroom for one of the cheapest rooms (room 34), although private, is out in the hallway past the friendly ghost.

El Pueblo Inn (896 W. Napa St., 707/996-3651 or 800/900-8844, www.elpuebloinn.com) is actually more of an upscale motel but offers a lot of rooms for a modest price and is just a 10-minute walk from the plaza. It's also one of the few places with no weekend minimum-stay requirements. The cheaper Adobe rooms all have air-conditioning and are $89–149 in winter, $150–219 the rest of the year, while two-room suites are available for as little as $150. Although they still hint at the 1950s motel rooms they once were, they now open onto a courtyard rather than a parking lot. The larger, more luxurious Sonoma rooms, added during a 2001 reconstruction, feel more hotel-like, with DVD players and high ceilings, but generally cost $20–30 more per night. All rooms have access to the small outdoor pool and landscaped gardens.

Most B&Bs in this area tend toward plenty of Victorian frills, but the **Sonoma Chalet** (18935 5th St. W., Sonoma, 707/938-3129 or 800/938-3129, www.sonomachalet.com) goes beyond the chintz to a fabulously over-the-top Swiss Family Robinson–meets–Wild West theme, with its alpine murals, dark wood accents, antiques, and colorful fabrics. There are four individually decorated rooms in the main Swiss-style farmhouse: The two cheapest ($125) share a bathroom, while the larger of the other two ($160–180) has a fireplace and balcony. Several small cottages on the three acres of wooded grounds have claw-foot tubs

and wood-burning stoves and cost from $185 per night. The leafy location on the edge of Sonoma is peaceful but a fairly long walk to most of Sonoma's shops and restaurants.

Although located in the relative no-man's land of Boyes Hot Springs just north of Sonoma, the **Sonoma Creek Inn** (239 Boyes Blvd., 888/712-1289 or 707/939-9463, www.sonomacreekinn.com) is one of the cheapest nonchain hotels in the valley, with rooms starting at $89–159 midweek, depending on the season, and $139–199 weekends. In this price range it's more common to see IKEA furniture, but the furnishings here are delightfully quirky, and some look like spoils from local antique stores. The 15 rooms are small and laid out in motel style; all are clean and have air-conditioning, and some have tiny private patios.

$150-250

The Chapel Suite with its vaulted ceilings and skylight above the bed is one of the more unusual rooms at the **Cottage Inn & Spa** and the neighboring **Mission B&B** (310 1st St. E., 707/996-0719 or 800/944-1490, www.cottageinnandspa.com), just a block north of Sonoma Plaza. This self-styled "micro resort" with its mission-style architectural flourishes is an oasis of calm and style, with a wide range of rooms for all tastes and wallets. The cheapest are the plain but comfortable Courtyard rooms ($150–220 per night midweek, $25 more on weekends), but for not much more money some of the quirky junior suites like the Chapel Suite ($225–365) come into play, many with private patios and fireplaces. The South Suite ($225–355) has a double-sided fireplace, the Vineyard View Suite ($300–440) is over 700 square feet of cathedral ceilings and panoramic views, while the three-room North Suite ($300–415) includes a full kitchen.

Just a bit further up the street and a step up on the luxury scale is the five-room B&B **Bungalows 313** (313 1st St. E., 707/996-8091, www.bungalows313.com). As the name implies, this is a cozy collection of bungalows around a peaceful courtyard fountain. Each suite is decorated in Italian country style with modern luxuries like sumptuous linens, an LCD television, and a DVD player. All are spacious, with seating areas, a kitchen or kitchenette, and private patio, yet all are unique in some way. One has a fireplace, another a jetted tub, and the largest is 1,200 square feet. Prices vary wildly from season to season, starting at $160–275 midweek in the winter and jumping to $239–379 in late summer. Weekend rates are $210–469. Beware of the 14-day cancellation policy.

A teddy bear slumbering on the bed greets everyone staying at the **Inn at Sonoma** (630 Broadway, Sonoma, 888/568-9818 or 707/939-1340, www.innatsonoma.com). It is one of Sonoma's newest hotels, and what it lacks in historic charm it makes up for in functionality, price, and convenience, being only a few blocks from the plaza. The 19 guest rooms are furnished in slightly pastiche, flowery Wine Country style but have a full range of modern amenities, including fireplaces, DVD players, and luxury bathrooms. The smallest Quaint Queen rooms are $205–270 per night. The larger queen and king rooms that cost $215–300 per night also have small patios.

A historic inn dating from 1843 is now home to the newly renovated **El Dorado Hotel** (405 1st St. W., Sonoma, 707/996-3220, www.eldoradosonoma.com), offering stylish 21st-century accommodations for not much more money than a pricey Wine Country motel. The lobby exudes the style of a classy boutique hotel but the luxurious spaciousness of the lounges doesn't quite make it upstairs to the 23 smallish guest rooms. They are instead decorated with simple modern furnishings and earth tones that give a nod to the hotel's mission-era history. A decent list of amenities includes CD players, flat-screen televisions, and wireless Internet access but doesn't stretch to bathtubs—only showers—or room service. The courtyard swimming pool looks nice but is somewhat pointless unless you like to swim or sunbathe just yards from diners spilling onto the patio from the hotel's bar and restaurant. Still, for $155–175 per night midweek, depending on

the season ($20 more on weekends and for the four bungalow rooms), and a location right on the plaza, it's hard to complain. All have a view of some sort from their small balconies—the best overlook the plaza, although they suffer from some associated street noise.

The two dachshunds and Nutmeg, the cat, help provide the welcome at the ◖ **Glenelly Inn** (5131 Warm Springs Rd., Glen Ellen, 707/996-6720, www.glenelly.com), a B&B tucked away behind Glen Ellen in a former railroad inn. The seven guest rooms and suites with private bathrooms are relative bargains for such a historic B&B, costing $119–229 per night. All are decorated in cottage style with plenty of floral prints and are relatively small except for the Valley of the Moon room, which has a wood-burning stove. There are also two small cottages for $269–299 per night with private porches and whirlpool tubs. As with most well-priced historic B&Bs, the soundproofing is minimal, none of the basic rooms has a television, and most have no air-conditioning. Breakfast is served outside in the pretty gardens during the summer, and there's also an outdoor hot tub.

Also near Glen Ellen, the **Beltane Ranch B&B** (11775 Sonoma Hwy., Glen Ellen, 707/996-6501, www.beltaneranch.com) looks like a little piece of the Deep South landed in the vineyards. The Victorian-era house with its New Orleans–style wraparound veranda and lush gardens sits in the middle of the valley at the end of a long driveway, far from the madding crowds of Highway 12. The five tastefully furnished, white-paneled rooms ($150–240 per night) evoke a bygone era without going over the top, and all open onto the veranda. The ranch is actually 1,600 acres of vineyards, pasture, and woods at the bottom of the Mayacamas Mountains, with miles of hiking trails and a tennis court for guests.

$250-350

MacArthur Place (29 E. MacArthur St., Sonoma, 707/938-2929 or 800/722-1866, www.macarthurplace.com) touts itself as a historic Victorian inn. What it doesn't tell you is that by expanding and transforming itself into an exclusive seven-acre spa resort in 1997 it came to resemble more of a luxury executive-housing development. Nevertheless, the cookie-cutter faux-Victorian cottages and landscaped gardens that now fan out from the original 1850s building provide 64 luxurious and spacious guest rooms, making it one of the larger hotels in Sonoma. High season rates start at $349–399 for the queen rooms and rise to $650–699 for the garden spa suites. All rooms are sumptuously furnished in a cottage style that makes it seem more like a luxurious B&B, and all have the usual modern conveniences for this price range. Other amenities include an outdoor pool, free DVD library, breakfast, evening cheese and wine, and the onsite steakhouse and martini bar, Saddles. Suites and cottages also come with a fireplace and decadent hydrotherapy tub. Try to avoid the rooms on the south side of the complex that overlook the neighboring high school or those bordering the street to the west.

An alternative to the big-name luxury resorts in the valley is the luxuriously appointed and fantastically Zen **Gaige House Inn** (13540 Arnold Dr., Glen Ellen, 707/935-0237 or 800/935-0237, www.gaige.com), where the serene setting is complemented by contemporary Asian-inspired furnishings, gourmet breakfasts, a big outdoor pool, and indulgent spa treatments to help soften the financial blow. The cheapest of the 23 rooms and suites in the main Victorian house start at $260 midweek and $360 weekends during the summer, and as the price increases the features include fireplaces and small private Japanese Zen gardens. The more expensive suites include fireplaces and truly indulgent bathrooms, while the Creekside rooms add a private patio overlooking the Calabazas Creek to the package. Vaulting into the next price category are stunning, Asian-minimalist spa suites added in late 2004, each with its own freestanding granite soaking tub, sliding glass walls, and contemporary furnishings. They cost from $460 per night.

Over $350

The **Ledson Hotel** (480 1st St. E. on Sonoma Plaza, Sonoma, 707/996-9779, www.ledson-hotel.com), a sibling to the Ledson Winery up the valley, made the Hot List of *Condé Nast Traveler* magazine in its first full year of operation, 2004. The Victorian-style brick building looks as old as the plaza itself, despite the fact it was built in this century. The six ornately decorated guest rooms ($350–395) are all named after previous generations of owner Steve Ledson's family, and all are on the second floor. Three have balconies looking onto the plaza, and all include just about every luxury feature possible, from state-of-the-art entertainment systems and high-speed Internet access to marble bathrooms with whirlpool tubs. Unusually for a hotel in this category, there is no dedicated reception area; guests either check in while sipping wine at the bar downstairs in the Harmony Club restaurant or slip in through a side door.

At the other end of the scale to the intimate Ledson Hotel is the 228-room **Sonoma Mission Inn** (100 Boyes Blvd., Sonoma, 707/938-9000, www.fairmont.com/sonoma), which dates from 1927 and is now owned by Fairmont Hotels. It is luxurious, even by Fairmont standards. The well-heeled are drawn by the 40,000-square-foot full-service spa, use of the exclusive Sonoma golf club next door, and one of the best (and most expensive) restaurants in the valley, Santé. Many of the rooms have tiled floors and plantation-style wooden shutters to complement their colonial-style furnishings, some have fireplaces, and they generally cost from $300 in the summer. The 60 suites, including the newest Mission suites, are priced upward of $500. Despite the exclusivity, the in-room amenities are typical of chain hotels, albeit a high-end chain.

Cottages

For a more private getaway, or for groups of more than two people, there are a lot of cottages available for rent in the valley, many owned by wineries. Although most charge an extra small fee for more than two people, they usually have full kitchens and still work out cheaper than booking multiple hotel rooms.

Even with only one or two occupants, some cottages cost less than some mid-priced hotels or B&Bs.

Some of the wineries listed earlier in this chapter that have rental properties on their grounds or nearby include **Sebastiani Vineyards & Winery** in Sonoma, the **Kaz Winery** near Kenwood, and **Landmark Vineyards** next door to Kaz. A couple of the local inns also have rental management companies, including the **Glenelly Inn,** with some 10 local cottages on its books, and the **Gaige House Inn,** which manages several local properties, including one on the **Andelssa Estate Winery** estate.

Camping

With cheap rooms at a premium in the valley and not a drop of rain falling for about five months of the year, camping starts to look attractive, especially when the campground also happens to be just 10 minutes from many wineries and a stone's throw from some of the best hiking trails in the area.

The year-round **Sugarloaf Ridge State Park** campground (2605 Adobe Canyon Rd., Kenwood) is the only one in the valley and has a lot going for it if you can stand the summer heat (it does get cooler at night). It's a somewhat typical state park campground, with a small ring road serving the 49 mostly shady sites for tents and small RVs (up to 27 feet), drinking water, restrooms, fire pits, and picnic tables.

Sites 1–11 and 26–28 back onto a small creek, across which is the start of a popular hiking trail. Most of the rest of the sites are at the foot of a hill and get the most shade, although none can be described as truly secluded. Year-round reservations can be made through www.reserveamerica.com or by calling 800/444-7275. Fees are $30 year-round.

FOOD

Sonoma's food scene has gradually been transformed over the years from rustic to more stylish, but the change has not been nearly so dramatic and universal as in some other Wine Country towns. Some high-profile chefs have been sent packing in recent years after their restaurants flopped. A foie gras eatery didn't last long, and even the Viansa Winery's once-successful Sonoma Plaza outpost, Cucina Viansa, eventually closed. Many of the most successful establishments are small and relaxed, retaining a degree of intimacy that some of their cousins in the Napa Valley seem to have lost. The key to a restaurant's longevity here seems to be honesty, modesty, and reasonable prices.

There's a strong European theme to food in the valley, but ingredients will likely be fresh and local, representing the giant produce basket that is Sonoma County. Expect to see menus change throughout the year as vegetables, fish, and meats come in and out of season. Sonoma itself offers a huge variety of places to eat, from cheap to chic, while most of the other notable restaurants are up-valley, in and around the scenic little town of Glen Ellen.

Downtown Sonoma

Ask any of the valley's winemakers where they like to eat and the list will likely include the family-owned Italian trattoria **Della Santina's** (133 E. Napa St., 707/935-0576, lunch and dinner daily, dinner entrées $12–18). The big outdoor patio and the simple Italian country food garner consistently good reviews, so reservations are usually essential despite the casual atmosphere. Prices for the pastas, daily fish, and spit-roasted meats run $10–18, and if the excellent local wine list does not satisfy, there's a $12 corkage fee, lower than the $20 charged by many other restaurants. Right next door to the restaurant is the wine bar and wine shop **Enoteca Della Santina** (127 East Napa St., 707/938-4200, Wed.–Thurs. 2–10 P.M., Fri. 2–11 P.M., Sat. noon–11 P.M., Sun. and Tues. 4–10 P.M., closed Mon.), which serves 30 Californian and international wines by the glass accompanied by appetizers at its copper-topped bar. It's a great place for a predinner drink while you wait for your table at a nearby restaurant or a late glass of port to end your day.

If a table is hard to come by at Della Santina

or you simply fancy some Thai food, right next door with an equally nice outdoor patio space is the popular **Rin's Thai** (139 E. Napa St., 707/938-1462, lunch and dinner Tues.–Sun., dinner entrées $10–14). Fresh local ingredients feature strongly in the classic Thai dishes that include curries, noodles, and Thai-style barbequed meats, and the elegant Zen interior of the old Victorian house and the pretty patio are far from the usual hole-in-the-wall atmosphere of Thai restaurants. Rin's also offers takeout and delivery (minimum $35) for those craving some gang dang (spicy red curry) or tom yum (spicy and sour soup) in their hotel rooms.

Almost opposite Della Santina is another trusted and well-loved restaurant, **Café La Haye** (140 E. Napa St., 707/935-5994, dinner Tues.–Sat., entrées $17–30). Local ingredients are the backbone of the simple yet polished dishes like house-smoked wild salmon ($8), pan-roasted Wolfe Ranch quail ($25), and a daily risotto ($18), while the wine list is dominated by smaller wineries from all over Sonoma and farther afield. The uncluttered, split-level dining room is small, so either book well in advance or be prepared to sit at the bar in front of the tiny kitchen. The café is part of La Haye Art Center, which contains studios and the work of several local artists.

◖ **The Girl & the Fig** (110 W. Spain St., 707/938-3634, www.thegirlandthefig.com, lunch and dinner daily, brunch 10 A.M.–3 P.M. Sun., dinner entrées $17–25) is somewhat of a valley institution, having moved to the Sonoma Hotel on the plaza from its previous home in Glen Ellen, spawning a cookbook and also a wine bar in its old Glen Ellen digs. The French country menu includes main courses like free-range chicken and seafood stew, Sonoma rabbit and *steak frites,* an excellent cheese menu, and delicious salads, including the signature arugula, goat cheese, pancetta, and grilled fig salad. The Thursday evening Plat du Jour menu is a bargain at $32 for three courses, or $40 including a three-wine flight or paired wines. To match the Provençal cuisine, the wine list focuses on Rhône varietals, with many from local Sonoma producers. There's not a cabernet to be

© PHILIP GOLDSMITH

Good food is never far away in Wine Country.

seen. The restaurant usually closes at 10 P.M., but a smaller brasserie menu is also offered until 11 P.M. on Friday and Saturday.

Hearty Portuguese food in rustic, Mediterranean-inspired surroundings are the hallmarks of **La Salette,** just off the plaza (452 1st St. E., Suite H, 707/938-1927, lunch and dinner daily, dinner entrées $16–26). The menu reflects Portugal's seafaring colonial history, with traditional dishes such as the Portuguese national soup, *caldo verde* ($7), complementing international influences like pan-roasted Mozambique prawns, and the filling Brazilian stew *feijoada completa.* The wine list includes a wide range of both local and Portuguese wines, plus a dozen madeiras and 19 ports.

Every Wine Country town worth its salt seems to have a restaurant started by an alum of the French Laundry in Napa Valley's Yountville. Sonoma's arrived in 2005 when the sleek **El Dorado Kitchen** (405 1st St. W., 707/996-3030, lunch and dinner daily, dinner entrées $20–30) opened in the historic namesake hotel that itself had undergone a transformative renovation. Seasonal farm-fresh fish and meat dishes are given modern twists in keeping with the sleek surroundings that make this a unique addition to the Sonoma dining scene. Many consider this one of the top restaurants in Sonoma, and executive chef Justin Everett, a former sous-chef at French Laundry, has become something of a celebrity in cooking circles. Inside the restaurant is all cool dark wood and slate minimalism, while outside by the pool the casual dining scene is more Miami than Sonoma and is one of the nicest locations for Sunday brunch in town.

It's not the best place for a relaxed dinner, but for wine, light evening food, and outstanding people-watching opportunities, the **Ledson Hotel & Harmony Lounge** (480 1st St. E., 707/996-9779, 11 A.M.–9:30 P.M. daily, $6–14) on the plaza can't be beat, with a beautifully detailed and ornate (but faux) Victorian-style dining room that spills out onto the sidewalk. Small plates of internationally inspired food, ranging from fries to dishes like tropical lobster salad and beef tenderloin carpaccio, can be washed down with Ledson wines that are available only here and at the winery itself.

Pay attention after ordering anything at the **Basque Boulangerie Café** (460 1st St. E., Sonoma, 707/935-7687, 7 A.M.–6 P.M. daily), because customer names are only called once when food is ready. The line to order often snakes out the door at lunchtime, but it usually moves fast. The wide selection of soups, salads, and sandwiches can also be bought to go, which is handy because table space inside and out is usually scarce.

There are more seating options at the colorful **Sunflower Caffe** (421 1st St. W., 707/996-6645, 7 A.M.–5 P.M. daily) across the plaza. It sells a fairly basic selection of cheap beverages and sandwiches, but the real gem is a big patio hidden down the side passageway at the back of the neighboring historic adobe home of Captain Salvador Vallejo (brother of General Vallejo), an oasis of greenery with plenty of tables.

Glen Ellen and Kenwood

The intimate and cozy **Saffron** (13648 Arnold Dr., Glen Ellen, 707/938-4844, dinner Tues.–Sat., entrées $16–25) describes its daily menu as "eclectic," but the emphasis is firmly on Sonoma with a hint of Spain. Main course options might include saffron-laced paella alongside roasted pork with winter vegetables. The wine list is certainly eclectic, with both Californian, Spanish, and other international wines together with an unusual selection of beers.

Some of the most reasonably priced food in the valley, together with free corkage all the time, can be found just down the street at **The Fig Café and Wine Bar** (13690 Arnold Dr., Glen Ellen, 707/938-2130, dinner daily, brunch weekends, dinner entrées $12–20). It is the North Valley offshoot of the popular The Girl & the Fig restaurant in Sonoma and serves up some of the same fig-accented French dishes in its colorful tiled dining room. The emphasis here is on lighter (and cheaper) food: thin-crust pizzas (including one with figs), sandwiches, and main courses like braised pot roast. The Sonoma-dominated wine list is also more compact, but markups are modest enough that you might not even decide to take advantage of the free corkage—a generous policy, but one that's slightly curious for a wine bar.

Eating outdoors right next to the vineyards is one of the attractions of the **Kenwood Restaurant and Bar** (9900 Sonoma Hwy., 707/833-6326, lunch and early dinner Wed.–Sun., dinner entrées $15–28). The simple country decor inside is pleasant enough, but the outdoor patio that's open during the summer is one of the most idyllic places to eat in this part of the valley, overlooking vineyards and surrounded by flowers. The small plates and main courses are simple and unpretentious combinations of local ingredients like goat cheese with red beets and grilled lamb chops with mushroom ravioli. The wine list is also dominated by locals and includes wines from almost every valley winery as well as the rest of Sonoma, plus a few bottles from Napa, France, and Italy for good measure.

One of the more unusual menus in this part of the world can be found at the quirky **Doce Lunas Restaurant** (8910 Sonoma Hwy., Kenwood, 707/833-4000, lunch and dinner Wed.–Sun., dinner entrées $16–21). The small menu is farm-fresh Californian with plenty of Asian and European influences, representing the heritage and globe-trotting culinary career of chef and co-owner Alex Purroy and his wife Jackie. Dishes like Nakayama Katsu can be found alongside more traditional steak au poivre and the signature dessert sticky toffee pudding. The location doubles as an antique store, creating an eclectic atmosphere that is made all the more quirky by the random plates on display as homage to the places all over the world where Alex has cooked. The four tables outside on the peaceful patio are perfect for summer evening dining.

Casual Valley Dining

Sonoma's Italian heritage is not only represented by fancy trattorias. **Mary's Pizza Shack,** founded by Italian New Yorker Mary Fazio in 1959, has been around longer than many other Sonoma restaurants and now has 15 branches throughout the North Bay. It might now be a chain, but you will at least be eating in the town where it all started. The traditional or build-your-own pizzas (starting at $12 for a medium) are consistently good, and there's a big selection of traditional pasta dishes ($11–15), including spaghetti with baseball-sized meatballs. Local branches are on the plaza (8 W. Spain St., 707/938-8300) and in Boyes Hot Springs (18636 Sonoma Hwy., 707/938-3600). Both are open for lunch and dinner daily.

Some inventive red (with tomato sauce) and white (no tomato sauce) pizzas at **The Red Grape** (529 1st St. W., Sonoma, 707/996-4103, lunch and dinner daily) include a pear, gorgonzola, and hazelnut pizza ($12), and another using local Sonoma Sausage Company meat ($12). There are plenty of less inspiring, but cheap, pizza and pasta options, and it's worth looking for a seat on the patio. The restaurant is named after a type of particularly sweet tomato.

For a monster burrito to soak up excess wine or to refuel after a long bike ride, try the roadside Mexican diner **Juanita Juanita** (19114 Arnold Dr., 707/935-3981, 11 A.M.–8 P.M. daily, entrées $6–12, cash only) on the west side of Arnold Drive just north of Sonoma. Although it isn't the cheapest Mexican food in Sonoma, it has come to be known as some of the best in this part of Sonoma County, and the ramshackle building with a patio is as colorful as the food. Choose one of the favorites listed on the menu, like the Jerk in a Blanket chicken, and you can't go wrong. Some of the food can be mind-blowingly spicy. Indeed, the menu warns: "Food isn't properly seasoned unless it's painful to eat."

With no microbreweries in this part of Sonoma, the next place to find beer is **Murphy's Irish Pub** (464 1st St., 707/935-0660, 11 A.M.–11 P.M. daily, 11 A.M.–midnight Fri.–Sat.) just off the plaza behind the Basque Boulangerie. It's one of the few places in the valley where beer trumps wine and live music, usually of the Irish variety, gets people dancing four nights a week. The food includes pub standards like fish-and-chips, shepherd's pie, and Irish stew, as well as sandwiches and a kids' menu. Nothing comes in over $18, and many dishes are under $10. Unfortunately, the pub also stays true to its Irish roots with its beer selection, which includes international favorites but little in the way of Northern Californian brews.

If you have a bear of an appetite but a bare wallet, head for the friendly, no-nonsense **Black Bear Diner** (201 W. Napa St., 707/935-6800, breakfast, lunch, and dinner daily, dinner entrées $7–17) a few blocks from the plaza. The portions are huge, from the Hungry Bear breakfast to the steaks and other comfort foods at dinner, all of which include salads and sides. The casual, fun atmosphere is family friendly too, offering entertainment for kids and discounts for seniors.

Up-valley in Kenwood, **Café Citti** (9049 Sonoma Hwy., Kenwood, 707/833-2690, lunch and early dinner daily) is a roadside cottage known for its rustic Northern Italian food, particularly the moderately priced rotisserie chicken dishes and risottos. The tasty focaccia sandwiches and pizzas also make it a popular lunch stop for winery workers in the area. Buy food for a picnic, or hang out on the patio with a tumbler of the cheap and tasty house wine.

Just south of Glen Ellen in Jack London Village you can buy gourmet soups, salads, sandwiches, and entrées at **Olive & Vine** (14301 Arnold Dr., No. 3, 707/996-9150). Owner and chef Catherine Driggers has cooked at numerous local wineries and restaurants, so don't be surprised to find luxurious picnic options like parmesan basil picnic chicken with fresh peach chutney on the seasonal menu. The cavernous room has a few tables inside, but the best place to eat is the big shady deck out back overlooking Sonoma Creek, where you might be able to pick some wild plums during summer.

Picnic Supplies

The Sonoma Valley is like one giant picnic ground. Many of the wineries have large open spaces or picnic tables, and the more adventurous can drive or hike into one of the many parks in the valley, such as the outlook above Sonoma, Jack London State Park, or up into the western hills in Sugarloaf State Park.

Many wineries now offer a limited selection of deli-style food in their visitors centers or gift stores, but some offer more than most, including the **Ledson Winery,** with its pungent selection of cheeses, and **Chateau St. Jean** in Kenwood.

Good bread can usually be found at most delis, though many places run out by lunchtime. Two bakeries supply most of the valley's bread, both centrally located. The **Basque Boulangerie Café** (460 1st St. E., Sonoma, 707/935-7687, 7 A.M.–6 P.M. daily) on the plaza sells not only sandwiches and salads to go ($5–8) but also freshly baked breads. It is one of the leading suppliers of bread to grocery stores in the area. The other big local bread supplier is **Artisan Bakers** (720 W. Napa St., 707/939-1765, 7 A.M.–4:30 P.M. Mon.–Sat.,

7 A.M.–2 P.M. Sun.), in a nondescript building about half a mile from the plaza. It also sells a picnic-worthy selection of sandwiches, salads, and pizza.

Three good cheese shops are around the plaza. On the north side is the **Sonoma Cheese Factory** (2 Spain St., 800/535-2855, 8:30 A.M.–5:30 P.M. daily), which is easy to spot: just look for the ugliest building, a brutal 1940s edifice that stands in stark contrast to the Victorian character of the rest of the plaza. It is the home of Sonoma Jack cheese and also sells other strangely flavored cheeses (which, thankfully, you can usually taste first) as well as a limited selection of salads and fancy sandwiches. A less-crowded place to buy cheese is the historic **Vella Cheese Company** (315 2nd St. E., 707/938-3232 or 800/848-0505, 9:30 A.M.–6 P.M. Mon.–Sat.), a block north of the plaza in a former brewery building. It's the latest incarnation of the cheese store opened in the 1930s by Thomas Vella.

Other places to stock up on some delicious gourmet sandwiches for well-traveled roads include the **Vineburg Deli & Grocery** (997 Napa Rd., 707/938-3306, 6 A.M.–6 P.M. daily) just south of Sonoma not far from the Gundlach Bundschu Winery. At the north end of the valley are **Olive & Vine** (14301 Arnold Dr., No. 3, 707/996-9150) and **Café Citti** (9049 Sonoma Hwy., 707/833-2690), both of which sell a big selection of picnic-ready food in addition to being great sit-down dining destinations.

Perhaps the easiest option for getting everything in one place is to visit one of the valley's excellent general grocery stores. The **Sonoma Market** (500 W. Napa St., 707/996-3411), not far from the plaza, and the **Glen Ellen Village Market** (13751 Arnold Dr., Glen Ellen, 707/996-6728) are both owned by the same partners and sell a wide variety of basics, including a decent local wine selection. Each has an extensive deli that includes hot and cold foods, sandwiches, and a salad bar. Both are open 6 A.M.–9 P.M. daily.

Fresh Produce

A well-known Californian oil producer with

ties to the Sonoma Valley, the **Figone Olive Oil Company** (9580 Sonoma Hwy., Kenwood, 707/282-9092) has been in the family olive oil business since the early 1990s and has become well known in the state's burgeoning olive oil industry. Figone's makes its own oils from olive groves in the Central Valley and Sonoma Valley and also presses oil for some other well-known oil suppliers, including winemaker Bruce Cohen here in the Sonoma Valley. The B. R. Cohen oils are sold in the tasting room along with Figone's own oils, some in hand-marked bottles. There are usually several oils to taste (for free) against a backdrop of the shiny equipment (some of it hand-me-downs from the Figone's Italian cousins) in the glass-walled olive press room.

Seasonal produce from the organic Oak Hill Farm and some fabulous freshly cut flowers are sold in an old dairy barn known simply as the **Red Barn Store** (15101 Sonoma Hwy., Glen Ellen, 707/996-6643, 10 A.M.–6 P.M. Wed.–Sun. April–Christmas), off Highway 12 just north of Madrone Road near Glen Ellen.

The Sonoma Valley's prolific farmers congregate at the **farmers market** in Depot Park, a block north of the plaza on 1st Street West, every Friday morning year-round. April–October there's an additional market in front of city hall on Tuesday evenings, 5:30 P.M.–dusk.

INFORMATION AND SERVICES

First stop for visitors to the Sonoma Valley should be the **Sonoma Valley Visitors Bureau** (453 1st St. E., Sonoma, 707/996-1090, www.sonomavalley.com, 9 A.M.–5 P.M. Mon.–Sat., 10 A.M.–5 P.M. Sun.) in the Carnegie Library building in the middle of the plaza right next to city hall and across from the Sebastiani Theatre. It publishes a free valley guide, and its staff is happy to dispense all sorts of local information for nothing more than an entry in the visitors book. There's a branch of the visitors bureau just through the gates of the Viansa Winery in Carneros.

If you're staying in the valley, be sure to pick up a copy of the **Sonoma Index-Tribune** newspaper, which has been published for more than 100 years and now comes out twice a week. It is full of local news, gossip, event information, and reviews.

For wine-related information, including events at individual wineries, check the website of the **Sonoma County Wineries Association** (www.sonomawine.com), which represents all of Sonoma's wineries, including those in the valley. The **Heart of Sonoma Valley Association** (www.heartofthevalley.com) represents only those wineries around Glen Ellen and Kenwood and organizes plenty of local events throughout the year.

Los Carneros

Replace the vineyards with grass, throw in a few more cows, and the Carneros area would probably look a lot like it did 100 years ago. *Carneros* is Spanish for sheep or ram, and grazing was the mainstay of the region for hundreds of years. In fact, it has more of a Wild West feel to it than most of the Wine Country and was home to the annual Sonoma Rodeo until 1950. These days it's car and bike racing at the Infineon Raceway that draws adrenalin addicts, but even here the area's bovine history is celebrated by the snarling

supercharged cow that sits atop the giant raceway billboard.

In addition to the grazing land that used to dominate the Carneros area, there were also fruit orchards growing every type of soft fruit. The first vineyards were thought to have been planted in the 1830s, and by the end of the 1800s the advent of the ferries and railroad had made Carneros a veritable fruit and wine basket.

Phylloxera and Prohibition wiped out the small wine industry in Carneros in the early

SOUTHERN SONOMA

LOS CARNEROS

To Napa

To Truchard Vineyards and Napa

29 121

OLD SONOMA RD

HENRY RD

DEALY LN

ARTESA VINEYARDS

FOLIO WINEMAKER'S STUDIO

THE DI ROSA PRESERVE

CARNEROS INN/ BOON FLY CAFÉ

CUTTINGS WHARF RD

SOUTH AVE

ETUDE WINES

MOORE'S LANDING

Napa River

CUVAISON

DOMAINE CARNEROS

DUHIG RD

MCKENZIE-MUELLER WINERY

ACACIA WINERY

LAS AMIGAS RD

BUCHLI STATION RD

BOUCHAINE WINERY

12 121

NICHOLSON RANCH WINERY

NAPA RD

RAMAL RD

RD

RAMAL RD

Vineburg

RAMAL RD

HOMEWOOD WINERY

BURNDALE RD

VINEBURG DELI & GROCERY

Schellville

8TH ST E

FREMONT DR

MILLERICK RD

LARSON FAMILY WINERY

ANGELO'S WINE COUNTRY DELI

CONERSTONE FESTIVAL OF GARDENS

VINTAGE AIRCRAFT COMPANY

JACUZZI FAMILY VINEYARDS

VIANSA WINERY

121

ARNOLD DR

Sonoma Creek

DENMARK ST

NAPA RD

5TH ST E

BROADWAY

12

VINEYARD INN

FRUIT BASKET

MEADOWLARK LN

CLINE CELLARS

To Glen Ellen

To Sonoma

W WATMAUGH RD

BONNESS RD

STAGE RD

GULCH RD

116

ROBLEDO FAMILY WINERY

GLORIA FERRER WINERY

To Infineon Raceway and Hwy 37

© AVALON TRAVEL

N

1 mi

1 km

0

0

CHAMPAGNE CENTRAL

The French fiercely guard the word *Champagne*, and over the last few decades they have forced much of the rest of the world to accept that a sparkling wine can only be called Champagne if it comes from the Champagne region of France, just east of Paris. Their hardest won battle was with the United States, and it wasn't until 2006 that the U.S. government agreed to prevent American wineries from using traditional French regional names like Burgundy and Champagne on their labels.

The agreement was part of broader trade talks, but there was a small catch for the French: American wineries already using the term *Champagne* on their labels could continue to use it. Most Californian wineries, however, have long stuck to the term *sparkling wine* to describe their bubbly and *méthode champenoise* to describe how it's made.

Champagne-style wines have popped up all over the world over the centuries, from the sophisticated cava wines of Spain that have been made for hundreds of years to the more recent rise of sparkling wines in California, where Carneros is the center of it all.

In the 1980s and 1990s, the world's top producers of cava and champagne saw the potential of Carneros to produce world-class sparkling wines, and many set up shop in the area. The two biggest cava makers in Spain, Freixenet and Codorníu, are represented by the Carneros wineries Gloria Ferrer and Artesa, while Domain Carneros is the American outpost of champagne house Taittinger.

The local wineries of many other big French champagne houses, including Mumm, Krug, and Moët & Chandon, might be located in the nearby Napa Valley, but all grow a large proportion of their champagne grapes in Carneros.

The cool climate of Carneros is ideally suited for growing the two most important champagne grape varietals, chardonnay and pinot noir. Brisk winds and overcast summer mornings might not be the best conditions for touring with the top down, but a taste of some crisp local champagne more than makes up for the morning chill.

1900s, and it didn't get back on its feet again until the 1960s. By then the fruit growers had moved elsewhere, and the march of the vineyards across the pastureland began.

Today, the western part of Carneros primarily resembles grazing land, and huge marshes still merge at the edge of the bay with the low-lying flatlands. Drive east and the low rolling hills are now covered with vineyards as far as the eye can see, a sign that cows will probably not return anytime soon.

The Wines

The 39,000-acre Los Carneros appellation borders San Pablo Bay and straddles the county line dividing Napa and Sonoma Counties, though the majority of its vineyards are actually on the Sonoma side of that line. Hence it's included in this chapter and not in the Napa Valley chapter, although both regions claim it as their own. The cool winds that blow off the

bay and the murky cloud cover that often takes half the morning to burn off in the summer help make this one of the coolest appellations in California, ideal for growing pinot noir, chardonnay, and other grapes with a flavor profile that makes crisp, aromatic, and well-balanced wines.

Not surprisingly, those two varietals fill 85 percent of the vineyards, but more winemakers are now discovering that very distinctive wines can be made from syrah and merlot grapes grown here. Carneros is about as cool as it can be for merlot to ripen completely, and the resulting wines have a greater structure and subtlety than their hot-climate cousins.

Despite its cool, damp appearance, Carneros actually gets less annual rainfall than any other part of Napa or Sonoma County. In addition, the fertile-looking topsoil is usually only a few feet deep and sits on top of a layer of dense cold clay that is unforgiving to vines and forces them to put more energy into producing fruit than leaves.

There are far fewer wineries in the Carneros region than its size might suggest. Its prized cool growing conditions mean that most of the vineyards seen from the road are either owned by, or sell their grapes to, wineries based outside the area. Those that are open range from international champagne houses to tiny family-owned businesses where you're more likely to experience informative (and occasionally free) tasting sessions that used to be the norm in Napa and Sonoma but are, alas, no more.

Finding some of the wineries can be a test, best taken when sober. Plenty of big white signs mark the vineyard owners, but they're of absolutely no help in actually finding a winery, so a sharp eye is needed to spot the tiny signs tied to trees and posts. Most of the bigger wineries are fairly obvious from the main road, however, and there are few back roads on which to get lost.

EASTERN CARNEROS WINERIES
Artesa Vineyards & Winery

A sure sign of how close this part of Carneros is to the Napa Valley, both geographically and culturally, is the marriage of wine, art, and design at Artesa (1345 Henry Rd., Napa, 707/224-1668, www.artesawinery.com, 10 A.M.–5 P.M. daily, tasting $10–20), an outpost of the historic Spanish sparkling wine producer Codorníu. The grass-covered winery was designed by Barcelona architect Domingo Triay to blend in with the surrounding land, and to a certain extent he succeeded: Driving up tiny Henry Road through the vineyards, the only sign of the winery's presence is that one of the low hills happens to be peculiarly square-shaped.

Art is everywhere, from the sculptures and reflecting pools around the parking lot up to the gallery-like interior of the winery, and much of it was created by the winery's artist-in-residence, Gordon Huether, who also has his own gallery in Napa. The airy tasting room has a spacious indoor seating area and large (if

breezy) patio overlooking the Carneros vineyards, and a small museum gives some history of champagne making and the Codorníu family.

Like those of most Carneros wineries, Artesa's 350 acres of vineyards are planted primarily with chardonnay and pinot noir, and the wine list reflects this. The winery also makes cabernet sauvignon, merlot, and syrah from Napa and Sonoma County grapes. Despite being owned by one of the world's great producers of cava sparkling wines, however, Artesa doesn't make any sparkling wine here, although it does offer tasting of some from Spain.

There are several tasting options in the sleek tasting room with its adjoining patio overlooking the vineyards. You can try the lower tiers of wines or the limited releases. Alternatively, a horizontal tasting of pinots from both Carneros and the Russian River Valley illustrates the subtle differences inherent to the wines from each region. Overall, however, the tasting options don't quite match the architectural and artistic scope of the winery, but tours are offered at 11 A.M. and 2 P.M. daily ($20). Perusing the art is free.

Folio Winemaker's Studio

Just down the road from the fake hill of Artesa, in a homey yet modern farmhouse, is a tasting room that can be either inspiring or intimidating, depending on your mood. Folio (1285 Dealy Ln., Napa, 707/256-2757, www.folio-winestudio.com, noon–5 P.M. Mon.–Tues., 11 A.M.–5 P.M. Fri.–Sun., tasting $10–20) is the home of no less than 35 different wines under seven different labels, all linked through some sort of family tie to the founder of Folio Fine Wine Partners, Michael Mondavi, who was long considered the less successful of the three children of famed winemaker Robert Mondavi. His son, Rob, is winemaker for many of the labels, which include one named for his wife, Isabel.

The seven different labels account for about 35,000 cases of wine per year, which might sound like a lot but is actually only an average 1,000 cases per wine. To complicate things further, however, there are three additional wine brands you can taste here that use the Folio facility to produce their "custom crush" wines. The result is a dizzying array of wines on the tasting menu, many with names that offer no clue as to their style or origins. They are organized by varietal, which might sound helpful, except it means you might end up tasting a Carneros pinot alongside one from Oregon. Be sure to question the server thoroughly before deciding which of the wines to taste. That will help ensure you're less intimidated and more inspired by one of the more diverse tasting lineups in Carneros.

If you can afford it, go for the more expensive "artisan" tasting, which includes pinots from some of the best West Coast pinot growing regions and a nice selection of old-vine zinfandels. If it's a quiet day and the weather's nice, then also be sure to make a beeline for the verandah at the back of the house through the door to the right of the main tasting bar. Piped music aside, it's a peaceful and cozy space overlooking a small secluded vineyard. Bring your own food and buy a bottle of rosé at the bar for a relaxing lunch.

◖ Domaine Carneros

The French heritage of one of California's premier champagne houses is obvious when you see the ornate château and its formal gardens on a low hill next to the main road. The Domaine Carneros estate (1240 Duhig Rd., Napa, 707/257-0101, www.domainecarneros. com, 10 A.M.–6 P.M. daily, tasting $15) was built in the style of the 18th-century Chateau de la Marquetterie, home of one of the winery's principal founders, Champagne Taittinger. The sweeping staircase leading from the parking lot and the palatial interior leave no doubt about the winery's fancy French pedigree. It all feels a little over-the-top, particularly when contrasted with the rustic, windswept Carneros landscape on a foggy day. With some sun on a less crowded day, however, it can feel almost magical. Be warned, however: Less crowded days in the middle of summer can be rare.

When it opened in 1990 it was the first Carneros winery devoted to champagne production and now produces more than 40,000 cases per year of sparkling wines, including a regular brut, brut rosé, and the flagship Le Rêve blanc de blancs that is made from 100 percent

Domaine Carneros, a taste of French glamour in Carneros

chardonnay and considered one of California's top champagnes. The most interesting sparkler, however, is the LD (late-disgorged) brut, which has an extra creaminess and crispness that comes from leaving the lees in the bottle for longer before it is disgorged, essentially slowing down the bottle-aging process.

In 2003, Domaine Carneros achieved another first when it opened the first Carneros wine-making facility dedicated to pinot noir production right behind the château. The solar-powered facility was designed to look like a carriage house to fit with the château theme. It produces about 15,000 cases of the winery's three pinot noirs. All the Domaine Carneros wines are made using grapes from the 300 acres of organically farmed vineyards around the winery.

There are three informative tours per day (11 A.M., 1 P.M., and 3 P.M.) that let visitors peer into the squeaky-clean, modern production and bottling areas after first sitting through a rather tiring PR-laden DVD presentation. At $25 per person, the tours offer the best value because they include a tasting of four wines along the way and you get to keep the tasting glass. Alternatively, one can simply chill on the huge terrace overlooking the vineyards and let the bubbles do their work, perhaps with some caviar or a cheese plate to help the wines go down. The tasting flight of three sparkling wines (including the Le Rêve flagship) or all three pinots is $15. Wines by the glass start at $6 and come with a few morsels to eat.

Cuvaison Estate

Right opposite the entrance to Domaine Carneros and its fancy French architectural excesses is the modern and minimalist home of Cuvaison (1221 Duhig Rd., Napa, 707/942-2455, www.cuvaison.com, 10 A.M.–5 P.M. daily, tasting $15), a winery that (rather ironically) takes its name from an old French term describing the part of the winemaking process that gives red wine its color. The contrast between the two neighboring wineries could not be starker: Where Domaine Carneros surrounds visitors with ornate luxury that almost

seems to enhance their luxurious sparkling wines, Cuvaison lets nature do the talking with an airy and contemporary concrete, wood, and glass indoor-outdoor tasting lounge from which you can almost reach out and touch the vines.

Also unlike its neighbor, Cuvaison is a bubble-free zone, and the portfolio of still wines here reflects the history of the winery. It was founded in the late 1960s at the northern end of Napa Valley near Calistoga (where the winery's second tasting room is located), but changed ownership in the 1970s and underwent a dramatic expansion, buying up hundreds of acres of land in Carneros, where the bulk of its estate vineyards and this tasting room are located today. In the late 1990s a prime vineyard on nearby Mount Veeder was bought, making Napa Valley cabernet as important a part of the portfolio as the Carneros-grown pinot, chardonnay, merlot, and syrah.

Although the tasting room only opened in 2009, the winemaking facility across the parking lot was up and running five years earlier, and a few years before that a new winemaker and new management arrived on the scene. By all accounts, this makeover of Cuvaison over the last decade had a big impact on the quality of the wines. The chardonnays and pinots here are as good as any in the area, particularly the pricier single-block versions, and they regularly get high ratings from the critics (chardonnay accounts for about two thirds of the winery's annual production of 60,000 cases). The syrah and merlot are also nicely made and offer a change from the usual Carneros varietals.

The real treat, however, is the Mount Veeder cabernet sauvignon, which is about as far from a fruit-bomb as a Napa cabernet can get. This is very much an Old World style of cabernet, with a balance, concentration, and structure typical of wines made from mountain-grown fruit.

Although Cuvaison advertises this tasting room as appointment-only, there's usually no problem rolling up unannounced. It's worth calling ahead if you can, however, because it can get crowded at certain times of the day.

Bouchaine Vineyards

Before turning in to the palatial grounds of Domaine Carneros, continue on Duhig Road for about a mile into the flatlands, turn left on Las Amigas Road, and then right on Buchli Station Road to get to this historic spot out on the scenic flatlands of Carneros close to the bay.

The current Bouchaine winery (1075 Buchli Station Rd., Napa, 707/252-9065, www.bouchaine.com, 10:30 A.M.–4 P.M. daily, tasting $15–30) was established in 1981, but there has been a winery on the site since 1934, when the Garetto Winery was established, and grapes were first grown here way back in 1899. Not much remains of the old winery following a 1990s renovation, although the old redwood tanks were recycled to create the sidings of some of the current buildings. The cozy tasting room is refreshingly free of Wine Country paraphernalia, and for a little more money you can taste the wines with cheese and olives on the veranda overlooking the vineyards with San Pablo Bay in the distance.

The winery's picnic area, however, is reserved for its club members and those who preorder a "Table for Two" picnic lunch, which includes a wine tasting, freshly prepared food, and a bottle of wine. At $75 for two people, it's as good a way to have lunch as any in Carneros, particularly if the sun is out. The lunch option is offered May–October and must be booked at least a day in advance. Bouchaine is also a popular stop for bikers who relish the quiet, straight, and flat roads of the area.

Bouchaine grows pinot noir, chardonnay, and a small amount of pinot gris in its 90 acres of Carneros vineyards and also sources grapes from neighboring vineyards for the 30,000 cases of wine produced annually. Pinot noir and chardonnay account for much of the production and include the pricey estate versions, blends from multiple Carneros vineyards, and some limited-production Bacchus Collection wines. The cheaper Buchli Station–labeled wines are generally not sourced from the Carneros region, however.

The estate wines are certainly good, but some of the more interesting wines are in the Bacchus Collection. They include the popular Chene d'Argent, a crisp and fruity chardonnay made with no oak contact at all, and a light, flowery pinot meunier, a varietal that is normally used as a blending grape in champagne production. There's also a spicy syrah sourced from northern Sonoma vineyards and a good gewürztraminer from Mendocino's Anderson Valley.

The appointment-only tour of the winery is worth taking just to see the old concrete open-top fermenters that are used instead of more modern stainless steel to ferment the pinot noirs.

Homewood Winery

Just a mile or so from the grandeur and glitz of Domaine Carneros, halfway down tiny Burndale Road, is the down-home atmosphere of Homewood Winery (23120 Burndale Rd., Sonoma, 707/996-6353, www.homewood-winery.com, 10 A.M.–4 P.M. daily, free tasting), where owner and winemaker Dave Homewood produces just 3,000 cases of reasonably priced wines from grapes he buys all over Napa, Sonoma, and often far beyond. A couple of acres of pinot noir right outside the tasting room were recent additions and started producing wines for the 2005 vintage.

The focus here is on small batches of a variety of mainly red wines like zinfandel, merlot, syrah, and bordeaux-style red blends sourced from vineyards elsewhere in Sonoma and Napa. There are also some excellent Napa and Carneros chardonnays available, and a couple of bottlings of pinot noir sourced from a neighboring Carneros vineyard. Most wines are very reasonably priced, with the best bang for the buck being the Flying Whizzbangers, a zinfandel-dominated red blend.

The staff will happily spend an hour or more with visitors in the tiny tasting room explaining the wines, conducting some vertical tastings, and teaching some tasting tricks, like how to identify the oak used in the barrels. That is, if no big groups arrive; otherwise the small indoor tasting area can quickly get claustrophobic, and it's best to spill out onto the back porch "lounge" if it's open. Be sure to check out the olive oils also sold at the winery.

Wineries by Appointment

Tucked away off the well-beaten path of the Carneros Highway are some notable appointment-only wineries that give more opportunities to discover some hot wines from the cool Carneros region.

The **McKenzie-Mueller** winery (2530 Las Amigas Rd., Napa, 707/252-0186, www.mckenziemueller.com) is the family-run operation of Napa Valley wine veterans Bob and Karen Mueller. From their 50 acres of estate vineyards they produce only 2,500 cases of wine, encompassing many varietals, including merlot, pinot noir, and cabernet sauvignon. Standouts include a steel-fermented pinot grigio and an aromatic cabernet franc, which is made with fruit from both Carneros and Napa Valley's Oak Knoll appellation. A large proportion of the vineyard grapes are sold to other wineries. The winery is on Las Amigas Road at the junction with Buchli Road, just up the road from Bouchaine.

Just down Las Amigas Road from McKenzie-Mueller is **Acacia Vineyard** (2750 Las Amigas Rd., Napa, 707/226-9991 or 877/226-1700, www.acaciavineyard.com, by appointment 10 A.M.–4 P.M. Mon.–Sat., noon–4 P.M. Sun.), a much larger winery that has produced pinot and chardonnay wines since 1979 and now owns 150 acres of local vineyards. The rather inelegantly named but powerful-tasting Marsh chardonnay is worth buying just for the fact that proceeds support the restoration of the nearby Napa-Sonoma Marsh. Acacia is on Las Amigas Road near the junction with Duhig Road.

At the eastern end of Carneros close to Napa is **Etude Wines** (1250 Cuttings Wharf Rd., Napa, 707/257-5300, www.etudewines.com), which is well known for its refined but pricey Carneros pinot noir. It also produces pinot blanc and pinot gris from local Carneros vineyards together with some Napa Valley merlot

and cabernet. The winery is owned by the multinational Fosters Wine Estates and offers tastings by appointment 10 A.M.–4:30 P.M. daily.

The highly acclaimed wines made by **Truchard Vineyards** (3234 Old Sonoma Rd., Napa, 707/253-7153, www.truchardvineyards.com) come from its huge 270-acre Carneros vineyard, where 10 varietals are grown, including cabernet, tempranillo, and zinfandel grapes that reflect the vineyard's location near the border with the warmer Napa Valley. Truchard sell most of its estate grapes to other wineries, using around 20 percent to make its 15,000 cases of premium limited-release wines, the best of which are the elegant syrah and pinot noir. A tour and $15 tasting also provides the chance to see the winery's 100-year-old barn.

WESTERN CARNEROS WINERIES
Nicholson Ranch

Though just outside the Los Carneros appellation boundary by literally a few yards (it's technically in the Sonoma Valley appellation), the mission-style Nicholson Ranch winery (4200 Napa Rd., Sonoma, 707/938-8822, www.nicholsonranch.com, 10 A.M.–6 P.M. daily, tasting $10) is perched on a small hill above the intersection of the Carneros Highway and Napa Road, putting it on the route of most visitors to Carneros or anyone heading to or from Napa beyond.

The winery, opened in 2003, was built by the Nicholson family on land where Socrates Nicholson, a first-generation Greek immigrant, had spent decades raising the other major Carneros agricultural product: cows. His daughter and her husband are the brains behind the winery, and dotted around the hillsides are Greek flourishes that hint at the family's heritage, including a small temple near the visitor parking lot.

Nicholson Ranch is predominantly a pinot and chardonnay producer, and those two varietals account for much of the 10,000 cases of wine made each year. The chardonnays, and in particular the flagship Cuvée Natalie, garner some good reviews from critics, and bottle

© PHILIP GOLDSMITH

A roadside sign in Carneros extols the virtues of the humble grape.

prices are generally reasonable. The winery also makes small quantities of syrah and merlot from local vineyards, both of which exhibit the classic aromas and restraint of cool-climate wines. Tasting is $10, but you can usually sample two or three vintages of some of the five chardonnays and four pinot noirs available, all worth trying. For just $5 more, you can take an appointment-only tour of the winery caves and winemaking facilities with a couple of extra tastes thrown in along the way.

The bright and spacious tasting room oozes sophistication, with limestone floors and a cherrywood central tasting bar topped with granite. Cheap gifts are nowhere to be seen, but a modest selection of picnic supplies are sold, including a cheese plate that can be paired with one of the half bottles of chardonnay available to create a nice lunch for two. There are tables on the veranda overlooking the surrounding hills and a grassy area next to the pond for those days when the weather's cooperating. The tasting room is open later than most in the area, even in winter, so those on a hectic schedule should make this their last winery of the day.

Larson Family Winery

To get to this historic patch of land, you must turn off Highway 121 and head towards the wetlands, down a small country road almost as far as dry land will take you. Only the whimsical, hand-painted signs along the way suggest there's civilization at the end of the road. The Larson Family Winery (23355 Millerick Rd., Sonoma, 707/938-3031, www.larsonfamilywinery.com, 10 A.M.–5 P.M. daily, tasting $5) is situated next to Sonoma Creek at the edge of the San Pablo Bay, near what was once call Wingo, where steamships from San Francisco docked in the mid-1800s and disgorged their Sonoma-bound passengers. It's a pretty part of the world, but being surrounded by wetlands has its disadvantages. The area is prone to flooding during winter rains, and summer days can be a bit chilly this close to the water.

A 100-acre plot of land and farmhouse were bought in 1899 by Michael Millerick, the great-grandfather of winery owner Tom Larson. The Millerick Ranch found local fame for decades as the site of the Sonoma Rodeo until, in the

1970s, it succumbed to the steady advance of vineyards across Carneros.

The Larson family has been a big player in the Carneros wine scene ever since. The Larson Family Winery rose, phoenix-like, from the financial ashes of the Sonoma Creek Winery, which filed for bankruptcy in 2003 some 25 years after it was formed by Tom and his father. The Sonoma Creek brand and inventory was eventually sold and the creditors paid off, leaving Tom Larson free to start on his latest winemaking venture.

Today, the winery produces about 4,000 cases of wine from its 70 acres of Carneros vineyards, as well as a far larger amount under contract for the new owners of the Sonoma Creek brand. Despite the relatively small production of Larson wines, the portfolio is large and dominated by cool-climate Carneros wines including pinot noir, barrel-aged chardonnay, and a gewürztraminer. Standouts among the reds include an unusual (and cheap) house blend of cabernet, merlot, and pinot noir, a petite sirah made using fruit from both Sonoma and Amador County in the warm Sierra foothills, and an award-winning estate cabernet sauvignon, which is one of the only wines sealed with a cork rather than cheaper screw-caps. The small production does mean that some wines might be sold out by late summer, however.

You won't find Larson wines on many reviewers' lists, but part of the fun of visiting here is the unique location and the down-home family-farm atmosphere that'll be a hit with kids and provide a refreshing contrast to the fancier wineries all around. The winery tasting room is in an old redwood barn with a small enclosure of goats and sheep right opposite and usually a couple of the winery dogs, Pete, Bubba and Sonny, lounging nearby. You might also be lucky enough to see the pet llama.

There's also a regulation-sized boccie ball court and a grassy picnic and play area behind the tasting room to enjoy a bite to eat with a bottle of Larson's Wingo White, a tantalizing blend of chardonnay, sauvignon blanc, and gewürztraminer. Jeep tours of the surrounding vineyards and wetlands are also sometimes available through an unaffiliated company—just look for the bright green Jeep in the parking lot.

Cline Cellars

Originally established across the bay in Contra Costa County, Cline (24737 Hwy. 121, Sonoma, 707/940-4000 or 800/546-2070, www.clinecellars.com, 10 A.M.–6 P.M. daily, free tasting) has come to thrive in southern Sonoma much like the lush, spring-fed garden oasis it calls home. The winery moved here in 1991 and brought its East Bay emphasis on Rhône varietals, planting syrah, viognier, marsanne, and roussanne instead of the more usual Carneros varietals, pinot noir and chardonnay. Cline is now one of Sonoma's biggest makers of Rhône-style wines and produces about 200,000 cases of wine a year from vineyards all over the Bay Area.

Despite being a relatively new member of the winery set in Carneros, Cline sits on some historic land. The tasting room is in a modest farmhouse with wraparound porch that dates from 1850. It sits on land that was once the site of a Miwok Indian village and later used by Father Altimira as a forward camp while investigating a site for what would become the Sonoma mission. Natural springs feed the three ponds and help sustain the giant willow trees, magnolias, and colorful flower beds surrounding small patches of lawn that are ideal for picnics. The tasting room contains a small deli, and the wines include several picnic-friendly options, including a light and fruity blend of chardonnay and pinot grigio and a dry mourvèdre rosé.

The winery's colorful history comes alive in the three tours offered daily at 11 A.M., 1 P.M., and 3 P.M. Celebrating the site's history as a temporary Spanish mission, the California Missions Museum is located in a barn right behind the tasting room and displays intricately detailed scale models of every single Californian Mission, from the first in San Diego to the last just north of here in Sonoma. They were created by two German cabinetmakers for the 1939 World's Fair in San Francisco and all bought by the Cline family in 1998 to keep the collection together.

SOUTHERN SONOMA

The wines are a pleasant change from the Carneros staples of pinot and chardonnay, and most are pleasantly priced at $20 or less. Standouts among the whites include a full-bodied yet dry blend of marsanne and roussanne, two traditional varietals from France's Rhône region, and the fun, fruity chardonnay–pinot grigio blend. All the red Rhône varietals sourced from Cline's East Bay vineyards are worth tasting, particularly the Cashmere, a velvety blend of grenache, mourvèdre, and syrah; a bright and flavorful carignane; and a dark, brooding mourvèdre. The Sonoma wines include some nice examples of cool-climate syrah and zinfandel, the best of which are the single-vineyard versions that cost $1 each to taste.

Jacuzzi Family Vineyards

Right across the road from Cline Cellars is another Cline family venture in the form of a giant Tuscan farmhouse, an homage to the family's Italian heritage. Jacuzzi Family Vineyards (24737 Arnold Dr., Sonoma, 707/940-4031, www.jacuzziwines.com, 10 A.M.–5:30 P.M. daily, free tasting) was opened in mid-2007 and is modeled after the Jacuzzi family home in Italy—the same Jacuzzi family that invented the eponymous bubbling bathtubs. In that sense it could be considered as another Carneros producer of bubbly.

Valeriano Jacuzzi, the grandfather of Fred Cline, immigrated to the United States in 1907 and eventually found his way to California, where he established an aeronautical engineering firm with his brothers—hence the giant airplane propeller on display in the main courtyard. Over the decades, that same company went from making aircraft to water pumps and filters, and eventually invented various hydrotherapy devices that morphed into the prototype Jacuzzi bathtubs in the 1960s. During the Depression, Valeriano also planted a vineyard in Contra Costa County, the same vineyard that is the source of Cline's Ancient Vine Rhône varietals today.

The Cline connection with Jacuzzi is not heavily publicized at the winery (and neither is the Jacuzzi connection to bathtubs), but Jacuzzi-label wines were being made for several

years before the winery opened and are sourced from Cline family vineyards across Sonoma. They include the classic Italian varietals nebbiolo, primitivo, and pinot grigio as well as the more common varietals in this part of the world like chardonnay, pinot noir, and merlot. The flagship red wine is named after Valeriano and is the winery's version of a super-Tuscan blend, albeit one incorporating the rather unusual combination of cabernet, malbec, barbera, and merlot. The flagship white is named after Valeriano's wife, Giuseppina, and is a mellow example of a Carneros chardonnay.

Jacuzzi is also the new home of Sonoma olive oil producer **The Olive Press** (www.theolive-press.com), which used to be based up in Glen Ellen. Its small tasting room is on the right as you enter the winery (for wine, turn left) and is the place to discover that olive oils can be as diverse in taste as wines. A small tasting bar usually features oils ranging from a light and grassy taste up to a rich, mellow one, with flavors generally determined by the olives used and where they're grown (sound similar to wine-grape lore?). The Olive Press is also a functioning production center, processing olives from growers across Northern California, and it sells a full range of oil-related gifts, from cookbooks and oil containers to soaps.

From a distance, the giant stone structure surrounded by lush gardens containing mature fig and olive trees looks distinctly marooned on the windswept Carneros flats. Up close, however, the imposing building with its huge courtyard overlooking the wetlands is impressive and another example of just how much money is sloshing around this part of the Wine Country. Thankfully visitors will not have to slosh around much of their own money, because tasting is free, although that could change once the winery becomes better known and a regular stop for tour buses. Some parts of the winery were still being completed as this edition went to press, so check the website for information about tours.

Robledo Family Winery

If you ever wondered about the fate of the laborers who hand-pick the grapes throughout the Wine Country, a visit to this winery will provide one answer. In the 1970s, Mexican immigrant Reynaldo Robledo was one of those laborers working in local vineyards, a job that was the beginning of his path to realizing the American Dream. He eventually formed a successful vineyard management company and finally created his dream winery, making his first commercial vintage in 1998.

The Robledo Family winery (21901 Bonness Rd., Sonoma, 707/939-6903, www.robledofamilywinery.com, by appointment 10 A.M.–5 P.M. Mon.–Sat., 11 A.M.–4 P.M. Sun., tasting $5–10) is a low-key affair down a sleepy, semirural residential street off Highway 116 (Arnold Drive) just north of the busy junction with Highway 121. Despite the lack of architectural flourishes of the big wineries nearby, the small tasting area with a giant oak communal table at its center is located in the barrel room, providing a wonderfully cool and intimate atmosphere in which to sample the wines surrounded by towering racks of barrels. You're also likely to be served by one of the Robledo family, so be sure to ask about the story of Reynaldo.

Grapes for the merlot, pinot noir, and chardonnay come from Robledo's three separate estate vineyards in Carneros, totaling 30 acres. There's also the chance to try cabernet sauvignon and sauvignon blanc from Robledo's Oak Ranch vineyard in the much warmer Lake County region north of the Napa Valley—not wines that are often found on tasting menus in this part of the world. Production is about 20,000 cases a year, making this a small winery by local standards but fairly large considering its family roots.

Gloria Ferrer

At one end of Carneros is Artesa, the California outpost of one of the giants of cava production in Spain. At the other end is Gloria Ferrer (23555 Carneros Hwy., Sonoma, 707/933-1917, www.gloriaferrer.com, 10 A.M.–5 P.M. daily), representing the other global Spanish bubbly producer, Freixenet, now the largest sparkling wine producer in the world. The fact that both these Spanish companies joined the largest French champagne houses in Carneros

over the years is simply further testament to the ideal growing conditions here for the chardonnay and pinot noir grapes used to make classic sparkling wines.

Gloria is the wife of José Ferrer, latest in a long line of Ferrers to have made Spanish champagnes, and they opened their little piece of Spain here in 1986. The winery is styled much like a Spanish farmhouse, with stucco walls, tiled floors, and a large terrace that has sweeping views south over San Pablo Bay and far beyond. It can get crowded, but if you can snag a terrace table and it's not too foggy, there are few better places in Carneros to enjoy an early evening aperitif.

It now has the largest selection of champagnes in Carneros, priced from a modest $20 for the classic Brut or lively and aromatic Va de Vi up to $50 for the flagship Carneros Cuvée in a distinctly curvaceous bottle that matches its smooth elegance. In addition to the champagnes, the winery also makes an increasing quantity of still wines. There are four pinot noirs, including several highly regarded single-vineyard versions, as well as several chardonnays and small quantities of both syrah and merlot. In all, more than 100,000 cases of wine are now made here from almost 400 acres of Carneros vineyards.

The informative daily tours ($10) take in the long, cool cellars in the hillside behind the winery and are as good a lesson in how to make champagne as you'll find at any other sparkling wine producer (call for times). Alternatively you can relax on the terrace with your choice of wine. The set up is more wine bar than tasting room— buy a glass of champagne, prices of which range $5–10 per glass, or taste the still wines in generous two-ounce pours for $2–3 each.

The visitors center shop is not only the place to buy wines but also to pick up all sorts of edibles, from picnic supplies and Spanish cooking ingredients to cookbooks and striking, pop art–inspired posters for some of the wines. You can also bring your own food, although you'll have to buy some wine if you want to eat it here and be happy sitting at a table—the only patch of picnic-worthy grass is essentially in the parking lot next to the entrance steps, a hectic position likely to give you indigestion.

Viansa Winery & Italian Marketplace

When a family dispute forced Sam Sebastiani out of his family's historic winery in Sonoma in the mid-1980s, he and wife, Vicki, founded their own operation down in Carneros and used a contraction of their own names (Vicki and Sam) to christen it. The Viansa winery (25200 Arnold Dr., Sonoma, 800/995-4740, www.viansa. com, 10 A.M.–5 P.M. daily, tasting $5–10) and its pretty gardens are perched on a windswept knoll overlooking the wetlands of Carneros, and the Italian heritage of its founders is obvious from the Tuscan-style architecture of the terra-cotta–roofed villa and from the 55,000 cases of Cal-Ital wines made there each year.

Although the winery was sold in 2004 shortly after Sam and Vicki divorced and the new owners have struggled, Viansa remains as popular as ever, with its 15,000 dedicated wine club members swallowing up much of the wine production and the giant parking lot regularly filled to overflowing with cars and tour buses.

Tuscan themes abound at Viansa Winery & Italian Marketplace.

© PHILIP GOLDSMITH

Cabernet sauvignon, merlot, and chardonnay are about the only non-Italian wines you'll find here. The long tasting menu is instead filled with red Italian varietals like sangiovese, barbera, dolcetto, nebbiolo, and freisa, and whites including pinot grigio, arneis, and vernaccia. Most of those grapes are grown in Viansa's own estate vineyards and elsewhere in Sonoma.

If you've never heard of most of those grapes, the $5 tasting of four wines will be a good introduction. The premier tasting option ($10) includes reserve cabernet sauvignon and the Samuele cabernet franc, named for the founder of the Sebastiani wine-making heritage in Sonoma.

As your mouth waters from the crisp, food-friendly reds and whites, the vast array of deli foods also sold in the tasting room will seem all the more appealing. (As it is such a popular destination for busloads of visitors, however, you might end up feeling more like a Mediterranean sardine yourself.) Many of the wines are also a perfect accompaniment (and price) for a picnic, and you can buy most by the glass from the tasting bar.

The neighboring 90-acre wetlands built by Viansa with the bay in the distance make a fine view from the numerous picnic tables on the long terrace, marred only by the constant drone of traffic and the sometimes-brisk winds. In the spring (Feb.–May), two-hour **wetland tours** are offered every other Sunday for $15, or for $25 with lunch. Call the winery for more details and reservations. Tours of the winery itself are offered twice a day at 11 A.M. and 2 P.M. and are free with the $5 tasting fee.

MacRostie Winery & Vineyards

Just south of Sonoma, MacRostie (21481 8th St. E., Sonoma, 707/996-4480, www. macrostiewinery.com) makes 20,000 cases of highly regarded and elegantly understated chardonnay, pinot noir, and syrah from vineyards all over Carneros, including Steve MacRostie's own local Wildcat Mountain vineyard, a windswept hillside that he first planted in 1998. The winery is open for tastings 11 A.M.–4:30 P.M. Saturday, or call for an appointment Monday–Friday.

SIGHTS
◖ The di Rosa Preserve

When writer Rene di Rosa sought rural tranquility in 1960 and bought some old grazing land in Carneros, locals might have thought they were as likely to see cows walking on water as the eventual creation of the biggest collection of Northern Californian contemporary art and one of the largest regional art collections in the country. Thirty years later, they saw both.

The di Rosa Preserve (5200 Carneros Hwy./Hwy. 121, Napa, 707/226-5991, www.dirosaart.org) opened to the public in 1997 and now has more than 2,000 works on display throughout its 217 acres, including a colorful cow that has floated on the 35-acre lake since 1989, although it occasionally tips over.

When he bought the land, di Rosa restored a turreted former winery building as his residence and eventually planted 250 acres of vineyards on the land where grapes were once grown until disease and Prohibition killed the wine industry. The art first came from local artists, often through barter arrangements, and di Rosa eventually sold off the vineyards to focus purely on his passion for collecting art.

The Winery Lake vineyards are now owned by Sterling Vineyards (the Winery Lake name can be seen on some of Sterling's premium merlot, pinot noir, and chardonnay wines), and the old winery building is now one of the four indoor galleries on the grounds of the preserve.

Di Rosa himself lives in an apartment above the neighboring tractor shed and still actively collects art from up-and-coming artists all over the Bay Area to add to the huge collection of works that date from the 1950s. Visiting the preserve is to enter an eclectic, artistic wonderland, where giant sculptures march up into the hills, a car hangs from a tree, and every indoor space is crammed with photographs, paintings, and video installations of sometimes mind-bending strangeness. Even nature seems to do its part to maintain the sense of whimsy as the preserve's 85 peacocks (including two albinos) strut, screech, and occasionally crashland around the galleries.

Don't expect labels to help make sense of the art because there are none, just a numbered catalog in each gallery. This is to ensure viewers approach each piece with no preconceptions. The only aspects that tie everything together are the Bay Area and di Rosa's love of maximal art over minimal. "The Bay Area is the pond in which I fish," he says. "The artists I like use the familiar as a hook to lead you into new realms. The best artists are like shamans who can take us to deeper truths."

The preserve is on the north side of the Carneros Highway (Highway 121) almost opposite the Domaine Carneros winery. Look for the two-dimensional sheep on the hillside. There are three tours you can take to see some or all of the collection, but they are only offered Wednesday–Saturday, so plan accordingly. You might be able to sign up for one of the tours on the day, but chances are you'll need a reservation, especially on Saturday. The one-hour introductory tour ($10) covers the main gallery and residence at 11 A.M. all year and additionally at noon during the summer. The 2.5-hour Discovery Tour (2 P.M. Wed.–Sat. year-round and also at 10 A.M. Wed.–Sat. summer, $15) is similar to the introductory tour but gives visitors more time to peruse the art and sculptures in the main galley, house, and surrounding lawns. The 2.5-hour Art & Meadow Tour ($15) takes in the main gallery and the acres of gardens teeming with sculptures but is only offered on Saturday at 10 A.M. during the summer months. For reservations call 707/226-5991 or visit www.dirosaart.org.

Some key pieces from the collection are on display at the Gatehouse Gallery, which can be visited free and without a reservation 9:30 A.M.–3 P.M. Wednesday–Friday and is still worth the time if you cannot get on a tour.

Cornerstone Sonoma

It's hard to classify this sprawling collection of shops, studios, cafés, tasting rooms, and gardens, but Cornerstone Sonoma (23570 Arnold Dr., Sonoma, 707/933-3010, www.cornerstonegardens.com, 10 A.M.–5 P.M. daily summer, gardens 10 A.M.–4 P.M. daily summer) should certainly be on the list of any architecture or gardening enthusiast. The centerpiece of Cornerstone is a nine-acre plot of land that's a showcase for several dozen well-known landscape architects, each of whom designed and planted separate plots. The result is a fascinating blend of traditional and contemporary gardens that make art and sculpture out of plants. Sadly the giant Monterey pine tree covered in blue plastic balls by Claude Cormier, which for years stood like a giant advertisement for Cornerstone, had to be removed before it fell down, but it has since been replaced by a smaller ball-covered tree. Tickets and a map for a self-guided tour of the gardens cost $9, but the price drops to $4 December–mid-March, when it's more often than not likely to rain.

To get to the entrance to the gardens, you have to navigate through an ever-growing collection of fancy shops, restaurants, and most recently, tasting rooms. The growing retail presence is no doubt a necessary moneymaker, and the landscaped outdoor spaces along with some unique shops make it far more pleasant than your average Wine Country retail experience. The downside is that it sometimes feels more like a crowded shopping center than a celebration of the outdoors, particularly if several tour buses have just disgorged their hungry passengers in search of sustenance.

The **Sonoma Valley Visitors Bureau** has a useful outpost here and is a first stop for many visitors to the region. **Sage Fine Foods & Provisions** is one of the best places in Carneros to pick up picnic supplies and sandwiches, and it also has a few tables inside and outside in the shade that can be relaxing if it's a fairly quiet day. The most fascinating of the shops and studios include **Artefact Design & Salvage,** which sells antiques and whimsical home and garden accessories made from salvaged materials (bar stools with a giant railroad springs in place of legs, for example) and **A New Leaf Gallery,** which is the showcase for some diverse sculptures from dozens of international artists.

In the last few years, tasting rooms have also found homes here. The current winery tenants include the irreverent **Roshambo,** tucked away around the corner from the entrance. This is currently the only place to sample Roshambo's broad selection of wines since it was forced to sell its contemporary Russian River Valley winery in late 2006 after overreaching with an ambitious expansion. A new winery is planned in the Dry Creek Valley, but as of press time there was no news about when it might open. Next to the visitors center is the often-packed tasting room of the **Larson Family Winery.** If you have the time, however, it's more enjoyable to visit the Larson Family's actual winery just a 10-minute drive away. Almost opposite the Larson outpost is the cavernous, contemporary space of the **Grange Sonoma** tasting room collective, which features wines from six Sonoma boutique wineries (Wed.–Mon., tasting $10). The sheer scale and starkness of the interior can feel a little unnerving if you're the only visitor, but there is some warmth to be found in the friendliness of the proprietor and staff, and in the sun at one of the outside tables near the entrance.

EVENTS

Both big and small wineries open their doors during the **April in Carneros** event, usually held on the third weekend in April. Just visit one of the participating wineries for a ticket ($40), which gets you a glass and access to special tastings and events at all the other wineries, including many that are not usually open to the public. Later in the year there's a similar event called **Holiday in Carneros,** usually held on the weekend before Thanksgiving. For a list of wineries and more information about the events, visit www.carneroswineries.org.

RECREATION
Infineon Raceway

Sleepy Carneros is the unlikely setting for one of the busiest racetracks in the country, the Infineon Raceway (29355 Arnold Dr., Sonoma, 800/870-7223), which usually has some sort of motorized vehicle racing round its two miles of track 340 days of the year. Born in 1968 as the Sears Point Raceway and rechristened in 2002 after San Jose–based Infineon Technologies bought the naming rights, the track is now part of the circuit for major national motor-sport events, including **NASCAR** in June (when the area is choked with traffic and best avoided in the late afternoon, when everyone leaves). It is also home to more than 70 motor-sport companies, from racing teams to parts suppliers.

The raceway is on the way from San Francisco at the turnoff for Sonoma and Napa, hidden behind the hill at the intersection of Highways 37 and 121. It's not hard to find—just watch for the turbo-charged cow atop the giant raceway billboard at the junction. The entrance is a few hundred yards north on Highway 121. A full list of events at the raceway can be found on their website (www.infineonraceway.com).

Those who prefer a more hands-on approach to motor-sports can try out the track through the **Russell Racing School** (800/733-0345, www.espnrussellracing.com), which is based at the raceway and offers driving, go-karting, and racing courses, most starting at about $500 for the day. Anyone worried about missing out on the Wine Country experience can buy a pricey Speed and Spa multiday package that includes racing instruction, a local hotel room, and spa services to soak out the smell of burned rubber.

Tubbs Island

When the tide comes in, large swaths of lower Carneros disappear underwater, so it's not surprising that the only hike in the area is through the wetlands at Tubbs Island, part of the San Pablo Bay National Wildlife Refuge. The path is on solid ground, so waders are not required, but it does get muddy in the winter. The eight-mile loop, open to hikers and bikers, is a dirt road that runs through farmland before reaching the edge of the bay and marshes.

It offers little in the way of memorable scenery or strenuous exercise, so the main reason to go is for the wildlife. Legions of migrating wetland birds call the tidal marshes home, particularly in the cold and wet winter months. Even in the slightly warmer summer months there are hawks, pelicans, and plenty of other interesting critters to see, including several endangered species, making the often bracing wind worth enduring.

The Tubbs Island gravel parking lot, where the trail begins, is on the south side of Highway 37, about 0.5 miles past the traffic lights at the junction with Highway 121 to Sonoma. Leaving the parking lot, you have to drive east almost all the way to Vallejo before you can turn around, so plan accordingly. For more information on the refuge, its wildlife, and the ongoing restoration projects, contact the Vallejo headquarters of the San Pablo Bay National Wildlife Refuge at 707/769-4200.

Flying

Elsewhere in the Wine Country, balloons might be the traditional way to see Wine Country from above, but Carneros has an altogether more adventurous way to take to the air. The **Vintage Aircraft Company** (23982 Arnold Dr., 707/938-2444, www.vintageaircraft.com, Thurs.–Mon.) offers rides in its fascinating collection of old planes, which include biplanes and a World War II–era training aircraft.

Simply pick your adrenaline level for the biplane flights, and the FAA-certified pilots can oblige. For a modest rush pick the 20-minute Scenic ride over the vineyards and mountains of the Sonoma Valley ($175, $270 for two people) or double the flying time (and price) for a trip out to the ocean. To really get the adrenaline pumping, try the Aerobatic ride with a few loops and rolls thrown in for fun for an additional $50. Longer trips of 35–40 minutes are also offered, with or without aerobatics, down to San Francisco, over the Napa Valley, or to the Pacific coast, starting at $300. Appointments are usually needed for the flight, but on weekends you might get lucky just by walking in.

The Vintage Aircraft Company's home is the Sonoma Country Airport, a thriving base for vintage aircraft restoration and flights. You'll probably see an old plane or two parked close to the Carneros Highway as you drive by.

ACCOMMODATIONS

As the drive through the endless vineyards and fields of Carneros might suggest, there's not much in the way of lodging in this part of Wine Country. Carneros thinks of Sonoma as its main

© PHILIP GOLDSMITH

Experience a different kind of barrel (roll) in one of the the Vintage Aircraft Company's old planes.

town, and that's where most of the "local" hotels can be found. There are, however, a couple of options at opposite ends of the price spectrum for those looking for either an out-of-the-way bargain or some out-of-this-world luxury.

$100-200

The recently refurbished **Vineyard Inn** (23000 Arnold Dr., Sonoma, 707/938-2350 or 800/359-4667, www.vineyardinnsonoma.com) is one of the best values in southern Sonoma. The Spanish-style former motel has 17 modern and comfortable rooms that cost from $159 per night just minutes from some of the biggest wineries in Carneros. The standard queen rooms are the cheapest, and the list of standard amenities includes private baths, satellite television, wireless Internet access, air-conditioning, breakfast, and use of the very small outdoor pool. The vineyard rooms in separate bungalows start at $249 midweek and have more space and additional features that include DVD players and fireplaces. Some rooms also have Jacuzzi tubs. There are also a handful of two-room suites and deluxe rooms starting at $269. One drawback is the inn's location at one of the busiest intersections

in Carneros, which makes some of the cheaper rooms at the front of the building a bit noisy. Other than the constant traffic and a gas station opposite, there's not much else around, so you'll have to drive to dinner; Sonoma plaza is only about 10 minutes away.

Over $200

The **Carneros Inn** (4048 Sonoma Hwy., Napa, 707/299-4900, www.thecarnerosinn. com) is a new development of 86 individual cottages surrounded by vineyards at the eastern end of Carneros, providing a dose of contemporary luxury on a 27-acre site that used to be a trailer park. As you drive past the place on the Sonoma-Napa Highway (U.S. 121), the tall, stark walls resemble those of a prison, but on the other side of those walls is a luxury planned community with its own manicured streets, a town square, and some privately owned three-bedroom houses that share the spa, infinity pool, vineyard views, and other amenities with the resort cottages. Not surprisingly, there's a hefty price to pay in the Wine Country for a personal cottage that's bigger than some apartments and boasts cherrywood floors, a plasma TV, a fireplace, an alfresco shower, and a private garden. The cheapest places start at $480 per night. The price rockets past $600 for a vineyard view and up to almost four figures for the 10 walled compounds they call suites. The popularity of the place also means that rates change very little with the seasons, although you might find some special deals in winter. One of the on-site restaurants is the highly regarded and remarkably cheap (for the inn, at least) Boon Fly Café, serving breakfasts that will make you feel instantly at home. The inn is only about a 10-minute drive from downtown Napa or Sonoma, but the often cool and breezy Carneros weather can make the cottage fireplaces and down comforters essential features even in the middle of summer.

FOOD

The bright red exterior of the 🄲 **Boon Fly Café** (4048 Sonoma Hwy., Napa, 707/299-4870, breakfast, lunch, and dinner daily, dinner entrées $10–20) brightens up the gray prison-like walls of the Carneros Inn on the Sonoma-Napa Highway. The food is rustic and full of fresh ingredients like those that might have been eaten by a local known as Boon Fly who used to farm the surrounding land. Breakfast and brunch are the fortes here and are priced low enough to make you want to fill up for the day, but it's also worth making a road stop in the evening to sample the flatbread pizzas or simple but elegant main courses, which are equally well priced.

Look for the sign to the Napa River Resorts a little farther east from Boon Fly and take Cuttings Wharf Road as far south as it will go, making sure you go left at the confusing fork in the road. There are no resorts at the river these days, but there is a popular juke-joint next to the boat ramp called **Moore's Landing** (6 Cuttings Wharf Rd., Napa, 707/253-7038, breakfast and lunch weekends, lunch Wed.–Fri., dinner Fri.–Sat., entrées $8–14). It serves American-Mexican comfort food to boaters, anglers, and the occasional stray winery visitor and has an idyllic deck right next to the

river. The winter hours tend to be erratic, so call first.

Picnic Supplies

Carneros is often chilly and windy compared to the Napa and Sonoma Valleys just to the north and so might not be the most inviting part of Wine Country for a picnic, but there are plenty of places to stop for supplies if the weather's nice or you're en route to warmer climes.

Angelo's Wine Country Deli (23400 Arnold Dr., 707/938-3688, 9 A.M.–5 P.M. daily), almost opposite the entrance to the Gloria Ferrer winery, is renowned for its smoked meats but also sells a wide range of other deli food and has become a bit of a Carneros institution. Despite being small, the store is hard to miss—there's a large model of a cow on its roof.

Just up the road is the **Fruit Basket** (24101 Arnold Dr., 707/938-4332, 7 A.M.–7 P.M. daily), which looks a little like a shack in the middle of its dusty parking lot but is actually a comprehensive open-air market and one of the best places to buy local in-season fruit and vegetables along with almost every other grocery staple, including bread, cheese, and a good selection of wine by the half-bottle. There's a second Fruit Basket on U.S. 12 in Boyes Hot Springs.

If you fancy a picnic without the hassle of finding the food yourself, give **Bouchaine Vineyards** (1075 Buchli Station Rd., Napa, 707/252-9065, www.bouchaine.com, 10:30 A.M.–4 P.M. daily) a call the day before and order one of its "Table for Two" picnic lunches. For $95, the winery includes a free wine tasting for two (worth $10), freshly prepared sandwiches and other treats, and a bottle of wine that can all be enjoyed at the scenic picnic area next to the winery.

At the other end of Carneros a popular picnic stop is the **Viansa Winery** (25200 Arnold Dr., Sonoma, 800/995-4740, www.viansa.com, 10 A.M.–5 P.M. daily), which sells a broad range of Italian-themed deli foods and sandwiches in its tasting room. There are some nice spots around the tasting room to eat, but when the winery gets crowded in the summer months, you'd do better to flee to somewhere more peaceful.

NORTHERN SONOMA

There's probably no other wine-producing region in California that has as much to offer visitors as northern Sonoma. Famed Victorian horticulturist Luther Burbank called this part of Sonoma the "chosen spot of all this earth as far as Nature is concerned," and he was pretty well traveled. For a man who tinkered with plants, this was paradise.

This is also a place where living off the land has always been, and still is, a way of life. That land provides some of California's best wine and food and countless recreational possibilities. You can mix wine with almost anything outdoors here: kayaking, mountain hikes, apple picking, camping, fishing, lounging on a sandy beach, flying, or even a safari.

While "Hop Country" and "Prune Country" don't have quite the same ring as "Wine Country," those crops and others once dominated the land but have long since vanished (at one point in the last century, a silkworm farm was planned, and a frog farm briefly found fame with its edible amphibians). There's even a major road named after the slowly disappearing Gravenstein apple. It would be easier to name crops that had not at some point been grown on these hills and valleys, helped along by the vast number of microclimates. There are probably more here than in any other part of the Wine Country—which is saying something in this climate-challenged part of the world. One day vines too might disappear, only to be replaced by the next big agricultural cash generator.

That's not to say that all is peace and rural tranquility; far from it. The freeway that was

HIGHLIGHTS

◖ **Hop Kiln Winery:** The towering hop kilns are so well preserved that this small winery could almost produce beer in addition to its unusual range of well-priced wines (page 197).

◖ **Korbel Champagne Cellars:** In a forest clearing in Victorian times, two Czech brothers started making wine, and the historic stone winery still makes sparkling wine fit for presidents and plebeians alike (page 199).

◖ **Iron Horse Vineyards:** An unassuming barn off the beaten track is home to some of the Russian River Valley's best sparkling wines and a view to die for (page 200).

◖ **Luther Burbank Home & Gardens:** Learn about the Victorian horticulturist who created hundreds of new plants in his greenhouses, and see many of those plants in the historic gardens (page 204).

◖ **Armstrong Redwoods State Reserve:** Take a break from the car and the heat on a short hike through the cool, damp redwood forest in this historic park (page 209).

◖ **The Russian River:** Rent a canoe for a day and drift through the trees on the Russian River, stopping at some of the many secluded beaches (page 210).

◖ **Ridge Vineyards:** This is a sister winery to its more famous sibling in the Santa Cruz Mountains. The building, made of rice-straw bales, takes the principle of organic wines to a whole new level (page 228).

◖ **Michel-Schlumberger:** Producing some of the best cabernet in a valley dominated by zinfandel, this winery is housed in a beautiful mission revival building tucked away down a scenic canyon (page 229).

◖ **Raven Performing Arts Theater:** Visit this historic theater for performance art, a movie, or simply a quick lunch, and support the artists that help keep Healdsburg real (page 238).

◖ **Alexander Valley Vineyards:** Incorporating part of the homestead of the valley's first settler, Cyrus Alexander, the grounds of this winery are peppered with historic buildings (page 257).

LOOK FOR ◖ TO FIND RECOMMENDED SIGHTS, ACTIVITIES, DINING, AND LODGING.

NORTHERN SONOMA

carved through the region in the 1960s has brought with it the kind of suburban sprawl and rush-hour traffic that sucked the soul out of the largest city, Santa Rosa. But while Santa Rosa continues to bulge outward, it doesn't take much to get back to the land and step back in time. Less than a half hour away, deep in the woods, are towns like Guerneville and Occidental that still retain some feeling of the frontier towns they once were, even as they become overrun in the summer by an unlikely mix of urbanites, hippies, bikers, and ranchers who all seem to coexist happily for a few months.

Even the Victorian town of Healdsburg has managed to keep in touch with its historic past, despite trying ever so hard to sell its soul to those marketing an imaginary Wine Country lifestyle.

The whole area is slowly being dragged up-market, however, as the burgeoning Bay Area population seeks out bigger backyards. At the southernmost edge of this part of the Wine Country, Sebastopol is starting to resemble a hip San Francisco neighborhood. Property prices everywhere are soaring, slowing down the mechanisms of change that have continually transformed the land since European immigrants first arrived here in the 1800s and carved out a life for themselves in the soil and forests.

Winemakers still produce wines to rival the best in the world, but as the cost of doing so rises, the conglomerates are beginning to take over, much as they've already done in the Napa and Sonoma Valleys. You increasingly have to be big to survive in the wine world here, and many new winemakers are looking farther north in Mendocino and Lake Counties for a chance to get in on the action.

Nevertheless, there's still plenty of life left in the northern Sonoma scene, with an amazing diversity of wine, scenery, and activities. There might be trouble in paradise, but it's still paradise to visit.

PLANNING YOUR TIME

Parts of northern Sonoma are easy to get around, others are not. The **Russian River**

Valley is definitely in the "not" category. This sprawling appellation encompasses forests and mountains, hills and dales, and has the navigational inconvenience of a large river cutting almost straight through the middle of it. A map is essential, as is a bit of planning to ensure you spend more time in wineries than backtracking on the roads. The Russian River Wine Road publishes one of the best maps, which can usually be found free at wineries.

The **Dry Creek** and **Alexander Valleys** are relatively straightforward to navigate by comparison, with most of the wineries strung along a few long, relatively straight roads. These valleys are almost like miniature Sonoma or Napa Valleys as far as climate, shape, and scenery, and it's easy to get a good feel for the area in a day or even a half day.

The three main appellations are like night and day when it comes to wine, which makes planning a wine route either exciting or daunting. Sample some velvety Alexander Valley cabernets, for example, before crossing into the Dry Creek Valley and tasting the subtly different cabernets there. Or try the warm-climate chardonnays in the Alexander Valley, then head down Westside Road to try some leaner, cool-climate versions in the Russian River Valley.

Alternatively, try to find your favorite Dry Creek zinfandel from the hundreds on offer in the valley, or hunt out the next big pinot noir in the Russian River Valley.

If all the possibilities just seem too overwhelming, there's always the option of staying in **Healdsburg,** which has enough tasting rooms to satisfy the most fussy wine drinker, as well as plenty of shops and restaurants to occupy those less curious about the region's wines. Healdsburg is also the most central town in the region, and the large number of good hotels and restaurants make it an almost essential staging post for any trip to this part of the world.

As in other parts of the Wine Country, wineries generally open late and close early, so don't expect to get started until late morning, and plan to be finished touring by about 5 P.M., closer to 4 P.M. during the winter.

Unlike the rest of Sonoma and Napa, free tasting is still fairly commonplace but is getting increasingly less so. Even when there is a fee for tasting regular or reserve wines, it will be far more palatable than in some other parts of Wine Country.

And of course, non-wine-related activities also abound. Check out the burgeoning Santa Rosa Arts District, or the multitude of hiking options in wilderness areas such as Armstrong Redwoods State Reserve.

GETTING THERE
The railroad came and left this part of Sonoma before most of us were even born, leaving the car and sporadic bus services as the only real options for getting around.

U.S. 101, which runs down the center of this region, might be a bit of an eyesore as it snakes up otherwise picturesque valleys leaving strip malls in its wake, but it's a pretty convenient way to get places fast. The drive time from San Francisco up the freeway to almost every major Russian River Valley town is usually not much more than an hour, to Healdsburg and beyond about an hour and a half.

From the freeway, Highway 116 (West) runs up through Sebastopol to Guerneville. In the Santa Rosa area, River Road runs west to Forestville, though it tends to get choked during rush hour. The Healdsburg Avenue exit leads straight into downtown Healdsburg, and the Westside Road exit is the entry to the Dry Creek Valley and Russian River regions. The next four exits serve Dry Creek and Alexander Valleys before the freeway reaches Cloverdale and then heads into the hills towards Hopland and Mendocino.

Although most people come to this part of the Wine Country by car, there are other transport options. Both Santa Rosa and Sebastopol are well served by **Golden Gate Transit** (415/923-2000 or 707/541-2000, www.goldengatetransit.org), which runs scheduled bus service to and from San Francisco hourly for much of the day. From Santa Rosa, **Sonoma County Transit** (707/576-7433 or 800/345-7433, www.sctransit.com) runs regular services to Healdsburg, Geyserville, and Guerneville. From Sebastopol there's service to Guerneville through Graton and Forestville. Things are so spread out in the Russian River Valley, however, that once you arrive there by bus you'll still need some mode of transport to see anything.

GETTING AROUND
The Russian River Valley is roughly square in shape, with an arm stretching from its northwestern corner up to Healdsburg. The major towns are Guerneville, in the northwest corner of the square, Sebastopol on the southern edge, Occidental on the western edge, and Santa Rosa on the eastern side. In the middle is a patchwork of farmland and vineyards, together with the hamlets of Graton and Forestville. Highway 116, also called the Gravenstein Highway, is the main road running north–south through them.

Wineries are spread mainly along Eastside and Westside Roads, which both run on either side of the river from Healdsburg down toward Guerneville, and throughout the patchwork in the middle of the area.

Many of the region's food and lodging options lie in Healdsburg and around the edge of this Russian River square. Unlike in the Dry Creek and Alexander Valleys farther north, roads here tend to meander as they follow the river and hills, often making driving times longer than anticipated.

By comparison, the Dry Creek Valley could be navigated with your eyes shut. Just two roads run the length of the valley, and the wineries are roughly spread out along them, making it the easiest part of northern Sonoma to visit in a day, even without a map.

Along the other side of the freeway is the longer and wider Alexander Valley. Even here, the wineries are concentrated along Geyserville Avenue on the western side of the valley and along Highway 128 on the eastern side.

Of course, driving is not the only way to get around. Wine Country would not be complete without cycling. The compact, flat Dry Creek Valley and relatively flat Westside Road from Healdsburg down into the Russian River Valley are two of the most bikeable routes. The Alexander Valley is also relatively flat, but distances between wineries are greater. In all areas, temperatures get high in the summer, so plenty of water is essential.

The best place to rent bikes is in Healdsburg, where there are several options. The friendly folks at **Spoke Folk Cyclery** in Healdsburg (201 Center St., 707/433-7171, www.spokefolk. com) can set you up on decent touring bikes for $30 per day. Nice road bikes and tandems cost from $50. They'll send you on your way with maps for biking routes that range from leisurely

12-mile loops in Dry Creek Valley to 40-mile adventures down to Guerneville. At the other end of town next to the Old Roma Station winery complex, **Wine Country Bikes** rents bikes from $33 for basic hybrids up to $55 for road bikes (61 Front St., 707/473-0610 or 866/922-4537, www.winecountrybikes.com). It also has plenty of options for organized tours, including a day tour of local organic farms and wineries during the spring and summer ($129) and a longer day tour for more avid bikers, which takes in scenery and wineries in both the Dry Creek and Russian River Valleys on its 45-mile loop ($149).

Russian River Valley

The Russian River Valley is one of Sonoma's largest and most diverse geographic regions. It covers about 150 square miles of forest, orchards, vineyards, and pastureland from trendy Sebastopol in the south to chic Healdsburg in the north and from the suburban freeway sprawl in the east to rural Occidental in the west. Running right through it is the mighty Russian River, shaping the climate, scenery, and recreational opportunities in the region.

The Russian River Valley attracted immigrants in the late 1800s to exploit its vast forests, and many of the towns that exist today were established as logging or railroad outposts. Once the redwood forests had been largely cleared, it was sheep ranches, cattle pasture, orchards, and even hop farms that took over the land. The Gravenstein apple, now an endangered piece of local agricultural history, was embraced as the region's very own, though its roots remain somewhat ambiguous.

It wasn't until the 1980s, when the cool growing climate was recognized as ideal for the increasingly fashionable pinot noir and chardonnay grapes, that the area's wine industry took off, and the Russian River Valley has long since been recognized as one of the best cool grape-growing regions in California. This is not an easy part of Wine Country to explore compared

to relatively self-contained valleys elsewhere in Sonoma, however. Roads wind through forests, over hills, and along the snaking river, making wineries sometimes hard to find. Large parts of the region are rural, dotted with small communities like **Forestville** and **Graton,** which hide their already small populations very well in the surrounding hills and woods.

The center of the action is **Guerneville** and neighboring **Monte Rio,** both slightly faded Victorian resort towns that are transformed each summer into a surreal scene of leather-clad bikers and plaid-clad outdoorsmen, hipsters, and hippies. Guerneville is something of a gay mecca and party town, and the rustic resorts and bars often pulsate with the beat of dance music and drunken hordes on summer evenings.

The eastern and western edges of the appellation could not be more of a contrast. The suburban sprawl of **Santa Rosa** is just outside the eastern boundary of the appellation and is almost a poster child for how not to grow a city. It is by far the biggest city in the region—a place where culture meets characterless malls—but a far cry from the peaceful and remote Bohemian Highway running along the appellation's western edge, where the picture-postcard town of **Occidental** exists in the midst of dense forests.

THE GRAVENSTEIN HIGHWAY

Although almost every imaginable fruit and vegetable seems to be grown in Sonoma, the most celebrated crop in the Russian River Valley (apart from grapes) is perhaps the apple, and in particular the small yellow and red Gravenstein with its strong aroma and taste.

Highway 116, which runs through Sebastopol and Graton, is also called the Gravenstein Highway for the large number of orchards it used to pass. The orchards are now disappearing, along with the Gravenstein apple itself, as growers favor bigger and more easily transported varieties of apple like Fuji and golden delicious.

At one point apple orchards covered 14,000 acres of Sonoma County, but by 2005 there were only about 3,000 acres left, and Gravensteins accounted for only one-third of that total. Slow Food Russian River, the local chapter of the Slow Food movement, is now campaigning to raise the profile of this humble little apple among consumers, retailers, and restaurants to slow any further decline.

Nothing specifically links the Gravenstein apple to this area – it is actually believed to have originated in Germany. It just happens to grow particularly well here and has been doing so for almost 200 years.

The Gravenstein is the earliest-ripening apple in the region, so look for it starting in late July. Other apple varieties tend to ripen August–December. Farms offering apples and other seasonal produce are generally clustered around Sebastopol and Graton. Many are open only during the summer and fall.

In Graton they include **Foxglove Farms** (5280 Gravenstein Hwy. N., 707/887-2759, Thurs.-Tues. July-Oct.), **Kozlowski Farms** (5566 Gravenstein Hwy. N., 707/887-1587, daily year-round), **Gabriel Farm** (3175 Sullivan Rd., just off Graton Rd., 707/829-0617, Sun.-Fri. Sept.-Oct.), and **Walker Apples** (10955 Upp Rd., off Graton Rd., daily Aug.-mid-Nov.), which sells a staggering 27 varieties of apple. Just south of Sebastopol on Pleasant Hill Road is **Twin Hill Ranch** (1689 Pleasant Hill Rd., 707/823-2815, Mon.-Sat. year-round), and halfway between Sebastopol and Occidental is **Ratzlaff Ranch** (13128 Occidental Rd., Sebastopol, 707/823-0538, Sun.-Fri. year-round), which grows Gravensteins along with other apples and pears.

Between Sebastopol and Graton on the Gravenstein Highway you will also likely find a bountiful supply of apples at the big roadside produce store called **Andy's Market** (1691 Gravenstein Hwy. N., Sebastopol, 707/823-8661, 8:30 A.M.-8 P.M. daily). Just south of Andy's on the other side of the road is the farm stand for local grower **Hale's Apple Farm** (1526 Gravenstein Hwy. N., Sebastopol, 707/823-4613, 9 A.M.-5 P.M. daily).

More information about all the fruits and vegetables grown here and the farms that sell them is available from **Sonoma Country Farm Trails** (707/571-8288, www.farmtrails. org). You might also see the free *Farm Trails* map and guide at wineries and farms in the region.

The Wines

Almost a third of all the grapes grown in Sonoma County come from the Russian River Valley, but there's the potential for it to be a far higher proportion. Only 12,000 acres, or about 10 percent, of the 125,000 acres in the valley are actually planted with vineyards. The rest is still pasture, forest, and the occasional town.

The river and the valley it carved through the coastal mountain ranges over millennia provide the region with the unique climate that is perfect for growing grapes that like cool conditions. There's enough strong sunlight each day to ensure the grapes ripen, but the air remains cool, often downright chilly at night, and keeps a lid on the fruit's sugar levels.

Pinot noir and chardonnay are the dominant varietals in this part of the Wine Country, but zinfandel is almost as important, and the resulting wines have a subtlety that is often lacking in the brawny zins from the warmer valleys to the north. Growers are also having increasing success with syrah and some other Rhône varietals, while gewürztraminer is also starting

NORTHERN SONOMA

Austin Creek State Recreation Area

To Dry Creek Valley and Healdsburg

CHRISTOPHER CREEK WINERY

FOPPIANO VINEYARDS

ACORN WINERY

Russian River

101

J VINEYARDS & WINERY

ARMSTRONG REDWOODS STATE RESERVE

C. DONATIELLO WINERY

WESTSIDE RD

WINDSOR RIVER RD

Riverfront Regional Park

Windsor

HOP KILN WINERY

EASTSIDE RD

STUMPTOWN BREWERY

KORBEL CHAMPAGNE CELLARS

THOMAS GEORGE ESTATES

GARY FARRELL WINES

SONOMA COUNTY AIRPORT

BOON HOTEL + SPA

WEST SONOMA INN

RIVER RD

Sunset Beach

WOHLER RD

TRENTON HEALDSBURG RD

Guerneville

APPLEWOOD INN

Steelhead Beach

THE RAFORD HOUSE

CREEKSIDE INN

THE RUSSIAN RIVER

BURKES CANOE TRIPS

FERN GROVE COTTAGES

RIVER RD

HARTFORD FAMILY WINERY

FARMHOUSE INN AND RESTAURANT

RIVER RD

MARTINELLI WINERY

116

GUERNEVILLE HWY

MIRABEL RD

Forestville

JOSEPH SWAN VINEYARDS

LAGUNA RD

OLIVET RD

116

MOSAIC RESTAURANT

To Bodega Bay

VILLAGE INN

KOZLOWSKI FARMS

GRAVENSTEIN HWY

MARTIN RAY WINERY

ZAZU

Monte Rio

IRON HORSE VINEYARDS

FOXGLOVE FARM

SEBASTOPOL VINEYARDS

WILLOW WOOD MARKET CAFÉ

PAUL HOBBS WINERY

GABRIEL FARM

FREI RD

Graton

BOHEMIAN HWY

UNDERWOOD BAR & BISTRO

116

HANNA WINERY

WALKER APPLES

MILL STATION RD

GREEN HILL RD

ANDY'S MARKET

OCCIDENTAL RD

GRATON RD

HALE'S APPLE FARM

BALLETTO VINEYARDS/ DUTTON GOLDFIELD

Occidental

INN AT OCCIDENTAL

RATZLAFF RANCH

FERGUSON RD

HEALDSBURG AVE

RAGLE RD

STARLIGHT WINE BAR

12

OCCIDENTAL RD

K&L BISTRO

HOPMONK TAVERN

FRENCH GARDEN RESTAURANT

BODEGA HWY

BODEGA AVE

Sebastopol

LUTHER BURBANK GOLD RIDGE FARM

0   2 mi

0   2 km

OSMOSIS SPA

TWIN HILL RANCH

RUSSIAN RIVER VALLEY

to make more of an appearance. The ubiquitous cabernet sauvignon and merlot are largely absent, however, except on the warmest eastern hills of the region.

The cool layer of damp marine air from the Pacific Ocean just a few miles west is the region's natural air-conditioner and was a big factor in the granting of the Russian River Valley's AVA status in 1983. Marine fog rolls down the river valley during the summer, snaking into gullies and canyons and keeping the temperature here lower than any other inland portion of Sonoma County. As the ripening process slows, the fruit can gain in complexity and retain enough acidity to keep the wines interesting. Grapes are usually harvested several weeks later here than in some hotter Sonoma regions.

The river is also responsible for the area's unique soils, depositing deep, well-drained sandy and gravelly sediments over million of years. The combination of relatively cool microclimates, no summer rain, and a patchwork of soils is a grape-grower's dream and a reason there are so many styles of pinot made here.

Within the southwest corner of the Russian River appellation, closest to the ocean, is the even cooler Green Valley AVA. This is just about as cool as a climate can be and still ripen grapes, and it is the source of some of Sonoma's best pinot noir.

WINERIES

Many of the Russian River wineries are south of Healdsburg down the meandering Westside Road, which has been dubbed the Rodeo Drive of Pinot Noir due to the number of high-end pinot producers strung along it. Once Westside Road reaches River Road, a map is an essential tool to find the hidden gems around Forestville, Graton, and beyond.

Foppiano Vineyards

The first major winery south of Healdsburg on the Old Redwood Highway is also one of the few historic wineries that continued to operate right through Prohibition. Foppiano Vineyards (12707 Old Redwood Hwy., Healdsburg, 707/433-7272, www.foppiano.

com, 10 A.M.–4:30 P.M. daily, free tasting) remains a family-owned affair, and a relatively small one compared to some of its corporate neighbors, producing about 40,000 cases of wine a year under a couple of labels.

Giovanni Foppiano founded the winery in 1896, and the fourth generation of Foppianos today runs the business and its 200 acres of estate vineyards. You could well bump into one of the two Louis Foppianos in the cozy tasting room that shares the parking lot with barns and other winery buildings. For most of its existence over the last century, the winery sold wine in bulk and made cheap and cheerful jug wines. It wasn't until the 1970s that the wines went upmarket and Foppiano put its product into bottles.

Today, Foppiano is best known for its powerful, inky petite sirah, which has been very highly rated in recent years and accounts for about a third of the winery's total production. Other wines include pinot noir, cabernet sauvignon, and merlot from Russian River Valley grapes, plus sangiovese and zinfandel sourced from vineyards elsewhere in Northern Sonoma.

All are well worth tasting, and not only because tasting is free. Unusually, most are aged in American oak barrels that impart a stronger tannic punch than the French oak more commonly used by Russian River wineries. The tannins will mellow over time, but those who are impatient should try the softer Reserve petite sirah, which is the only Foppiano wine aged in French oak. White wines including sauvignon blanc and chardonnay are sold under the cheaper Riverside label.

Although there are no official tours, visitors are free to wander off into the vineyards on a self-guided tour, leaflets for which can be found in the tasting room.

J Vineyards & Winery

Just south of Foppiano, the giant parking lot shared with the neighboring Rodney Strong Winery can be a magnet for busloads of tourists, but there's a relative oasis and some delicious food to be found inside the sleek and modern J Winery (11447 Old Redwood Hwy., Healdsburg, 707/431-3646, www.jwine.com,

11 A.M.–5 P.M. daily, food and wine tastings $20–60).

Food pairings are part of the tasting experience here—a unique but expensive proposition. At the main tasting bar, $20 buys generous pours of five wines from the lengthy menu of red, white, sparkling, and dessert wines. If the spacious tasting room is overrun, a common occurrence on weekends, the more exclusive Bubble Room (four seatings per day Fri.–Sun.) takes the tasting experience (and the price) up a notch with comfy seating, table service, heartier food samples, and the chance to taste more expensive sparkling and single-vineyard wines. Each of the six wines (two red, two white, and two sparkling) is paired with food, such as pinot noir with pan-seared Alaskan halibut, or viognier with French mussel soup. Despite its $60 cost, the Bubble Room is popular, and the six-course menu is pretty filling, so it's best to make reservations during the summer. If it's already booked up, there's a similarly structured but slightly less indulgent tasting menu available on the outdoor terrace Thursday–Monday during the summer.

J specializes in sparkling wines and pinot noir from the Russian River Valley. Its portfolio of bubbly includes a late-disgorged brut and the flagship Vintage Brut, which is the signature wine here. It was the only wine that owner Judy Jordan (hence the name "J") made when she started the winery in 1986 as a spin-off of the Jordan Winery in the Alexander Valley, and the swooping yellow J on the bottle is unmistakable. The sparkling wine-making process is the focus of the appointment-only tours that finish with a food and wine tasting.

About half the 65,000-case production here is still wine and includes chardonnay, pinot gris, and three excellent pinot noirs, of which the best is arguably the limited-production Nicole's Vineyard version. There are also a couple of limited-production winery-only wines, including a Russian River Valley zinfandel and viognier from the Alexander Valley.

C. Donatiello Winery

The wine's not bad, but a visit to C. Donatiello

(4035 Westside Rd., Healdsburg, 707/431-4442 or 800/433-8296, www.cdonatiello.com, 11 A.M.–5 P.M. daily, tasting $7–12) might well have you raving about aromas of a different kind—those from the wonderfully scented culinary and medicinal herb gardens that surround the rustic redwood winery buildings in a maze of terraces. There's probably a medicinal cure for a hangover in there somewhere. More usefully, there are countless plants with aromas that mimic those found in the wines made here, enabling a stroll through the gardens to become an education in identifying wine aromas.

The winery was established in the early 1980s by the investment banker and philanthropist William R. Hambrecht, and for many years it was run as the Belvedere Winery. In 2008, wine industry executive Christopher Donatiello took over the facilities and, with backing from Hambrecht, transformed the winery into a smaller and leaner operation producing about 10,000 cases of high-end pinot noir and chardonnay from local Russian River Valley vineyards. The relaxing, contemporary tasting room and shady patio overlooking the estate

are in keeping with the quality of the wines that have been getting some rave reviews from the critics. Hambrecht, meanwhile, continues to operate the smaller **Bradford Mountain Winery,** tucked behind C. Donatiello. It makes a wide range of wines from Russian River and Dry Creek vineyards, and is open for tasting by appointment at the weekends (707/431-4433, www.bradfordmountain.com).

Most of the production at C. Donatiello is accounted for by the blended Russian River Valley pinot and chardonnay, which retail for about $40 and $25, respectively. From that starting point, the prices and accolade increase with the single-vineyard and single-clone versions of the wines. The best values are arguably the mid-priced Maddies Vineyard bottlings, sourced from the vineyard right in front of the winery.

【 Hop Kiln Winery

A few miles south of Healdsburg is one of Sonoma's best-preserved old hop kilns, a towering wooden building where hops were once dried before being used to make beer. The hop

Hops, not grapes, were once processed in the building that's now Hop Kiln Winery.

vines of Sonoma have long since been replaced by grapevines, but the Hop Kiln Winery (6050 Westside Rd., Healdsburg, 707/433-6491, www.hopkilnwinery.com, 10 A.M.–5 P.M. daily, tasting $5) has kept much of the cavernous interior of the 1905-era building intact, including the old stone drying ovens.

Belying its giant home, the winery itself is a fairly small operation, producing about 12,000 cases a year of reasonably priced zinfandel, cabernet sauvignon, chardonnay, and some interesting blends. The winery is set to grow, however, following its acquisition in 2004 by a Seattle-based investment company. New plantings and a new winemaker are likely to liven up the rather homey-feeling winery, and already there is a new HK label for some higher-quality estate wines.

King of the cheaper wines is Big Red, which is as big as its name suggests—a rambunctious blend of zinfandel, cabernet, and syrah. A Thousand Flowers is a more delicate white blend of chardonnay, gewürztraminer, and riesling. The once-common Napa gamay red grape is also represented under its more accurate name of valdiguié. Very few wineries still make it, and it's an acquired taste.

There are plenty of picnic tables around the building, including some next to a rather murky pond. The winery stocks a host of vinegars, oils, and mustards, but not much in the way of more filling picnic fare, so you'll have to bring your own.

Thomas George Estates

Opened in 2009 in the former Davis Bynum winery, Thomas George Estates (8075 Westside Rd., Healdsburg, 707/431-8031, www.thomas-georgeestates.com, 11 A.M.–5 P.M. daily, tasting $5) has brought some Canadian blood and new ideas to the Westside Road scene. The winery came about after one of the best-known pinot producers in the area, Davis Bynum, opted to retire. He sold his brand and inventory to the owners of Rodney Strong Vineyards, but the physical winery and the small estate vineyard were bought by the Toronto-based Baker family (the winery is named after the patriarch,

Tom). They sank a small fortune into refurbishing both the winery and some of the vineyards, brought in a veritable who's who of the pinot world as consultants, including Gary Farrell, and poached the winemaker from the nearby Christopher Creek winery. All this suggests the Bynum legacy is in good hands. Only time will tell.

Bynum originally established a winery here in the 1970s in a former hop kiln and worked with many of the region's pinot pioneers as the area became established. Among the secrets to his success were the agreements he made to buy grapes from some of the best growers in the area. Thomas George Estates will still buy grapes from some well-known local growers as they ramp up production to a planned 15,000 cases, but they also bought a couple of additional vineyards in the Russian River Valley to complement the estate Baker Vineyard that was acquired from Bynum.

Several different pinots and chardonnays are poured in the tasting room alongside zinfandels from Dry Creek and a Sonoma Valley viognier. In early 2010, as this edition went to press, the winery completed construction of new caves and what promised to be a nice picnic area, which promise to make the visitor experience as much about the hillside surroundings as the wine.

Gary Farrell Wines

The last winery on Westside Road before it reaches River Road, Gary Farrell Wines (10701 Westside Rd., Healdsburg, 707/473-2900, www.garyfarrellwines.com, 10 A.M.–4 P.M. daily, tasting $10–15), is also one of the newest. The spacious tasting room at the end of a long driveway (easy to miss when driving east) was completed in 2001, and its huge picture window overlooks some of the Russian River vineyards from which some acclaimed chardonnay and pinot noir are made.

Farrell made his name as the winemaker at nearby Rochioli Vineyards and Davis Bynum, both regarded as among the best pinot makers in the area. He set up his own winery in the 1980s to pursue his pinot passion. Since

2004 the winery has been owned by multinational wine companies (first Allied Domecq, now Ascentia Wine Estates), but it retains a low-key atmosphere, and Gary Farrell stayed on as a consulting winemaker for a number of years before establishing his current pet pinot project, Alysian Wines, in nearby Forestville in 2009 (that winery is not open to the public). The current winemaker was Farrell's former Associate Winemaker.

Most of the wines made here are pinots and chardonnays, both appellation-specific versions from the Russian River Valley and beyond to the pricier vineyard-specific bottling sourced from some well-known local vineyards that are part of the more expensive Limited Release tasting. Those two varietals account for more than half the 17,000-case annual production. Don't overlook the beautifully structured cabernet sauvignon and zinfandel, however, which all have the same understated elegance.

☕ Korbel Champagne Cellars

This is one of the most impressive of the 19th-century wineries in Sonoma—a collection of solid, imposing stone and brick buildings at the edge of redwood forests. If you're a fan of sparkling wines, it's a place worth visiting—it might not have the acclaim of top producers like Iron Horse, but Korbel (13250 River Rd., Guerneville, 707/824-7000, www.korbel.com, daily 10 A.M.–5 P.M. summer, 10 A.M.–4:30 P.M. winter, free tasting) offers perhaps the best value for money among sparkling wine producers and has a fascinating history.

Three Korbel brothers, immigrants from the Bohemia region of what is now the Czech Republic, founded the winery in 1882 after making their money in the local redwood lumber business. They continued making redwood tanks and boxes even after planting vines and among the stumps of some of the cleared land. But wine production gradually took over from their other businesses as the quality of their sparkling wines and brandies improved and word spread.

Now the winery makes close to 1.7 million cases of the fizzy stuff a year in a dizzying array of styles. It has also added some respectable table wines to its portfolio, as well as brandy and port, all of which can only be bought at the winery.

The Korbel family connection is long gone, but Korbel wines remain the tipple of both presidents and plebeians alike. The champagne has been poured at five presidential inaugurations, and is claimed to be the most popular premium champagne in the United States.

From the bone-dry top-of-the-line Le Premier to the sweeter Sec, Korbel's 10 or so champagnes are eminently affordable, as are the cabernet, pinot noir, chardonnay, and zinfandel table wines, and even the barrel-aged port. After the tasting room bubbles have gone to your head, the prices look even better. It's hard to leave without at least a couple of bottles.

How the bubbles get into the wine and how the Korbel brothers got into the wine business are both covered in an entertaining tour offered five times a day—buy tickets in the little shack at the opposite end of the parking lot from the tasting room. A tour of the sweet old rose garden is offered twice a day, Tuesday–Sunday mid-April–mid-October, and after all that touring you can lounge on the deck of the small delicatessen, shaded by redwood trees with a gourmet sandwich and even a beer.

Hartford Family Winery

A little off the beaten track about a mile up Martinelli Road and surrounded by lush gardens and redwood forest is the big white barn-like winery and mansion of this pinot noir and chardonnay specialist. Hartford (8075 Martinelli Rd., Forestville, 707/887-1756 or 800/588-0234, www.hartfordwines.com, 10 A.M.–4:30 P.M. daily, tasting $5) makes about 20,000 cases of some serious point-scoring regional and single-vineyard wines from the Sonoma Coast, Russian River Valley, Carneros, and (unusually) Marin County to the south.

Although it is touted as a down-home family winery sort of place, you'd be forgiven for thinking it is just a bit too big, smart, and formal for the average wine-making family. That's because the part-owner Don Hartford has some very nonaverage family connections. He's married to the daughter of Jess Jackson, founder of the Kendall-Jackson wine empire that also owns the majority of Hartford.

The portfolio of wines is very compact, however, comprising only pinot noir, chardonnay, and zinfandel, all from cool-climate vineyards and all well worth tasting. Chances are that many of the best vineyard-designate chardonnays and pinots made under the Hartford Court label will be sold out, but you're still likely to find a few winners on the tasting list. The slightly cheaper Hartford-labeled wines are well worth trying and include four zinfandels from some of the oldest vineyards in the Russian River region.

Sebastopol Vineyards/Dutton Estate Winery

The modest tasting room (8757 Green Valley Rd., Sebastopol, 707/829-9463, www.sebastopolvineyards.com, 10 A.M.–5 P.M. daily, tasting $10–15) of the Dutton family, just off Highway 116, barely hints at the renown of their Dutton Ranch in the Green Valley AVA for producing highly rated, limited-production wines.

Dutton Ranch is not a single vineyard but a collection of 10 vineyards and a few apple orchards totaling more than 1,300 acres, all farmed by the family and supplying grapes to wineries across the region. Indeed, most of the grapes are sold to other wineries, but enough are used in the two wineries in this region to bear the Dutton name. Joe Dutton produces about 10,000 cases of wine under the premium Dutton Estate label and slightly cheaper Sebastopol Vineyards label. (His brother Steve is a partner in the nearby Dutton-Goldfield Winery.)

Chardonnay, pinot noir, and syrah are the only wines made here, but there are lots of different versions of them made from specific vineyards and sometimes specific blocks within a vineyard. Discovering some of the nuances of the tiny Green Valley subappellation with the more expensive vineyard-specific wines entails

a higher tasting fee, but there is also a wine and cheese pairing offered for $20.

◖ Iron Horse Vineyards

One of the southernmost wineries in the Green Valley appellation, Iron Horse Vineyards (9786 Ross Station Rd., Sebastopol, 707/887-1507, www.ironhorsevineyards.com, 10 A.M.–3:30 P.M. daily, tasting $10), is also well off the beaten track down Ross Station Road (off Highway 116), a one-lane road that winds through orchards, over a creek, and (perhaps) past some wild turkeys before climbing up the palm-lined driveway to the winery.

The rustic simplicity of the barnlike building and its indoor-outdoor tasting bar belies the pedigree of the sparkling wines made here—they have been served to presidents and won numerous accolades from wine critics over the past 30 years. Tours are offered by appointment weekdays only, but with such panoramic views over the valley from right behind the tasting area, you might be content just to sit back and relax in the bucolic setting.

a bottle of Benchmark wine from Iron Horse Vineyards

© IRON HORSE VINEYARDS

Today the winery is still run by the Sterling family that built it in the 1970s and makes about 20,000 cases of sparkling wines a year, most priced at $30 and up. They include the ever-popular Wedding Cuvée and a series of late-disgorged wines, including the flagship Brut LD, which are bottle-aged for four or more years in contact with the lees to give them a rich aroma and flavor. All the grapes for the sparkling wines are sourced from the winery's vineyards in the surrounding Green Valley AVA, the coolest part of an already cool Russian River Valley appellation.

It's an ideal place to grow chardonnay and pinot noir, both of which Iron Horse also bottles as outstanding still wines that are worth tasting. Try the unoaked chardonnay—one of the best examples of this new breed of food-friendly chardonnays. A wide range of mainly red wines are also made from the winery's T-bar-T vineyard in the warmer Alexander Valley, including a juicy sangiovese and a petite verdot, normally a blending grape but also capable of producing a plush wine in its own right. Worth noting is that Iron Horse closes far earlier than most in the area and is a five-minute drive off the main road, so get there early.

Martinelli Winery

One of the most noteworthy zinfandels made in the Russian River Valley comes from the Jackass Vineyard of Martinelli Winery (3360 River Rd., Windsor, 707/525-0570 or 800/346-1627, www.martinelliwinery.com, 10 A.M.–5 P.M. daily, tasting $5), planted in the 1800s and still going. That notable vineyard's name has absolutely no historical significance, instead referring to the sort of farmer who would consider farming such a steep and rugged slope.

The Martinellis have been a fixture here since the early 1900s as grape and apple growers. In fact, apples can be found alongside the wines and other gourmet food in the rather chaotic winery gift shop inside the big red barn, a former hop barn. (This Martinelli apple-and-wine clan is, however, unrelated to the Martinelli clan that supplies cheap apple cider to your local supermarket.)

The family only started making wines in the late 1980s from their vineyards and only got noticed more recently when it hired renowned consultant winemaker Helen Turley to tame the Jackass vineyard. Since then the accolades have poured in for the wines, particularly the powerhouse Jackass zinfandel together with several syrahs and chardonnays from Russian River Valley vineyards.

Not much of the popular, if expensive, Jackass zin is made each year, however, so chances are it will have sold out. There are plenty of other wines to try in the huge portfolio. So many different wines are made here that it's hard to believe total production is only about 10,000 cases. The portfolio of pinot noir stretches to more than a half-dozen wines, most sourced from the Russian River Valley or Green Valley and most being big, earthy, and full-bodied affairs. Others worth tasting include an off-dry, exotically flavored gewürztraminer and an intensely aromatic muscat, both unusual wines for this area.

Hanna Winery

From humble beginnings in the 1970s, Hanna (5353 Occidental Rd., Santa Rosa, 707/575-3371, www.hannawinery.com, 10 A.M.–4 P.M. daily, tasting $5) has grown to become one of the larger privately owned wineries in northern Sonoma, making 35,000 cases of wine at its modest Home Ranch winery here in the Russian River Valley and set to grow even larger following the completion of a new 100,000-case winery at its Alexander Valley location (9280 Hwy. 128, Healdsburg, 707/431-4314).

Hanna's specialty is crisp, steel-fermented sauvignon blanc that is usually a hit with critics, but it has a full portfolio of wines from the 250 acres of vineyards it owns around its two winery locations and high up in the Mayacamas Mountains at its Bismark Ranch vineyards above Sonoma Valley—claimed to be the highest-elevation vineyard in Sonoma.

The Bismark red wines, including cabernet sauvignon, nebbiolo, and zinfandel, are powerful and often highly rated by critics. At the other end of the scale is the fruity rosé made from petite sirah and zinfandel, an ideal accompaniment to a picnic on the pretty patio overlooking the vineyards.

Balletto Vineyards & Dutton Goldfield Winery

An industrial-looking modern building is an unlikely setting for two wineries with deep roots in the grape-growing business in the Russian River Valley. Both only recently started making wines from their renowned vineyards, and together they offer a remarkable range of Russian River Valley wines in terms of both price and style in their new tasting room.

The Balletto family (5700 Occidental Rd., Santa Rosa, 707/568-2455, www.ballettovineyards.com, 10 A.M.–4:30 P.M. Mon.–Fri., 10 A.M.–5 P.M. Sat.–Sun., tasting $5) started out as fruit growers in the 1970s, then became grape growers, and finally began making small quantities of wines from their four Russian River Valley vineyards in 2001. The new winery was completed in 2006 and now produces a modest 5,000 cases of Balletto wines, although higher production is planned. Pinot noir and pinot gris account for much of the output, with zinfandel and chardonnay making up the balance. All are decent enough and made all the more palatable by their reasonable prices—the pinot noir is the most expensive at $25. The best of the four are undoubtedly the two reds.

The vineyards are also home to the Dutton-Goldfield Winery (tasting room at 3100 Gravenstein Hwy. N., 707/827-3600, daily 10 A.M.–4:30 P.M., tasting $10), which makes limited-production wines positioned at the other end of the price spectrum. Founded in 1998 by Dan Goldfield, a well-known winemaker, and Steve Dutton, a member of the family that farms the renowned vineyards that make up the Dutton Ranch, the winery produces about 5,000 cases of high-end wines that garner some glowing reviews.

To a certain extent, the quality of the wine is to be expected. Goldfield knows the area well, having made wines at some well-known pinot

producers in the Russian River Valley. He now has some of the best fruit in the region to work with, sourced from the 1,200 acres of Dutton Ranch vineyards that are regarded as some of the best in the valley.

Pinot noir accounts for most of the production, both a blended Russian River Valley version and several exquisite single-vineyard bottlings that are made in such limited quantities and win such stellar reviews that they usually sell out fast. Chardonnay, zinfandel, and syrah make up the balance of the production. The syrah and zinfandel, in particular, are elegant and earthy cool-climate examples of the varietals and well worth trying.

Martin Ray Winery

Although housed in the oldest continually operating winery in Sonoma and named after one of California's pioneering modern winemakers, the Martin Ray Winery (2191 Laguna Rd., Santa Rosa, 707/823-2404, www.martinraywinery.com, 11 A.M.–5 P.M. daily summer, 11 A.M.–4 P.M. daily winter, tasting free or $5) is actually a relatively modern operation with few links to the site's historic past or the man after whom it is named. Nonetheless, it makes some good wines from mountain fruit and has some fascinating historic features and heritage that make it worth visiting.

The winery itself dates back to the late 1800s, and a few of the massive redwood fermenting tanks from the early 1900s are still on display outside the modest tasting room at the end of the long driveway. Since then it has undergone countless transformations, first as a maker of sacramental wines during Prohibition, then as the Martini & Prati Winery making wines under historic labels like Paul Masson and Fountain Grove, and eventually as a custom crush facility in the 1990s.

It was reinvented again in 2003 when current owner Courtney Benham acquired the property. He had already bought the rights to the Martin Ray name a decade earlier and set about reintroducing it more than 100 miles from where Ray originally found fame, in the Santa Cruz Mountains. Martin Ray was equally beloved and reviled in the 1950s for his fanatical devotion to making high-quality varietal wines from his mountain vineyards when the rest of the industry was still churning out bland, blended bulk wine. He made some phenomenal wines, by all accounts, but made many enemies as he urged the introduction of more honest wine labeling practices.

The winery today makes several hundred thousand cases of wine, a size that's evident from the huge warehouses and water tower on the site. The wines cover just about every major varietal and growing region in northern California, with an emphasis on mountain fruit. From a historic and quality perspective the most interesting are the expensive reserve cabernet sauvignons from vineyards in the Santa Cruz Mountains, Martin Ray's old stomping ground, and Diamond Mountain in the Napa Valley. Both are intensely flavored mountain wines, each with the distinctive character of its region. They're worth paying the modest reserve tasting fee to try. The best pinot noir in the lineup, from the Russian River Valley, is also a reserve wine. The cheaper nonreserve Martin Ray wines include a nice Russian River chardonnay and Mendocino pinot gris along with a series of less unique wines from Napa Valley vineyards.

Cheaper wines sold under the Angeline label account for the vast majority of total production here and are good value but not in the same league as the reserves. Most fun is the fruity one-liter jug wine, a blend of tempranillo, syrah, and cabernet sauvignon that costs just $15.

Wineries by Appointment

Tucked away inside an anonymous unit in the middle of an industrial estate on the northern edge of Santa Rosa, **Siduri Wines** (980 Airway Ct., Suite C, Santa Rosa, 707/578-3882, www.siduri.com, by appointment 10 A.M.–3 P.M. daily) has quietly carved out a huge reputation for its single-vineyard pinot noirs sourced from just about every great pinot-growing region on the West Coast. Owners Adam and Dianna Lee have followed a dream of making

their favorite wine fervently, since they first left their native Texas in their twenties. After years gaining experience working for small wineries, they leased their first acre of vineyards, made their first 100 cases of wine in 1994 and, through a chance meeting with critic Robert Parker, won what would be the first of countless stellar ratings.

The key to Siduri's success is buying fruit from some of the best pinot growers and best vineyards in California and Oregon. The portfolio runs to more than 15 single-vineyard pinots sourced from the Willamette Valley in Oregon all the way down to the Santa Rita Hills near Santa Barbara. Anywhere from a few hundred to 1,000 cases are made of each wine, but all are richly extracted and regarded as among the cream of West Coast pinots. The big news is when Siduri *doesn't* receive a 90-plus point rating for one of its wines, which generally cost $30–50 per bottle. Visiting the winery is a refreshing change from Wine Country chintz—in such an industrial setting you can't help but focus solely on what's under your nose, which might well be one of the keys to Siduri's success. That and perhaps the fact that the winery is named after the Babylonian goddess of wine.

The setting does make finding Siduri challenging, however. From Piner Road just west of U.S. 101 go north on Airway Drive, into what looks like (and is) a light industrial area. The first road on the right is Airway Court, and Siduri is in the warehouse right at the end of the street, through the gates, on the right.

Another winery renowned for Russian River pinot but with a far longer history is **Joseph Swan Vineyards** (2916 Laguna Rd., Forestville, 707/573-3747, www.swanwinery.com, 11 A.M.–4:30 P.M. Sat.–Sun., by appointment weekdays). Joseph Swan got into the wine-making game when he bought a run-down farm in Forestville in the late 1960s with a plan to grow grapes and make wine during his retirement. He went about it with such a perfectionist passion and with so many good wine-making connections, however, that he became one of a small group of pinot pioneers in the Russian River Valley—a group that helped put the region firmly on the world pinot noir stage. Today his son-in-law continues Swan's legacy, producing beautifully crafted single-vineyard pinots as well as an excellent-value Russian River Valley blend called Cuvée de Trois, which usually sells out fast. Also worth trying are the equally elegant single-vineyard zinfandels. The small, rustic winery tasting room is off the beaten path, down tiny Trenton Road at the northern end of Laguna Road, and is open without an appointment on weekends, by appointment only during the week.

From Healdsburg via Argentina to Graton might seem like a tortuous route for a wine-maker, but the founder of **Paul Hobbs Winery** (3355 Gravenstein Hwy. N., Sebastopol, 707/824-9879, www.paulhobbswinery.com) picked up some valuable wine-making experience along the way from Simi Winery near Healdsburg and Vina Cobos winery in Mendoza, Argentina, before establishing his wine label in 1991. As he built up his vineyard holdings during the 1990s, his wines were made at other Sonoma wineries, including Kunde; a dedicated facility in Graton was opened in 2003. Now Hobbs makes highly rated, vineyard-designate chardonnay and pinot noir from Russian River vineyards, and a cabernet sauvignon using Napa fruit. Prices of the wines, like their ratings, are high.

Acorn Winery (12040 Old Redwood Hwy., down a gravel driveway just south of Limerick Ln., Healdsburg, 707/433-6440, www.acorn-winery.com), with its modest tasting bar in the corner of Bill and Betsy Nachbauer's garage, couldn't be further from the wine-making behemoths of Rodney Strong and Foppiano nearby. The Nachbauers are former corporate lawyers who bought their 26 acres of vineyards here in 1990 and started making their own wine six years later using equipment at other wineries but barrel aging (and tasting) in their garage. Production now is about 3,000 cases a year and a thoroughly Italian affair. Wines include zinfandel, sangiovese, dolcetto, and field blends including Medley, a blend of 15 varietals that redefines the term "complex." Being

popular, however, most of the wines sell out fast each year.

Most Italian wine families in northern Sonoma can trace their roots back over a century, but Giuseppe Battaglini and family arrived in the 1950s with the same dream of recreating his memories of the Italian Wine Country right here in Sonoma. **Battaglini Estate Winery** (2948 Piner Rd., Santa Rosa, 707/578-4091, www.battagliniwines.com) has the advantage of owning vineyards planted by one of those early Italian immigrant families in the 1880s that supply grapes for the intensely flavored zinfandel and petite sirah wines. A more recent planting of chardonnay brought total production up to about 2,100 cases. It's all very much a family affair, and visitors will probably bump into a Battaglini family member in the tasting room in a small barn.

SIGHTS

The Russian River Valley is full of beautiful natural sights, from rivers to fir-covered mountains, but most of the cultural sights in the region are clustered around Santa Rosa, which has made a big effort in the last decade to nurture a small but growing arts scene. In the 1990s, the city designated a large chunk of the downtown area as the **Santa Rosa Arts District** in an effort to encourage investment in public art and institutions. The district is bounded by College Avenue to the north, Sonoma Avenue to the south, and Railroad Square to the west, and it incorporates the best cultural and historic sites (listed below) along with a growing collection of public murals and sculptures, with more planned. It is by no means a tourist-friendly district because everything of interest is so spread out. More information and a map of the current and planned art-related locations can be found at the City of Santa Rosa website (ci.santa-rosa.ca.us/departments/recreationandparks/programs/artsandculture/artsdistrict).

◖ Luther Burbank Home & Gardens

Apples and pears, grapes and hops, plums

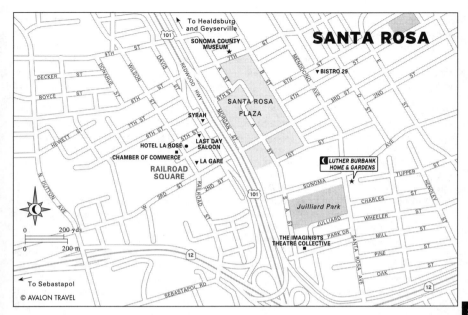

To Healdsburg and Geyserville

SONOMA COUNTY MUSEUM

SANTA ROSA

BISTRO 29

SANTA ROSA PLAZA

SYRAH

LAST DAY SALOON

HOTEL LA ROSE

CHAMBER OF COMMERCE

RAILROAD SQUARE

LA GARE

LUTHER BURBANK HOME & GARDENS

Juilliard Park

CHARLES ST

WHEELER ST

THE IMAGINISTS THEATRE COLLECTIVE

MILL ST

PINE ST

OAK ST

To Sebastopol

SEBASTOPOL RD

© AVALON TRAVEL

0   200 yds
0   200 m

and peaches—as Sonoma County's rich agricultural history suggests, pretty much anything will grow here. Pioneering horticulturist Luther Burbank recognized this when he made Sonoma County his home in 1875.

Burbank's cross-breeding experiments at his Santa Rosa and Sebastopol greenhouses are credited with creating more than 800 new strains of flowers, fruits, trees, and other plants over his 50-year science career, including the big white Shasta daisy, a spineless cactus, the blight-resistant Burbank potato, and the plumcot, a cross between an apricot and a plum.

He was well connected in scientific circles of the time, counting Thomas Edison and Henry Ford, among others, as friends. Ford sent him the first tractor off the company's production line as a gift in 1918.

Santa Rosa was proud to have Burbank, and he in turn was happy to be part of the city's self-promotion. A Santa Rosa promotional brochure in the 1920s described him as "California's best citizen," and borrowed one of his many famous Sonoma quotes: "I would

rather own a piece of land the size of a good healthy house lot in Sonoma County than an entire farm anywhere else on earth."

Burbank's own healthy house lot, where he lived until 1906, is preserved along with a small greenhouse and the gardens as part of the 1.6-acre State Historic Park in Santa Rosa (on the 200 block of Santa Rosa Ave. at Sonoma Ave., just across the street from City Hall, 707/524-5445, www.lutherburbank.org).

The gardens contain many of Burbank's horticultural creations and are open 8 A.M.–sunset every day. The museum and greenhouse (10 A.M.–4 P.M. Tues.–Sun. Apr.–Oct., $4) include some of his tools and explain the significance of his work. Guided tours are available during the summer months.

Also open about a half mile west of downtown Sebastopol is the 15-acre **Gold Ridge Experiment Farm** (7781 Bodega Ave., Sebastopol, 707/829-6711, open daily year-round, cottage open Wed. 9 A.M.–noon), where Burbank did many of his horticultural experiments and where there is now a historic collection of some of his creations. The replica cottage (the original was destroyed in 1906) and gardens have a rather unflattering modern setting in the middle of a retirement community. Take a self-guided hike or join a docent-lead tour (by appointment year-round).

Railroad Square

There's a hopping restaurant, shopping, and entertainment scene around the historic Railroad Square district in Santa Rosa, encompassing 3rd, 4th, and 5th Streets downtown, just west of the freeway. The center of the Railroad Square district is the **Northwestern Pacific Railroad Depot,** a small stone station house built in 1904 to replace an earlier wooden structure that burned down. Like many of the basalt stone buildings in the surrounding blocks, the depot is as solid as it looks and withstood the 1906 earthquake that leveled much of downtown Santa Rosa.

Its claim to fame was acting as a backdrop in the Alfred Hitchcock film *Shadow of a Doubt,* and it is now home to the **Santa Rosa Convention & Visitors Bureau** (9 4th St., Santa Rosa, 707/577-8674 or 800/404-7673, 9 A.M.–5 P.M. Mon.–Sat., 11 A.M.–5 P.M. Sun.).

Pick up a historic walking map from the visitors bureau to see some of the other historic buildings made from the locally quarried basalt stone. The buildings now house dozens of **antique stores, jewelry stores,** and other boutiques; 4th Street is particularly rich in historical storefronts.

Old Towne Jewelers (125 4th St., Santa Rosa, 707/577-8813, 10 A.M.–5:30 P.M. Mon.–Sat.) specializes in glamorous vintage jewelry and watches from Victorian and Edwardian to mid-century and 21st century periods.

Whistlestop Antiques (130 4th St., Santa Rosa, 707/542-9474, 10 A.M.–5:30 P.M. Mon.–Sat., 11 A.M.–5 P.M. Sun.) is a collective of dozens of antique dealers worth visiting not least because of its antique home—a 1911 brick-and-steel building that won the city's first merit award for historical preservation and is typical of much of the surrounding edifices.

Over the road, **Gado Gado** (129 4th St., Santa Rosa, 707/525-8244, 11 A.M.–6 P.M. daily) is simply worth visiting if you happen to need an antique statue of a Buddha or, indeed, any other Asian artifact. The store is an ethnic wonderland of Asian and African antiques and Asian-inspired home furnishings, all imported by the owners themselves. The retail business is just part of the story—a few blocks away is the company's huge warehouse, chock-full of everything from giant Indonesian gazebos to tiny Buddhas.

Museums

Santa Rosa has only a modest number of cultural attractions, but being the biggest city in Sonoma County does mean it's the rightful home of the **Sonoma County Museum** (425 7th St., Santa Rosa, 707/579-1500, www.sonomacountymuseum.org, 11 A.M.–5 P.M. Tues.–Sun., $5). Located in the city's historic former main post office building, the museum includes permanent exhibits of historic artifacts and photos that help tell the story of the county alongside temporary local art and photography exhibits. There's also an unlikely collection of art from the world-famous artists Christo and Jeanne-Claude that was donated to the museum in 2001 by their longtime assistant Tom Golden, who's from nearby Freestone.

In 2005, the Sonoma County Museum and the **Sonoma Museum of Contemporary Art** decided to merge after determining the city could not sustain two separate institutions. The MOCA, as it was known, was relatively small but claimed to be the only museum between San Francisco and Portland, Oregon, dedicated to contemporary art. Over the coming years the Sonoma County Museum will open additional gallery space to try to cram in some of the former MOCA exhibits, eventually creating a more balanced art and history museum.

A slightly offbeat cultural attraction is the **Charles M. Schulz Museum** (2301 Hardies Ln., off W. Steele Ln., 707/579-4452, www.schulzmuseum.org, 11 A.M.–5 P.M. weekdays, 10 A.M.–5 P.M. weekends summer,

11 A.M.–5 P.M. Mon. and Wed.–Fri., 10 A.M.–5 P.M. weekends fall–spring, adults $10, kids $5), also slightly off the beaten track just north of downtown Santa Rosa, which might explain why visitor attendance has been a little lackluster since it opened. You'd better like Snoopy if you come here, as this museum is dedicated to the Snoopy creator, who lived in the city until his death in 2000. Exhibits of original cartoons by Schulz and his peers are on display alongside Snoopy-related art and other dog-related exhibits. The gift shop, of course, sells every conceivable Snoopy toy as well.

ENTERTAINMENT

Santa Rosa's entertainment scene is somewhat dispersed, but the city does have a well-established local theater group. **The Imaginists Theatre Collective** (461 Sebastopol Ave., Santa Rosa, 707/528-7554, www.theimaginists.org) puts on an eclectic series of original and imaginative plays year-round at a small theater once home to an auto-repair shop. The evening performances are usually concentrated in a two-week stretch each month. Check the website for a performance schedule.

One of the most popular live music venues in the city is the **Last Day Saloon** in the Railroad Square area (120 5th St., Santa Rosa, 707/545-2343, www.lastdaysaloon.com, bar and restaurant Thurs.–Sat. until late, and other times when a show is scheduled). It's a fairly big and somewhat grungy venue with a decent bar and basic restaurant at the front, but most people come here for the DJs or the live music—generally rock and blues with some fairly big-name bands sometimes appearing. It also boasts the biggest dance floor of any venue in the area, which is not saying much. Check the website for upcoming shows and other events.

Guerneville and Sebastopol are two other local towns to go for some late-night fun. Guerneville and its environs have probably the most diverse entertainment scene in the Russian River Valley, befitting the eclectic population that swells in the summer with an influx of both gay and straight revelers. Sebastopol's action is a little more mainstream.

Much of Guerneville's nightlife caters to the gay scene with a curious mix of rustic bars enhanced with Day-Glo furnishings, all open late (and a few open unusually early too) and all along a three-block stretch of Main Street downtown. **The Rainbow Cattle Company** (16220 Main St., 707/869-0206, 6 A.M.–2 A.M. daily) is one of the oldest, with a big outdoor patio and legendary quarts of Long Island iced tea to get patrons in the mood. The poolside bar at the **Russian River Resort** (16390 4th St., 707/869-0691, www.russianriverresort.com, from 11 A.M. daily), also known as the Triple-R, is a popular drinking location for the gay masses and has some form of entertainment on weekend nights during the summer and Friday nights during the winter.

A few miles east of Guerneville and almost an institution in the area is the **Rio Nido Roadhouse** (14540 Canyon 2 Rd., off River Rd., Rio Nido, 707/869-0821 www.rionidoroadhouse.com), which combines a rustic bar, restaurant, and poolside entertainment. Here you can lounge on a lawn next to bikers and aging hippies, surrounded by redwoods while soaking up the alcohol and the last rays of sun while tucking in to some freshly barbecued ribs and listening to a local blues band. It can be quite a trip, even for Guerneville. Bands play most weekend evenings throughout the year, and the pool is open Memorial Day–Labor Day.

About 15 minutes west on Highway 116, Monte Rio is a sort of miniature Guerneville on acid, a self-proclaimed Vacation Wonderland with more going on than its scrappy cluster of downtown buildings suggests.

Hard to miss is the brightly painted, neon-signed hump of the **Rio Theater** (20396 Bohemian Hwy., at Hwy. 116, Monte Rio, 707/865-0913, www.riotheater.com, daily summer, Wed.–Sun. winter), an old World War II–era Quonset hut, one of 170,000 churned out for emergency housing and warehousing in the 1940s. The theater now shows a program of current films that would put any big-city independent theater to shame. The weekend matinees ($6) start late afternoon, and the main

NORTHERN SONOMA FESTIVALS AND EVENTS

Whatever the time of year, there's always some sort of festival or wine-related event going on in this part of the world.

JANUARY
Wineries have to think of something to bring in customers in the depths of winter. Hence the **Winter Wineland** event (707/433-4335, www.wineroad.com), held around the middle of the month. More than 100 of the region's wineries take part. For the ticket price of $40-50, visitors get the VIP treatment and samples of limited-release wines. There's even a special designated-driver ticket price of $10.

MARCH
The region's annual **Barrel Tasting** (707/433-4335, www.wineroad.com), held on the first two weekends of the month, is a great excuse to visit as many wineries as possible in a day and sample wines straight from the barrel, whether you're interested in buying wine futures or not. Tickets are $20 in advance, $30 at the door.

APRIL
The **Passport to Dry Creek Valley,** held on the last weekend of the month, gets visitors into almost every winery in the valley, even those usually open by appointment only. Every one of them has some sort of theme for the weekend and puts on quite a party, with plenty of food and, of course, wine. The mock passports are stamped at every winery, though numbers are limited so book early. Contact the Winegrowers of Dry Creek Valley (707/433-3031, www.wdcv.com) for more information.

MAY
At the end of the month, on Memorial Day weekend, Healdsburg's antique sellers set up shop on the plaza for the one-day **Healdsburg Antique Fair** (707/433-6935, www.healdsburg.org). May is also the month that farmers markets all over Northern Sonoma dust off the stalls and start their summer season, which lasts through October or November.

JUNE
Before wine there was the Wild West, which is celebrated every year at the **Russian River Rodeo** (707/865-9854), held the first weekend of the month at the Duncans Mills Rodeo, a 15-minute drive west of Guerneville. Over in Healdsburg, the beginning of June marks the beginning of the annual **Healdsburg Jazz Festival** (www.healdsburgjazzfestival.com), a weeklong series of concerts at venues around the city.

AUGUST
They named a highway after this apple, so why not have a festival in its honor as well? The **Gravenstein Apple Fair** (800/207-9464, www.farmtrails.org) in Sebastopol is held around the middle of the month at the town's Ragle Ranch Park. It celebrates the increasingly rare little apple that is still grown in orchards along the nearby Gravenstein Highway. The event includes music, crafts, and plenty of apple-flavored fun.

SEPTEMBER
The big blowout wine event of the year is the **Sonoma Wine Country Weekend** (800/939-7666, www.sonomawinecountryweekend.com), a three-day wine, food, and arts extravaganza held during the beginning of the month at the region's wineries. The main event is the **Taste of Sonoma County,** which is usually held at a winery near Healdsburg.

Celebrate the end of summer on the beach in Guerneville at the **Russian River Jazz and Blues Festival,** usually held the weekend after Labor Day. Top jazz musicians, fine wine, late summer sun, and the option of simply floating on the river all combine to make a unique experience. Tickets for the weekend event are available starting in April from the festival organizers (510/869-1595, www.omegaevents.com).

NOVEMBER
With all the creative names for food and wine events apparently exhausted for the year, this month's reason to eat and drink to excess is called simply **A Food & Wine Affair.** Many of the region's wineries match their wines with all sorts of food on the first weekend of the month. All you have to do is get from one winery to another. Tickets ($40-60) and information are available from the Russian River Wine Road (707/433-4335, www.wineroad.com).

daily show time is 7 P.M. in winter, 7:30 P.M. in summer ($8). Check the website or call the theater for the regularly changing schedules.

If you think a movie theater satiates the cultural requirements of tiny Monte Rio, think again. Monte Rio is also home to an active nonprofit theater group, the **Pegasus Theater Company,** established in 1998 by some veteran regional actors. It puts on plays and readings during the year, most from well-known playwrights (except the holiday variety show). Each runs for about six weeks at the 90-seat Pegasus Theater (20347 Hwy. 116, Monte Rio, 707/522-9043, www.pegasustheater.com).

Live local bands, DJ dance nights, and the occasional open-mike night are the main forms of entertainment at the **Hopmonk Tavern** (230 Petaluma Ave., 707/829-7300, www.hopmonk. com, daily until late) in Sebastopol. There's something going on nearly every night, particularly in summer when the dance action can also sometimes spill out onto the patio. Check the website for upcoming events. Covers for live bands range $5–30, and most come on around 8 P.M. There's also a late-night menu for anyone looking for some food to wash down the microbrews made here.

RECREATION

Two big wilderness areas, miles of river, tracts of forest, and a limited population make almost any sort of outdoor pursuit possible in the Russian River Valley, whether on land, on water, or in the air.

◖ Armstrong Redwoods State Reserve

This 805-acre reserve is just a few miles up Armstrong Woods Road from the center of Guerneville and is, as its name suggests, home to some neck-twistingly tall redwoods. The shady and damp forest provides welcome relief from the summer heat and is now the largest remaining old-growth redwood forest in Sonoma.

Some of its trees survived the region's vast 19th-century logging operations and were ironically saved by a lumberman—Colonel James

© PHILIP GOLDSMITH

Redwoods are almost as common as vines in the Russian River Valley.

Armstrong—who bought the land in the 1870s to preserve the last tracts of the very same forest he profited from.

Visitors with little time or energy can make a short trek on groomed paths from one of the three parking lots to some fine redwood specimens, including the 308-foot-tall Armstrong Tree, which is believed to be about 1,400 years old. If craning your neck is too strenuous, relax at one of the picnic tables scattered among the trees.

The more adventurous can choose from any number of longer hikes up out of the redwoods to the oak and madrone forests on the ridges higher up and continue on into the Austin Creek State Recreation Area, which is north of the reserve.

One such hike is a relatively quick loop (2.2 miles) that illustrates the wide range of vegetation and microclimates. The **East Ridge Trail** climbs steeply from just behind the visitors center up to a warm ridge that ducks in and out of the sun before descending back into the redwoods (head down the hill at the first sign-posted trail junction, or the hike will become a half-day ordeal). Once back in the redwoods it's an easy walk down the road or the **Pioneer Trail** back to the visitors center.

Another moderate loop is the 2.3-mile **Pool Ridge Trail,** which climbs 500 feet up a series of switchbacks before looping back down into the forest.

The reserve is open sunrise to sunset, and there's a $8 day-use fee for cars. Alternatively, park at the visitors center (17000 Armstrong Woods Rd., Guerneville, 707/869-2958, 11 A.M.–3 P.M. weekdays, 10 A.M.–4 P.M. Sat.-Sun.) and walk in on the road or a trail to avoid the fee. Dogs and bikes are not allowed on any trails. For more information, call 707/869-2015.

Austin Creek State Recreation Area
More adventurous outdoorsy types might want to drive straight through the Armstrong reserve up the steep switchbacking road (no trailers and vehicles over 20 feet) to this 5,700-acre wilderness with 20 miles of hiking trails, chaparral and oak woodlands, rolling hills, and meandering creeks (17000 Armstrong Woods Rd., 707/869-2015, day use $8).

The road ends at the Bullfrog Pond campground but stops at several trailheads on the way up, including the **Gilliam Creek Trail,** which dives down to Schoolhouse Creek and toward a handful of primitive creek-side campgrounds. The closest of these is almost four miles, so allow plenty of time.

Horseback riding is allowed on all of the Austin Creek trails, but unless you own your own horse the only option for getting on one is with **Armstrong Woods Pack Station** concession (707/887-2939, www.redwoodhorses.com), which operates by reservation only from down in the Armstrong Redwoods reserve. Two-hour rides to full-day trips are available year-round (weather permitting) from $80. There's usually a four-person minimum for the rides, though if there are not enough riders

booked, there's also the option of a two-person ride for double the normal price.

Riverfront Regional Park
About three miles south of J Vineyards on Eastside Road, this park is the perfect retreat to stretch your legs or sit in the shade of a redwood grove next to the parking lot and enjoy a picnic. The former gravel-mining operation here left behind a series of small lakes that look very inviting on a hot summer day but are strictly off-limits to swimmers. Several miles of trails around the 300-acre park give plenty of chances to see the wildlife on and around the lakes, however, and fishing for bass in the lakes is allowed with a current license. A new picnic area opened at the end of 2007 (along with permanent restroom facilities) about a half mile from the main parking lot. Just beyond that is the Russian River, where you can swim if you're brave enough. There's no official river access and no real beach, but it's easy enough to get down to the water if you're desperate to cool off. The park is open sunrise to sunset, and there's a $6 day-use fee.

(The Russian River
With the Russian River gently snaking through the vineyards and forests towards the sea, it's not surprising that canoeing and kayaking are popular summer activities here. The river flow is relatively smooth this far downstream, even in the winter when the water is higher and faster, so don't expect any adrenaline-pumping rapids. Do expect to have to slather on the sunscreen on a hot summer day, however, and not to care if you tip over and take an unexpected dip in the river.

The least strenuous way to experience the river's meandering pace is to rent a canoe at **Burkes Canoe Trips** (8600 River Rd., Forestville, 707/887-1222, www.burkescanoeetrips.com, May–Sept., $60 per day). Paddle or simply float 10 miles downriver, stopping at the many secluded beaches along the way, to Guerneville, where courtesy shuttles run back to base every half hour all day long.

For a slightly more strenuous option

RUSSIAN RIVER BEACHES

It can get hot in this part of Sonoma in the summer – too hot for even a chilled chardonnay to take the edge off. Luckily, the cool waters of the Russian River are always only a short drive away, though perhaps best experienced without being inebriated.

Native Americans had a good name for the river – Long Snake – and as it snakes its way down the Alexander Valley, loops around Fitch Mountain in Healdsburg, then barrels past Guerneville to the ocean, there are ample opportunities to take a dip.

As summer temperatures soar and the water level falls, the river is relatively calm and benign compared to the swift torrent it can become in the winter and spring, fed by the rains and melting snow hundreds of miles away in the mountains. Don't be fooled, though: It's still fairly cold with plenty of hidden obstacles underwater.

The dozens of small beaches exposed as the water level falls in the summer are technically public land, but getting to them usually involves crossing private or restricted areas. That puts many out of reach unless you're floating down the river in a canoe – the best way to experience some summer river fun.

It is still possible to get to some key beaches from the road, however.

In the Alexander Valley west of Geyserville on Highway 128 is the **Geyserville Bridge,** with space for a few cars to park off the side of the road at both ends. The easiest way down to the river is a short trail at the southwest end of the bridge that leads down to a gravelly beach area and stretches for quite a ways downstream.

A better place for swimming in the area is **Memorial Beach** at the southern end of Healdsburg, just across the Memorial Bridge. This is a more family-friendly beach with a swimming lagoon and concession stands for renting canoes. There's a $5 fee for parking in the lot, which can fill up quickly in the summer. Finding free parking anywhere near the beach is usually tough. The best alternative is to park on 1st Street in Healdsburg and walk back over the bridge.

As the river snakes its way down toward Guerneville the beaches become less plentiful and some of the visitors less modest. Don't be surprised at the occasional nude sunbather, especially at some of the more secluded sunning spots.

The historic **Wohler Bridge** on Wohler Road (just off the southern end of the Westside Rd.) has a small parking lot and boat ramp at the west side of the bridge and some limited parking along the road. Walk back to the other side of the bridge, hop over the steel gate, and follow the gravel trail for about a half mile, past the Water Agency yard and bearing right at a small fork until you reach the meadow and generally sandy beach just beyond. This is a popular beach with nude sunbathers and has recently gained a reputation as a gay cruising area.

Continue southeast on Wohler Road, past the Raford House B&B, and turn right on River Road. About one mile further, on the right, is the entrance to **Steelhead Beach** ($5 day-use fee). The large parking lot and boat ramp at the main beach hint at the spot's popularity for fishing and canoeing. A couple of trails heading east from the parking area lead to a more secluded stretch of beach that is better for swimming.

Farther along River Road, just west of the junction with Westside Road, is **Sunset Beach** (also known as Hacienda Beach), a popular spot with locals but easy to miss. Look for tiny Sunset Avenue off the south side of River Road next to a cluster of old wooden buildings. Parking on Sunset is illegal unless you live there, but there's usually plenty of space on the wide shoulder along River Road. At the first bend on Sunset Avenue there's a dusty trail off to the right leading down to a wide, gravelly beach and a good swimming hole. From there you can walk further downstream to additional, more secluded beaches.

Another good family beach is **Johnson's Beach** in the middle of Guerneville, just a few hundred yards off Main Street, where a makeshift dam is set up each summer to create a lagoon for swimming or paddling around in a rented canoe. It's crowded in summer, but the big parking lot is free, the food plentiful, and the atmosphere fun. The beach is also the site of the town's Fourth of July bash and the annual Jazz on the River festival.

© ROBERT JANOVER

Take a dip in the cool Russian River on a hot summer day.

involving real "sit on top" touring kayaks rather than the glorified aluminum cans that most places rent, go to **Russian River Outfitters** (behind the old railway depot building on Moscow Rd., 707/865-9080), farther downstream in the old logging town of Duncans Mills, about five miles west of Guerneville. From here it is six miles to the ocean at Jenner, where a shuttle can pick you up by prior arrangement, or simply paddle upstream to the beach at Monte Rio and back.

Single kayaks cost from $55 for a half day and doubles from $75. This less-populated section of the river downstream from Guerneville is where you're less likely to see garbage and old tires, and more likely to see some of the river's wildlife, including otters, herons, and an occasional turtle sunning itself.

Kayaks and canoes can be rented for a day or more from **Kings Sport & Tackle** in Guerneville (16258 Main St., 707/869-2156, www.guernevillesport.com, open daily). Single kayaks cost $30 per day, doubles are $50, and aluminum canoes cost $55. From Guerneville's

Johnson's Beach, it's four miles to Monte Rio downstream or eight miles to Forestville upstream. Make it a round-trip or pay $15 for the store to send a shuttle for pickup or drop-off (9 A.M.–2 P.M. only).

Fishing for the river's bass, bluegill, catfish, and winter salmon is also popular from a rented canoe or one of the many beaches, though a California fishing license is required. Two-day and longer licenses can be bought at Kings Sport & Tackle in Guerneville (which also rents fishing equipment) and most other tackle shops in the area. Also ask about the myriad rules and regulations. Barbed hooks cannot be used, for example, and only artificial lures (no bait) are allowed during the summer.

Ballooning

While not as plentiful as in the Napa Valley area, there are still plenty of opportunities to take to the air in this part of the Wine Country, and, arguably, the aerial views of vineyards, mountains, rivers, forests, and the distant ocean are more impressive than in less scenically diverse Napa.

Taking to the air in Wine Country, of course, usually means ballooning, which entails getting up before the crack of dawn (balloons typically take off not long after sunrise), spending several hundred dollars, waiting around as the balloon is set up, and having little idea of which way it will drift once it does get airborne. Almost everyone thinks the reward, however, is worth it, as the initial adrenaline surge from lifting off yields to a sense of relaxation from being in a still and silent world thousands of feet above the stress of daily life.

Flights usually last about an hour, but expect the whole experience, including a post-flight brunch, to take up about half a day. Also expect to have to make reservations up to a month in advance during the summer and be held to a strict cancellation policy. Full directions to the meeting place along with any flight-related updates are provided once you make a reservation.

Wine Country Balloons (707/538-7359 or 800/759-5638, www.balloontours.com, $225 pp) usually flies from the Sonoma County airport near Santa Rosa and meets passengers at a nearby restaurant. **Up and Away** (707/836-0171 or 800/711-2998, www.up-away.com, $235 pp) also meets passengers at the Sonoma County airport, though balloons may take off elsewhere, depending on the weather. Both companies' balloons fly year-round and usually carry 6–8 people, though private flights can also be arranged for a lot more money.

Golf
Stroll among the redwoods without donning hiking boots at the **Northwood Golf Club** in Monte Rio, just west of Guerneville (19400 Hwy. 116, Monte Rio, 707/865-1116). The historic par-36, nine-hole course was conceived by members of the exclusive gentlemen's retreat Bohemian Grove, just across the road, designed by famous course architect Alistair McKenzie (who also designed the Augusta National course), and completed in 1928.

Weekend greens fees start at $28 for nine holes, $43 for 18.

Russian River Spas
The spa destination in the Russian River Valley is as alternative as its remote location on the Bohemian Highway just south of Occidental suggests. The mud baths at **Osmosis** (209 Bohemian Hwy., Occidental, 707/823-8231, www.osmosis.com, 9 A.M.–8 P.M. daily) are of the dry variety, in which hundreds of enzymes are mixed with rice bran and ground-up evergreen leaves to ferment the impurities out of the skin. The warm, relaxing treatment is best enjoyed before consuming the local fermented grape juice, however; otherwise an early hangover might be the only result. The enzyme baths cost from $75 each for couples ($85 for a single person) and include a pretreatment tea service in the peaceful Zen garden. Massages and facials are available to complete the rejuvenation process, and full packages incorporating two or three treatments start at $190.

ACCOMMODATIONS
The main city in these parts is Santa Rosa, and it has perhaps more rooms than any other town, although mostly in chain hotels. But the bohemian resort town of Guerneville and the surrounding area offer the widest range of accommodations, from so-called river resorts that have seen better days to some classier and reasonably priced inns and B&Bs.

As usual, camping is by far the cheapest option, and there's plenty of the great outdoors to choose from, including the wilds of the backcountry and the relative comforts of the grounds of some of those resorts along the river.

If all else fails, there are usually rooms to be found in the string of motels along the freeway and to the south in Sebastopol. Just be sure to drink a glass of wine to remember that this is indeed Wine Country and not some random freeway exit to Anywhere, USA.

Under $100
The **Creekside Inn** (16180 Neely Rd.,

Guerneville, 707/869-3623, www.creeksideinn.com) is indeed right beside the creek otherwise known as the Russian River. It is just a few minutes' stroll to Guerneville's main street but also even closer to noisy Highway 116. Nevertheless, the rooms in the main house are cheap, starting at $98 for those with rather plain furnishings and increasing to $175 for the more sumptuously decorated suites with their own decks that can sleep four. The several acres of grounds include a pool and eight cottages, from studios to two-bedrooms, starting at $130 per night, and a handful of new solar-powered Nature Suites starting at $200 per night that come with fully equipped kitchens and can sleep four.

Rather like a funky Guerneville version of an 1830s resort, **Fern Grove Cottages** (16650 Hwy. 116, Guerneville, 707/869-8105, www.ferngrove.com) offers equal measures of tranquility and activity among the redwoods at the far western end of town. The collection of well-spaced cottages includes studio, one-bedroom, and two-bedroom accommodations starting at less than $90 per night during the week, $110 per night on weekends, plus some twists including wet bars, hot tubs, and fireplaces. They are relative bargains, though the somewhat sparse decor is a reminder that they were built in the 1920s as a cheap family resort. On-site amenities include a pool, a bar, and a giant picnic area that's a hive of activity in the summer.

$100-200

Another refreshing change from the rustic nature of many cheap lodging options in the area is the **West Sonoma Inn** (14100 Brookside Ln., Guerneville, 707/869-2470 or 800/551-1881, www.westsonomainn.com). The 36-room self-styled resort and spa is surprisingly cheap considering its relatively central location in Guerneville and the modern decor and amenities that include down comforters, fireplaces in most rooms, luxury bathrooms, and nice views. It would almost fit in to the chic Healdsburg scene. The cheapest are the two Vineyard rooms and two Creekside rooms

($109–169). The best value is the Deluxe Vineyard or Courtyard rooms ($119–179), which are more spacious and have either panoramic views or a cozy fireplace. More expensive suites range in price $139–299.

In a pretty part of the valley en route to Armstrong Redwoods State Reserve is a new hotel that adds some much needed style to the Guerneville accommodation scene, the **Boon Hotel + Spa** (14711 Armstrong Woods Rd., Guerneville, 707/869-2721, www.boonhotels.com). The new owners have transformed a tired old resort into a sleek modern hotel with 14 rooms furnished in contemporary style. Many of the rooms have fireplaces and decks, and all are appointed with luxury fixtures, high-end electronics, and quality linens, including bath robes that are ideal to wear while sipping a cocktail beside the solar-heated saline pool and hot tub. Downtown Guerneville is about a half mile away, which is easily walkable but best navigated using one of the hotel's cruiser bikes that can be rented for a modest daily or half-daily fee. The cheapest junior queen rooms without fireplaces or decks are $145–195. Rooms with a private deck cost $10–15 more, and rooms with both a fireplace and a deck start at $165–225, rising to $230–290 for the biggest king suites that can sleep four.

A few miles west of Guerneville in Monte Rio is the **Village Inn** (20822 River Blvd., off Bohemian Hwy., Monte Rio, 707/865-2304, www.villageinn-ca.com), a tastefully restored Victorian home set in the redwoods on the south bank of the river not far from the infamous Bohemian Grove, an exclusive country club for America's elite and powerful. All 11 rooms have private bathrooms and a view of something, whether trees or the river. The bargains here are the three queen studios in the main inn (all $180), which have comfy club chairs and views of the river from their private balconies. The cheapest rooms are in the separate lodge and start at $125, while the most expensive deluxe king studio ($215) has a big private deck overlooking the river. Amenities include TVs and VCRs, wireless Internet access, and mini-fridges so you can chill a bottle of Russian River chardonnay to enjoy on the balcony.

Standing sentinel at a sharp bend in Wohler Road just half a mile south of Wohler Bridge is the historic (**Raford House** (10630 Wohler Rd., Healdsburg, 707/887-9573 or 800/887-9503, www.rafordhouse.com), once part of a huge hop-growing estate in its Victorian heyday but now a charming hotel with verandahs overlooking acres of vineyards. All six rooms have private bathrooms and are decorated in a tasteful and fairly restrained Victorian style. The smallest of the six are $150–180, while the biggest rooms ($205 and up) have their own fireplaces. The largest of all, the Bridal Room, has a private covered porch overlooking the valley. Rooms at the front of the house have the best views. Standard amenities include a CD player–radio, wireless Internet access, and an evening wine reception.

One of the larger nonchain hotels in Santa Rosa is the **Hotel La Rose** (308 Wilson St., Santa Rosa, 707/579-3200 or 800/527-6738, www.hotellarose.com), an imposing basalt stone building that's part of the historic Railroad Square development downtown, within walking distance of many of the city's sights and restaurants. The 49 guest rooms in the main building and Carriage House across the street (built in 1985) cater to the tourist and business crowd alike and so are well equipped and businesslike with minimal frills on the Victorian-style decor. Standard rooms start at about $130 in winter, $150 in summer, and top-floor rooms in both buildings are the most interesting, with either vaulted or sloping ceilings.

Over $200

A bit like staying on a French country wine estate, the **Vintners Inn** (4350 Barnes Rd., Santa Rosa, 707/575-7350 or 800/421-2584, www.vintnersinn.com) sprawls amid 50 acres of manicured gardens and vineyards just a few miles north of Santa Rosa. It's ideally located for exploring the Russian River Valley, and quick access to the freeway (River Road exit) gives easy access to Healdsburg and beyond

(though also some freeway noise). All 44 rooms and suites are cozy and luxurious, some with fireplaces and all with either balconies or patios. Rates start at $195 for the patio rooms and just over $300 for the junior suites but rise rapidly in the summer and on weekends to $330–420. Breakfast is always included in the room rates, but on weekends you could also indulge with a sumptuous brunch at the Inn's renowned **John Ash & Co.** restaurant, one of the eateries credited with starting the Californian "Wine Country cuisine" style of cooking that so many other restaurants now mimic.

A little off the beaten track is the neat former railroad town of Occidental, and just off the main road on the edge of the forest is a delightfully rambling Victorian homestead that is now the (**Inn at Occidental** (3657 Church St., Occidental, 707/874-1047, www.innatoccidental.com), a quirky yet luxurious bed-and-breakfast. None of the 16 whimsical rooms and suites are alike, although all have fireplaces and are stuffed with odd pieces of folk art, as are many of the inn's common areas. Rates drop close to $200 for a few of the smaller rooms during winter, but most usually cost $250–350.

A little piece of the Mediterranean landed in the redwoods just south of Guerneville in the form of the **Applewood Inn** (13555 Hwy. 116, Guerneville, 707/869-9093 or 800/555-8509, www.applewoodinn.com). Three salmon-pink villas are nestled around a manicured central courtyard, the oldest of which is the 1922 Belden House with the cheapest (and smallest) rooms, starting at just under $200. The more modern Piccola Casa and Gate House, built since 1996, both contain the bigger and more expensive rooms, costing over $300. At those prices, the tranquil surroundings, swimming pool, in-room luxuries, and available spa therapies are to be expected. The big building at one end of the courtyard houses an outstanding restaurant offering classy Mediterranean-influenced Californian food and an extensive local-wine list. Alternatively, order a gourmet picnic basket for $50 and head for the hills.

Just a stone's throw from the Russian River,

the Farmhouse Inn

tucked away in the woods just off busy River Road, is the **Farmhouse Inn and Restaurant** (7871 River Rd., Forestville, 707/887-3300 or 800/464-6642, www.farmhouseinn.com), which has recently undergone a complete renovation and expansion to take it further up-market than it already was. Brightly painted cottages nestled among the trees house the 10 cheapest rooms with rates that start at just under $300 for the smallest (rooms 3 and 5) and rise to $345–575 for the largest suite or luxury king rooms with their own fireplaces and saunas or steam showers. A new barn was added on the site in 2007 containing seven more luxurious guest rooms that start at $525 and include every amenity you could imagine, from radiant heating and fireplaces to steam showers and jetted tubs. The restaurant is considered one of the best in the Wine Country.

Camping

There are plenty of resort campgrounds along the Russian River, but many cater to summer crowds and RVs and usually charge a premium price for the extensive services and facilities

they offer. In all cases, reservations are essential during the busy summer months.

One of the more reasonable is **Burkes Canoe Trips** (8600 River Rd., Forestville, 707/887-1222), hidden in the redwoods right next to the river (and the road) just north of Forestville. The full-service campground, open May–October, has 60 sites for tents or RVs for $10 per person per night. This is also a popular place to rent canoes. The year-round **Hilton Park Family Campground** (10750 River Rd., Forestville, 707/887-9206, www.hiltonparkcampground.com) is one of the smaller of the riverside resort campgrounds, with 49 open or secluded sites for tents ($35 per night, $40 for the premium riverside sites) and small RVs ($45), all in a lush, woodsy setting. There are also eight "camping cottages" that just about sleep two people and have space for a tent outside, but cost a relatively steep $65 per night.

The more scenic campgrounds are generally off the beaten track—well off the beaten track in the case of the primitive but scenic creek-side campgrounds high up in the **Austin Creek State Recreation Area.** The road up into the park through Armstrong Redwoods State Reserve ends at the **Bullfrog Pond Campground,** with 23 sites ($15), toilets, and drinking water. No vehicles over 20 feet long are allowed into the park, so the camping experience here is relatively free of humming RVs.

From Bullfrog Pond it's about a three-mile hike to the **Tom King Trail** and **Gilliam Creek Trail** primitive campgrounds, and about four miles to **Manning Flat** campground. A water purifier or filter is essential if you want to drink the creek water, which you probably will in the summer when it can get very hot. The required backcountry camping permits ($15 on a first-come, first-served basis), together with maps, can be picked up at the Armstrong Redwoods park office (17000 Armstrong Woods Rd., Guerneville, 707/869-2958, 11 A.M.–3 P.M. weekdays, 10 A.M.–4 P.M. Sat.–Sun.) on the way up into the Austin Creek area.

FOOD

The food scene in the Russian River Valley is one of the most varied in northern Sonoma, as would be expected from a place that is effectively the produce basket of Northern California.

It certainly has its share of pricey, stylish establishments, particularly in the many inns hidden away in the woods. But since it's a down-to-earth, outdoorsy sort of place, there are also plenty of cheap and homey establishments where the lack of an uptight reservation system can make the experience instantly relaxing.

Guerneville

Being the hub of the region, Guerneville should be the first stop for those desperate for a quick and easy meal. There might be a bit of a wait in the busy summer months, particularly on festival weekends, but there are plenty of places to cater to the ravenous hordes.

This is not a five-star resort town, so don't expect five-star restaurants. Instead, most places are the caliber of the landmark **River Inn Grill** (16141 Main St., 707/869-0481, breakfast and lunch 8 A.M.–2 P.M. daily, breakfast $6–$13, lunch entrées $9–13). Its cozy booths, acres of Formica, hunks of ham, and piles of pancakes seem right out of a 1950s movie.

A California town would not be complete without its cheap Mexican restaurant, and one of Guerneville's most popular is the spacious **Taqueria la Tapatia** (16632 Main St., 707/869-1821, lunch and dinner daily, $5–12) serving decent quality food at the western end of town. More daring Mexican food connoisseurs might want to check if Guerneville's taco truck is parked in front of the Safeway parking lot for a more authentic street food experience. Right next door to the Taqueria is **Spliffs Organic Espresso** (16626 River Rd., 707/869-2230). Only in alternative Guerneville can hemp, organics, and coffee be inspiration for a name (and a big sign), though don't expect anything more potent than caffeine in the coffee.

Coffee, sandwiches, and other snacks are also available at the **Coffee Bazaar** (14045 Armstrong Woods Rd., 707/869-9706, 6 A.M.–8 P.M. daily), just around the corner from Main Street. The cool cavernous hangout is about as laid-back as things get in this part of the world, and there's a fascinating little used bookstore to browse through right next door.

With a modern, minimalist interior that looks like it belongs more to the trendy Healdsburg restaurant scene than in rustic old Guerneville, **Boon Eat & Drink** (16248 Main St., 707/869-0780, dinner and lunch Thurs.–Mon., dinner entrées $14–25) is a popular new bistro related to the nearby (and equally hip) Boon Hotel, where some of the vegetables are grown. It checks all the right boxes of a modern Wine Country bistro—organic, sustainable, and locally-produced ingredients prepared in imaginative small plates and main dishes with international influences. The small wine list is dominated by Russian River wines from small local producers.

One of the few saviors of beer drinkers in this part of Wine Country is the **Stumptown Brewery and Smokehouse** just east of Guerneville in Rio Nido (15045 River Rd., 707/869-0705, lunch and dinner Wed.–Sun.), which serves juicy ribs, brisket, and sandwiches for less than $15. Its heady microbrews, like Red Rocket and Racer 5, will get you drunk as fast as their names suggest and are best enjoyed while chilling on the giant deck out back.

Just south of Guerneville things get classier and more romantic at the 🄲 **Applewood Inn** (13555 Hwy. 116, 707/869-9093 or 800/555-8509, www.appplewoodinn.com, dinner Tues.–Sat., entrées $24–34). Seasonal dishes like braised rabbit with olives and Humboldt Fog cheese are inspired by local produce and classic French cooking. As would be expected, the wine list is a who's who of local growers and regularly wins *Wine Spectator*'s Award of Excellence.

Monte Rio and Duncans Mills

About a 15-mile drive west of Guerneville in the two-block hamlet of Duncans Mills is the **Cape Fear Café** (25191 Hwy. 116, Duncans Mills, 707/865-9246, breakfast and lunch daily, dinner Fri.–Wed., dinner entrées $16–24), where Sonoma seafood meets Southern soul food. Many dishes in this cozy restaurant have a Cajun twist, and the grits make it worth an early morning drive for breakfast or a weekend brunch.

A scenic place to grab a bite halfway between Guerneville and Duncans Mills is the **Village Inn Restaurant** (20822 River Blvd., off Bohemian Hwy., Monte Rio, 707/865-2304, dinner Wed.–Sun., entrées $14–25) in Monte Rio. The beautifully restored building and its dining patio peek out from the redwoods onto the banks of the river. Most of the bistro-style main courses are well under $20 and can be washed down with wine from the award-winning list.

Forestville

You would not expect world-class food to find a home out in the woods east of Guerneville, but that's fast becoming the reputation of the restaurant at the luxurious **Farmhouse Inn and Restaurant** (7871 River Rd., 707/887-3300 or 800/464-6642, www.farmhouseinn.com, dinner Thurs.–Mon., dinner entrées $28–42). Chef Steve Litke, a proponent of the Slow Food movement, lets the veritable treasure trove of local produce do the talking here, with dishes like oven-roasted bluenose sea bass, or roasted red kuri squash and mascarpone ravioli. With main courses averaging $30 or more and a cheese cart to die for, however, this slow food will quickly empty your wallet. The exception is the three-course prix fixe menu that is often offered on Sunday and Monday nights for a more modest $45.

Behind a modest storefront in sleepy Forestville, the **Mosaic Restaurant & Wine Lounge** (6675 Front St., 707/887-7503, lunch and dinner daily, dinner entrées $21–34) has energized the local food scene since it opened in 2005. The decor is rustic chic, with concrete floors, brick walls, and plenty of dark wood that is a perfect foil for the exuberant modern food, like the signature coffee-crusted filet mignon with chocolate-cabernet sauce and mashed potatoes. There are also simpler dishes

executed with the same flair and a wine list that includes plenty of reasonably priced local wines. If you're just after more modest sustenance or a quiet drink, head to the cozy wine bar nook at the back of the restaurant. One look at the leafy patio, however, and you might be ready to make a dinner reservation.

Graton

Halfway between Forestville and Sebastopol is the tiny rural town of Graton, home to some big names in Russian River Valley dining. The best known is the **Underwood Bar & Bistro** (9113 Graton Rd., just west of Hwy. 116, 707/823-7023, lunch Tues.–Sat., dinner Tues.–Sun., dinner entrées $19–27), where lots of dark wood, plush red booths, and a nickel-plated bar add some unique luxury beyond the rustic exterior. The Mediterranean-inspired bistro menu features tapas plates (the oysters are popular) and hearty main dishes like Catalan fish stew and Moroccan-spiced lamb. There's a late-night tapas menu served after 10 P.M. on weekend nights.

Across the road (and sharing the same owners) is a rustic local gathering spot that doubles as a country store, the **Willow Wood Market Café** (9020 Graton Rd., 707/823-0233, 8 A.M.–9 P.M. Mon.–Sat., brunch and lunch Sun.). The well-priced breakfast, lunch, and light dinner menu is always popular with locals, and the polenta ($11–15) is legendary in these parts. It is becoming a victim of its own success, however, with lines that snake out the door on the busiest lunchtimes, although the back patio provides a bit more space. On a Sunday morning, this is where those in the know come for a brunch of Willow Wood Monte Cristo washed down with a mimosa.

Sebastopol

Sebastopol is chock-full of places to eat, though many of them cater to Bay Area urban commuters and don't particularly stand out. A few are worth navigating the town's one-way street system to visit, however.

Wine is the main attraction at the ◖ **Starlight Wine Bar** (6761 Sebastopol

Ave./Hwy. 12, 707/823-1943, dinner Tues.–Sun., dinner entrées $10–29), inside a 1950s Southern Pacific railroad car now permanently stationed at the Gravenstein Station mall. The many small plates of tapas or cheese might be enough to satisfy as you explore the fascinating and reasonably priced wine list from the comfort of a booth. More filling fare comes in the form of pizzas and southern-influence comfort food like gumbo or chicken pot pie. If you think this gloriously restored railroad relic resembles a movie set, you will not be surprised to learn that the co-owners of the restaurant are former Hollywood visual effects artists.

If something more filling is needed, the popular **K&L Bistro** (119 S. Main St., 707/823-6614, lunch Mon.–Sat., dinner Mon.–Sun., dinner entrées $13–26) serves classic French-style bistro food, including French fries that are probably the best in the region. Equally suited to the relaxed, if slightly cramped, setting is K&L's famous mac and cheese, which can be ordered either as a main dish or a side.

On the western edge of town, the **French** **Garden Restaurant** (8050 Bodega Ave., 707/824-2030, lunch and dinner Wed.–Sun., entrées $25, three-course prix fixe $28 Sun. only) offers some French sophistication in an unlikely setting. The appeal here is the simple, beautifully crafted Mediterranean-inspired food that takes full advantage of the wide range of produce grown on a neighboring 16-acre farm run by the restaurant owners. The ambience in the main dining room is as awkward as the faux-Renaissance building, which formerly housed a family-style Italian restaurant, might suggest. Outdoors on the large patio is the best place to ask for a table, or you can order some of the filling appetizers from the full menu in the cozy bar warmed by a large fireplace. Sunday Brunch here is accompanied by a farm stand selling much of the same produce used in the restaurant.

The comfort food goes very well with the microbrews in the classy dining room or on the patio of the **Hopmonk Tavern** (230 Petaluma Ave., 707/829-7300, lunch and dinner daily, dinner entrées $10–19). The menu is filled with the greatest hits of pubs, such as meatloaf, fish-

NORTHERN SONOMA

© CARLYN PARKS-STALLMANN

K&L Bistro on Sebastopol's Main Street

and-chips, grilled chicken, and burgers, but the main draws are entertainment and beer, both in-house and domestic brews. The entertainment ranges from open-mike nights to DJs and live music. There's also a late-night menu. If you go for the New York steak from the menu, there's a modest wine list with plenty of middle-of-the-road wines at reasonable prices to help wash it down.

Occidental

At first glance, picture-postcard Occidental would seem to be the sort of town teeming with celebrated chefs ready to turn its sleepy Victorian charm into the next big food destination. Instead, the rural counterculture is alive and well here and so, evidently, is the Italian culture. There are almost as many Italian restaurants here as organic-labeled eateries and services (organic housecleaning, anyone?).

Find mountains of cheap Italian comfort food and surroundings in need of some updating at **Negri's** (3700 Bohemian Hwy., 707/823-5301, lunch and dinner daily, entrées $9–15). Specialties include the "world-famous" homemade ravioli, made from an old family recipe, alongside plenty of other pasta, chicken, and fried seafood dishes.

Similar family-style food with pizza thrown into the mix can be found in the homey dining room of the historic **Union Hotel** (3731 Main St., 707/874-3444, lunch and dinner daily, dinner entrées $12–20), which curiously also offers free overnight RV parking with dinner.

A breath of garlic-free fresh air is provided by the tiny French-inspired **Bistro des Copains** (3782 Bohemian Hwy., 707/874-2436, dinner daily, entrées $19–23). Classic bistro dishes include pan-seared halibut on a potato pancake with cherry tomato beurre blanc or braised cloverdale rabbit in mustard sauce with butter noodles, while a wood-fired oven ensure pizzas, breads, and roasted meats turn out perfect. The wine list is dominated by Russian River Valley and Sonoma Coast wines, including more than a dozen pinot noirs, and if you bring your own bottle of

Sonoma wine on Tuesday, the normal $15 corkage fee is waived.

Santa Rosa

With vast expanses of Napa and Sonoma Counties to explore, there are few reasons to head into Santa Rosa. One reason, however, is the city's burgeoning restaurant scene, in particular French restaurants, which might eventually persuade people to linger for longer downtown.

Some of the best restaurants are around the historic Railroad Square development near downtown. The location was obviously an inspiration when naming **La Gare** (208 Wilson St., 707/528-4355, dinner Wed.–Sun., entrées $19–44), which serves simple but sophisticated French-Swiss food, including some lavish steaks, in an old-school setting of starched white tablecloths (the French influence) and mountain ambience (from Switzerland). It was established in 1979, and such longevity is rare for a Sonoma restaurant, which means it must be doing something right.

As the French grape varietal syrah becomes more popular in Northern California, it seems only fitting that the French-American restaurant **Syrah** (205 5th St., 707/568-4002, lunch and dinner Tues.–Sat., dinner entrées $17–34) found its roots and is now a popular fixture with an impressive cheese menu. Not surprisingly, syrah and shiraz dominate the red wine portion of the wine list, but there are plenty of other California and international wines to choose from, all well-priced.

One of the most popular new restaurants on the Santa Rosa scene is **Bistro 29** (620 5th St., 707/546-2929, lunch Fri., dinner Tues.–Sat., dinner entrées $19–26). The food is inspired by Breton regional cuisine from northwestern France (29 is the number of the Département, or district, called Finistère in Brittany) and includes dishes like *fromage blanc* buckwheat gnocchi à la Bretonne, sautéed Alaskan Halibut with cauliflower-lobster risotto, and old French standbys like cassoulet and *steak frites*. The modern decor hints at French country style, and the wine list also gives a nod to French regional wines with choices from Bandol, the Rhône, the Loire, and Languedoc complementing the extensive Northern Californian options. Ask about the three-course prix fixe dinner menu ($29) that is offered midweek.

During the day, the schizophrenic **Hank's Creekside Bistro** (2800 4th St., at Farmer's Ln., 707/575-8839, breakfast and lunch daily) belongs to all-American Hank, who flips burgers and pancakes and pours coffee in a rustic diner-style atmosphere.

A favorite if slightly out-of-the-way breakfast and lunch spot for locals is **Chloe's French Café** (3883 Airway Dr., Suite 145, 707/528-3095, breakfast and lunch Mon.–Fri., sandwiches $7–9) tucked into an anonymous unit at the back of a medical building on the northern edge of the city. It has a plain-looking commercial café interior, but the gourmet cold and grilled sandwiches made from fresh local ingredients are what draw legions of fans. Chloe is not the owner but the name the Pisan family gave to their trusty old Citroën truck that they shipped over from France.

Also just north of Santa Rosa, **Willi's Wine Bar** (4404 Old Redwood Hwy., just south of River Rd., 707/526-3096, lunch Tues.–Sat., dinner daily, $7–15) is another player in the burgeoning small-plate scene, where sipping wine or cocktails is as much a part of the fun as eating. Willi's shares the same owners as Willi's Seafood and Raw Bar in Healdsburg and has a relaxed New Age ambience that creates a perfect backdrop for the globally inspired small dishes, few of which are over $10. There are so many dishes to choose from that they almost outnumber the wines.

What was once the much-loved Willowside Café reopened in 2002 as **ZaZu** (3535 Guerneville Rd., Santa Rosa, 707/523-4814, dinner Wed.–Sun., brunch weekends, dinner entrées $16–25), a stylish, compact roadhouse about three miles east of Graton that serves California-inspired northern Italian cuisine. Enjoy familiar seasonal dishes with special touches, like flat-iron steak with Point Reyes blue cheese ravioli, at copper-topped tables overlooking the vineyards.

Picnic Supplies

There is no shortage of supermarkets, including organic ones, in most of the region's towns, but a few smaller stores are worth searching out for more unusual options.

The **Korbel Delicatessen** (13250 River Rd., Guerneville, 707/824-7313, 10 A.M.–4:30 P.M. daily fall–spring, 10 A.M.–5 P.M. daily summer), right next door to the winery's tasting room, makes fat sandwiches and gourmet salads to go. Eat on the small deck outside or head off into the wilds.

The **Kozlowski Farms** store in Forestville (5566 Hwy. 116, 707/887-1587, www.kozlowskifarms.com, 9 A.M.–5 P.M. daily), hidden down a driveway a few yards north of Ross Station Road, has a deli and offers a different kind of tasting—the countless jams, jellies, sauces, and chutneys it makes. A little further toward Sebastopol is the barnlike **Andy's Market** (1691 Hwy. 116, Sebastopol, 707/823-8661, 8 A.M.–8 P.M. daily), which is part organic produce market and part grocery store. In addition to the piles of fresh produce, the market sells breads, cheeses, olives, and sandwiches. In late summer it's the place to find countless varieties of local apples, and throughout the summer you'll often find a barbeque fired up outside.

The **Duncan's Mills Wine and Cheese Company** (25179 Hwy. 116, 707/865-0565, noon–6 P.M. Wed.–Mon. summer, noon–6 P.M. Fri.–Mon. winter) is the first little building on the north side of the road from Guerneville, next to the cows, and offers not only a great selection of local wines (with regular tastings) but also an equally impressive selection of local cheeses.

And in Guerneville, almost thumbing its nose at neighboring 24-hour Safeway, is the little organic grocery store **Food for Humans** (1st St. at Mill St., 707/869-3612, 9 A.M.–8 P.M. daily), an eminently better place to buy produce.

In Santa Rosa, head to **Chloe's French Café** (3883 Airway Dr., Suite 145, 707/528-3095, breakfast and lunch Mon.–Fri., sandwiches $7–9) just north of downtown for gourmet sandwiches to go. In the heart of the downtown area, **Arrigoni's Deli** (701 4th St., Santa Rosa, 707/545-1297, 7 A.M.–4:30 P.M. Mon.–Fri., 7 A.M.–3:30 P.M. Sat., sandwiches $7–10) has a good selection if sandwiches and other deli items needed for a gourmet picnic.

There is also no shortage of tranquil places to have a picnic, from the beaches of the Russian River to the shade of the redwoods at the Armstrong Redwoods State Reserve just north of Guerneville. Or head to one of the many picnic-friendly wineries and pick up a bottle of wine to go with lunch. Some of the better picnicking wineries include Davis Bynum, Hop Kiln, and Foppiano.

Farmers Markets

With so many small towns in this agricultural region, there's a farmers market almost every day of the week, usually from Memorial Day to Labor Day. On Fridays (4 P.M.–dusk June–Oct.) it's **Occidental**'s turn, downtown in front of the Howard Station Café. **Sebastopol's** farmers market is held on Sunday morning (until 1:30 P.M. Apr.–Nov.) at the Downtown Plaza, and **Duncan's Mills** has its own on Saturday (11 A.M.–3 P.M. May–Oct.) behind the Blue Heron Restaurant on Steelhead Boulevard.

Santa Rosa has two farmers markets worth checking out. The **Santa Rosa Downtown Market** includes chef demonstrations and other entertainment alongside farm stands. It is held on 4th Street from Mendocino Avenue to E Street on Wednesday evenings 5–8:30 P.M., Memorial Day–Labor Day. The more traditional **Santa Rosa Farmers Market,** without the fun and games, can be found on Wednesday and Saturday mornings, 8:30 A.M.–noon, in the parking lot of the Veterans Building at 1351 Maple Avenue just south of the downtown area.

INFORMATION AND SERVICES

The most important tool for visiting the Russian River Valley is the excellent free map published by the **Russian River Wine Road** (707/433-4335 or 800/723-6336, www.wineroad.com), an organization representing wineries and other businesses throughout northern Sonoma that is based in Healdsburg. The map is pretty easy to find at all major wineries and covers all the major roads in the Russian River Valley and up into the Dry Creek and Alexander Valleys.

More detailed and specific information about the Russian River Valley can be found in the free guide published by the **Russian River Valley Winegrowers Association** (707/521-2534, www.rrvw.org), also widely available. Neither organization has offices open to the public.

Maps and other information about the region are available at the drop-in office of the **Russian River Chamber of Commerce** in the center of Guerneville (16209 1st St., at the old bridge, 707/869-9000 or 877/644-9001, www.russianriver.com, 10 A.M.–5 P.M. Mon.–Sat., 10 A.M.–3 P.M. Sun.). There's also an outpost at the Korbel winery in the old station house that is now the ticket office.

In downtown Santa Rosa, the **Santa Rosa Convention & Visitors Bureau** (9 4th St., Santa Rosa, 800/404-7673, www.tastesantarosa.com, 9 A.M.–5 P.M. Mon.–Sat., 10 A.M.–5 P.M. Sun.) offers countless maps and brochures about accommodation, food, and wine, and activities in the city and surrounding regions.

Also worth noting is that there are virtually no gas stations west of Sebastopol and Guerneville, so fill up in Forestville or Sebastopol if you plan to venture out to the coast.

Dry Creek Valley

This compact valley is perhaps one of the easiest parts of northern Sonoma to visit in a day, and certainly one of the easiest to get around by car or bike.

At its southern end is the Victorian town of **Healdsburg,** with plenty of Wine Country frills but still relatively crowd-free even on summer weekends. It also has a staggering number of downtown tasting rooms, so many in fact that you can't help but wonder whether they'll all survive. You could tour northern Sonoma wines, never venturing more than a few blocks from the plaza, but that would mean missing out on the rustic charms of places like the Dry Creek Valley.

Although Healdsburg is the only place to shop, stay, or eat, getting out of the town is essential if you plan to experience the area. At its hot northern end, the Dry Creek Valley is dominated by the huge Lake Sonoma Recreation Area, which offers some of the best outdoor recreation opportunities in Sonoma County. Between Healdsburg and the lake, there are vineyards, barns, and small wineries full of character, many run by eccentric characters.

Although the wine industry got an early start here when French and later Italian immigrants planted grapes in the late 1800s, Prohibition killed everything off, and for much of the 20th century the valley was full of plum and pear orchards. It was not until the early 1970s that grape growing started to pick up again, and the 7,000 acres of prune orchards that once filled the valley with their bounty shriveling in the hot sun are now long gone.

During that agricultural transition, little else apparently changed in the valley, and the only development seems to have been winery related. Just two main roads run up the valley, on either side of Dry Creek itself: West Dry Creek Road and the original Dry Creek Road, which eventually becomes Skaggs Springs Road and heads off over the coastal hills to the ocean. Apart from a couple of roads traversing the valley and cutting through the eastern hills to the freeway and Alexander Valley beyond, that's about it.

Development did significantly change one

NORTHERN SONOMA

© PHILIP GOLDSMITH

© CREDIT

rural charm in the Dry Creek Valley

NORTHERN SONOMA

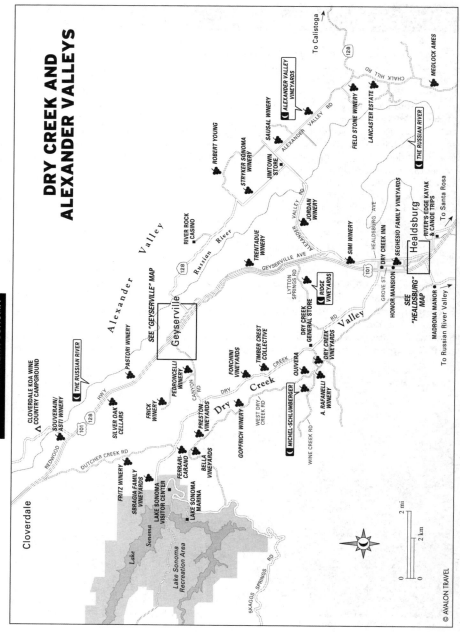

DRY CREEK AND ALEXANDER VALLEYS

Cloverdale

To Calistoga

MEDLOCK AMES

CHALK HILL RD

128

ALEXANDER VALLEY VINEYARDS

◄ THE RUSSIAN RIVER

FIELD STONE WINERY

LANCASTER ESTATE

SAUSAL WINERY

ROBERT YOUNG

STRYKER SONOMA WINERY

JIMTOWN STORE

ALEXANDER VALLEY RD

Alexander Valley

RIVER ROCK CASINO

Russian River

128

SEE "GEYSERVILLE" MAP

Geyserville

TRENTADUE WINERY

GEYSERVILLE AVE

JORDAN WINERY

SIMI WINERY

HEALDSBURG AVE

SEGHESIO FAMILY VINEYARDS

Healdsburg

RIVER'S EDGE KAYAK & CANOE TRIPS

To Santa Rosa

DRY CREEK INN

GROVE ST

SEE "HEALDSBURG" MAP

HONOR MANSION

MADRONA MANOR

To Russian River Valley

LYTTON SPRINGS RD

RIDGE VINEYARDS

ALEXANDER VALLEY RD

DRY CREEK GENERAL STORE

DRY CREEK VINEYARDS

Dry Creek Valley

101

PASTORI WINERY

PEDRONCELLI WINERY

CANYON RD

FORCHINI VINEYARDS

TIMBER CREST COLLECTIVE

DRY CREEK

QUIVERA

A. RAFANELLI WINERY

◄ MICHEL-SCHLUMBERGER

WEST DRY CREEK RD

WINE CREEK RD

FRICK WINERY

PRESTON VINEYARDS

GOPFRICH WINERY

REDWOOD HWY

128

SILVER OAK CELLARS

SOUVERAIN/ ASTI WINERY

CLOVERDALE KOA WINE COUNTRY CAMPGROUND

◄ THE RUSSIAN RIVER

DUTCHER CREEK RD

FRITZ WINERY

SBRAGIA FAMILY VINEYARDS

FERRARI-CARANO

BELLA VINEYARDS

LAKE SONOMA VISITOR CENTER

LAKE SONOMA MARINA

Lake Sonoma

Lake Sonoma Recreation Area

SKAGGS SPRINGS RD

2 mi

2 km

0

0

© AVALON TRAVEL

thing: the valley's eponymous creek. Dry Creek used to dry up to nothing more than a few puddles by the end of the summer, like the many smaller creeks running down the valley sides still do today. Since the dam that created Lake Sonoma was completed in the 1980s, however, Dry Creek has become wet year-round.

The Wines

Dry Creek is perhaps best known for its zinfandels, which can sometimes take on an overbearing, jammy style in the hotter parts of the valley. But zinfandel vines do not dominate the valley as much as the wine's prevalence might suggest and account for only about a quarter of the almost 10,000 acres of vineyards in the Dry Creek AVA. That's a big total acreage for such a small and narrow valley, especially when you consider the sprawling Russian River Valley AVA to the south only contains a few thousand acres more.

About 4,000 acres in the Dry Creek Valley are planted with cabernet sauvignon and merlot, particularly on the cooler western hillsides around places like the renowned Bradford Mountain. The hotter valley floor with its richer, alluvial soils grows excellent sauvignon blanc and, increasingly, semillon. Other varietals hint at the valley's French and Italian heritage, with syrah and petite sirah coexisting with small amounts of sangiovese and carignane.

The ideal mix of growing conditions for so many grape varietals results from the two ranges of low mountains that flank the valley—the 1,500-foot coastal hills on the valley's western side and the lower hills on the eastern side that separate it from the Alexander Valley. These hillsides have thousands of acres of benchland and canyons where growers can usually find just the right degree of heat needed for ideal ripening of most grape varietals. The hills also shield the valley from direct influence of the cold coastal air, yet just enough cool air and fog is funneled up from the Russian River Valley to prevent things from getting too hot and sticky, particularly at night.

At the far northern end of the valley, on the

hot rocky ridges overlooking Lake Sonoma, is the aptly named Rockpile AVA, established in 2002. Don't expect to be visiting wineries here, though, because there are none. In fact, there are few paved roads. The 200 acres of vineyards are planted predominantly with zinfandel and cabernet, producing intensely flavored wines for the few wineries lucky enough to own land here.

WINERIES

This part of the world offers perhaps the most eclectic mix of wineries, from rustic homespun operations of families that have been making wine for generations to the splashier newcomers reflecting the increasing popularity of the Dry Creek Valley as a major wine destination. Most wineries (even some newcomers) are fairly small and many still offer some sort of free tasting, although more are now charging a modest fee for a basic tasting, usually $5. Nearly all the wineries also have some sort of outdoor space for picnics.

Fritz Winery

Unlike many wineries in the valley, Fritz (24691 Dutcher Creek Rd., Cloverdale, 707/894-3389 or 800/418-9463, www.fritz-winery.com, 10:30 A.M.–4:30 P.M. daily, tasting $10) has actually become smaller with age after slashing its annual production by two-thirds in the mid-1990s as part of a business reorganization. Production has since crept up to almost 20,000 cases after a new vineyard was acquired in the Russian River Valley, but it is still well below 1995 levels, and the winery has recently started to focus on producing only single-vineyard wines rather than regional blends.

The estate and other Dry Creek Valley vineyards provide grapes for zinfandel, sauvignon blanc, and cabernet, including a rich cabernet from the tiny Rockpile appellation just north of here. The Russian River wines include chardonnay and pinot noir, both of which have become as highly regarded as some of the Dry Creek wines. Don't miss the two tasty Vino Valpredo–labeled proprietary blends—one a cabernet and zinfandel blend and the other sauvignon blanc and chardonnay.

The winery building itself, buried in a hillside north of the Frick Winery (with which it's sometimes confused), owes its *Jetsons*-like styling in part to the energy crisis of the late 1970s when it was built by Jay and Barbara Fritz. The patio and domed tasting room are above two levels of winery workings deep underground, so no pumps, coolers, or air-conditioning were needed, saving power and adding to its modern-day green credentials.

Sbragia Family Vineyards

This northernmost winery in the valley, with sweeping views south, couldn't help but be a success thanks to some useful family connections. Sbragia Family Vineyards (9990 Dry Creek Rd., Geyserville, 707/473-2992, www.sbragia.com, 11 A.M.–5 P.M. daily, tasting $5–10) was created by Adam Sbragia and his father, Ed, who also happens to be the winemaker at Beringer Vineyards in the Napa Valley, where he produces some of Napa's greatest cabernets.

Ed's skill at creating highly extracted yet elegant wines, together with his connections to some of the best growers in Sonoma and Napa, gave his latest family venture quite a leg up. All the wines made here are single-vineyard versions from both the family's own vineyards and other growers.

The Sbragia connection with Dry Creek Valley is a long one. Adam Sbragia was raised in the valley, and Ed worked in his father's vineyards near Healdsburg as a child. The Sbragia family still lives in the area, but their new winery is located in the former Lake Sonoma Winery facility.

Much of the wine is sourced from estate vineyards in the Dry Creek Valley and includes a merlot and a highly rated chardonnay from the 20-acre Home Ranch vineyard in the southeast part of the valley. The Gino's Vineyard zinfandel is a quintessentially spicy and jammy Dry Creek zin from the vineyard named after Ed's grandfather, and the cabernet sauvignon comes from the benchland Andolsen Vineyard owned by the family's doctor.

The Sbragias also make some limited-production wines from elsewhere in Sonoma and Napa using grapes sourced from renowned vineyards. There's an intense cabernet from Monte Rosso vineyard atop the Mayacamas Mountains above Sonoma Valley, for example, and a powerfully flavored chardonnay from Gamble Ranch in the Napa Valley. More outstanding vineyard sources are constantly being added to the portfolio, mainly cabernet in the Napa Valley, where Ed still has his day job at Beringer. They include the Rancho del Oso vineyard on Howell Mountain and the Wall vineyard on Mount Veeder, both in the Napa Valley. All the cabernets can be tasted for $10 at the winery, or choose from three of five wines for the cheaper tasting option.

Ferrari-Carano Vineyards and Winery

Ferrari-Carano (8761 Dry Creek Rd., Healdsburg, 707/433-6700 or 800/831-0381, www.ferraricarano.com, 10 A.M.–5 P.M. daily, tasting $5–15) might sound like it was established by one of the old Italian wine-making families of northern Sonoma, but this is actually the flagship winery of a hospitality empire built up by the Carano family in the last 40 years. Sister businesses include the Eldorado Hotel and Casino in Reno and the Vintners Inn in Santa Rosa.

Despite its lack of historic pedigree, the pink Italianate mansion known as Villa Fiore (which translates to House of Flowers, a fitting name when the spring bulbs are in full bloom) and the acres of manicured gardens evoke a grandiose past, albeit one that's a little out of sync with the rustic charm of most Dry Creek wineries. Equally grandiose is the huge vaulted cellar that can house up to 1,500 barrels of aging wine down the grand stairs from the main tasting room. As you wander in the lush gardens, be careful not to trample any of the flower beds, or you might meet the same fate as a wild boar that once did and is now memorialized by a statue outside the tasting room.

The 160,000 cases of wine made each year are sourced from the 1,200 acres of vineyards

© GEORGE ROSE

Villa Fiore at Ferrari-Carano Vineyards and Winery

that Carano owns throughout Sonoma, including its rapidly growing Alexander Valley mountain estate. They include a whole raft of highly rated single-vineyard chardonnays and a wide range of reds from single varietals to blends including the Bordeaux-style Tresor blend. There are also two decadent dessert wines, including the Eldorado Noir, made from black muscat.

Those are among the best wines that can be tasted downstairs (for a price) in the Enoteca Lounge, a sumptuous den opened in 2006 that is effectively the winery's reserve tasting room. It provides respite from the bustling, Mediterranean-style main tasting room and the somewhat unexceptional wines poured there. Among the best of the cheaper lineup are the fumé blanc and an unusual blend of sangiovese, cabernet sauvignon, and malbec called Siena.

Frick Winery

Proceeds from the sale of a '57 Chevy helped get Bill Frick started in the wine business in 1976 near Santa Cruz. He moved to this small hillside winery at the end of sleepy Walling Road at the far northern end of Dry Creek Valley in the late 1980s.

The six acres of estate vineyards at Frick Winery (23072 Walling Rd., off Canyon Rd. or Dutcher Creek Rd., Geyserville, 707/857-1980, www.frickwinery.com, free tasting) are mainly planted to Rhône varietals, and owner Bill Frick is perhaps Dry Creek's most ardent Rhône Ranger. The 3,000 cases of wine produced each year include syrah, viognier, cinsault, and C-Squared, which is a blend of cinsault and carignane. More unusual still is the Grenache Blanc, a white version of this varietal that is rarely seen in California.

The cottage tasting room is open noon–4:30 P.M. weekends, but by appointment only during the week.

J. Pedroncelli Winery

It no longer sells jug wines like it did up to the 1950s, but Pedroncelli (1220 Canyon Rd., Geyserville, 707/857-3531 or 800/836-3894, www.pedroncelli.com, 10 A.M.–4:30 P.M. daily) still produces some very approachable wines for the masses at the slightly ramshackle cluster of buildings on Canyon Road. None of the wines sell for more than $25 and most are under $15, making this a good place to buy a picnic wine or stock up with some everyday drinkers.

The winery has been a family affair since John Pedroncelli bought the rundown former Canota winery and 90 acres of vineyards in 1927. The 75,000-case production includes zinfandel, chardonnay, sangiovese, petite sirah, and cabernet sauvignon, all made in the style of robust, easy-drinking table wines. Nearly all the wines are sourced from Dry Creek Valley vineyards with one notable exception—a Russian River Valley pinot noir that's pretty good for its modest price.

Some more unusual wines include vintage port and a zinfandel rosé that is bone-dry compared to its distant cousin, the nasty "white zin" found at supermarkets. Zinfandel is something of a specialty here, and the portfolio includes the Mother Clone zin, sourced from clones of Victorian-era vines.

In addition to the cheap wines, a boccie ball court, a nice picnic area, and regular exhibitions by local artists make this an entertaining place to visit.

Forchini Vineyards & Winery

The Forchini family has been growing grapes in the Dry Creek and Russian River Valleys since the 1970s but only started making wines in the mid-1990s, and production hasn't grown much since then. As a result, the Forchini winery (5141 Dry Creek Rd., Healdsburg, 707/431-8886, www.forchini.com, 11 A.M.–4:30 P.M. Fri.–Sun., tasting $5) has a charming homey character that makes you feel like a privileged guest.

The 3,000 cases of wine made each year use only about a quarter of the fruit from the family's 90 acres of vineyards; the rest is sold to other winemakers. The well-balanced Dry Creek cabernet sauvignon is, unusually, blended with 10 percent carignane; the zinfandel is a typically intense Dry Creek style; and the Russian River vineyards are represented by a big, rich chardonnay and a more reserved pinot noir. The cheap and cheerful

Papa Nonno blend, made in the style of easy-drinking Tuscan table wine, is primarily zinfandel and makes a great picnic wine.

The small tasting room in the main house is open weekends only (or by appointment during the week) and has a small deck next to the cabernet vines lining the driveway.

(Ridge Vineyards

Not just the wines here but the entire building is organic. The new barrel and tasting rooms at Ridge (650 Lytton Springs Rd., Healdsburg, 707/433-7721, www.ridgewine.com, 11 A.M.–4 P.M. weekdays, 11 A.M.–5 P.M. Sat.–Sun., tasting $5) were constructed using only sustainable materials, although the contemporary design and solid feeling of the building barely hint at just how unusual the building materials actually were. The thick walls of the winery are made of rice-straw bales and a natural plaster, both chosen for their superior insulating properties. In fact, the building was the largest commercial straw-bale building when it was completed in 2003. Recycled lumber was used for the framing, flooring, and siding, and even the facing on the tasting room bar is made of pieces of old oak fermentation tanks. To cap it all off, 400 solar panels on the roof provide most of the winery's power.

The building is new, but Ridge has been active in the region for more than 30 years. It started buying grapes from the surrounding vineyards in 1972 and eventually acquired the former Lytton Springs winery property and its vineyards in 1991 to add to many other vineyards it owned throughout Northern and Central California.

Ridge is the king of zin, some years making more than 13 different versions that account for the majority of its 85,000-case annual production. Two-thirds of the zinfandel vineyards are in northern Sonoma, which makes the Lytton Springs outpost the company's Zinfandel Central, though it also makes syrah, petite sirah, and grenache. Even those who are not partial to zinfandel are likely to find at least a couple of wines to like here.

Ridge has another winery in the Santa Cruz

Mountains that is more famous for its outstanding cabernet and chardonnay, and some of those wines can often be tasted here too.

Dry Creek Vineyards
Built in 1973 not far from Dry Creek itself, this ivy-clad winery was the first to be built in the valley since the repeal of Prohibition. Although it is by no means the oldest in the valley and is far more commercial than most neighbors, the Dry Creek winery (3770 Lambert Bridge Rd., Healdsburg, 707/433-1000 or 800/864-9463, www.drycreekvineyard.com, 10:30 A.M.–4:30 P.M. daily, tasting $5) has, without doubt, played an important role in transforming the valley from prune orchards to vineyards. What it lacks in homey charm it makes up for by producing some of the best white wines in the valley.

Owner David Stare planted the valley's first sauvignon blanc vines and is now a cheerleader for the varietal. Unusually for the Dry Creek Valley, the flagship wine here is the fumé blanc, although zinfandels like the Heritage Clone are still well worth tasting. Together those two wines account for almost half the winery's annual production of 120,000 cases. A full range of other reds and whites are also made from grapes grown in the estate vineyards and throughout Sonoma, including cabernet sauvignon, chenin blanc, a meritage blend, and even a zinfandel grappa.

The nautical theme on all the wine labels and in the cavernous tasting room hints at Stare's other passion, sailing. Grab a bottle of the bargain-priced Regatta white blend or Chenin blanc and relax at a picnic table on the shady, grassed picnic area while planning the rest of your day.

◖ Michel-Schlumberger
In a beautiful mission-revival building surrounding a tranquil courtyard, Michel-Schlumberger (4155 Wine Creek Rd., off W. Dry Creek Rd., Healdsburg, 707/433-7427 or 800/447-3060, www.michelschlumberger.com, tour and tasting $15–30) is tucked away up Wine Creek Canyon and surrounded by 100

acres of undulating benchland vineyards that create a multitude of different growing conditions, from the cool heights of nearby Bradford Mountain down to the hotter canyon floor.

Unusually for the Dry Creek Valley, zinfandel is notably absent from the wine portfolio here, but that's for good reason, according to the winemaker. Good zins come from old vines, he says, and Schlumberger currently has only young zinfandel vines. The cooler hillsides do, however, favor cabernet sauvignon, merlot, pinot blanc, chardonnay, and pinot noir. The cabernets, particularly the Reserve, are outstanding illustrations that the Dry Creek Valley is good for growing more than just zinfandel. Some young-vine zinfandel does sometimes make it into the plush and popular Maison Rouge blend, however.

The cheaper wines in the portfolio are sourced from Schlumberger's 90 acres of vineyards outside the valley, including a syrah and various components of the Maison Rouge. All told, the winery produces about 20,000 cases of wine per year. Tours of the winery and vineyards followed by a wine tasting are offered twice a day by appointment at 11 A.M. and 2 P.M. for $15. Longer tours into the vineyards to learn about organic farming principles followed by an outdoor tasting are offered at 10:30 A.M. Thursday–Saturday for $30.

Quivira Vineyards
Although the winery is named after a mythical place where Spanish explorers expected to find untold riches in the 1500s, there's nothing mythical about the qualities of the vineyard-designate zinfandels and the flavorful sauvignon blanc made by biodynamic Quivira (4900 W. Dry Creek Rd., Healdsburg, 800/292-8339, www.quivirawine.com, 11 A.M.–5 P.M. daily, tasting $5, tours $15).

Those wines are Quivira's specialties, but it also makes several Rhône-style wines, including a syrah, a mourvèdre, and the highly regarded Steelhead Red blend, taking total production to about 25,000 cases annually. Quivira is also one of the few Sonoma wineries to have its vineyards certified biodynamic, and its green credentials were given a further boost in 2006 with the addition of vast array of solar panels on the winery roof that provide all its electricity.

The mythical land of Quivira shows up on many of the 16th-century maps of the Pacific region collected by the Wendt family, which founded the winery in the 1980s. They are also heavily involved in local environmental projects, including the restoration of nearby Wine Creek, said to have earned its name during Prohibition when it ran with the confiscated wine found by the authorities. The creek is a spawning ground for steelhead trout, hence the Steelhead name for the red blend. Learn more on an appointment-only tour.

Bella Vineyards

This rising star of the Dry Creek Valley was founded in the mid-1990s just up the road from Preston Vineyards as a grape supplier to other wineries, but owners Scott and Lynn Adams soon decided to start making wine themselves and have since expanded their vineyard holdings in the Dry Creek Valley and neighboring Alexander Valley. Bella (9711 W. Dry Creek Rd., Healdsburg, 707/473-9171 or 866/572-3552, www.bellawinery.com, 11 A.M.–4:30 P.M. daily, tasting $5) is now known as a producer of outstanding single-vineyard zinfandels and syrahs.

The best zinfandels are sourced from old vines in each of Bella's three vineyards, including the robust and complex Lily Hill zinfandel from the vineyard around the winery. There's also a sweet late-harvest zinfandel and a limited-production Rhône-style blend of zinfandel, syrah, and grenache called the Hillside Cuvée.

Syrah was a fairly recent addition to the portfolio, and in addition to a version made from both Dry Creek and Alexander Valley grapes, there are two very distinctive but limited-production single-vineyard versions. The best is the smoky and dense Big River Ranch syrah. Even more site-specific versions of zinfandel and syrah were released in 2007 from specific vineyard blocks.

The farm-like setting of the winery

Bella Vineyards: Taste your wine under the vines it grew on.

© SONOMA COUNTY TOURISM BUREAU

overlooking the valley is pretty enough, but the pristine caves completed in 2004 with vines growing literally right above the entrance add a touch of class to the tasting experience. Tasting wines underneath a vineyard certainly is a cool summer diversion at this hot northern end of the valley.

Preston Vineyards

Dry Creek's ubiquitous zinfandel falls way down the list of interesting wines at Lou Preston's idiosyncratic establishment. Like Fritz, this is another of Dry Creek's incredible shrinking wineries. Founded in the mid-1970s, the annual production at Preston (9282 W. Dry Creek Rd., Healdsburg, 707/433-3372, www.prestonvineyards.com, 11 A.M.–4:30 P.M. daily, tasting $5) eventually grew to 30,000 cases in the late 1980s but is now down to about 8,000.

This is probably to allow Lou and wife Susan to pursue their other varied Wine Country passions, from bread making (there's a commercial bakery on-site) to olive-oil production from the small olive grove at the winery, and even an annual boccie tournament on the winery's two boccie ball courts. The selection of locally-produced foods here rivals that in some delis and makes this an ideal place to buy everything you need for an impromptu picnic next to the boccie courts in the company of the winery cats.

The organic wines are just as varied. Zinfandel is produced here, but the list is dominated by Rhône varietals, including a highly regarded petite sirah, syrah, cinsault, carignane, mourvèdre, and an unusual blend of syrah and petite sirah (called, naturally enough, Syrah Sirah). Also worth trying are the spicy barbera, the grassy sauvignon blanc, and the cheery Guadagni Red jug wine, a robust blend of zinfandel, malvoisie, and carignane made in tribute to the Guadagni family, which established some of the best of Preston's 110 acres of vineyards in the late 1800s.

Timber Crest Collective

The distinctive red barn up the hill next to Dry Creek Road marks the location of a collective wine-making facility, shared by some of the valley's best small wineries, Timber Crest Farms (4791 Dry Creek Rd., Healdsburg, 11 A.M.–4:30 P.M. daily). The driveway is marked by a well-populated signpost next to the road. Four wineries make wines and have modest tasting rooms here—in some cases just a counter propped on barrels. Tasting is more about the wine and the unpretentious vibe than the surroundings. Indeed, the wineries are small enough that it's likely to be the winemakers themselves doing the pouring.

After decades of making wine for other valley wineries, Rick Hutchinson started his own **Amphora Winery** (707/431-7767, www.amphorawines.com) in 1997 in a small barn just down the hill from Michel-Schlumberger and recently moved his operation across the valley to this site. He makes a little over 2,000 cases of vineyard-designate zinfandel, cabernet, syrah, merlot, and petite sirah. Pottery is Hutchinson's other passion, in particular the creation of the amphorae that inspired the winery's name and appear on the wine labels.

Another long-time Dry Creek producer, Fred Peterson, moved his winery here in 2006 after 20 years making his wines up-valley, and his son has now taken over most of the wine-making duties. The **Peterson Winery** (707/431-7568, www.petersonwinery.com, tasting 11 A.M.–4:30 P.M. Sat.–Sun., weekdays by appointment) makes small lots of about a dozen different wines, with total production around 5,000 cases annually. There are several very good and well-priced zinfandels, but it is some of the more unusual (and unusually named) blends that stand out here, including a powerful cabernet-syrah blend called Shinbone and a cheap and cheerful Rhône blend called Zero Manipulation. You also can't go wrong with any of the single-vineyard wines (cabernet, syrah, and zinfandel) sourced from Fred's Bradford Mountain vineyard in the southwest corner of the valley.

The **Papapietro Perry Winery** (707/433-0422, www.papapietro-perry.com, tasting $5) was formed by two former San Francisco newspaper men, Ben Papapietro and Bruce Perry, in

1998 and has established quite a reputation for its more than half dozen pinot noirs sourced from Russian River Valley and Anderson Valley vineyards along with a more recent addition to the portfolio, a trio of zinfandels—two from nearby Dry Creek vineyards and one from the Russian River Valley. Although not all the vineyard- and clone-specific pinots are likely to be available to taste, there will still be a dizzying array of wines for any pinot or zin lover to taste.

The fourth winery at Timber Crest is a relative newcomer to this area. **Kokomo Winery** (707/433-0200, www.kokomowines.com) is the brainchild of Eric Miller, originally from Kokomo, Indiana, who makes a varied portfolio of elegant, understated wines with the help of longtime local grower Randy Peters. The Dry Creek wines include zinfandel, cabernet sauvignon, sauvignon blanc, and syrah. There are also a couple of pinot noirs, a chardonnay, and a malbec made using fruit from a vineyard to the south that straddles the Russian River Valley and Chalk Hill appellations.

Seghesio Family Vineyards

Another of the old Italian family wineries that helped define the northern Sonoma wine industry over the past hundred years is about a 20-minute walk (or five-minute drive) from Healdsburg Plaza in a building dating from the 1890s. Although it is not surrounded by bucolic vineyards and fields, the ample gardens at Seghesio (14730 Grove St., Healdsburg, 707/433-3579, www.seghesio. com, 10 A.M.–5 P.M. daily, tasting $5) make it the best place to picnic and play a game of boccie within easy reach of the plaza.

Although the winery is now in a leafy residential area rather than farmland, it remains very much a family affair, run by the grandchildren of founder Edoardo Seghesio, who arrived in the region from Italy in 1886, planted his first vines in 1895, and established the winery in 1902. The wines are very much Italian as well, sourced from 400 acres of vineyards throughout the Russian River, Alexander, and Dry Creek Valleys.

About half the winery's 80,000-case production is just one wine—the excellent and bargain-priced Sonoma County zinfandel. Even with so much made, however, it often sells out after receiving its almost-standard rave reviews in the press. At the opposite end of the zin scale are the limited-production and age-worthy San Lorenzo and Cortina zinfandels as well as one from the tiny Rockpile appellation at the northern end of the Dry Creek Valley.

Sangiovese is the other dominant varietal here and an important component in Omaggio, a blend of cabernet and sangiovese that is Seghesio's version of a super-Tuscan. The limited-production Venom is sourced from the oldest sangiovese vines in the United States and named for the rattlesnakes that thrive in the hilltop vineyard. Also represented are the Italian varietals barbera and the unusual arneis, a grape that has roots in the same Piedmont region of Italy as the Seghesios.

The best way to experience the varied portfolio of wines here is with a wine and food pairing ($35) that is offered by appointment several times a day for most of the year except in winter. Five wines are served with Cal-Ital appetizers like fettuccine primavera with prosciutto and braised chicken with black olives and porcini mushrooms at one of the winery's giant redwood-topped banquet tables.

Wineries by Appointment

Up a long driveway off West Dry Creek Road, just south of Wine Creek Road, is where the fourth generation of Rafanellis now makes its limited-production wines at the **A. Rafanelli Winery** (4685 W. Dry Creek Rd., 707/433-1385). An intense zinfandel accounts for more than half the 11,000-case annual production, and the rest is cabernet and merlot sourced from the hillside vineyards. All the wines have attained an almost cultlike status, so the winery tends to attract those serious about their zins. The views from the vegetable garden next to the old redwood barn are also pretty spectacular, which along with the difficulty getting an appointment only adds to the slightly exclusive atmosphere.

There is more than the family's German heritage to the **Göpfrich Estate Vineyard and**

Winery (7462 W. Dry Creek Rd., 707/433-1645). In addition to limited-production cabernet, zinfandel, and syrah wines from the Dry Creek estate, Göpfrich also sells limited quantities of fragrant, late-harvest German white wines including riesling, huxelrebe, and silvaner from its sister winery in the Rheinhessen region of Germany.

HEALDSBURG TASTING ROOMS

Being located at the junction of the three most important northern Sonoma appellations makes Healdsburg a good jumping-off point to visit them all. Westside Road heads down into the Russian River Valley, Dry Creek Road to its namesake's valley, and Healdsburg Avenue heads north into the Alexander Valley.

But it's just as easy to ditch the car and sample wines from those appellations and many more in the numerous downtown tasting rooms and wineries, all within walking distance from the plaza. There are more wineries represented here than most people can comfortably visit in a day and more than in any other Wine Country town. They might lack the rustic, rural charm of wineries surrounded by vineyards, but visiting these urban tasting rooms at least saves you from having to hop in and out of a hot car all day.

All opening times listed below are for the summer months through October. In winter, many tasting rooms close an hour earlier.

La Crema

One of the first tasting rooms you come to on entering Healdsburg from the south is this fancy new outpost of a well-established Russian River Valley winery. La Crema (235 Healdsburg Ave., 707/431-9400, www.la-crema.com, 10:30 A.M.–5:30 P.M. daily, tasting $5) has long since been absorbed into the Kendall-Jackson wine empire and turns out huge volumes of sometimes mediocre wine but still makes some nice examples of cool-climate pinot noir and chardonnay.

Look for the wines from the Russian River Valley, which tend to be better (and more expensive) than those from the larger Sonoma Coast region. La Crema also makes some nice pinot from other cool-climate appellations including Los Carneros and the Anderson Valley in Mendocino. The flagship wines are the limited-production pinot and chardonnay made under the Nine Barrel label, but they are not usually available to taste.

Instead the free tasting menu rotates through the La Crema portfolio, changing regularly but usually including a couple of the Russian River wines along with the cheaper Sonoma Coast versions.

Thumbprint Cellars

Touting itself as a "micro-winery," Thumbprint (102 Matheson St., 707/433-2393, www.thumbprintcellars.com, 11 A.M.–6 P.M. Sun.–Thurs., 11 A.M.–7 P.M. Fri.–Sat., tasting $5–10) was started as a hobby for winemaker Scott Lindstrom-Dake in the late 1990s and has rapidly grown to become a member of the boutique brigade. It now makes more than 3,000 cases of mainly warmer-climate, fruit-forward wines from the Alexander and Dry Creek Valleys and further north in Lake County.

The small, relaxed tasting room has a vibe that's about as far from the corporate airs of Kendall-Jackson around the corner as you can get. Try the Threesome—a sexy blend of cabernet franc, cabernet sauvignon, and syrah—or any of the other lush red wines that include syrah, zinfandel, and cabernet sauvignon. The Russian River pinot noir is one of the few cooler-climate wines but just as approachable as the others. The lone white wine is a sauvignon blanc from Lake County, and it is a veritable flavor explosion.

Both Scott and his wife are vegetarians and make all their wines without animal-based fining agents, so they're fit not only for vegetarians but also vegans. You might also pick up some interesting ideas for pairing wines with vegetarian food.

Toad Hollow Vineyards

The toad in this hollow is actually owner Todd Williams, the half brother of comedian Robin,

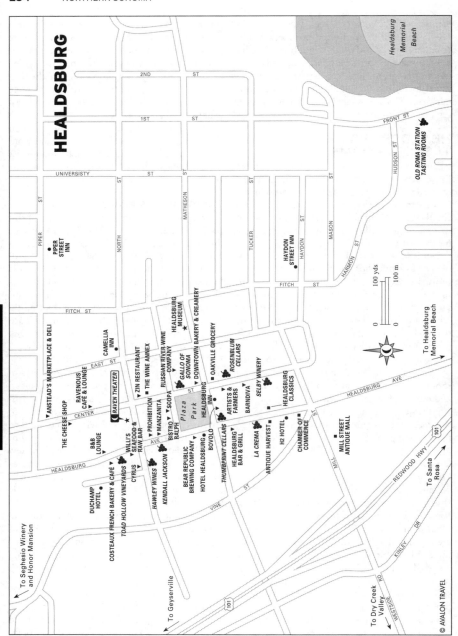

HEALDSBURG

Healdsburg Memorial Beach

2ND ST

1ST ST

FRONT ST

OLD ROMA STATION TASTING ROOMS

UNIVERSISTY ST

HUDSON ST

PIPER ST

NORTH ST

MATHESON ST

TUCKER ST

MASON ST

PIPER STREET INN

HAYDON ST

HAYDON STREET INN

HARMON ST

FITCH ST

100 yds

100 m

To Healdsburg Memorial Beach

FITCH ST

HEALDSBURG MUSEUM

ANSTEAD'S MARKETPLACE & DELI

CAMELLIA INN

EAST ST

RAVENOUS CAFÉ & LOUNGE

ZIN RESTAURANT

THE WINE ANNEX

RUSSIAN RIVER WINE COMPANY

GALLO OF SONOMA

DOWNTOWN BAKERY & CREAMERY

OAKVILLE GROCERY

ROSENBLUM CELLARS

SELBY WINERY

RAVEN THEATER

THE CHEESE SHOP

CENTER ST

B&B LOUNGE

PROHIBITION

MANZANITA

SCOPA

BISTRO RALPH

Plaza Park

HEALDSBURG INN

ARTISTS & FARMERS

BARNDIVA

HEALDSBURG CLASSICS

HEALDSBURG AVE

WILL'S SEAFOOD & RAW BAR

HEALDSBURG AVE

CYRUS

HAWLEY WINES

KENDALL JACKSON

BEAR REPUBLIC BREWING COMPANY

HOTEL HEALDSBURG

BOVOLO

THUMBPRINT CELLARS

HEALDSBURG BAR & GRILL

LA CREMA

ANTIQUE HARVEST

H2 HOTEL

CHAMBER OF COMMERCE

MILL STREET ANTIQUE MALL

MILL ST

REDWOOD HWY

To Santa Rosa

DUCHAMP HOTEL

COSTEAUX FRENCH BAKERY & CAFÉ

TOAD HOLLOW VINEYARDS

VINE ST

To Seghesio Winery and Honor Mansion

To Geyserville

101

To Dry Creek Valley

WESTSIDE RD

KINLEY DR

© AVALON TRAVEL

who has sported the amphibious nickname since his youth. This downtown tasting room is the only public face of the Russian River Valley winery where you can taste its unusual selection of red, white, rosé, and sparkling wines at the gnarled redwood bar.

Toad Hollow (409A Healdsburg Ave., 707/431-8667, www.toadhollow.com, 10:30 A.M.–5:30 P.M. daily, free tasting) is best known for its oak-free chardonnay, sourced from the 103 acres of estate vineyards, but also makes estate pinot noir and merlot, a Central Coast zinfandel, and one or two unique (and uniquely named) wines, including the popular Eyes of the Toad, a bone-dry pinot noir rosé, and a cheaper red blend called Erik's the Red, which is made from a staggering 15 different types of grape. The two sparkling wines are not local, however, but imported from France.

If the wines don't entertain, their colorful labels, painted by San Francisco artist Maureen Erickson, might. Serious wines sport a very conservative-looking toad while the fun wines see the toad in party mood.

Hawley Wines

John Hawley certainly knows the area, having been a winemaker at the giant Clos du Bois and Kendall Jackson wineries since he started his wine-making career in the 1970s. In the mid 1990s he started making small quantities of wine under his own label, and along with help from his sons has since expanded his portfolio to about a dozen varietals sourced from a wide variety of northern Sonoma vineyards, including the family's own estate on Bradford Mountain in the Dry Creek Valley.

From overseeing the production of a several million cases of wine at Kendal Jackson, he now focuses on making a few hundred cases of each of his own wines today. Hawley's Russian River wines include pinot noir and chardonnay. Wines from the estate vineyard in the Dry Creek Valley include an acclaimed barrel-fermented viognier, a classic Dry Creek zinfandel, and a merlot from the Bradford Mountain estate that usually sells out fast. Two cabernet sauvignons are also made, one

from Dry Creek fruit and one from Alexander Valley fruit.

Hawley (36 North St., 707/473-9500, www.hawleywine.com, 11 A.M.–6 P.M. daily, tasting $5) completed a new wine-making facility just a few miles away in 2000. This new downtown tasting room opened in late 2009 and is as much a showcase for the family's wines as for its resident artist, Dana Hawley. Her striking figurative work and impressionist paintings of vineyards and other Northern California landscapes add a splash of color and class to the elegant tasting room.

Rosenblum Cellars

Although the winery itself is in industrial Alameda just across the bay from San Francisco, Rosenblum (250 Center St., 707/431-1169, www.rosenblumcellars.com, 11 A.M.–6 P.M. daily, tasting $5–8) is best known for its big, bold, highly praised zinfandels sourced from vineyards in the Dry Creek Valley and Rockpile appellations, hence the tasting room in Healdsburg next to the Oakville Grocery.

Zinfandels might dominate the 100,000-case annual output, but Rosenblum also makes a lot of other wines from vineyards all over California. These include some rich muscat dessert wines and the fun Coat du Bone blends sold under the Chateau La Paws label—a tribute to the veterinarian roots of founder Dr. Kent Rosenblum.

The tasting room is through a vine-draped pergola just a few yards down Center Street from the Oakville Grocery and shares its space with a small art gallery.

Selby Winery

Down Center Street from Rosenblum and almost opposite the police department is the tiny tasting room of the Selby Winery (215 Center St., 707/431-1288, www.selbywinery.com, 11 A.M.–5:30 P.M. daily, tasting free or $5), which has its production facility in a nearby warehouse.

The 10,000 cases of wine Selby makes each year come from vineyards all over Sonoma, with an emphasis on the nearby Russian River

Valley, Alexander Valley, and Dry Creek Valley. The Russian River Valley chardonnay is perhaps the best wine here and one that regularly wins praise from the critics. The reserve chardonnay has even been served at the White House.

Other wines include a Russian River pinot noir, a couple of nicely structured syrahs, including a dry syrah rosé, and some nice zinfandels, including a juicy port. Most of the red bordeaux varietals are also in the winery's large portfolio, including a nice malbec from the nearby Chalk Hill appellation.

All can be tasted free in the relaxed and usually very quiet tasting room, where you're as likely to see a few locals hanging out as you are visitors. There's a nominal charge for trying the reserve wines.

Gallo of Sonoma

It might be part of the largest privately owned wine company in California, and the largest landowner in Sonoma County, but Gallo of Sonoma (320 Center St., 866/942-9463, www.gallosonoma.com, 11 A.M.–5 P.M. Sun.–Wed., 10 A.M.–6 P.M. Thurs.–Sat., tasting $5–15) has a remarkably modest, café-style tasting room on the plaza that only opened in 2002.

Also remarkable is the fact that this is the only place that the public can taste Gallo's best wines, made under the Gallo of Sonoma label. None of the countless historic wineries acquired by Gallo over the years, including the nearby Frei Brothers winery in the Dry Creek Valley, are open to the public. A local supermarket is the place to pick up some of Gallo's 57 other labels of cheap and cheerful brands.

The premium wines poured here include the full range of reds, including the Italian varietals barbera and sangiovese. Whites are represented by chardonnay and pinot gris, and some of the wines, most notably the cabernet and chardonnay, are available in more expensive vineyard-specific and estate forms.

The stalwart Sonoma County cabernet and chardonnay are consistently highly rated and a good price. And with so many wines to taste, Gallo has created a series of fun and educational tasting flights that range in price from nothing to $15.

You can do a horizontal tasting (sample wines of the same varietal from different vineyards or regions), a vertical tasting (different vintages of the same wine), a cabernet tasting, and even an oak tasting that compares white wines that have had different oak treatments, from barrel fermentation to no oak contact. Or you can simply pick three of the single-vineyard wines and watch the world go by on the plaza.

Kendall-Jackson

If Gallo is the largest landowner in Sonoma County, then the Kendall-Jackson (337 Healdsburg Ave., Healdsburg, 707/433-7102, www.kj.com, 10 A.M.–5 P.M. daily, tasting $5–15) empire can boast the county's highest acreage of vineyards.

The Healdsburg tasting room of this Sonoma wine titan is a cavernous but chintzy place that offers tastes of some of the bewildering array of wines for $5, including not only Kendall-Jackson wines but also some from the numerous other wineries the company owns in California and Australia. Tasting the reasonably priced reserves and other high-end wines costs $15.

If there is a specific wine not available for tasting here, it might be offered at the main visitors center (5007 Fulton Rd., Healdsburg, 707/571-7500, 10 A.M.–5 P.M. daily), a French-style château next to U.S. 101 at the Fulton Road exit, a short drive south of Healdsburg. Before you go to either tasting room, visit the winery's website, where there's often a coupon that can be printed for a free tasting.

Old Roma Station

A dozen small wineries have tasting rooms in the Old Roma Station (Front St. and Hudson St., Healdsburg, www.oldromastation.com), an old complex of warehouses on the southern edge of town right across from the Russian River, a pleasant 10-minute walk from the plaza. This was once home to the Roma Winery, a Victorian-era winery that shipped

© SONOMA COUNTY TOURISM BUREAU

Kendall-Jackson

fortified wines by rail from its own station before the trains were halted by Prohibition. After finding various uses throughout the rest of the 20th century, the complex was renovated a few years ago and is once again home to wineries, often referred to by locals as the Front Street Wineries. Most offer tasting every day, but some are appointment-only, and a few are closed for a few days midweek. Whatever time you visit, however, you're sure to taste some unique wines from unique wineries, the most notable of which are listed below.

The tiny tasting room of the boutique **Camellia Cellars** (57 Front St., Healdsburg, 707/433-1290, www.camelliacellars.com, 11 A.M.–6 P.M. daily) makes less than 2,000 cases per year of sangiovese, cabernet, and its super-Tuscan Proprietor's Blend.

Dry Creek zinfandels and cabernets are the specialties of **Pezzi King Vineyards** (707/431-9388, www.pezziking.com, tasting by appointment). It makes a half dozen zins, including several nice single-vineyard and old-vines versions sourced from the estate vineyard. The estate zinfandel and cabernet sauvignon are standouts, along with a nice Russian River Valley chardonnay.

Sapphire Hill Vineyards (707/431-1888, www.sapphirehill.com, 11 A.M.–4:30 P.M. Thurs.–Mon.) produces several thousand cases of Russian River Valley chardonnay, syrah, pinot noir, and four single-vineyard zinfandels, including a late-harvest version. The best value is a juicy blend of syrah and zinfandel called Harlot. Also ask about the infamous limited-release zinfandel called VineAgra that is only available in (you guessed it) magnums rather than those regular-sized bottles.

J. Keverson Winery (707/484-3083, www.jkeverson.com, 11 A.M.–5 P.M. Thurs.–Mon.) makes a couple of very good Dry Creek and Russian River zinfandels, but is also well known for its Carneros chardonnays. Also worth trying is a light and vibrant sangiovese from Mendocino.

SIGHTS

Healdsburg is one of the more appealing Wine Country towns, with the right mix of history, modernity, shops, and wine, and a population

(11,000) that's large enough to prevent the town's economy from lurching too far in favor of wine tourism.

There is still plenty of Wine Country paraphernalia here, however, and there are often-voiced concerns that the town is being "St. Helena-ized," but it remains decidedly less frenetic than that smaller Napa Valley town. This could be partly thanks to some of its active cultural counterweights, including the loose collective of local artists called Stark Raving Beautiful, who have the motto "Help Make Healdsburg Weird" and a desire to prevent the town from becoming a "bourgeois play-land."

The town has a history as storied as any other in the region. It was established in the mid-1800s by an enterprising former gold miner from Ohio, Harmon Heald, who eventually bought enough parcels of land to lay out the town around a Spanish-style plaza and sell plots to other businessmen. He bought the land from Captain Henry Fitch, who was granted most of the surrounding area by the Mexican government and whose name lives on in Fitch Mountain, the small hump at the bend in the Russian River just east of the town.

Healdsburg was incorporated in 1867 and boomed after the railroad arrived in 1871. Like many of the region's towns, it went through a slump brought on by the 1906 earthquake, the Great Depression, and Prohibition, but returned to prosperity after Prohibition, when the region's agriculture and wine industry took off.

The modest-looking **Healdsburg Museum & Historical Society** (221 Matheson St. at Fitch St., 707/431-3325, www.healdsburgmuseum.org, 11 A.M.–4 P.M. Wed.–Sun., free), a few blocks from the plaza, is a treasure trove of information and photos illustrating the town's Victorian heyday and its Native American roots. Serious history buffs can pore through oral histories, official records, and newspapers going back to the 1860s.

Ask for a pamphlet about historic homes and visit some of the many Victorian buildings around town. The library itself is in one of Healdsburg's most notable neoclassical

buildings, and the **Healdsburg Plaza** has been constantly reinvented since it was created in 1873.

The plaza was donated to the city by Harmon Heald in the 1850s, but nothing much was done with the patch of glass and oak trees until the 1870s, when it was cleared and fenced and the diagonal paths were laid out. Over the following decades features came and went with the fashions of the times—first a bell tower in the middle of the plaza, then a gazebo, and finally a bandstand. Most of the mature trees in the plaza today were planted between 1897 and 1900, including Canary date palms, orange and lemon trees, and a rare dawn redwood from China that is deciduous.

The bandstand survived until 1960, when the modern plaza finally took shape, with a new fountain in its center and new landscape design based around the mature trees. The last addition of note is the pavilion on the east side of the plaza, which was built in 1986 and resembles (in postmodernist style) the gazebo that had stood on the plaza a century earlier.

ENTERTAINMENT
◖ Raven Performing Arts Theater

Hats off to Healdsburg's fiercely independent Raven Performing Arts Theater (115 North St., 707/433-6335, www.raventheater.org) for keeping it real in the middle of Wine Country.

Believe it or not, there are four movie theaters squeezed into the **Raven Film Center** (415 Center St., 707/522-0330, www.srentertainmentgrp.com) behind this historic building (though one is about the size of an average living room), so there's usually a combination of mainstream, independent, and documentary films showing 3–5 times every day (entrance on Center St., admission $9, matinees $6). For a more unique Wine Country movie experience, opt for a Hollywood & Vine ticket, which costs $11.50 but includes snacks and a glass of wine that you can drink at your leisure.

The theater is owned by a performing arts cooperative, ensuring an eclectic mix of live performances, most of which revolve around

© PHILIP GOLDSMITH

The independent Raven Performing Arts Theater helps keep Healdsburg real.

music, from Broadway musicals to jazz, classical, and rock. Local artists feature as strongly as national and international acts, particularly in the occasional theater productions put on by local groups and ensembles. Check the website for a full calendar of events or stop by the theater a block away from the plaza to check the listings and catch a movie.

Nightlife

A couple of local hangouts keep the bar scene in Healdsburg real too, staying open all day, every day until 2 A.M. Both **John & Zeke's Bar & Grill** (111 Plaza St., 707/433-3735) and the **B&B Lounge** (420 Healdsburg Ave., 707/433-5960) have a no-nonsense attitude and grumpy bartenders, and they shun Wine Country frills for good old-fashioned barroom entertainment like jukeboxes, pool, and darts. The B&B is more popular with locals and slightly less of a dive.

At the other end of the drinking spectrum

are places like **Barndiva** (231 Center St., Healdsburg, 707/431-0100) and **Willi's Wine Bar** (4404 Old Redwood Hwy., just south of River Rd., 707/526-3096), where cocktails are often the drink of choice, the Hawaiian shirt is the clothing of choice, and the entertainment revolves around fancy food and people-watching. Both have nice patios outside that are the best places to nurse a drink on a warm summer evening.

A novel addition to the upscale Healdsburg bar scene, **Prohibition** (340 Healdsburg Ave, 707/473-9463, 11 A.M.–9 P.M. daily) opened in early 2010. As the name suggests, it's a bar that celebrates the secret speakeasy joints that flourished in the area during prohibition in the 1920s. Pass through a secret door in a corner phone booth at the back of a harmless-looking shop selling wine-related knick-knacks and enter a world of exposed brick, wood, and leather where it's not home-brewed hooch but cocktails and fine wines from small, high-end local producers that is served. The wine bar was the idea of the owner of the local Grape Leaf Inn who fondly remembers his grandfather's stories about running a real Prohibition-era speakeasy.

As Healdsburg slowly goes upscale, jazz is fast becoming the evening music of choice. The poster child for upscale, the swank **Hotel Healdsburg** (25 Matheson St., 707/431-2800) usually has some sort of live jazz in its lobby on Friday and Saturday evenings from 7 P.M. during the summer.

The best place to escape the Wine Country scene and nurse a cold beer at a small hole-in-the-wall bar is, ironically, right among the wineries of Dry Creek Valley. The **Dry Creek Bar** (3495 Dry Creek Rd., at Lambert Bridge Rd., 707/433-4171) at the Dry Creek General Store is open daily from 3 P.M. Grab a beer, sit outside, and watch the wine tasters drive by. Closing time varies and usually depends on how many people are left propping up the bar.

SHOPPING

Wine is about all you'll be buying in most of the Dry Creek Valley, except in Healdsburg, a

NORTHERN SONOMA

town of boutiques and antiques. Most of the treasures have long gone and many of the old antique stores have gone too as rents increased, but it's still fun to rummage through the handful of stores that remain along Healdsburg Avenue just south of the plaza.

The barnlike antiques cooperative **Healdsburg Classics** (226 Healdsburg Ave., 707/433-4315, 10 A.M.–5 P.M. daily) features the wares of more than 20 small dealers and is fun to rummage around in. There's another antiques cooperative a short distance away at the **Mill Street Antique Mall** (44 Mill St., just off Healdsburg Ave., 707/433-8409, 11 A.M.–5 P.M. daily). It boasts more than 20,000 square feet of floor space that is home to numerous local dealers and craftspeople.

Possibly the best place in town to buy a unique gift is **Artists & Farmers** (237 Center St., 707/431-7404, 10 A.M.–5 P.M. Mon.–Fri., 10 A.M.–6 P.M. Sat.–Sun.), a cavernous space in what used to be part of the town's opera house that is part studio and part marketplace, featuring artistic gifts and home furnishings together with unusual foods and fresh-cut flowers. It is a spin-off of the Barndiva restaurant next door, and it sells some of the same locally sourced foods as well as glasses and dishes used at the restaurant. It's far from just a cynical marketing exercise for Barndiva, however, and has developed more of a showcase of weird and wonderful artistic creations from local and global artisans. Wine Country clichés are nowhere to be seen among the products, and prices of many of the unique creations are not as expensive as the hipper-than-thou atmosphere suggests.

Other shopping highlights include the **Russian River Wine Company** (132 Plaza St., 707/433-0490, 11 A.M.–4 P.M. Tues.–Fri., 11 A.M.–6 P.M. Sat.), which sells wine from all over the area, not just the Russian River, and specializes in smaller producers. The space also doubles as the Healdsburg tasting room of **Sunce Winery,** a small Russian River Valley winery that specializes in small-lot wines from the region, most notably some lean chardonnays and a rich, age-worthy Meritage red blend. Right next door is the cool tranquil

space of the **Plaza Arts Center** (130 Plaza St., 707/431-1970), which showcases varied, mainly contemporary art from its local-resident artists, one of whom will likely be staffing the front desk.

There are several other wine shops in town, perhaps the most novel of which is **The Wine Annex** (340 Center St., 707/433-6488, 11 A.M.–7 P.M. daily), a combination tasting room and retail store. Behind the long tasting bar are dozens of wines on tap from all over California, and a few from elsewhere in the world. From the regularly changing tasting menu you can buy everything from one-ounce tastes of individual wines ($1–6, depending on the retail price of the wine) to a larger taste or an entire glass. If you find something you like, you can buy a bottle safe in the knowledge that you probably won't find a cheaper price. The Wine Annex is an outpost of the popular Santa Rosa wine shop, The Bottle Barn, which is widely known for its discount prices and regular generous sales.

RECREATION
Lake Sonoma Recreation Area

When the Army Corps of Engineers completed the Warm Springs Dam at the northern end of Dry Creek Valley in 1983, the resulting lake not only made Dry Creek's name obsolete by providing a year-round source of water but also became one of the best regional recreation areas.

Controversially, Lake Sonoma flooded some sacred sites of the Pomo people, now represented in a small exhibition in the **Milt Brandt Visitor Center** (3333 Skaggs Springs Rd., Geyserville, 707/433-9483, 8:30 A.M.–5:30 P.M. daily), right at the end of Dry Creek Road. Despite protests during the drawn-out planning stages in the 1970s, the flood control, water supply, and recreation advantages created by the dam won the day, and it was finally completed more than 20 years after first getting approval.

The 17,000 acres of hot oak-studded hills of the Lake Sonoma Recreation Area have more than 40 miles of trails for hikers, bikers, and

© HENG LING TIE/123RF.COM

Lake Sonoma is a camping and boating mecca.

riders, the region's best bass fishing, and plenty of open water (about 2,700 surface acres, to be precise) for swimming and boating.

The main access points to the lake and trails are Stewarts Point Road, just south of the bridge; Rockpile Road, north of the bridge; and the grassy **Yorty Creek Recreation Area** (from S. Cloverdale Blvd., turn left on W. Brookside Rd., left on Foothill Rd., and right onto Hot Springs Rd.), which is on the eastern side of lake and is accessible from Cloverdale.

A couple of the easier and more accessible hiking trails start at the South Lake Trailhead (on Stewarts Point Rd. about 0.5 miles south from its junction with Skaggs Springs Rd., just before the marina turnoff). From there it's a quick jaunt up the hill to the **Overlook,** with great views of the lake. Or take the **South Lake Trail** for a longer hike, ducking in and out of groves of madrone and pine along the way. At about two miles, head right; it's then about 0.75 miles down to the Quicksilver campground, where you can duck into the lake for a swim, if you come prepared. Alternatively,

go left and stay on the South Lake Trail for as long as you want. Other trails start at another trailhead across the bridge off Rockpile Road. A trail map is available at the visitors center.

Mountain bikers will have to be content with just one loop on the **Half-a-Canoe Trail,** which starts at the No Name Flat Trailhead, about 1.5 miles north of the bridge on the left. The loop is about 4.5 miles of mostly fire road with a short section of single-track.

You might notice that it gets hotter as you drive up Dry Creek Valley. Temperatures around the lake regularly top 100°F in the summer, so take plenty of water, whatever you do (the lake water is not drinkable). Other natural hazards include the occasional rattlesnake, disease-carrying ticks, and poison oak. You might be lucky enough to see the odd jackrabbit, a wild pig, or a rare peregrine falcon.

Fishing

The **Congressman Don Clausen Fish Hatchery** (behind the recreation area visitors center) was built to beef up the steelhead, chinook, and coho salmon populations in the Russian River and its tributaries and to mitigate some of the detrimental effects caused by construction of the Warm Springs and nearby Coyote Valley Dams. Tours are offered during the January–April spawning season (call 707/433-9483 for information). The main fishing draw on the lake is the healthy stock of largemouth bass, which love the submerged trees that were left in the Dry Creek arm of the lake when it was flooded.

The bass record stands at just over 15 pounds, though most reportedly weigh less than 10 pounds. There are also smallmouth bass, catfish, crappies, sunfish, perch, and numerous other species, including some landlocked steelhead.

When the water is clearest, during the summer, sight fishing is possible in the shallower waters close to the shore, as is bank fishing, particularly at the Yorty Creek Recreation Area. The lake is primarily a boat-fishing lake, however, and boats can be rented at the **Lake Sonoma Marina** (100 Marina Dr., 707/433-2200, $25–45 per hour for fishing boats, depending on the season, or $70–90 per hour for larger powerboats), just off Stewarts Point Road about 0.5 miles south of Skaggs Springs Road.

Other Water Activities

There are three places to launch boats on Lake Sonoma—a trailer ramp at the Lake Sonoma Marina ($10 to launch), a big public ramp just across the bridge ($3), and a car-top launch area at Yorty Creek ($3). Check with a ranger for the boating rules. If fishing or high-octane boating doesn't appeal, paddleboats can also be rented at the marina.

Unless you're fortunate to be camping at one of the hike-in or boat-in campsites, there are not many places with decent shoreline access for swimming on the lake, however. The only official swimming beach is at the Yorty Creek Recreation Area.

Further south, in Healdsburg, the Russian River provides a few water-related recreation opportunities. On the south side of town, just beyond the Old Roma Station complex and over the bridge, is **Memorial Beach,** a stretch of sandy and rocky shoreline along the river with a swimming area and concession for canoe rental. Parking at the beach costs $5, but the lot is often so crowded that a better option is to park on the other side of the bridge in a residential area and walk back to the beach. Alternatively, it's about a 15-minute walk from downtown Healdsburg.

During the summer (generally May–Oct.), canoes or kayaks can be rented at Memorial Beach from **River's Edge Kayak & Canoe Trips** (13840 Healdsburg Ave., 707/433-7247, www.riversedgekayakandcanoe.com). Prices are $10–15 per hour, or you can sign up for a half-day or full-day river adventure through Alexander Valley.

The best aspect of renting a kayak or canoe for even a couple of hours is the access to more beaches. Paddle upstream under the railroad bridge toward the small hump of Fitch Mountain, and you'll find a whole host of little beaches and swimming holes. The public is allowed on all the beaches along the Russian River that fall below the winter high-water mark—basically every beach you see during the summer.

Golf

Touting itself as a Wine Country golf course, the **Tayman Park Golf Course** (927 S. Fitch Mountain Rd., Healdsburg, 707/433-4275, www.taymanparkgolfcourse.com) is actually in a Healdsburg residential area, a five-minute drive from downtown, but it does have some nice views west toward Dry Creek and the Russian River Valley. It's a nine-hole course that can also be played as an 18-hole par-68 course. Green fees are $14–24 for nine holes, depending on the time of the week, and $18–31 for 18 holes. Golf-cart rental starts at $9. Drive east on Matheson Street from Healdsburg Plaza; the road becomes Fitch Mountain Road and heads up the hill to the club.

ACCOMMODATIONS

Take one look at the expanses of vineyards and hills dotted with the occasional winery and it's clear that the Dry Creek Valley is not a part of the world that's chock-full of hotels. Pretty much every accommodation option is in the town of Healdsburg, where Victorian frills still dominate the scene, though some contemporary style has recently crept in. As would be expected in a premium Wine Country destination town, prices are not low, regardless of style.

Under $150

Few options exist for those on a budget other than chain hotels and motels. Cheaper lodging is available to the north in the Alexander Valley and south in the Russian River Valley, but the town of Healdsburg itself seems to work hard to retain its sense of exclusivity.

One of the better among the chain lodging options is the **Dry Creek Inn** (198 Dry Creek Rd., Healdsburg, 707/433-0300, www.drycreekinn.com), a Best Western property less than one mile from the plaza but perilously close to the freeway at the Dry Creek Road exit. The hotel underwent a renovation in 2006, and most of the comfortable but ultimately plain rooms start at around $125, even in peak season. Amenities that include free wireless Internet access, a large pool, and a free tasting coupon for Simi winery make the stay a little more bearable.

$150-250

This could be classified as the Victorian frills price category, into which fall the many small family-owned inns and B&Bs in often historic houses. There might be some inflexibilities inherent to such small establishments (check whether smoking or pets are allowed, for example, and ask about the sometimes-strict cancellation policies), but the advantage is that the owners usually know the area like the backs of their hands and can offer great local insights and, of course, a great local breakfast.

One of the relative bargains in a crowded local field of frilly B&Bs is the **Camellia Inn** (211 North St., Healdsburg, 707/433-8182 or 800/727-8182, www.camelliainn.com). Flowers abound on the walls and fabrics inside

the elegant 1869 house and in the gardens, which contain more than 50 varieties of camellia, some planted by renowned horticulturist Luther Burbank, who was a friend of the original owners. Unusually for a small B&B, there is air-conditioning in all rooms as well as a small swimming pool. Four of the nine guest rooms have gas fireplaces. Rates start at $129-149 for the tiny budget room but jump to $199-249 for the queen rooms and the single suite. The Lewand family owns both the inn and the **Camellia Cellars** winery, which has a tasting room not far away on Front Street. Wine shows up in the Victorian parlor most evenings, and you can chat with the innkeeper and winemaker himself, Ray Lewand.

There's a little more chintz on show at the **Haydon Street Inn** (321 Haydon St., Healdsburg, 707/433-5228 or 800/528-3703, www.haydon.com) on a quiet residential street about a 10-minute walk from the plaza. The Queen Anne-style house was built in 1912 as a private residence and briefly used as a convent before becoming a B&B in the 1980s. The six rooms in the main house cost $190-290, and all have private baths (across the hallway in the case of the Blue Room). Two additional deluxe rooms are in a separate cottage on the manicured grounds and cost upward of $300 depending on the season.

Other standouts in the crowded Victorian B&B scene include six-room **Calderwood Inn** (25 W. Grant St., Healdsburg, 707/431-1110 or 800/600-5444, www.calderwoodinn.com), not far from the Seghesio Family Winery. The Queen Anne Victorian boasts gardens that were laid out by famed horticulturalist Luther Burbank and has a beautifully (and tastefully) restored interior, right down to the reproduction Victorian wallpaper. The spacious rooms all have garden views and cost $210-300 depending on the season.

Filling a gaping hole for reasonably priced, Victorian frill-free accommodation is the hip **H2 Hotel** (219 Healdsburg Ave., 707/922-5251, www.h2hotel.com), which opened in 2010 just down the block from its sister establishment, the Hotel Healdsburg. As seems to be the norm for trendy new hotels, the green credentials of the sleek new building are impeccable, from the undulating grass-covered "living" roof to the solar heating and water collection system and right down to the furniture in each room, made from reclaimed wood or sustainable bamboo. The hotel was on the verge of opening as this edition went to press, so full details were not available, but it promises a rustic yet modern aesthetic with balconies or private patios for the 36 rooms and suites and an impressive list of luxury features, from high-definition TVs to custom organic bathroom amenities. Complementary bike rentals, a fireside lounge and bar, and a new restaurant are also promised. Rates for the hotel's opening summer started at $195–215 midweek and from just under $300 on weekends. Expect winter rates to be about $50 lower.

The town of Healdsburg might have a surplus of historic Victorian houses, but the ⓒ **Madrona Manor** (1001 Westside Rd., Healdsburg, 707/433-4231 or 800/258-4003, www.madronamanor.com), just outside the town at the southern end of the Dry Creek Valley appellation, puts them all in the shade. This enormous pile of Victorian opulence is the centerpiece of an eight-acre hilltop estate dating from the 1880s and is on the National Register of Historic places. Not surprisingly, the Manor's movie-set looks make it a very popular wedding location, and they also attracted the attention of director Francis Ford Coppola, who bought the estate in 2006.

The elegantly furnished rooms and common areas contain plenty of genuine and reproduction antiques as well as most amenities, except for televisions, which is probably fine since no children under 12 can stay here anyway. Any bored adults can watch the fire burn or the sun set from the private decks of some of the 21 rooms and suites that are spread among five buildings.

Room rates are not as high as the opulence suggests, but with such high-profile new ownership of the Manor they could rise in the coming years. Summer rates start at $210–250 for the cheapest rooms in the Carriage House and

manor house itself and rise to more than $350 for the suites. Winter rates are sometimes as low as $180. If the romantic setting, landscaped grounds, and swimming pool aren't enough to keep guests from ever leaving during their stay, then the manor's renowned restaurant might be. It serves the sumptuous breakfast included in the rate and a stylish, though pricey, dinner (on the big porch in the summer) with an outstanding wine list that leans heavily on the local appellations.

Over $250

In this price range, Victorian frills start to yield to more contemporary style, nowhere more so than at the ⓒ **Hotel Healdsburg** (25 Matheson St., Healdsburg, 707/431-2800, www.hotelhealdsburg.com), the centerpiece of the decidedly un-Victorian hunk of modern architecture that dominates the western side of the plaza. Strategically placed design elements and luxurious furnishings successfully soften the angular concrete minimalism of the interior, both in the rooms and the starkly minimalist lobby area. Such Manhattan style doesn't come cheap, however, even in sleepy Healdsburg. The smallest of the 49 rooms start at about $275, though they include the usual luxury amenities, including an iPod dock, a walk-in shower, and high-speed Internet. Add a tub and a few more square feet, and the rate jumps to more than $350. All guests have access to the tranquil outdoor pool and small fitness room, while the minimally named **The Spa** offers a wide range of spa treatments and massages for $110 and up. Downstairs is the pricey and equally contemporary restaurant, the **Dry Creek Kitchen.** A similar modern aesthetic at a lower price is offered by the hotel's new sister property just down the road, the H2 Hotel.

Slightly more reasonable rates but a slightly less contemporary feel can be found at the **Healdsburg Inn on the Plaza** (112 Matheson St., Healdsburg, 707/433-6991 or 800/431-8663, www.healdsburginn.com). The inn is part of the Four Sisters hotel chain and was recently renovated, so comfort and a reasonable level of amenities are guaranteed (as well as the signature teddy bear on each bed). All rooms have nice bathrooms, bay windows or balconies, and simple modern decor that blends with the original features of the Victorian building to create a sort of contemporary-lite character. Rates for the standard rooms start at $275, rising to more than $325 for some of the larger rooms. Afternoon cookies and wine are usually on offer, and the inn will also lend you bikes, although being right on the plaza you might not need them.

Even more luxury, tranquility, and contemporary style can be found at the even more expensive **DuChamp Hotel** (421 Foss St., Healdsburg, 707/431-1300 or 800/431-9341, www.duchamphotel.com), a short walk from the plaza and voted one of the top 25 hot new hotels by *Condé Nast Traveler* in 2001. Where the Hotel Healdsburg sometimes feels like it's trying a bit too hard to be hip, the DuChamp feels effortlessly chic, from the low-key minimalism of the six pool- and creek-side villas starting from $350–425. There's every luxury amenity you can imagine and a few you can't, such as a 50-foot lap pool, private terraces, and its private-label champagne (made by Iron Horse Vineyards). Private tastings can also be arranged at the nearby DuChamp Estate Winery (which makes only syrah).

A few Victorians offer some healthy competition to the high-end modern newcomers, not least the **Honor Mansion** (14891 Grove St., Healdsburg, 707/433-4277 or 800/554-4667, www.honormansion.com). At this gloriously indulgent establishment the unusual antiques and period architectural features do the talking without an excess of applied frills, giving some rooms at the self-styled "resort inn" an almost artistic feel. The 13 rooms and suites don't come cheap ($230–600) but do come with all amenities, including CD players and VCRs, as well as some fun features ranging from double-headed showers and ornate four-poster beds to private patios and giant fireplaces. There's even a two-story suite inside an old Victorian water tower. The three acres of verdant grounds contain a swimming pool, a koi pond, boccie and

tennis courts, and a croquet lawn. The two- or three-course breakfast can be enjoyed out on the dining patio, weather permitting.

Camping

Lake Sonoma Recreation Area, at the northern end of Dry Creek Valley, is a tent-camping mecca, especially if you have a boat. There are more than 100 hike-in or boat-in primitive campsites along its 50 miles of shoreline, most of them on the Warm Springs arm of the lake. The most easily accessible on foot are the Island View or Quicksilver campgrounds, though the heat and terrain make the 2.5-mile hikes to them fairly strenuous during the summer months.

Most of the campgrounds are small, with an average of about 10 tent sites. None have drinking water, but all have fire rings and chemical toilets. Apart from the usual wildlife warnings (look out for rattlesnakes and ticks that carry Lyme disease), visitors should also keep an eye out for feral pigs, descendants of domestic pigs brought by early white settlers.

Also worth noting: Some campsites are located on lake areas designated for waterskiing, and the constant drone of power boats and Jet Skis can spoil an otherwise idyllic scene. More peace and quiet can be found near parts of the lake designated as wake-free zones (marked on the free map available at the visitors center). Island View is the quieter of the two most accessible hike-in campgrounds.

Reservations cost $14 during the summer months (877/444-6777, www.reserveusa.com). Even with a reservation, all backcountry campers must first get a permit from the hard-to-miss **visitors center** (3333 Skaggs Springs Rd., Geyserville, 707/433-9483), which also has trail maps. More information about the campsites is also available at the Army Corps website (www.spn.usace.army.mil/lakesonoma/index.htm).

For car campers, there's just one developed drive-in campground: **Liberty Glen** (877/444-6777, www.reserveusa.com). About a mile across the bridge from the visitors center, it has 95 sites for tents and RVs (no electrical

SONOMA

hookups) that cost $10. Worth noting is that during the summer the gates to the site are closed to cars at 10 P.M., so don't plan on any late-night reveling.

FOOD

With Dry Creek largely devoid of shops and restaurants, it is left to Healdsburg to supply most of the food. In keeping with the town's breezy atmosphere, the culinary scene is also fairly relaxed. Restaurants generally never seem to be trying as hard as in some other Wine Country destination towns.

There are a few exceptions, and well-known regional chefs have had their eye on the place for some time. Some big-name establishments have taken hold here, like Manzanita, with input from Bizou in San Francisco, but they lack the big-city attitude (and, reportedly, the polished big-city service). Dinner reservations, though usually not needed, are nearly always recommended, especially in summer.

Fine Dining

The dining destination in Healdsburg and indeed most of the Northern Sonoma these days is **Cyrus** (29 North St., Healdsburg, 707/433-3311, dinner daily spring–fall, Thurs.–Mon. winter, 5–8 courses $102–130). The intimate restaurant with its vaulted ceilings and dark-suited waitstaff has been flatteringly compared to the famous French Laundry in Yountville for its contemporary and elegant food, fixed-price menus, and collection of Michelin stars. It has a more relaxed atmosphere, however, and diners actually get a choice for each of the courses from a small selection on the menu, a flexible system that still allows the kitchen to focus its efforts on a handful of dishes. Main-course choices might include Thai marinated lobster with avocado or mango roulade of lamb with porcini mushrooms and sangiovese sauce. Matching a wine to such simple yet sophisticated dishes is made more challenging by a wine list that runs to many hundreds of different Californian and international options, so be sure to make use of the reportedly excellent sommelier. For a cheaper dining option with

fewer frills (and a greater chance of getting a seat) head to the small bar area, where many of the appetizers and entrées on the regular menu can be ordered separately along with a half dozen different caviars. Seats at the bar are on a first-come, first-served basis.

It's no surprise that almost half the wines available at **Zin Restaurant** (344 Center St., Healdsburg, 707/473-0946, lunch Mon.–Fri., dinner daily, dinner entrées $14–28) are zinfandels. More surprising is that chef Jeff Mall manages to match many of the dishes on the menu to one style of the wine or another, highlighting just how flexible the humble zinfandel grape really is. Of course, you don't need to be a zinfandel lover to enjoy the postindustrial interior, with its concrete walls and exposed beams, or the elegantly understated but exquisitely executed dishes made with seasonal local produce. Wines from all northern Sonoma regions are represented, and in addition to the reasonably priced main courses there are cheaper blue plate specials on many days of the week, depending on what's available down on the farm.

Bistro Ralph (109 Plaza St., Healdsburg, 707/433-1380, lunch and dinner Mon.–Sat., dinner entrées $15–29) is everything a cozy local bistro should be, with whitewashed brick walls, white-clothed tables, and giant plates of cheap fries. Owner Ralph Tingle kicked off Healdsburg's culinary resurgence with this bistro in the early 1990s, and it still serves sophisticated Cal-Ital food in a relaxed, if cramped, environment right across from the leafy plaza. Dinner can get pricey, but lunch remains a relative bargain.

The big red barn housing **Barndiva** (231 Center St., Healdsburg, opposite the police station, 707/431-0100, lunch and dinner Wed.–Sun., dinner entrées $12–40) looks very Wine Country from the outside but inside is more Manhattan. This being a rural part of the world, the clientele doesn't quite match the contemporary interior, but it's still a fun and unusual scene, albeit one that sometimes gets a bit full of itself. Barndiva opened in 2004 and bills itself primarily as a cocktail lounge, though one that also serves stylish Asian-influenced food and a huge selection of wine from a menu that is best examined while sober. The dinner menu is arranged according to mood, the wines by their flavor profile, so it takes a while to decide whether you're in a spicy, passionate mood or are feeling light and clean. Service is reportedly a bit spotty, perhaps because the waitstaff are as confused as diners about the menu.

Another newcomer to the small-plate phenomenon is **Willi's Seafood and Raw Bar** (403 Healdsburg Ave., Healdsburg, 707/433-9191, lunch and dinner daily, small plates $8–13), a few blocks north of the plaza. This is a sister establishment to the popular Willi's Wine Bar just south of Healdsburg and suffers from the same pleasant problem—there are just too many of the small plates of food to choose from. Most are under $10, so just try them all if

BEER BEFORE WINE

It's hard to imagine a time before vineyards in Sonoma, but another type of vine was once the mainstay of the agricultural economy in the Russian River Valley. From Sebastopol to Healdsburg and up into Mendocino, hop vines rather than grapevines once lined the roads and covered the hillsides. All that is left to remind us now are the tall hop kilns that rear up over the landscape from Guerneville to Hopland, some long since converted into wineries.

The conditions were perfect here for hop growing. Rich alluvial soils and the cooling influence of the fog favored the hop vines just like they favor chardonnay and pinot noir grapevines today. Hops were first planted in the region around 1880, and by 1930 almost 3 million pounds were harvested each year. That's enough to make more than 100 million gallons of beer, by some estimates.

The small green fruit, resembling a miniature pine cone, was harvested, dried (or "toasted") in the giant kilns, and used in the making of beer. A resin-like substance from the hops called lupolin is what gives beer its distinctive bitter taste.

Market forces, disease, and (ironically) a mechanical invention by a local hop grower all spelled doom for the local hop industry. After World War II, demand and prices for hops plummeted as the public started to prefer less bitter beer (call it the Budweiser effect). Adding to growers' misery, downy mildew started to thrive in the damp, foggy air and infected the soils in the 1950s, killing vast tracts of hops.

The final nail in the hop growers' coffin was the invention of an automated hop harvesting machine in the 1940s by Santa Rosa grower Florian Dauenhauer. It quickly made the small, hand-harvested growing lots that were common in Sonoma far less economical. Growers sought out bigger plots of land elsewhere in California and the Pacific Northwest that could be machine-harvested, and by the 1960s the Sonoma hop industry was dead.

All that is left of the beer-related industry in northern Sonoma these days is a handful of brewpubs, many of them now buying hops from the Pacific Northwest or further afield. In Healdsburg, the **Bear Republic Brewing Company** (345 Healdsburg Ave., Healdsburg, 707/433-2337, www.bearrepublic.com) is right behind the Hotel Healdsburg and has a quiet, sunny outdoor patio. In Guerneville, the **Stumptown Brewery** (15045 River Rd., Guerneville, 707/869-0705, www.stumptown.com) offers such potent-sounding microbrews as Red Rocket and Death and Taxes.

Over in Santa Rosa, the **Third Street Ale Works** (610 3rd St., Santa Rosa, 707/523-3060, www.thirdstreetaleworks.com) challenges drinkers to get their mouths around names like Drunken Weasel Dunkelweizen and Goat Rock Doppelbock. A few blocks away is the **Russian River Brewing Company** (725 4th St., Santa Rosa, 707/545-2337, www.russianriverbrewing.com), which was actually founded by a winery (Korbel) in 1997 but now goes it alone, brewing dozens of ales and lagers with names that probably sound funnier when drunk, like Hop 2 It, Pliny the Elder, and Blind Pig IPA. Down in Sebastopol the beer legacy is kept alive by the **Hopmonk Tavern** (230 Petaluma Ave., Sebastopol, 707/823-7837, www.hopmonk.com) and its modest portfolio of four brews.

you're peckish. This is also the place to experiment with food and wine pairing, particularly as most wines are available by the glass or half bottle. Although the decoration in the dining room is straight from Cuba, the inspiration for the food seems to come from all over the world.

An unassuming house opposite a strip mall a block from the plaza is home to the flagship of perhaps one of Healdsburg's most successful restaurant partnerships, Joyanne and John Pezzolo. Their ◖ **Ravenous Café & Lounge** (420 Center St., Healdsburg, 707/431-1302, lunch and dinner Wed.–Sun., dinner entrées $11–25) was moved here from its previous pint-sized location next to the Raven Theater (they transformed that former space into an equally successful lunch spot, Ravenette). Inside, the Ravenous Café feels as homey as the exterior suggests and serves generous portions of sophisticated bistro food from the ever-changing menu, though the trademark Ravenous Burger is always on the menu. On summer evenings, the tranquil garden dining space is as much the star of the restaurant as the food.

If you want a Victorian setting for dinner, there is probably no better option than the restaurant at **Madrona Manor** (1001 Westside Rd., Healdsburg, 707/433-4321, dinner Wed.–Sun., entrées $17–30) just outside Healdsburg. Eating here is as much about the sumptuous five-room Victorian setting and candlelit table decorations as the food, though the very expensive and stylish modern cuisine gets rave reviews.

Casual Dining

Although most of Healdsburg's many bistros serve very reasonably priced lunches, there are plenty of even cheaper places to grab a quick bite. At the back of the Plaza Farms market hall and offering a unique take on casual Italian dining is **Bovolo** (106 Matheson St., 707/431-2962, 9 A.M.–4 P.M. Mon.–Thurs., 9 A.M.–8 P.M. Fri.–Sat., 9 A.M.–6 P.M. Sun.). The self-serve style restaurant was created by the chefs behind Santa Rosa's successful ZaZu and features a smorgasbord of Italian treats, from wood-fired pizza and cured salamis to gelato and cheap carafes of house wine, all made

from local ingredients. The restaurant gets its name from the Italian for a type of snail, a symbol for the "slow food" movement that encourages people to grow, prepare, and enjoy their own creations at a leisurely pace rather than eat and run. That's no doubt why you have to order and carry your own food to your own table, although the patio on a summer day is reason enough to linger.

Unpretentious and delicious Italian small plates, pizza and pastas along with a energetic yet intimate vibe have made **Scopa** (109A Plaza St., 707/433-5282, dinner Tues.–Sun., antipasti dishes $5–10, entrées $13–17) wildly popular since it was opened in 2008 by the former chef of Geyserville's award-winning Santi restaurant. Antipasti dishes like grilled calamari and Venetian-style sardines won't necessarily win awards for inventiveness but have won accolades for perfect execution and very reasonable prices. Main courses include pizzas, pastas, and simple meat dishes that exude the same rustic yet gourmet quality, and the wine list offers just as many regional Italian wines as northern Sonoma options. Being so popular makes securing one of the tables wedged into the long, narrow industrial-looking space a challenge, however, so consider eating at the small bar instead.

A block from the plaza is the younger sister to the successful Ravenous Café, **Ravenette** (117 North St., 707/431-1770, dinner Fri.–Sat.). The eight-table café with leopard-print seats and barely enough room to swing a cat is in the annex of the Raven Theater and serves seasonal food as eclectic as its location and decor suggests.

At the other end of the casual dining spectrum from the likes of Ravenette and Scopa is the spacious **Healdsburg Bar & Grill** (245 Healdsburg Ave., Healdsburg, 707/433-3333, lunch and dinner daily), with as many tables inside its saloon-style interior as outside on its shady patio. As its name and the giant outdoor barbecues suggest, this is paradise for lovers of big hunks of char-grilled meat, and they form the basis of the classic pub menu. There's a half decent wine list too.

There's more saloon-style dining and food just around the corner at the **Bear Republic Brewing**

Company (345 Healdsburg Ave., Healdsburg, 707/433-2337, lunch and dinner daily), right behind the Hotel Healdsburg. The many microbrews are the main attraction, however, and can be enjoyed right in the shadow of stainless steel brewing tanks on the patio outside.

The southwest corner of Healdsburg's plaza is dominated by the bustling **Oakville Grocery** (124 Matheson St., Healdsburg, 707/433-3200, 8 A.M.–6 P.M. daily). Go there for deli food with that added Wine Country flair (and price) to stock up for a picnic or to eat at one of the shaded tables on the large patio overlooking the plaza.

Adding some European flair to the deli scene is the **Costeaux French Bakery & Café** (417 Healdsburg Ave., Healdsburg, 707/433-1913, 7 A.M.–4 P.M. Mon.–Thurs., 7 A.M.–5 P.M. Fri.–Sat., 7 A.M.–1 P.M. Sun.). It sells the usual crusty bread and other bakery fare together with some tasty breakfasts and deli lunches that can be enjoyed on the big patio next to the sidewalk, a few blocks north of the plaza and considerably calmer than Oakville's. It also offers a light dinner and wine on Friday and Saturday evenings. Filling breakfasts and decadent pastries are the specialty of the **Downtown Bakery & Creamery** on the south side of the plaza (308A Center St., 707/431-2719, 7 A.M.–5:30 P.M. Mon.–Sat., 7 A.M.–4 P.M. Sun.).

Picnic Supplies

The **Oakville Grocery** (124 Matheson St., Healdsburg, 707/433-3200) is also picnic central, and it has just about everything, including wine, needed for either a gourmet alfresco feast or just some simple bread and cheese. Don't forget the sandwiches and bread available at the **Costeaux French Bakery** (417 Healdsburg Ave., Healdsburg, 707/433-1913, 7 A.M.–5 P.M. Tues.–Sat., 7 A.M.–4 P.M. Sun.).

Artisanal cheeses from all over the world, together with bread and other potential picnic fare, is available nearby at **The Cheese Shop** (423 Center St., 707/433-4998, 11 A.M.–6 P.M. Mon.–Tues. and Thurs.–Sat.). Also ask about cheese tastings and guest lectures by local cheese makers.

© PHILIP GOLDSMITH

The Dry Creek General Store is the only place to buy a beer and sandwich in the valley.

If you're heading up to the Alexander Valley or Dry Creek Valley, **Big John's Market** (1345 Healdsburg Ave., just north of W. Dry Creek Rd., 707/433-0336, 8 A.M.–8 P.M. daily), a bakery, deli, and grocery store all in one, is on the way.

Once in the Dry Creek Valley there's really only one place to buy food, and that's the **Dry Creek General Store** (3495 Dry Creek Rd., at Lambert Bridge Rd., 707/433-4171, 6 A.M.–6 P.M. Mon.–Sat., 7 A.M.–6 P.M. Sun.), which has existed in some form or another since the 1880s and continues to supply modern-day picnickers and peckish winery employees with deli sandwiches and groceries. Locals also like to hang out at the neighboring **Dry Creek Bar** (3495 Dry Creek Rd., 707/431-1543) to sip a cool beer while contemplating the wine business. The bar opens at 3 P.M. Monday–Thursday and noon Friday–Sunday, and usually closes whenever the last person falls off a stool.

Farmers Market

If you're after something really fresh, the **Healdsburg Farmers Market** is held

9 A.M.–noon Saturday mornings May–November in the parking lot of the Plaza Park (North St. and Vine St.), a few blocks west of the plaza itself. Those in the know say it's one of the best farmers markets in this part of Sonoma. On Tuesday evenings from June through October (4–7 P.M.) the market sets up on the main plaza downtown.

INFORMATION AND SERVICES
Comprehensive information about the wines and the winemakers of the Dry Creek Valley is available from the **Winegrowers of Dry Creek Valley** (www.wdcv.com, 707/433-3031). The association does a sterling job of ensuring the area's wineries get national attention and organizes the sell-out Passport Weekend event, a two-day party involving nearly all the valley's wineries on the last weekend in April.

Wine buffs can do even more research at the Healdsburg Public Library, which houses **Sonoma County's Wine Library** (Piper St. and Center St., 707/433-3772, Mon.–Sat.), a small annex crammed with every conceivable wine book, including plenty on local and California wine history.

More information about Healdsburg and its amenities can be found at the **Healdsburg Chamber of Commerce & Visitors Bureau** (217 Healdsburg Ave., 707/433-6935, www.healdsburg.com, 9 A.M.–5 P.M. weekdays, 9 A.M.–3 P.M. Sat., 10 A.M.–2 P.M. Sun.), a few blocks south of the plaza.

Alexander Valley

Most people speeding north on the freeway might glimpse vineyards as they cruise past the Alexander Valley. Some might even stop to visit some of the valley's biggest wineries that are close to off-ramps. Finding the true character of this part of the Wine Country and many of its smaller wineries requires a little more time navigating U.S. 128, however. The road runs from Geyserville through some rather alarming 90-degree bends and down into the rustic Chalk Hill and Knights Valley appellations. From there it's only a short drive to Calistoga at the northern end of the Napa Valley.

The 20-mile-long Alexander Valley stretches from Healdsburg in the south to the cow town of Cloverdale in the north. In between there is only one town of note: the hamlet of **Geyserville**, which for years has been destined to become the next big Wine Country resort town, only to stubbornly remain its old sleepy self.

Geyserville wasn't always so quiet. Back in the late 1800s the nearby geysers drew visitors from far and wide, and the resulting influx of money helped build the town's grand Victorian homes. Now the only signs of the area's underground hot water supply are the clouds of steam sometimes visible from the 19 geothermal plants in the hills east of Geyserville (an area known simply as The Geysers). The area is one of the world's largest geothermal energy sources.

As with many other parts of the Wine

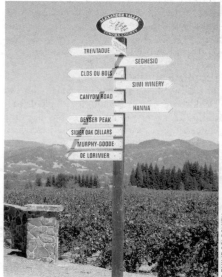

Navigating the Alexander Valley is a cinch.

Country, this valley was once dominated by cattle pasture and fruit orchards. The cows still hold sway around **Cloverdale** and farther north, where dairies are still more common than wineries, but the vineyards are spreading. Cloverdale marks the end of Northern California's most famous wine regions and the beginning of the new frontier of wine-making in Mendocino County. The Anderson Valley and Hopland are only short drives from Cloverdale but a world apart.

How many Wine Country visitors will venture north beyond Napa and Sonoma is yet to be seen, but Cloverdale optimistically opened its Wine and Visitors Center in 2000, clearly anticipating a northward shift in wine-making attitudes and winery visitors.

The Wines

The Alexander Valley is the northernmost appellation in Sonoma and also one of the hottest, despite the fact that the Russian River flood plain is wide enough to allow some of the more persistent fog to creep this far north on summer nights. Summer temperatures in Geyserville can often be 10 degrees higher than in Healdsburg just a few miles south. Cloverdale is hotter still.

With the ripening power of the sun and heat, together with the rich alluvial soils deposited by the Russian River over millions of years, it's relatively easy to guess what style of wine can be made here—big and opulent. Indeed, Alexander Valley cabernets have a softness and suppleness that they attain in few other places. There was good reason why the cabernet specialist Silver Oak Cellars chose this valley in 1993 for its first vineyard and winery outside the Napa Valley.

Sometimes the wines can get a little too soft and undistinguished. In general, however, Alexander Valley cabernets are characterized by soft tannins and lush fruit with hints of dark chocolate, making them perhaps the easiest drinking in California, if not necessarily the most complex or long-lived.

Other varietals grown here include chardonnay, which ripens easily to make rich and flavorful wines, along with merlot, zinfandel, and increasing quantities of syrah and sangiovese.

The appellation expanded in 1990 to include

the vineyards creeping up the hillsides, particularly on the eastern side of the valley where the mountains climb to more than 2,500 feet. As growers experiment with the cooler hillside vineyards, subtler styles of wine are being created than the blockbusters from the fertile, sun-drenched valley floor.

At the southern end of Alexander Valley, east of Santa Rosa, is the Chalk Hill appellation, which derives its name from soils that contain chalk-like volcanic ash, similar to those at the northern end of the Napa Valley. It's directly in the path of the cooler Russian River Valley air and is mostly contained within the easternmost part of the Russian River appellation. The few wineries here are perhaps best known for some tangy chardonnays.

Sandwiched between the eastern parts of Chalk Hill and Alexander Valley, with the border of Napa County to the west, is the Knights Valley appellation, a primarily grape-growing region with just a couple of small wineries.

Millions of years ago the Russian River ran down the Alexander Valley, through Knights Valley, and into the Napa Valley, depositing gravelly soils ideal for growing grapes. Knights Valley soils are also part volcanic, deposited during the volcanic eruptions that eventually changed the course of the river westward to its present-day path past Healdsburg and Guerneville to the ocean.

Completely shielded from the cool ocean air, Knights Valley is the hottest of Sonoma's appellations, providing ideal conditions for sauvignon blanc and cabernet sauvignon. Look for the Knights Valley appellation in the wines from Napa Valley's Beringer Vineyards, which owns about half the vineyards here.

WINERIES

From the north end of the valley at the historic Asti winery, home of Italian-Swiss Colony (no longer open to the public), the Alexander Valley stretches southeast, past Healdsburg down to the Chalk Hill Road.

Most major wineries are on Geyserville Avenue, which runs parallel to the freeway between Healdsburg and Cloverdale, and on Highway 128, which runs southeast from Geyserville.

Pastori

One of the northernmost wineries open to the public is also one of the quirkiest and among the smallest in the valley. The primitive, cinderblock tasting room of Pastori (23189 Geyserville Ave., Cloverdale, 707/857-3418, open whenever there's someone there, usually 9 A.M.–5 P.M. daily, free tasting), squeezed into one of the old warehouses at the side of the road, is a throwback to the old days of wine making when locals would come and fill up their jugs for a couple of bucks.

Frank Pastori is one of Sonoma's old-timers, and his family has been making wine here since the early 1900s. If the tasting room is open at all (it seems to have no regular hours) he's likely to be the only one there and will happily spin yarns about the good old days of wine making and perhaps try to convince you that white wine is "not real wine."

He offers good old prices for his zinfandel wine and port, and jug wines (bring your own jug). Don't expect much more than basic table wines, but do expect an unusual Wine Country experience.

Souverain

After selling its old winery property in Geyserville, Chateau Souverain dropped the "chateau" from its name and moved operations to the historic Asti winery, which is owned by its parent company, Fosters Wine Estates. Most of the winery's vineyards were also retained, so production continued uninterrupted. It is the latest move for a winery that has a history of transformations.

Souverain (26150 Asti Post Office Rd., Cloverdale, 707/265-5490 or 866/557-4970, www.souverain.com, 10 A.M.–5 P.M. daily, tasting $5–15) was originally a Napa Valley winery when it was established in 1944, but it moved to the Alexander Valley when its founder sold to the Pillsbury food company in 1973 and became known as Souverain Cellars, and later as Chateau Souverain when the next owner,

THE ITALIAN CONNECTION

It is not by chance or climate alone that there is a preponderance of Italian names among the wineries of the Dry Creek and Alexander Valleys. In the 1880s an Italian immigrant named Andrea Sbarboro, a financier by trade, had the bright idea of starting a sort of grape-growing cooperative, or colony, to provide worthwhile work and lodging to the many other Italians arriving by the boatload in San Francisco.

He and his financial backers, including several Swiss businessmen, bought about 1,500 acres of land just south of Cloverdale and called the place Asti, after the town in the Piedmont region of Italy that was (and still is) famous for its wines. The Italian-Swiss Agricultural Colony, later shortened to Italian-Swiss Colony, was born.

The idea was that workers recruited to work there contributed a small portion of their salary each month in exchange for food and lodging, and to buy shares in the venture, thus making some money for Sbarboro and giving workers a sense of ownership.

Things didn't go quite to plan. Workers were suspicious of Sbarboro's financial intentions and didn't want to share the risk. The falling price of grapes soon meant the colony had to build its own winery to remain viable.

But the colony and its winery eventually became a huge success. By the turn of the 20th

century it was both profitable and said to be the biggest producer of table wine in California. By 1910 it was making more than 14 million gallons of wine per year.

Early generations of many local wine families came to work at the colony. Edoardo and Angela Seghesio met there, and Ed went on to create the Seghesio Family Vineyards in the early 1900s, for example. Ferrari, Martini, and Rossi are other Italian names once associated with the colony that have been influential in the local wine world over the last century.

Pietro Rossi was Sbarboro's first winemaker, and the Rossi family bought the winery during Prohibition, keeping it alive as the Asti Grape Products Company before reentering the commercial wine business after repeal. It was eventually sold in the 1940s, and after changing hands a few more times it was finally bought by Fosters Wine Estates in 1988.

The old winery at Asti has been well preserved even after Fosters invested in new wine-making equipment for its Souverain and Cellar No. 8 brands that are made there today. After being closed to the public for over a decade, Fosters reopened the winery to the public in 2009 and now offers daily tours that allow visitors to see once again the grandeur of the old buildings and grounds along the bank of the Russian River.

Nestlé, came along in the 1980s. Half a century later, it has its original name back.

It may have an unsettled history, but there's nothing unsettled about the wines, which include consistently high-scoring Alexander Valley cabernet and merlot together with chardonnay, sauvignon blanc, viognier, syrah, and zinfandel. Some grapes are sourced in the Dry Creek Valley and elsewhere in Sonoma County.

All told, Souverain produces about 300,000 cases of wine, more than a third of which is cabernet and chardonnay. Winemaker Ed Killian also keeps the best grapes for the Winemaker Reserve cabernet, merlot, and chardonnay wines, available only at the winery and well priced considering their reserve status. Wines from another

Fosters brand, the cheap and cheerful Cellar No. 8, are also made here and available to taste.

Perhaps the best reason to trek this far north in the Alexander Valley, however, is to see the parts of the historic Asti property, home of the Italian-Swiss Colony that was established in the late 1800s and was once the biggest winery in California before Prohibition ended its run. The tour ($15) takes in the original winery building, since retrofitted for modern production; the huge barrel room; and the old Victorian villa on the bank of the Russian River that was once home to the founder of the Colony, Andrea Sbarboro.

Silver Oak Cellars

On just the other side of the freeway from

Pastori is a temple for red-wine lovers, the Sonoma outpost of Silver Oak (24625 Chianti Rd., Geyserville, 800/273-8809, www.silveroak.com, 9 A.M.–4 P.M. Mon.–Sat., appointment-only tours at 1:30 P.M. Mon.–Fri., tasting $10), which makes just one wine—cabernet sauvignon. If you like cabernet, you'll undoubtedly like Silver Oak's powerful, velvety version that some say has an unusual aroma from being aged for years only in American oak barrels. You might not like the price, however.

The 50,000 cases made here are produced from the winery's 200 acres of vineyards in the Alexander Valley, Russian River Valley, and Chalk Hill appellations. A further 10,000 cases of cabernet are made at Silver Oak's original Oakville winery in the Napa Valley, which was recently rebuilt after a fire destroyed the facility in 2006.

The Alexander Valley winery was established in the early 1990s more than a decade after the Napa Winery. Both facilities have legions of die-hard fans that line up each year to buy the new release, despite its ready availability, a testament to the loyalty of Silver Oak crowd and the quality of the wine. Some less adoring fans, however, think this cult status makes the wines more expensive than they perhaps deserve to be.

The Alexander Valley cabernet is $70 per bottle, and the Napa version is over $100. Not surprisingly, there's a $10 tasting fee, although you can keep the glass. Another option for $10 is to take the tour offered weekdays only at 1:30, which culminates in a tasting of both Silver Oak wines and a Napa Valley merlot from sister winery Twomey (but no free glass). You might also be able to taste the more moderately priced port that's only available at the winery.

Geyser Peak Winery

Just down Chianti Road from Silver Oak is the giant ivy-clad home of one of the region's biggest wineries. Geyser Peak (22281 Chianti Rd., Geyserville, 707/857-2500 or 800/255-9463, www.geyserpeakwinery.com, 10 A.M.–5 P.M. daily) turns out hundreds of thousands of cases of mediocre wines and a few very good ones.

There has been a winery on the site since 1880, but the Geyser Peak name dates from 1911. Through the 1980s it was a bulk wine producer, making up to 1 million cases of cheap wines per year, and only became known for premium wine in the late 1990s; it proudly boasts being named Best U.S. Wine Producer at the 2003 International Wine & Spirit Competition. For more than a decade Geyser Peak has been owned by various big corporations and was most recently acquired in 2008 by Ascentia Wine Estates.

A dizzying selection of wines makes up the 350,000-case production, including cabernet, merlot, zinfandel, shiraz, sauvignon blanc, and chardonnay, nearly all available as regular, reserve, and vineyard-designate wines. Expect to see more than two dozen wines on the tasting list. The cheaper wines in particular can be good value, but the winery is perhaps best known for its concentrated Alexander Valley cabernets and red blends that compared well with some of the best in the valley. One of the more unusual wines worth trying (although it's an acquired taste) is the Alexander Valley tannat, a varietal more commonly seen in Uruguay and southwestern France.

The giant tasting room is big enough to cope with the vast number of wines and crowds but has an understandably corporate vibe, and you won't necessarily learn much about the wines from the inexperienced staff. Five of the lower-end wines can be tasted for $5, while four of the better single-vineyard wines can be tried upstairs in the more relaxing reserve tasting room overlooking the barrel room for $10.

Trentadue Winery

In keeping with the Tuscan heritage of the founding family, Trentadue (19170 Geyserville Ave., Geyserville, 707/433-3104 or 888/332-3032, www.trentadue.com, 10 A.M.–5 P.M. daily, tasting free or $5) was one of the first wineries in this region to grow sangiovese grapes and now produces a cluster of sangiovese-based wines. The flagship La Storia Cuvée 32 wine (*trentadue* is Italian for the number 32) is a super-Tuscan style blend of sangiovese, merlot, and cabernet. Sangiovese even makes its way into the Old Patch Red blend, named for a 100-year-old block of zinfandel vines.

Trentadue also makes some of the best-value wines in the valley. The limited-production La Storia wines regularly score over 90 points in the press yet start at well under $30. The cheaper Trentadue wines are rarely over $20. Many of the wines are produced in small lots, however, so they sell out quickly.

About one-fifth of the winery's 20,000-case production is merlot, but sauvignon blanc, viognier, zinfandel, cabernet, and mourvèdre are also made here. You can also taste a flight of the red and white ports in the Mediterranean-style tasting room for the same price as the reserve wine tasting.

Jordan Vineyard and Winery

While Judy Jordan focuses on bubbly and pinot noir at the J Winery in the Russian River appellation, father Tom crafts rich cabernet sauvignon and chardonnay at this château-style winery just north of Healdsburg, making about 90,000 cases of supremely drinkable wine.

The beautifully manicured Jordan Vineyard estate (1474 Alexander Valley Rd., Healdsburg, 707/431-5250 or 800/654-1213, www.jordan-winery.com, open daily for sales, tours and tastings by appointment only 11 A.M. Mon.–Sat. fall–spring, Mon.–Sun. summer, tasting $20, tour tasting $30) is perhaps the most picturesque winery setting in the valley and is best appreciated on the hour-long tour that culminates in a tasting of wines and the estate olive oil together with some tasty morsels of food. Cabernet lovers might want to opt for the library tasting, which includes current releases of red and white wines along with several older vintages of the estate cabernet sauvignon, accompanied by a cheese plate.

Two-thirds of the production at Jordan is the cabernet, which has a style typical of the Alexander Valley's soft and fruit-forward red wines, and the rest is a crisp chardonnay from the Russian River Valley.

Simi Winery

Brothers Pietro and Giuseppe Simi came from Tuscany in the 1860s and set themselves up as winemakers and traders in San Francisco before moving to the current site of Simi Winery (16275 Healdsburg Ave., Healdsburg, 800/746-4880, www.simiwinery.com, 10 A.M.–5 P.M. daily, tasting $5–10), just north of Healdsburg, in 1881.

Back then the winery was called Montepulciano, after the Simis' Tuscan homeland. The Simi name was adopted after the repeal of Prohibition, but by the 1970s the family connection had ended and the winery was bought by a subsidiary of multinational conglomerate Constellation Brands in the 1990s.

In its heyday, the winery boasted Sonoma's first public tasting room—a 25,000-gallon redwood tank set up at the side of the road by Isabelle Simi Haigh, the second-generation owner of the winery. It was evidently a roaring success, but the current tasting room is a more modern affair inside the historic stone cellar building, which dates from the late 1800s.

The winery is best known for its chardonnay, sourced from the 120 acres of Russian River Valley vineyards, and its cabernets, from 600 acres of Alexander Valley vineyards. Those two varietals alone account for more than two-thirds of the 300,000-case annual production, and both garner consistently good reviews. Other wines in the portfolio include sauvignon blanc and merlot sourced from a variety of vineyards in Sonoma County.

Tastings are $5, for reserve wines $10, and $3 extra buys an informative tour of the gardens, which include a stand of redwood trees planted by Isabelle Simi. Tours followed by a tasting are offered twice daily at 11 A.M. and 2 P.M.

Stryker Sonoma Winery

The name is appropriate considering the new Stryker Sonoma winery (5110 Hwy. 128, Geyserville, 707/433-1944 or 800/433-1944, www.strykersonoma.com, 10:30 A.M.–5 P.M. daily, tasting free or $5–10) is housed in one of the most striking buildings in the Alexander Valley, a contemporary glass, wood, and concrete structure that won an architectural award when it was completed in 2002.

The huge glass-walled tasting room overlooks

26 acres of estate vineyards that provide some of the grapes for the 8,000 cases of wine made each year—mainly cabernet, merlot, zinfandel, and chardonnay plus some interesting blends.

The cabernets are the standouts and range from the intense version from the Monte Rosso vineyard high in the Mayacamas Mountains further south to the plush estate version, which is a fine example of an Alexander Valley cab. There are also other cabernets from the Knights Valley and Dry Creek valley. Many are only available in the tasting room.

There is an even more bewildering array of zinfandels from up and down Sonoma, including an estate version and a couple of bright, cool-climate zins from Russian River Valley vineyards. One of the more unusual red wines to try, however, is the inky and pungent Petite Verdot, normally used as a blending grape in Bordeaux-style wines.

The portfolio of whites is tiny, by contrast, but includes a couple of nice Russian River chardonnays and a chardonnay-semillon blend with an enticing mix of citrus and tropical fruit flavors. There are usually four of the cheaper wines to taste free, but flights of the pricier single-vineyard zinfandels, cabernets and blends will cost $5–10 to taste.

Sausal Winery

Some of the first zinfandel vines planted in the valley are part of the winery's 120 acres of vineyards, and Sausal (7370 Hwy. 128, Healdsburg, 707/433-2285 or 800/500-2285, www.sausalwinery.com, 10 A.M.–4 P.M. daily, free tasting) takes full advantage of them. The bulk of the 10,000 cases of wine made each year is zinfandel, and much of that is made using grapes from these old vines. The resulting Century Vines zinfandel is arguably the best wine in the portfolio.

Other wines range from the affordable Private Reserve zin down to cheap, summer-drinking Cellar Cats Red, named for the winery's two feline residents and perfect for a picnic in the shade of the old oak trees on the grounds.

This is still the Alexander Valley, however, so a rich, age-worthy cabernet sauvignon gets a look in too. The sangiovese that goes into the robust Sogni d'Oro blend along with zinfandel is a

Sausal Winery, perfect for a picnic

nod to the Italian heritage of the current owners of the winery, who are third-generation relatives of some of the valley's pioneering winemakers.

Leo Demostene, son of a first-generation Italian immigrant, bought this former prune and pear farm in the 1950s and started making bulk wine after working for many years at Abele Ferrari's historic Soda Rock Winery and marrying Ferrari's daughter, Rose. The current winery, which includes a converted prune dehydrator, was completed in the 1970s after Leo's death by the current Demostene generation and is one of the more rural and relaxed wineries in the valley, perfect for a picnic.

Robert Young Estate Winery

Chardonnay dominates among the 14 varietals grown on the 320 acres of Alexander Valley vineyards owned by the Robert Young winery (4960 Red Winery Rd., Geyserville, 707/4331-4811, www.ryew.com, 10 A.M.–4:30 P.M. daily, tasting $5), and a rich, full-bodied version of this varietal is what the winery is best known for. In fact, there is a Robert Young clone of the chardonnay grape. Much of the rest of the estate is planted with merlot and cabernet, both of which go into the flagship Scion blend. Only about 4 percent of the grapes are used to make the 4,000 or so cases of wine; the rest are sold to other wineries.

The Young family first settled this part of the world in 1858, but it was Robert Young who planted grapes here in the 1960s, slowly transforming what had been prune orchards and grazing land into hundreds of acres of vineyards, planting the very first cabernet sauvignon vines in the valley in 1963, and chardonnay in 1967. Robert died in 2009 at the ripe old age of 91, but there are still plenty of other Youngs who call the beautiful estate home, including Fred Young, who established the wine-making operations, and Jim Young, who is the vineyard manager.

◀ Alexander Valley Vineyards

It shares the name of the historic valley for good reason. In the 1960s the founders of the winery bought a large chunk of the original homestead once owned by Cyrus Alexander, the mountain man who became a ranch manager and finally a landowner credited with planting the valley's first vineyards in 1846.

Whether Alexander ever made wine from those grapes is not known, but today's vineyards provide the grapes for the 100,000 cases of mainly red wines that Alexander Valley Vineyards (8644 Hwy. 128, Healdsburg, 800/888-7209, www.avvwine.com, 10 A.M.–5 P.M. daily, free tasting) produces. About half that volume is cabernet and merlot, with another quarter accounted for by chardonnay and the two decadent zinfandel blends, Sin Zin and Redemption Zin.

Other varietals include chardonnay, pinot noir, sangiovese, syrah, and viognier, together with some interesting red blends, including the flagship wine called Cyrus, a Bordeaux-style wine honoring the winery's namesake.

Historical sites pepper the current estate, including a wooden schoolhouse built by Alexander in 1853 and the Alexander family gravesite up the hill behind the winery. Educational tours of the expansive wine caves are also available by appointment.

Field Stone Winery

Built from stones unearthed during construction in 1977, the small Field Stone winery (10075 Hwy. 128, Healdsburg, 707/433-7266 or 800/544-7273, www.fieldstonewinery.com, 10 A.M.–5 P.M. daily, tasting $5), cut into a dusty valley hillside, was one of the first of a wave of modern underground wineries built in the Wine Country, but it had a tumultuous early life.

Wallace Johnson, a former mayor of Berkeley, founded the winery to test his newly invented mechanical grape-harvesting system, but he died just two years later. The winery then passed to his daughter, Katrina, and son-in-law, the Reverend John Staten, giving it a unique claim of being the first (and perhaps only) winery managed by a Presbyterian minister.

Grapes from the 50 acres of estate vineyards, together with some from the Russian River Valley and Mendocino, go into the 10,000 cases of wine made each year. Reds include cabernet, merlot, sangiovese, and the winery's signature, petite sirah. Whites include a limited-production viognier, sauvignon blanc, chardonnay, and gewürztraminer. Some of the proceeds from the sale of the Convivio line of lower-priced wines are donated to a local clinic serving farm workers.

Oak trees shade two small picnic areas outside the small tasting room, sometimes shared with the local wild turkeys, and staff might be willing to take you on an impromptu tour if it's not too busy.

Locals Tasting Room

Opened in 2003, this charming tasting room cooperative on Geyserville's main street pours wines from 10 of northern Sonoma's boutique wineries. It is a broad mix of wineries representing wines from as far south as the Central Coast up to Mendocino and most points between. Locals (Geyserville Ave. at Hwy. 128, 707/857-4900, www.tastelocalwine.com, 11 A.M.–6 P.M. daily, free tasting) also has its own wine club incorporating most of the wineries represented here, making it one of the more varied and worthwhile clubs to join.

They include the Russian River region's **Eric Ross** winery as well as several small Dry Creek Valle producers that include **Peterson Winery, Martin Family Vineyards,** and **Ramazzotti Wines,** the Mendocino syrah specialist **Saracina,** and **Laurel Glen Vineyards,** which makes a couple of nice mountain-grown cabernets as well as several versions of malbec sourced from vineyards thousands of miles away in Argentina's famous Mendoza region.

Wineries by Appointment

You might miss the turnoff from Highway 128 to Chalk Hill Road, but you won't miss the striking modern gates of the **Lancaster Estate** (15001 Chalk Hill Rd., Healdsburg, 707/433-8178 or 800/799-8444, www.lancaster-estate.com). This small but exclusive maker of cabernet sauvignon offers a free tour of the vineyards, state-of-the-art wine-making facility, and caves before retiring to what seems like a private salon for tastings of the Bordeaux-style red wines, which range from the limited

production Nicole's Vineyard blend to the flagship Lancaster Estate cabernet.

Make sure to get detailed directions to **Medlock Ames** (13414 Chalk Hill Rd., Healdsburg, 707/431-8845, www.medlock-ames.com), about a mile off the Chalk Hill Road down what seems like an endless dirt driveway. Take a wrong turn and you might end up in a neighbor's driveway. Take the right turn and you'll find the striking new stone and steel winery building surrounded by manicured lawns, organic vineyards, and perhaps some stray wildlife. Medlock Ames was started by two thirty-something friends with money to invest and a passion for the Wine Country lifestyle. Newly minted winemaker Ames Morrison and moneyed business partner Chris Medlock James have produced limited production merlot, cabernet, and chardonnay from the 55 acres of organic vineyard since 1999. The current 5,000-case production could eventually reach 20,000 cases, as revealed by an informal tour of the huge but still relatively empty barrel room.

SIGHTS
Cloverdale Historical Museum

The modest Cloverdale Historical Museum (215 N. Cloverdale Blvd., Cloverdale, 707/894-2067, 11 A.M.–3 P.M. Fri.–Sun. Nov.–Feb., 11 A.M.–3 P.M. Thurs.–Mon. Mar.–Oct., free) is actually the meticulously restored Gothic revival-style Gould-Shaw Victorian house and headquarters for the nonprofit Cloverdale Historical Society.

The house itself is one of the oldest dwellings still standing in Cloverdale, and almost everything in it, from the iron crib to the pump organ, is from the same era, donated or borrowed from other historic homes in the area. It also houses the society's research center, with archives going back to the late 1800s, and you can pick up a guide for a short walking tour of some of the other historic Victorian homes in the town.

ENTERTAINMENT

If you can ignore the ugly concrete scar it creates halfway up the otherwise unspoiled hillside, the **River Rock Casino** (3250 Hwy. 128, Geyserville, 707/857-2777, www.river-rockcasino.com, open 24 hours) provides one of the more unusual recreational opportunities in the county. That is, if you call winning or losing money recreation.

The casino is jointly owned by a Nevada gaming company and the Dry Creek Band of the Pomo Indian tribe, which has suffered at the hands of white people since the first settlers arrived in the 1800s. The Pomo tribe's 85-acre Dry Creek Rancheria, on which the casino is built, is a far cry from the vast territory of mountains and valleys in the region they used to call home.

The casino has sweeping sunset views over the vineyards of the Alexander Valley, as well as the usual array of modern amenities to help visitors part with their money, including restaurants, bars, 1,600 slot machines, and 16 tables. It's also easy to find—the entrance is right off Highway 128 about three miles south of the bridge over the river, just past the red barn on the left.

RECREATION

Some of the best outdoor pursuits can be found in the neighboring Dry Creek and Russian River Valleys, but the Alexander Valley and Chalk Hill areas do have their own unique possibilities. Although most opportunities to float on the river are focused south of Healdsburg, the stretch of Russian River between Cloverdale and Healdsburg is long, straight, and probably one of the easiest to navigate. It's also a pretty route through the vineyards.

River's Edge Kayak & Canoe Trips (13840 Healdsburg Ave., 707/433-7247, www.riversedgekayakandcanoe.com, Apr.–Oct. only), at the bridge in Healdsburg, offers a whole host of options for trips starting from either the top of the valley near Asti or halfway down and floating downstream to the beach in Healdsburg or beyond. There are a few rough patches of water but nothing worse than feeble Class I rapids. Later in the summer it will probably be a totally smooth float downstream.

The full day trips are 11–15 miles, which usually takes 4–6 hours and gives plenty of time for stopping at swimming holes along the way. The shorter trips are about half that. In all cases the price includes the rental of the kayak ($55 per day) or canoe ($85 per day) and a free shuttle ride upriver to start the adventure. Double kayaks are $85 per day. For a few extra dollars you can buy one of the packages that include everything from lunch to sunscreen.

Kayaks and canoes can also be rented on an hourly basis ($10–15) from the company's concession stand at Healdsburg's Memorial Beach at the eastern end of the bridge.

Safari West

Cruising around the Alexander Valley in a rental car might not exactly bring to mind the savannas of Africa, unless you happen upon this little animal oasis of cheetahs, zebras, and giraffes that happily laze away in the sun just over the hill from many of Chalk Hill's wineries.

The Chalk Hill appellation is the unlikely setting for the 400-acre Safari West wildlife preserve (on Porter Creek Rd. at Franz Valley Rd., 707/579-2551 or 800/616-2695, www.safariwest.com), home to a wide variety of endangered species from around the world, including many from central Africa. Whether the weather in Africa is similar to northern Sonoma is somewhat irrelevant considering the apparent happiness of the animals.

This is not a zoo or safari in the regular sense of the word, however. Instead, it started out in the late 1980s as a private ranch and preserve dedicated to saving endangered species from around the world. Humans were only admitted in 1993.

Seeing the magnificent beasts requires a reservation for one of the three-hour tours that set off three times a day (twice a day in winter) on a customized old jeep. They cost $68 for adults, $30 for kids under 12. The more adventurous might consider sleeping overnight in one of the luxurious tent cabins ($225–245 for two people, each extra guest $25) or cottages ($300 for two people). Lunch and dinner are available at the on-site café; wine is served, but antelope steaks are not.

Because it's a working preserve, visitors get easy access to the wildlife experts who work there and who are happy to reel off fascinating facts about the animals. This little corner of wild Africa in Sonoma also provides a welcome escape from the wilds of Wine Country tourism.

ACCOMMODATIONS

The Alexander Valley has more places to stay than its rural setting and tiny towns might suggest. Most of the B&Bs are clustered up at the far northern end of the valley in the quiet cow town of Cloverdale, but there are a few worthwhile places to consider around Geyserville to the south.

Under $100

With all the B&Bs in the valley costing well over $100, it is once again left to the motels to accommodate those with tight budgets or an aversion to Victorian inns. The biggest concentration of motels (all totally unexceptional) in this area is just off the freeway on Cloverdale Boulevard (take the Citrus Fair Dr. exit) and includes the **Cloverdale Oaks Motel** (123 S. Cloverdale Blvd., 707/894-2404) and the **Garden Motel** (611 N. Cloverdale Blvd., 707/894-2594). Best Western and Holiday Inn also have properties in the area.

$100-200

At the lowest end of the price range is the conveniently located **Geyserville Inn** (21714 Geyserville Ave., Geyserville, 707/857-4343 or 877/857-4343, www.geyservilleinn.com), a modern two-floor building resembling an upscale motel at the northern edge of Geyserville. Request an east-facing room to get a view of the vineyards and mountains rather than the freeway, which is a little too close for comfort. The smaller of the 38 rather plain guest rooms start at $110-119. The larger rooms, all of which have a fireplace and most of which have a balcony or patio, go for $149-249. Next door is the homey **Hoffman House Café,** which serves breakfast and lunch every day.

Driving through Geyserville, it's easy to miss two bargain B&Bs among the homes along the main road, but slow down and the historic elegance of the two Victorian-style **Hope Inns** (21253 Geyserville Ave., Geyserville, 707/857-3356 or 800/825-4233, www.hope–inns.com) becomes more obvious. The richly decorated interiors were restored in painstaking detail by the Hope family in the 1980s, and they put many of the historic Healdsburg B&Bs to shame.

There are eight guest rooms ($150-290) in the **Hope-Merrill House,** an 1870 Eastlake-style Victorian that features silk-screened wallpapers, coffered ceilings, and original woodwork. This is where the dining room (where breakfast is served), pool, and registration desk are located. Across the street is the Queen Anne–style **Hope-Bosworth House,** which has four guest rooms ($150-200) featuring the more restrained furnishings of that period. Only one room, the sumptuous Sterling Suite in the Hope-Merrill House, has a television, though others have some features that more than compensate, from fireplaces and chaise longues to whirlpool and claw-foot tubs. Free wireless Internet access was recently added.

The huge brick fireplace in the lobby of the **Old Crocker Inn** (1126 Old Crocker Inn Rd., Cloverdale, 707/894-4000 or 800/716-2007, www.oldcrockerinn.com), just south of Cloverdale, gives a hint of the Wild West roots of this charming lodge. It was built in the early 20th century by railway magnate Charles Crocker, founder of the Central Pacific Railroad, as a grand summer house, and the current owners have recreated the rustic character that it must originally have had—an odd blend of the Wild West and Victoriana.

The biggest guest room is the namesake Crocker room ($155-295), with a massive mahogany four-poster. The other four guest rooms ($130-185) in the main lodge building are named after Crocker's railroad partners. There are also three small cottages ($130-215), two of them able to comfortably sleep four people. All the rooms have old and modern features alike, including claw-foot tubs, gas fireplaces, TVs, and Internet access. The peaceful five-acre property also has an outdoor pool and feels like it's far from the madding crowds of the Wine Country. The complimentary gourmet breakfast is served in the lodge's spacious dining room.

Camping

The valley's main campground is the **Cloverdale KOA Wine Country Campground** (1166 Asti Ridge Rd., across the River Rd. bridge from Geyserville Ave., 707/894-3337) next to the hamlet of Asti. It might be part of the KOA chain, but it is a clean, easily accessible, and family-friendly option when the sites at nearby Lake Sonoma in the Dry Creek Valley are full. It also has a well-stocked fishing pond, bicycles for rent, and a big swimming pool.

There are 47 tent sites that cost from $35, and over 100 RV sites from $55. Reserve at 800/368-4558 or online (www.winecountrykoa.com). The rustic little one- and two-room **Kamping Kabins** ($72–82) might also be an alternative if the local B&Bs are full, though you have to supply your own bedding. Better still are the so-called **Lodges** dotted around the hillside. Each is like a luxury mini cabin with one bedroom plus a futon sofa, a full kitchen, and a barbeque outside (but no linens or towels). They cost from $175 and will comfortably sleep four with no extra charge.

Those with an aversion to developed campsites would do better to head 20 minutes west to Lake Sonoma in the Dry Creek Valley, where there are dozens of more primitive campsites, including many hike-in or boat-in sites.

FOOD

Most valley dining options are in nearby Healdsburg, but there are some notable exceptions. With the closure in 2010 of the renowned Taverna Santi in the center of Geyserville, the job of keeping the Italian food flame alive in the town was handed off to the less luxurious but no less delicious sister restaurant **Diavola Pizzeria & Salumeria** (21021 Geyserville Ave., 707/814-0111, www.diavolapizzeria.com,

lunch and dinner daily, pizzas and antipasti $13–16, dinner entrées $18–24). This is very much a restaurant for meat eaters, specializing in house-cured salamis and wood-fired pizzas, but also crafting a dozen or so antipasti plates of seasonal Italian-inspired food served on rustic copper-topped tables in a historic brick-walled building. The list of two dozen wines has as many Italian wines as local wines.

A little farther north on Geyserville Avenue is the **Hoffman House Café** (21712 Geyserville Ave., Geyserville, 707/857-3264, until 2 P.M. daily), with a big outdoor patio and a reputation for great brunches. It also sells gourmet boxed lunches, ideal for picnics.

For more food on the go, and some of the best picnic supplies around, the bright yellow and green **Jimtown Store** (6706 Hwy. 128 at Alexander Valley Rd., Healdsburg, 707/433-1212, 7:30 A.M.–5 P.M. daily), with its bright-red vintage pickup truck parked outside, is a valley fixture and seems to sell a bit of everything, including its own label wine. The boxed lunches alone are worth a detour and include a fat gourmet baguette sandwich, cookies, salad, and fruit, all for less than $11.

INFORMATION AND SERVICES

More information about this area's wines together with a comprehensive winery map can be found on the **Alexander Valley Winegrowers Association** website (www.alexandervalley.org).

More information about the history and businesses of Cloverdale and Geyserville can be obtained from their respective chambers of commerce. The **Geyserville Chamber of Commerce** (707/857-3745, www.geyservillecc.com) is not open to the public but has an excellent website. The **Cloverdale Chamber of Commerce** (105 N. Cloverdale Blvd., 707/894-4470, www.cloverdale.net) also contains the **North Coast Wine & Visitors Center** (9 A.M.–5 P.M. weekdays, 10 A.M.–4 P.M. weekends), which has maps, guides, and discount vouchers for anyone planning to explore northern Sonoma and Mendocino wineries.

NORTHERN SONOMA

BACKGROUND

The Land

GEOLOGY

Some 150 million years ago, probably long before vines had evolved from the primordial jungles, what we today know as Napa and Sonoma Counties was at the bottom of a giant ocean lapping up against massive volcanoes that eventually formed California's Sierra Nevada mountain range about 100 miles east of today's Napa Valley.

Much of modern-day California did not come into existence until the tectonic plates that make up the earth's crust had played their game of geological push and shove, generating massive creases in the earth's surface that pushed up the sea floor, creating mountains and shifting and splitting ancient continents to create the map of the world we recognize today.

From a winemaker's point of view, the geological history of California is ultimately what makes this area such a great wine-growing region. The ancient soils, valleys, and mountains combine into some of the most perfect places on earth to grow grapes.

Franciscan Formation

The section of the earth's crust that ended up

© SHERRI CAMP/123RF.COM

creating California is the Farallon plate, immortalized in the tiny Farallon Islands that lie about 20 miles off the coast of San Francisco. Where the plate pressed against its neighbor, the massive North American continental plate just west of the Sierra Nevada, it lost the shoving battle and ended up being forced under its larger neighbor in what is known in geological terms as a subduction zone.

As the Farallon plate was squeezed closer to the hot core of the earth under immense pressure, it generated huge quantities of molten rock, fueling prehistoric volcanoes that over millions of years built the mountains we know today. The process is continuing today all around the Pacific Ocean, and further north in Washington there's a reminder of the continuing tectonic activity every time Mount St. Helens sparks into life.

Geologists believe that as those prehistoric mountains got bigger and heavier from spewing out lava over the course of millions of years, they literally squashed the earth's crust and created a surrounding bulge hundreds of miles wide, much like pushing the edge of your finger into soft mud will cause the goop around it to bulge up.

That big undersea bulge then acted like a giant spatula, scraping off big chunks of the Farallon plate as it dived under its neighbor in the subduction zone and depositing them over millions of years to create what we now know as modern coastal California, including Napa and Sonoma. These geological scrapings are known as the Franciscan formation and form the bedrock of Northern and Southern California.

Volcanoes

The mountains and valleys of coastal California are altogether more recent additions to the Franciscan formation: recent at least in terms of geological timelines. About 5 million years ago, fissures in the bedrock opened up all over the land and spawned violent volcanoes that spewed out lava, ash, and giant boulders, rearranging the surface of the land and blanketing it with deep layers of volcanic rock and ash.

In the Napa Valley, evidence of these ancient volcanoes is easy to see. Mount St. Helena is an ancient volcano that once blew its top, flattening nearby trees that were buried, fossilized, and eventually resurfaced in the area where Calistoga's Petrified Forest is today. Nearby, Calistoga's hot springs, geyser, and the volcanic mud that visitors submerge themselves in are reminders of the cauldron that still bubbles deep underground, and just southeast of Calistoga is an area called Glass Mountain, so called because of the lumps of the black glass-like volcanic rock called obsidian that's found in the soils.

While the volcanoes were adding their own ingredients to what would become the complex mix of soils in the Wine Country, enter the giant geological blender known as the San Andreas Fault, a huge gash in the earth's crust.

The mountains and valleys of Napa and Sonoma were formed in the last 3 million years as the Pacific plate, another giant chunk of the earth's crust under the Pacific Ocean, slid northward along the San Andreas fault, eventually breaking up the Farallon plate in front of it. As it progressed, unleashing an earthquake with every sudden move, it slowly compressed the edge of the neighboring North American continental plate and buckled the land on the other side of the San Andreas fault line over millions of years, pushing up ridges of the Franciscan bedrock through the deep volcanic deposits covering it and creating the series of coastal mountain ranges and valleys that today define this part of Northern California.

The Mayacamas Mountains between the Napa and Sonoma Valleys, for example, were formed by this buckling, as was the coastal range of mountains on which the best Santa Cruz wines are grown. The plates are still moving today, ever so slowly, and the only reminders we have of this ongoing evolution of the planet's geology are the occasional earthquakes that rattle California.

The Franciscan and volcanic soils were further mixed up over the millennia by rivers and streams that carved their way down through the rocks, picking up sediment and dumping it miles away. The resulting patchwork of Franciscan, volcanic, and sedimentary soils is a winemaker's dream and helps explain why Northern California's Wine Country can turn out so many diverse styles of wine. Napa Valley alone is said to have up to 150 distinct types of soil.

CLIMATE

The soils aren't everything, of course. The mountains, hills, and valleys that make the geographical patchwork of the region also create a patchwork of climates, sheltering some areas from cool ocean winds, channeling the cool air to others, and exposing different slopes to different amounts of sunshine throughout the day. Throughout Napa and Sonoma and indeed much of the greater San Francisco Bay Area, microclimates are the norm. It might be a cool, murky August morning in San Francisco, but just 10 miles away the sun will be out and the weather balmy. Even within one sunny valley the temperature can vary widely in just a few miles.

The average maximum temperature in the city of Napa in July and August (the hottest months of the year) is about 82°F, according to historical climate data. In St. Helena, halfway up the Napa Valley, it averages about 89°F, and in Calistoga, far away from the cooling influence of the San Francisco Bay air, it averages 92°F. Carneros, meanwhile, is right next to the bay and usually only reaches the mid-70s at best.

Elsewhere in the area the extremes are just as great. On the eastern side of the Santa Cruz Mountains, sheltered from the ocean air, Los Gatos swelters in average high temperatures of 86°F in July, while on the other side of the mountains Santa Cruz relaxes at 74°F. In northern Sonoma, Cloverdale in the Alexander Valley bakes in average temperatures of nearly 92°F in July, while down in the fog-bound Russian River Valley, Occidental chills out at about 75°F.

For a winemaker, different climates are measured using a method called heat summation (also known as the Winkler Scale), which categorizes climates into regions on a scale from 1 to 5 depending on how hot the average daily temperature is during a vine's main growing season from April to October. Different grapes grow and ripen best in each climate region.

If California were a country, it would be one of the few on earth that have areas corresponding to all five growing regions. Northern California's Wine Country alone contains four of the five regions (though some say it has only three), which means there's an ideal climate for almost any type of grape.

Winemakers also have an easier job here than their colleagues in many other parts of the world, particularly in Europe, because rainfall is almost nonexistent for much of the summer, so grapes can ripen in the plentiful sun and avoid damp-related fungal disease like mildew. Similarly, hail and damaging winds are almost unheard of here during the summer. Most rain falls between November and April, and apart from the rare summer thunderstorm or late spring showers, it is generally dry from late May through October.

Fog

One of the defining aspects of the weather along the Northern California coast is the fog—damp, chilly marine fog creeps—sometimes charges—inland from the cold Pacific Ocean during the summer through every gap it can find in the mountains.

Perhaps no aspect of the weather here is more important. It takes the edge off the sometimes vicious summer heat and sun, keeps the nights cool, and slows the ripening of grapes in many places to a perfect tempo. It also generates the damp conditions in which California's famous coastal redwoods thrive, from Santa Cruz to Mendocino and nowhere more so than in the Russian River Valley, which is essentially a fog freeway, providing a direct channel from the ocean through the coastal hills and inland.

The factors that generate the fog, however, actually start hundreds of miles away in the sun-baked Central Valley of California. As the temperature there rises on summer days, so does the hot air, lowering the atmospheric pressure near the ground. Something has to replace all that rising air and even out the pressure. Imagine, then, a giant sucking noise as cool air is pulled in from the ocean to do just that.

Because the ocean is so cold, thanks to some

chilly Alaskan currents, it actually condenses water from the air (much like cold air does to your breath), forming a deep bank of fog that sits, menacingly, just off the coast. The onshore winds generated by the inland sun drag that fog onto the coast.

How far inland it gets depends on all sorts of factors, from the time of year to the prevailing atmospheric pressure. During summer days it usually hugs the coast. At night it can advance inland as far as the southern part of Napa Valley, Dry Creek Valley, and even the Livermore Valley, burning off rapidly as the sun heats things up.

Many additional factors have recently been found to influence fog formation, from weather over the Rocky Mountains to the currents in the South Pacific. But all the winemakers care about is that the fog helps make a great bottle of wine.

UNIQUE VINEYARD CONDITIONS

The combination of diverse soils and diverse microclimates offers just about everything a winemaker could want. There are very few grapes that have not been able to grow somewhere in California, and the current diversity of grape varietals (or lack thereof) has more to do with marketing than weather.

The French have a term for the unique conditions of a place that a grape is grown: *terroir*. It describes the combination of geological, geographical, and climate-related aspects of the land, including the soil, the slope, elevation, sun exposure, wind levels, and temperature patterns. California has a vast number of distinct *terroirs*.

Terroir explains why grapes grown in one vineyard will make a wine that tastes different from that made from grapes in a neighboring vineyard. So-called vineyard-designate wines sourced from one specific vineyard rather than multiple vineyards take advantage of that difference. There can even be a difference in the wine made from different sections, or blocks, of an individual vineyard.

It explains why the Napa Valley's Stag's Leap Wine Cellars can make very different wines from different blocks of one of its vineyards, for example, and why Stags Leap District cabernets as a whole taste different from those produced in the Rutherford District just a few miles up the road.

Best Soils and Climate

Almost without exception, the best soils for growing wine grapes are well drained and relatively infertile. Drainage is important to prevent the vines and grapes from getting too damp and potentially rotting, and also to encourage the vines to grow deep roots in search of a stable source of water. Some of the oldest vines have been known to send roots down as deep as 100 feet.

Drip irrigation systems are common sights in Californian vineyards, but they often have more to do with producing a financially viable quantity of grapes per acre than keeping the vines alive. Without some artificial water the vines might well survive but would not look nearly so lush with leaves and plump grapes by the end of the summer.

Fertility (or the lack of it) is a less important factor, although it's not by chance that some of the world's most distinctive and flavorful wines come from vineyards that thrive on fairly barren, rocky land, including steep mountainsides where even native plants struggle to grow.

Ultimately, grape growers are trying to produce a stressed vine—one that has to relentlessly search for water and survive on meager nutrients. This is not exactly the aim of most gardeners, who water and feed their plants to make them as big and lush as possible.

The theory goes that a stressed vine will produce fewer and smaller grapes but they will have a far more concentrated flavor. The same principle (taken to an extreme) explains why a shriveled raisin has a far more concentrated and powerful flavor than a plump Thompson seedless grape grown with the aid of plenty of watering and fertilizer.

Climate plays an equally important role in how a wine turns out, determining how quickly a grape ripens and the level of ripeness it is ultimately able to reach as measured by its sugar content. Temperatures during the day and night are affected by sun exposure, wind patterns, and countless other factors. Climate helps explain why a cabernet produced from vineyards on the west-facing slopes of a valley side that gets sun much of the warmest part of the day will taste slightly different from that made from a vineyard on an east-facing slope that might get less sun due to morning fog.

Appellation or AVA?

The diversity of grape growing conditions is recognized around the world in various national systems of defining geographical regions based on their specific soils and climate. Such systems have given rise to the names of famous types of wine all over the world, from Bordeaux to Burgundy, Chianti to Barolo. In the United States, such regions are called **American Viticultural Areas,** or AVAs, though many people simply call them appellations, after the French word meaning almost, but not quite, the same thing.

An appellation describes a geographical area, like an entire state or even a country. An AVA is based on a unique growing region only, one that can be shown to have conditions (soils, climate etc.) that make it stand apart from other areas around it. An appellation can be an AVA, but not all are. If wine were an appellation, then specific types of wine would be the viticultural areas. In the same vein, California is an appellation, and the Napa Valley is an AVA.

The federal Bureau of Alcohol, Tobacco, and Firearms (ATF) is the arbiter of AVAs and dishes them out only when wineries in a specific area have been able to prove that theirs is a unique place to grow grapes. Such proof usually comes in the form of an analysis of soils, climate, and physical features of the land. The petitioning and granting of an AVA takes many years, as is typical of most federal government processes, and is usually led by one or a group of wineries. Wine-making politics often complicates matters, especially when some wineries don't want to be included in an AVA for some marketing reason

or another, leading to some very drawn out application processes and sometimes arbitrary AVA boundaries.

The first AVA was established in 1980 in, of all places, Augusta, Georgia, and they are still being established today. The biggest in the country in terms of area is the Ohio River Valley, covering 26,000 square miles in parts of four different states. The smallest is Cole Ranch in Mendocino County, California, covering about a quarter square mile.

In Northern California there was a rush to get AVA status in the early 1980s by most of the major wine regions, and by 2009 there were 108 AVAs in California, a figure that is constantly growing. The first AVA in Northern California's Wine Country was the Santa Cruz Mountains, created in early 1982, followed shortly thereafter by the Sonoma Valley in the same month and Livermore Valley later that year. In 1983 the Napa Valley and Dry Creek Valley gained their AVA status, and since then there has been a steady stream of applications.

There can also be AVAs within AVAs, often called subappellations (again a technically incorrect term in some cases, but often used anyway). The Napa Valley AVA, for example, contains a patchwork of 15 smaller AVAs, each producing its own distinctive style of wine. The appellation of Sonoma County contains 11 AVAs, some of which overlap. If defining the land is so complicated, it's no wonder that the wines are so varied.

One interesting pattern exists in the Napa Valley. Since 1989, thanks to an arcane labeling law designed to protect the exclusivity of the Napa Valley name, no Napa County viticultural areas can fall outside the Napa Valley AVA. That's why many of the smaller AVAs in the Napa Valley, such as Mount Veeder and Spring Mountain, end abruptly at the county border. The one exception is the Los Carneros AVA, which sprawls across the southern portion of the Napa Valley and west into Sonoma County. It defies Napa Valley borders only because it was created before the 1989 law was enacted.

History

Northern California is widely regarded as the historic center of the state's wine industry, but it was not always so. In the early 1800s, Southern California was where all the wine-making action took place.

CALIFORNIA'S EARLY WINE INDUSTRY
Spanish Missions

California's missions played a crucial, though controversial, role in California's history, including its wine-making history. Their inexorable march northward from Mexico to Northern California introduced important wine-making skills thanks to the demand for sacramental wines. The missions also marked the beginning of the end for the lifestyles and cultures of the region's Native Americans, who had lived off the land for thousands of years.

The most important mission in Northern California was the 21st California mission and the last one built—Mission San Francisco de Solano in present day Sonoma. It was established by Father Jose Altimira, who arrived in the Sonoma Valley in 1819. Once the mission had been dedicated in 1824, the missionaries quickly set about their religious purpose. With the aid of the Mexican army, Native Americans were converted to Christianity whether they wanted to be or not. Within six years the mission had also established a big farming operation, with thousands of head of sheep and cattle, and had planted some of the region's first vines.

The new mission was founded not only to continue the spread of Christianity but also to provide food for the ailing missions in present-day San Francisco and San Rafael, which were struggling to sustain themselves. It was also the first and only mission in California created under Mexican rule, and it's likely that part of its purpose was to help prevent any expansion of a trading outpost established by Russian hunters nearby on the Sonoma coast at Fort Ross.

Just three years later, trouble rode into town in the form of a 25-year-old Mexican army lieutenant, Mariano Guadalupe Vallejo, who was sent north from the Presidio in San Francisco to rattle some sabers at the Russians and establish a military post at Sonoma. Vallejo would remain in Sonoma for the next half century and play a pivotal role in the creation of modern California.

When the missions were secularized by the Mexican government in 1835, Vallejo's garrison at Sonoma was well established and had created a Mexican-style plaza (present-day Sonoma Plaza) as a parade ground. He was ordered to take over the mission, and he promptly started to divide the buildings and land between friends and relatives. Meanwhile, the garrison and the town started to grow in importance, and Vallejo was promoted to colonel, the highest rank he ever achieved (despite this, he somehow became commonly known as "General Vallejo," a title that sticks to this day). As the military importance of his garrison in peaceful California slowly dwindled, he started living the good life, amassing land and planting vineyards.

The Land Grants

As the military commander and later Director of Colonization in Mexico's Northern Frontier, Vallejo controlled much of the land in today's Napa and Sonoma Counties and was under orders to dole it out to Mexican citizens for development. In reality he doled it out to friends, relatives, and business associates.

The land was snatched up by names that would eventually become a big part of modern wine history, including Agoston Haraszthy, a Hungarian immigrant who planted some of the earliest European vineyard cuttings and is credited with dragging the California wine industry from its missionary roots into the modern era through his Buena Vista Winery in the Sonoma Valley.

Over in the Napa Valley, Edward Bale was

granted a huge swath of land in 1844 near present-day St. Helena by way of marriage to Vallejo's niece. He planted some vines, and friend Charles Krug, a Napa wine pioneer, made wine for him. Another Napa valley pioneer, George Yount, was granted the 18-square-mile Rancho Caymus in the Napa Valley in 1836, an area that today includes Yountville. He built up a huge agricultural business and is credited with planting the first grapes in the Napa Valley. He made small quantities of wine but never became one of the valley's big early producers.

Up at the northern end of the Sonoma Valley, in 1859, Scotsman Charles Stuart bought some of Vallejo's land and named his home and ranch Glen Ellen, after Ellen, his wife. The name was eventually adopted by the town that developed in the area, and Stuart's ranch was renamed Glen Oaks. It still exists today. Captain Henry Boyes was another beneficiary of Vallejo's land and would go on to establish his mineral baths, Boyes Hot Springs, another name that eventually became a town.

Also in northern Sonoma, Captain Henry Fitch was granted 48,000 acres of land around present-day Healdsburg, about a quarter of which he later gave to Cyrus Alexander (after whom Alexander Valley is named) in recognition of the help that the former mountain man had been in managing Fitch's huge acreage.

As the early agricultural pioneers got started on these vast new swaths of land, the stage was set for an even bigger catalyst for change in California's early history—gold. The gold rush that started in 1848 brought a tidal wave of European immigrants to California, many of whom made their fortunes not from gold but by supplying the massive new economy with agricultural products.

The sheer scope of the immigrant influx is staggering. The nonnative population of California was believed to have been around 15,000 people in 1848 when gold was first discovered in the Sierra Nevada Mountains. Five years later it was an estimated 300,000, and most of those people were under age 40. Some of Napa and Sonoma's early pioneers were among them.

The Bear Flag Revolt

It was around this time that more American settlers were crossing the mountains to Northern California and letting everyone know about it. The Mexican government became apoplectic and tried to round up these American illegals and dissuade others from coming to California, an ironic reversal of roles compared to today's flow of Mexican migrant workers into California. Near Sacramento, Captain John Sutter was welcoming the new immigrants at his fort, riling the Mexican government even more. Not helping matters was the arrival of U.S. Army captain John C. Frémont in California on a mapping expedition.

As the tensions rose, Vallejo tried to stay neutral, walking a fine line between supporting various parties in the increasingly fragmented Mexican government and remaining friendly with the new American immigrants.

Soon tensions boiled over. In 1846, word came that Mexican general Castro was planning to drive out the Americans at Sutter's fort. Some of the settlers believed that Vallejo, who had met with Castro several times, was part of the plan to reexert Mexican authority, and they launched a preemptive attack on Vallejo's small garrison at Sonoma.

A ragtag group of about 30 men rode the 120 miles from Sacramento to Sonoma on the night of June 13, 1846, and barged into Vallejo's unprotected residence, La Casa Grande, to arrest him. He was taken the next day to Sacramento, where he remained under arrest until August. That day the members of the raiding party made a flag for their newly declared California Republic, and that Bear Flag replaced the Mexican emblem over Sonoma Plaza.

The U.S. Navy, which had a ship off the coast, soon stepped into the power vacuum created by the Bear Flaggers and raised the Stars and Stripes over Sonoma Plaza on July 9, 1846, claiming California for the United States with little in the way of a fight. Coincidentally, a few months earlier, U.S. president James Polk had declared war on Mexico after his request to buy Texas and California had been rejected. News

THE "BARE" FLAG

The flag of the great State of California, symbol of strength, courage, and freedom, started out as a crudely painted rectangle of fabric incorporating a woman's red petticoat. At least, that's one version of events back in 1846 when it was first raised over Sonoma Plaza.

The ragtag group of men behind the short-lived Bear Flag Republic needed something for their symbol. A loose committee finally decided that it should incorporate a bear, symbolizing strength and courage, and a star, inspired by the newly minted flag of Texas. So the saddle-stitchers and painters in the group set about making their new flag.

One member supplied the red fabric that some say was part of his wife's petticoat, although others maintain it was actually a flannel shirt. This was sewn to some bleached fabric onto which was painted the bear, the star, and the words "California Republic," the bear apparently looking more like a squat pig.

When it was finally done, the paint still wet, the flag was raised and flew for the 25 days it took the U.S. Army to march into town. The handmade Bear Flag was replaced by the Stars and Stripes on July 9, 1846. The flag was destroyed in the San Francisco earthquake and fire in 1906, but in 1911 the design was adopted as the official state flag, and today it flies above almost every public building in the state.

shape the region for the next 100 years arrived by the boatload.

By now, the missionaries, General Vallejo, and the early wine pioneers had shown that the region was well suited to growing just about everything, including grapes. The twin catalysts of the Mexican land grants and the Gold Rush had just given a huge boost to California's agricultural industry. The next few decades would see wine production surge as all the newly-arrived Europeans put their wine making and wine drinking experience to use.

By 1876 the Sonoma Valley alone was producing 2.3 million gallons of wine a year, and Northern California had overtaken Southern California as the biggest wine-producing region in the state. Around this time many of the immigrants that would shape the Napa and Sonoma wine industry had started to arrive from Europe, lured by the early successes of pioneering winemakers in the Napa and Sonoma Valleys like Charles Krug, Jacob Gundlach, and the Beringer brothers.

Outlying areas like the Alexander Valley and Dry Creek Valley were being planted with vines; the Italian-Swiss Colony, a wine-making cooperative, was established near Cloverdale; and down in Santa Cruz the first vines were planted on land freshly cleared of redwood forests.

Then the scourge of phylloxera struck. It is a devastating disease caused by a small aphid-like insect that attacks the roots of vines and slowly kills them by preventing the plant from absorbing water and nutrients. Phylloxera wiped out many vineyards in Europe in the late 1800s but is actually native to the United States. In fact, California's wine industry was doing so well in the late 1800s in part because the devastation in Europe wiped out exports and left Americans on the East Coast gasping for wine from other sources.

It would only be years later, after most Californian vineyards had themselves been decimated, that vines with resistant rootstock were replanted in Northern California by Gundlach, one of the Sonoma Valley's early wine pioneers.

of the war didn't reach California until mid-July. Two years later when the war was over, California and other Southwest states were officially ceded by Mexico.

The Early Wine Boom

When Vallejo was released, he returned to Sonoma and, over the next decade, became a big player in the region's politics. As Northern California's importance and wealth grew during that period, helped by the Gold Rush, the entrepreneurs and immigrants that would

Not long after Northern California's wine industry had started to recover from phylloxera and was once again booming, it took another economic hit, one from which it barely recovered.

Prohibition

The 18th Amendment of the United States Constitution, which ushered in the era of Prohibition in 1919, was born not out of government meddling but of an increasingly powerful temperance movement that had its roots in the puritanical beliefs of the country's founding fathers. Not helping matters was the increasing drunkenness of American society during the 1800s, which resulted in widespread public disgust and calls for change.

By some estimates, average Americans were drinking almost three times the amount of whiskey and other spirits in the mid-1800s as they do today. The more people drank, the more temperance movements tended to spring up all over the country in response. Eventually, the so-called "Drys" gained the political clout to pass laws in many states that banned public drinking, finally getting the Volstead Act, and with it Prohibition, passed in Congress. Winemakers had hoped that, being an upper-class drink, wine would be exempt from the legislation. In the end, the commercial production, sale, and transportation of any form of alcoholic drink was banned.

As with any piece of legislation, it doesn't take long for people to find the loopholes and to take advantage of weak enforcement. Bootleggers and gangsters set up a huge underground liquor network, and the wine industry got in on the act. Despite all commercial wine being banned, there were more acres of vineyards in existence during Prohibition than before it, and the price of grapes actually increased even as the quality of the grapes generally declined. Grape juice concentrate or bricks of compressed grapes were shipped all over the country, sometimes even accompanied by yeast tablets, for individuals to make their own wine behind closed doors, which was perfectly legal.

Although many grape growers flourished, wineries did not, and many closed. The few that remained open did so by making sacramental wine, which was still legal (as wine historians like to say, a lot of people found religion during Prohibition) or wine for government functions, also legal. After all, leaders still had to be able to entertain foreign dignitaries with fine wine even when the rest of the country had to do without.

In many ways, Prohibition marked the end of one chapter of California's wine-making history. In some areas, like the Santa Cruz Mountains and Livermore Valley, virtually all the wineries closed, never to reopen. Fruit trees replaced vines in many of today's wine-making valleys and held sway until relatively recently.

In Napa and Sonoma, a handful of wineries continued to operate during Prohibition, making sacramental wines, including Beringer Vineyards (the oldest continuously operating winery in the Napa Valley), Beaulieu Vineyard, Buena Vista Winery (its Carneros facility is the oldest continuously operating winery in California), and Sebastiani Vineyards. Still others turned to farming or supplying grapes until Prohibition was repealed, then resumed wine-making, while a few wineries continued to make wine and store it in the hope that Prohibition would soon end.

It took 14 years for Prohibition to come to an end; it was finally repealed in 1933, when the 21st Amendment was passed by Congress. In those 14 years, California's wine industry had been gutted. Most wineries had closed, important wine-making skills had been lost, and the public had lost the taste for fine wines, instead preferring homemade hooch. Making matters worse, the few remaining wine producers emerged from the shadow of Prohibition and into the gloom of the deepest economic crisis in American history, the Great Depression.

Picking Up the Pieces

Following repeal, winemakers were left with broken wineries, vineyards that had been planted with grapes that shipped well rather than grapes that made good wine, and a nonexistent domestic market for wine. For an industry in such a dire state, recovery was surprisingly fast.

In some ways the wine industry took several steps back after repeal, turning out bulk and fortified wines of far lower quality than the world-class wines made by the new European immigrants some 30 years earlier. The few big wineries that did survive, especially those in the Napa, Sonoma, and Livermore Valleys, continued to make some high-quality wines, but they too joined the bulk bandwagon.

They were joined by former grape growers who made a tidy profit during Prohibition, including the Gallo brothers who, in 1933, established a winery that would morph into the world's largest wine producer half a century later. Other new wineries prospered from the sale of massive quantities of cheap wines. Fine-wine production remained a rarity and the preserve of the modest number of old-school wineries that had largely been left behind in the new wine-making environment, where size mattered.

After all booms come busts, and it was no different for the booming Californian wine industry. By the end of the 1930s the industry was suffering a monumental postrepeal party hangover as the market imploded under the weight of too much bad wine. Prices crashed and the number of wineries dramatically declined, but there was a silver lining. The formation of two important marketing organizations in the 1930s, the Wine Institute and the Wine Advisory Board (the board has long since been disbanded), would give California's wine industry some much-needed strategic direction as it once again picked itself up after the war.

The Modern Era

The Californian wine industry emerged from the frugal war years as production of cheap wines sourced from cheap grapes once again soared as it had after Prohibition The difference this time was that improved marketing had created more buyers of cheap wine than in the 1930s, but important figures in the industry still recognized the need to improve quality and

wean the public onto finer wines. This was the period when the pioneers of California's modern wine industry would start to appear—figures like Martin Ray in the Santa Cruz Mountains region, André Tchelistcheff at Beaulieu Vineyards in the Napa Valley, Herman Wente in the Livermore Valley, and perhaps most importantly, the Mondavi family.

One of the key figures in the start of the modern age of fine wine making was Robert Mondavi in the Napa Valley. His father, Cesare Mondavi, was one of the many producers of bulk wine in the Napa Valley after Prohibition, and his two sons, Robert and Peter, were already getting some experience helping run the bulk business. When Cesare bought the old Charles Krug winery in 1943, the family's attention increasingly turned to fine wines, but following a family feud after Cesare's death, Robert was forced out of the family business.

With wine already in his blood, he started his own Robert Mondavi Winery in 1966, the first new winery to be built in Napa since the repeal of Prohibition. It proved to be one of the most important symbols for growth in the fine wine industry in the region, and Mondavi is often cited as one of the figures who proved that a dream of starting a great winery from scratch could become reality. Whether by luck or by design, Mondavi's venture coincided with a surge in the popularity of fine wines, and in the following decade hundreds more wineries were established by dreamers hoping to catch the same wave, including many of today's biggest wine-making names.

From the 1940s to the 1970s the number of wineries in California steadily declined as production of fine wine slowly replaced massive output of cheap wine. In 1945 there were just over 400 wineries in the state. By 1970 that number had dwindled to about 240 wineries. The industry had reached another nadir by 1970, but it would rise yet again, this time with a strategy that would last. By the end of the 1970s the number of wineries had more than doubled to more than 500, and every region covered in this book was firmly established on the wine map of California.

There was no single person or event that helped usher in this modern wine era in California. Instead, it has been linked to the more general growth in modern technology. The world became smaller as air travel and television introduced millions to previously unknown cultures and ideas. There was a population boom in the United States and an economic boom that introduced the modern consumer age. And, it seems, the wine industry's marketing efforts finally started to click.

The Judgments of Paris

The reputation of California's modern wines was cemented at an international wine-tasting event in Paris in 1976. British wine writer and critic Stephen Spurrier, already familiar with the rising quality of California's wines, suggested a taste-off between what he regarded as the best Californian and best French wines in an event to celebrate the American bicentennial.

Five Californian chardonnays and five cabernet sauvignons were pitted against the same number of French white Burgundies and red Bordeaux wines. The all-French panel of esteemed judges had to taste blind in case the French national disdain for New World wines at the time influenced their conclusions. Having set all this up, Spurrier must have been pretty confident the Californian wines would do well, but he reportedly did not expect them to win.

The tasting panel placed a 1973 cabernet sauvignon from Stag's Leap Wine Cellars in the Napa Valley at the top of the reds, followed by the three Bordeaux wines and a cabernet from Ridge Vineyards. The Californian whites did even better. A 1973 Chateau Montelena chardonnay was judged to be the best white wine, and two other Californian chardonnays were placed in the top five (from Chalone Vineyard and Spring Mountain Vineyards).

The shockwave of the French being beaten at their own game reverberated around the wine world. The French were gutted. California winemakers never looked back.

The French tried to salvage some pride, suggesting that Californian wines might well taste better upon release but they would not age as well as their French counterparts. That theory was disproven when the tasting was recreated 30 years later. The so-called Judgment of Paris was retried in 2006, when the same 1970s vintage wines were pulled from cellars and tasted again. Once again the Californian wines trounced the French, perhaps more decisively so than in the original tasting. The top five reds were all from California, led by the 1971 Ridge Monte Bello cabernet sauvignon and the 1973 Stag's Leap cabernet.

Marketing types proclaimed that this proves Californian wines can age as well as the best Bordeaux. Critics suggested it was simply a gimmick, and the wines of 30 years ago bear no resemblance to wines made today. It was a fun exercise nonetheless, even if it only proves that California can indeed make good wines (as judged by the French).

The events leading up to the 1976 tasting were recounted in the 2008 movie *Bottle Shock*. The producers of the film were accused by Stephen Spurrier of taking too much artistic license in the name of entertainment, and he was particularly annoyed at his depiction in the film, but it nonetheless provided an entertaining portrayal of an important turning point in California's wine-making history.

CALIFORNIA'S MODERN WINE INDUSTRY
Economy

The wine industry is to the Napa and Sonoma Valleys and large parts of northern Sonoma what the movie business is to Los Angeles—an integral part of the cultural and social fabric. Everyone seems to have some link to the wine business, whether directly or indirectly, and given the industry's sheer size it's hardly surprising.

If California were a country, it would be the fourth-largest producer of wine in the world after Italy, France, and Spain. The state's wine industry made 620 million gallons of wine in 2008, according to the Wine Institute, or more than 90 percent of all the wine produced in the United States. That makes California's wine industry about an $18 billion industry in terms of U.S. retail sales, but it brings a lot more money to the state in other ways.

An estimated 20 million tourists visit many of the state's almost 2,900 bonded wineries each year, and the wine industry accounts for more than 300,000 jobs in California directly and indirectly. All told, the value of the wine industry to California's overall economy was estimated at more than $60 billion in 2008, and the economic impact on the U.S. economy was more than $120 billion, according to one research report.

Napa and Sonoma dominate California's wine industry, though not by sheer size; Santa Cruz and other parts of Northern California's Wine Country are bit players by comparison. Together the two counties contain almost half of all the wineries in the state, even though they account for less than one-fifth of the state's total acreage of wine-grape vineyards. The important factor is quality. Huge quantities of cheap wines are churned out in the Central Valley of California, but Napa, Sonoma, and other important Northern California wine regions produce a big proportion of the state's premium wines, the fastest-growing category of wines that sell for premium prices.

Consumption Trends

Luckily, the rest of the world likes to drink wine, because Americans apparently don't. Although an impressive 750 million gallons of all types of wine were consumed in the United States in 2008, much of it made in California, consumption per person is only about 2.4 gallons, or about 11 bottles, per year.

Per capita consumption in the United States is actually about the same today as it was in the mid-1980s, but it has been increasing at quite a pace. Still, by 2006 people in the United Kingdom were drinking about twice as much wine on average as their U.S. counterparts, the Germans almost three times more, and the French a whopping six times more. Even Slovaks, Finns, and Swedes drink more wine than the average American. And the top per-capita wine consumer in 2006? Vatican City.

wine barrels in a storage cave at a winery in Napa Valley

UNSUNG HEROES

They pick the grapes, prune the vines, and help manage the vineyards, but the workers toiling away during the long hot summers in Northern California are largely the unsung heroes of the wine industry, ensuring winemakers have the best vines and grapes to work with but rarely remembered when the cork is pulled.

As is the case in much of the rest of the state's agricultural sector, most of these workers are migrants from Latin America. They do the work that locals usually won't touch for the money offered, which in many cases is barely above the state's minimum hourly wage.

The political debate continues over their legal status – it's a thorny issue that will probably never be fully resolved. But without question, the migrant labor pool is a valuable competitive asset for California's winemakers and the state's agriculture industry as a whole.

Despite the low wages paid to workers, it still costs almost double the amount per ton to harvest grapes and maintain vines by hand than by machines. Increasing mechanization has drastically reduced the number of vineyard workers in the past few decades, but they remain a critical part of the wine industry, particularly in the premium growing areas like Napa and Sonoma, where hand-picking of the valuable grapes is much preferred over letting a machine bludgeon its way through the vines. Steep mountain vineyards in Northern California also pose problems for machines and require the human touch to manage and harvest them.

By some estimates, 98 percent of the vineyard workers in California are from Mexico, so it's no surprise that after decades of toiling in the vineyards, an increasing number of Mexican American families are cashing in on the skills, knowledge, and contacts they have developed.

Since the early 1990s, more than a dozen Mexican families have started their own wineries in Sonoma and Napa. Former migrant worker Reynaldo Robledo, for example, started working in California's vineyards in the 1960s, later established his own vineyard management company, and finally realized his dream to make his own wine. He founded the Robledo Family Winery in Carneros, which became the first Mexican American winery to open a public tasting room in 2003.

His story and those of the numerous other newly minted Mexican American wine-making families are just part of the latest chapter in California's wine industry, which owes a historical debt to immigrants from all over the world, from the Victorian pioneers like Charles Krug and Samuele Sebastiani to the Gallo and Mondavi families, who helped put California's wine industry on the international map after Prohibition.

It's not that Americans in general don't drink much wine, just that most Americans don't drink any at all. Nearly all the wine consumed is drunk by less than one-fifth of the population (and Californians drink about a fifth of all the wine consumed in the United States). A wide range of factors might explain the country's low rate of wine consumption, including its puritanical roots, the legacy of Prohibition, and even the climate.

One important factor is simply that the U.S. population does not have a great wine-making legacy. Wines have only been made in California in commercial quantities for 150 years, which might seem like a long time but is the blink of an eye when you consider that the Romans fueled their orgies with the stuff some 2,000 years ago. Moreover, the waves of recent American immigrants from Central America and Asia also tend to have little previous exposure to wines.

Europeans have been making wine for thousands of years, and it is as much a part of the culinary culture in many European countries there as, say, apple pie is in the United States. American consumers tend to view wine as a special-occasion drink, something to be enjoyed once in a while rather than every day.

While it's true that high-quality wine might be a little too expensive for most people to open a bottle every day, consider that wine in an open bottle can remain fresh for 4–5 days if stored correctly. If you prefer to save an expensive wine for a special occasion, consider stocking up with "house wine," which still tastes good but at a price far more inviting for an everyday drink.

Chardonnay remains the most popular wine, even though that popularity has waned slightly in recent years. Merlot, cabernet sauvignon, and white zinfandel are not far behind in popularity. Those four varietals together accounted for just over half the wines sold in U.S. food stores in 2006, and overall sales of red wines were about the same as sales of white.

The Power of Marketing

Take a trip to wineries in Napa and Sonoma and you'd be lucky to find any wine for sale under $30, which might give the impression that wine is generally an expensive drink. But those pricey wines account for only a fraction of the wine made in California. A trip to the local supermarket or liquor store will confirm that most wine sold in the United States is of the cheap and cheerful kind, usually in big 1.5-liter bottles or casks. In fact, about two-thirds of the wine sold in the United States in 2004 cost less than $7 per bottle, according to the Wine Institute. That represents about the same alcoholic bang for the buck as beer.

So-called premium wine, costing over $7 per bottle, is where the big money is for the wineries, however, so that's where the marketing dollars tend to get spent. It's also the fastest-growing segment of the wine industry in the United States, although there are signs that the 2009 recession has slowed the growth in sales of the most expensive wines.

Wineries in the best wine-making regions of Northern California have high costs to recoup. Land for vineyards in the Napa Valley costs about $120,000 per acre. It then costs $25,000–50,000 per acre to prepare and plant it with vines. Add the costs of managing that vineyard and actually making, bottling, and distributing the wine, and some wine prices start to seem justified.

But it's also in a winery's best interests to try to wean consumers onto the expensive stuff because then they'll probably be consumers for life. Research shows that once your palate is used to a $50 cabernet, you're highly unlikely ever again to choose a jumbo bottle of $5 generic red wine to go with dinner. You'll buy as much of the $50 wine as you can afford.

Gaining and retaining consumers is a tough balancing act for the wineries from a marketing point of view. On the one hand they want to lure new premium wine consumers into the fold by promoting their wines as an easy entry into some sort of elite Wine Country lifestyle. But as wineries push pricey wines and all the pretensions that go along with them onto non–wine drinkers, they risk scaring the uninitiated away altogether. Just visiting the Napa Valley, with its $25 tasting fees, can be enough to scare some people off.

The industry sometimes doesn't seem to help itself either. One new winemaker in Sonoma recounted asking some industry colleagues how he should price his new wine. He was told not to price it too low or no one would take it seriously. It goes to show that price is not necessarily a firm measure of quality but is just one of many indicators.

Fortunately, the wine industry sometimes gets some marketing help from unlikely places. Touting the health benefits of moderate amounts of wine has always been a surefire, if temporary, way to get more Americans to drink the stuff. The increasing marketing of food and wine together is also helping to push up consumption—cooking shows now routinely feature advice from wine experts.

More recently, the Oscar-winning 2004 movie *Sideways,* a comedy-drama that follows two aging bachelors on a voyage of self-discovery through the Santa Barbara Wine Country, did wonders for sales of pinot noir. As the movie's characters waxed lyrical about the joys of a good pinot, American consumers apparently decided to discover the joys themselves, and sales of pinot noir in California jumped by a third in the year leading up to the 2005 Academy Awards compared to the previous year, according to statistics from A. C. Nielson, which monitors sales at retail outlets. Although Santa Barbara pinots were the stars of the movie, Northern California's pinots benefited just the same.

The 2008 movie *Bottle Shock,* about the famous 1976 Judgment of Paris, had less of an effect on overall wine sales, but did reportedly bring more tourists to the already-popular Napa Valley and reminded the world how good California wine can be.

Wine and Health

In 1991, CBS aired a *60 Minutes* program titled "The French Paradox," which reported that the French population has a far lower incidence of heart attacks than the American population despite getting less exercise, eating more fatty foods, and smoking more. According to some medical experts, this apparent health paradox could be explained by the fact that the average French person drinks a lot of wine.

The American wine industry could not have asked for better publicity. In the month following the broadcast, wine sales reportedly jumped by 44 percent compared to the same period a year earlier. Although the sales spurt didn't last, and research has since suggested that the French paradox is far more complex than can be explained simply by higher wine consumption, the wine industry gained a new marketing angle for its wines.

Wine and some other alcoholic beverages have been shown to indeed have health benefits. In the case of the French paradox, however, it is thought that the health benefits have as much to do with overall lifestyle and food consumption patterns as they do with drinking wine.

Low stress (the French take far more vacations than most Americans) and a Mediterranean diet rich in fish, fresh vegetables, and oils, for example, could be factors. Regular wine drinkers also tend not to be binge drinkers, avoiding all the potential health hazards associated with overconsumption of alcohol.

The jury is still out on whether alcoholic beverages, and wine in particular, have direct effects on long-term health. Statistical studies performed all over the world suggest that moderate wine drinkers (those that drink 1–2 glasses a day) seem to suffer from lower rates of heart diseases and certain cancers, but no one yet knows exactly why or what other factors might be involved.

Some research has focused on a family of chemicals found in the skins of red grapes (and therefore only in red wines) called polyphenols, which are believed to be natural antioxidants. Some polyphenols have specifically been shown to reduce the likelihood of arteries getting clogged in laboratory tests.

As is the case with many health-related issues, there seems to be a new study done every year that in some way contradicts results from the last. It's enough to give anyone a headache even before drinking too much wine.

In one study published in the science journal *Nature* in 2005, for example, researchers in Denmark reported that levels of "good" cholesterol increased in test subjects who drank red wine and not in those who drank grape-skin extract rich in polyphenols or water. That seemed to suggest lifestyle or simply alcohol content are more important factors than chemicals in the wine. Then, in 2006, a Harvard Medical School study found that another naturally occurring substance in red wine called resveratrol could offset the bad effects of high-calorie diets in mice.

Yet another study published in 2006, this time in the United Kingdom, suggested another family of chemicals found in wine, procyanidins, could help lower the risk of heart attacks by blocking a chemical signal in the body that normally constricts blood vessels. Moreover, wines from southwest France and southern Italy were found to contain higher levels of procyanidins, perhaps lending credence to the supposed benefits of the Mediterranean diet.

Whether research will ever be able to discover the secrets behind the French paradox, if indeed there are any, is anyone's guess. While much of the media focus has been on the supposed beneficial effects of drinking wine, there are some less-well-publicized downsides to drinking wine, even in moderate amounts, aside from the headaches, impaired driving ability, and worse things that everyone knows about.

As anyone who has drunk several glasses of a Napa cabernet with dinner will probably have discovered, red wine stains the teeth. But it does more than just this temporary cosmetic damage; the acids in both red and white wines wear away the protective enamel on teeth (white wines are the worst offenders), making them more susceptible to decay. For wine tasters who often swill hundreds of wines around in their mouths each week, it is a very significant problem, and regular fluoride treatment is often recommended to replace minerals lost from the teeth.

But even for the occasional wine drinker there can be an effect, not least because wine is consumed over several hours, giving those acids plenty of time to start working on the teeth. Recommendations to prevent damage range from drinking plenty of water to help dilute the acidity and get your saliva flowing to eating cheese at the end of the meal. Cheese neutralizes acids, and it has been suggested the calcium in cheese might even harden the enamel weakened by the wine's acid.

Wine 101

CALIFORNIA GRAPE VARIETALS

The diversity of California's wine industry and the multitude of growing conditions are illustrated by the vast number of grape varietals grown in the state. There are more than 30 types of red wine grapes grown in almost 300,000 acres of vineyards, and 25 types of white wine grapes grown in almost 200,000 acres of vineyards. It's a dizzying array of varietals but is dominated by just a handful.

Certain grapes will only grow in certain conditions, while others will grow anywhere. Chardonnay, for example, is the everyman's grape, able to grow happily almost anywhere in the Wine Country. Pinot noir is fussy and will only grow in a narrow range of cooler climates—and makes good wine in an even narrower range.

Red Wine Grapes

Cabernet sauvignon is by far the most important red wine grape in California, accounting for about a quarter of all red grapes grown in the state. It is easy to ripen in the Californian sun and capable of making both powerful, tannic wines in hotter climates and lighter, more austere wines in cooler mountain regions, all of them usually capable of long-term aging if they are well-made and all having the telltale aromas of cassis (blackcurrant), blackberry, green bell pepper, cedar wood, and leather.

Merlot is the second most widely planted red wine grape in California, though its popularity peaked in the 1990s and is now waning. It is usually blended with cabernet sauvignon in Bordeaux wines, but in California is often made into an easy-drinking wine that is less tannic and more plump than most cabernet sauvignons. Sometimes its more subtle flavors can be lost, resulting in a bland wine, but a well-made merlot has just as much structure as other reds.

Zinfandel is not far behind merlot in terms of total acreage planted and is often considered a California native, though recent genetic studies have shown it probably originally came from southern Europe. Zinfandel can come in many styles, from intense, jammy, and tannic wine to a more subtle, spicy wine with cherry and berry flavors and nice structure—typical of cooler-climate styles. A characteristic of zinfandel vines is that individual grapes can vary dramatically in size within bunches, so they ripen at different speeds. This can result in some being overripe when picked, leading to high sugar levels and even higher alcohol levels in the wines, together with an almost raisiny

© PHILIP GOLDSMITH

grapes on the vine

Rhône-style wines in cooler parts of California, exhibiting telltale black pepper and chocolate flavors and an almost purple color. It makes a much denser, more powerful wine when grown in hotter climates, including parts of California and in Australia, where it is commonly known as **shiraz.**

Petite sirah is normally used as a blending grape, particularly in zinfandels, but it is also increasingly bottled on its own. The resulting wine is one of the darkest colored you'll see and has a trademark intensity with plenty of dark fruit and peppery flavors that can (and often do) support some fairly robust tannins. It can age well but is at its best when blended with Rhône varietals to give it a little more complexity. Despite the different spelling, petite sirah is genetically related to syrah, although most of the petite sirah grown in California has actually been found to be a varietal called durif, which is itself a cross between petite sirah and another varietal called peloursin. The confusion is yet another example of how California's pioneer winemakers were often a little too casual or simply inaccurate when documenting newly planted grapes.

flavor. Old vines tend to have a smaller crop with more uniform grape size and are favored by winemakers—some zinfandel vines are over a century old.

Pinot noir is a distant fourth in terms of acreage due to its finicky nature, which limits the areas where it can be successfully grown. It is said to have the most complex flavors and be able to communicate the unique properties of the *terroir* like no other grape, but only if grown in the right conditions—not too hot, yet just warm enough to ripen the grapes sufficiently. Classic pinot flavors and aromas include cherry, raspberry, strawberry, violet, and any number of earthy overtones. Cooler parts of California are some of the few areas of the world where great pinot noirs are made, the most famous being the Burgundy region of France. It is also one of the most important grapes for making champagne.

Syrah is the rising star of California's red wines and the fifth-most-planted red grape in the state. Its traditional home is the Rhône region of France, and it is often made into

White Wine Grapes

Chardonnay is the king of white grapes in California. It accounts for almost 100,000 acres, or more than half the total acreage planted with white varietals, and about a quarter of all wine made in California in 2005. It grows almost anywhere and can be made into wines of a multitude of styles to suit almost every palate, depending on the wine-making process. Overoaking is a common fault of Californian chardonnays, as is an overreliance on high levels of malolactic fermentation, which give the wines a sweet, buttery, and slightly generic flavor. Chardonnay is also one of the most important champagne grapes.

Chenin blanc is the grape that chardonnay eclipsed, and the acreage planted to this varietal in California has been declining steadily since the 1980s. It makes an equally easy-drinking (some say plain) wine as chardonnay, full of fruity flavors, but it is most commonly used as a blending grape.

Sauvignon blanc is one of the most important white grape varietals in Bordeaux, where it is usually blended with semillon, and it is growing in popularity in California. In cool climates like its home in France and parts of California it makes a refreshingly crisp, aromatic wine, often with unusual aromas of grass and herbs. In warmer climates it makes a more intense style of wine from which winemakers sometimes coax richer, more tropical fruit flavors. These richer styles are often called **fumé blanc** but are still made from the same sauvignon blanc grape.

Viognier is an increasingly fashionable white varietal originally from the Rhône region of France that exploded onto the California wine scene in the 1990s. In 1992 there were just 100 acres planted of this varietal; by 2002 there were 2,000 acres. It does well in California's warm climate, where it ripens enough to create full-bodied, elegant wines with a distinctive exotic, floral aroma and rich texture. It is sometimes used in small quantities as a blending grape in red wines. Watch out for sometimes excessive levels of alcohol (often over 15 percent) that can give the wine a "hot," or overly alcoholic, taste.

Riesling is regarded as the king of white wines on its home turf in Germany and is increasingly popular in California thanks to its ability to make different styles of wine depending on the climate and wine-making process. Some rieslings are too sweet and lack structure, but the best wines from places like the Anderson Valley in Mendocino have a unique balance of acidity, tropical fruit flavors, powerful aromas, and a lightness that makes them some of the most complex in the white wine world. Also look for a delicious dessert wine made from so-called botrytized grapes, which have been infected by the botrytis mold either naturally on the vine or artificially after harvest. The mold has the effect of dehydrating the grape, concentrating the sugars and flavors into an uncommon intensity.

Gewürztraminer is another Alsatian grape that has found a home in the cooler parts of California, most notably the Anderson Valley in Mendocino, and produces wonderfully complex wine with a telltale floral aromas and a refreshing acidity that makes them great with food. Most gewürztraminer is made in a dry style, but grapes are also often harvested later than usual to make a rich and equally complex dessert wine.

HOW WINE IS MADE

For thousands of years civilizations have made wine, and the chemical process of fermentation that turns the sugar in grape juice into alcohol in wine is the same as it's always been. The actual process of making wine has changed drastically, however, particularly since the science behind fermentation was first discovered in the mid-1800s. Since then, wine making has become ever more refined to get the best out of particular grapes and to make different styles of wine, some for aging and others for mass consumption.

The year that appears on a wine bottle, known as the wine's vintage, is the year that the grapes are harvested and wine making begins. The processes used to make red and white wines are similar but with a few important differences. One of the most important is that red wines are made by fermenting the juice in contact with the skins of the grapes. The skins contain the pigments that make red wine red; juice from virtually all grapes, whether red or white, is relatively colorless. Cut a red grape in half, scoop out the flesh, and it will be almost identical in color to flesh from a white grape.

Grapes are brought from the vineyards to the crush pad at the winery, where they are unloaded onto a conveyor and fed into a **crusher-destemmer,** a machine that chops off the stems but lets the grapes through, gently crushing them in the process so the juice can seep out. In the case of the best grapes destined for more expensive wines, human sorters often pull out withered, unripe, or otherwise unworthy grapes and stems from the conveyor so only the best get through. Once grapes are crushed and destemmed, the wine-making process begins.

Although red and white wine-making

techniques differ in many ways, they both involve a fermentation stage during which naturally occurring yeasts on the skins of the grapes, often supplemented by the addition of other yeast strains for certain flavor characteristics, get to work on the grape juice and turn the naturally occurring sugar into alcohol. Fermentation can be carried out in giant wooden tanks (the old fashioned way), temperature-controlled stainless steel tanks (the modern way), or even open-top concrete tanks (old-fashioned but still widely used in California for some wines, like pinot noir).

Almost as important as the type of fermentation vessel used is how the wine gets in and out of it. A lot of modern wineries use standard food-grade pumps and pipes to move the wine between each stage of wine making. The more traditional method of moving the liquid around is gravity flow—literally letting gravity do the work. This is how it used to be done before the age of modern pumps and electricity. Many old (and an increasing number of modern) wineries are designed around the gravity flow principle, whereby each stage of the wine-making process is at a progressively lower level of the winery. Purists argue that gravity-flow wine making minimizes the amount of contact the wine has with processing equipment and the heat it generates. It also saves a considerable amount of power.

Californian wine making differs from that in some other parts of the world in that winemakers cannot add any sugar to the wine (known as chaptalization). Luckily, the weather is hot enough and the sun strong enough that ripening grapes to their necessary sweetness is generally not a problem in California. Very little else can be added to wines during fermentation either, except for yeast and clarifying agents, but winemakers have plenty of ways to manipulate wines after fermentation. More sugar can be added in the form of additional grape juice, acid levels can be increased with the addition of tartaric or citric acid, and alcohol levels can be lowered if necessary using a process called reverse osmosis. Such manipulation of the finished product is more common than wineries and winemakers want you to believe.

HOW MANY GRAPES IN A GLASS?

Understanding the wine-making process is a bit easier if it's brought down to a personal scale – how many grapes go into the bottle of wine you're drinking. The Sonoma County Grape Growers Association has helpfully worked it out for us.

An average vineyard yields about 5 tons, or 10,000 pounds, of grapes per acre (it's actually far less for the best vineyards and most expensive wines). All those grapes make about 13.5 barrels of wine, which is 797 gallons, or 3,985 bottles.

Do the math and it turns out that one bottle of wine is made using about 2.4 pounds of grapes, so one glass comes from just under 10 ounces of grapes.

This is little more than a back-of-an-envelope calculation, however, and will depend on all sorts of factors, from the type of grape to the style of wine being made.

The Napa Valley Vintners Association has slightly different figures. It says a ton of grapes makes on average 720 bottles of wine, so each bottle contains about 2.8 pounds of grapes. It also helpfully calculates that one average vine plant produces enough grapes to make 4-6 bottles of wine each year.

Alcohol and many naturally occurring chemicals act as preservatives in bottled wine, but a chemical that is usually added for its additional preservative action is sulfur dioxide, and this is responsible for the statement on wine labels that a wine "contains sulfites." Sulfur dioxide is added to wines before bottling to prevent the growth of bacteria that could spoil the wine, and it is also sometimes added at the beginning of the wine-making process to kill naturally occurring yeasts, some of which might impart slightly funky flavors to a wine. In most cases, however, natural yeasts are an important part of the wine-making process, though often supplemented by other strains of yeast, all of which create wines with slightly different characteristics.

The headaches that some people claim are caused by sulfites in wine, particularly cheap wine, could also be due to naturally occurring histamines. Some people experiment with taking an antihistamine before drinking wine.

Making Red Wine

After destemming and crushing, the grapes are either pumped or flow by gravity into the fermentation vessel, where fermentation begins and usually continues for a couple of weeks.

During fermentation, the grape skins, seeds, and remaining small pieces of stem float to the top and form a thick crust that has to be constantly broken and remixed with the fermenting wine to ensure all the pigments in the grape skins and the other desirable chemicals like tannins are leached out of this "cap" of crud. These days the wine from the bottom of the fermentation tank is usually pumped over the cap and filters back down through it, or a giant mixer-like system keeps all the skins and stems constantly circulating through the fermenting wine.

Traditionally, the cap was broken up and pushed back down into the wine by hand using a big wooden paddle, and this punching-down technique is still used in some smaller wineries today, especially to produce pinot noir—a wine that requires more work to extract the color from the grape skins.

Once the winemaker determines that enough pigment and tannins have been extracted from the skins and fermentation has gone on long enough, the liquid is transferred into barrels or stainless steel storage tanks. This is known as the free-run juice and goes into the best wine. Sometimes the free run is blended with some of the more concentrated and tannic press wine, generated when the leftover skins and other mulch in the cap are pressed to extract all the remaining juice, which is then stored separately. In some cases fermentation is stopped by chilling the wine and filtering

out the yeast, but fermentation will also stop naturally when alcohol levels rise high enough to kill the yeast—usually about 15 percent by volume.

The blending of the free-run wine and the press wine is just part of the important **blending** process. Wines from different vineyards, sometimes from different parts, or blocks, of the same vineyard, are usually made and stored separately and will have slightly different characteristics. They are blended together at a later stage by the winemaker, often together with small quantities of wines made from different grapes, to make the final product. Labeling laws determine how the final wine is described on the bottle.

Most of the premium wines made in Napa, Sonoma, and Santa Cruz are aged in oak barrels once they have been blended—the barrels you often see stacked on giant racks in caves or cool storage rooms of wineries. This barrel aging not only lets the wine continue to develop its taste and aroma through ongoing chemical reactions but also imparts new flavors and aromas that come from the barrels themselves. It is also when most red wines undergo **malolactic fermentation,** which is not fermentation at all but a bacterial reaction that converts the tart malic acid in a wine to the softer lactic acid.

Buying the barrels and storing them is expensive and reserved for the best wines that can command premium prices. Cheaper wines made to be drunk right away are bottled straight from the stainless steel tanks in which they were blended. Sometimes oak chips are added to those tanks to impart some of the important oaky flavors, a method still frowned upon by European winemakers.

Before wines are bottled or left to age in barrels, they are purified using a process called **fining,** which uses a coagulant to remove all the particles of dead yeast, excess tannins, and other crud suspended in the liquid. The coagulant can be anything from types of clay to egg whites or gelatin and is simply dropped into the wine, where it attaches itself to particles and pulls them down to the bottom of the barrel or tank. In fine wines that need to age further, the freshly cleaned wine is siphoned off into clean barrels to ensure this gunk does not interfere with the aging process, a process known as **racking.** After usually six months or a year (longer for the very best age-worthy wines) the wine from barrels will be bottled, often after being filtered to remove the last of the sediment. Cheaper wines stored in stainless steel tanks are usually bottled soon after fining.

Some more expensive red wines are made without the crusher-destemmer step; instead, whole bunches of grapes with the biggest stems removed are left to ferment using the yeasts naturally occurring on the skins. The grapes eventually burst and the fermented juice escapes.

Making White Wine

White wine production leaves out many of the steps involved in making red wines and is an altogether quicker process. The speed of the wine making and the fact that most Californian white wines are not aged for long (if at all) before bottling explain why a bottle of white wine often has a much more recent vintage date on the label than a red.

Winemakers don't want white grape juice to sit in contact with grape skins and stems for long because that would introduce all sorts of bitter flavors, so the grapes often go through not only the crusher-destemmer but also a press, which gently squeezes the juice out. The first juice out of the grapes is the best and is often reserved for the best wines, much like the best olive oils are the "first cold-pressed." The last juice to be squeezed out picks up some of the bitterness from the skins, seeds, and stems and is destined for cheaper wines.

Most Californian white wines are fermented in giant stainless steel vessels, and fermentation is carefully controlled using giant refrigeration jackets incorporated into the outside of the tanks to ensure a wine retains some sweetness—white wines, even dry whites, generally contain more residual sugar and have less alcohol than most reds. Because of this extra refrigeration the fermentation time for white wines is usually longer than that of reds.

During fermentation, dead yeasts and other particles, known as the **lees,** will slowly drop to the bottom and are sometimes left in contact with the fermented wine to add distinct yeasty, toasty aromas. This is often the case with more expensive white wines that are fermented and aged in barrels.

Once fermentation is complete, the wine is fined and filtered and either bottled or transferred to barrels for aging, which adds the oakiness that Californian chardonnays are so famous for. White wines often undergo some degree of malolactic fermentation, which turns a crisp white wine into a rich, buttery-tasting one. If a winemaker does not want malolactic fermentation to occur, the wine undergoes some additional filtering and might also be treated with sulfur dioxide to kill the bacteria responsible for the reaction.

Making Champagne

The cool climate of Carneros and the Russian River Valley is ideally suited for growing the two most important champagne grape varietals, chardonnay and pinot noir. A few other grapes are also often used, including small amounts of pinot blanc and pinot meunier (producers of the Spanish sparkling wine, cava, use totally different grapes more suited to the local Spanish climate).

Most Californian champagne-style wines are blends of both pinot noir and chardonnay, with some exceptions. A blanc de blancs champagne is made only from chardonnay grapes and has the lightest, most delicate style. A blanc de noirs is still a white wine but made exclusively from dark-skinned grapes like pinot noir, giving it a fuller body. Somewhere in between the two is rosé, or pink, champagne, which is made by adding a small amount of red wine to the white blend.

The key to making champagne is to bottle the wine while it is still fermenting so the yeast will continue to do its work and generate both alcohol and the all-important gas that creates the fizz, carbon dioxide.

The fizziness was likely discovered by accident when the cold winters of the Champagne

FIVE FIZZY FACTS

- **Champagne making is a high-pressure business.** The pressure inside a champagne bottle created by the dissolved carbon dioxide gas (carbonic acid) is about 90 pounds per square inch, or about three times the pressure in a car tire. That's why the glass of champagne bottles is so thick and the cork can shoot so far.

- **Champagne isn't just for celebration.** More than 80 percent of sparkling wine sales occur between November and January, but it is a style of wine that can be enjoyed at any time of year and with a wide range of foods. Try it as an aperitif or instead of chardonnay at the beginning of a meal.

- **Not all bubbles are created equal.** The more expensive the champagne, the smaller the bubbles and the smoother and creamier it feels in your mouth. The priciest French champagnes barely taste fizzy at all. The cheapest supermarket sparklers feel like fizzy water or soda in your mouth.

- **Champagne gets you tipsy more quickly.** The carbonation in sparkling wine is thought to relax the valve between your stomach and small intestine, where alcohol is absorbed by the blood more quickly. So while still wines stay in the stomach longer, champagne enters the small intestine more quickly and really does go to your head faster.

- **Better champagne glasses make for better bubbles.** The tall, slender champagne glasses, known as flutes, help keep the wine sparkling for longer and show off the bubbles better. Most good-quality flutes have a small etching at the bottom that encourages the bubbles to form. That's why you'll usually see a long, straight line of bubbles rising from the very bottom of the glass.

region stopped barrel fermentation in its tracks before the wine was bottled. Once the wine was bottled and the weather warmed up, fermentation started again, only this time inside the sealed bottle, where the carbon dioxide (dissolved in the liquid as carbonic acid) had nowhere to go. As pressure built up the corks popped off (and the fizzy wine was immediately drunk by people assuming it had gone bad) or the bottles simply exploded from the immense pressure.

English merchants taking delivery of barrels of French wine were probably the first to experience this peculiar phenomenon of exploding wine. At the time, back in the late 1700s, England was also home to a state-of-the-art glass-blowing industry, so once the wine sellers understood what was going on with the wine, they were able to develop bottles thick enough to contain it.

The full potential of this new style of fizzy wine was quickly realized, and modern champagne production began. The biggest challenge for the early champagne houses was to remove the sediment of dead yeast and other by-products of fermentation from the bottle without losing the fizz; otherwise the champagne would end up murky.

The process developed in 1805, known as *méthode champenoise,* is still largely unchanged today. Bottles of half-fermented champagne are stored neck-down in large racks and were traditionally turned on an exact schedule over many months to get the sediment to work its way down to the cork, a process known as riddling. Today, of course, the riddling is all done by computer-controlled machines (despite what many champagne houses would have you believe).

Then comes the process of disgorging, during which the sediment is carefully removed. In today's automated version, the neck of the bottle is frozen, the cork is removed, and the compressed gas in the wine shoots the frozen plug of muck out. Finally comes dosing, when the bottle is topped off with wine and some sugar (more sugar for the sweeter wines, less for the dry styles) before being recorked and allowed to continue fermenting in peace.

It's a precise and expensive process, which is why it's reserved for the high-end champagnes. Cheaper sparkling wines are today more likely to be made in large stainless steel tanks that are pressurized to keep the carbon dioxide dissolved in the wine before it is filtered and bottled.

Making Port

Dark, juicy ports have become increasingly popular in recent years, and some sort of port can now be found at most wineries. Not all of it is good, however. Some is nothing more than an overly sweet red dessert wine that has about as much complexity as concentrated, alcoholic grape juice. Others approach (though don't yet reach) the sophistication of the best ports made in the country where they were invented—Portugal. The name is derived from the Portuguese coastal city of Oporto from where the wines were shipped to their main market, England.

Traditional ports are made using the Portuguese grape varietals tinta barroca, tinta roriz, tinto cao, and touriga, though a lot of Californian ports use more common regional varietals, particularly zinfandel and syrah.

The process starts out similar to the red wine–making process, but the fermentation is stopped in its tracks when the wine is poured into a fortified spirit like brandy, which has enough alcohol to kill the yeast that was turning the wine's sugar into alcohol. The result is a half-fermented wine still containing plenty of unfermented sugar but with a high alcohol level (usually around 20 percent) thanks to the addition of the brandy.

Because fermentation of red wine is stopped halfway, the winemaker has to work hard to ensure that enough color has been extracted from the grape skins before the wine is poured off into the brandy. In Portugal that is still often achieved by the age-old custom of crushing the grapes with bare feet to thoroughly grind up the skins. Not many Californian wineries will admit to that.

The best ports in the world are aged for many years in barrels, sometimes many

decades, and eventually attain a pale, tawny color. These are the most expensive tawny ports. Most Californian ports are made to be drunk relatively young, although they can also be aged in the bottle just like regular wines.

Wine Barrels

Oak was traditionally used for making barrels because it was strong, had a fine grain and so was watertight, and was plentiful in the forests of Europe. Early winemakers also discovered that wines picked up some pleasant flavors and smells when stored in oak barrels, which is why oak has remained the most desirable wood to use when aging wines.

Most barrels used in wine making today are made of oak, but not all oak is the same when it comes to making wine. Just as different varietals of grape have different flavors and smells, different types of oak also have different characteristics that a winemaker can incorporate into the wine-making process. Even oak from different forests can have distinct properties.

French oak is the most highly prized because of the soft, subtle flavors it gives a wine. It is also the most expensive. A typical French oak barrel costs a winery $600–800, compared to about $300–500 for a barrel made from American oak, which tends to add more pronounced flavors to a wine. As French oak is priced out of the market, the oak from Eastern Europe, particularly Hungary and Slovakia, is becoming more popular and has some of the same characteristics as its French cousin but at far less cost to the winery.

Some of the most distinctive flavors and smells added to a wine by aging it in oak barrels include vanilla, leather, tobacco, cloves, and cedar. Those flavors will be stronger the newer the barrel is. Wineries often age wine in a mixture of new and old barrels, both to save money and to get the right mixture of strong and mellow flavors from the oak. They will also often use a mixture of American and European oak to get the right balance of flavors and aromas.

When barrels are made by a cooper (an art in itself) they are usually **toasted** by lighting a fire inside the half-finished barrel to create a thin layer of burnt wood. This toasted wood imparts its own set of flavors and smells to the wine, including the rich, chocolate, caramel, and nutty characteristics typical in barrel-aged wines, particularly reds.

The Wine-Making Year

A winegrower's year is a busy one, and January is about the only time they can take significant time off for a well-earned vacation. Most of us have more flexible vacation time and can choose when to visit Wine Country based on all sorts of factors, including the weather, the scenery, events, and where the winegrowers are in their year-long process of creating great wines.

January: The vineyards are bare, the weather is cool and wet, and the Wine Country is at its quietest. This is also the time of year that the vines are pruned. Straggly bare stems are cut back to the thick branches and trunks of the vine. In the cellar, racking of the red wines is underway.

February: More vineyard maintenance and pruning are carried out, but the wet weather has by now started all the wildflowers blooming, including cover crops like the bright yellow wild mustard that fills the rows between vines in many parts of the Wine Country between now and April. Racking and blending the wines for barrel ageing continues.

March: New vines are planted, and bottling lines at wineries spring into action, bottling wines designed to be drunk young (like many whites) that were made the previous year.

April: Buds are open on the vines and the new growing season begins in the vineyard as the weather finally starts to dry out and warm up. The danger of late frosts often gets the giant wind machines going to keep the air moving and prevent ice from forming on the delicate shoots.

May: Vines are now growing vigorously, and wineries are gearing up for the summer rush of tourists.

June: The vines are tied to the wires and posts of the trellises to make sure the grapes get as much sun as possible later in the year.

The vines also start flowering, so rain is an unwelcome, though rare, disruption. Bottling of older wines begins before the heat of summer sets in.

July: Flowering is over, and grapes are starting to form. Spraying with organic or other chemicals starts to safeguard the developing grapes from pests and diseases.

August: This is the first month that red grapes will really start to look red as they continue to grow. Pruning of excess leaves sometimes takes place to ensure grapes are not shaded and can fully ripen. Smaller, less-developed clusters of grapes might also be cut off so the vine can concentrate all its energy and nutrients into the remaining grapes. Wineries start to clear space for the imminent harvest.

September: The first harvesting begins, with the earliest-ripening grapes in the hottest areas picked first (in particularly hot years or those with an early summer, harvesting sometimes starts in August). Most grapes in Northern California's premium growing regions are picked by hand, usually by migrant workers. This is the best time to surreptitiously taste just how sweet wine grapes are if you see any dangling over the shoulder of country roads. Wineries themselves are hives of activity as tons of grapes start to be brought in by truck.

October: Harvesting finishes, and the vineyards start to look a little more bare, though the vines will keep their leaves for another month or so. The crush is well underway at wineries, and steel tanks rapidly fill up with wine.

November: The vineyards start to turn shades of red and yellow as the weather starts to cool, and the leaves finally drop when the nights get cold enough. In wineries, the wine is starting to be transferred from the fermentation vats into barrels to begin aging.

December: Many wineries offer barrel tasting of new wines, and the winemaker will start to plan the blends that will ultimately be bottled.

Reading Wine Labels

Thanks to strict labeling regulations overseen by the federal Bureau of Alcohol, Tobacco, and Firearms it is tough for wineries to mislead consumers about what goes into a bottle of wine, but there is a little more to a wine's content than might meet the eye.

The year on the bottle is the **vintage date** and indicates the year in which at least 95 percent of the grapes that went into the wine were harvested.

Usually underneath the vintage is the **appellation of origin,** which is where the dominant grapes in the wine were grown. It is usually a geographical area (appellation) like California or Sonoma County or a specific American Viticultural Area (AVA) such as Rutherford, Napa Valley, or Dry Creek Valley. In the case of an appellation, at least 75 percent of the grapes in the wine must have come from that area. In the case of an AVA, at least 85 percent of the grapes must be from the area identified on the bottle.

The type of grape the wine is made from, or **varietal designation,** is usually displayed above or below the appellation of origin. If a specific grape varietal is identified (cabernet sauvignon or sauvignon blanc, for example), then at least 75 percent of the grapes the wine is made of must be that named varietal. That leaves a lot of leeway for winemakers to blend small quantities of other grapes into a wine to add to its character; sometimes these blending grapes will be identified elsewhere on the label, other times not.

If less than 75 percent of the grapes in a wine are one varietal, then a winery will either simply call it red or white wine or will come up with a snappy and unique name to describe the blend. Such a wine is known as a **proprietary wine** or blend. Meritage (rhymes with heritage) is a name unique to the United States that is sometimes used to describe a blend of Bordeaux varietals, either red or white.

The final words to look for on labels are **estate bottled,** which means that all of the grapes in a wine came from land owned or controlled by the winery, and the wine was made and bottled on the winery premises. So-called estate wines tend to be among a winery's best and most expensive. Sometimes a wine is made using grapes from only one vineyard, in which case the vineyard is identified on the label (although it doesn't have to be) and the wine is known as a single-vineyard or vineyard-designate wine.

HOW TO TASTE WINE

The involved process of thoroughly smelling and tasting a wine is one reason why aficionados love the stuff and a big reason that novices tend to be intimidated. Some people seem to regard wine almost as an intellectual pursuit. Others just like the taste or want to get drunk.

On one level, it seems ludicrous to spend so long detecting every nuance of flavor in a wine. After all, when a plate of food arrives in a restaurant we don't sit for five minutes smelling it to try to detect every ingredient and how they were cooked. Then again, there is probably no other drinkable liquid on earth that can pack as many complex aromas and flavors into a glass as wine can, and certainly no other food product that can reflect so completely the place that it came from.

With the magic worked by winemakers, simple grape juice can be transformed into wines that mimic the smells and tastes of a remarkable range of fruits, vegetables, and countless other substances. From a scientific point of view, however, there's no magic involved—grapes actually contain many of the same chemicals that give other fruits and vegetables their distinctive smells. Wine reviews often read like a shopping list for the produce department at a local supermarket.

Wine appreciation cannot be taught. It has to be learned by experience. One reason that many people are confused by those slightly pretentious-sounding reviews is that they cannot actually recognize many of the smells or tastes being referred to. Someone who has never smoked a cigar, for example, is not gong to understand what a reviewer is referring to when he describes a cabernet sauvignon as having an aroma of "cigar box." Everyone knows what chocolate tastes and smells like, though, so a "chocolaty" cabernet will instantly ring a bell in most people's minds.

The sort of diverse smell and flavor database that critics use takes time (and an extremely varied diet) to develop. Patience is the best way to learn—it takes a while to develop a palate that can detect the subtle nuances of wine and years to build up a useful tasting memory that you can draw on to recognize and describe wines or their aromas.

When in doubt, simply listen to how everyone else describes the wine, or just ask whoever is pouring the wine at a winery what exactly you are supposed to be smelling or tasting. On a few occasions you might not get much help from a harried staffer, but usually they are happy to give a quick description.

Alternatively, an intensive wine-tasting course can shorten the process of learning all the smells and tastes by setting out every imaginable fruit, vegetable, and other organic substance in dishes, allowing students to directly match flavors from the foods to the aromas in wines (something you can also do at home with whatever you have in your kitchen).

Of course, the world of smells and tastes is unique to each individual. There are some fairly standard categories of the basic flavors and aromas of wines. Beyond them, it's fine to make up your own comparisons and the more recognizable they are the better. For fun, make up your own personal wine descriptions every day—pinot noir can sometimes smell a little like a traffic jam on the St. Helena Highway on a hot summer afternoon, for example. Alternatively, just ignore all the fancy words and simply say "it smells and tastes good." Just never use the word "Yummy."

The fact that critics don't always agree with each other illustrates just how subjective the art of describing wines really is. Take these three excerpts from reviews in three major wine magazines of a 2001 merlot from Pride Mountain Vineyards. All three have a few common threads, but they could equally be describing totally different wines:

Possesses gorgeous aromas of creosote, damp earth, sweet black cherry as well as currant fruit, and a chocolaty aftertaste.

Rich in spicy currant, exotic spice, and ripe blackberry fruit, turning spicy and exhibiting pretty mocha-scented oak.

Smoky aromas of black raspberry, coffee, and nutty oak. Lush, fat, and sweet, with layered flavors of black raspberry and sweet oak.

Looking at Wine

There's no denying it: wine looks inviting. Whether it's the pale yellow of a sauvignon blanc, the golden hue of chardonnay, or the deep purple of a syrah, the purity of color in wines is striking. How a wine looks in the glass can also give some clues about what you're about to drink. Try to look at it against a white background (the tasting room menu, for example). Overall the wine should be crystal clear and a bright, vivid color. Any hint of cloudiness is generally not a good sign.

White wines range from a pale yellow in young and light wines like sauvignon blanc to a darker gold in some heavier whites like some styles of chardonnay that have been aged in oak. White wines darken as they age; a hint of brown might be a sign of a well-aged wine, but for most Californian whites it's usually the sign of a wine that's past its prime.

Red wines have a much wider range of colors, ranging from deep red in the case of cabernet sauvignon to deep purple in a young syrah and a paler brick red in pinot noir. The color of red wines fades as they age and the pigment molecules react with other chemical components of the wine, so the deeper the color, the younger the wine.

Smelling the Wine

There's no other drink that can match the array of aromas in a wine, and experiencing all those smells is one of the great pleasures of tasting wine. Trying to identify and describe them is one of the great challenges. Wine glasses are designed to concentrate the aroma of a wine and channel it straight to your nose. Most of what we taste is actually what we smell, so smelling a wine is the key to enjoying it and discovering its complexities.

Professionals smell the wine to learn more about it, such as the main grape varietals it contains and the region it came from, especially in blind tastings that are designed to be as objective as possible. Most people smell wine just to enjoy and appreciate the glorious aromas before drinking it. Identifying those aromas is really nothing more than a bit of fun that might one day be useful if someone asks you to identify a wine with no label.

Swirl the glass two or three times to help release the aromas, and then take a deep sniff and try to identify all the aromas. Take as many sniffs as you want. Some wines have an intense smell, others more subtle ones.

Most of the up-front smells are the aromas that come directly from the fruit in the wine, and such fruity smells are the biggest category of aromas in the world of wine tasting. Another big category of aromas is vegetative, or anything that smells like it came from a plant, whether grass, bell pepper, or tobacco. Some of the most enticing aromas are those of exotic flowers.

Classic aromas for white wines include apple and pear, citrus fruits, tropical and stone fruits, grass, bell pepper, honey, and melon. For red wines there might be aromas of any number of berries, cherries, raisins, plums, licorice, and black pepper. The lists are almost endless. Some of the more subtle, underlying smells come from the barrel, yeasts, and other winemaking factors. They include vanilla, oak, nuts, butterscotch, and chocolate.

Wine aromas are supposed to be pleasant, but sometimes bad smells creep in and are an indicator of a wine gone bad. Most are pretty obviously bad, like the rotten egg smell of hydrogen sulfide, the vinegary smell of oxidized wine, or the sherry-like smell of cooked, or maderized, wine.

A corked wine—one that has been contaminated by mold on the cork—can sometimes be harder to detect. Often the characteristic musty or mildewed smell is so fleeting that it might be missed and quickly overpowered by other aromas. Another indicator of mold contamination is a strong smell of wet cardboard.

Tasting the Wine

Taking a sip of wine will be the ultimate test of whether to buy it or not. Most wine smells pleasant enough (unless you have an aversion to fruit or the wine is bad), but not all wines will taste good to everyone. This is where subjectivity becomes most evident.

More aromas than you initially smelled might be detectable once a wine is in your mouth as the body's heat vaporizes chemicals that you could not previously smell. The "flavors" of fruit are actually aromas hitting the back of your nose—most of what we think we taste is actually an aroma.

Our taste buds can only detect four fundamental tastes—sweet, sour, bitter, and salty—but those four are enough to determine whether a wine is in balance and ultimately good to drink. There's also a fifth element that taste buds can detect, known as umami, which can best be described as a savory character. What complicates matters is that everyone has a different threshold for those five tastes. Sweet to one person might be sour to another—it all depends on the structure of our mouths and the wiring of our brains.

The amounts of alcohol, tannin, residual sugar, and acid in a wine can all be detected by swirling it around in your mouth for about 10 seconds, making sure it coats every part of your mouth to hit all the different taste buds.

The sum of these tastes is more important than each one individually. How they all interact together is a reflection of a wine's balance, yet another highly subjective measurement of overall quality. Some people prefer sweeter wines; others prefer a little more acidity to make their mouths water. Some don't like the astringency of tannins, while others like the solid taste they can give to a powerful wine. Generally, however, people describe a wine as balanced when all these tastes are about equal to each other.

Aftertaste (the pleasant kind) is almost as important as the main taste. Poor wines have no aftertaste, and once the wine is swallowed, that's it. Good wines leave your taste buds tingling for anywhere from a few seconds to almost a minute, and aromas will waft around in your mouth almost as long.

Another aspect of a wine that is worth noting is its body. Much like water will feel lighter in your mouth than milk, a light-bodied white wine will have a different presence in your mouth than a full-bodied red like a zinfandel.

The Aroma Wheel

Recognizing smells is always easier than naming them, which is why tasting wine is more fun when you know what you're supposed to be smelling. The wine's label or a winery's description will often include a list of aromas the winemaker has identified in the wine, which can be useful, but the ultimate tool to train yourself to recognize aromas is the Aroma Wheel.

An educator at the University of California at Davis created the Aroma Wheel, and even professionals use it when describing wines. It broadly categorizes aromas and bouquets, then subcategorizes them and gives specific examples. If you smell something fruity, for example, the wheel will break down fruity smells into categories such as citrus, berry, and tropical fruit, then break each of those subcategories down further into examples of specific fruits.

Aroma Wheels are often sold among the wine paraphernalia in the tasting rooms of large wineries or can be bought online (along with Aroma Wheel T-shirts for those who live for wine) at www.winearomawheel.com. The website also includes information on how to use the wheel.

WINE AND FOOD

Probably as intimidating to many people as the smelling and tasting wine is the question of how to match a wine with food, or vice versa. Like everything else to do with wine it ultimately boils down to personal taste and personal experience, but there are some underlying principles worth knowing about.

Learning from scratch how your favorite wine interacts on your palate with your favorite foods will increase your appreciation for both the wine and the food. Along the way you'll probably discover the few combinations that really are best avoided and a few others that make your taste buds sing.

There really are no rules to pairing food and wine, despite what some connoisseurs might say. Instead, think of any advice you are given as merely guidelines that will help make the voyage of discovering your favorite food and wine combinations quicker and easier.

These guidelines are constantly in flux. Cuisine trends change and so do wine-making trends. The old adage of white wine with fish and red wine with red meat is somewhat irrelevant. It all depends on the style of a particular wine, how the meat or fish is prepared, and what goes into the accompanying sauces and dishes.

One guideline to pairing food and wine is based on sensory adaptation. An acidic wine will taste less acidic if paired with a fairly acidic food. Vinaigrette dressing on a salad, for example, will mellow out a wine that would otherwise taste too tart. Similarly, a sweet wine will taste less sweet if drunk with a dessert, which is why dessert wines taste far too sweet if drunk on their own.

Some food and wine interactions are more confusing. Saltiness of food has a profound effect on how a wine tastes, for example. A salty dish will give the impression of neutralizing some of the acidity of a particularly tart wine, making it taste smoother and fruiter. Foods with some inherent bitterness, such as green vegetables, can actually enhance the bitterness of some wines.

Perhaps one of the classic pairings is a bold red wine with steak, and for good reason. The concentrated protein in red meat serves to soften the taste of tannins in wine, taming what would normally be an astringent, tannic monster into a softer and fruiter beast altogether. A barrel-aged Napa cabernet, for example, would be perfectly balanced with a steak but would taste like a hunk of wood if you still have some left over when the crème brûlée arrives as the sugar in the dessert overpowers the fruit in the wine, leaving just those woody tannins to dominate.

For a thoroughly educational experience, try drinking just one wine, white or red, with a multiple-course meal to see how its taste dramatically changes with each course. It might not be fun for some courses, but the basics of food and wine interaction very quickly become evident.

Some of the simplest foods can prove to be the hardest to find a good wine match. Cheese, for example, does not (as many people believe) go terribly well with many red wines. Try port for rich cheeses like Stilton or a dry white wine like sauvignon blanc for sharper cheeses like goat cheese.

Wine in Restaurants

If you've ever wondered how restaurants can justify charging more than $40 for a wine that you just bought in a tasting room for $20, the answer is fairly simple, even if it's hard to swallow.

The markup helps restaurants cover their overhead costs, especially those related to the wine. It pays for the salary of a sommelier (so make sure you use his services), some of the salaries of the waitstaff, spoilage of wine (by some estimates, about 5 percent of all restaurant wines go bad before being opened), the cost of storing wine (wine cellars cost a lot of money), and all sorts of other costs of doing business, from the electricity bill to broken wine glasses that can cost a restaurant thousands of dollars a year to replace.

In general, cheap wines have higher markups, percentage-wise, than expensive wines. Those from well-known regions or made from popular grape varietals also tend to have higher markups because they're guaranteed sellers. The pricing ploys can be cynical, but there is a way to beat them.

One way to save money on wine in restaurants is to bring your own. Corkage fees (the fee charged by the restaurant for you to bring and open your own wine) vary but are generally

about $15 in Napa and Sonoma restaurants. It sounds pricey, but it's worth considering if you plan to drink an expensive wine. Some places offer free corkage on certain days of the week, however, and many others offer free corkage on one bottle of your own wine for every bottle you buy from their wine list. Ask about the corkage policy of the restaurant when making a reservation.

Having ordered a bottle in a restaurant, there is yet another wine ritual to go through. The smelling and tasting ritual is all about finding those wines you like; this restaurant ritual is all about finding those wines that you don't want to drink.

When a server brings a bottle of wine to the table and shows it to you like some trophy, double-check that it is in fact the wine you ordered. Take note of the vintage because it's not uncommon for a restaurant to receive new vintages and forget to update its wine list.

When the wine is opened, the cork will often be handed to you or placed gingerly on the table. It might make a nice souvenir but is actually given to you to check whether it's in good condition. A good cork should feel springy and soft. A dried out and hard cork suggests that the wine was not stored well and should be a warning to pay close attention when you taste the wine. Don't bother smelling the cork—it will just smell of cork. And don't bother doing anything at all with synthetic corks, other than perhaps bouncing them off the ceiling for fun.

Finally, the server will pour a tasting-room quantity of wine into your glass. The idea is to check that the wine is the right temperature and that it is not oxidized or corked. If you simply don't like it, you're stuck with it, though many wines will sometimes taste a bit rough when first opened. Always give the wine a few minutes in the glass before drinking to let it open up and show off its full range of aromas and tastes.

Restaurants are usually pretty good about chilling white wines before serving, but red wines can sometimes feel like they have been stored above a hot oven in the kitchen. In those cases it's fine to ask for an ice bucket to cool the bottle down. After all, red wine is generally best drunk at 60–70°F, not 85°F.

AGING WINE

The whole point of aging wine for some people is to make it more valuable. For most of us, however, aging wine is all about making it taste better after a few years of development. Youthful wine is like a youthful person— brash, unsure of itself, and a bit awkward. Like us, a wine mellows, gets more complex, and becomes a more well-rounded individual the older it gets. At least that's the theory.

As wine ages it undergoes a complex chemical process that only scientists fully understand. For the rest of us, the aging of wine is a process full of mystery and myths. One common myth is that all wine gets better as it ages. Sadly, that's not true, so don't start stocking a cellar with $10 bottles of cabernet. A poorly made wine that is not in balance when young will not turn into a finely balanced masterpiece after a few years.

A wine almost has to be designed to be aged by the winemaker. Moreover, a wine capable of aging for a decade or more might taste a little unappealing when young. A wine made to be drunk young will probably taste flat and generally awful after 10 years.

Another myth is that age-worthy wine gets better and better as it gets older. While that's almost true for some of the most famous Bordeaux wines, most modern wines are created to be drunk relatively young and will reach a peak after a certain number of years, then go downhill fast. Wineries don't help matters by making sweeping statements that a wine will "continue to improve for 10–15 years." It all depends on how it's stored. In many cases that wine will be barely drinkable after 10 years unless stored under almost perfect aging conditions.

Unfortunately, winemakers and wineries are the only sources of information on how a wine might age, because there are no hard and fast rules. One way to get a fairly good idea of how a particular wine will age is to taste some so-called library wines, those from previous vintages that are kept by wineries in part so they themselves know how their wines change with age. Most good wineries either offer library tasting to the public for a fee or will happily oblige if it will likely result in the sale of a case of expensive wine.

In California, virtually no white wines are made to be aged, and they should be consumed within a couple of years. Some that are more age-worthy tend to be chardonnays from mountain vineyards like those on Mount Veeder in the Napa Valley, and those in the Santa Cruz Mountains.

It's harder to determine which Californian red wines will age well. In very general terms, good quality red port will happily age for the longest, followed by a decent cabernet sauvignon, syrah, zinfandel, merlot, and finally pinot noir, which is often at its peak after a couple of years.

Price can also offer a hint at a wine's aging potential, though this test sometimes falls foul of marketing and overpricing. A $100 bottle of Napa Valley cabernet will probably only be bought by serious collectors, for example, who are unlikely to crack it open that night but will instead cellar it for years to either enjoy themselves or sell for a profit to another collector. Winemakers and wineries often have that sort of buyer in mind when they craft the style of wine.

STORING WINE

Research has shown that most American consumers drink wine very soon after buying it, so storage is not a big issue. Aging wines, even for a few years, however, requires a little care to ensure it does not spoil. A pretty iron wine rack on top of a fridge opposite a sunny kitchen window will be useless for anything but short-term storage.

Wine likes to be dark, still, and kept at a fairly constant temperature somewhere from 50–70°F, conditions found in most basements or even a dark interior closet in many homes. The most ideal storage conditions will also be cool (below 60°F) and damp (over 60 percent

BOTTLE SIZE MATTERS

If you're wondering how the regular wine bottle came to be the size it is (750 milliliters — and one of the few beverages in the United States measured in metric units), it is because this was the approximate size a Victorian glassblower could blow with one deep breath. The size was then standardized by European winemakers. There are some bottles smaller — the half-bottle and the split or quarter bottle handed out on some airlines — but most people tend to notice the bigger bottles on display at some wineries.

Bigger bottles are actually better when it comes to aging fine wine. Aging is directly affected by how much of the liquid is exposed to the small gap between the wine and the cork, known as the ullage. The lower the proportion of wine there is in contact with the ullage, the longer the aging process will be. Since even giant bottles generally have necks almost as narrow as regular bottles, they also have a proportionately smaller ullage. Big bottles don't stop at the common magnum size either. There are some true giants that hold enough wine to keep a big party going all night long.

Bottle sizes are named after ancient, mythical kings. No one really knows why, but the theory is that such names convey greatness, grandeur, and longevity. They increase in size as follows:

- **Magnum:** 2 standard bottles (1.5 liters)
- **Jeroboam:** 4 bottles (3 liters)
- **Methuselah:** 8 bottles (6 liters)
- **Salamanazar:** 12 bottles (9 liters)
- **Balthazar:** 16 bottles (12 liters)
- **Nebuchadnezzar:** 20 bottles (15 liters)

And the biggest bottle ever? It was a one-time-only creation that held 130 liters of wine, the equivalent of 173 regular bottles or 1,200 glasses of wine, commissioned by the Morton's Steakhouse chain in 2004 to celebrate its 25th anniversary. That giant bottle was 4.5 feet tall and filled with Beringer Private Reserve cabernet sauvignon, a quintessential steak wine that is also a quintessentially expensive Napa Valley wine. The retail value of the wine in that bottle was a staggering $17,000, and the bottle eventually sold at auction in late 2004 for almost $56,000, giant corkscrew not included.

relative humidity), though these last two requirements can be tough to achieve without digging your own cave or buying some sort of specially designed storage cellar.

Although excessive heat makes wines age a little too fast to achieve their full potential, a constantly fluctuating temperature is the biggest enemy. As the temperature goes up and down during the day, the wine will expand and contract in the bottle, causing the cork to move in the bottle neck by a fraction and potentially suck in air. That air will gradually oxidize the wine and spoil it.

If a wine is stored in very low humidity, the cork might also dry out and expose the wine to air. Keeping the cork moist so it retains a good seal with the neck of the bottle is the main reason for storing wine sideways.

SHIPPING WINE

The 21st Amendment to the U.S. Constitution ended Prohibition in 1933 but still plagues the wine industry today because it allows states to continue to regulate the sale and distribution of all types of alcoholic beverages.

Since repeal, a patchwork of rules and regulations unique to almost every state has evolved. If you plan to buy wine at a Californian winery or on the Internet and have it shipped to your home state, you might be out of luck, although an important U.S. Supreme Court decision in May 2005 on interstate shipping laws is slowly reshaping the archaic laws all across the country.

Before May 2005, there were 23 states that banned any direct shipping of wine and other alcoholic drinks from out of state to consumers (Alabama, Arkansas, Connecticut, Delaware, Florida, Indiana, Kansas, Kentucky, Maine, Maryland, Massachusetts, Michigan, Mississippi, Montana, New Jersey, New York, Ohio, Oklahoma, Pennsylvania, South Dakota, Tennessee, Utah, and Vermont). Even buying the wine yourself and sending it home in a FedEx box to avoid having to carry it was illegal. Many of those states allow shipments from producers within the state, however, and some allowed wine shipments from out of state as long as it came through designated in-state distributors.

That discrimination between in-state and out-of-state wineries was the basis of the May 2005 Supreme Court decision that struck down such shipping laws in both New York and Michigan. The court ruled that such discrimination against out-of-state businesses was in violation of the Commerce Clause of the U.S. Constitution, which ensures free trade between states. Although the ruling only affected two states, by definition it called into question the laws in the other states that similarly ban out-of-state wine shipments.

Importantly, however, the Supreme Court left the 21st Amendment untouched in its ruling, so many of those states are still free to enact legislation to either ban or put restrictions on all distribution of alcoholic beverages, whether from within or outside the state.

They could go the route of the 13 states (Alaska, Arizona, Georgia, Louisiana, Nebraska, Nevada, New Hampshire, North Carolina, North Dakota, Rhode Island, South Carolina, Texas, Virginia, and Wyoming) that, along with the District of Columbia, allow direct shipping but with restrictions. Though all stop short of an outright ban, the restrictions vary state by state and can be complex. Some allow shipment of only limited quantities of wine, others leave the rules up to each individual county within the state, and still others limit shipments from individual wineries. These rules also change regularly. Texas, for example, lifted many restrictions on shipments in May 2005 as a result of an earlier lawsuit.

The remaining states allow wine shipments from out of state but only on a reciprocal basis, meaning that shipments are only allowed from states that in turn allow shipments to be made to them.

Luckily, California wineries are on top of the ever-changing situation, and as of 2009 they will generally be able to ship wine for personal consumption to all states except Alabama, Arkansas, Delaware, Iowa, Kentucky, Maryland, Massachusetts, Mississippi, Montana, New Jersey, New Mexico, Oklahoma, Pennsylvania, South Dakota, and Utah. Be sure to ask your favorite winery about the latest laws, because everything might well have changed again by the time this book is published.

International shipping tends to be prohibitively expensive and involves considerable taxes, though some wineries will oblige. If you plan to take wine overseas yourself, be sure to check the liquor import laws of the countries in question. Unfortunately, taking wine on a plane yourself became much harder when airlines banned carriage of liquids in cabin baggage. Packing a few bottles of wine in checked luggage is an option, but make sure the bottles are well protected from the sometimes rough baggage handlers. Most wineries will sell shipping boxes with plenty of padding.

WINE CLUBS

Chances are that you will be told about a winery's wine club while at the tasting room bar. Every winery has a wine club of some sort, and many dream up fancy names to make them sound more exclusive (some actually are exclusive and have long waiting lists to join).

Wine clubs are an important marketing tool for wineries and can be one of the only distribution channels for small boutique wineries. They can also be a great way for visitors to the Wine Country to get discounts on their favorite wines even if they live hundreds of miles away or when the wines are not widely distributed. Make sure you read the rules carefully, however. The small print sometimes commits new members to buying far more than they anticipate.

When new members sign up to a wine club and hand over a credit card number, they often get an on-the-spot discount on wines (this club discount varies, but it's generally 10–20 percent). More importantly for the winery, the new club members have also agreed to buy at least one (sometimes more) wine club shipment in the future before they are able to cancel their membership. Those shipments contain wines that the winery chooses, not the customer, and are subject to often sizable shipping fees that can more than offset the club discount (if you live near the winery, you can usually avoid shipping fees by collecting the wine yourself).

Wine club shipments are usually made once every three or four months, and there's often a choice of different tiers of membership, offering different styles (red or white) or quantities of wine in each shipment. There are also plenty of other "exclusive" membership privileges, from discounts on gifts to free reserve wine tastings, some more worthwhile than others, depending on how far you live from the winery.

OPPORTUNITIES FOR STUDY

Where better to get some professional wine training than in the heart of Wine Country? It's easy to learn a lot just by visiting wineries and talking to the staff, but to really come to grips with wine it might be worth taking one of the short courses at the Culinary Institute of America, just north of St. Helena.

They don't come cheap and last several days, but these courses will quickly get your wine knowledge up to professional levels. The best introductory courses are **Mastering Wine** (level 1), a five-day crash course in everything wine for $1,000, and **Sensory Analysis,** a two-day course for $450 that focuses only on developing your sensory skills to appreciate wine. For a full catalog of these and other courses, together with schedules, contact the Culinary Institute at 707/967-2568 or browse the Professional Wine Studies Program online at www.ciaprochef.com.

A less formal crash course in wine making and wine appreciation is offered through the popular **Wine Boot Camp** program organized by Affairs of the Vine. The one-day courses ($400) take place at one or more wineries in a different wine region each month, with much of the education provided by winemakers and other experts. Students even get to try their hand at making a wine blend. For more information and a calendar, contact Affairs of the Vine at 707/874-1975 or www.winebootcamp.com.

ESSENTIALS

Getting There

BY AIR

There are four major international airports within a few hours' drive of most parts of Napa and Sonoma Counties. San Francisco International Airport, Oakland International Airport, and San Jose's Norman Y. Mineta International Airport all serve the cities of the San Francisco Bay Area, and Sacramento International Airport serves its namesake city and parts of California's Central Valley.

The biggest airport by far is **San Francisco International** (650/821-8211, www.flysfo. org), known locally as SFO. It is served by 28 airlines at last count, about two-thirds of which are international carriers. All major domestic U.S. airlines serve SFO (United Airlines has by far the largest number of flights), as do a number of low-cost carriers, including Southwest Airlines, ATA, JetBlue, and Virgin America.

Driving from SFO to Napa or Sonoma takes about 1.5 hours if traffic is good but involves hitting San Francisco city streets for a few miles to reach the Golden Gate Bridge. In rush hour, add at least a half hour to that.

The Oakland and San Jose airports get their "international" tag from just a handful

© GEORGE ROSE

of international flights, and most of the airlines serving them are domestic. Flying into either can often be cheaper than going to SFO, but the drawback is that direct flights from major U.S. cities tend to be less common and connections might be necessary.

Oakland International Airport (510/563-3300, www.flyoakland.com) is just across the bay from San Francisco and is served by three of the big domestic airlines (United, American, and Delta) as well as major low-cost carriers (JetBlue, Southwest, and America West) and a handful of charter airlines. Driving time from Oakland's airport to Napa is about an hour. Driving to Healdsburg in northern Sonoma can take more than two hours.

San Jose's **Norman Y. Mineta International Airport** (408/277-4759, www.sjc.org) is served by the six major domestic airlines and low-cost carriers including Southwest and ATA. The airport is about a 45-minute drive south of SFO, putting it farther from Napa and Sonoma.

Sacramento International Airport is smaller than the three Bay Area airports and is really only an option for those visiting Napa, about a 1.5-hour drive.

In 2007, Horizon Air started service to the tiny **Sonoma County Airport** in Santa Rosa (800/547-9308, www.sonomacountyairport.org) and now offers daily or twice daily flights to and from Seattle, Portland, Los Angeles, and Las Vegas.

BY RAIL

The days of easily being able to get to much of Napa and Sonoma by train are long gone—about 100 years gone, to be exact. Railroads that brought Victorian visitors to Sonoma's lush forests and Calistoga's spa resorts were driven out of business by the car, which has since come to dominate transport in California.

Oakland is the only major Bay Area city served by rail service these days (technically the station is in Emeryville, right next to Oakland)

via Amtrak's California Zephyr service from Chicago and Denver. The service is not for those with limited vacation time, since it takes several days to cross the West, and to get from Emeryville to parts of the Wine Country requires transferring onto Amtrak bus services.

From the Emeryville station (5885 Horton St.) there are connecting bus services to San Francisco and some of the bigger Napa and Sonoma towns, including Napa and Healdsburg. There is both an Amtrak bus and train service (from Sacramento on the Capitol Corridor service) to San Jose.

Times and frequencies of all these services vary depending on the day and season, so contact Amtrak (800/872-7245, www.amtrak.com) for more information.

BY BUS

Most major cities in Wine Country can be reached by a combination of long-distance and local bus services (and Amtrak bus service, outlined above). Many of the smaller towns and most of the wineries, however, are off the beaten path and can be reached only with your own wheels, though it's certainly an option to go to Napa, Healdsburg, or Sonoma by bus and rent a bicycle for a couple of days of touring.

Getting to those cities by bus might take a while. The long-distance **Greyhound Lines** buses (800/231-2222, www.greyhound.com) serve only the major Bay Area cities of San Francisco, Oakland, and San Jose, plus Santa Rosa in Sonoma.

Local bus service from Santa Rosa on the **Sonoma County Transit** bus network connects to Guerneville, Healdsburg, Glen Ellen, and Sonoma. San Francisco is the best place to head for using Greyhound Lines for connections to Napa via the Vallejo ferry and local **Vine** bus service. More information on all these connection possibilities can be found in each destination chapter.

Getting Around

BY CAR

Almost everyone gets around by car in California, and it's no different in Napa and Sonoma, where public transportation links are even thinner on the ground than in urban areas. With so many people in cars, congestion is a constant problem.

The San Francisco Bay Area was ranked the second most congested part of the nation in 2005, beaten only by (where else) Los Angeles, and rush hour on the area's freeways has been stretched to 2–3 hours at each end of the day, even on weekends: 7–10 A.M. and 4–7 P.M., expect slow freeway traffic at almost any major junction, bottleneck, or bridge.

Up in the Wine Country the roads are smaller but are also often congested during rush hour, and especially on summer weekends when visitors from local cities flock to their favorite wineries.

The worst roads are in the busiest parts of Wine Country—U.S. 12 between Sonoma and Kenwood in the Sonoma Valley, and U.S. 29 between Napa and St. Helena in the Napa Valley. In northern Sonoma, the U.S. 101 freeway through Santa Rosa tends to get clogged during the rush hours almost every day, though mercifully the roads from the freeway into the Russian River Valley are far quieter, except sometimes the River Road (U.S. 116) through Guerneville, which can be a traffic jam on hot summer weekends or when there's an event in town.

You can help the traffic flow by making sure you know where you're going and driving at the same clip as other drivers. If you're being tailgated by more than one car on a narrow, winding road, pull over at the nearest turnout or turnoff to let the faster traffic pass. And on two-lane roads with a center turn lane, use that lane both for turning left to avoid holding up traffic behind you and also to merge into traffic when turning left onto that main road.

Gas in the San Francisco Bay Area is some of the most expensive in the nation due to a combination of higher state and local taxes, higher costs for gas stations, and tight supply of the special, cleaner-burning formulation that is required in the state. The most expensive gas by far is in San Francisco. Some of the cheapest is in the most unlikely places off the beaten track, like Forestville in the Russian River Valley and Kenwood in the Sonoma Valley. Although there's sometimes no rhyme or reason to explain the difference in prices between one gas station and the next, Arco usually offers the cheapest gas and will sometimes be matched by other local gas stations. The prevalence of gas stations generally means you'd be hard-pressed to run out of gas anywhere in Napa and Sonoma, but don't set off on a drive over a winding mountain road if the gas warning light is already on.

Much of Napa and Sonoma is within easy reach of a freeway. From San Francisco, take U.S. 101 north out of the city and over the Golden Gate Bridge ($6 toll, payable southbound only). About a 20-minute drive north of the bridge is U.S. 37 East, which connects with U.S. 121, which leads to Carneros, the Sonoma Valley, and the Napa Valley. Continue on U.S. 101 to Santa Rosa (about 45 minutes from the bridge) for jumping off points to the Russian River Valley, and drive a further 15 minutes for Healdsburg, the Dry Creek Valley, and Alexander Valley.

Driving from downtown San Francisco to Napa is often quicker via I-80 East, which crosses the Bay Bridge ($4–6 toll, payable westbound only) then turns north and crosses the Carquinez Bridge about 25 minutes later ($5 toll, payable northbound). Shortly after is the American Canyon Road exit, which leads to the southern end of the Napa Valley.

Rental Cars

All the major car-rental companies are represented at the three main Bay Area airports, and most also have locations in downtown San Francisco, Oakland, San Jose, Santa Rosa, and Napa. Prices vary wildly, although they tend to be more expensive in California than in other parts of the nation. Deals are always available, and it's worth noting that four-day rentals usually cost the same as weekly ones.

For current prices and availability contact **Alamo** (800/462-5266, www.alamo.com), **Avis** (800/831-2847, www.avis.com), **Budget** (800/527-0700, www.budget.com), **Dollar** (800/800-3665, www.dollar.com), **Enterprise** (800/736-8222, www.enterprise.com), **Hertz** (800/654-3131, www.hertz.com), and **Thrifty** (800/847-4389, www.thrifty.com). You can also get some good deals and make reservations through major online travel agencies, including **Orbitz** (www.orbitz.com), **Travelocity** (www.travelocity.com), and **Expedia** (www.expedia.com). Check whether there are any discounts from your airline too.

Always check what your own car-insurance policy, credit cards, or travel insurance will cover before renting a car so you don't buy unnecessary (and often pricey) car, medical, or personal possession insurance at the rental counter. Liability insurance is required by law for all drivers in California, so if you have no car insurance of your own, you'll have to buy it from the rental company. Credit cards will generally not cover it.

BY BIKE

Biking is a potentially fun way of seeing parts of Napa and Sonoma but one that few people seem to try, if the lack of bicycles on the roads is anything to go by. Choose your location well, however, and the rewards of experiencing the warm air and all the unique smells of Wine Country are many. Plan badly and you'll be cursing all day long.

The roads in much of Wine Country can make biking more exciting than you'd like. Small roads tend to be winding and narrow, with the ever-present danger of inattentive (or drunk) drivers failing to see cyclists or give them enough clearance. While accidents seem to be few, close shaves are more common, so be well aware of approaching cars and always cycle in single file as close to the edge of the road as possible.

Make sure you wear a helmet, and don't plan on drinking much. Biking drunk is illegal, and it increases your risk of having an accident, whether from being hit by a car or running off the road down a ravine.

Cycling is a great way to see parts of the Wine Country up close.

© PHILIP GOLDSMITH

Drinking and strenuous exercise is also a recipe for dehydration and heatstroke. Hot summer days might not be the best time to go biking in much of Napa and Sonoma, except in the cooler parts of the Russian River Valley and down in Carneros. If you do go in the summer, plan on taking a picnic and whiling away the hottest mid- and late-afternoon hours somewhere off the bike. Spring and fall are the best times to venture out on two wheels. Winter is out, unless you like wet-weather riding or happen upon one of the occasional warm, dry spells.

Bike Tours

Some of the best places to see wineries by bike include the Dry Creek Valley, a relatively flat and compact area crammed with small wineries, many just a few minutes' ride from Healdsburg's bike shop. Healdsburg is also the jumping-off point for rides down the Westside Road into the Russian River Valley and into the Alexander Valley, though distances are longer and wineries farther apart.

The handful of wineries and historic sites around the city of Sonoma are also perfect for a bike tour. They are close together and only a short ride from Sonoma's main bike-rental shop near the downtown plaza. From Sonoma it is a slightly longer ride down into Carneros, but once you're there the flatlands and wetlands are fun to explore on a bike. Wineries here tend to be farther apart, however, and the weather can be on the cool and murky side, even in summer.

The Napa Valley has some good areas for biking, but the size of the valley and the crowds mean you'll have to plan a route carefully to avoid traffic and long distances. Try sticking to the Calistoga area, for example, or the wineries along the Silverado Trail in the Rutherford appellation, just a few minutes' ride from St. Helena.

Tips for Travelers

CONDUCT

Despite seemingly endless official rules and regulations, there's a refreshing anything-goes attitude to life in Northern California. The multicultural population is so used to bizarre behavior by its fellow citizens that people barely bat an eye at characters who might leave outsiders staring in disbelief.

Californians might be tolerant of the stranger members of their society, but they are not necessarily as liberal and laid-back as people would like to believe. This is a hardworking state: People work hard to attain their personal Californian Dream and then work hard to keep it. They work hard to stay in shape and just as hard to enjoy themselves, whether through outdoor recreation or indoor wining and dining. All that hard work has created a multitasking population that is ironically under so much stress that it even works hard to try to unwind.

The Wine Country is generally a wealthy enclave in a wealthy part of California, a place where money talks and lifestyle is everything. Like the rest of California, it's also a place of sharp economic contrasts. Migrant workers in the vineyards harvesting grapes are at one end of the economic scale, corporate winery executives are at the other. As is the norm in California, each group seems to happily tolerate the other.

Dress

California virtually invented business casual attire, and it's rare to see a shirt and tie, especially in Napa and Sonoma. About the only places that require you to pay attention to what you wear are golf courses (collared shirt and appropriate shoes) and a handful of top restaurants (smart casual for women, jacket and tie for men).

Otherwise you can get by wearing just about anything, though you'll have to wear *something* because public nudity is illegal (though on some beaches officials turn a blind eye), and establishments of all kinds will generally not serve the shoeless or shirtless.

Smoking

Smokers will find California's environment far from tolerant. Smoking is banned in all bars and restaurants in the state and is usually not allowed in or near public buildings either. That includes many hotels and inns, which either have a property-wide no-smoking policy or will only allow smoking in outdoor areas.

Despite the rather stringent ban, there are a few bars where you might see people light up, probably because the bar owner tacitly approves (and risks a fine). In such cases, offended nonsmokers would do well to keep quiet, because any outsiders complaining may quickly find the wrath of the bar's local patrons bearing down on them.

Tipping

As is the case in the rest of the nation, tipping is a voluntary but necessary practice in restaurants, bars, taxis, and for services given by valets or hotel concierges. A 15 percent tip is average, though more is normal in this land where money talks. Most restaurants will automatically add a standard 18 percent gratuity to the bill for parties of more than six or eight people. If that's the case, you have no obligation to add any further tip when signing the credit card slip, even though there will still be a spot for one.

Tipping is definitely not necessary in winery tasting rooms. In fact, you risk offending the generally well-paid staff if you do try to slip them a fiver, however helpful they have been. If you feel a strong urge to return a favor, simply buy a bottle or two of wine.

TRAVELERS WITH DISABILITIES

California is one of the most progressive states in the country when it comes to access for people with disabilities, and its state laws often go beyond the requirements of the federal Americans with Disabilities Act, which requires that all new public buildings must be disabled-accessible and older ones must be retrofitted if readily achievable.

Major wineries that are open to the public without an appointment, together with museums and other sights, all generally have wheelchair access ramps and restrooms for disabled people. Appointment-only wineries often stay appointment-only partly because of the prohibitive cost of meeting the various building and safety codes required for commercial public buildings, including access for disabled people. Small B&Bs and inns often do not have to comply with the strict laws because their historic buildings cannot easily be made disabled-accessible.

Napa and Sonoma Counties are ostensibly rural areas, so access for disabled people is always going to be far from universal. One organization that can help people with disabilities plan visits within Northern California is **Access Northern California** (1427 Grant St., Berkeley, 510/524-2026, www.accessnca.com). It has specific information on accommodations and sights with access for the disabled. Also contact local chambers of commerce or visitors centers for more specific information.

TRAVELING WITH CHILDREN

Most, but not all, winery activities are geared toward adults. Wineries generally allow children onto the premises, but anyone under 21, California's legal minimum drinking age, cannot taste any wines. And wineries without wine tasting tend to be pretty boring places, especially for kids.

If there are children in tow, careful planning can avoid tears of boredom and frustration. Some wineries offer educational tours that can be fun for kids and adults alike. Others have other attractions, ranging from art to historic cars. In all cases double-check that children are welcome because some wineries, such as the Castello di Amorosa castle, that might seem to offer plenty of entertainment for kids have an age limit.

Plenty of sights and museums have something to offer inquisitive young brains. The Petrified Forest or Old Faithful geyser near Calistoga will delight and amaze children (though not necessarily adults), as will an adult-supervised ride in a canoe on the Russian River or a ride on one of the narrow-gauge railroads at Train Town in Sonoma.

Also worth noting is that a lot of higher-priced B&Bs and resorts do not allow children under a certain age, and some do not allow children at all. The reasons vary—in some cases the policy is to protect precious antiques, in other cases simply to ensure that the peace and tranquility that guests are paying top dollar for is not shattered by screaming kids. Always check the policy on young guests when booking a room.

TRAVELING WITH PETS

Wine Country might not be terribly kid-friendly, but it is most definitely not dog-friendly. Dogs are actively discouraged or banned in many wineries, even those that have their own resident winery pooch. They are also not allowed in rooms of many lodgings, though a few hotels and motels will accept pets for an additional nightly fee. On many hiking trails, dogs are either not allowed at all or must be on a leash at all times.

Worse still (from the dog's point of view), the hot summer weather makes cars thoroughly uncomfortable places to be even for short periods of time. Dogs should never be left for long periods in a car in the California sun, even with the windows slightly cracked.

MAPS

Beware the cartoonish maps in many of the free magazines that blanket the Wine Country. Many of them are highly inaccurate for anything other than determining the approximate location of wineries and other major sights. Even for that purpose they can sometimes be unreliable, putting wineries on the wrong side of the road, for example, or giving little idea of distances involved. As road maps they should certainly not be relied on. Many small roads are missing from them, and other roads turn out to be dead ends or are misnamed.

The most reliable road maps for planning a trip covering Napa and Sonoma are published by the veteran map companies. Most of these maps don't have wineries or other sights marked on them but are good for general navigation, especially when used in conjunction with this book or the winery maps published by local wine associations in each region (listed at the end of each chapter).

The **American Automobile Association** (AAA) publishes a specific *Sonoma and Napa Wine Country* map as well as more detailed road maps for Napa, Sonoma, and the greater San Francisco Bay Area. They are available from your local AAA office and are free for members. Check www.aaa.com for your local office and to order maps online.

Rand McNally publishes several excellent road maps covering Napa and Sonoma, including *North Bay and Wine Country,* as well as another map for the greater Bay Area that includes some but not all of the major wine regions. Rand McNally maps are usually available at bookstores and can also be ordered online at www.randmcnally.com.

Health and Safety

DRINKING AND DRIVING

Driving (and even cycling) under the influence of alcohol is a serious offense in California. Both state and local police are well aware that visitors to Wine Country might have overindulged, and they will often be on the lookout for erratic driving in popular wine-tasting areas on busy weekends.

The blood alcohol limit for driving in the state is 0.08 percent, a level you can reach very quickly in a tasting room. Most wineries will pour about one ounce of wine per taste (some might be stingier, but use one ounce as a guideline), which means that by visiting one winery and tasting (and swallowing) four wines, you will already be well on the way to that limit.

People weighing less than 150 pounds who taste another flight of four wines at another winery in a two-hour period will likely be at their legal limit already. Those over 150 pounds will have a little more leeway, but not much.

The penalties for a DUI conviction are severe, including a fine ranging $200–7,000 and time in jail, not to mention the potential loss of your driving license and a big jump in insurance premiums if you are able to get it back. If you are a driver involved in an accident that causes bodily harm while your blood alcohol is over the legal limit, the penalties are even stiffer.

Trying to calculate how much can be drunk before reaching the limit is a notoriously inexact science. It depends not only on how much alcohol is consumed but also the person's weight, gender, metabolism, and how much food he or she has eaten over the previous few hours. Drinking a lot of water while tasting might ward off headaches but will do little to lower the blood alcohol level.

The only way to guarantee you are safe to drive is not to drink at all. Instead, use a designated driver, or if that's not an option, learn to spit wine out after smelling the aromas and swirling it around your mouth. If you really want to experience the lingering aftertaste of a $100 cabernet, then swallow just one wine out of all those you taste. There are usually plenty of spitting containers on tasting room counters. Just double-check that it's not the water jug you're about to empty your wine into.

OUTDOORS

The Wine Country might be all about luxury pampering, but the wilds here are also a major draw for visitors and can be just as wild as anywhere else in California. Experiencing Napa and Sonoma is as much about experiencing the great outdoors as the wine, but there are some basic outdoor rules to be aware of, particularly if you've had some wine. Even a few tastes of wine can be enough to potentially impair your judgment.

On the hiking or mountain-biking trail, make sure you know where you're going, and never go alone in case you get into trouble. Also be aware that many of the trails in Napa and Sonoma might start off in cool, damp woods but will often climb up to scrubland with little shade and often searing heat in the summer. Sunscreen, sunglasses, and a hat are mandatory in California during the summer, far less important during the winter. Luckily, most large wineries sell baseball caps should your bare head be overheating.

On the water, whether the Russian River or the many lakes, take the usual water-safety precautions. Don't jump in unless you know what's under the water, especially in the Russian River, where all sorts of treelike debris washed downstream during the winter and spring might lurk just below the surface of the often-murky water. Always wear a life-jacket when in a boat, and avoid doing anything on or in the water when you've had too much to drink.

Lyme Disease

Potentially the most dangerous animal for outdoor hikers in many parts of California, particularly parts of Napa and Sonoma, is also one of the smallest. The diminutive deer tick, which thrives in most lowland hills and meadows, can transmit Lyme disease, one of the most common vector-transmitted diseases in the United States.

The good news is that Lyme disease is easily treated with antibiotics if caught early. The bad news is that it can be difficult to detect early, with many of the early symptoms (including fever, aches and pains, headaches, and fatigue) often mistaken for other ailments. If left untreated, Lyme disease can develop into a serious degenerative illness, and the longer it goes untreated the harder it is to cure with antibiotics.

The best protection is to wear long pants and sleeves to avoid picking the ticks up in the first place. Plenty of insect repellent also helps. If you are bitten by a tick and it is still attached, do not try to pull it off with your fingers because the head will likely stay embedded. Remove ticks with tweezers by grasping the tick's head parts as close to your skin as possible and applying slow steady traction. Do not attempt to get ticks out of your skin by burning them or coating them with nail polish remover or petroleum jelly.

Always check for ticks after being outdoors in woodland or grassy meadows and watch for the telltale circular rash that usually appears around tick bites from three days to a month after being bitten. Also be aware that any flu-like symptoms might be a sign of Lyme disease. If in any doubt, see a doctor.

Wildlife

Much of California's other wildlife is not a great danger for visitors. Mountain lions, also known as pumas or cougars, do live in many of the hills and forests around urban areas, especially those where deer (their favorite prey) are common, but they are rarely seen and usually stay well away from humans, especially big groups of noisy humans (one reason never to hike alone).

Attacks by mountain lions are extremely rare. In fact, you're more likely to get struck by lightning. Sightings are more common, though still relatively rare. If you do happen across a lion on a hiking trail and it doesn't instinctively run the other way, try to make yourself look as large as possible to scare it, then slowly back away. Mountain lions are big cats—males can weight up to 150 pounds and grow up to eight feet long from head to the tip of the tail—but they'd rather not pick a fight with something their own size. In the rare instance a lion does attack, fight it with whatever comes to hand, like rocks and sticks. It's a strategy that has saved plenty of victims.

One thing you should not do is turn and run—mountain lions can run faster. Dogs should be kept on a leash (it's the law in most wilderness areas) to avoid agitating mountain lions, and also for the well-being of the dog, which would be easy prey. If you see a big cat in the brush next to the trail, do not try to approach it. Remember that you are trespassing on their territory, so if you let them get on with their lives, you'll likely be left alone.

Another animal that can do some damage to humans but is rarely seen is the western diamondback rattlesnake, the most common of the eight varieties of rattler found in California. The snakes are brown with a triangular head and a dark diamond pattern running down their backs. They also have that distinctive rattle that should be a warning to walk the other way if you hear it.

Rattlesnakes live throughout Napa and Sonoma, preferring hot rocky or grassy areas. When tromping through such areas, always be aware of where you're stepping, and if climbing on rocky ledges, make sure you can see where you're putting your hands. If you are bitten, the venom is rarely fatal but can lead to a few days of discomfort and requires a visit to the local hospital.

Snakes will usually head the other way when they hear anyone approaching, but if you do see one and it refuses to budge, back off and give it a wide berth. Also be especially alert for rattlers in the spring when the snakes are just emerging from hibernation and tend to be groggy, hungry, and mean.

Poison Oak

Poison oak is a deciduous shrub, usually 2–4 feet tall, with glossy leaves resembling those of a real oak tree. The leaves are arranged in clusters of three and are tinged a rusty red color in the late summer and fall. Those leaves and stems contain an oil, similar to that in poison ivy, called urushiol, that causes an allergic skin reaction in an estimated three-quarters of the population, even after only brief exposure.

Even in the winter the bare stems remain just as dangerous to passing skin and can be hard to spot. Even burning a small amount of poison oak on a campfire generates dangerous smoke that, if inhaled, can lead to a potentially fatal inflammation of the lungs.

The plant is common all over California, particularly in shady lowland woods and meadows. You will almost certainly encounter it alongside hiking trails, and it's particularly abundant after wet winters. Learn to identify it and avoid it if at all possible.

Wear long pants and sleeves and wash both clothes and skin as soon as possible if you even *think* you have been in contact with poison oak. Rashes can take a few days to appear, but once they do there's little you can do to get rid of them, and they'll likely spread as your body's immune system battles to neutralize the poisons and becomes even more sensitized in the process. The oil stays active for months, sometimes years, on surfaces like hiking boots and clothes (and dogs) and can rub off on skin at any time and cause a rash, so wash these too if you think they have been contaminated. Any regular laundry detergent will remove the oil.

If you do get a rash, do not scratch it, and make sure it is covered to prevent infection. Contrary to popular belief, the ooze from the rashes cannot spread the toxins, but it can attract bacteria that will further irritate the skin. Mild rashes will usually go away in a few days. The more seriously afflicted could be driven mad for many weeks by a growing rash, and some might require treatment with anti-inflammatory steroids, though the application of readily available hydrocortisone cream is the usual treatment.

Some specialized cleansing products that will neutralize the toxic oils are worth using if you're highly allergic. They are sold under the Tecnu brand name and are available at most pharmacies.

Dehydration and Heatstroke

Dehydration is a perennial enemy for about half the year in Napa and Sonoma, whether from tasting too much wine or from any sort of exertion in the heat. Most of Northern California is warm May–November and can get downright hot July–September, especially in the inland valleys.

Parts of the Russian River Valley, Carneros, and coastal regions will often be cooler because of fog and cool ocean breezes, but even these areas can heat up quickly in the summer when the sun comes out or the breezes die. The other half of the year, November–May, is the rainy season, though even in November, April, and May there can be some very warm spells of weather.

Drink plenty of water, especially if hiking but even when frolicking on or in the water on a hot day. For serious hiking in hot weather, at least a half quart of water per hour is recommended (in small doses, not all at once). Wear a hat to help prevent both sunburn and heatstroke, a potentially fatal condition created when the body is no longer able to cool itself sufficiently, causing symptoms including headache, confusion, and muscle cramps.

The water you do drink should always come from a bottle or a tap. Most of California's rivers and lakes contain parasites and bacteria that, although not fatal, can play havoc with digestive systems for several days and might require treatment. If camping at a primitive site near a stream or lake, consider taking a water filter so you don't have to carry all your water in with you.

RESOURCES

Glossary

acetic acid All wines contain a minuscule amount of acetic acid (vinegar), but bad wine will have enough (over about 0.1 percent) to actually start smelling of vinegar – not a good thing.

acid/acidity The natural acids (citric, malic, tartaric, and lactic) in a wine create a tartness that is supposed to act as a counterpoint to sugary sweetness, balancing the wine.

aftertaste The flavors that linger on your palate after swallowing the wine. The longer the aftertaste, the better – sometimes you can still taste wines almost a minute after swallowing.

aging The process of storing a wine in barrels or bottles for a few months to many decades so it develops character and more desirable flavors. White wines tend to turn from a greenish hue in young wines to a yellowish caste/tone to a gold/amber color as they age. Reds usually have a purple tone when young, turning to a deep red (bordeaux wines and cabernet, for example) or a brick red color (burgundy wines and pinot noir, for example), detectable at the surface edge in a wineglass as they age.

alcohol The colorless and flavorless chemical created as a byproduct of fermentation that gets you drunk but also acts as a preservative for the wine. The higher the sugar content of the grape when picked, the higher the alcohol content of the wine. Californian red wines tend to have alcohol content of over 13 percent, sometimes as high as 16 percent in the case of some zinfandels.

angular Describes a tart wine with a sharp edge to its taste. The opposite of a round, soft, or supple wine.

appellation or AVA The specific area a wine comes from. Technically, appellation is a term simply to describe a geographic area. To be classified as an American Viticultural Area, or AVA, by the federal Bureau of Alcohol, Tobacco, and Firearms (ATF), an area must be shown to have unique soil, climate, or other growing conditions that will distinguish its wines from those grown in other areas. When an AVA, such as Napa Valley or Carneros, is named on the label, at least 85 percent of the grapes must have come from there (100 percent in Washington and Oregon). There can also be AVAs within AVAs. The Napa Valley, for example, is a single AVA that contains 13 other AVAs, commonly referred to as subappellations.

approachable An approachable wine is easy to enjoy and generally made to be drunk without aging.

aroma The smell of a wine that comes from the fruit or smells like fruit. As wine ages, some of the fruit-related smells dwindle and are replaced by more complex smells from chemicals created during the aging process, referred to as the bouquet.

aromatic Describes wines that have a strong flowery or spicy character.

astringent The rough, puckery taste that most people describe as sour and that often comes from a high tannin content. Astringent wines normally mellow with age.

austere Slightly hard and acidic wines that seem to lack depth of flavor. Such wines may soften a bit with age and develop more subtle complexity than fuller wines. Austere wines are often from cool growing regions, especially mountain areas.

Bacchus The Roman god of wine and a name sometimes seen in jokey marketing material.

balance A balanced wine is what winemakers strive to make, one in which no flavor or aroma overpowers another. Acid balances the sweetness, fruit against oak and tannin. You'll know a balanced wine when you taste one.

barrel A wooden vessel used to store wine before it is bottled, made of oak and charred (toasted) on the inside to impart specific flavors and color to the wine. On any winery tour you'll likely pass racks of oak barrels (sometimes called *barriques*) that are usually the standard size of 59 gallons or about 225 liters. American oak barrels cost more than $200 new. Highly prized French oak barrels cost more than $500 each. Barrels are usually used and reused for several vintages, then end up as planters or are discarded.

barrel fermenting The fermentation of wine in barrels to impart specific flavors and texture. It often gives a richer flavor to white wines, though is sometimes overused and will make a wine "over-oaked." In red wines, barrel fermenting will impart more tannins to the wine so it can age for longer. The increasingly common alternative is to age wines in stainless steel or concrete vats.

big Wine with a big, robust, and full-bodied character, usually because of high alcohol content. Dry Creek Valley zinfandel is an example of a "big" wine.

bitter One of the four basic tastes that your taste buds can detect. Some wines are supposed to have slight bitterness, but too much is a bad thing. It comes from unripe grapes or from too many stems being crushed with the grapes (that's why many wineries destem grapes first).

blanc de blancs Sparkling wine or champagne made purely from white grapes like chardonnay. Other white sparklers might contain the juice from the dark-skinned pinot noir grape and are called blanc de noirs.

blending The mixing of different types of wine

(cabernet, merlot, or syrah, for example) or of wines made from the same grape but from different vineyards. Blending different wines is part of the winemaker's art and is done to create a wine of particular character, much like different shades of paint are blended to create the desired tone.

body How heavy the wine feels in your mouth, a perception created by the alcohol, glycerin, and sugar content of a wine. An Alexander Valley cabernet sauvignon is a full-bodied wine, while a Santa Cruz chardonnay is lighter bodied.

Bordeaux blend A wine (usually red) made from a blend of some or all of the main grape varietals used to make wine in the French region of Bordeaux – cabernet sauvignon, merlot, cabernet franc, malbec, petit verdot, and carmenère in the case of red wine; sauvignon blanc, semillon, and muscadelle in the case of white. See also *meritage*.

botrytis A gray fungus (also known at noble rot) that attacks grapes in humid conditions, shriveling them up like raisins and concentrating the sugar and acid content. Wines made from affected grapes are sweet and complex, often sold as dessert wines.

bouquet Often confused with the aroma, the bouquet refers specifically to the scent in a wine that comes from the aging process in either the barrel or bottle, rather than from the fruit.

brawny Term used mainly to describe young red wines (especially in California) with high alcohol and tannin levels.

briary An aggressive, prickly taste in young wines, sometimes described as peppery.

brix A measure of the sugar content in a grape, used to determine when grapes should be harvested. The final alcohol content of a wine is often related to the brix reading of the grapes when harvested.

brut Refers to a dry (but not the driest) champagne or sparkling wine with less than 1.5 percent residual sugar.

burgundy A catch-all term to describe red and white wine from the Burgundy region in France. Real red burgundies are usually pinot noir. Cheap Californian burgundies are usually misusing the term for totally unrelated wine.

buttery An obvious taste often found in good white wines, particularly Californian chardonnay.

cava A sparkling wine from Spain made in a similar style to champagne but using different grapes.

Champagne A region in northern France best known for production of sparkling wine by a very specific method, known as the *méthode champenoise,* using chardonnay, pinot noir, and pinot meunier. Since 2006, American wineries are no longer allowed to call sparkling wines made this way "champagne."

chaptalization The addition of sugar to wine before or during fermentation to increase the final alcohol content. It is legal in France, where cooler weather often means grapes do not have enough sugar when harvested, but not legal (and not necessary) in California.

charmat method The process of making cheaper sparkling wines by carrying out the secondary fermentation (the one that creates the bubbles) in large steel vats under pressure rather than in the bottle like the more expensive *méthode champenoise* used to make fine champagnes.

chewy Usually used to describe powerful tannins in red wines like cabernet that give it an almost viscous mouthfeel, making you almost want to chew it before swallowing.

citrus An aroma and flavor reminiscent of citrus fruits, especially grapefruit, in many white wines, particularly those from cooler growing regions like Carneros and the Russian River Valley.

claret An old English term used to describe red wines from Bordeaux. In France, "clairet" is a particular bordeaux that is produced like red wine, but the wine must stay in contact with the skins for the first 24 hours during its making.

clone A genetic variation of a grapevine. In a wine and vineyard context, usually the specific genetic type of vine picked to match the local growing conditions or the desired style of wine.

cloudy Used to describe a wine that is a little hazy when viewed through the glass rather than crystal clear. Except in some rare occasions, a cloudy wine is not a good thing and might also have an unpleasant smell.

complex The ultimate flattery for winemakers is to call their wines complex. Everything from the aroma to the long aftertaste is in balance and harmony.

cooked Leave wine in a hot car for a day, open it, and it will probably taste odd. It has been cooked (see *maderized*).

cooperage All the containers a winery uses to store and age wine, including barrels, vats, and tanks. They are made by coopers.

corked The most common fault of restaurant wine, it is the brief taste or smell of wet cardboard in a wine that is caused by bacteria in a contaminated cork interacting with chemicals in the wine. It can often be very subtle, so many people might not realize a wine is corked, and it is harmless to drink.

creamy The silky taste and texture of a white wine that has undergone malolactic fermentation. Often accompanied by the faintest smell of creamy foods like crème brûlée.

crisp A definite but not undesirable tartness and acidity usually used to describe white wines and often accompanied by the aroma of citrus fruits. White wines from cool climates like Carneros are often crisp.

crush Literally the crushing of the grape skins to release the juice and start the fermentation process. Crush is the term also used to describe the process of harvesting and transporting the grapes of a particular year prior to making the wine.

cuvée A French term to describe the blend of wines from different grapes and different years that is used to make champagne and sparkling wines.

decanting The slow and careful pouring of aged red wine into a broad, shallow glass container to ensure the sediment from aging stays in the bottle and to then allow the wine to breathe, or start to release its aromas, before drinking.

demi-sec A slightly sweet sparkling wine or

champagne containing 3.5–5 percent residual sugar.

dessert wine A sweet red or white wine usually drunk in small amounts with dessert. The sweetness of desserts would mask the much smaller amount of sugar in a normal wine and make it taste bitter or acidic. Sweet dessert wines are often made from late-harvest grapes, picked when they are riper and their sugar content is higher. The botrytis fungus can also be used to make these sweeter wines.

dry Describes a red or white wine that has been fermented until less than 0.2 percent of the natural sugars remain. Although a dry wine will not taste sweet, it might still taste fruity.

dumb My favorite wine term — it means, literally, a wine with nothing to say. Flavors and aroma might have been muted by overchilling a white wine or simply because a red wine is at a certain stage of aging when it is in between youthfulness and adulthood (often when about 5–6 years old).

earthy Fine pinot noir is always earthy, possessing an aroma and/or flavor that could have come straight from the ground. Think of what a handful of damp soil smells like, and that's the earthiness. Different soil smells a different way, and the pros can often detect the type of soil or region a wine comes from simply by recognizing the smell of that earth. Or so they say. A lot of wines have the potential to be earthy, but other aromas and flavors often mask the distinctive smell.

elegant How to praise a well-balanced and graceful wine. The opposite would be "rustic."

enology The science and study of wine making, often spelled *oenology* outside the United States. An *oenophile* is someone who loves wine.

estate bottled Refers to wine made from vineyards that are both owned by the winery and in the same appellation or AVA as the winery. In addition, the entire wine-making process from fermentation to bottling has to occur at that winery. Nonestate wines are made from grapes bought from other growers or grown in another appellation.

fat Describes the texture of a full-bodied wine with lots of fruit. A full-bodied wine without enough acidity to balance the fruit is often called flabby.

fermentation The process that turns grape juice into wine. A biochemical process in yeast cells converts the sugar in grape juice into alcohol and carbon dioxide. Usually that gas is simply allowed to escape, but in the secondary fermentation process used to make sparkling wines it is retained in the wine under pressure and released as the bubbles when a bottle is opened.

filtering The easy way to remove particles from a wine to ensure it is clear before being bottled. Pumping wine through filters can, however, damage the flavor of a wine. Fining is a more laborious but better way to clarify wine.

fining The process of adding a natural, nonreactive substance like gelatin or crushed eggshell to a tank of wine to slowly remove suspended particles as it falls to the bottom. It takes longer than simple filtering.

finish Also sometimes called the aftertaste, this is the lingering impression of the wine on your palate after swallowing. It might be long or short (or absent), acidic or sweet. Generally, a longer finish denotes a better wine.

firm A wine that has some acidic astringency, much like firm unripe fruit. Like unripe fruit, a firm wine is usually young and will ripen with age, mellowing its acidity. But sometimes it won't.

flat Wines with too little acidity are said to be flat and uninteresting.

flowery A white wine that has an aroma reminiscent of flowers.

forward A forward wine is one that has all its best aromas and flavors right up front and screams "drink me now." You'll usually hear the term *fruit forward* used to describe cheap red wines in which the fruity flavors overpower all others (if there are even others present).

fruity A generic term used to describe whatever aroma and flavor comes from the grape itself. Strangely enough, wine does not usually smell of the one fruit used to make it but of everything from grapefruit to honeydew melon, depending on the type of grape and how the wine was made. Fruity wines are not necessarily sweet wines.

funky Believe it or not, this is a real wine-tasting term used to describe a certain unidentifiable yeasty aroma that some wines have. You'll have to be a professional wine critic to recognize the smell. Most people simply call any unidentifiable smell or taste "funky." Just don't say it in front of a winemaker.

grassy Sauvignon blanc is often described as grassy. Imagine the smell of freshly cut grass. Too much grassiness is not a good trait.

green A term often applied to sauvignon blanc. It describes the slightly leafy taste of a wine made with underripe fruit.

hollow When there's really nothing between the first initial taste of a wine and the aftertaste. Something's missing in the middle for any number of reasons.

horizontal tasting No, not drinking wine while lying down, but tasting the same type of wine from the same year but from different wineries. It's fun to line up a horizontal tasting of, say, cabernets from different Napa Valley appellations to learn how different growing conditions affect wine.

hot You'll know a hot wine when the back of your throat burns after swallowing, as though you just downed a shot of vodka. It's caused by too much alcohol in the wine and not enough of everything else. This is a normal character of fortified wines like port and sherry but a no-no in regular wines like cabernet sauvignon. Cheap, high-alcohol zinfandels are often hot.

jammy Word most often used to describe Californian zinfandel. Imagine the taste of a spoonful of blackberry jam.

late harvest Picking grapes as late as possible so their sugar content is as high as possible to make a sweeter wine, usually a dessert wine.

lean More body would be good, sort of thin in the mouth, often too much astringency; sometimes a compliment for certain styles.

lees The leftover yeast and other crud that falls to the bottom of barrels or fermentation tanks or is removed by fining. It is also sometimes called mud. Makers of white and sparkling wines sometimes leave it in the bottle so it can impart a yeasty, toasty flavor and smell to aged wine. That technique is called fermenting wine *sur lies.*

legs Spot the novice wine taster cracking jokes about "great legs." Swirl wine around the glass, then stop and watch clear rivulets cling to the side of the glass. They are the legs, and how fat or long they are actually has nothing to do with the quality of the wine. Instead they have everything to do with how much alcohol and glycerin there is in the wine, what the temperature is, and even how clean the glass is.

length Pretty much the same as finish, namely how long the flavors and aromas of a wine last on the back of your throat after swallowing; the longer, the better.

maderized What might happen to your wine if you leave it in a hot car for too long. It is a distinctive brown color and smell caused by exposure of wine to excessive heat and oxygen. Also sometimes called "oxidized." Even if you haven't smelled the Portuguese fortified wine madeira, you'll know when a wine has maderized. It doesn't smell like wine anymore.

malolactic fermentation A secondary chemical process (not technical fermentation at all) that nearly all red wines undergo and white wines are sometimes put through to give them a smoother, less acidic flavor (often described as creamy or buttery). It converts the harsh-tasting malic acid that naturally occurs in wine into the softer lactic acid plus carbon dioxide. Wineries often use the process to make a more popular style of easy-drinking chardonnay, though sometimes they overdo it and create a wine that lacks any sort of acidity at all and is just flat.

meritage Californian wines have to contain at least 75 percent of one grape varietal to be labeled as such, but some of the best red wines are blends of some of the five varietals used in bordeaux wine with no grape in the majority. Californian winemakers, not wanting to use the term *bordeaux blend,* instead came up with a new term to describe blended red wines: meritage.

It remains an uncommon term, however, and most wineries instead come up with their own proprietary names for their blends.

mouthfeel How a wine feels rather than tastes in your mouth. Use any description you want. Ones I use too much include "velvety" and "soft."

musty A flaw that makes a wine smell like your grandmother's dank old attic. It is caused by mold getting into the wine sometime during the wine-making or bottling process.

nonvintage Most wines are made with grapes harvested in a single year (vintage). Nonvintage wines are made by blending wines made in different years, and they have no year on their label. Some cheap red wines are nonvintage and made by using up surplus wine from different years. The best champagnes are also nonvintage so the winemakers can make sure the wine is of consistent high quality every year.

nose The most important tool for wine tasting, but in most cases used to describe the overall smell of a wine, a combination of the aroma and bouquet.

oaky The taste or smell of freshly sawn oak, toast, or vanilla that comes from aging wine in oak barrels that have usually been charred, or toasted, on the inside. A hint of oakiness in red wines is considered a good thing and is a matter of taste in white wines. Oak aromas and flavors should never overpower the fruit in a wine, as they do in some "over-oaked" chardonnays. There's an entire vocabulary used to describe oak smells and tastes, all of which depend on factors ranging from where the oak tree was grown to the size of the wood's grain.

open up/opening up Some bottled cellar-aged red wines possess the peculiarity that, when the cork is first pulled and the wine poured, the full flavors do not immediately make an appearance. However, after the passage of several minutes in an open glass goblet, the wine develops unsuspected flavor characteristics that can verge on the sublime. This phenomenon is referred to as "opening up." These flavors can disappear just as fast in just 30 minutes, leaving a subsequent impression of a flat, stale, over-the-hill, or mediocre wine.

overripe A grape precondition necessary for making certain styles of Californian zinfandel wines. Left on the vine to dry in the sun, certain grape varietals will develop the desirable raisiny character and concentrated sugar necessary for making specialty wines such as the Hungarian tokay.

oxidized As soon as a bottle of wine is opened, it is exposed to the oxygen in the air and starts to oxidize, usually a good thing for an hour or two. If it has been exposed to air for too long, however, either due to a leaky cork during storage or from being left open on a kitchen counter for a week, it will start to smell like cheap sherry and turn brown. At that point it is oxidized. With excessive heat as well it will become maderized.

peppery A term that usually goes hand-in-hand with *spicy* to describe the slightly pungent quality of wines like gewürztraminer and some styles of syrah.

phylloxera A small aphid-like insect that attacks the roots of vines and slowly kills them by preventing the plant from absorbing water and nutrients. It wiped out many vineyards in Europe in the late 1800s but is actually native to the United States, where it has periodically ravaged California vines, particularly in the early 1900s. Most vines are now grafted onto resistant rootstock, though some are not, and limited outbreaks still periodically occur.

Pierce's disease A virus that infects grapevines and kills them in 1–5 years. It is spread by a leafhopper-type insect called the glassy-winged sharpshooter. Though the disease is not yet endemic in Northern California's vineyards, authorities are worried it could soon be and have imposed strict plant quarantine laws to prevent its spread.

plump Almost a fat wine but not quite.

pomace The mashed-up residue of skin, seeds, stems, and pulp left after grapes are pressed to release the juice. In California it's often used as fertilizer. In Italy they distill it to make grappa.

racking A traditional method of wine clarification that involves transferring wine from one barrel to another to leave sediment and other deposits behind.

reserve wine The term *reserve wine* actually means nothing in California thanks to the total lack of official definition. In general, a reserve wine is made from the best grapes (they are reserved specially) and often aged for longer to create a higher quality wine than a winery's normal offerings. In practice the term is often as much about marketing as good wine. Some wineries give their best-of-the-best wines other labels like "special selection."

residual sugar The percentage, by weight or volume, of the unfermented grape sugar that remains in wine when it is bottled. The driest wines have less than 0.5 percent residual sugar, though many have slightly more to give them a fuller flavor.

rootstock The roots of a grapevine, which often come from a different species than the leaves. Many vines are a combination of two different plants. The stems and leaves might come from one, and they are grafted, or grown onto, roots from another chosen either for its suitability for certain growing conditions or resistance to disease.

rough If a wine feels like it's taking the lining off your throat with its tannins, it's described as rough. Some rough wines smooth and mellow with age.

Rutherford dust A slightly mineral flavor said to be present in some of the classic cabernets grown in the Rutherford appellation of Napa Valley.

sediment The small quantity of particulate matter often found at the bottom of well-aged red wines, generated during the aging process. Sediment includes a lot of the phenols that give wine its color, so as a wine gets really old the color literally starts dropping out of it. Sediment is harmless but best left in the bottle for presentation's sake.

soft A wine that has low acid or tannin content that has little impact on your taste buds.

sommelier The person responsible for the wine cellar, wine service, and wine list in a restaurant. If you have no clue which wine to order,

ask to speak to the sommelier, and he or she can usually help.

sour Almost a synonym for acidic. Implies the presence of acetic acid plus excess acid component. (It is also one of the four basic taste sensations detected by the human tongue.)

spicy Almost a synonym for peppery, but it implies a more nuanced flavor suggesting delicate Indian spices rather than those that get up your nose.

supple A red wine with a mouthfeel that lies somewhere between lean and fat; usually an easy drinker.

tannin The reason many people don't like red wines. Tannin is a naturally occurring chemical (a phenol) in grape skins, seeds, and stems as well as the wood of barrels. It gives red wines their backbone, helps preserve them, and has an astringent taste. Young wines, particularly those meant for aging, can be highly tannic but will mellow and soften with age. Other overly tannic wines taste rough or harsh and might never mellow. White wines generally contain very little tannin.

tartaric acid If you ever see what looks like small shards of glass in a bottle of white wine, they are probably crystals of tartaric acid, a harmless acid that is in all white wines and can crystallize under certain conditions.

terroir A French term for all the environmental characteristics of a vineyard, including every conceivable nuance of the soils, climate, and geography. The *terroir* is said to give the grapes grown there a unique flavor profile, and the best wine experts in the world can identify (allegedly) the exact vineyard that the grapes in a wine came from.

tobacco A common description of a flavor often found in cabernet sauvignon that refers to the smell of fresh tobacco leaves. *Cigar box* is a common term often used in its place. Like all those flavor descriptions, it's easier to identify if you have actually experienced the smell firsthand by smelling and smoking a cigar.

ullage The small gap between the wine in the bottle and the cork. It should be almost nonexistent and is formed by the evaporation of the wine through the cork or cork leakage. If the ullage gets too big, it will contain enough oxygen to start oxidizing the wine.

vanilla A desirable aroma and taste component of many red wines that comes from the compound vanillin in oak barrels. Newer barrels have more vanillin than older barrels. Smell a bottle of vanilla essence used in cooking to help identify the subtle equivalent in a wine.

varietal A wine made from a particular type of grape, such as pinot noir, chardonnay, cabernet sauvignon, and so on, that shows the distinct characteristics of that type of grape. A varietal wine must contain more than 75 percent of the grape variety identified on the label. Blended wines made from more than one type of grape, such as many European wines identified more by their region than the grape (bordeaux and chianti, for example), are not varietal wines.

vertical tasting Tasting a number of different vintages of one varietal of wine from the same winery, starting from the youngest and working to the oldest. Vertical tasting can help identify the best years for a particular wine and show how it changes as it ages.

vineyard-designate Describes a wine that is made using grapes from a single, named vineyard only. These wines are usually more expensive and higher quality than those made with grapes from multiple vineyards.

vintage The year grapes are harvested, which is the year on the bottle label. Making the wine and bottling it often takes several more years, so a 2003 wine might not be released until 2005 or beyond.

Vitis vinifera The main grapevine species behind all the great wines of the world, and one that is often grafted onto rootstock from other *Vitis* species. All the major varietal grapes are members of the *Vitis vinifera* species, including chardonnay, cabernet sauvignon, pinot noir, sauvignon blanc, and so on.

yeast Single-celled fungi that use enzymes to turn the natural sugars in grape juice into alcohol and carbon dioxide gas (and energy for themselves) through a biochemical process called fermentation. Different wild and genetically modified yeasts are used by winemakers, each performing differently and imparting a slightly different flavor to the wine. Wild yeasts often live naturally on grape skins, and winemakers will simply rely on them. A few wild yeasts can, however, give an undesirable yeasty odor to wines.

Suggested Reading

CUISINE

Don't expect to lose weight with cookbooks from Napa and Sonoma, though there's usually plenty of advice on pairing food with wines between their covers. Wine Country cuisine is all about using the freshest local produce, and recipes in many of the Wine Country cookbooks tend to rely heavily on the kind of ingredients you might not necessarily find in your local supermarket. Still, they make a nice reminder of what to strive for in recreating an idyllic Wine Country lifestyle and will probably be a fun reminder of memorable meals in the Napa and Sonoma restaurants that inspire many of them.

Bernstein, Sondra. *The Girl & the Fig Cookbook.* New York: Simon & Schuster, 2004. Simple recipes that reflect the culinary fun to be had in the Sonoma restaurant, from liquid meals of martinis through to full French-inspired bistro meals, not all requiring the trademark figs.

Brown, Carrie, and John Werner. *The Jimtown Store Cookbook.* New York: HarperCollins, 2002. The Jimtown Store is the little store that could, hidden away in the heart of the Alexander Valley but still managing to compile a no-nonsense collection of classically stylish yet simple Wine Country recipes that cross all culinary borders.

Chiarello, Michael, and Penelope Wisner. *The Tra Vigne Cookbook: Seasons in the California Wine Country.* San Francisco: Chronicle Books, 1999. The landmark St. Helena Italian restaurant is beautiful to look at and so is this book, though some of the recipes might have you out in the woods hunting for a particular wild mushroom that happens to be in season.

Jordan, Michele Anna, and Faith Echtermeyer. *The New Cook's Tour of Sonoma: 150 Recipes and the Best of the Region's Food and Wine.* Seattle: Sasquatch Books, 2000. A sort of greatest hits of Wine Country cooking, with recipes from all over Northern California and profiles of the people behind the famous produce of the region that defines the cuisine.

Keller, Thomas. *Bouchon.* New York: Artisan Press, 2004. If you can't afford to eat at French Laundry or would rather spend $200 on a case of wine, then buy this giant cookbook from the little bistro opened by the same owners just down the street in Yountville and learn how to make some simple yet sophisticated bistro-style food to go with your new wine purchase.

Pawlcyn, Cindy. *Mustards Grill Napa Valley Cookbook.* Berkeley, CA: Ten Speed Press, 2001. One of the more digestible Wine Country cookbooks from this famous Yountville restaurant, with plenty of relatively simple recipes based on hearty American fare with twists of sophistication. This is the restaurant credited with starting the Wine Country food scene.

Sone, Hiro, and Lissa Doumani. *Terra: Cooking from the Heart of Napa Valley.* Berkeley, CA: Ten Speed Press, 2001. This cookbook, from one of St. Helena's best restaurants, contains often sophisticated and tricky recipes drawing on French, Italian, and Japanese cuisine, but it helps makes their preparation as simple as possible with plenty of handy kitchen tips.

HISTORIC LITERATURE

Fisher, M. F. K. *The Art of Eating,* 5th edition. New York: Wiley, 2004. One of the Sonoma and Napa Valleys' most famous writers, who ended up living in Glen Ellen, Fisher was also one of the best-known food writers in the United States in her later years. This compilation of five of her books is a collection of autobiographical information and musings on food preparation, consumption, and nutrition. She was described by John Updike as "the poet of appetites."

London, Jack. *The Valley of the Moon.* Berkeley, CA: University of California Press, 1999. Although not one of this prolific Victorian author's better-known books (such as *The Call of the Wild*), this is a clear homage to the beauty of the Sonoma Valley, a mythical nirvana to the story's two protagonists, who try to escape their harsh working-class roots in Oakland for a simple country life. The story mirrors the life of London himself, who eventually moved from Oakland to live in the Sonoma Valley, a place he adored. First published in 1913.

Russack, Benjamin, ed. *Wine Country: A Literary Companion.* Berkeley, CA: Heyday Books, 1998. A collection of essays, poetry, travelogues, and fiction from almost two dozen writers spanning more than a century, all about or inspired by Napa and Sonoma. Includes works from Jack London, Robert Louis Stevenson, M. F. K. Fisher, Ambrose Bierce, Ursula Le Guin, and many other heavyweights.

Stevenson, Robert Louis. *The Silverado Squatters.* Rockville, MD: Wildside Press, 2004. The Victorian author is better known for his classic book *Treasure Island,* but he spent a few days of his honeymoon in a cottage at the abandoned Silverado Mine just outside Calistoga. He wrote an entertaining account of the colorful characters he met and places he visited in the surrounding area, including early wineries and some sights still there today. First published in 1884.

NAPA VALLEY

Conaway, James. *Napa: The Story of an American Eden.* Boston: Houghton Mifflin, 1990. With a compelling narrative style, author and journalist James Conway tells the story of the key people, families, and politics that helped make the Napa Valley what it is today—a land of dreams, obsessions, money, and wine.

Conaway, James. *The Far Side of Eden.* Boston: Mariner Books, 2002. James Conway picks up where his previous book, *Napa: The Story of an American Eden,* left off to chart the rise and impact of new money in the Napa Valley's recent social and wine-making history through the boom years of the 1990s.

Lapsley, James T. *Bottled Poetry: Napa Winemaking from Prohibition to the Modern Era.* Berkeley, CA: University of California Press, 1997. An entertaining analysis of the people, dreams, and marketing savvy that helped make Napa the great wine region it is today. More businesslike in its approach and style than Conway's books, but still as readable.

Mondavi, Robert. *Harvests of Joy: How the Good Life Became Great Business.* San Diego: Harcourt, 1998. No family has had more of an impact on the modern wine industry of the Napa Valley, and indeed California, than the Mondavis, and Robert Mondavi in particular. Here the man himself gives the inside information on what makes it all tick.

O'Rear, Charles. *Napa Valley: The Land, the Wine, the People.* Berkeley, CA: Ten Speed Press, 2001. *National Geographic* photographer O'Rear paints a picture of life in the Napa Valley through hundreds of color and black-and-white photos of the people and places that make it unique.

Swinchatt, Jonathan. *The Winemaker's Dance: Exploring Terroir in the Napa Valley.* Berkeley, CA: University of California Press, 2004. A dense book for wine or science enthusiasts only that explains how the Napa Valley came to be the way it is and how its geology and geography make it such a fine place to grow grapes.

SONOMA COUNTY

Barry, Jennifer, Robert Holmes, and Mimi Luebbermann. *Sonoma: A Food and Wine Lovers' Journey.* Berkeley, CA: Ten Speed Press, 2003. A coffee-table book with glorious photographs but also plenty of travel facts and recipes that highlight the food as well as the wine of this bountiful part of the world.

Deutschman, Alan. *A Tale of Two Valleys: Wine, Wealth and the Battle for the Good Life in Napa and Sonoma.* New York: Broadway, 2003. *Vanity Fair* contributing writer Deutschman continues where James Conway left off with his book *The Far Side of Eden,* chronicling the flood of dot-com wealth into both the Napa and Sonoma Valleys and the changes it wrought in Wine Country society. His style is brasher than Conway's and might not be to everyone's liking.

TRAVEL AND RECREATION

Brown, Ann Marie. *Moon 101 Great Hikes of the San Francisco Bay Area, 4th edition.* Berkeley, CA: Avalon Travel, 2011. The perfect companion for any avid hiker visiting the Wine Country or the Bay Area includes some of the best short and longer hikes in Napa and Sonoma, with thorough descriptions of each trail and directions to trailheads.

WINE REFERENCE

Kolpan, Steven, Brian Smith, and Michael Weiss. *Exploring Wine: The Culinary Institute of America's Guide to Wines of the World, 2nd edition.* New York: Wiley, 2001. This giant tome is a crash course in wine making, wine appreciation, and the wines of the world, with the added authority of being from the Culinary Institute of America, which offers some of the most highly regarded wine and food education courses in the country. That probably explains the unbelievably comprehensive chapter on pairing food and wine that, like many chapters, tends to read more like a textbook.

Kramer, Matt. *Matt Kramer's New California Wine.* Philadelphia: Running Press, 2004. Opinionated food and wine writer Kramer explains what has shaped and continues to shape the modern Californian wine industry with plenty of facts and information about key wineries and wines from every California wine-making region, including Napa and Sonoma. A vital book for California wine enthusiasts.

MacNeil, Karen. *The Wine Bible.* New York: Workman Publishing, 2001. A book to be found on many winery office desks, not least because MacNeil and her husband are Napa Valley winemakers themselves. It has an altogether more chatty, approachable style than the CIA guide and contains information on just about every wine and wine-related term you will come across, although it sometimes lacks depth.

Pinney, Thomas. *A History of Wine in America from Prohibition to the Present.* Berkeley, CA: University of California Press, 2005. A followup to Pinney's out-of-print volume covering pre-Prohibition history, this exhaustive tome details the characters, trends, and policies that shaped both the West and East Coast wine industries from the 1930s to the turn of the century.

Robinson, Jancis. *The Oxford Companion to Wine, 3rd edition.* Berkeley, CA: University of California Press, 2006. A massive tome that is widely regarded as the most exhaustive and accurate encyclopedia of everything you ever wanted to know about wine, from a well-known British wine writer and master of wine.

Sullivan, Charles. *A Companion to California Wine: An Encyclopedia of Wine and Winemaking from the Mission Period to the Present.* Berkeley, CA: University of California Press, 1998. Learn just about everything there is to know about California's wine industry, from its history to key facts and figures, in this fascinating reference book.

Internet Resources

All the following Internet resources are either totally free or at least have some useful information that is free. They supplement the more specific regional Internet resources listed in each destination chapter. Most major magazines are not included in this list because they operate subscription-based websites.

WINE
Vines.org
www.vines.org
A free if slightly clunky-looking site that is a giant database of all things wine. Its encyclopedic format is not ideal for browsing, but it will likely have an answer to any specific question you can throw at it.

Vinography
www.vinography.com
An entertaining and sometimes brutally honest blog from a well-informed San Francisco wine enthusiast.

Wine Business Online
www.winebusiness.com
All the latest industry news, events, jobs, and other business-related wine information for industry insiders.

Winefiles
www.winefiles.org
An authoritative, searchable database of wine, wine making, wine history, and grape growing from the Sonoma County Wine Library.

The Wine Institute
www.wineinstitute.org
The main lobbying organization for the national wine industry, with all the background you could want on wine-related laws, regulations, and statistics.

RECREATION
Bay Area Hiker
www.bahiker.com
Maps, photos, and information about some of the best hikes in the Bay Area and Wine Country from the author of a popular regional hiking book.

Index

List of Maps

Acknowledgments

You've never heard gossip like the gossip in the Wine Country. That's one secret I learned during the year I spent researching this book, visiting hundreds of wineries and tasting hundreds of wines while listening to entertaining stories from the folks that make, pour, or sell the stuff.

Those folks come from a tight-knit community of growers, winemakers, vineyard workers, and a cast of thousands working in tasting rooms and behind the scenes (winery dogs and cats included), who all seem to have a tale, a tip, some advice, or some gossip for this hapless writer with wine-stained teeth and a funny accent.

I'm grateful to all of the hundreds of people I met along the way who helped me tap into the sprawling Wine Country grapevine and taught me more than I ever thought I'd know about wine. In particular, Miryam Areas, Kate Jones, Michael Coates, and Monty Sander all introduced me to some fascinating wine-industry movers and shakers in Sonoma and Napa, and at the Culinary Institute of America John Buechsenstein tried his best to refine my belligerent palate.

I appreciate the time given by all my interviewees, including Steve Ledson, Bruce Cohn, Jeff Bundschu, Peter Marks, Daryl Sattui, and especially Bob Benziger, who redefined the term "Wine Country mover and shaker" with a white-knuckle ride through the Benziger vineyards in a golf cart, during which I miraculously managed to keep some wine in my glass.

Thanks also to the patient folks in Avalon's editorial, cartography, graphics, and marketing departments, who must have thought I was slumped in a wine-induced stupor as deadlines came and went without a word from me.

Closer to home, Nicole Phillips patiently listened to my frustrations, shared my dreams, endured my frantic all-night writing sessions, smiled gamely through endless winery visits, and managed to develop a wine palate more finely tuned than mine will ever be.

I should also mention the entertaining British wine critics, including Hugh Johnson, Jancis Robinson, and Malcolm Gluck, who helped pique my interest in wine decades ago in my home country. Their uniquely British combination of skepticism, humor, and bluntness helped demystify a subject that too many people still find intimidating. I hope their columns and books inspire many more people to explore the world of wine, and I hope my book encourages novices to explore Northern California's colorful Wine Country.

www.moon.com

DESTINATIONS | ACTIVITIES | BLOGS | MAPS | BOOKS

MOON.COM is ready to help plan your next trip! Filled with fresh trip ideas and strategies, author interviews, informative travel blogs, a detailed map library, and descriptions of all the Moon guidebooks, Moon.com is all you need to get out and explore the world—or even places in your own backyard. While at Moon.com, sign up for our monthly e-newsletter for updates on new releases, travel tips, and expert advice from our on-the-go Moon authors. As always, when you travel with Moon, expect an experience that is uncommon and truly unique.

MOON IS ON FACEBOOK—BECOME A FAN!
JOIN THE MOON PHOTO GROUP ON FLICKR

MAP SYMBOLS

▦	Expressway	◖	Highlight	✘	Airfield	⚲	Golf Course
▦	Primary Road	○	City/Town	✈	Airport	℗	Parking Area
▦	Secondary Road	⊙	State Capital	▲	Mountain	◢	Archaeological Site
▫▫▫	Unpaved Road	⊛	National Capital	✦	Unique Natural Feature	▮	Church
- - - -	Trail	★	Point of Interest			⛽	Gas Station
⋯⋯	Ferry	•	Accommodation	🗻	Waterfall	◌	Glacier
▬▬	Railroad	▼	Restaurant/Bar	▲	Park	▨	Mangrove
▥	Pedestrian Walkway	▪	Other Location	▣	Trailhead	▨	Reef
▦	Stairs	△	Campground	⛷	Skiing Area	▨	Swamp

CONVERSION TABLES

°C = (°F - 32) / 1.8
°F = (°C x 1.8) + 32
1 inch = 2.54 centimeters (cm)
1 foot = 0.304 meters (m)
1 yard = 0.914 meters
1 mile = 1.6093 kilometers (km)
1 km = 0.6214 miles
1 fathom = 1.8288 m
1 chain = 20.1168 m
1 furlong = 201.168 m
1 acre = 0.4047 hectares
1 sq km = 100 hectares
1 sq mile = 2.59 square km
1 ounce = 28.35 grams
1 pound = 0.4536 kilograms
1 short ton = 0.90718 metric ton
1 short ton = 2,000 pounds
1 long ton = 1.016 metric tons
1 long ton = 2,240 pounds
1 metric ton = 1,000 kilograms
1 quart = 0.94635 liters
1 US gallon = 3.7854 liters
1 Imperial gallon = 4.5459 liters
1 nautical mile = 1.852 km

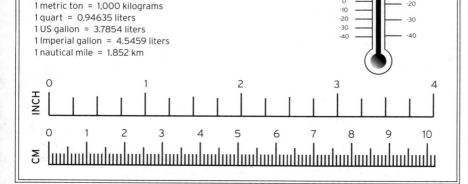

MOON NAPA & SONOMA

Avalon Travel
A member of the Perseus Books Group
1700 Fourth Street
Berkeley, CA 94710, USA
www.moon.com

Editor: Tiffany Watson
Series Manager: Kathryn Ettinger
Copy Editor: Christopher Church
Fact Checker: Nikki Ioakimedes
Production Coordinator: Elizabeth Jang
Graphics Coordinator: Kathryn Osgood
Cover Designer: Elizabeth Jang
Map Editor: Brice Ticen
Cartographer: Kat Bennett
Indexer: Judy Hunt

ISBN-13: 978-1-59880-596-3
ISSN: 2156-6526

Printing History
1st Edition – November 2010
5 4 3 2 1

Front cover photo: Vineyard with mustard and plum blossoms, Napa Valley © Ed Callaert
Title page photo: Courtesy of Up & Away Ballooning

Pg. 4, Sonoma Coast © Sonoma County Tourism Bureau; pg. 5 (top left) Merlot grapes ready for harvest at Ravenswood © Peter Griffith; (top center) cherryblock vines © Foley Family Wines; (top right) another inviting picnic spot © Philip Goldsmith; (bottom) oak and mustard in Sonoma County © Chris Willis/www.snapchris.com; pg. 6 (thumbnail) © Philip Goldsmith; (bottom) © Sonoma County Tourism Bureau; pg. 7 (top left) Jimtown in the Alexander Valley © Philip Goldsmith; (top right) blooming lavender © Susan & Neil Silverman; (bottom right) fall grape leaves at Sebastiani © Foley Family Wines; pg. 8 © Philip Goldsmith; pg. 9 © Sonoma County Tourism Bureau; pg. 10 © George Rose; pg. 11 (left) the Infineon Raceway sign © Philip Goldsmith; (center) at Viansa Winery © Philip Goldsmith; (right) blooming roses © Philip Goldsmith; pg. 12 © James Gateley; pg. 14 © Foley Family Wines; pg 16 © Thomas Barrat/123rf .com; pg. 17 Courtesy of Domaine Chandon; pg. 18 © Sonoma County Tourism Bureau; pg. 19 © George Rose; pg. 20 © Bryan Maleszyk

Printed in Canada by Friesens

KEEPING CURRENT

If you have a favorite gem you'd like to see included in the next edition, or see anything that needs updating, clarification, or correction, please drop us a line. Send your comments via email to feedback@moon.com, or use the address above.